The Complete Poems of

JAMES DICKEY

James Dickey, circa 1969. Photograph courtesy of Special Collections, Thomas Cooper Library, University of South Carolina.

The Complete Poems of

JAMES DICKEY

Edited with an Introduction by Ward Briggs

Foreword by Richard Howard

The University of South Carolina Press

© 2013 University of South Carolina

Published by the University of South Carolina Press
Columbia, South Carolina 29208

www.sc.edu/uscpress

Manufactured in the United States of America

22 21 20 19 18 17 16 15 14 13   10 9 8 7 6 5 4 3 2 1

LIBRARY OF CONGRESS CATALOGING-IN-PUBLICATION DATA
Dickey, James.
The complete poems of James Dickey / edited with an introduction by Ward Briggs ;
foreword by Richard Howard.
p. cm.
Includes index.
ISBN 978-1-61117-097-9 (cloth : alk. paper)
I. Briggs, Ward W. II. Title.
PS3554.I32 2012
811'.54—DC23   2012020573

PERMISSIONS

From *Buckdancer's Choice* by James Dickey © 1964, 1965 by James Dickey. Published by arrangement with Wesleyan University Press.

From *Drowning with Others* by James Dickey © 1958, 1959, 1960, 1961, 1962 by James Dickey. Published by arrangement with Wesleyan University Press.

From *The Eagle's Mile* by James Dickey © 1990 by James Dickey. Published by arrangement with Wesleyan University Press.

From *Helmets* by James Dickey © 1962, 1963, 1964 by James Dickey. Published by arrangement with Wesleyan University Press.

From *Poems 1957–1967* by James Dickey © 1958, 1959, 1960, 1961, 1962, 1963, 1964, 1965, 1966, 1967 by James Dickey. Published by arrangement with Wesleyan University Press.

From *The Whole Motion: Collected Poems, 1945–1992* by James Dickey © 1945, 1955, 1958, 1959, 1960, 1961, 1962, 1963, 1964, 1965, 1966, 1967, 1981, 1983, 1990, 1992 by James Dickey. Published by arrangement with Wesleyan University Press.

From *The Eye-Beaters, Blood, Victory, Madness, Buckhead and Mercy* by James Dickey © 1968, 1969, 1970 by James Dickey. Used by permission of Doubleday, a division of Random House, Inc.

From *Puella* by James Dickey © 1982 by James Dickey. Used by permission of Doubleday, a division of Random House, Inc.

From *Stolen Apples* by Yevgeny Yevtushenko © 1971 by Doubleday, a division of Random House, Inc. Used by permission of Doubleday, a division of Random House, Inc.

From *The Strength of Fields* by James Dickey © 1979 by James Dickey. Used by permission of Doubleday, a division of Random House, Inc.

From *The Zodiac* by James Dickey © 1976 by James Dickey. Used by permission of Doubleday, a division of Random House, Inc.

All other poems © by James Dickey. Used by permission of the Heirs of James Dickey.

For Bronwen, Chris, and Kevin

Poetry won't save your life—
But it will make your life worth saving.

James Dickey

Contents

1961–1967

1968–1973

1977–1997

POEMS OF UNCERTAIN DATE

POEMS FOR CHILDREN

FOREWORD

When James Dickey died in 1997, a rare and conflicted spirit was extinguished, though of course the poems are fulgent for good. Unlike the spirit which generated them, the poems themselves are neither rare nor conflicted: they are, as you can determine from the volume in your hands, a copious, clamorous amassment, and though they are frequently querulous, their quarrel is usually a conflict with one another; when Yeats said, or meant to say, that a man's quarrel with himself is poetry, he foretold *this man's* career, for even the most secluded covens of Dickey's verse are loud with multitudinous disputation. There were many collections of poems unanimous only in their insistence, and I suspect that the last cumulus (1957–67) of his earlier "movement," as he so appropriately described its collective genre, is the one chiefly admired today. For there is a sense (or a folly) in which James Dickey grew too big for mere poetry; the energy and intensity of his powers spilled (surely the right word) into fiction, into criticism, as well as into a curious form of prose commentary packed into several volumes of self-interviews which he teased or tormented into an autonomous genre.

The rage to disarm and then confront one's (presumably helpless) humanity governs or subverts what I am tempted to call the "bulk" of this poet's last-ditch production, its celebration of life and death on earth and the convulsive figures he imagined for them. Though Dickey's is a poetry charged with justice to the visible world rendered by a divining conscience, and though the work echoes with a version of morality collected from instances of natural order, it inveterately identifies every subject, indeed every subjection of identity, to some wilder form of chthonic energy, to that possession by the gods Dickey has owned up to throughout his work; and though most of the later poems still (occasionally) possess "a certain music, order and repose," they also possess a savage dissidence from those so often rejected virtues, an heroic outrage for which the poet was latterly reproached by the very admirers of his old hieratic stance, his initial Heraclitean status.

Yet it is a mistake to admonish the poet for precisely what he knew he was created to do: his titanic choice was to recast the entire burden of utterance ("as though to be born, to be awakened, to be what one is / were to be carried"), transforming what is recurrent and therefore changeless to what is, merely, real and released. No poetry

xvii

of our time is so determined upon exaltation; no poetry of our time is so exposed to debasement. The wonder of it, and the reward, is the success in submission, the assent which turns to ascent; the assumption of rage, torment, darkness which positively "enables" transfiguration.

In an unfallen world, to which Dickey's poems always allude, which they sometimes approach, and which they even, at appalling moments, create; in the risen world, then, hunting and warfare—his chosen actions—become search and struggle. That is the consummation of these later violent texts which insist upon anguish and madness, which in their very dispersal on the page rehearse mortality. It has been Dickey's ultimate exploit to see the risen world "through" the other one, through what he calls "an enormous green bright growing NO / that frees forever."

Richard Howard

Preface

This book is a *labor amoris*. I am a classicist by trade and certainly not a specialist in modern American poetry. I undertook this project in partial payment to my friend Jim Dickey for a friendship of nearly thirty years, continual enlightenment and entertainment at every meeting throughout that time, and a demonstration of utter courage in the face of physical collapse. I can also thank him for insights and analysis of the work of virtually every important modern poet, except for his own. If I ever brought up one of his poems in conversation, except to thank him for writing it, I cannot remember it. He certainly never volunteered to discuss one of his poems with me: he was far happier, with me at least, discussing the poetry of anyone but himself.

This edition presents a systematically edited text of the 331 poems James Dickey (1923–1997) published during his career, for the most part in chronological order of publication, and an apparatus criticus that establishes the first publications of the poems; lists later anthologies and Dickey collections in which the poems were reprinted; identifies people, places, and references in the poems; and lists textual variants and author's revisions to different versions published under Dickey's authority.[1] Where it is significant, I also include in the apparatus criticus variants in his final typescript copy. Undatable poems are included in the section "Poems of Uncertain Date." His two poems for children follow this section.

In his edition of Robert Penn Warren's poems, John Burt described the two chief aims of a volume of collected poems: the collection can be a kind of "author's autobiography, representing the author's career as it looked from the end of it, with all of the blind alleys and false turns elided. . . . Or it can be like an author's diary, representing the author's intellectual life as it unfolded, with no certainty, but with many provisional intuitions, about how each event will fit into the big picture."[2]

Dickey provided the first type of collection with *The Whole Motion* (1992) by selecting and arranging 238 poems (some previously unpublished) at virtually the end of his career. Throughout his career, he maintained a strict control over the style, format, and order in which his poems were presented. He carefully arranged the poems in each of his collections, and it was so with *The Whole Motion*. He chose not to include thirty-eight previously uncollected poems, twelve poems that had been previously collected, and his two children's poems. In addition twelve poems from *Puella* were omitted, some because of a publisher's error. I include the poems omitted from *The Whole Motion* as well as twenty-four poems written in the 1950s (ten previously unpublished) and collected after 1992 in *Striking In* and six poems published after 1992 in various venues.

Dickey hoped that his career as a poet would be judged by *The Whole Motion* as he arranged it. Unfortunately he and the publisher did not produce a volume worthy of his poetic legacy. Apart from the omission of many *Puella* poems, *The Whole Motion* contains more than fifty typographical errors, more than one in every five poems. Providing a clean text of his poems is therefore a major aim of this collection.

The present work aims to be the second of Burt's types. The poems presented in chronological order (albeit of publication, not necessarily composition) provide a kind of poetic autobiography emphasizing the poet's development, his poetic innovations and experiments, his shifts in style and subject matter, and his great successes as well as his failures. Dickey would never have authorized a complete edition of his poems and would never have agreed to this chronological ordering.[3] I beg his pardon and hope that he would eventually have seen the value of the present arrangement.

The primary sources for this book are his twelve major collections, one bibliophile edition of previously unpublished verse, and three volumes of translations.[4] For many poems my copy text represents Dickey's intentions with regard to format, punctuation, and spelling in his collected volumes. I have not included previously unpublished poems. At his death Dickey had manuscripts that he thought were ready for publication (some submitted to journals, some not), which others have published, notably "For a Ballet," and "The Crusader's Dream," both from 1950,[5] and "Rain in Darkness."[6] I respect the biographer's prerogative, but to include some of these unpublished manuscript poems in a work such as this would oblige me to include them all. Since dating Dickey's drafts and manuscripts is almost impossible, the guesswork involved would not significantly improve our understanding of Dickey's development as a poet.

Like most poets, Dickey, in the course of his public readings, regularly introduced each poem with a comment on the personal experience or artistic intention that gave rise to the poem.[7] Often the background story that accompanied a reading was a wild exaggeration or fantasy. To a group of advertising executives, for instance, he introduced "False Youth: Autumn" thus: "I was in this tough district of Columbia, South Carolina, where I live. It's a weird place called Harden Street, where it's kind of a mixture of redneck toughs and hippies and so on. . . . I went into this barbershop to get a trim or something. And there were the toughest guys I've ever seen in my life. I mean you couldn't even have gone into the pool hall next door and found any tougher ones than those fellows. They were kind of like the two guys in *Deliverance,* you know, on the river bank, not too much different."[8]

Harden Street is the central axis of the college-bar area in Columbia. There is a mix of college types and townspeople, but no one would call it "weird" or say that it was full of "redneck toughs." Dickey's barber shop, the Carolina Barber Shop, was in fact on Devine Street and had no pool hall next door.

Dickey was less likely to exaggerate in print and slightly less likely to do so in interviews. I have nevertheless cited Dickey's published views on his poems in my notes, both to supply the factual incidents from which some poems arose and to present the poet's intentions when writing the poems.

He explained himself so frequently to the press that his friend George Garrett wrote that Dickey was "one of the most interviewed and monitored writers in literary history."[9] In 1970 Dickey took the unusual step of publishing *Self–Interviews,* in which he was at pains to clarify the background of many of the poems in *Poems 1957–1967,* among others. Such self-explanation may be interpreted as a friendly gesture of outreach to his readers or as a nearly unprecedented attempt to manipulate the reader's response: something either descriptive or prescriptive. Five years later he concluded, "I think of all American poets, I've explained myself overly much, and it probably doesn't do very much for anybody for me to keep on doing it more and more and more."[10]

With such an unusual amount of information provided by the author, it seemed natural that a secondary aim of this edition should be to reproduce as many published remarks by Dickey on his individual poems as possible. Readers are free to accept as much of what Dickey said as they may choose, but it should be understood that my inclusion of these comments is intended not simply to show the poems as distortions of real events (which of course all poems are) but to illuminate how art is made out of mundane experience. There will be no voice here but Dickey's (however reliable that voice may be) to specify personal background or literary explication of his work.[11] I have identified allusions and corrected errors of spelling and fact when they are known to me.[12] I mention the recurrence of such subjects as snakes, sharks, the death of his brother, and the color white, but I leave it for others to interpret their meanings.

I have made free but cautious use of Henry Hart's capacious biography, *James Dickey: The World as a Lie* (New York: Picador USA, 2000),[13] for specific points of fact. I have also profited greatly from Gordon Van Ness's admirable *The One Voice of James Dickey* (2 vols., Columbia & London: University of Missouri Press, 2003), *Crux: The Letters of James Dickey,* edited by Matthew J. Bruccoli and Judith S. Baughman (New York: Knopf, 1993), and *James Dickey: A Descriptive Bibliography,* by Bruccoli and Baughman (Pittsburgh: University of Pittsburgh Press, 1990).

Dickey's own varying accounts of his life—many factitious, many fictitious—have tended in the eyes of some to diminish his poetic achievement. The James Dickey I knew probably suffered from a benevolent form of *mythomanie,* not so severe as that of fictional fabricators Don Quixote or Tartarin de Tarascon or of real-life frauds such as Mary Baker (Princess Caraboo) (1791–1864) and Sir Edmund Blackhouse (1873–1944). Dickey's imagination was at work twenty-four hours a day, manipulating reality to entertain himself and others, his family, his friends, his students, or perfect strangers. The most frequent subject of his fabrication was his war service. He bitterly regretted not qualifying as a pilot, and, like Faulkner, he lied about his military record, claiming at one point in print that he "shot down seven enemy planes, received two Distinguished Flying Crosses and a Silver Star."[14] His biographers have cataloged many of his exaggerations and "lies" and more will surely do so in the future. Though my notes identify persons and places mentioned in his poems and sort fact from fiction as necessary, such distinctions are wholly irrelevant to the value of the poet and his poems.

Though Dickey said that his life was "more complicated and unknowable than that of Lawrence of Arabia,"[15] for an understanding of his poems beyond their texts, perhaps no more is needed than Dickey's own brief autobiographical sketch:

And so if anybody asks you how Jim Dickey became a poet, starting from Buckhead, you can say that one day he got off the bench at North Fulton High School, but instead of going into the football game, he got on a red motorcycle belonging to Ed Van Valkenburg and rode off into North Georgia. Tell whoever asks you, that Jim Dickey listened to a lot of jazz with Walter Armistead, that he took guitar lessons from Sam Worley because he couldn't wait any longer than age forty to learn to play. Tell him that the man fought in a war in airplanes, reading Plato between missions, that he got a desperate education at Vanderbilt, worked in some ad agencies, drank whiskey with Dave Sanders, hunted deer unsuccessfully with Lewis King, shot some rapids with Al Braselton, looked at pictures with Jarvin Parks, and watched Bess Finch dance, and that he published, in the end, some poems based on these things.

And so, if you can imagine me, looking as I do now, as a skinny blond boy in an unstained football uniform, riding on a red Harley-Davidson through Fannin County, carrying with him a load of people—his particular artistic community: weight-lifters, archers, writers, drunkards, musicians, housewives, poets, painters, anarchists, tennis players, village atheists and business men—well, that'd be me.[16]

1. I have not recorded variants from versions of Dickey's work that were not published under his authority (see the apparatus criticus). In the latter part of his career, he worked on two long poems: "The Indian Maiden," which sprang from his affair with Robin Jarecki (see "Adultery"), and "Two Poems on the Survival of the Male Body" (see "The Drift-Spell"). "The Indian Maiden" is lost (though, as the apparatus points out, an echo or two exists in Dickey's published work). It would be possible to construct a version of "Two Poems on the Survival of the Male Body" from the many manuscripts of that work that exist in the Department of Special Collections, Washington University Libraries, St. Louis, and in the Manuscripts, Archives, and Manuscript Library, Emory University, Atlanta, but I limit myself here only to poems published by Dickey.

2. *The Collected Poems of Robert Penn Warren*, edited by John Burt (Baton Rouge: Louisiana State University Press, 1998), 625.

3. When Gordon Van Ness suggested publishing Dickey's poems of the 1950s for just such a purpose as mine, Dickey declined; see *Striking In: The Early Notebooks of James Dickey,* edited with introductions by Gordon Van Ness (Columbia: University of Missouri Press, 1996), 239. In *The Whole Motion* Dickey grouped previously unpublished poems in sequences involving war ("The Place of the Skull"), peacetime, and the family ("Seeking the Chosen"), but he arranged them in the order in which the events they describe occurred in his life, not in the chronological order of the poems' composition.

4. The major collections are *Buckdancer's Choice; Drowning with Others; The Eye-Beaters, Blood, Madness, Buckhead and Mercy; The Eagle's Mile; Falling, May Day Sermon, and Other Poems; Helmets; Into the Stone and Other Poems; Poems 1957–1967; Puella; The Strength of Fields; Striking In;* and *The Whole Motion.* (*Poems 1957–1967* and *The Whole Motion* also reprint previously collected poems). The bibliophile edition is *Veteran Birth.* The translations are *Head-Deep, Stolen Apples* (with others), and *Värmland.* For full citations see the apparatus criticus.

5. Published in Henry Hart, *James Dickey: The World as a Lie* (New York: Picador USA, 2000), 158–59.

6. Published in Gordon Van Ness, *The One Voice of James Dickey*, 2 vols. (Columbia & London: University of Missouri Press, 2003) 1:66.

7. Those who want a taste of the introductions Dickey gave at his readings are directed to his two recordings, *The Poems of James Dickey (1957–1967),* Spoken Arts SA 984, 1967, and *James Dickey Reading His Poetry,* Caedmon TC 1333, 1971.

8. "Words That Work," *Papers from 1973 Annual Meeting of the American Association of Advertising Agencies (May 19, 1973)* (White Sulphur Springs, W.Va.: Greenbrier, 1973), 5.

9. "'Liar, Liar, Pants on Fire': Some Notes on the Life and Art of the Late James Dickey," *Virginia Quarterly Review* 77 (Winter 2001): 31.

10. *Unmuzzled Ox* 3, no. 2 (1975): 74; republished in *The Voiced Connections of James Dickey: Interviews and Conversations,* edited by Ronald Baughman (Columbia: University of South Carolina Press, 1989), 84.

11. According to Garrett, "Dickey . . . hardly ever told the truth about anything. He lied about everything even when there was no reason not to tell the truth. There is a certain amount of fun in seeing Dickey get away with this" ("'Liar, Liar, Pants on Fire,'" 31).

12. My emendations are few, as in "Spring-Shock" (line 18) and "Mexican Valley" (line 10).

13. I refer many times in the apparatus criticus to Hart's biography and occasionally correct Hart's facts or his interpretation of them (for example, of Doris Holbrook in "Cherrylog Road").

14. Program for Dickey's lecture "Hart Crane and the Peripheral in Poetry," Twenty-Fourth Peters Rushton Seminar in Contemporary Prose and Poetry, University of Virginia, February 7, 1962.

15. *Sorties: Journals and New Essays* (Garden City, N.Y.: Doubleday, 1971), 89.

16. *Night Hurdling: Poems, Essays, Conversations, Commencements, and Afterwords* (Columbia & Bloomfield Hills: Bruccoli Clark, 1983), 188–89. For Van Valkenburg, see "Cherrylog Road"; for Armistead see "Walter Armistead." Sam H. Worley (1918–2008) taught guitar at the Rhythm City Music store in Buckhead; David E. B. Sanders, Jr. (1921–1982) worked in his father's construction company and lived near Dickey's brother Tom. Sanders and Dickey regularly drank together on Friday nights in Atlanta (Hart, *James Dickey,* 217–18). Edward Lewis King was Dickey's canoeing partner and the model for Lewis Medlock in *Deliverance* (see Hart, *James Dickey,* 244). For Dickey's fellow ad man, drinking friend, and canoeing partner Braselton, see "Drifting." Jarvin L. Parks (1931–1967) was an eccentric Buckhead artist and poet who worked as a display director at a library. Mae Bess Finch (b. 1921) was a childhood friend who may be the "Elaine Shields" in Dickey's short story "The Eye of the Fire," 64.

Acknowledgments

I have neither asked for nor received grants, graduate assistance, technical expertise, office space or supplies from anyone for the research, travel, or production costs associated with this book. I have, however, asked repeatedly for assistance, and it has been readily granted by a great number of friends new and old.

My chief debt is to the late Matthew J. Bruccoli, Dickey's literary representative, who encouraged my undertaking of this project, advised me expertly at every stage, and offered warm approval of much that I showed him. The Dickey family, first and foremost Christopher Dickey, but also Bronwen Dickey, Kevin Dickey, Deborah Dickey, Patsy Hamilton Dickey, Trent Dickey, Dorian Dickey, Katie Dickey Marbut, and Michael Allin, have been characteristically generous with memories, facts, and encouragement from the beginning. That beginning would not have been possible without the support and assistance of Jane H. Che. I owe a major debt to Steve Enniss and the staff at the Manuscripts and Rare Books Library of the Robert W. Woodruff Library at Emory University. My colleagues at the University of South Carolina have been enormously helpful, and I have relied on their expertise and their devotion to Jim, who was their colleague also. Judith S. Baughman painstakingly read the proofs and corrected many errors. Don Greiner and Patrick Scott have given support and wisdom throughout the life of the project, read parts of this book, and saved me from numerous embarrassments; I hope I save them any embarrassment that arises out of being associated with this project. Joel Myerson advised me on textual matters. Elizabeth Sudduth and the staff of Rare Books and Special Collections at the Thomas Cooper Library at the University of South Carolina were especially helpful as were Robin Copp and the staff of the South Caroliniana Library. My warm thanks are owed to Vitaly Rassolov, Thomas J. Brown, Arlyn Bruccoli, Bradford Collins, John Ferguson, Michael Jasper, Dave Smith, D. Reece Williams, and Benjamin Franklin V for more help with this project than they realize. Experts on Dickey outside the university have been of great help, particularly Gordon Van Ness, Ernest Suarez, and James R. Mann, Jr. I am also grateful to John F. Miller of the University of Virginia and Mortimer Chambers of UCLA.

I have met wonderful people in the course of this project and I am grateful to Mary Bookwalter, Al Braselton, Jeannie Braselton, Lewis King, Dr. William C. Roberts, W. Cliff Roberts, and Mrs. Thomas Grindstaff.

Lastly I am very grateful to Brandi Lariscy Avant for the painstaking care she took in designing and typesetting this book and to Karen L. Rood for her diligence and expertise in editing the manuscript and seeing the book through the production process.

I hope that whatever errors remain in this work will not diminish the generosity of those mentioned here or my appreciation of it.

INTRODUCTION

The issues involved in determining an accurate text for each of James Dickey's poems may be found in a brief review of the various modes in which Dickey's career unfolded. A few biographical divagations, with remarks on his various experiments with forms, will illuminate the central textual difficulties. I attempt no assessment of his career, merely a discussion of the features of his career that influenced my editing.

Dickey said that he was, in Wordsworth's phrase, a poet of "the second birth," not one who, like Rimbaud or Dylan Thomas, had a natural instrument for poetry.[1] The way a "made" poet such as Dickey catches up to a "born" poet is, "if at all, by years of the hardest kind of work, much luck, much self-doubt, many false starts, and the difficult and ultimately moral habit of trying each poem, each line, each word, against the shifting but finally constant standards of inner necessity."[2] It could be said that Dickey brought a kind of athleticism to his work, with an athlete's dedication to a perfected performance that he recognized in the story of football player Jim Marshall: determination is more important than physical gifts.[3] Dickey's preferred analogy for his process of composition was the mining of "low-grade ore." "I work like a gold-miner refining low-grade ore: a lot of muck and dirt with a very little gold in it. Back-breaking labor! Infinite! But when this kind of worker gets what he's after, he has the consolation of knowing that the substance he winds up with is as much real gold as it would be if he had just gone around picking up nuggets off the ground."[4] Poets of the second birth often bloom late, and so it was with Dickey.

"Sports and girls: that was it for me, until the war. Sports, girls and motorcycles." Dickey's letters and biography make clear that an unstudious, unartistic, reserved, and girls-and-sports-obsessed southern boy "with no more talent for poetry than Joe Louis" was transformed into a poet by World War II.[5] Dickey enlisted in 1942 but saw combat only from January 1945 to the end of the war, flying as a radar observer in thirty-eight combat missions over the Philippines (for which he received five Bronze Service Stars), Borneo, Japan, and China with the 418th Night Fighter Squadron. Poetry came alive to him as he read Ernest Dowson in his radar navigator's seat during long and frightening night flights or Yeats on his camp cot after witnessing the crashed Liberators and corpses brought in from nearby battles.[6] Poetry took him out of battle and away from the strange tropical jungle, where he found himself a world away from his home in the comfortable Atlanta suburb of Buckhead, and it took him away from the monotony of military life and the horror of combat death. What Dickey did in the air and what he saw on the ground endowed him with the guilt of both the survivor ("The Performance" [1959]) and the destroyer ("The Firebombing" [1964]). Thus war gave him a set of experiences he drew on in poetry and novels for the rest of his life. "I have come, pretty much, to look at existence from the standpoint of a survivor: as someone who is alive only by the inexplicable miracle of chance."[7]

Dickey took an especial interest in minor poets who did not survive, including Edward Thomas ("To Be Edward Thomas" [1957]), killed in World War I two years after discovering his poetic gifts; Hendrik Marsman ("The Zodiac" [1976]) and Alun Lewis ("The Strength of Fields" [1977]), both killed during World War II; Robert Bhain Campbell ("For Robert Bhain Campbell"[1960s]) and Trumbull Stickney ("Exchanges" [1970]), both dead at an age before Dickey's career even got started. Dickey devoted limited parts of his career to ruminations on his dead brother Eugene, the illness of his mother, his gamecock-keeping father, the care and protection of his children, his extramarital loves, the imagined childhood of his second wife, and the growth and potential of his daughter; but the war and his survival of it were the overarching preoccupations of his career. Harold Bloom correctly noted that when Dickey said the fragmentary parts of "Drinking from a Helmet" (1963) are set between the battlefield and the graveyard, he gave "no inaccurate motto for the entire cosmos of what will prove to be the Whole Motion, when we have it all."[8]

The war over, Dickey's generation "had our lives; then came the problem of living them."[9] "I was never really young, because my generation went into the war. I found my true youth in middle age, and it is better than the actual youth that I had."[10] Dickey's juvenilia was thus written in his midtwenties when he was a veteran, a husband, and a father, and his apprentice work began when he was well into his thirties, rather late for any poet, much less a lyric poet. His early influences were George Barker, Kenneth Patchen, Dylan Thomas, Hart Crane, and particularly Theodore Roethke.[11] Dickey's undergraduate efforts (often in the Vanderbilt magazine the *Gadfly*) played with traditional forms and recherché vocabulary ("inchmeal," "cordonnet," and "sighflown" in "The Shark at the Window"; "discharted" in "Sea Island"; "therianthropic" in "King Crab and Rattler"). "He was working at his own poetry in those days regularly trying different line-lengths, rhythms, casting widely for imagery."[12] Dickey's early work is also heavily informed by his college studies in anthropology, particularly, in the words of one of his teachers, Monroe Spears, "rituals of initiation, rites of passages, myths of the hero, confrontation with fear and violent death,"[13] all helpful, Dickey wrote later, in "mythologizing my own experience."[14] Under the influence of Ezra Pound, with whom he carried on a correspondence until 1957, Dickey tried to develop mental images into poetry but fit the image into appropriate language, "the wording or *voicing* of the perception."[15] Later in life he described this period: "My problem was that I felt my imagination could . . . override anything. And that I could take any subject and make something good. I can't. And so before I would give in I wasted years trying to salvage, by sheer invention, subjects that weren't salvageable, that never could have worked, never. Nobody could make 'em work, least of all me. But when I did give in, when I admitted that, I began to write much better because it enabled me to pick, to pick what would work or that at least had some sort of chance to work."[16]

"Although I didn't care for rhyme and the 'packaged' quality which it gives even the best poems, I did care very much for meter, or at least rhythm."[17] The poems of the late 1950s are defined largely by sound and rhythm, imposed by Dickey's "thump-loving American ear," which led him to a kind of incantatory anapestic verse, a signature of his early work, beginning with his first collection, *Into the Stone* (1960).[18] "Most of the poems of *Into the* Stone are in variations of a dactylic or anapestic rhythm—depending on where you start the count—whether you think of it as a rising or a falling rhythm."[19] "I moved over from that into more of a three-beat organization which was less heavily rhythmical."[20] His editor John Hall Wheelock called Dickey's rhythm "rising trimeters" while Dickey called it "A night-rhythm . . . felt in pulse not word."[21] He found the heavy accent "rhythmically compelling, almost coercive. . . . Suppose you were able to get some valuable poetic insight into the meter; you would have this compellingness, this hypnotic effect which lots of poetry does not have."[22] The lines in these poems are generally end-stopped, and the narrative persona is almost invisible.

Near the end of his life, Dickey described his process of composition, with specific reference to a poem of this period, "A Dog Sleeping on My Feet" (1962):

> "A Dog Sleeping on My Feet" was written more or less as I write most things I do, including novels and screenplays. . . . It begins with an image, something I see in my mind's eye. . . . It could be a photograph. It could be something real that happened. I would emphasize that the poet works with whatever comes to him. If you ask him if he works from experience, a real poet would have to say that you must define experience, because experience is anything and everything that has ever impinged on your imagination. It can come from things that have actually happened to you, or things that someone has told you about: stories, anecdotes, jokes. It could be something you just made up or something you saw in a movie; or a painting or a photograph could have suggested it to you. . . . But the main thing the poet must remember is, never to be bound by facts because he's not trying to tell the truth. He's trying to make it.[23]

The characteristics of the "Wesleyan" phase of his career, beginning with the period 1959–64 ("The Early Motion"), were an interest in poetic form and tribal ritual that led Dickey to seek the truths of the world by means of communion with the darker mysteries of nature. He expanded his use of classical rhetorical devices, which would be a mainstay throughout his career: chiasmus ("Dover" [1958], line 10);[24] zeugma ("Kudzu" [1963], lines 80–81); oxymoron ("Mercy" [1969], lines 72–73, 94–95, and "False Youth: Autumn: Clothes of the Age" [1971], line 4); tricolon ("Drinking from a Helmet" [1963], line 168); anaphora ("Uncle" [1960], line 56, and "Fog Envelops the Animals" [1961], line 35);[25] and asyndeton ("Drinking from a Helmet," line 168).[26] In this period he wrote his only poem in rhymed couplets ("The Island" [1960]). In the same year he invented a slant-rhyme couplet for "Sleeping Out at Easter" and a constantly changing rhyme scheme for "The Prodigal." He also began to play with the appearance of the lines on the page with "Wall and Cloud" (1962). In 1963 he began to use quotations from other poets as the last lines of poems (Walt Whitman in "Drinking from a Helmet").[27]

The "night-rhythm" continued to be the grounding point in *Drowning with Others* (1962): "First I heard, then I wrote, and then I began to reason; when I reasoned, I wrote more of the same."[28] "I edged toward the end of sound over sense,[29] toward the foreordained hammering of ultra-rhythmical English, and tried to make the concepts, images, and themes of my life conform to what the night-rhythm had caused to come through me."[30] Dickey began, like Thomas Hardy, to create his own forms, such as the semicouplet in "The Underground Stream" (1960) or the refrains gathered in the final stanzas of "On a Hill below the Lighthouse" (1959) and "Sleeping Out at Easter" (1960).[31] "In some of the early poetry that I wrote I would start out with the most difficult problem I could think of: to invent a rotating refrain, for example. But I saw, before I did more than one book's worth, that each of the pieces that I tried to write this way was getting to be more of a game than a poem, so I shied away from doing things that way."[32]

He continued to experiment with the long, multipart poem as he had with "Dover: Believing in Kings" (1958), moving into the woods for "The Owl King" (1961–62). That poem also exemplifies his use of different narrative perspectives, particularly the viewpoint of the animal, a feature of such poems as "The Sheep Child" (1966).

For *Helmets* (1964) Dickey continued to write long poems such as "Approaching Prayer" (1964) and "Drinking from a Helmet" but with more lightly stressed rhythms: "In *Helmets*, though I still relied on the night-rhythm, the sound-before-meaning, I also wanted to give more play to narrative movement, the story-value of what was being said, and consequently I toned down the heavy bombardment of stress and relied more on matter-of-fact statement and declaration."[33] Toward the end of *Helmets,* Dickey was clearly breaking away from the regular stanzaic structures and end-stopped lines of his earlier work, a process embodied in the movement of "Approaching Prayer" and previously seen in "The Being" and "Breath" (both 1963).

If any phrase defines the shifts and slides of Dickey's verse making it might come from "Turning Away" (1966): "Change; form again." According to Dickey, "The trouble with most American writers is that they are afraid to make a mistake—they get a little inch that they can peddle pretty effectively and they just cultivate that inch forever. I will throw away something that has been successful for me. I will throw away the anapestic rhythm, I will throw away the margin-to-margin organization, I will eventually throw away the balanced poem and go on to some other thing that I think would be interesting to try."[34]

He appreciated Dylan Thomas and thought Thomas had an original voice, but only one, and the unfortunate result was a brilliant and original monotony.[35] Thus, even after Dickey had found a successful medium for his voice, whether it was a rhythm, a form, or the arrangement of words on the page, he continually tried, in his friend Ezra Pound's words, to "make it new."[36] "My primary consideration is to change. I dare not use the word grow; there may or may not be growth involved, but to change."[37]

By 1964 Dickey was "A middle-aged, softening man / Grinning and shaking his head / In amazement to last him forever."[38] Part of his amazement stemmed from the limitless formal possibilities of poetry. With *Buckdancer's Choice* (1965) he began the experiments that he later decided "to go all the way with."[39] He set aside the thumping anapestic trimeter and lengthened some of his lines to five and six beats ("Sled Burial, Dream Ceremony" [1965]) in which, recalling the classical odes of Catullus and Horace (whom Dickey read in translation), the effect is created not by stress accent but by the juxtaposition of a five-beat line with a three-beat line. He began to experiment with free verse in long lines, in the manner of Whitman, Robinson Jeffers, and Roethke. "For 'Reincarnation (I),' I simply wrote as far across the page as the typewriter would go, and that was essentially the line."[40] The title *Buckdancer's Choice*, drawn from an old folk song, indicates his movement to softer rhythms and linear narrative. The poems were largely written at Reed College (January 1963–May 1964), when Dickey and much of the rest of the country were caught up in the folk-music revival. If an athletic vigor marks the thumping rhythms of his earlier works, now the lighter touch of a finger-picked (not strummed) guitar can be heard (a technique he had just learned from Al Braselton) to accompany the narrative of a folk song, giving a lighter stress on accent and an increased concern with "the story-value" of the poem. His career, scarcely a decade in progress, was crowned with the 1966 National Book Award for *Buckdancer's Choice*.

Dickey was shaping the general poetic profile that he described at the end of the decade: "I have three modes of poetry that I am working in now. One is the narrative-dramatic mode that most of my work heretofore has been in. Second is the so-called 'new metric.' The third, the one that I have done least writing in and least experimentation in is what I call 'country surrealism.' . . . The point is, though, to write different things in different modes, and to bring them together, at times, *very* cautiously."[41]

Since Dickey was trying other experiments in the second part of his Wesleyan University Press career (1965–67), a background note is in order. In 1961 Dickey had disparaging words for *The Maximus Poems* (1960) of Charles Olson (1910–1970), whose book on Herman Melville, *Call Me Ishmael* (1947), was popular about the time Dickey was writing his M.A. thesis on Melville's poetry at Vanderbilt in 1950.[42] Olson, the rector of Black Mountain College, had his own salon of younger poets: Robert Creeley (1926–2005), Robert Duncan (1919–1988), and Denise Levertov (1923–1997), an editor of *Buckdancer's Choice* (1965). Olson's essay "Projective Verse" declared that the poet, freed from metrical constraints, "can declare, at every moment, the line its metric and its ending—where its breathing, shall come to, termination."[43] In addition, said Olson, the typewriter was the poet's ally—as E. E. Cummings, Pound, and William Carlos Williams had demonstrated—because "due to its rigidity and its space precisions," it can "indicate exactly the breath, the pauses, the suspensions even of syllables, the juxtapositions even of parts of phrases, which he intends."[44] Dickey noted that what Olson called "projective verse" actually derived from the French critic René Nelli (1906–1982), author of *Poésie ouverte, poésie fermée* (1947), and thus Dickey called Olson's technique "nothing very new"[45]: "What Olson's notion of 'open' verse does is simply to provide creative irresponsibility with the semblance of a rationale which may be defended in heated and cloudy terms by its supposed practitioners."[46] Nevertheless Dickey, in his restless search for new forms of expression, adapted Olson's approach to midline pauses, free metrics, and typewriter-aided poetic architecture.

In 1964 Dickey published "Mary Sheffield," the first of his poems to employ what he called "burst writing," "the grouping of words with space between them and no punctuation," which grew out of his trimeter line.[47] This technique could be used onomatopoetically, as in "May Day Sermon" (1967), where line 249—"he stands up stomps   catches   roars"—effectively imitates the starting of a motorcycle.[48] But Dickey had another use for the technique: "I wanted to keep that memorability factor that the three-beat line has, to keep that compression where you would remember which words went with which to create an effect, but you would also be writing in a way that approximates the way in which the mind associates."[49] The words on the page may have come from his knowledge of musical phrasing or his experience reading his poems dramatically, but it was clear that he intended the spaces in the poem, where there were no words, to be part of the poetry too.[50] The words on the page certainly resembled Olson's "breath units," as the number of words spoken naturally in a single breath, but Dickey wished to imitate not the limits of the lungs but the processes of the brain in what became known as his "split line technique": "I evolved the split line to try to do what I could to reproduce as nearly as I could the real way of the mind as it associates verbally. The mind doesn't seem to work in a straight line, but associates in bursts of words, in jumps. I used this technique for 'Falling' in a more pronounced form and wrote such poems as 'Slave Quarters' and 'The Firebombing' in a more modified form."[51] Elsewhere he explained, "What I intended, though, was to try to conceive a use of the poetic line which would be like a small line within a large line, to set the lines apart not by printing them one above the other, or one below the other, but by putting them parallel and leaving white spaces between them. Because this seemed to me more nearly to approximate the way the human mind really does work and associate. It goes in jumps instead of a regular linear progression."[52]

In the same year as "Mary Sheffield," he published "Reincarnation (I)" (1964), his first poem to employ a visually expressive technique he called "a shimmering wall of words" or "block format,"[53] which he developed as a showcase for his "split-line technique": "I wanted to present the reader with solid and all but impenetrable walls—a wall of language where you have these interstices of blank spaces at irregular places. It's a wall you can't get over, but you have to descend, climb down, in a way."[54] Dickey declared this experiment the counterpart of *Color Fields,* a series of paintings by artist Mark Rothko (1903–1970), which dates from this period,[55] as does the "wall of sound" created by record producer Phil Spector (1940–).

Though he had begun his experiments by cutting and rearranging words on cardboard, Dickey came to appreciate Olson's use of the typewriter as a structural tool: "I began to build the walls directly on the page from the typewriter, and spent more and more time erecting them and pushing against them, and trying to peer through them at the place that let the light through."[56] The interstices in the split lines were where the light came through. Three 1965 poems—"The Fiend," "The Shark's Parlor," and "Coming Back to America"—all use this technique, but it is most effective in "Falling" (1967), where the mass of long lines gives the effect of slowing down the stewardess's descent. The last poem in this form was "The Eye-Beaters" (1968).

For Dickey the 1960s were the high-water mark of critical success and limitless possibility: "There doesn't seem to be any end to what I can think up these days; some of it is crazy, some of it is rather classical in form, some of it is like nothing ever heard or seen by God or man before."[57] His greatest triumph was *Poems 1957–1967,* which contains more than half the poems of *Into the Stone,* two-thirds of *Drowning with Others,* nearly all of *Helmets,* and all of *Buckdancer's Choice,* plus some extraordinary previously uncollected poems, including "For the Last Wolverine" and "The Sheep Child" (both 1966) and "Falling" and "May Day Sermon" (both 1967). Richard Howard called the three hundred pages of poetry, "a decade's work, a lifetime's achievement."[58] Dickey was the subject of a big spread in *Life Magazine,* and Peter Davison in the *Atlantic Monthly* crowned Robert Lowell and Dickey the only major poets of their generation.[59] Following two terms as poetry consultant for the Library of Congress (today the poet laureate) in 1966–68, Dickey was employed at a generous salary (relative to poets) for the rest of his life by the University of South Carolina.

Dickey had fashioned himself into a neoromantic, which despite all his talent and originality, put him out of step with such contemporaries as Robert Lowell, James Merrill, and Allen Ginsberg. Dickey expressly distinguished himself from what he called Lowell's "confessional" poetry, "the solipsistic world of a single person." What Dickey attempted was something "essentially impersonal. It may have personal references in it, but the effect of the Lowell-type poetry is to close down the arena of the poem to one person's experience, that of the poet. . . . I wanted something different, larger, more inclusive."[60] The outsized split lines, the edifice of words on the page broken by dramatic gaps, were all tools to free himself from the "claustrophobia" of "locked-in verse": "I want, mainly, the kind of poetry that opens out, instead of closes down."[61]

Thus, despite his great success, he relentlessly tried to "make it new." The title of his next collection, *The Eye-Beaters, Blood, Victory, Madness, Buckhead and Mercy* (1970), illustrates that he was even less constrained by conventional forms, lengths, or diction. In "Blood" and "Pine" (both 1969) he composed more free verse, and he created even a kind of rhythmical prose in another 1969 poem, "The Cancer Match." He honed his technique of "associational imagery," as at the beginning of Pine": "Low-cloudly it whistles" and "so landscape is eyelessly / Sighing."[62] Dickey left behind "thumping" anapests,[63] vatic autobiographical moments, and traditional forms (including the repeated use of refrains) and tried once again to "make it new."

By 1968 Dickey was famous enough that Doubleday offered him a large bonus to sign with them. From the perspective of format, the poems in *The Eye-Beaters* differ more from their magazine appearances than those in any of his previous books. Dickey began to experiment with the appearance of text on the page with spacings that can be almost like dramatic directions, telling the reader how to read the poem aloud ("May Day Sermon"), or they can indicate action, such as the flight of butterflies ("Messages" [1969]). His new editors eventually agreed to an unusual oblong format for his volumes *The Zodiac* (1976) and *Strength of Fields* (1979).[64] Such features as the integral black page in the first part of "Apollo" (1969) were further proof of the visual importance of the page for the substance of Dickey's poems.[65] Yet, when the poems appeared in *The Eye-Beaters,* many of the spaces that had so distinguished the magazine forms of the poems were missing. It is not clear why magazines added these spaces, but Dickey's intentions are clear from the typescripts he sent to his publishers and from the final versions in his collections.

The year 1970 was truly an *annus mirabilis* for Dickey. In addition to a volume of verse, *The Eye-Beaters,* he published an account of his life and work, *Self-Interviews,* and the classic novel *Deliverance*. In 1971 came his journals and some essays, *Sorties*. These two years appear in retrospect as the watershed of his career.

Dickey became enraptured with the success of *Deliverance* both as novel and as movie (for which he wrote the screenplay[66] and in which he memorably appeared onscreen). Later in life he said, "I think sometimes that *Deliverance* was a mistake for me ever to have written."[67] To the envy of many he became too public a poet, too ready to sell his services to *Life* to memorialize officially the Apollo missions to the moon, or to write Jimmy Carter's inaugural poem ("The Strength of Fields"), or celebrate the 1983 inauguration of Richard W. Riley as governor of South Carolina ("For a Time and Place"). Dickey was the talk-show guest of Johnny Carson, Dick Cavett, Mike Douglas, Tom Snyder, and William F. Buckley, hawking his books and telling cornball stories. *Self-Interviews* and *Sorties* seemed to go out of their way to insult the contemporary poetic establishment (Robert Penn Warren had found Dickey as a critic "one of the roughest around"),[68] on top of which Dickey still suffered from the false charge, courtesy of Robert Bly, that he was a violence-prone pro-Vietnam racist pervert.[69]

The resentment of his colleagues did not bother Dickey, who, after the success of his novel—rather like Warren after the success of *All the King's Men*—laid his poetry aside awhile. He devoted himself to writing screenplays (*The Call of the Wild* [1976]) and commercially successful coffee-table books (*Jericho* [1974] and *God's Images* [1977]), reinforcing the negative opinion of his wounded contemporaries.

The glitter of Hollywood was replaced by the glow of Washington when Dickey's fellow Georgian Jimmy Carter was elected president in 1976. Dickey was once again on stage as part larger-than-life poet, part outsized personality.

In 1975 he had turned to a translation of a Dutch poem by Hendrik Marsman, another casualty of the war, a translation that appeared in the *Sewanee Review* in 1947 while Dickey was in college (see "The Zodiac"). Dickey's version is his own. Apart from its other characteristics, it employs the familiar play with format and the dramatic use of space on the page that characterized much of Dickey's recent work. So integral was the wide format that Doubleday changed the shape of the book from the 6" × 9" of *The Eye-Beaters* to 8.25" wide by 5.75" long to accommodate the long lines. The "wall of words" was no more, eliminating the need for a long page to "climb down."

Doubleday used the same format for *The Strength of Fields* (1979), in which "Some of the poems . . . employ a principle which I roughly refer to as 'balance.' . . . I try to 'true' things up, and give the poem a feel of hanging there, suspended: only precariously there."[70] The vast majority of the poems of the Doubleday phase of his career are centered on the page.

To the three modes of poetry Dickey described in *Sorties* (1971), he now added a fourth: "translation work and *mis*readings, from, say the German."[71] Dickey's only proficiency in a language other than English was in French, and his knowledge and love of modern French poetry were substantial. He had been fascinated by French poets and had been translating them since he was asked to provide some translations for Robert Bly in the early 1960s.[72] With *Head Deep in Strange Sounds* (1979) he finally collected his translations of his admired Lucien Becker, André Frénaud, and others, as well as translations of poets from Finland, Hungary, China, and elsewhere, many of whom he translated from French versions in books he had purchased in Paris in 1952. Dickey greatly admired the work of French poets such as André du Bouchet (see "Form"), Yves Bonnefoy, and other poets of the movement that became *poésie blanche* (white poetry) associated with the journal *L'Ephémère*, published between 1966 and 1973. White poetry, especially in the hands of du Bouchet, consisted of a few words or lines set unusually on the page with the intention of exploding the black letters off the stark white page into the mind of the reader. Dickey did not go as far as du Bouchet, but he clearly admired this new form and was influenced by it in his own experiments ("Messenger" [1969]).

His major period of celebrity over, Dickey settled into home life with his second wife, Deborah. "I got to thinking about the subject of young girls because I had married one, in my own late middle age. The marriage brought in a whole new set of possibilities to write about."[73] He claimed that he was "experience-oriented, rather than word-oriented. Or rather, I have been up until now. I'm sort of interested in trying the other way to see what there might be in that. . . . [*Puella*] has at least partly that approach to it."[74] He republished only eight of the twenty poems from *Puella* (1982) in *The Whole Motion*.[75] He had frequently narrated in the guise of another character, such as the Indian in "Remnant Water," the sheep child, a Dutch sailor in "The Zodiac," and women, particularly the stewardess in "Falling" and the female preacher in "May Day Sermon." By now "I had been writing poetry of the versified anecdote, as I called it. I thought I had not given enough primacy to the language itself in the sense that Hart Crane would have, or in some ways that Wallace Stevens would have. So I thought I would move over to the other side of things and try to write some poems that concentrated on language more than situations."[76]

Deborah Dickey was Catholic, and the flavor of the priest Gerard Manley Hopkins (1844–1889) runs from the epigraph to the unusual compound words, the fragmentary images, and the strange syntax:

poetry is not exciting to me to write if I take a subject in which I know I can use the same perspective and same kind of approach I have in others which have been accepted, printed, paid for and so on by the *New Yorker* or some such publication. That becomes a trick, hardly more than a tic, a conditioned reflex, a knee jerk. When the exploratory sense dies out of it, the sense of adventure, the excitement, it is just a routine and that's the last thing it should be. It was not going to become that to me. I don't know whether *Puella* is a great book of poems—whether it is successful—the main thing to me is that it is different, and a lot of possibilities opened up for me as a result of writing it that would not otherwise have been there. You have got to be prepared to fail or to take a chance, to gamble.[77]

Dickey returned to dactyls and anapests for some of the *Puella* poems, but unfortunately for him Doubleday returned to the traditional 6" × 9" format for this book, and the results did not always please him. For example, in "The Surround" (1980) line 8 was printed as a full line in its original appearance of the poem in the *Atlantic Monthly* earlier in the year, but it is broken at the end of *Puella* because of the book's format. Dickey complained of another setting: "In 'Ray-Flowers' it is not only desirable but necessary that the units presented in opposition to each other 'true-up' on the page as they do in the manuscript I sent. Some of the effect of balance I intended is undone by displaying the poem as it appears in the Doubleday version. There should not have been any difficulty in typography here, for there was none when the poem was printed as desired in the *Kenyon Review,* nor was there any trouble in the gift edition that our friend out in Arizona, Janet McHughes, had done for the occasion last May."[78]

Dickey began to rely almost exclusively on the visual effect of the words on the page, sometimes in the ancient Greek style of the *technopaegnion.* He had centered poems on the page as early as "The Courtship" and "Breath" (both 1963) and continued with "The Moon Ground" (1969). In *The Eagle's Mile* (1990) he manipulated words to create visual effects—as he had with "Messages" (1969)—and returned to the practice of centering poems on the page. To serve the purpose once met by rhythm or "word-bursts," he added stress marks to the words he intended the reader to emphasize.[79] Centering his split lines as if they were one line proved a continual challenge for typesetters, and Dickey was especially grateful to editors who got it right.[80] After *Puella* he focused again on translating, largely his French poets and the Spaniard Vicente Aleixandre. Nearly half of the poems after *Puella* were "collaborations" with these poets. His final poems show a renewed commitment to formal expression as he dealt with the death of his brother Tom and (finally) his first wife, Maxine, who had died in 1976.

ACQUIRING THE TEXTS

My first business was to gather all the known copies of the poems published by Dickey. I scanned all the poems in *Into the Stone; Drowning with Others; Helmets;*

Buckdancer's Choice; Poems 1957–1967; The Eye-Beaters, Blood, Victory, Madness, Buck-head and Mercy; The Strength of Fields; Puella; Night Hurdling; The Eagle's Mile; The Zodiac; and *The Whole Motion.* (Full citations of these and other books by Dickey may be found at the beginning of the apparatus criticus.) I also scanned all the poems in the Wesleyan reprint volumes *The Early Motion* (*Drowning with Others* and *Helmets*), *Falling,* and *The Central Motion* (*The Eye-Beaters, The Zodiac, The Strength of Fields,* and *Head Deep in Strange Sounds*). I have not scanned British or Australian editions as they were all set or pirated from the American editions. I then scanned bibliophile volumes of textual significance, such as *Veteran Birth, Head-Deep in Strange Sounds, Scion,* and *Striking In,* but not those of the bibliophile *Puella* or *Intervisions* as they were not produced under Dickey's control. Finally I scanned poems first published in translations of other poets (such as *Stolen Apples*), newspapers (the *New York Times*), obscure journals (such as *Corradi*), broadsides, and ceremonial printings (for example "The Drift-Spell") of textual significance. I then scanned all the first appearances of these collected poems in their various forms, usually in small limited-circulation literary journals or in important popular magazines. All scans were checked by eye for errors and corrected.

I began the collation process by comparing by eye the various print versions of each poem, from its first appearance, against its subsequent appearances in first editions of Dickey collections. I corrected textual errors observed in this fashion and then collated each poem electronically against each of its subsequent appearances in Dickey collections. At this point I constructed the initial form of the "variants" portion of each poem's apparatus, listing the preferred reading of the most reliable text first, then variant readings. The final step was a last collation by eye, checking and correcting the text and lists of variants.

THE PROBLEMS

Every editorial policy must address the particular difficulties of the author's texts. In trying to arrive at Dickey's settled intention at the period of his career with which each poem is most readily identified, nearly all the substantial problems arise not in the transition from manuscript to first publication but from magazine appearance to book. The problems are grouped below as 1) errors, 2) format, 3) revisions, and 4) double titles, rewrites, and "coupled poems."[81]

Errors

A small number of errors appear in each of Dickey's volumes up to *The Whole Motion* (1992). By some lights, the author's last intentions as expressed in his final publication of any given poem should be the basis for an authoritative edition of a text. In Dickey's case, however, this is difficult because *The Whole Motion* (1992) is full of defects. That there should be errors in *The Central Motion* (1983), which Wesleyan University Press transcribed from the books originally published by Doubleday,[82] is to be expected, but that the same press that originally published *Drowning with Others* and *Helmets* for *The Early Motion* (1981) and the poems from *Poems 1957–1967* in *Falling* (1981) should make errors in reprinting their own editions is startling. *The Whole Motion,* which represents the third time Wesleyan had printed many of these poems and the second time for others, should by then have been relatively error free.

Though Dickey might have had little incentive to proofread reprints, as was his normal practice ("I don't do anything in proof but look for typos because I've already worked on it so much that when I send in a typed copy it's exactly as I want it, else I don't send it"[83]), he nevertheless made a valiant effort to check the 475-page text of *The Whole Motion* and sent his editor a list of fifty-six errors in the proof copy.[84] Despite his attention to the text, *The Whole Motion* contains at least forty-three unique typographical errors.[85] Surprisingly nineteen of these come from books originally published by Wesleyan,[86] twelve from Doubleday books,[87] and twelve from other sources.[88] Particularly inexplicable are the seven errors introduced from correct printings in *The Early Motion*.[89] In addition there are eight typographical errors in *The Whole Motion* that are repeated from other prior collections for a total of at least fifty-one typographical errors.[90] Thus the rate of typographical errors in *The Whole Motion* is one for every 4.76 poems, an unacceptable rate.

Alterations in *The Whole Motion* not attributable to error—and therefore considered revisions—are few but problematic. The minor emendations are mostly improvements,[91] but major ones seem more like marginal comments than verse: at line 33 of "From Time," Dickey added "You bet." At line 481 in "The Zodiac," he added "I've said this somewhere."

As may be clear, Dickey's general practice was to rely on the presumed infallibility of the typesetter. He caught some errors at the proof stage in each of his books, but significant errors in the early collections continually escaped his attention and must be corrected here.[92]

Format

Poems employing the "wall of words," "word-burst," and "split-line" techniques have far longer lines than Dickey's previous poetry and were better suited to the magazine formats of the *New Yorker* and the *Atlantic Monthly* than to the normal octavo book. Many of the intentional and meticulously designed spaces presumably demarcating "word-bursts" that appeared in the *Atlantic Monthly, Harper's,* and especially the *New*

Yorker are absent from the book versions, thus creating difficulty for the editor. [93] This problem is evident in poems as early as some in as *Buckdancer's Choice* ("The Shark's Parlor") and continues in *The Eye-Beaters* ("Diabetes"). The unusual format of *The Zodiac* and *The Strength of Fields* helped but made oddly shaped volumes. When Doubleday returned to the normal 6" × 9" format for *Puella,* some lines intended to be whole broke to form turnover lines, such as line 4 of "In Lace and Whalebone."

Given Dickey's movement away from the heavily and regularly stressed beats with which he began, to the visual representation of thought process (split lines), to the purposefully created appearance of the poem on the page, be it a solid wall or a delicately balanced centerpiece, it is clear that intentional or unintentional alterations of format (the placement of blank lines or the placing of spaces between word groups within a line and even the use of punctuation) must be considered substantive changes or errors (assuming one makes the distinction between substantives and accidentals), because they alter the tone, rhythm, or meaning of the sequences in which they occur.

Punctuation issues parallel the problems of format change from magazine to book. While most magazines respected Dickey's spelling (such as "marvellous") as much as his formats, some publications, especially the *New Yorker* (in which Dickey published sixty poems), employed more conventional spelling and heavier punctuation than those used in the typescripts Dickey submitted to the editors. Dickey was quick to change his texts back to his own preferred spellings and punctuation for his collections, and thus I employ Dickey's punctuation and spelling as gleaned from each poem's first collected appearance. These changes represent his final intentions for the poems at the point in his career when the poems made their greatest impact.

Punctuation and format difficulties become especially problematic in the collections beginning with *The Eye-Beaters.* No published text captured what seemed to be the poet's intention: to have the format of the magazine appearances with the spelling and punctuation of the collected versions.

To resolve this problem, even though this edition concerns itself only with published versions of the poems, it might seem to have been useful to consult the staggering number of drafts available in the Dickey archives at Washington University in St. Louis and Emory University in Atlanta. Ideally Dickey would have kept a meticulous notebook recording each stage of each poem's composition in the manner of Philip Larkin. Less ideally one would have the advantage John Burt had of being able to discuss Robert Penn Warren's poetry with the author over a period of years. Unfortunately neither is possible in this case. In the entire Emory collection, for example, only one version of any poem bears an inscribed date (and the hand is not Dickey's),[94] and only a few drafts in either the Washington or Emory collections give clues to their chronology. True to his practice, Dickey did not even append specific dates to his journal entries in *Sorties* or *Striking In*. Apparently he believed that his intentions for a poem were expressed in the printed versions only and that his manuscripts exist merely to bear witness to his "mining of low-grade ore" approach to making verse.[95] Thus the closest and most consistent indication we have for the composition chronology of his poems is their date of publication.[96] This conclusion is surely a problematical way to proceed, but in Dickey's case it is the only option. Undated poems published long after their time of composition are among those included in a separate section titled "Poems of Uncertain Date."

Fortunately the Dickey Collection at Emory University contains the setting typescripts for *Into the Stone, Drowning with Others, The Eye-Beaters, The Strength of Fields, Puella,* and *The Eagle's Mile.*[97] When Dickey worked in advertising (1956–61), his wife, Maxine, did much of the final typing of his poems for publication. He had no direct secretarial support during his university appointments in 1963–66, though he had office help at the Library of Congress in 1966–68 and could afford a full-time personal secretary once he arrived at the University of South Carolina in 1968. Nevertheless, the uniformity of the copies and the continued use of carbon copies after the advent of Xeroxing and computerized word processing leads to the conclusion that either Dickey or his wife likely typed the first two books and that, when he began his experiments with spacing and centering on the page, he continued to type the final copies himself.

The carbons are arranged for the most part in the order in which the poems appear in their respective collections, making it likely that these poems were retyped by Dickey or his wife after their initial magazine appearances. Over the decades the typist(s) continued to follow conventions with regard to punctuation, placing two spaces after periods, colons, and semicolons, which often came near the middle of the line. This same typist regularly indicated the spaces between Dickey's "word-bursts" by three or four spaces. On first looking at the typed carbons, the reader may not find immediately obvious the distinction between two spaces after punctuation and three after "word-bursts"; that is, it appears that extra spaces are wanted after the punctuation marks. Closer examination reveals the typist's consistency over the years, and a perusal of the apparatus criticus makes it clear that almost all the spaces-in-the-line discrepancies between magazine and book appearance follow punctuation.[98] If the typescripts Dickey submitted to the magazines resembled these carbons, then one would almost be tempted to say that the magazines were in error, since Dickey wrote that the gaps in his lines were to appear with "no punctuation"; indeed the "spaces between the word groups would take the place of punctuation."[99] If the gaps in the line were to serve as a kind of punctuation, then a punctuation mark itself should serve the same function and a gap following it is extraneous. These carbon-copy setting typescripts, where available, are the best indication of Dickey's intentions with regard to format, punctuation, and spelling. I have relied on them for settling my copy text. I have not maintained or noted variants in the lineation of Dickey's relatively few long titles. [100]

Revisions

Dickey's poems seem to have been published fairly promptly,[101] especially by such journals as *Poetry*, to which Dickey contributed thirty-three poems, and the *New Yorker*, where poems by Dickey appeared in seven issues in the thirty-two weeks between May 21 and December 24, 1960, and seven times in the twenty-four weeks between June 24 and December 2, 1961.

Once published, the poems were often collected within a year or two up through the appearance of *Poems 1957–1967* in 1967. While Dickey often restored his original spelling and punctuation when necessary (especially in poems initially published by the *New Yorker*),[102] he changed titles less often.[103] He corrected errors[104] and occasionally made either substantial revisions[105] (as in "A Saying of Farewell," "In the Child's Night," and "Slave Quarters")[106] or rewrote an entire poem (such as "Springer Mountain" and "Purgation"). In general, however, once a poem was published in a collection supervised by Dickey, it was not subsequently changed in later printings overseen by him.[107] Though I have tended to read the author's carbon copies of typescripts sent to the book publisher as reliable indicators of the author's intention for each poem *at that stage in his career,* one must still consider the version collected by the author as primary.

There is, however, a group of poems that Dickey did revise more aggressively than others. These are his juvenilia (*Veteran Birth* [1978]) and apprentice work (*Striking In* [1996]). To print revised versions of a poem thirty to forty years after its initial publication would defeat the purpose of the chronological arrangement of the poems. Had Dickey made continual revisions throughout his career, as did Auden and Warren, for instance, a different editorial policy might have been called for.

Double Titles, Rewrites, and Coupled Poems

Dickey changed titles,[108] but he also recycled them: "I often write poems on the same theme. I feel like I didn't get out of it the first time. I had the wrong approach, and there's nothing says I can't go around and try again. It's like when the tower waves you off on a landing, you go around the pattern and come back again. You try it another way. Any subject has an infinitude of possibilities, and if I'm not satisfied with the way I did the first time, I just take the whole thing and start in from another angle."[109]

Dickey wrote two poems titled "Under Buzzards" (1963 and 1969 as the second part of "Diabetes") and two labeled "Springer Mountain" (1962 and 1964).[110] He also wrote two poems called "Reincarnation" (both 1964), and he published two versions of "Purgation" (1979 and 1980). The title of "Amputee Ward: Okinawa, 1945" (1948) is repeated as a tag line at the heads of "The Work of Art" (1957) and "The Contest" (1950s). "A Beginning Poet, Aged Sixty-Five" (1958) and "To Landrum Guy, Beginning to Write at Sixty" (1960) treat a similar subject.

In collected volumes after 1967, Dickey began to gather two or more poems together—as in "On the Coosawattee" (1962–64), "The Owl King" (1959–60 and 1961–62), "Two Poems of Flight-Sleep" (1970 and 1973), "Apollo" or "Two Poems of Going Home." This coupling of poems may have begun with his publication in the *New Yorker* of "Poems of North and South Georgia" (1962) or in the calligraphic bibliophile version of "The Firebombing" and "Reincarnation (II)" as *Two Poems of the Air* (1964).[111] In most cases these coupled poems were written within a year or two and gathered within a year after that.[112] In other cases, however, the poems were written years apart and represent significantly different-in-time responses to a similar situation: "Two Poems of Flight-Sleep," for example, describe training for combat ("Camden Town") and memories of combat ("Reunioning Dialogue"). Some coupled poems were written within a short time period and make no distinct thematic statement together that they do not make separately. "For the First Manned Moon Orbit" and "The Moon Ground" were published in January and July 1969 and coupled as "Apollo," with an added epigraph. In trying to determine the forms of the poems that had the most meaning for Dickey's career, I generally kept joined poems such as "Apollo" as one poem while poems he grouped as separate poems (for example "Two Poems of Flight-Sleep") as individual poems.

I was recently discussing this project with a sophisticated and well-connected literary friend in New York. At one point he said, "I did not know James Dickey wrote poetry *also*" (emphasis added). That *Deliverance* has become an American classic novel and film has certainly obscured Dickey's renown as a poet. For all his grandstanding and barnstorming for poetry, Dickey felt, as he once told Johnny Carson, that his natural home was in the back pages of small literary magazines, not in the glare of the media. While no edition can perfectly reflect an author's process of composition, his artistic development, or even his own wishes for such a collection, one hopes at least to do justice to a good man and a long career in the service of literature by projecting as accurately as possible the arc of a poet who rose to extraordinary prominence and sank away into near oblivion, his books out of print, his poems barely anthologized, his biography a welter of stories of outsize charm, hilarious repartee, and scandalously inappropriate behavior. Perhaps a reconsideration of his work will overcome the focus on his personality, and Dickey will be like the beasts in his "Heaven of Animals": "They fall, they are torn, / They rise, they walk again."

NOTES

1. William Wordsworth, "The Prelude," 10:83. Dickey also named W. S. Graham, Theodore Roethke, and John Berryman as poets of the second birth.

2. "The Second Birth," in *The Suspect in Poetry* (Madison, Minn.: Sixties Press, 1964), 55.

3. "For the Death of Lombardi," lines 27–31.

4. Terry Roberts, "Getting to the Gold," *Arts Journal* 7 (May 1982): 114; republished in *Night Hurdling: Poems, Essays, Conversations, Commencements, and Afterwords* (Columbia & Bloomfield Hills: Bruccoli Clark, 1983), 241. See also *New York Quarterly* 10 (Spring 1972): 33; *Texas Review* 5 (Spring/Summer 1984): 81.

5. *Night Hurdling*, 185.

6. William Heyen and Peter Marchant, "A Conversation with James Dickey," *Southern Review*, n.s. 9 (January 1973): 135–56; republished in *Night Hurdling*, 287.

7. *Night Hurdling*, 186.

8. Harold Bloom, introduction to *Modern Critical Views: James Dickey* (New York: Chelsea House, 1987), 13.

9. Roberts, "Getting to the Gold," 43; republished in *Night Hurdling*, 232.

10. *Sorties: Journals and New Essays* (Garden City, N.Y.: Doubleday, 1971), 122.

11. Monroe K. Spears, "James Dickey's Poetry," *Southern Review* 30 (Autumn 1994): 752.

12. Calhoun Winton, "James Dickey at Vanderbilt: A Memoir," in *Critical Essays on James Dickey*, edited by Robert Kirschten (New York: G. K. Hall, 1994), 76.

13. Ibid.

14. *Self-Interviews*, recorded and edited by Barbara and James Reiss (Garden City, N.Y.: Doubleday, 1970; reprinted, Baton Rouge: Louisiana State University, 1984), 85.

15. *The Water Bug's Mittens: Ezra Pound—What We Can Use* (Columbia & Bloomfield Hills: Bruccoli Clark, 1980); republished in *Night Hurdling*, 31.

16. P. Ivan Young, "A Day on the Razor's Edge: An Interview with James Dickey," *Yemassee* 5 (Winter/Spring 1998): 12–13.

17. *Babel to Byzantium: Poets & Poetry Now* (New York: Farrar, Straus & Giroux, 1968), 283.

18. *Self-Interviews*, 84. "I think it's because I had kind of a thump-loving American ear. I like heavy rhythms. There seems to be a sound going on all the time in my head, all night, even in my sleep, what I call the night rhythm. It has that basic sound to it. It's an anapest, I guess. I know from reading poetry that this is frowned on as a kind of basic rhythm for a given poem. People constantly cite Poe, for example. That is, it has such a mechanical sound, a conveyer belt kind of tendency where the meaning is just sort of loaded onto the meter and the meter just carries it along like a conveyer belt. But that rhythm, that powerful, surging rhythm, is so strong. Suppose the material you were dealing with was good, was imaginative in its own right. That meter would

give it such force, such a hypnotic quality, that it might be worth trying. So I tried it and wrote the first book, a couple of books, mainly in that. I never regretted it. I'd do it again." (Donald J. Greiner, "Making the Truth: James Dickey's Last Major Interview," *James Dickey Newsletter* 23 [Fall 2006]: 8).

19. Heyen and Marchant, "A Conversation with James Dickey," 145; republished in *Night Hurdling*, 286. "The Performance" is an exception.

20. Ibid.

21. *The Early Motion* (Middletown, Conn.: Wesleyan University Press, 1981), vii; republished in *Night Hurdling*, 113.

22. Paul Christensen, "Ritual Magic: An Interview with James Dickey," *Lone Star Review* 3 (July/August 1981): 4; republished in *Night Hurdling*, 222.

23. Greiner, "Making the Truth," 22.

24. See also "Reincarnation (II)," line 206.

25. See also "The Being," lines 11–12; "Cherrylog Road," line 85; "The Firebombing," lines 82–88; "The Eye-Beaters," lines 5–6; "Madness," line 103; "The Lifeguard," line 60; and "Messages," line 4 (four repetitions). For triple anaphora of a phrase, see "Them, Crying," lines 31–32; "Angina," lines 58–59; "Rein-carnation (II), lines 158–59; "Adultery," lines 24–25; and "Camden Town," lines 29–30. For multiple anaphora see "False Youth: Summer," lines 41–43, and "Pine," lines 11–12.

26. See also "The Lifeguard," line 60.

27. He ended "Bread" (1967) with a line from Coleridge, "The Strength of Fields" (1976) with a quotation from Alun Lewis, and his essay "Enemy from Eden (Blowjob on a Rattlesnake)" (1978) with Christopher Smart's "Determined, Dared, Done."

28. *The Early Motion*, vii; republished in *Night Hurdling*, 113.

29. "An ear and an appetite for these sounds of sense is the first qualification of a writer, be it of prose or verse. But if one is to be a poet he must learn to get cadences by skillfully breaking the sounds of sense with all their irregularity of accent across the regular beat of the metre" (Robert Frost to John T. Bartlett, July 4, 1913; see also Frost's letter to Sidney Cox, January 19, 1914, in *Robert Frost: Selected Letters,* edited by Lawrance Thompson (New York: Holt, Rinehart & Winston, 1964), 80, 107.

30. *The Early Motion*, viii; republished in *Night Hurdling*, 114.

31. On Dickey's use of the refrain in general, see "The String" (1959).

32. "Play for Voices," *Night Hurdling*, 195.

33. *The Early Motion*, viii; republished in *Night Hurdling*, 114.

34. Christensen, "Ritual Magic," republished in *Night Hurdling*, 225; see also *Night Hurdling*, 313.

35. "Play for Voices," 191.

36. Pound, *Make It New* (London: Faber & Faber, 1934). See Dickey's *The Suspect in Poetry* (Madison, Minn.: Sixties Press, 1964), 9: "To follow a current style is effrontery."

37. Bruce Joel Hillman, "At Home: The Voices of James Dickey," *Writer's Yearbook 1981* 52 (1981): 33; republished in *Night Hurdling*, 321.

38. "Springer Mountain [b]" (1964), lines 96–98.

39. *Falling*, viii; republished in *Night Hurdling*, 118.

40. *Self-Interviews,* 140.

41. *Sorties,* 107–8. "Country surrealism" refers to poems composed of "violence and the grotesque."

42. "The Death and Keys of the Censor," *Sewanee Review* 69 (Spring 1961): 322–24; republished in *Babel to Byzantium,* 136–39; see also "Confession Is Not Enough," *New York Times Book Review,* July 9, 1961, 14. For Dickey's thesis and its importance in his poetry, see notes to "Reincarnation (II)" in the apparatus.

43. "Projective Verse," in *Selected Writings,* edited by Robert Creeley (New York: New Directions, 1967), 19. For Olson "breath is the new principle that liberates poetry from set meters, the sounds of language free the poem from the strict conventions of syntax and logic." Paul Christensen, *Charles Olson, Call Him Ishmael* (Austin: University of Texas Press, 1979), 78.

44. "Projective Verse," 22.

45. *Babel to Byzantium,* 136–37.

46. Ibid., 137–38.

47. Letter to James Boatwright, November 3, 1963, *Crux: The Letters of James Dickey,* edited by Matthew J. Bruccoli and Judith S. Baughman (New York: Knopf, 1993), 207.

48. "Craft Interview with James Dickey," *New York Quarterly* 10 (Spring 1972): 29; republished in *Night Hurdling,* 305.

49. Christensen, "Ritual Magic," 4. See in particular, "Drinking from a Helmet."

50. Dickey was fond of citing Mozart's saying that the finest music was no music, that is, the pauses between notes, where the sensitive ear anticipated the next note and reflected on the last.

51. *Self-Interviews,* 184–85.

52. *The Writer's Voice: Conversations with Contemporary Writers,* conducted by John Graham and edited by George Garrett (New York: Morrow, 1973): 231. See also *Falling,* viii; republished in *Night Hurdling,* 117–18; and "An Interview with James Dickey," *Eclipse* 5 (1966): 8, where he said, "It's a kind of impressionistic technique which as nearly as I can tell approximates as close as I myself can get to the way the mind really associates, and it doesn't really associate in sentences so much as it does in word clusters."

53. *Sorties,* 65; *Self-Interviews,* 140.

54. Christensen, "Ritual Magic," 5; republished in *Night Hurdling,* 224.

55. *Falling,* vii; republished in *Night Hurdling,* 116.

56. Ibid.

57. Dickey to James Bexley, September 4, 1969, in Hart, *James Dickey,* 416.

58. Richard Howard, *Alone with America* (New York: Atheneum, 1969), 96; republished in Bloom, ed., *Modern Critical Views: James Dickey,* 59.

59. Paul O'Neill, "The Unlikeliest Poet," *Life* 61 (July 22, 1966): 68–70, 72–74; Peter Davison, "The Difficulties of Being Major: The Poetry of Robert Lowell and James Dickey," *Atlantic Monthly* 220 (October 1967): 116–21.

60. Christensen, "Ritual Magic," 3; republished in *Night Hurdling,* 219.

61. *Sorties,* 8–9.

62. Well explained by Ronald Baughman in *Understanding James Dickey* (Columbia: University of South Carolina Press, 1985), 17–18.

63. *Self-Interviews,* 48.

64. *Tucky the Hunter* (1978) was published by Crown in a similar oblong format.

65. For example "Victory" (1968) represents the twining snake winding around the body. The lines take the shape of body parts.

66. *Deliverance* (Carbondale & Edwardsville: Southern Illinois University Press, 1982).

67. Thorne Compton, "Imagination at Full Stretch: An Interview with James Dickey," *James Dickey Newsletter* 20 (Fall 2003): 41.

68. See Franklin Ashley, "James Dickey: The Art of Poetry XX," *Paris Review* 17 (Spring 1976): 70.

69. Robert Bly, who had previously praised Dickey in "The Work of James Dickey," *Sixties* 7 (Winter 1964): 41–57, attacked "*Buckdancer's Choice*" in "The Collapse of James Dickey," *Sixties* 9 (Spring 1967): 70–79.

70. *Night Hurdling*, 224.

71. *Sorties*, 108.

72. See Dickey to Robert Bly, June 30, 1962, *Crux*, 184–89.

73. *Night Hurdling*, 233.

74. Ibid., 313.

75. Because of a typesetting error discovered only at the proof stage, at least six *Puella* poems were not included in *The Whole Motion*. Dickey omitted six others. In all twelve poems from *Puella* were not included: "Deborah Burning a Doll Made of House-Wood," "Deborah, Moon, Mirror, Right Hand Rising," "Deborah and Deirdre as Drunk Bridesmaids Foot-Racing at Daybreak," "Veer-Voices: Two Sisters Under Crows," "Deborah in Ancient Lingerie, In Thin Oak Over Creek," "Heraldic: Deborah and Horse in Morning Forest," "Ray-Flowers I," "Ray-Flowers II," "The Lyric Beasts," "The Surround," "Summons," and "Deborah in Mountain Sound: Bell, Glacier, Rose." See Dickey's letter to David Havird, June 9, 1992, in Van Ness, ed., *The One Voice of James Dickey,* 2:483.

76. Greiner, "Making the Truth," 15.

77. Compton, "Imagination at Full Stretch," 34.

78. Letter to his former student Shaye Areheart, a Doubleday editor, December 13, 1982, in Van Ness, *The One Voice of James Dickey*, 2: 388. The letter refers to a 1982 limited edition of *Puella* produced by the Pyracantha Press at Arizona State University in Tempe.

79. A practice begun with "Patience: In the Mill" (ca. 1957).

80. He complimented the editor of the *Amicus Journal* for setting up "The Olympian" "better than anyone else has ever done one of these 'balanced' poems of mine" (*Crux*, 424).

81. That is, two or more poems grouped under a collective title, such as "Two Poems of Flight-Sleep."

82. *The Eye-Beaters, The Zodiac,* and *The Strength of Fields*, along with *Head-Deep in Strange Sounds.* Dickey maintained some errors and introduced one in "Diabetes" at line 93 and another in "Looking for the Buckhead Boys" at line 61, which remained uncorrected in *The Whole Motion*.

83. Greiner, "Making the Truth," 24.

84. Letter of September 12, 1983, to Jeanette Hopkins at Wesleyan University Press, *The Whole Motion* file, box 123, Manuscripts, Archives, and Manuscript Library, Emory University.

85. As Sidney Lew wrote in his review of *The Whole Motion*, "It seems scandalous that a poet of Dickey's stature should have a volume of collected poetry in which no dates for prior

collections appear, and in which there is no index of first lines or titles. . . . And it seems even more scandalous that faulty proofreading is so commonplace" (*Georgia Review* 47 [Fall 1993]: 609). I do not include as typographical errors broken lines, inserted blank lines, or some revisions that may in fact be errors.

86. *Drowning with Others:* 6 errors, *Helmets:* 2, *Buckdancer's Choice:* 3, *Poems 1957–1967:* 4, *The Eagle's Mile:* 4.

87. *The Eye-Beaters:* 5 errors, *The Zodiac:* 0, *The Strength of Fields:* 7, *Puella:* 0.

88. Two errors occur in poems appearing in The *Whole Motion* for the first time: "The Baggage King" and "The Place of the Skull."

89. "Antipolis," line 21; "The Change," line 1; "Summons," line 1; "A Screened Porch in the Country," line 6; "Snow on a Southern State," line 26; "The Being," line 44; "Goodbye to Serpents," line 6.

90. One error was introduced in *Buckdancer's Choice* and continued in *Poems 1957–1967* and *The Whole Motion:* "The Fiend," line 12. Two errors introduced in *Poems 1957–1967* are present in *The Whole Motion:* "Into the Stone," line 5, and "Kudzu," lines 52–53. One error introduced in *Poems 1957–1967* remains in *Falling* and *The Whole Motion:* "Reincarnation (II)," line 37. One error in *The Strength of Fields* persists in *The Central Motion* and *The Whole Motion:* "For the Death of Lombardi," line 13. One error in *The Central Motion* recurs in *The Whole Motion:* "Diabetes," line 93.

91. At line 15 in "When," *The Whole Motion* has "I'll" while every other version has "I." In "From Time," line 28, "Bach" is changed to "Mozart" in *The Whole Motion*, then at 32 "the past" becomes "Bach and his gist." In "The Firebombing," line 70, "that" is changed to "this."

92. Errors introduced in *Poems 1957–1967* that continued in later editions are at line 5 in "Into the Stone," lines 52–53 in "Kudzu," and line 37 in "Reincarnation (II)." The misspelling of "Nitschke" at line 13 in "For the Death of Lombardi" was introduced in The *Strength of Fields.* An error at line 93 of "Diabetes" was introduced in *The Central Motion.*

93. For example "Mercy" in the *Atlantic Monthly* (1969), "Haunting the Maneuvers" in *Harper's* (1970), and "Camden Town" in *Virginia Quarterly Review* (1970).

94. "False Youth Spring: The Olympian" (Emory, box 97, folder 2) is inscribed (not in Dickey's hand) "finished 2/26/82."

95. For example, on "Sleeping Out at Easter," see Janet Larsen McHughes, "From Manuscript to Performance Script: The Evolution of a Poem," *Literature in Performance* 2 (November 1981): 26–49, and on "The Flash," see "James Dickey: Worksheets," *Malahat Review* no. 7 (July 1968): 113–17.

96. *Crux* includes some letters in which Dickey described working on various poems (such as "The First Morning of Cancer" and "The Red Bow," 102).

97. The Emory file for *Drowning with Others* is missing "Dover: Believing in Kings."

98. For example see lines 11 and 25 of "Root-Light, or the Lawyer's Daughter" in the *New Yorker.*

99. *Babel to Byzantium,* 290.

100. "To Landrum Guy, Beginning to Write at Sixty," "Hunting Civil War Relics at Nimblewill Creek," "For the Nightly Ascent of the Hunter Orion Over a Forest Clearing," "A Poem about Bird-Catching by One Who Has Never Caught A Bird," "May Day Sermon to the Women of Gilmer

County, Georgia, by a Woman Preacher Leaving the Baptist Church," "Deborah Burning a Doll Made of House-Wood," "Deborah, Moon, Mirror, Right Hand Rising," "Heraldic: Deborah and Horse in Morning Forest," "Springhouse, Menses, Held Apple, House and Beyond," "Deborah in Mountain Sound: Bell, Glacier, Rose," "Deborah in Ancient Lingerie, in Thin Oak over Creek," Deborah and Deirdre as Drunk Bridesmaids Foot-Racing at Daybreak."

101. Once submitted for publication a poem might sit on an editor's desk for a while. "The Shark at the Window" was accepted by the *Sewanee Review* in 1947 or 1948 but was not published until 1951 (Spears, "James Dickey's Poetry," 752–53).

102. The *New Yorker* regularly altered Dickey's compound words printing "junk yard" for "junkyard" ("Cherrylog Road," line 102), "half-track" for "halftrack" ("The Driver," line 15), "ice cap" for "icecap" ("Pursuit from Under," line 20). This also happened with other journals, such as the *Southern Review* ("Sled Burial," line 20) and the *Virginia Quarterly Review* ("Gamecock," line 10). The *New Yorker* also liked the dramatic dash (as in "The Common Grave," line 42, and "Them, Crying," line 64). The magazine also imposed new commas ("Orpheus before Hades" or "The Salt Marsh"), swapped colons for semicolons, and capitalized ("Snow on a Southern State"). Dickey did sometimes change his own punctuation; "The Being," for instance, is punctuated differently in *Early Motion* than in *Helmets*, with the poet deleting commas in the last line (69) to reflect his post-*Helmets* graphic representation style.

103. "Below the Lighthouse" (1959) became "On the Hill below the Lighthouse" (1960); "To a Beginning Poet, Aged Sixty" (1960) became "To Landrum Guy, Beginning to Write at Sixty" (1962); "At Darien Bridge, Georgia" (1962) became "At Darien Bridge" (1964); "Sled Burial: Dream Ceremony" (1965) became "Sled Burial, Dream Ceremony" (1965); "False Youth: Summer" (1965) became "Summer: Porch-Wings" (1983), and "False Youth: Winter" (1966) became "Winter: Thumb-Fire" (1983); "The Sheep-Child" (1966) became "The Sheep Child" (1967); "May Day Sermon to the Women of Gilmer County by a Lady Preacher Leaving the Baptist Church" (1967) became "May Day Sermon to the Women of Gilmer County, Georgia, by a Woman Preacher Leaving the Baptist Church" (1967); "For the Death of Vince Lombardi" (1971) became "For the Death of Lombardi" (1971); "Water-Magic in Sunlight: The Voyage of the Needle" (1978) became "The Voyage of the Needle" (1979)

104. He corrected "nipa" to "napa" in "The Enclosure" and "Euclid" to "Diogenes" in "The String." In "Cherrylog Road" he changed the name of the girl the protagonist meets for sex in the junkyard from Charlotte Holbrook, the name of a high-school acquaintance and his boss's wife, to Doris Holbrook.

105. As, for example, Robert Lowell famously altered the ninth stanza of "Waking Early Sunday Morning" between its initial appearance in the *New York Review of Books* in 1965 and its republication in *Near the Ocean* (1967).

106. The most heavily redacted of his *New Yorker* poems is "Slave Quarters," portions of which were not printed by the magazine. For its appearance in *Buckdancer's Choice,* Dickey restored the cuts and even deleted a portion of the published poem. This poem also is unusual in that there are substantial differences between its first book publication in *Buckdancer's Choice* (reprinted in *The Whole Motion*) and its appearance in *Poems 1957–1967.* Dickey radically altered the end of "Breath" from its *New Yorker* publication for its appearance in *Helmets*, changing the poem's meaning. The end of "Horses and Prisoners" was also altered from its first appearance, in the

Hudson Review. Nineteen of the thirty-six lines of "In the Child's Night" were changed from that poem's initial publication in the *Virginia Quarterly Review* (for the broadside version, see the apparatus criticus).

107. For example, after "Dover: Believing in Kings" was published in *Drowning with Others,* he changed line 59 for *Poems 1957–1967* and changed line 160 after the poem appeared in *Poems 1957–1967.*

108. For example, "Wetlands Bridge" was changed to "Meadow Bridge." For consistency I use the title found in the first collected edition, thus the poem titled "At Darien Bridge, Georgia" in the *New Yorker* is "At Darien Bridge," as in *Helmets.*

109. *The Voiced Connections of James Dickey,* 80.

110. In *Striking In* he grouped "The Contest" and "The Work of Art" together as "Two Versions of the Same Poem."

111. I do not count "Two Poems" in *Poetry* 82 (June 1953): 137–39 ("The Child in Armor" and "The Anniversary").

112. "The Owl King" (1962) comprises "The Call" (1959) and "The Owl King" (1961); "On the Coosawattee" (1964) comprises "By Canoe through the Fir Forest" (1962), "Below Ellijay" (1962), and "On the Inundation of the Coosawattee Valley" (1963); "Fathers and Sons" (1965) comprises "The Second Sleep," (1964) and "The Aura" (1965); "False Youth: Two Seasons" comprises "False Youth: Summer" (1965) and "False Youth: Winter" (1966). In *The Eye-Beaters* Dickey grouped two poems under one title four times: "Apollo" (1970) comprises "For the First Manned Moon Orbit" (1969) and "The Moon Ground" (1969); "Two Poems of Going Home" (1970) comprises "Living There" (1969) and "Looking for the Buckhead Boys" (1969); "Diabetes" (1969) comprises "Sugar" (1969) and "Under Buzzards" (1963); "Messages" (1970) comprises "Butterflies" and "Giving a Son to the Sea"; "Pine" (1970) comprises "Pine: Sound," Pine: Smell" (1969), and "Pine: Taste, Touch and Sight" (1969). In *Strength of Fields* "Two Poems of the Military" comprises "Haunting the Maneuvers" (1970) and "Drums Where I Live" (1969); "Two Poems of Flight Sleep" comprises "Camden Town" (1970) and "Reunioning Dialogue" (1973).

1947–1960

Christmas Shopping, 1947
1947

Wingless, wayworn, aging beneath a perpetual
folded sun, despair unsounded in the eyes' drum,
these wheel in lax processional
past the cold counter and listless stall;
desire in rayon, in cellophane the dream.   5
Outside, the day, the frozen intercourse of streets;
glass placid, grave glitter of guilt and gift
bear single witness to the bartered birth, recall

the lip, the sponge, the God-swung temple-lash.
But here the current of the five wounds fails,   10
the igneous cross no longer lights the mesh
and marrow of the hugely living. The bulging present fills
all calendars with gowns and tumbling clowns who fall
to end the sting. I think of chestnut waters
linked back to back with autumn floating leaves,   15
the flow of stallions over cloud-white hills.

Sea Island
1948

One harbor's history is the beam
Swung from a searchlight's heavy dream,
Where shrimpers ride from painted docks
And night has water-killed the clocks.

Once more the tide-trimmed shadows run   5
Afearing to the sunken sun,
But kelp-thick meadows do not heed
The winter bunching star and seed.

Like energies divorced from maps
The glossy misspent waves collapse.   10
Discharted and sold out to sleep
They twist a hush with froth-cold creep.

A watcher on these mirror sands
Grows Himalayan, understands
Why jasmine birds in opal trees   15
Assemble futures at his knees.

––––––––––

King Crab and Rattler
1948

A page that makes a simple counterfoil
Of cages in this stall of August heat
Spreads on an unused lectern of the mind:
Collusive crab and rampant snake defeat
All enterprise, enisled and spectre-blind,   5
And mythic shapes embroil
The quick.

Escape is *in,* shell-harbored flight,
To such a one, humped in his armored dark.
The snake, involved and weaving to his mark,　　　　10
Brute-fangs a death through amber drifts of light.
Only the acts are human, never the wills.

Contusion or decay of rationale
Locks love in hermit skull, deploys
In therianthropic dusk along canal　　　　15
The unsuspecting breast the tooth destroys
Or loving kills.

Also our deaths are cage-kept: Waves
Clash over crab at throat and kelp-cold wrist.
The rattler coils, (a tongue and pliant twist)　　　　20
His toxic ring on monumental graves.

————————

Reflections in a Bloodstone Ring
1948

This moveless anonymous sector,
Seagarnished and vein-flecked, grows past the shade
And rapt insouciance of classic head, and holds
The chaliced face in structures of regret.
The darkling eye, thrust through supernal screen　　　　5
Or window in the hovering fog of breath,
Stands open to the winter of the will
Or climbs carved rungs of spine to find its end.

A fatal process, like beckoning to the blind,
Bends blood and ivy round a sunless glen.　　　　10
Death's diamond delves the socket of the rose,
And perfect love subsists without a kiss.

Amputee Ward
Okinawa, 1945
1948

Displayed in acreages of crackling light
More hopeless than the spatulate cross
Thrust by a withering sea, they lie
In the immaculate percentage of their loss.

One plunges like a porpoise; his furrowed face,   5
The shape of rotting blood, leaves him forever.
One winnows sheets like thorns, and water-crazed,
Explores extravagant jungle-trails of fever.

Here each is desperate duchy in the floes:
An angelus of anguish bells their fall   10
As photographs betray them; gifts and girls
Perfect a fearful violence, worst wound of all.

The medics in their sterile winter-world
With hands like guttering fountains underground
Are sightless nomads, and leaves of shaken breath   15
Vast cacti in the desert of a wound.

Their blood drives all their debtors from the clock
In tides that move beyond a kissproof dawn.
Locution fails. To traverse this lost ground
Past poem's periphery: transfixion of the swan.   20

Whittern and the Kite
1949

In the old 5th Air Force, three hundred combat hours entitled a pilot to return to the states.
After all his time had been logged there was nothing for the pilot to do but wait for orders.
Some of them, like Whittern, were hard put to find anything to do during this period.

Here where the Bird-of-Freedom birds unloft
To blood the blood sun down its Shinto white,
The Spirit o' Whittern trembles, wags to lift
A casual strand into stark, manned light.
Whittern, malarial, his final mission bland   5
On the yellow sheets, squints from his beaked shade
Up past soft-writhing tents and limed clay flats
Sun-overborne but somehow baseline-lined
By boys who play queer pasts against a raid
Or trudge to the chutestack with their sewn-in kits   10

All pause, look up. The exile's sapient nod
Lends to the handled air such guileless grace
That bursts of metal rising to the Rod
Are patched with humor to a boyish place.
Our Clausewitz colonel, pledged and Undefiled,   15
Gut sunk in battle-lure, and of a mind
Inimical to kites, stares like a loon:
This war is leashed, prolapsed and waving—mild,
As if Headquarters jeeped bombed glades to find
Girls talking lilacs on the fiery noon.   20

The Shark at the Window
1951

for my brother's marriage

I

Driving home from your wedding in light-
blunting fog, the road I inchmeal held
Dropt instantly, I could not guess it, great
White sail-settled and drew, and I gained there
A sanctum of midnight cloud, a float of trusts.   5

More than the repartitions of the womb, my brother,
That pilgrim-place has cast our centered bloods:
Renewal, oneness are there; our semblances fail.
We enter to find ourselves the same in love,
In kinship, as the tussled cloth about   10
A river-reed's needle, a stitching snag, can
Never alter, but renders Platonist and caddis
Fly the selfsame cordonnet, as of point-laced, ancient,
Vital hair, though the water move
More calmly than the waters of a grape, or mull   15
Sienna-spread and vastly wild
Under ephemerae of mule and leaf.

II

Brother in the window welcome,
Welcome brother at the seatrap
Glass. Near ghost, your lacquered   20
Shade drops off and waits—
Aqueous, breathclouded, seeming.
Our centers meet.

III

Flesh that would have stood in finished grainfields
(The round hard thumb, the eye, the wheaten hair)   25
In the pollened, trampled fore of Tartar horse,
And to the slung and sighflown spin of blade have
Sung, as it brownly, brightly cropped
Matted and cruel lives
                   stood off from you once   30
In aquarium glass. We watched it from our uncertain place,
And watched its next-to, brotherly image, and the fraught
Protected waters for a sign.
                   Balanced,
A huge and casual leaf   35
Fall, through shivered trays of stacked
Autumnal light
Our symbol subsided to us.
We marked behind our shapes of breath
The smeared and old man's mouth, the slatted   40
Gills, the absolute and unknown terror,
The closest conch that might be trembled into.

It was fear first pressed
Us through that pearled and helical threshold where
No adumbrations pass.   45

Expecting the dark, we found the shapen cupping
Resplendent with the light we made.

Gray and pink volution wore
Our whispers back in rounds.

A single voice became in those one-weltered sounds.   50

In the shell of the bridal
Chamber, in the still sump of midnight,
Know without fear

This with her.

Of Holy War

1951

O sire, I dreamed
You danced with greaves
Afire (it seemed)
At Acre, or leaves
In Caen gave on   5
A peregrine:
Coal under plume
Penumbrally seen.

That phoenix watched.
Rood and gate   10
Embered and percht
His spreaded weight.
Sire, flee this shadow.
I grass his meadow.

———————

The Child in Armor

1953

On such a day I see him at a window
Or a casement, urging shut
The sky in which the sun is caught
Above the stone enclosing that precise
Gray with which my fantasy is bought,   5
Not turning, but feeling with his mace,
That lifts itself, how
Free the outer air is, and of what pace.

On his light breast shine
Lion's paw, pine cone, in a crest   10

I cannot wholly take for mine.
His arms are weighted with a thought he has not furnished;
That which moves them is part me,
Part of my time and his, letting the burnished
Innocent falconry of arms   15
Ride the green fields, and burn or rest in them.

His face is shut from me,
A light and grated anvil. It is all lovely.
Somewhere a hound barks, and suddenly the window
Is green with moss, the sun is out,   20
The helm is opening. He lifts now
A sword with no will but his own,
And I sit here in the light, gazing not at his visor
But at my ancient son, with nothing but his armament renewed.

—————

The Anniversary
1953

She is who,
Aligned to joy,
A candle's blue
And quiet alloy,
Took me as wonder   5
Far into summer,
Allayed the ear
Come down through fear,
Broke clear as hazard
And perisht hard   10
Against the breast
The sun not help
Nor moon destroy,
Left whole the beast
And bled the boy.   15

By lights and signs
Beneath the arch
And breach of loins
We lay from other
And coined a stitch   20
To lace the river
An inch from sight,
And soaring brother
From that odd night.
Warm in such braces,   25
Mentioning grasses,
Grinning disgraces
And opulent faces,
We led each other
Two golds together,   30
That else would've been
No hue of the scene.

Now this is a stranger,
And letting the strings
Out over the river,   35
The slow grass ring
The hell of the ear,
I splay the guitar,
Bleeding my faces
Out of disaster   40
And into disgraces,
And kneel in time
Deep as a look
Where none may shine,
Shaping the book   45
The heart deceives,
Folding a tongue
In five dead leaves.

Utterance I

1953

for my wife

One cry behind hunger
Roils like a harp
Drawn full to the head. The father listens
In his own voice.
Deliveries and saints   5
Of actual fever bring
Verb unto verb into feature.

Now may imagination
Step up into the sun
Sustained and blooded in its dream   10
That she in this wise be broke
Partial, as she must live,
Into the whole wish of my words,
Letting all skill
Fall from prayer to save the voice.   15

Your clay has seen, mother
Of images, the flagrant beast
Wander the brake to love, and called the hawk
Onto the whisper's bough.
Lady, withdrawn and tender,   20
Calm in your leaves through toilsome birth,
I am of Thee mindful.

No syllables more flown
Than these, or any other
Statement or will or walk of words   25
Shall be this poem;
Toward that new place,
Immanent, maintained,
Our soft child is, let it
Gesture and fail.   30

From his clear frost
Of shellèd light, globed, situate
And to be lost, descend
The difficult way from the child;
Enter and enter into my breath 35
Forever dying out of each new sound
That he may your peace, my praise
Breed and outleap.

———————

The Ground of Killing
1954

The heron's shade:
Black beak for orange.
Doubles God willed.
Wind riffles both,
Water, one. The scream 5
Of fish swells light
And blind and sharp
What neither cries.
The glow from opening
Sun takes white from 10
Feathers, spreads it upward,
Loses it weightward.
The waters think down
A coral port, temper
Of bells, joining of cords, 15
Eyes drawn over font.
Who, deafening, kneels
Through lust to cold,
Lungs beating bright,
Comes at this weather 20
Under stone sail.

The diver enters
A weaving casement:
With level trident,
Warm mind for lamp,   25
Changes his skin
Passing the bill
Of the sentinel bird.
A pasture opens
Downward, under glass.   30
He hangs more ironly
To answer shade;
He tongues a dying mouth.
The striped fish in the last
Slant shuttle of light   35
Fans as muscle gathers
Its throat of arrows.
As the prongs drive slowly
From the thin hilt
Of blood, like metaphor   40
From soundless sleep,
The eye of the heron
Enters precisely the side
Of the fish and passes
Into the red village.   45

—————

The Sprinter's Mother

1955

She is, she must be lying
Under a wreath like holly.
It is sick
With lightning, here; the sparks grow;
There is her face, momentarily,   5
Against the hard leaves

Says the sun, alive in a diagram
Of fountains maintaining the dead
By overflowing hilltops
And choking: by dust-clayed leaves,   10
By chunks of rock laid endwise, flat,
Among each other, ghosted and smoked with weeds.

Whether interrupting or completing, the boy
Should take the roses from his hand
With his other hand, and put them forward   15
Onto the cocked murmuring of the ground.
At the second hill, rain falls,
But the cut-out, preyless shadow
Of his mother's eagle rests between his arms
Struggling rawly with the light,   20
And the planed hill drifts to meet the cloud
Enough to hold him up
Beside her grave, which is blue
Slate. She would plead for the roses.
He holds them in his breath,   25
His mouth shucked. What music there
Of lightning thrown into sunlight,
Lightning like vines stripped
By a forgotten intensity of the moon,
Should be sounded, is looking for a way   30
To put his flowers down.
His legs are sleeping among the works
Of the great lock of daylight: it is terrible
For her to watch, to be rigid, to wait

For the staggered lanes, the boys crouching.   35
The shadow of the stone eagle
Explodes, the leaves at her forehead shimmer,
Dissolve: he stretches for the turn,
His legs and mind and backbone
All one jarring radiance   40
Forward: a light comes on in his mouth:
The strings of his teeth ache with her voice
Opening for him: the turn leans: she is rising

To touch the flowers: at his shoulder, a body,
Half, a tinge: he is alone: he is tying up: 45
The crowd surges together, in:
He must get his head down: No! the tape
Is there. He puts down the roses.
A bird streams thickly into song.
The dark roses are singing under the bird   50
To the rain, with speed and quiet;
Among the petals, half-hidden like rich drops,
Her cries are shyly balanced,
As if taken back to blood.

And, panting, blowing, he understands   55
How it is all proved, by childishness.
No small part of his body feels
The sun, light blue under the cloud:
Only the chest, back, and legs,
Warmed with excitement,   60
Glow over the graves in the changing light,

As she turns
Slowly into his face, not as a heelprint,
But as a held look he lets his breath
Gather to sustain, and the world   65
Flowed together in a new way, trembles,
Comes back at him, touches at his hair.

———————

The Angel of the Maze
1955

I. THE MAZE

At mid-morning her wheel-chair seems to rock
Softly, plaited and varnished, free
Of the light held thick with clearness

Under the sill. The lawn of ivy rustles.
As he sits and reads, hand on wicker table,   5
Light passing over his wrist and sleeve
And fingers composedly trembling
As if raised, not sure, nor yet in appeal
From an animal partially withdrawn,
Ivy moving together in one heaped, gently   10
Flaking sound, an angel comes to pay
Him for his wife. He knows with what
Inflections the spirit relievedly smiles
Through the braced shuttle of the blind
Hung with its side-faced and deepening coin.   15
He feels his palm glance into the small
Cambricked light, and the other burns off,
Not seen, past the window: the stripes turn
For one closed furious shock of sun, black,
Or solid light, and behind them something runs,   20
Pattering rapidly over the ivy leaves,
Then stands.
                    He takes his cap and cane
And goes out the bright door, down
The three stairs into the garden,   25
For a moment looking up at the house
Like a cliff, forty years old, white,
The back as pretty as the front.

In the summerhouse mired in roses
He pins a rose-leaf with his cane,   30
And hears the intricate circle glide
Form within form toward perfect
Silence, order, place, and sun.
Here, he imagines the statue of a boy,
Or a girl, it is sexless with youth,   35
On a pedestal: just the warm head
And unfinished shoulders. Leaves,
The small-squared light, shower it
With motion, and lay the shadows
Bare against the hesitant sweet mouth.   40
He wraps his fingers on the cane, shifts,

And tries to think. Beside, before
His trying, inside the hedges, the green
Lattice-work, on gravel, the head stands,
A cloud breathed dazzling about its unknown   45
Rain, conceived like thirst, not moving,
Never giving up, fiercer, more perfect—
Unchanged. Toward the slender lips, his voice
Brims like a harp, and is still.

Day after day the edges of the mouth   50
Hold more, to keep the smile the same,
As though the sculptor, having placed a hand
In the clean spring of his childhood,
With the other flowered stone to dream
His mother's face. It is healed forever   55
Into shadows: it need not speak,
It need not lift into noon, nor to his face:
He has nothing but to believe
In the silver light coming through it,
And out of the harmless wild of the eyes   60
Altering, and altering back
So fast there is no change, and he must run
Still and deep to his gaze as stone
To make the bright rooms stop
Upon him here, their flowers close   65
Him down among the cut paths of the sun.

At night each leaf of ivy trembles
As though it grew sharply, lightly,
Over a mouth. All night, upstairs,
He thinks of wandering, lifting his hand   70
Upon his chest, feeling it solidly
Hold him there, as he turns in the leaves
And corners of the paths of the centerless
Garden. *Subtly the hedges are changed*
Out of a mind exhaustless, clear, struck whole   75
Into its open gaze prefigured deviously
In crossing wheels and limits of the sight
Through fire, in forests grown amazed and mild

About recurrent passage. The ivy scatters,
Bending to moon-white, as a low wind breasts.   80
Scott? Falcon? Falcon Scott? Such cold
To hover trackless, for miles, he did not wish—
He came again upon
                    his dead soul,
Leaning forward out of the air   85
Of the circle, touches him, and the circle parts
To his lifted hand at the same place,
But the place itself is changed
Over with suns through different, more
Radiant brush, perfect, beginning again,   90
Marvelling painlessly—
                 for a moment
He is confused by a stone figure
Of his mother's: a boy with a straw
Marble hat. He grins into the dark   95
Like an old young man, and the timbers
Of a fiery wood fall dead together
About him, into his cool-breathing house,
And he sleeps, and the angel wakes.

II. The Angel

Steadily in the thinning dark   100
His sleep forms on the pane,
Delicate, blurred into one
Renewing continuous white
Stride of breath toward morning.
The broad walls of his room   105
Swim in tentative flowers.

As he wakes, as his gray mind cramps
Drowning on the unshaped weight
Of air, I am deeper into marble
Fractured, again and again   110
Broken back to hold his waning head
In conclusive mystery he feels
As awe, as something properly done

He cannot grasp, appointing entire
The low siege of ivy, brush,   115
Roses like two hands caught
Together and seen through an artery,—
Beginning to hold out of air
Features mask-like and bearable,
Humbly smiling, prettily forlorn.   120
Down the white seethe of marble
The sun is limed upon my breast;
The particles boil coldly
Circling into place, and
The ancient summer closes   125
In a storm of corruptible leaves
Upon the ruins of heaven.
The sun kills his breath through glass.
From the blue print of sunlight
On his page, he bends to walk   130
After the dazzling solitude of wings
He cannot think, or that he would,
If he could, believe as trailing
Awkwardly underfoot, like oars,
And sits where their snow-graved feathers   135
Warmly danced over by depth
Fold tremorless into the child.
His gaze falls earnestly,
Changing through my head
Into the earth, whereon I lie,   140
A virgin, still in the slender hail
Of roses, wedded to die
Again, be broken eagerly
Across the altar scented
Of rockery stone and fern,   145
And the dumb, first breath
Of the entering angel plays,
Deepening, unsteady,
With stumbling force blares
Heavily, silently, until the child   150
Rises to the gold and humming
Of the leaves. Here, where purity

Sharpened upon my age, and, scraped
By cloth to bleed, one eye
Pulled empty by the lights   155
Of every room, the other burning
Near a snow, a stone, a child
Weeping into its teeth, I struck
Into the bent and whirling spokes
To labor down your halls   160
Onto the porch, and see the garden
Made, Ervin, you sit steadily
Holding the great crushed bow
Of your blood, among the grasses,
In the soft deadfall of sun   165
Where the white image grinds with fury
Of life to make your mortal limits
One, draw in, be near. Breathe,
Nod, Ervin. Your peace is inescapable:
Each moment brings to leaf   170
A deepening order of change
Perpetually renewed
In decisive, unattainable
Ceremony, which is the dead.

———————

The Confrontation of the Hero

1955

—April, 1945—

Claw-hammer, hay, and grease,
We club the engine from its crate,
Swinging, and harness the nacelle.
The dog's head blown from earth
By propeller blast, then buried, then   5
Stencilled to hem the nosewheel in its jaws,
Looks off between us at quiet,

Increasing, until there is a sound.
I drag on the hemp and chain of the pulley,
But the engine grinds into coral.   10
Line astern through a smoked first sketch
For swans, the craft come over.

You place your foot, still, forward
Sleeping in its flesh, road by road
Into the island, and the coral shudders,   15
Gives way, turns easily, a zodiacal wheel,
And the beasts step from their stars over you
And disappear in the sea and earth of noon.
For a second you seem to move among them,
Sewn as a flower on the Ram's light horn.   20
You grow, then soar from the matted head
And stretch toward night, swelling and foaming
Into sparks, your leg-bone traversed
By an incandescent angle of the pattern,
Blue-white and fixed. The rest drops off.   25
Down the long road where the aircraft break
From dust, and wedge their wheels,
There is no violence, and under the stumps
Of the plantain wood you turn like stars,
And a spring forces suddenly open,   30
Shining and groaning, at your ear.
A bulldozer moves with the sun downhill,
Mice racing softly before the blade.
In, where wire-meshed bulbs are set,

I hear the right hand of the sky   35
Purl, withheld. Searchlights brim through heads
Of horses masked and run in a field of flowers
To the knife, on the shell of canvas:
Men running, wading the leaves of shadow
Strongly with their eyes. From hour to hour   40
Medics bandage-roll and thread my calf
Into the sea. Their needles buckle, slash,
And hold to count; my nostril jerks at its hose;
Light fastens to my shin. His blade

Strikes on the sun let down through walls   45
A man is putting up leaf by leaf.
His whirring feathers fill my ears;
His wolf-hound's skull lights up
Around my serum; he swings his shield
Flashing and streaming down the aisle of beds   50
To cut his sight from mine, but I rise
From cotton, aluminum, rubber, gauze, tin,
And creep out on a leg like a double exposure's:
Out, as the wind dives still,
And the light from the high sword falls   55
To the roads through my leg
In dim and complex joy. My foot breaks
New, as with throat-heat, down smashing the records
Shed, slamming into tents, over bunkers.
He dances like dust, low in the chalk fields   60
As I sprint the beach past landing-craft,
Fuel drums, crates, revetments, stars
Waiting in delicate rain to fix my form at night
To the north. In gold flats of sun, he hangs,
Not sure, because of the speed that takes my head   65
Lashing from side to side on guano'd rocks.
My eyes close in unforgiving pity

On his dwindling shield. I sleep
And wake. My loins draw in: I relax
And stream all day and night   70
As rocks, sea, sun, above the landing beach.
A truck blasts through with a load of coral.
About that spirit burning emptily
Darkness lowers the coals into the nut grove,
Where we blew on the soil, and licked with flame,   75
Mud, from the fortified tombs. Looped with cartridges,
With foresters' gear, dug in, I sprawled
In the enfilade: the urn-shaped gun-pits rocketed
Through my sights, and the island sang
Glory for glory into my shadow,   80
For the field lay clear to the sea,
And the aircraft rose. I woke and knelt

Over the ward, then crept, knee, fist, and stump,
Into a crab-grassed, brambled gulley
Where was a cow. Its eyes rolled   85
And fell back. For a while I lay with my side
Touching in and out of the earth,
Until the dark boys formed in ranks around,
And from above, as at a sign, all raised to their lips
Thistle, and blew a long soft mirror-clouding breath   90
In which something shook to come back,
Or to go on, but could not, in the huge light snow
Like a face advancing to its counterparts:
The mouth toward hunger to be made serene,
The eyes to enchanted marble, the ears, the sea,   95
All through my eyeholes floating still.
In my horns I held the short-haired
Or crab-back-thorned sun, far off,
Listening. Round metal cleared.
My grinning serpents flew at his feathered heels,   100
Beat down, and Spring tore off their skins.
He placed his armor on the stair of light
And bent to take my yellowed head,
His muscles gliding naked in the mirror
Of the air, his face warm as a man's   105
Who shall hold at his breast the look
To freeze his untroubled cities to the stone
Lamp of every room, though over plotted graves
He bear it in trembling gentleness, till it be richened
With the stars between the ships of all the bays,   110
And nail it to the ground in secret weeping.

The Vigils

1955

It is time for the trees in motionless flight in a ring
Through the shaken powder of fatigue,
For the dogs, nosing their rippled bodies,
And for the shadow of a burning table
Reversing, into the lake,   5
To lift from the heart of the urn
Of water a man limbed all in metal,
His visor dazzling, that his iron lips
Describe in excessive silence as he moves
Skyward, the blue hilt of space   10
Buried in the lake, and its handlers
Tangled in the roots of the ceremony he makes clear.
A shout knocks and blazes; water destroys the wood with light.

But the two boys sit quietly
In the cure or vigil of their fallen dusk,   15
And the shining-flat of the ring
Of pines on the yellow window
Is slow and intense as wheels
Silked close with turning-speed.
The sun cannot blow white enough to flower   20
Their breath in the lidded lake
More still. Though they must try to rise
To their feet, and aim the long spark of the blade
Through the sun, and with it cross
The heart of the voice of a fasting choir,   25
Though with their bodies they must shape the water
Until the ebbing needles of their heat
Spring, nail them to holy armor from within,
They cannot quite bring sound
The figure haunting the latent sky: 30
He wavers between them, his mailed feet
And hands nearly living, nearly
Shaded out of dust, drifted,

Rocking, as the pines clear
Continually from the depth. 35

Once more their father calls.
A squirrel banks off high through sticks
That should be winter's but have flowered,
And the water shakes under the dogs,
Their jaws unearthly warmed, and their eyes, 40
Half holy with fear of the dream
Of sunlight crossing the open lake,
Descend, stop at the reeds, turn back
In a mist of boiling glass and flying

As he tries to step down from the death 45
Of the knight: from the barbed leaves
At his elbows licking the sun,
From the untouched, immobile cloud
With its water trembling to be lit
By his passing face, to the full purity 50
Of the world fed blindingly, and legendless,
The unaltered feast: but his eyes blur
In the sweat of the marvelling iron:
The sun-marked dazzle floods
Over his hidden face, his scaled, rustless fingers 55
Raised from the head of the living dog into cloud,

He being half the ritual of the dead,
And that sustaining. Virgin, Lion, Pale Horse, Dove:
Their veiled, historied waiting is now,
To have always been, the lake 60
Between their breaths, and he, come
Burning like a locust, a raised power of light
Helpless in leaves and reeds above the lake
Not quivered by his voice spread blown away,
Alone unceremonious, and of a falling bright. 65

The Flight

1956

Come to stand, the hawk
Holds out his share of the moth:
In summer already is
Another place, and snow become
The listening of a myth,   5
Having dispersed the body from the stone.

Here among this green your child
Has broken the famine of statues.
Through the immovable dream of the air
He feels with the bird the stone drawn   10
By high-pencilled rocks from his feet.
The summer begins to shine without its eyes.

There is only the hawk's way to plunge
Into the universe, a field at course
Drumming with flowers,   15
Past the wire-dipped cloud of the cage.
You point the branching hammer of gravity
Toward him, as snow falls down invisibly onto shape,

And at the center of the falling,
Where dark has slept the white wound,   20
Divided undiscoverably, into the passing cliff,
You look to see him, turning his arms

In speculation, but he is not yet there.
He is floating in his last drink of water
Like the world-driven breath of the sea.   25
He plucks the sex from the sleeping horse
Who drinks from the brilliant river.
There, the bill of the pitcher balances
At your throat, that of the clearest

Raging drinker. You see him as the rain   30
Must raise its limits to the inner crown,
To fall white, in summer, through the mind.
The cage, renewing and trembling,
Goes over the small, broomed grass,
Floating its bones where the mouse sleeps.   35
One by one we are all together

In the massed, airy effect of the bars,
And the glade shimmers, intense, there,
Its stripes gliding inward as the wings grow
Over the heel-drafted, harlequin bed. Come: 40
Think your hand the tree

Where that bird might settle,
Having killed thus freely from his cage.
At every imagined touch, a branch may wander loose
Swaying inside the light. Your hand is like your face.   45
As the claws touch there, your roots release
The victim; dark strikes your heart in the child.

It is the way the animals lie there,
Bearing the earth, not able to ride it out.
The air-dead are on fire   50
With unknowable suspension, and from their wonderment,
Like that of targets, the summer begins again to snow

For the lost hawk. Beneath, your cry breaks
Into the tongue of a healing wilderness.
In clear summer there is light   55
Beaten with thickets, smoked with thorns,
Wherefrom he rises like a ghost through the floors
Of an expanding home. Your heart looms

Impassibly and truly in your blood.
Distance changes the bright, flickering bruise   60
Under the eyelids of the dead,
And is nearing; the crystal cemeteries hang.
You look for your childhood buried in air,

But the small animals dance in flood,
In the open depth of shadow, increasing in judgment.   65

Here the hawk in one of your pupils
Finds one of his wings, and stares across
At the other, branching your brows together
Head to head with the child beside you in fury
Over the light victim. But the mouse is lost in snow,   70
In imagination come standing fully round
In nothing at all but white:
But the cage enveloping snow.

He is flying there. Snow: white, conjectural solidity:
King-headed hydra, sifting   75
Brow and crown. Something loiters into its stride,
And you begin to sprint the paths of the park,
Your child beside you, padding swift,

Freezing with murder, a knife you have given him
In either hand: you are blazing green,   80
He is white and lost, you the season
Of killing, and he blind with chance
In the closed center of morning.
And as you go, the watching eye

Is suddenly nature's, from a bole,   85
From the slow ascent of a leaf
Falling upward unnoticed through Heaven,
The first trance of a shorn lamb.
Your face is the mediocrity of a bush
Writing the wind in its head.   90
Your child whistles out into light
And scores with his eyes a brilliant right and left
Through snow into snow

Where you stop, with the cage panting round you,
And in the distance, diminishing,   95
Is the small shape with its mind lit

From the heart of nothing, its hands aflash,
Beautiful, low, and speeding. Turn your eyes

Like balanced coins, and on their outer side
The bird sits, the cage is falling like rain,   100
The dazed archer's mind of snow has brought
From itself the green of a beautiful prey
Immobilized and flowering everywhere,
Whose height the child marks in your side.
To be at all is to haunt the world.   105

———————

The Father's Body
1956

   His father steps into the shower;
In the rising lamp of steam
Turns his fatted shoulders on.
The boy is standing, dry and blue,
Outside the smoke-hole of water,   5
The ink-cut and thumb-ball whorl of planks
About him like the depth in a cloud
Of wire, dancing powerfully.

Back to back with the sea,
Light hovers out the shadow of the sun.   10
The father's hair breaks down
Warmly under the shining.
He has come up from the river-bed, never seen,
Beneath the flowing of mirrors.
In the sterile, cross-lit grass   15

Of water, something descends into the man
Of ruined, unarrestable statuary
Not made by men: stone, blind

With the mule's gaze, sleeps itself awake,
And, before anything, is on the man's face   20
And through the boy's loins, and past,
Burning hairs up out of the earth.

The child watches the clean, shameful sight.
There in the moth-killing, trembling pine,
He thinks the frail moon of day is snowing   25
With silver readiness, the man
Up from the floor. His father's head
Is dark white, his mouth bell-shaped and drinking.
The boy steps into the water,

Re-shimmering its loaded height.   30
A movement comes down on his hair
As the stiff, bright headdress of fever.
In one immortal, preliminary posture
After another, he is cast
Down a ray of water. And knowing,   35
As a rain surrounds itself, how prayer
Kills out its breath, and beats, he bears

All of him in to his father.
They ride there, in beginning.
He takes a long drink of velocity   40
Shucking his face.
It keeps wearing out there,
Its pointedness keeps running down,
So that his closed eyes pelt back at it, and see,
Uncontrollably, a wood   45

Where nothing pours. Grass comes gently
Down into being, in a ring.
He steps forward, deeper,
In the descended brow-light of a shell
Spreading the nerves of sound into itself.   50
Echo shouts slowly with the miracle.

In there, it is all intense
And mild, with flowers growing solid as a ball
And floated warm. As he looks into trees
Sheering the sun, his father asks   55

For his hands, and binds on the glittering chains.
Each ritual has the heartbeat of the first:
He lies then with his heart
Eating the center of the ring, his feet together.
His father at the edge of the fair field   60
Is uncertain, in his blue bathing-trunks.
Then the man is over him, as at night.

He is seen through gauze to be
Very faint; he reaches in where the boy's ribs
Are unformed, where they are wavering   65
Like the ribs of sand in water.
Sleep yells from ear to ear; his organs rise,
Lash clear, as from his mouth,
And he is overtaken from within
By weightlessness. His father draws his tongue out   70
With two fingers, and the syllabled dark from his throat.
("Soul," he cries after it with his last word).

He is all beamed blood, with light between;
All matterly, but connected like a cloud.
The girl beside him, who is still wet   75
With him, screams: she kicks and squeals
As his father, his eyes closed,
Kneeling, molds her body.
He builds her freely
Strange, as the aging of a prophetic glass   80
Where all of historied time she is
Becoming the first and last of images,

And then, alone, the last.
In the backward of silver depth
The weather blooms out tempered, as from warmth itself.   85

The boy begins to breathe without his soul,
Lying there voiceless, pierced by a sprig of holly
Between the single freshness of his legs.
Her face moves from within. They are laid together.

The wedding blazes up all around.   90
She lies against him, glowing his mouth
To sweat like a glass of milk.
The bust of his father burns from his neck
Like a fountain waked in by a god;
His inner and unknown face,   95

Of a singing animal, breaks through.
Above them, his father's eyes are aging
With the sky, dancing about them
A pattern swum from wood, watched luminous from silk,
And he feels his father rise   100
Through his own slight, helpless loins
Into the frankness of space.
He falls through her from there, and her eyes change.

The shadow of the cross
Of a sword-hilt held awkwardly by his father   105
Imprints itself on his back, floating and burning.
He parts the girl's terrible legs; he shouts
Out silence; his waist points
And holds and points, empowered
Unbearably: withheld: withheld—   110

A loom is flooded with threads,
Showing him stretched on the nails
Of the inward stars of noon, released.

He has died, and his father flickers out
In the lengthening grass where he and the girl   115
Have been crowded down and crowned.
A little blood subsides into his heart,
And is his heart. Its word brings the girl's lips balanced

Through like water, and the multiple sleep
Of a shuddering herd calms over them.   120
She has leapt to the roots of his beard.
His father dies, and snaps the water off:

Snaps the descended and hypnotized leaves
Off in midair, and the warm ring of the wood.
They all three have been shining.   125
Yet the boy stands in the stall of the cottage,
His face thought up
By speechlessness, bright with death,
And his father, withdrawing as he stands
Deeper in the grove, alone,   130
Breastward in the springing dream of seed,
In the bestial completion of sunlight
Hid up and down, branchingly sings.

—————

The Swimmer
1957

The river stands, a shadow balanced open.
I stand. My skull makes a motion of closing
Over stems, between upward and downward—
Closed, it is pressed white
Listening to thirst graze formally among its vectors,   5
And lifted down, and the girl,
Each muscle of her body near a voice
Plucked and set beating harp-metal by the wedged sun
Between leaves and strings,
Falls from the opposite bank.   10

Toward the swinging paint of her shadow
Paired with a tongue that might be arched

And caught forever singing out
The dead intensity of the river
From the sleep of a blue mouth, brightening,   15
Yet is all sidling silence,

My head dips past its print, and the flesh goes,
And my eyes through the river's rain
(A wall burned gently from its nails) pass
From sun to moon: from sun to moon   20
Light of nausea, her hair dancing
Under the day-moth's dancing
Small step of suspension,
Ceases to shape back,

And under the water where I have loved   25
I touch it with the echo of my face,
And feel my legs, tuned to the river's magnet, follow,
Hum solid, changingly, like urns struck hard
Being filled, and light from the porch of a headless god
Binds down the trees of the abyss.   30

Behind my throat, a Presence
Is hooded out with bones, is trembling with whiteness
As white as the bones, between the bones:
In that dry, sparkling field under daylight,
Under the half-watered air   35

Of the strangling swimmer,
The current throws scars from the heart of lightning
Into the Hunt, and I leap
Up the branched channels of a vertical wind.
Death flickers light and broken: the thickets stream: 40
Above, her legs are shattering right, she pulls:
Form and Vigor
Tear out her saliva and rope it to the banks.
A hound passes its tongue through my shoulder—
My horns lift him, he staggers, his legs flail   45
The dancing sun of water, and I stand, at last,

In hiding, my antlers tuned to the dark of the wood,
And the sprinters with their lances pass,
Cleansed with young steam and honey,
As she beats back panic through the slow, clear wall: 50

Where my new, flowing flesh stares up,
She flogs toward the bush of the drinking deer
Whose stripped shadow under the stream, moveless,
Ceremonial, hung with dead leaves and dry
Sparkling, carbon and moonlight,   55
Draws with his patient gaze
Her lines of force from the spring
To the sea, through her nipples,
And through the kick of her arms
His stone ear runs and runs   60
Over the whole river, and a wheel
Meshes emptily there, with colorless flowers.

I feel at my brow the sleeping deaf
Press their violent foreheads up
To touch her, sowing greatly, in the lungs.   65
And as the crest of her geometry fires
And falls over the river, and vanishes into a bird
As she walks out, the lances of the sprinters,
The foam of the deer

Float unimaginably still. Tradition holds her safe,   70
Though we who made it,
The hunters and the hunted in her form,
Seethe in the current, cold, and things touch us:
My great eyes look at me from the air,
And I set my powerful, numb head   75

And hold through my stone ribs
The water carefully, but where she slept
Is past. I am stiller and not leaping
Back to my face and body rained to death
By the sun, where the spiritless eyes no longer   80

Are vacant, but know: her naked walking shakes them,
But onto me like no leaf
Falls, in the perfect gloom and body

Of the dark faultless field where shadows move
The forms of darkness dazzlingly,   85
And take no body back, that ever comes
To touch the bones of his bestial face
To the murmuring wall, late after love.
Turn back: stare in, through the multiple heart
Of proven water. Let your throat re-form.   90
God sheds the cloth of air.
Silence turns its following weight
Mindless, to rest Him freshly in the leaves.
Helen! Incorruptible extreme!
We have the blue eyes of prisoners.   95

The First Morning of Cancer
1957

    The first morning of cancer he awoke
And went with his eyes half all the way
From their grave room, as it wore in two.
All night in the dream of his mouth he had held
His life, by the tongue drawn down   5

To the sand brim, where the hourglass hears the whirlwind from its toe
Sing itself clear of the ground.
Upward of the bed, he passed, again,
The sense of floating brightly in a maze.

All two honest shapes   10
Of light, either one invisible, he lay there face-
to-face, in both the shadow's men: the Fallen,

And the Risen-from-the-Sun.
In the smell of bread-making flames he kept hearing,
"The thing that you are you have done." 15

Almost awake, he had the serpent's
Measure, of lying long, along
Each felled position of his life
In Light, prodigious casting of a center.
Halfway through the sun, he knew. 20
He closed his eyes, and suddenly he was one
Of an army of panting men.

His fear passed off, intact. Abandoned, sustained,
A loose chair came and rode
Partly down under his clothes. His shoes on the floor 25
In a kind of mooring swayed, by their weight slowly signed, again.
To where he was, he had come, his slight hair folded

Wrong, from the very beginning, about his naked brain.
He laid the sheet aside, and softly entered his hand, and with it fell
Upon his chest, spellbound with what it was doing. 30
As it drew air, he seemed to dip inside, at once,
All of the miles of breath upon the earth.

He thought what he would say.
All night he had heard the bed
About him, in the fluttering of a bush, be used 35
And flaked away, and on the saved-up word
To be said to his son out of sleep, had felt his lungs
The covering of his voices with a sack, and slept again
Headlong into a sound.

And now he looked, and the child was gone 40
He had called, and a posture with jackstrawed hair
Fled outward, not gaining, through sleep.
Something, a pain, came out of him
And was shimmering by the inch and mile, at once.

Across his temperate skin, the child's flesh deeply blew,   45
An uncorrected gentleness of air.
Through this he stepped, and turned,
And in the window was immersed.

Alone above the bed, he saw his son
Taken by leagues of sunlight from behind.   50
Much like his earlier fear, the pain passed off.
Slowly he filled with the blue hulk of his eyes
Gazing from love. It could not, then, be other.

He looked, out past himself and behind.
The wet crept up to the house, and the tended grass   55
Went on and under,
Beyond. Moment after moment out of air
His youth arrived. He began to dance in his blood.

The sun came over him, in a stroke of life.
His guts were burning with hunger.   60
His lawn on the very wings
Of Possession beat, and raised him, where he swayed
With the world's good pulse: the wings of a bird
In flight, which must shut
The bird each instant from falling.   65

His hair dumped over his forehead, he dumped it more,
And took off his shirt, and sat in the little of wind.
The chapped skin on his back stretched close
And bloomed like a great hedge in the light.
The cancer rose in his brain, and yet therein   70
Made no dramatic stand upon an image.

A fathomless shawl on his back, he stooped
And took a double handful of the room
Out of the slept-in air. He dispersed the ball of his hands,
Having learned not a thing, but happiness,   75
Over again. Through the crawl of bloom on his back,
Slowly his soul from its watchful night came in,

Still lapping the bricks of the house. Anew, and doubly, he looked down
Where the lives of his wife and son streamed on,
Unlimited, into their crimson lids.   80
A stirring stopped. Nothing before

He moved had moved. A shell somewhere broke water:
An armored slug, a king-crab in a wig,
A turtle sparkling mossily from its back,
In its twilight of weight gone mad.   85
He was found in the window, and the universe struck like flint
Unreasonable eyes of prey.

About him in his yard, each paid-for rock
Shortened its shade, pulled on it like a scab.
Uneasily, he let his breath curve out around   90
The end of the sun, in his room,
The whole God, in a mask like a green-house, behind him.

A soundless cry went up and stood
In amazement between the beds, as if it felt the sun
Flattened on stone, of moonlight, then   95
Come back. He remembered he had shone himself all night
Into a helpless hanging-there of boughs.

He drowsed, and tried again. Along his arms
Some hidden branches came afloat. He kicked and pled.
They took him from the tree, and closed his sleeping body in the hill   100
Of light. He screamed in all his face
And it was singing from the rocks.
The air blew hard, and was a fire of dust

On all the roads. The bone of blindness turned
Among his brows, until it struck the light. The mountain moved.   105
He shrilled, and brought a man, his size, of sweat,
Superb, from the flight of the sun.
Beyond all light, his shadow shed
Through all of him to the wall. His son said,

"I will help." He heard. He set himself to call,   110
But broke. A thing, that instant, had grown
In the way a child, being lost in another's house,
Will fall to its knees and creep.

Astonished, the son rose up.
A knitted shape the size of two great ironing-boards, was pulled   115
To feathers on his back.
Vibrant as the haze of a propeller, from his miraculous head, one eye
Opened, and was followed by the moon's. In his light, inside the light
Of the first morning, he stood by the stone, and could hear,
Beyond, the death from the nearest of flesh,   120
In its basket of hands, nailing one
To another, and deadly, self,
Up and down and across from within.

Upon him, all his waking came to be
Where he strove with the starry stone,   125
His milled nails torn to mica by the weight,
And moving the rock not an inch.
Half dead from imagined screaming, he yelled out wide once more,
"And they found the stone rolled away."

Yet when the child arose   130
Beside the window's cave, the Being
Dropped from his breast, from sleep, into the sun
Wearing the soldier's dreaming mail,
The angel wept, as the child remembered
His father. For a moment the man saw brightly   135

Dilated through stone, the cross, an olive-tree,
Close with the Foe-within-Light, to ruin him into leaf.
From the boy he was
The distance where the soul appears, and all their eyes

Ablaze with intelligence, their face the face the horseman feels   140
Ascend to his, from the sprinting horse.
The boy came to him, and the cancer found

Life, in the motion of a woman unbinding
Her hair all the way to the bone.
It billowed about them like seaweed, and the man   145
Descended. God gave him up,
And smiled across his breastbone, in the light:
On his, like a crown, the candle-

dancing head of unconsciousness placed. It was all in the fear
Of waking, returned in full, immense as the angel's   150
Alone in the sun, first watching the silent earth
From fire and shadow be made. There, he had come to be,
Unmystical, Love's pure bare Looking-On,
Not to notice, on pain of expulsion, who
In the world it was, the child gripped,   155
Trembling, by one hard healthy foot.

To Be Edward Thomas
1957

In under a flock of shade
Wired loosely into light, a generalized swaying of moss,
Those faceless beards with the breath of water
Stirring, I stooped with the old New England man

Between the leaves let down there,   5
The sun sitting patched and almost dead
In the white board chairs
We had left, to walk up and down a furlong of the sea's
Inviolable nakedness, in all its shining-level with the grave.

Just inside Florida we took our seats.   10
A bird's cry broke into four.
All around, mimosa, hibiscus,

Palms, the self-choking matted grass: slowly,
Where we were, we were inside

A shadow listening deeply to the light   15
Come out of a tree of yarn, the wild-wire gentle glowing.
I glanced at Frost, in him all loved old men
Composed, eroded, in the world's despairing search
For the time-born, original, singing and featureless face
That moved upon the making of its waters,   20

And thought, how vulnerable they are, the old,
Whose body in every motion is
Extending back through time: how valuable,
The good ones: how unafraid

As a wind blows out of the sun's dying   25
Increasing forge-red stroke
Down sea, down the great wild trembling shape
Saw-edged from water risen. Feeling the saw-edge in the wind,
In the air going over us, a rocking from side to side,

The body warm from the sun shining into the brain,   30
I saw that a part of light would not
Be there, as it was, without three words:
"The team's head-brass." On the sea, from my mind,
Or another's, two horses, a horse,
His head with ornament alive,   35

Stood, on the quick soil of ripples, there. It was not Frost had said,
But Edward Thomas, whom he had known.
The sun gave out. I could not tell if I
Could see the horse, or if he were, with

No light for bright head-gear, for hide,   40
And thinking instead of Thomas, poor, indeterminate, bare,
Writing acceptable prose, from cottage gone
To cottage with his family, and no work nearest his heart,
And seeing the old man silent, in the gray dark straining with wind

Watching me, asked then like a body-blow from the soul   45
What it might be
To come to one's self, near the end of life in a war,
Under just this look:
To be brought forth by this.

From living in such friendship Thomas said   50
Gravely his old and laboring breath away.
He bent upon a tree, a horse,
A look that drew off Time, and put about the thing
Its end and its beginning, like a church. Its Being blazed
With reverence, upon head-brass and hide, or twigs,   55

Bark, wind in the interlaced boughs: these, beyond thought, at last,
What they must surely be: leaves, limbs, beasts, in their holy reasons:
Determined by him, but given by the world.
In his new poems the brooks and fields
Kept hearing the sound of their making: it was   60

As silence, and all restraint become
The classic restraint of tears, to let him speak:
Who brought also axes, hop-poles,
Hay-forks, shovels, in, and all
So still, put down just after work, or   65

Not used in years, whose men in the heat are drowsing,
Deep in the brown ring of the land, or dead
As drowsing. He drew close to cattle and plants,
And saw with unparalleled joy each thing his life required
Grow whole, in what he said.   70

Low mist lay in on water, where we were.
A tower no one had noticed
Made light, and none of it thrown,
But passed around, intact. We watched the double-handled hole
In dark, go by,   75

Brought off, brought on, brought off.
I looked up levelly. The beam came into my head
Through my nose, or brows. In the momentary face,
Unblinkable, of light, I floated like powder
Assembling. Dark. Then light   80

Again, and a long-stemmed flash
Through the nose of the skull, of deep, precarious bright.
A battle-field framed in a key-hole.
Gone. Once more I waited, still. Shadow
Ignited, and behind it the whole   85
Light, full out of the blind of the brain.
In the gold-filled arch of bone,

Wire. White heat, not hot,
Spat, arced leaping among the harp-strung graven hills
About the fragment of an outline of a man   90
Struggling, in planetary blue. The dead,

Who inhabit the white of the eye,
Show forth, when shone upon.
This was Vimy Ridge, where Edward Thomas died.
Each time the mowing light went past, I watched him, after it,   95

From his death, as grass behind wind,
Rise, never getting all the way to his feet, as the lamp-swung hall
Left him, seeming to sigh like a prow.
To be killed is suddenly to feel the self
Without the body, flash: 100

To fall wherever you can, upon the ground
Of shell-holes moved in a whorling drift, as from an oar,
And enter with the closeness of your eyes
The presence of many grains.

Killed many times, and risen off   105
Alive, alert, into dark, we got up at last
In our bodies, and stood on the long sea-wall
For one more look. The bright flag floated over.

There, in the wilderness glow
And moss of stones, a thicket of little fish. 110
Light shone them into being:

In the quick of it, from all one side of their weightless herd
Their collected vision swayed
Like dust among them: we could see the essential spark
Travel from eye to eye. 115

Closed in the dark, till the other arm
Rode out of the lamp, we stood: they had not turned:
A whiff out of bright: fire full of them
Swept, and their bush of inlaid burning
Quivered, once. They were gone with molecular swiftness. 120

You cannot choose whatever thing shall mean.
Out of the whole of chance it must occur,
The meaning felt, escaped into your head, requiring speech.
Fish, cold in the flight of fire
That speckled the sea with their eyes, may be recast, 125
And known, and memory rise like the dead,

Assembling the full of sense, as slowly the drowned recall
What profound, entire grip they had
With their hands, on the sea, when rowing.
The words may yet be said. 130

Around me, in the flower-lifted room
Of open dark, from the heavy, luminous man
Who had not said a word: from sight, from memory
From air and fire and water,
A personal permanence, something to say 135

To myself from every side,
Grew, as having. I thought what friends of mine, known
Or unknown, as yet in the army of the brother
Lost, might serve me so.
As Frost, Edward Thomas, or whom so I might serve. 140
Back to the house in the wind

Walking, I would believe therefrom
In field, fish, dark, light, the bundle-bodied grave
To be seen in no outlying flash: to be seen
As the dead see, in the living, the bright horse known in life   145
And come back from the sun

In a silence like Being, wherein you gently hold
What you have witnessed, and thence must love, as utter
Intimate invaluable strangeness:
As it is, as you have made it,   150
Alive with what human light?

————

The Work of Art

1957

—Amputee Ward, Okinawa, 1945—

There, burned
By imagination slowly

Out of the hulk of leaning,
The walls of the tent begin to glow.
His heartbeat continually fires   5
True, for his leg, and misses.
The wind blows the island on
Under a gentle shoulder of sun in the air.

An arm moves, filling temperately with land.
He says, with his head to the sand sheets,   10
"My courage is the inside of bright light,"
And a singled muscularity opens, in weight
Beginning to rain, a wildening space of God.
He steps back with his strange left foot
Into the blue-eyed floating of the soul.   15

On a skylight aging the smell of lawns,
The figures, in their stacked sparks
Of thread, are standing together.
Given the mica of their coats,
The hunters have gained, for years,   20
Their stiff, elected limbs;

The boar is stitched in fever from his life
Where the precious leaves have grouped his place.
The amassed geometer whispers
Into the sea, "The Lord of Tapestry is maimed."   25
His leg is mired to the thigh
In Creation, and lies on him breathing in threads.
"The Sword shall devour the Sun,
And there be no less light."

It hangs about him, all its rays   30
Constellated equal, killing its craftsmen with age.
He thinks the yeast of cloth is called
"Resurrection," death has everywhere so much
The shine of reliefless artistry.
In the place in him quivering dead in length   35
The shotted threads are moored.

And when the Limb, resplendent
In castle-green and black,
In the God-eaten white of cloud
And the canvas-gold of bone implied   40
Through the scarlet spool of the wound,
Hangs deathlessly, and the work is given to men,
What of the man himself, when the leg shocks out its gilt
How deadly still, into the still museum?
How to say that its unfigured man,   45
Forgotten by the cloth, has not yet died;
Has but devoured

In sleep the thread of the labyrinth?
He shouts between two screams.

The bubble of color   50
Rings mindlessly, in answer.
A hunting wall of sun
Comes down on the veil of the amateur.

Shines, like a marsh, the sun
On the crossed brow of listening.   55
He beats his empty hands on his ears, and twists
All around his leg, white, edged gold, sewn flat
Beside a hooded falcon burned in grass.
A procession of knights and hunters
Is watched around him into cloth.   60
He feels the move among the craftsmen's minds
Pull him up terribly to sit,

Facing, over his seed-pearled leg
The green and blinding thicket of the boar.
He braces his free foot on the sheets   65

And reaches through the weaving-bright of stillness,
Ablaze with meditation in his arm.
The silver sun

Catches one turn of thread alive
About his thumb, and begins to fall,   70
Unravelling, falling through the woven world
Into an upraised blade.
He feels its snowing vibrancy
Create his hand, its jewels hilt his palm, the blade

Shimmer in the bodiless stone of air: 75
The whole cloth burning and swinging, he yells,
"Pour la Reine," and brings it down,
Halving the green blaze, rippling
Across his thigh. The Work for an instant shines
For bright miles down the animal,   80
Fibrous moonlight of his nerves

As the leg begins its life.
His two hands cramping his thigh
Close from the rushing of the world,
He sees a Unicorn, a Serpent, and a Poison Tree   85
Flicker stilly from the void into the place
Which has been, until now,
Their absence by miracle. Before him,
The young hunter dies
Forever, asway in his silken cage.   90
The eye of Heaven grows,

Embroidered unsparingly, into the years of weaving,
Focussed where the sword fell
Historyless as cloud.
Not yet thought by the craftsmen, an angel's form   95
Is drugged by the green string of the hill.
It wavers on the tent-wall,

Seen gold through the bone of his brow.
He fades it helplessly back,
Increased, into the dance.   100
The tent feels his dampened flesh fall on
As the sun feels the backs of a herd through mist.
He smiles and licks his skull.
Memory and the Secret come apart
Upon the hovering fly.   105

––––––––––

The Red Bow
1957

On side-showering wheels afloat, well off
I stopped from them, my bicycle leaning in-
side one tiring pleasant leg, as they came down

From the clear house, holding up bows.
Beneath us the fern forest weighed,   5
The light on leaves as brightness moves
Somewhere along the pulling of a chain.
                                           The lawn dropped
As they crossed, the game and grace of the child
Gone somberly forth upon, and the first of the upper trees.   10

To hunt, I saw that one must see,
When approaching, the unmanned wood
As one stroke of life from the heart. I waited there,
Waiting for my heart, as the father moved,
The boy with his small vivid bow   15
Following. Each quick look from his head was out
Of the round gold smoke of the sun.

Small serpents, sparrows, insects, mice
Lay close, in their whole cloth
Of shovelled shade, but the child was making a thing   20
To be fallen upon in a sovereign blur from above:
Among the blinding sensitivity of stars
Countersunk by the sun through leaves, not blood
But death, a run- or flown-down shape come green and full
Into trembling to stop and be struck there.   25
Slowly by their advance the prey

Began to be built among the trees. The leaves
Shook seriously, and the wood neared the whole sound
Of the secrecy of insects in the light,
A zone of fanatical grazing—   30
Yet on a sudden fining of the ear, the stand
In sound of a single fly was borne.

A hush caved in: went rising round
The balanced Game, whose heavy bush was blue
With the holding of years of breath.   35
There, going into the trees, one understands
The dancing of the world, mistaken for the leaves',

And the sense of dissolving
Forward, into the last great stone.

Deeply the dark bird sighed   40
Under watching, and a breeze fell short—
Then the ferns, nocked with drops, were still,
Again, with the only stillness.
At once more strongly: endless
Piling, the spring-loaded green   45

And ply of whole branches moved.
Near their feet, the leaves of a fern blew wrong-
side-out, and toiled, and knit once more
In the pattern of the muscles of a back.
A dead limb churned, breaking off something else in its fall.   50

There is no way first to place your foot
Inside the wood while the wind blows, and the trees,
Not equal to themselves, unearth from the very roots
The half-used, whelmèd postures of a god.
Uncertain, the father picked an arrow   55

As one he might as well lose, and crossed it with his bow.
A leaf turned brightness over in the wind.
He leaned back, pulling wide,
Until the quick of feathers touched his face, and powerfully let go
Around them a mixture of little pines   60
In a shuddering brain-wave of needles went, and stood
The shade of the wood on end.
                              A small
And yet a smaller and blacker stick, the arrow rose
And burned out a nerve of sunlight as it fell   65

Over into falling, off in height.
From there in a slow return
Of size, it came. Had one looked only then, it had appeared
Brought to bear by Heaven,
Not so much to fall, as fired with all intent   70

Level into the trees. A still cloud passed.
The blinding wood of stars went out, and shadow profoundly
Opened all the way to the sun:

Out of the dimming piece-work of the ground,
Color, a butterfly, small, close, and unforeseen,   75
Flurred and stood up as it would
Just off the center of sight.

Light came up again
Around it, from the grass. The fern swept in and died;
The ribs of all of us   80
From the spine were beautifully swayed. Excited, released,
The father pulled his bow. In the nervous, strong
Sharing of cord and wood, the hulk of air
Drew, huge upon itself, the tension of a bundle—
The green earth leapt; the butterfly rose   85

Off warmly into light, resettled aimlessly,
Was followed. There, where the wings
Moved among grass, exhorting the ground to breathe,
The father pulled the bowstring to his eye. Thin color blew
Away as the arrow shocked; the earth drove its quivering up   90
To balance in the shaft.

They went on, the man giving life after life
Waiting inside himself in line
In vigorous bronze, a chance to shoot,
While at his side, enseamèd air   95
In geometrical violence gave and danced
In the sound of a million marks of leaves being made
By shadow, restored, on light.

I saw them as lids
Asleep in the sun see   100
Blood shed alive upon the sight, and men in clouds
Come there, beyond Time, to Act.
Seeing, I began to see
With something not in myself, the father drop his bow,

And kneel, and take up his son in his arms,   105
Sending me no reason at all for this

To be the time, and a shining breath across
My breast laid cruciform.
With the child, I stood looking
Into the wood, past the grounded arrow,   110
And knew, with him, at last,
The sun between trees can be ridden like a beast.

Suddenly the trembling Game, bright-black and red,
Was pinched upon the feather of the shaft.
Forgetting, forgetting, the man picked up his bow   115
And poised again, one knee set forward,
Like a centaur to pull the string,
And the son watched the hidden muscles rise
In themselves in ferns to take
His father from behind,   120
Drawing the shaken curve of the bow
By the strength of his right arm out of myth.

Behind his widened, humming hands
His face and chest split open like a bean: he fled
Into the wood, a vibrant field hung up in afternoon   125
Upon dilation and fatigue: half-dark,
Half-singing, half-burning with a sky.
Beside him the butterfly woke
On its wings, from a sleep in which something had pounded
Its shoulders into gold-leaf in a hole.   130

He stopped, and fully he was clothed
In all the floated shine and nourishment of sweat.
He knelt down there, and lay. Above, the butterfly danced
To the sun, singing above sound.

Warm dark, bright cold through the little sticks, he watched, 135
As the soul sees the bars of the rib-cage
Glow into Being, around,
A long exhalation of moss

He made, bring dry from his honest form
The connected shape of weather of the years.   140
A moth crept beating in
And shifted down upon.

He heard a hill of grass go round the world
Day after day, year after year be made, and die:
Be made. And there some wind   145
Hulled among leaves and stalled,
As a step

Unseen, brought him the child with the red bow
Turning a single way among the trees.
Every branch lived dead   150
Against conceptionless waiting,

As the boy placed one foot forward. He aimed
Directly at the wings, and
Pulling back the cord, drew the blaze of color
Out of the breath of his father.   155
The man sensed a sailing of arrows

Far off, in shimmering flight: a rain
Of eyelashes, or, as the grey leaves of the willow are
By river-water shown, a glitter of pencil-marks.
All those were lost, beyond. Each tree was filled   160
With a brave and fragile earnestness of speed.
The son took on in a rush what was always his: the power,
Where only his father was concerned, of striking
Out of an infinitude of light.

Yet he above some mortal in the bush,   165
A tomb, an unset boundary-mark
Of Man, a nest where bones of hares
Were trembling, trembled still,
Put forth his hand upon his father's brow,
His own as pale as a hanging of gnats is made, and makes   170
A transparent hole in air.

Below the spread of limbs, no leaf
Ever moved, the arrow was,
Come down. Out of the blur of floating
It opened its wild, stiff bud, and fell   175

Through the child through the heart, as he lay and wept
Above, trying his best to protect, and not to do
The living he must, of a thing to death:
Through the wings, which leapt alive, and into the mould of leaves
As it held to a vibrating shape, consumed. The father rose   180

To himself with the bow at the grasses' edge,
Whose man was the body of joy.
A crown of whispering came
All to be moved by trees. The boy got up to hear
The syllables of his name take place   185
Within that endless brink of sound.
They walked back over the lawn.

Holding the bones of motion in my legs,
A skinned-out form of metal and honed wires, I waited,
Waiting for my heart, until the room-lights leapt   190
And brought the windows of the House of Earth
Gold from the grass, laid flat to the dampening ground.
Under the moon's small broken loaf

In my seventeenth year, I kept watching
For the one step the fireflies took   195
On light, then to go on in darkness.
They were all about me in depth, and much dark,
And I loved my dead father like beauty,
And with sheer, bright, bodiless steps went down

To the wood, and the coming of all my sons.   200
"The trees show the shape of Nothing,
Moved. The moon stirs weakly, until the Day of age,
The place where one may make a bed of constant love
Of his own panting shadow. The dust in you has stood,

And next will sing, then watch again,   205
Having run. Who enters the trees
Has entered also the house, and been whole among those
Whose best-loved has not told his name."

————————

The Sprinter's Sleep

1957

    Among the shades, it is he,
Beginning to warm up. About them all,
The stadium a little seems to fill
One of its sides with a flaking and almost falling
Of faces lowering down the wall,   5

Until a light is out of the moon on grass
And a weightless frosted rain has taken place.
In the radiant cool, they jog, by two's and three's
Passing together. All drawing and letting of breath becomes

More strong, more regular as they run.   10
Terrific quietening from the sound
Falls and rises, so that the temperate starter cannot speak.
They know they must undress

Themselves to a glaze of sweat beneath the moon,
Six of them, there, lined up,   15
And see their shadows stand, arms crooked, and shaking out
The muscles of their legs,
Dancing for warmth upon their ribbon lanes
Where the glimmering tape is stretched across the end.

He bends upon his blocks. Across the army cot the moonlight lies   20
With him inside. The hall of the boxcar gym
Is faint, with the bright steam of their sleep,

And he can see them all,
The other five, arisen, luminously dead,
Bunch down their nervèd shadows on the line,   25
As dreading as he to spring, this night.

———————

The Cypresses
1958

It is not as if it were painted
Between the cypresses, for they,
In only the hair between their limbs,
Nod, one time a day
In a wind   5

That might have been there all the time.
The dust of it stirs, and comes round.
It is a stillness to be walking here
Out of the shadow,
Out of the sun,   10

And to think, at the same time drawing the hot
Cow-breathed breath of the wind.
Who is your keeper, now,
In the white, stiff road
Not painted   15

Between the cypresses? A brother?
A father? Your child, who loiters with you,
Kicks at the dust, which hangs
Back, and waits for the one wind
To come again   20

And spring from the stillest of trees.
Is it up to you to become
As a little child, as the child

Must try to become as his father?
Is it that   25

Here, your son and you,
He mistakenly, you certainly in dread,
Have entered a kind of brotherhood?
His eyes are those of a brother
Belovèd   30

In this bright, silent place.
He shall dress himself
In the warm, mossed beard
Of a tombstone,
And shall walk   35

Beside you, wherever you go,
In your real, deep-growing beard
Which holds the pose of the last wind
From the far-off sea.
You are the man   40

Who has drawn him from nothing, and shown
The motion of earth, and of death
Going into the sun.
No brothers may look so lost
Once, each day: 45

He has, in the fallen wind,
Already the grave in his eye
You gave. It stops the speech on your face
As you would speak, as you cross
From shadow   50

To sun, again, on the thready ground:
Who, sleep-walking the double form
Of love, would shape a sound of your breath
As come from God and the common dead
At once, one time.   55

Poem [a]

1958

There were powerful strides in his sighing.
He rose. His body made a centaur of the bed.
    With him, four-square,
Death stood on wooden legs. He swayed about in its form.
He looked for a way out of dying   5

Like a myth and a beast, conjoined.
More kinship and majesty
    Could not be,
And nothing could look away.
Shrunk to my heart, I clung there,   10

Feeling how the walls of the room
Would disappear from around him
    And confer on his only kinsman
The shape of a beast and a statue,
A god's naked treasure of form.   15

His last long breath, drawn up
All the way from the legs of the bed,
    Like Apollo blew on my mind.
I felt the sun turn mortal in the air.
He fell from his fabulous mount.   20

Thirty years, more slowly than cancer,
You fall from there, Uncle,
    Upon my growing son,
Unfolding your face in his features,
Turning knowledge and power of dying   25

To childish, appalling play. I look,
And I am unchecked and rising
    To speak out in praise
Of the child, as he takes on a dead man's visage.
This is the face, transformed,   30

I drew from the death-room's center
Down the dark stair, as it became
    The whole of my mind:
Which I bore—luminous, weightless—over
The gritting calm of the driveway   35

Under the oak-trees, and with it sat
Looking down through the bubbling creek-bed,
    And saw, in time,
Through the sun-bearing muscle of water,
A raw, dead stone give up   40

A look like a burst of power
As squarely unchanged and unchanging
    As the gaze come out
Of a new, dead, loving mind.
Uncle, I grieved and delivered   45

Your deep features up to the child
Unknown to both of us, where now
    They move, and smile
To explode with the main-strength of shining
Of the centaur's eye, where his animal's body burns through it   50

In a gaze from a stone under water
Or through my child, from yourself. Or was I,
    In the room
Where you swayed, upright within cancer, and am I now
Death, you smile in the face of, who look like neither?   55

A Beginning Poet, Aged Sixty-Five
1958

    This at my age this night
I do, and do by out-listening God.
    All over the house is amazed.
    The table shines, as if blindly
Thinking, on my hand, immersed in the ground   5
Of patience. *It falls, it falls.*

    Yet the two or three images
Make all of that sound with their being.
    These must become as a child
    Who three years lived as my son,   10
And a horse my older brother owned,
Which stood, floated out of a field,

    Cut off at the knees
From the earth, by a rolling ground-fog.
    A cricket seizes slowly on my ear.   15
    Part of that word I can use
For the silence won from the dead. It says
A river would move like a smoke.

    It does, and then I think it.
Animals in it would stand, and this would change   20
    Their eyes, as their thin lower legs
    Dissolved. Their words on the page
Have no breath. Stand out, all things, to hear me
Call to the dead. Perpetually I see

    The light of the sun strike stone   25
In space, and fall to the summer ground
    Outside my house, stone dead
    And bright. Amazedly down
Quietly under the wind, I speak, and under the moon
Light and insect, as my hair falls out from the quick   30

In a waterfall's shuddering sound.
Do not move from the cloud-top of earth
    Where you kneel without knowing it, horse.
    Child, do not believe to change
From death. Light, I am trembling fast   35
Asleep, in the ray where the moon holds on

    To throw the sun
To the ground, each second, around me.
    I write *the child and the animal,*
    And now my staring son   40
Has mounted the river's horse.
I see all their eyes as the same

    As in unbelievable flight.
Now they shall *move within death.* Almost it is said.
    Stay silent, son: one word, or two   45
    Together, more, and you ride
A pale, tall horse down the river
Of Heaven. I have come for the living and the dead.

————

Genesis

1958

    When car-lights turn
The inside corner of the room
I wake to come singing up.
    I watch a woman burn

    Who of myself is made   5
In the sun, and turned by her heart
Into the sea. Half-buried is she
    In water, on legs of shade,

In the world's deep grave
Of dancing. Her look goes bluely out   10
Through the force of brow
    Of the new wave:

Of a sudden, I know God
Himself, when the dewy man lay down,
Could not but flesh His hand   15
    In Adam's side

I, remembering,
Can catch the movement of woman
Back to the sea, who feel one rib,
    Bent in the ring   20

Of others, touched
Like a tuning-fork, and singing curvèdly.
She springs; the wave bites down on its window;
    Her body, new-hatched,

Glides trembling over   25
The dead. In the heavy, draughting water
She lies alone, in divine, inessential life,
    And dreams of a wounded lover.

Each time I think, she is born.
A man beats broken music from his ribs   30
Where she smiles, now, into the sea, and sleeps
    Face-down, upborne.

Joel Cahill Dead

1958

The farmer, fighting busily for his home,
Heard, in the pouring sound of fire,
    From the blackened bushes something run
Straight up the back of his neck into the air.
Through smoke, he saw a stiff-winged shape   5
Smash into earth, and a great flame come from flame.

    Like a man sent for, he ran,
Waving his arms, and yelled through his sooty kerchief
    In a curving voice around
The boy who stood, amazed, beside the plane,   10
Exhaled in fire, his shirt at the shoulders smoking,
Who got then down upon one ragged knee.

    The farmer threw his hat away
As if it would take fire, and knelt beside the boy,
    Who then, by opening his own,   15
Opened the farmer's champing mouth
To speak. Between them, missing their hands,
Blood fell, and seemed to splash up from the heart

    Of stone. The wind around them changed.
Over and through them, invisible in midair,   20
    Fire leapt, from leaf to leaf.
From the other side of the house, the farmer's wife,
Expressionless, came. They picked the boy between them
Up, and stumbled him inside, where he lay down.

    He lay on top of a peacock quilt   25
And gave off a fragile steam. Above him,
    A lantern on a nail
Showed him nothing but the toothy edge of light.
He smiled, not having to breathe,
But stiffened, then, remembering the Colonel,   30

To whom he must affirm
That he had less than no excuse to lie
    Alone, in a carven bed, to hear a woman weep,
To fade in and out of his open eyes,
And see a forest, blazing, in the teeth   35
Of a cock's-combed, motionless flame,

Turned down, to bother no one while he slept
In its fluted veil of glass.

————

Dover
Believing in Kings
1958

As we drove down the ramp from the boat
The sun flashed once
Or through hand-shieldedly twice;
In a silence out of a sound
We watched for channel swimmers dim with grease,   5
Come, here, to the ale of the shallows.
Within a wind, a wind sprang slowly up.
Birds hovered where they were.
As they were there, the airstream of the cliffs
Overcame, came over them   10
In the sackcloth and breast-beating gray
The king wears newly, at evening.
In a movement you cannot imagine
Of air, the gulls fall, shaken.

No stronger than the teeth in my head   15
Or a word laid bare
On chilling glass, the breathed stone over us rode.
From its top, the eye may sail,

Outgrowing the graven nerves
Of the brow's long-thought-out lines,   20
To France, on its own color.
From a child's tall book, I knew this place
The child must believe, with the king:
Where, doubtless, now, lay lovers
Restrained by a cloud, and the moon   25
Into force coming justly, above.
In a movement you cannot imagine
Of love, the gulls fall, mating.

We stopped; the birds hung up their arms
Inside the wind   30
So that they heeled; above, around us,
Their harp-strung feathers made
The sound, quickly mortal, of sighing.
We watched them in pure obsession.
Where they did move, we moved   35
Along the cliffs, the promenade,
The walls, the pebble beach,
And felt the inmost island turn,
In their cross-cut, wing-walking cries,
To a thing, as weeping, sensitive,   40
And haunted by the balancement of light
The king wears newly, in singing.

We wandered off from the car
In the light, half-sun,
Half-moon, in a worn-down shine out of stone,   45
And the taste of an iron ladle on the wind.
In the moon's grimed, thumbprint silver
The anchor spoke through the bell,
Far out, the hour that hung in the sea.
I threw a slow-flying stone; it dropped   50
Inside the brilliant echo of a light.
In a great, clustered, overdrawn sigh
The gulls went up, on a raiment of wings
The king wears newly, in panic.

In a movement you cannot imagine   55
Of error, the gulls rise, wholly.

We climbed a wall they had flown.
Each light below
On water, shook like a thing in a lathe.
In the heron crest of a lamp,   60
Among lights, in their treading motion,
The head of my reflection seemed to sing
A dark, quickened side of the truth.
I touched my wife. I saw my son, unborn,
Left living after me, and my Self,   65
There, freed of myself,
In a stricken shade dancing together,
As a wave rolled under the water,
Lifted and rode in our images
The king wears newly, redoubling.   70

Where we went in, all power failed the house.
I spooned out light
Upon a candle thread. My wife lay down.
Through the flaming, white-bread nerve
I peered from the eye of the mind.   75
No child from the windowed dark came forth
To the hand, in its pure-blooded fire,
But the basket glow of the crown.
The glass fetched white to a breath; I understood
How the crown must come from within: 80
Of water made, and a wheel,
And of the thing in flame that seems to pant.
In a movement you cannot imagine
Of mirrors, the gulls fall, hidden.

I lay in bed. One hand in its sleeve   85
Lay open, on my breath.
My shadow dancing stilly beneath me,
Rose, through my form. I heard the bell,
In mist, step backwardly onto the waves.

The wind fell off, as candle shade   90
Unraveled our walls like knitting, and I,
Undone, outstretched through the trampled shining
Of thousands of miles of the moon,
And the fallen king
Breathed like a nosebleed, there,   95
Two men wear newly, in hiding.
In a movement you cannot imagine
Of bloodshed, the gulls fall, inward.

I listened for the coming of a barge.
In a cat's-cradling motion   100
Of oars, my father rocked, in the mist. He died;
He was dying. His whisper fell,
As I, beneath the grave. Below the drowned
I panted, in the pig-iron taste of my beard.
I yelled, as out of a bucket,   105
Through my fettered mask, before the dawn
When my arms, my big-footed legs would hang
From pothooks, strange and untimely.
The stone beat like a gull; my father's voice
Came to life, in words, in my ear.   110
In a movement you cannot imagine
Of prison, the gulls turn, calling.

Believing, then, astoundedly, in a son,
I drew from tufted stone
My sword. I slew my murderer, Lightborn, on the stair: 115
With the flat of steel, I flashed
Him dead, through his eyes high-piled in the hood.
When the tide came in, I rose
And onto the curded dark climbed out.
In the cliffs, where creatures about me swam,   120
In their thin, slain, time-serving bones,
The heavy page, the animal print of the chalk,
With wounds I glittered, dazzling as a fish.
In my short-horned, wool-gathering crown
I came from the beasts to the kingdoms   125
The king wears newly, in passing.

The sun fell down, through the moon.
The dead held house.
I hove my father to my back
And climbed from his barrow, there. 130
Pride helped me pick a queen and get a son.
The heroic drink of the womb
Broke, then, into swanlike song.
One came with scepter, one with cup,
One goatlike back'd, and one with the head of a god. 135
My mask fell away, and my gyves.
Through my sons I leapt in my ghost
The king wears newly, on fire.
In a movement you cannot imagine
Of birth, the gulls fall, crying. 140

In the cloudlike, packed, and layered realm
I wept, when I would sing.
I laid my father down where he must lie,
And entered, again, in my passion,
An older, incredible shape 145
Becoming young, as the cliffs let fall within stone
Their shadow green down from the crest.
I stood on the cliff top, alone.
My father's body in my heart
Like a buried candle danced. I saw it shed on the sea, 150
On the flats of water, far out:
A rough, selected brightness
Exchanging a flame for a wheel
The king wears slowly, in measure.

Birds drifted in my breath as it was drawn 155
From the stressing glitter
Of water. Where France becomes
Another blue lid for the eye,
I felt my green eyes turn
Surpassingly blue, of one great look upon distance. 160
The sword dissolved, in my hands; wings beat.
I watched them rise from my arms, and stood
Excited forever by love. I saw the child's eye shine

From his book, a wave of justified light.
The prisons like organs moaned. In a death like life   165
I sang like a head on a pole.
In a movement you cannot imagine
Of emblems, the gulls fall, silent.

One foot shone to me, from the sun.
I felt the sun's   170
Mortality increase. In the blown,
Brow-beating light, I woke, and saw the room
Arise like a yeast from the floor,
The window come down like a bee.
In the long-legged, warm-bodied bed   175
I thought of him who would tell
To himself, arising in his candle-cast bones:
Every man, every man
Not a king. It is I
The king wears newly, in lasting.   180
In a movement you cannot imagine
Of spells, the gulls fall, listening.

How shall the stranger wake
Who has issued from dark
With the king? With gulls asleep   185
In the blue-burning grass? And on the sea,
A blaze that is counting itself,
The white birds holding
Still, on the field of the cloth of gold,
On the self and soul of the air?   190
Who stands, big-footed with glory, yet,
With the sound falling out of his voice
And his voice halfway to his son
Whose breath Time holds, in a woman?
In a movement you cannot imagine   195
Of silence, the gulls fall, waiting.

Why not as a prince, who, as
From a distance, wakes?
Who turns from the regular mirror

To watch, at the flawing pane,   200
Pale fire on a hairspring still burning
In the puddled socket, and the fishing flash
On the shuffled rock of a wave
Overturn, in an inlaid crash
In the window's half-mirror, half-air   205
As he steps through this room from the sea?
A tossed, green crown on his head,
He combs down the hair of his spirit,
Which is dead, but for the eyes
The king wears newly, at thirty: 210

Yet who is *he?* Whom does he face, in reflection?
The stained-glass king,
Or the child, grown tall, who cried to earth and air,
To books and water: to sun and father and fire
And nothingness to come and crown him, here?   215
Or are they, both of them, and neither,
This straw-headed knave, in blue-printed blue jeans appearing:
Who, in exultant tenderness upon a woman's sleep
Onlooks, then leaps out the door out of that
Up onto the seaside path, and when the sheep track dies,   220
Two late and idle lovers in the grass
Kicks into love, and goes up the cliffs to be crowned?
In a movement you cannot imagine
Of England, the king smiles, climbing: running.

————————

The Falls

1959

Upon the light, bare, breathless water
To step, and thereby be given a skiff
That hangs by its nose to the bank
And trembles backward:

To stand on those boards like a prince   5
Whose kingdom is still as a cloud,
And through it, like a road through Heaven
The river moves:

To sink to the floor of the boat
As into a deep, straining coffin,   10
And in one motion come from my mother,
Loose the long cord:

To lie here timelessly flowing
In a bed that lives like a serpent,
And thus to extend my four limbs   15
From the spring to the sea:

To look purely into the sky,
As the current possesses my body
Like a wind, and blows me through
Land I have walked on,   20

And all in a pattern laid down
By rain, and the forces of age,
Through banks of red clay, and cane-fields,
And the heart of a forest:

And at dusk to hear the far falls   25
Risingly roaring to meet me,
And, set in that sound, eternal
Excitement of falling:

And yet, strangely, still to be
Upheld on the road to Heaven   30
Through the changing, never-changed earth
Of this lived land:

And now in all ways to be drunken,
With a mind that can lift up my body
In all the grounded music of the dead   35
Now nearer their rising:

To do nothing but rest in my smile,
With nothing to do but go downward
Simply when water shall fall
In the mineral glimmer   40

Of the lightning that lies at the end
Of the wandering path of escape
Through the fields and green clouds of my birth,
And bears me on,

Ecstatic, indifferent, and   45
My mother's son, to where insupportable water
Shall dress me in blinding clothes
For my descent.

————————

The Other

1959

Holding onto myself by the hand,
I change places into the spirit
I had as a rack-ribbed child,
And walk slowly out through my mind
To the wood, as into a falling fire   5
Where I turned from that strength-haunted body
Half-way to bronze, as I wished to:

Where I slung up the too-heavy ax-head
And prayed to my thunderous ear-drums
That the deep sweat fall with the leaves   10
And raise up a man's shape upon me,
Come forth from the work of my arms
And the great, dead tree I hit down on:
That the chicken-chested form I belabored

Might swell with the breast of a statue   15
From out of the worm-shattered bole,
While I talked all the time through my teeth
To another, unlike me, beside me:
To a brother or king-sized shadow
Who looked at me, burned, and believed me: 20
Who believed I would rise like Apollo

With armor-cast shoulders upon me:
Whose voice, whistling back through my teeth,
Counted strokes with the hiss of a serpent.
Where the sun through the bright wood drove   25
Him, mute, and floating strangely, to the ground,
He led me into his house, and sat
Upright, with a face I could never imagine,

With a great harp leant on his shoulder,
And began in deep handfuls to play it: 30
A sail strung up on its spirit
Gathered up in a ruin in his arms,
That the dog-tired soul might sing
Of the hero, withheld by its body,
Upsprung like a magical man   35

To a dying, autumnal sound.
As I stood in the shadow-ruled clearing,
Wind died, all over a thicket.
Leaves stood everywhere within falling,
And I thought of our taking the harp   40
To the tree I had battered to pieces
Many times, many days, in a fever,

With my slow-motion, moon-sided ax.
Reason fell from my mind at a touch
Of the cords, and the dead tree leapt   45
From the ground, and together, and alive.
I thought of my body to come;
My mind burst into that green.
My brother rose beside me from the earth,

With the wing-bone of music on his back   50
Trembling strongly with heartfelt gold,
And ascended like a bird into the tree,
And music fell in a comb, as I stood
In a bull's heavy, bronze-bodied shape
As it mixed with a god's, on the ground,   55
And leaned on the helve of the ax.

Now, owing my arms to the dead
Tree, and the leaf-loosing, mortal wood,
Still hearing that music amaze me,
I walk through the time-stricken forest,   60
And wish another body for my life,
Knowing that none is given
By the giant, unusable tree

And the leaf-shapen lightning of sun,
And rail at my lust of self   65
With an effort like chopping through root-stocks:
Yet the light, looming brother but more
Brightly above me is blazing,
In that music come down from the branches
In utter, unseasonable glory,   70

Telling nothing but how I made
By hand, a creature to keep me dying
Years longer, and coming to sing in the wood
Of what love still might give,
Could I turn wholly mortal in my mind,   75
My body-building angel give me rest,
This tree cast down its foliage with the years.

The Vegetable King

1959

Just after the sun
Has closed, I swing the fresh paint of the door
And have opened the new, green dark.
From my house and my silent folk
I step, and lay me in ritual down.   5

One night each April
I unroll the musty sleeping-bag
And beat from it a cloud of sleeping moths.
I leave the house, which leaves
Its window-light on the ground   10

In gold frames picturing grass,
And lie in the unconsecrated grove
Of small, suburban pines,
And never move, as the ground not ever shall move,
Remembering, remembering to feel   15

The still earth turn my house around the sun
Where all is dark, unhoped-for, and undone.
I cannot sleep until the lights are out,
And the lights of the house of grass, also,
Snap off, from underground.   20

Beneath the gods and animals of Heaven,
Mismade inspiringly, like them,
I fall to a colored sleep
Enveloping the house, or coming out
Of the dark side of the sun,   25

And begin to believe a dream
I never once have had,
Of being part of the acclaimed rebirth
Of the ruined, calm world, in spring,
When the drowned god and the dreamed-of sun   30

Unite, to bring the red, the blue,
The common yellow flower out of earth
Of the tended and untended garden: when the chosen man,
Hacked apart in the growing cold
Of the year, by the whole of mindless nature is assembled   35

From the trembling, untroubled river.
I believe I become that man, become
As bloodless as a god, within the water,
Who yet returns to walk a woman's rooms
Where flowers on the mantel-piece are those   40

Bought by his death. A warm wind springs
From the curtains. Blue china and milk on the table
Are mild, convincing, and strange.
At that time it is light,
And, as my eyelid lifts   45

An instant before the other, the last star is withdrawn
Alive, from its fiery fable.
I would not think to move,
Nor cry, "I live," just yet,
Nor shake the twinkling horsehair of my head,   50

Nor rise, nor shine, nor live
With any but the slant, green, mummied light
And wintry, bell-swung undergloom of waters
Wherethrough my severed head has prophesied
For the silent daffodil and righteous   55

Leaf, and now has told the truth.
This is the time foresaid, when I must enter
The waking house, and return to a human love
Cherished on faith through winter:
That time when I in the night   60

Of water lay, with sparkling animals of light
And distance made, with gods
Which move through Heaven only as the spheres

Are moved: by music, music.
Mother, son, and wife   65

Who live with me: I am in death
And waking. Give me the looks that recall me.
None knows why you have waited
In the cold, thin house for winter
To turn the inmost sunlight green   70

And blue and red with life,
But it must be so, since you have set
These flowers upon the table, and milk for him
Who, recurring in this body, bears you home
Magnificent pardon, and dread, impending crime.   75

———————

The Jewel
1959

Forgetting I am alive, the tent comes over me
Like grass, and dangling its light on a thread,
Turning the coffee-urn green
Where the boys upon camp-stools are sitting,
    Alone, in late night.   5

I see my coffee curving in a cup,
A blind, steeled, brimming smile
I hold up alive in my hand.
I smile back a smile I was issued,
    Alone, in late night   10

A man doubled strangely in time,
I am waiting to walk with a flashlight
Beam, as a third, weak, drifting leg
To the aircraft standing in darkness,
    Alone, in late night.   15

Who packs himself into a cockpit
Suspended on clod-hopping wheels,
With the moon held still in the tail-booms,
Has taken his own vow of silence,
   Alone, in late night.   20

Across from him, someone snaps on
The faceted lights of a cabin.
There, like the meaning of war, he sees
A strong, poor diamond of light,
   Alone, in late night,   25

And inside it, a man leaning forward
In a helmet, a mask of rubber,
In the balance of a great, stressed jewel
Going through his amazing procedure,
   Alone, in late night.   30

Truly, do I live? Or shall I die, at last,
Of waiting? Why should the fear grow loud
With the years, of being the first to give in
To the matched, priceless glow of the engines,
   Alone, in late night?   35

————

The Game

1959

In the world, or behind the world,
My child nearby is concealed:
Among the high free-ranging plants
At the edge of the bluff,
Or, on the red stone-crop below,   5
Dead, immortally hidden from view.
A cloud comes over;
Seeking a child within leaves,

Or a child whose home is the cloud,
I feel the sun strongly divide   10
Into life and death.
Lightly, at the change, someone laughs.
More charged than this wind not to speak,
Lest he fall from his life on the sound
Of my voice, I come   15
Into his waiting game.

It is filled with blue water. Upon it
Is the blank, baseless shape of the cloud.
At the edge I stand up and seek him,
Forgetting he might be, now,   20
Everywhere, his body on the rocks
Having given a child to the wind
In my ear. The sea comes forth;
The grass hovers clear of the shadow,

And I feel the crossed sun give off   25
The green earth that holds me, by burning.
A great ragged angel of sunlight
Returns its wild shape to the sea.
Lifting out of the waves, the rocks
Shine and are born again.   30
No sound may now come from another.
A laughter springs up at my feet.

My blind son stands up beside me,
The wind, at the quick of his hair,
Silent, and hiddenly blowing,   35
His eyes turning round toward my voice.
I stoop, and see the world living on darkness,
And no more danger, there,
Than the blind upon earth have beheld,
While others reached the limits of their breath,   40

And broke them, weeping only
For a stone in the sea, or the sun
Swapping light for a shade in midair.

So shall he live, whose world can show
No thing to hurt him: but in that place shall be   45
What another must seek in his terror,
And kneel to in wide-eyed thanksgiving,
That both may rise up and be found.

———————

The Landfall
1959

Blue water; upon it two possible movements.
For hours I put them together.
My shoulders shut and were opened,
And the land fell out of the world.
In my parallel hands I turned   5
The huge sea over and over,
And looked in her eyes as I rowed,
Seeing there no promise of landfall,
But only my head set its jaw,

Flame up in her mind, and burn out,   10
And I turned in my ribs, and beheld,
Far back in the whaling glitter,
A place in the sun, a bar
Of sand, a province of shadowless trembling.
We rowed round it, bringing our presence.   15
In sand we drew a circle for a bed.
Beside it we posted an oar,
And felt, as it rooted in burning,

All fish struck around us down
To the floor of the sea by the sun.   20
Our garments fell from us like grave-cloths.
Her hair shone on me and hurt me.
I entered her man-killing image;
The oar-stock burst into leaves.

My shoulder-blades hovered above me   25
Like wings, as we moved with each other.
In her eyes I flew like a gull

On the strength of two possible movements.
And yet, at the height of that motion,
We could not shade one another   30
In any position we measured.
Pain stitched my white back to the sun.
Her face changed color beneath me.
I dragged the boat onto the bar,
Overturned it, and we crept under.   35
Each fought to give breath to the other,

As the boards sprained apart in the heat,
And one fiery crack pursued us
Down the hull, where it died on her breast.
A wind reached the air. Another   40
Thing shone. In the cool-bodied water we knelt,
And righted the boat, and embarked.
We stepped through the moonlight for hours
On wood I waved thinly through water.
At midnight I turned from the ocean,   45

Up a still, mossed canal between roadways,
With trees broad as lawns leaning over
Our crusted, salt-glittering heads,
And lights going out within houses
As the wind turned around,   50
And we rose up at last in the boat
By two banks of land balanced strongly,
And touched one another,
Come back from the unrelieved kingdom

To kiss with black lips in the city,   55
To dream of mild sleep in a bed
Swept clean with a broom of its sand-grains,
Where the frame of a window upon us
Would hold, first a tree, and then features

Emerging from dark into presence   60
Above the bed's bearable glow, wherefrom
That child, never touched by the rays of the sun,
Might rise, because of love.

————

The Signs

1959

—Recovery Room, Georgia Baptist Hospital, 1958—

If he should lift his hand
I knew my one son lived beyond recall,
Back-to-back with his stretched-out shadow
    No longer, like Janus into sunlight and moonlight
    Singing. I knew the listening dead   5
    Raised up, in their assembled arms,
        Farewell, farewell, as he.

If he should turn his head
Around, in its blasted hair,
I knew he was alive, but bore the deadly king   10
    Upon his back: a shadow black and deep
    As space, in a helmet glowing with spines:
    That, prone in the body of the athlete,
        Achilles had escaped from the dead.

If he should raise his lids   15
    I knew that love was halfway in his brain,
Looking like water: that the world of death is full
    Of springs and streams, and lakes,
    Each stiller than the last, where warriors wander,
    Their breast-plates beating frankly   20
        With their hearts.

Those waters see no more
Than air, than sun, than stone,
And stare it blind: in love, in love. I held his hand.
A window like the sun went round   25
The room. Ether dissolved in a sweat.
A wandering smile broke out
Beneath his face.

As though for a brother,
He smiled: for a being who lives forever,   30
In the dead as well as the quick, in a fever of waiting.
He smiled as a cunning creature
Abandoned to time, and a hero
Who cannot die, where he looks
Like a pond on the sun,   35

Where he lies in an animal
Music. If he should tell me how
He saw his unborn brother's face
Shudder in light, I should believe him,
For I know, more than he, those lakes.   40
Before he came to life
I was father to all the dead.

I know those clip-wing'd corselets,
The helmets brittle as paper, shining like flame
And like sun, and the helpless heroes cut   45
From the spiritless air of hell,
And wild for the usage of flesh,
As they watch the sick athlete come
Awaver on fumes of gas,

To sit in their frenzied council,   50
To dance with a bee-singing sword
Among the yews and the ilex, till the golden warrior creep
On hands and knees to leap upon his back
To save his soul. My brain has glowed,
Before my son showed form,   55
To pick a son from the dead,

Alive with Apollo's shape.
That hope shed a man of light.
I could feel how a woman's womb
Would flash like a brain, with his image. Awaiting now   60
Another child, I sit with my mending son
In Spring, and watch for the dead to say
Good-bye to another of mine,

As the trees free-fall
Into their green, and the brass-bound creek   65
Hurls its bed down onward through the hills.
It is true the dead and I
Are powerfully bewildered this season
By signs of life in the loins
And those in the spirit's   70

Poor timeless flesh.
I shall ask of them what they can give me:
What contract the drunken athlete,
Wounded, sick and sleeping on his bed,
Has made with them, for a brother,   75
Below the surface of thought,
Below the ground.

Like the dead about to be
Born, I watch for signs: by kings
Escaping, by shadows, by the gods of the body   80
Made, when wounded skillfully,
And out of their minds, descending
To the dead. These I shall see, and shall answer
Too late, for they have chosen.

The Enclosure

1959

Down the track of a Philippine Island
We rode to the aircraft in trucks,
Going past an enclosure of women,
Those nurses from sick-tents,
With a fume of sand-dust at our backs.   5
We leapt to the tail-gate,
And drew back, then,
From the guards of the trembling compound,

Where the nailed wire sang like a jew's-harp,
And the women like prisoners paced.   10
In the dog-panting night-fighter climbing,
Held up between the engines like a child,
I rested my head on my hands;
The drained mask fell from my face.
I thought I could see   15
Through the dark and the heart-pulsing wire,

Their dungarees float to the floor,
And their light-worthy hair shake down
In curls and remarkable shapes
That the heads of men cannot grow,   20
And women stand deep in a ring
Of light, and whisper in panic unto us
To deliver them out
Of the circle of impotence, formed

As moonlight spins round a propeller,   25
Delicate, eternal, though roaring.
A man was suspended above them,
Outcrying the engines with lust.
He was carried away without damage,
And the women, inviolate, woke   30
In a cloud of gauze,
Overhearing the engines' matched thunder.

Then, the voice of the man, inmixed,
Seemed to them reassuring, unheard-of
Passing out softly into the hush   35
Of nipa-leaves, reeds and the sea,
And the long wind up from the beaches,
All making the nets to be trembling
Purely around them,
And fading the desperate sound   40

To the whine of mosquitoes, turned back
By the powdery cloth that they slept in,
Not touching it, sleeping or waking,
With a thing, not even their hair.
The man sat away in the moonlight,   45
In a braced, iron, kingly chair,
As the engines labored
And carried him off like a child

To the west, and the thunderstruck mainland.
It may have been the notion of a circle   50
Of light, or the sigh of the never-thumbed wire,
Or a cry with the shape of propellers,
Or the untouched and breath-trembling nets,
That led me later, at peace,
To shuck off my clothes   55
In a sickness of moonlight and patience,

With a tongue that cried low, like a jew's-harp,
And a white gaze shimmered upon me
Like an earthless moon, as from women
Sleeping kept from themselves, and beyond me,   60
To sweat as I did, to the north:
To pray to a skylight of paper, and fall
On the enemy's women
With intact and incredible love.

The Performance

1959

The last time I saw Donald Armstrong
He was staggering oddly off into the sun,
Going down, of the Philippine Islands.
I let my shovel fall, and put that hand
Above my eyes, and moved some way to one side   5
That his body might pass through the sun,

And I saw how well he was not
Standing there on his hands,
On his spindle-shanked forearms balanced,
Unbalanced, with his big feet looming and waving   10
In the great, untrustworthy air
He flew in each night, when it darkened.

Dust fanned in scraped puffs from the earth
Between his arms, and blood turned his face inside out,
To demonstrate its suppleness   15
Of veins, as he perfected his role.
Next day, he toppled his head off
On an island beach to the south,

And the enemy's two-handed sword
Did not fall from anyone's hands   20
At that miraculous sight,
As the head rolled over upon
Its wide-eyed face, and fell
Into the inadequate grave

He had dug for himself, under pressure.   25
Yet I put my flat hand to my eyebrows
Months later, to see him again
In the sun, when I learned how he died,
And imagined him, there,
Come, judged, before his small captors,   30

Doing all his lean tricks to amaze them—
The back somersault, the kip-up—
And at last, the stand on his hands,
Perfect, with his feet together,
His head down, evenly breathing,   35
As the sun poured up from the sea

And the headsman broke down
In a blaze of tears, in that light
Of the thin, long human frame
Upside down in its own strange joy,   40
And, if some other one had not told him,
Would have cut off the feet

Instead of the head,
And if Armstrong had not presently risen
In kingly, round-shouldered attendance,   45
And then knelt down in himself
Beside his hacked, glittering grave, having done
All things in this life that he could.

———————

The String

1959

Except when he enters my son,
The same age as he at his death,
I cannot bring my brother to myself.
I do not have his memory in my life,
Yet he is in my mind and on my hands.   5
I weave the trivial string upon a light
Dead before I was born.

Mark how the brother must live,
Who comes through the words of my mother.
I have been told he lay   10

In his death-bed singing with fever,
Performing with string on his fingers
Incredible feats of construction
There before he was born.

His Jacob's Coffin now   15
Floats deeply between my fingers.
The strings with my thin bones shake.
My eyes go from me, and down
Through my bound, spread hands
To the dead, from the kin of the dead,   20
Dead before I was born.

The gaze of genius comes back.
The rose-window of Chartres is in it,
And Euclid's lines upon sand,
And the sun through the Brooklyn Bridge,   25
And, caught in a web, the regard
Of a skeletal, blood-sharing child
Dead before I was born.

I believe in my father and mother
Finding no hope in these lines.   30
Out of grief, I was myself
Conceived, and brought to life
To replace the incredible child
Who built on this string in a fever
Dead before I was born.   35

A man, I make the same forms
For my son, that my brother made,
Who learnt them going to Heaven:
The coffin of light, the bridge,
The cup and saucer of pure air,   40
Cradle of Cat, the Foot of a Crow
Dead before I was born.

I raise up the bridge and the tower.
I burn the knit coffin in sunlight

For the child who has woven this city: 45
Who loved, doing this, to die:
Who thought like a spider, and sang,
And completed the maze of my fingers,
Dead before I was born.

———————

On the Hill below the Lighthouse
1959

Now I can be sure of my sleep;
I have lost the blue sea in my eyelids.
From a place in the mind too deep
For thought, a light like a wind is beginning.
    Now I can be sure of my sleep.   5

When the moon is held strongly within it,
The eye of the mind opens gladly.
Day changes to dark, and is bright,
And miracles trust to the body,
    When the moon is held strongly within it.   10

A woman comes true when I think her.
Her eyes on the window are closing.
She has dressed the stark wood of a chair.
Her form and my body are facing.
    A woman comes true when I think her.   15

Shade swings, and she lies against me.
The lighthouse has opened its brain.
A browed light travels the sea.
Her clothes on the chair spread their wings.
    Shade swings, and she lies against me.   20

Let us lie in returning light,
As a bright arm sweeps through the moon.

The sun is dead, thinking of night
Swung round like a thing on a chain.
    Let us lie in returning light. 25

Let us lie where your angel is walking
In shadow, from wall onto wall,
Cast forth from your off-cast clothing
To pace the dim room where we fell.
    Let us lie where your angel is walking, 30

Coming back, coming back, going over.
An arm turns the light world around
The dark. Again we are waiting to hover
In a blaze in the mind like a wind
    Coming back, coming back, going over. 35

    Now I can be sure of my sleep;
    The moon is held strongly within it.
    A woman comes true when I think her.
    Shade swings, and she lies against me.
    Let us lie in returning light; 40
    Let us lie where your angel is walking,
    Coming back, coming back, going over.

———————

Into the Stone

1959

On the way to a woman, I give
My heart all the way into moonlight.
Now down from all sides it is beating.
The moon turns around in the fix
Of its light; its other side totally shines. 5
Like the dead, I have newly arisen,
Amazed by the light I can throw.
Stand waiting, my love, where you are,

For slowly amazed I come forward
From my bed through the land between,   10
Through the stone held in air by my heartbeat.
My thin flesh is shed by my shadow;
My hair has turned white with a thought.
No thing that shall die as I step
May fall, or not sing of rebirth.   15
Very far from myself I come toward you

In the fire of the sun, dead-locked
With the moon's new face in its glory.
I see by the dark side of light.
I am he who I should have become.   20
A bird that has died overhead
Sings a song to sustain him forever.
Elsewhere I have dreamed of my birth,
And come from my death as I dreamed;

Each time, the moon has burned backward.   25
Each time, my heart has gone from me
And shaken the sun from the moonlight.
Each time, a woman has called,
And my breath come to life in her singing.
Once more I come home from my ghost.   30
I give up my father and mother;
My own love has raised up my limbs:

I take my deep heart from the air.
The road like a woman is singing.
It sings with what makes my heart beat   35
In the air, and the moon turn around.
The dead have their chance in my body.
The stars are drawn into their myths.
I bear nothing but moonlight upon me.
I am known; I know my love.   40

Awaiting the Swimmer
1959

Light fails, in crossing a river.
The current shines deeply without it.
I hold a white cloth in my hands.
The air turns over one leaf.
One force is left in my arms   5
To handle the cloth, spread it gently,
And show where I stand above water.

I see her loosed hair straining.
She is trying to come to me, here.
I cannot swim, and she knows it.   10
Her gaze makes the cloth burn my hands.
I can stand only where I am standing.
Shall she fail, and go down to the sea?
Shall she call, as she changes to water?

She swims to overcome fear.   15
One force is left in her arms.
How can she come, but in glory?
The current burns; I love
That moving-to-me love, now passing
The midst of the road where she's buried.   20
Her best motions come from the river;

Her fear flows away to the sea.
The way to move upon water
Is to work lying down, as in love.
The way to wait in a field   25
Is to hold a white cloth in your hands
And sing with the sound of the river.
Called here by the luminous towel,

My rib-humming breath, and my love,
She steps from the twilit water.   30
At the level of my throat, she closes

Her eyes, and ends my singing.
I wrap her thin form in the towel,
And we walk through the motionless grasses
To the house, where the chairs we sit in   35

Have only one force in their arms.
The bed like the river is shining.
Yet what shall I do, when I reach her
Through the moon opened wide on the floor-boards?
What can I perform, to come near her?   40
How hope to bear up, when she gives me
The fear-killing moves of her body?

————

Orpheus before Hades

1959

The leaf down from the branch,
Swirling, unfastened, falls;
Halfway from there to the ground
Is hypnotized, and stays.
No leaf is as still as that.   5
The earth-colored forest sways
Whose leaf is the center of waiting.

A great gray cloud lets fall
Its leaves, like the eyelids of fossils,
To a great stone skin on the ground.   10
I stand in the frozen field
In tow-sacks and burlap arrayed.
My breath disappears overhead
And white is the center of waiting.

The Spring comes out of the ground.   15
A wood shades into the air.
Each bough is as light as a fern;

All of life comes in on a breath.
My eyes turn green with the silence
Of the thing that shall move from the hillside   20
Where love is the center of waiting.

My tongue is of cloth, and I sing
As she would be singing, like water,
In a land where the cricket is flaking,
Yet chirrs, on the copper grassblade   25
The sunlight is thinking of woman,
And black is the world, in its body,
When flesh is the center of waiting

    God add one string to my lyre
    That the snow-flake and leaf-bud shall mingle   30
    As the sun within moonlight is shining:
    That the hillside be opened in heartbreak
    And the woman walk down, and be risen
    From the place where she changes, each season,
    Her death, at the center of waiting.   35

————————

Reading Genesis to a Blind Child
1960

I am hiding beside you to tell you
What the world itself cannot show,
That you walk with an untold sight
Beyond the best reach of my light.
Try as you can to bear with me   5
As I struggle to see what you see
Be born of the language I speak.

Claw, feather, fur, and beak,
The beasts come under your hand
As into the Ark, from a land   10

That a cloud out of Hell must drown,
But for you, my second-born son.
The sheep, like your mother's coat,
The bear, the bird, and the goat

Come forth, and the cunning serpent.   15
I am holding my right arm bent
That you may take hold of the curve
Of round, warm skin that must serve
For evil. Now, unbreathing, I take
A pin, for the tooth of the snake.   20
You gravely touch it, and smile

Not at me, but into the world
Where you sit in the blaze of a book
With lion and eagle and snake
Represented by pillow and pin,   25
By feathers from hats, and thin
Gull-wings of paper, loosed
From pages my fingers have traced

With the forms of free-flying birds,
And these are the best of my words.   30
If I were to ask you now
To touch the bright lid of my eye
Might I not see what you see?
Would my common brain not turn
To untellable vision, and burn   35

With the vast, creative color
Of dark, and the serpent, hidden forever
In the trembling right arm of your father,
Not speak? Can you take this book
And bring it to life with a look?   40
And can you tell me how
I have made your world, yet know

No more than I have known?
The beasts have smelled the rain,

Yet none has wailed for fear.   45
You touch me; I am here.
A hand has passed through my head,
And this is the hand of the Lord.
I have called forth the world in a word,

And am shut from the thing I have made.   50
I have loosed the grim wolf on the sheep;
Yet upon the original deep
Of your innocence, they lie down
Together; upon each beast is a crown
Of patience, immortal and bright,   55
In which is God-pleasing delight.

Your grace to me is forbidden,
Yet I am remembering Eden
As you sit and play with a sword
Of fire, made of a word,   60
And I call through the world-saving gate
Each word creating your light:
All things in patient tones,

Birds, beasts, and flowering stones,
In each new word something new   65
The world cannot yet show.
All earthly things I have led
Unto your touch, have been fed
Thus on the darkness that bore them,
By which they most mightily shine,   70

And shall never know vision from sight,
Nor light from the Source of all light.
The sun is made to be hidden,
And the meaning and prospect of Eden
To go blind as a stone, until touched,   75
And the ship in a greenwood beached
Not rise through the trees on a smoke

Of rain, till that flood break,
The sun go out in a cloud
And a voice remake it aloud,   80
Striving most gently to bring
A fit word to everything,
And to come on the thing it is seeking
Within its speaking, speaking.

———————

A Child's Room

1960

I lay in a twelve-barred cage.
My mother turned the silence of a wheel.
The sun moving over the floor
Moved with it, and carried a winding sound.
Across the wall, the light   5
Stretched onto my face, and the sound
Reached into the sea, and spoke.
   It was the river, running.

The moon through the bars of my bed
Stared my eyes wide open, not waking.   10
Along the dim wall, my mother
Lay stiffly, with eyelids of plaster.
I felt, in the night, my new blood
Come back from the tips of my fingers.
I reached for the light, as it reached me.   15
   It was the still sun, shining.

The cage door fell, and they drew me
Through the room with the river and sunlight,
Past the round spinning-wheel and the daybed,
Through the white, ghostly wall of my dwelling   20
To a place where the sun, turned loose,
Flamed wildly on terrible water.

The grass and the leaves burned my brain.
I heard my wrong voice, singing.

I lay in my twelve-barred bed   25
With the things of the world in their places.
My mother beside me sat spinning.
The moon changed itself into sunlight,
And I tempered my tongue night and day,
And fitted my voice to a wheel,   30
To sing, in their proper relation,
The sun and the river, turning.

The Wedding

1960

During that long time, in those places,
Courage did no hard thing
That could not be easily lived-with.
There, as I watched them have it,
One of them leaned   5
Low in the bell-tent,
Sewing a tiger's gold head

To the scarred leather breast of his jacket.
Another pounded softly, with a hammer,
A Dutch coin, making a ring for his wife.   10
In the late afternoon, they placed
The mallet by the pole
Of the slack tent,
And put on the tiger's head, blazing

Over the heart. Among them I moved,   15
Doing the same, feeling the heavenly beast,
Without a body, attempt in pure terror to move
His legs, as if to spring from us,

His lips, as if
To speak for us,   20
As we rode to the black-painted aircraft,

And climbed inside and took off.
Many are dead, who fell battling
The gold, helpless beast that lay
Bodiless, on their breaths   25
Like an angel
In the air,
Who wore their silver rings upon

Their gloved, sprung little fingers,
So precious had they become,   30
So full of the thought of their wives
That the scratched, tired, beaten-out shining
Was more
Humanly constant
Than they. Years later, I go feeling   35

All of them turn into heroes,
As in the closed palm of my hand,
And am strangely delighted to find
That they are, to history also,
Heroes as well,   40
Though nameless,
As the tiger dies, folded over itself in the attic,

As the moon-glowing, center-bored rings
We made good before the dark missions,
Softly pounding our handful of money,   45
Have been given safely to children,
Or nothing,
Or to the sea,
The human silver, essential to hope in the islands,

Now never worn by woman in its life.   50

Near Darien

1960

It may be the sea-moving moon
Is swayed upon the waves by what I do.
I make on the night no shade,
But a small-stepping sound upon water.
I have rowed toward the moon for miles,   5
Till the lights upon shore have been blown

Slowly out by my infinite breath,
By distance come slowly as age,
And at last, on the heart-shaken boards
Of the boat, I lie down,   10
Beginning to sleep, sustained
By a huge, ruined stone in the sky

As it draws the lost tide-water flat,
And the wind springs into the sea,
And for miles on the calming surface   15
The moon creeps into its image.
Inside the one flame of that stone
My breath sheds the light of the sun,

All water shines down out of Heaven,
And the things upon shore that I love   20
Are immortal, inescapable, there.
I know one human love,
And soon it must find me out.
I shall float in the mind of a woman

Till the sun takes its breath from my mouth,   25
And whispers to my wife upon the land,
Who, like this unbalancing light,
When the half-eaten stone in the sky
Pulls evenly, and the wind leaps out of its life,
Assembles upon this place,   30

And finds me exultantly sleeping,
My ear going down to the floor
Of the sea, overhearing, not fish,
Their gills like a bracken all swaying,
But man and wife breathing together.   35
I shall row from the sun to the beach,

Where she shall have risen from darkness,
From her vast, shining place in the moonlight,
Where a man slaved for hours to reach her
And lie in the quick of her image.   40
She shall stand to her knees in her shadow,
Gazing outward, her eyes unshaded,

As I ride blindly home from the sun,
Not wishing to know how she came there,
Commanded by glorious powers: 45
At night by the night's one stone
Laid openly on the lost waves,
By her eyes catching fire in the morning.

———————

The Scratch

1960

Once hid in a fiery twist
Of brier, it binds my wrist.
In this marked place, on a stone,
I watchfully sit down
To lift it wisely, and see   5
Blood come, as at a play,
Which shall fall outside my life.
It knows neither stone nor leaf
Nor how it has come from my heart
To find its true color in light.   10
The glaze of my death is upon it

In the shadowy sun, and yet
A merciful rust shall set in
To kill, not me, but my pain.
My arm opened up by a thorn,   15
I feel the no-soul of the rock;
I hear, through the trees, the cock
Shout out his long-necked cry.
My patience comes over the wood,
And, caught in the silence of blood,   20
The wind in the leaves stands still
And delivers its green to my will.
I raise my other-armed sleeve,
And wipe, in a kind of love,
The wellspring of love from its bed,   25
And, glancing about for the dead,
Look distantly off at my blood
As it forms upon air, as if
It were the first blood of my life,
And the last thing of earth that I owned.   30
I conjure up sons, all crowned,
Who this drop shall not inherit,
And women who shall not share it,
Who might have borne me that son
To sit on a moss-backed stone   35
And master the kingdom of silence
Forever: as I do, once.
I feel more alive thereby
Than when the same blood in my eye
Of sleep, brought my real son,   40
Or my wife, that heavenly one.
I have had no vision but this
Of blood unable to pass
Between father and son,
Yet wedding the brain and the stone,   45
The cock's cutting cry and the thorn,
And binding me, whole, in a wood,
To a prince of impossible blood.
The rock shall inherit my soul.

The gem at my wrist is dull,   50
And may or may never fall.
Which will be, I do not know.
I shall dream of a crown till I do.

———————

Uncle
1960

All around, they hiddenly hear him.
The matched, trim, saddle-shaped leaves
Scramblingly nod without wind,
Now a lake, now a clamoring chorus
Of turned-green, insolent ears   5
Pricked up inside a deep pain
That covers everything upon the earth.
If he does not move, he can live

With himself, though if he does,
His joints flash punishing fires.   10
If it were only for this,
He still would get to his feet,
Toss his hound-headed cane away,
And dance an old, rich-man's dance
Up and down on the ears of the ivy,   15
Swaying upon their deep

Unearthly, earth-bound cloud,
With rusty sparks from his knees
And elbows flying about him,
Till he seemed to cavort in the sky,   20
A human fire-works, or were
The Great Bear dancing in Heaven
In broad daylight, for joy.
Yet this way joy is the same

As if he were dancing alone;   25
The pain is almost the same,
Though he does not move any joints,
Though he keeps his long cane at his side.
He is watching the ivy grow,
Devouring his weak-kneed grass.   30
He is watching it wait to wave
Its unclaimed, ravenous heads:

Though he could walk on that water,
Or lie in it singing forever,
He had rather think of its drawing   35
Unkillable force from his ground,
To be all his wealth shall apportion
To this unbequeathable spot.
He feels that his tongue will turn
Green as an angel's one word   40

When the wings of his house disappear
Deep into a crawling cloud,
And the wide upper windows sense
The forced, triumphal approach
Creeping upward, brick by brick,   45
Like the eyes of a cat,
Till ivy festoons the rafters,
Covers each wall like a thicket,

And lifts his marriage- and death-bed
Clear of the floor, gently swinging.   50
Slowly, dancingly, he says to himself
What the taste of his shadow tells him.
The leaves rise up in his eyes,
And he may be sitting there saying
A word as alive as an angel's   55

Increase, increase, increase.

The Island

1960

A light come from my head
Showed how to give birth to the dead
That they might nourish me.
In a wink of the blinding sea
I woke through the eyes, and beheld   5
No change, but what had been,
And what cannot be seen
Any place but a burnt-out war:
The engines, the wheels, and the gear
That bring good men to their backs   10
Nailed down into wooden blocks,
With the sun on their faces through sand,
And polyps a-building the land
Around them of senseless stone.
The coral and I understood   15
That these could come to no good
Without the care I could give,
And that I, by them, must live.
I clasped every thought in my head
That bloomed from the magical dead,   20
And seizing a shovel and rake,
Went out by the ocean to take
My own sweet time, and start
To set a dead army apart.
I hammered the coffins together   25
Of patience and hobnails and lumber,
And gave them names, and hacked
Deep holes where they were stacked.
Each wooden body, I took
In my arms, and singingly shook   30
With its being, which stood for my own
More and more, as I laid it down.
At the grave's crude, dazzling verge
My true self strained to emerge
From all they could not save   35

And did not know they could give.
I buried them where they lay
In the brass-bound heat of the day,
A whole army lying down
In animal-lifted sand.   40
And then with rake and spade
I curried each place I had stood
On their chests and on their faces,
And planted the rows of crosses
Inside the blue wind of the shore.   45
I hauled more wood to that ground
And a white fence put around
The soldiers lying in waves
In my life-giving graves.
And a painless joy came to me   50
When the troopships took to the sea,
And left the changed stone free
Of all but my image and me:
Of the tonsured and perilous green
With its great, delighted design   55
Of utter finality,
Whose glowing workman stood
In the intricate, knee-high wood
In the midst of the sea's blind leagues,
Kicked off his old fatigues,   60
Saluted the graves by their rank,
Paraded, lamented, and sank
Into the intelligent light,
And danced, unimagined and free,
Like the sun taking place on the sea.   65

Sleeping Out at Easter
1960

All dark is now no more.
This forest is drawing a light.
All Presences change into trees.
One eye opens slowly without me.
My sight is the same as the sun's, 5
For this is the grave of the king,
Where the earth turns, waking a choir.
    All dark is now no more.

Birds speak, their voices beyond them.
A light has told them their song. 10
My animal eyes become human
As the Word rises out of the darkness
Where my right hand, buried beneath me,
Hoveringly tingles, with grasping
The source of all song at the root. 15
    Birds sing, their voices beyond them.

    Put down those seeds in your hand.
These trees have not yet been planted.
A light should come round the world,
Yet my army blanket is dark, 20
That shall sparkle with dew in the sun.
My magical shepherd's cloak
Is not yet alive on my flesh
    Put down those seeds in your hand.

    In your palm is the secret of waking. 25
    Unclasp your purple-nailed fingers
    And the wood and the sunlight together
    Shall spring, and make good the world.
    The sounds in the air shall find bodies,
    And a feather shall drift from the pine-top 30
    You shall feel, with your long-buried hand.
    In your palm is the secret of waking,

For the king's grave turns him to light.
A woman shall look through the window
And see me here, huddled and blazing.   35
My child, mouth open, still sleeping,
Hears the song in the egg of a bird.
The sun shall have told him that song
Of a father returning from darkness,
    For the king's grave turns you to light.   40

    All dark is now no more.
    In your palm is the secret of waking.
    Put down those seeds in your hand;
    All Presences change into trees.
    A feather shall drift from the pine-top.   45
    The sun shall have told you this song,
    For this is the grave of the king;
    For the king's grave turns you to light.

————————

The Prodigal
1960

"See!" he cried, "the dead dust turns
To green, in Umbria! It burns
To lift my steps on the road
To Heaven, stride on stride!"
He is that one I let out   5
On the old, unwavering, flat
Track that walks to Assisi.
Of a child alone in this country

I had no knowledge, but only
Great fear, and creative awe,   10
Yet knew I must let him go
Forth, on the April plain,
Believing dust-devils a sign

Of life, where plodding cows
Drew stubborn, time-killing ploughs   15
Slowly, to raise the spring

From Etruscan tombs, that it sing.
All day I sat in the door.
The wall and I sweated with fear,
Looking out the gate down the road.   20
Then slowly, up from my side,
One arm of mine stretched out
Toward that high crumbling gate,
And, poised as the dead, I saw

I beckoned, not him, but dry   25
Beggars, the halt and the lame,
Those men most immune to time
My guide-book had not allowed:
Who shambled to me in a crowd
Of eternal gestures, tossed   30
Away upon sunlight, and lost
To all living creatures but me,

Who sensed their identity,
And mine, with cattle and birds,
And the holiest movement of words,   35
Though none of these was my son,
And I had been brother to none.
Among them, I wondered if he
Were now of such company,
Or if he would come driving sheep,   40

His blond, living image deep
In their eyes, or holding a cock
On his wrist, to sell me
For sharp-edged American money.
He came at dusk, and leaping   45
Like a child released by the spring
From a tomb. At the sill he sat
Smelling of sun, and of what

Is gone when the sun is gone
To dust, somewhere between 50
This place and a holy town.
A farmer had set him astride
A bull's earthen neck, to ride
Through chickens and goats and pigs,
Moving deeply in time with the legs 55
Of a patient beast, to the church

Below the steep mountain-side
Where a saint's light whispered in shade.
He had clambered alone through the wood
And sat on the knotted bough 60
Whose birds are still pondering how
They may live by the sermon they heard
Preached there in the leaf-like mother
Tongue, by their human brother.

He had come back onto the plain 65
Into dust, and the dusty green.
"Something turned in my mind," he said.
"I walked up a hill from the road,
And where I had stumbled alone
Were my many steps arising alone 70
Into air, and porous with sun,
Each feather-foot standing alone:

And then the whole space of a wind
Moved; for miles my footprints danced
Without me, and I with them. 75
I climbed the vast tree of the air
And leapt in my footsteps, where
They were dancing like leaves, over sheep
And goats, at the heart of my life,
And a saint whole-heartedly sang 80

Through animals, making the spring
Abound. What to do, if cast among

The beasts and birds of that song
In the dead's frail, many dusts,
Raised up from the singing beasts   85
In my own resurrected stride
Through the chanting, holy word,
I have come to myself, at last,

Thick-plastered with animal dust,
Before this house, and find   90
The poor of this country around
My earthly father, who hands me
Handfuls of American money,
And grins as he gives it away
Right and left to the halt and the lame,   95
With a cock on his timeless arm,

With a strange mote of dust in his eye,
With beggars and children about him
Silent as leaves, all of whom
He seems to be blessing with silence: 100
What to do, when out of that dance
Of birds, I have fallen to earth,
Whose steps on the white road knew
How to bear my wild body to Heaven,

And I have walked home, forgiven,   105
Instead, and found my father
And beggars and blind goats together
Grinning, while a dead wall drips
Human sweat as it keeps
Shining without any sun,   110
And the last of the money is gone,
And the cock on his shoulder hops

To mine, as my body drops
Beside him down on the sill:
How shall I know who I am,   115
And how can I tell it to him?

Shall I sing like a bird or a bull,
Or dance upon light, or fall
Like a leaf, now I can give
More human love than I have?"   120

———————

To Landrum Guy,
Beginning to Write at Sixty
1960

One man in a house
Consumed by the effort of listening,
Sets down a worried phrase upon a paper.
It is poor, though it has come

From the table as out of a wall,   5
From his hand as out of his heart.

To sixty years it has come
At the same rate of time as he.
He cannot tell it, ever, what he thinks.
It is time, he says, he must   10

Be thinking of nothing but singing,
Be singing of nothing but love.

But the right word cannot arrive
Through the dark, light house of one man
With his savage hand on a book,   15
With a cricket seizing slowly on his ear:

One man in a house cannot hear
His ear, with his hair falling out from the quick.

Even to himself he cannot say
Except with not one word,   20
How he hears there is no more light
Than this, nor any word

More anywhere: how he is drunk
On hope, and why he calls himself mad.

Weeping is steadily built, and does not fall   25
From the shadow sitting slowly behind him
On the wall, like an angel who writes him a letter
To tell him his only talent is too late

To tell, to weep, to speak, or to begin
Here, or ever. Here, where he begins.   30

———————

The Underground Stream
1960

I lay at the edge of a well,
And thought how to bury my smile
Under the thorn, where the leaf,
At the sill of oblivion safe,
Put forth its instant green   5
In a flow from underground.
I sought how the spirit could fall
Down this moss-feathered well:
The motion by which my face
Could descend through structureless grass,   10
Dreaming of love, and pass
Through solid earth, to rest
On the unseen water's breast,
Timelessly smiling, and free

Of the world, of light, and of me. 15
I made and imagined that smile
To float there, mile on mile
Of streaming, unknowable wonder,
Overhearing a silence like thunder
Possess every stone of the well 20
Forever, where my face fell
From the upper, springtime world,
And my odd, living mouth unfurled
An eternal grin, while I
In the bright and stunned grass lay 25
And turned to air without age.
My first love fingered a page
And sang with Campion.
The heart in my breast turned green;
I entered the words afresh, 30
At one with her singing flesh.
But all the time I felt
The secret triumph melt
Down through the rooted thorn,
And the smile I filtered through stone 35
Motionless lie, not murmuring
But listening only, and hearing
My image of joy flow down.
I turned from the girl I had found
In a song once sung by my mother, 40
And loved my one true brother,
The tall cadaver, who
Either grew or did not grow,
But smiled, with the smile of singing,
Or a smile of incredible longing 45
To rise through a circle of stone,
Gazing up at a sky, alone
Visible, at the top of a well,
And seeking for years to deliver
His mouth from the endless river 50
Of my oil-on-the-water smile,
And claim his own grave face

That mine might live in its place.
I lay at the edge of a well;
And then I smiled, and fell.   55

————————

Walking on Water
1960

Feeling it with me
On it, barely float, the narrow plank on the water,
I stepped from the clam-shell beach,
Breaking in nearly down through the sun
Where it lay on the sea,   5
And poled off, gliding upright
Onto the shining topsoil of the bay.

Later, it came to be said
That I was seen walking on water,
Not moving my legs   10
Except for the wrong step of sliding:
A child who leaned on a staff,
A curious pilgrim hiking
Between two open blue worlds,

My motion a miracle,   15
Leaving behind me no footprint,
But only the shimmering place
Of an infinite step upon water
In which sat still and were shining
Many marsh-birds and pelicans.   20
Alongside my feet, the shark

Lay buried and followed,
His eyes on my childish heels.
Thus, taking all morning to stalk

From one littered beach to another,   25
I came out on land, and dismounted,
Making marks in the sand with my toes
Which truly had walked there, on water,

With the pelicans beating their shadows
Through the mirror carpet   30
Down, and the shark pursuing
The boy on the burning deck
Of a bare single ship-wrecked board.
Shoving the plank out to sea, I walked
Inland, on numb sparkling feet,   35

With the sun on the sea unbroken,
Nor the long quiet step of the miracle
Doing anything behind me but blazing,
With the birds in it nodding their heads,
That must ponder that footstep forever,   40
Rocking, or until I return
In my ghost, which shall have become, then,

A boy with a staff,
To loose them, beak and feather, from the spell
Laid down by a balancing child,   45
Unstable, tight-lipped, and amazed,
And, under their place of enthrallment,
A huge, hammer-headed spirit
Shall pass, as if led by the nose into Heaven.

———————

Trees and Cattle
1960

Many trees can stand unshaded
In this place where the sun is alone,
But some may break out.

They may be taken to Heaven,
So gold is my only sight.   5

Through me, two red cows walk;
From a crowning glory
Of slowness they are not taken.
Let one hoof knock on a stone,
And off it a spark jump quickly,   10

And fire may sweep these fields,
And all outburn the blind sun.
Like a new light I enter my life,
And hover, not yet consumed,
With the trees in holy alliance,   15

About to be offered up,
About to get wings where we stand.
The whole field stammers with gold;
No leaf but is actively still;
There is no quiet or noise;   20

Continually out of a fire
A bull walks forth,
And makes of my mind a red beast
At each step feeling how
The sun more deeply is burning   25

Because trees and cattle exist.
I go away, in the end.
In the shade, my bull's horns die
From my head; in some earthly way
I have been given my heart: 30

Behind my back, a tree leaps up
On wings that could save me from death.
Its branches dance over my head.
Its flight strikes a root in me.
A cow beneath it lies down.   35

A Birth
1960

Inventing a story with grass,
I find a young horse deep inside it.
I cannot nail wires around him;
My fence posts fail to be solid,

And he is free, strangely, without me.   5
With his head still browsing the greenness,
He walks slowly out of the pasture
To enter the sun of his story.

My mind freed of its own creature,
I find myself deep in my life   10
In a room with my child and my mother,
When I feel the sun climbing my shoulder

Change, to include a new horse.

Between Two Prisoners
1960

I would not wish to sit
In my shape bound together with wire,
Wedged into a child's sprained desk
In the schoolhouse under the palm tree.
Only those who did could have done it.   5

One bled from a cut on his temple,
And sat with his yellow head bowed,
His wound for him painfully thinking.
A belief in words grew upon them
That the unbound, who walk, cannot know.   10

The guard at the window leaned close
In a movement he took from the palm tree,
To hear, in a foreign tongue,
All things which cannot be said.
In the splintering clapboard room   15

They rested the sides of their faces
On the tops of the desks as they talked.
Because of the presence of children
In the deep signs carved in the desk tops,
Signs on the empty blackboard   20

Began, like a rain, to appear.
In the luminous chalks of all colors,
Green face, yellow breast, white sails
Whose wing feathers made the wall burn
Like a waterfall seen in a fever,   25

An angel came boldly to light
From his hands casting green, ragged bolts
Each having the shape of a palm leaf.
Also traced upon darkness in chalk
Was the guard at the rear window leaning   30

Through the red, vital strokes of his tears.
Behind him, men lying with swords
As with women, heard themselves sing,
And woke, then, terribly knowing
That they were a death squad, singing   35

In its sleep, in the middle of a war.
A wind sprang out of the tree.
The guard awoke by the window,
And found he had talked to himself
All night, in two voices, of Heaven.   40

He stood in the sunlit playground
Where the quiet boys knelt together
In their bloodletting trusses of wire,

And saw their mussed, severed heads
Make the ground jump up like a dog.   45

I watched the small guard be hanged
A year later, to the day,
In a closed horse stall in Manila.
No one knows what language he spoke
As his face changed into all colors,   50

And gave off his red, promised tears,
Or if he learned blindly to read
A child's deep, hacked hieroglyphics
Which can call up an angel from nothing,
Or what was said for an instant, there,   55

In the tied, scribbled dark, between him
And a figure drawn hugely in chalk,
Speaking words that can never be spoken
Except in a foreign tongue,
In the end, at the end of a war.   60

Drowning with Others
1960

There are moments a man turns from us
Whom we have all known until now.
Upgathered, we watch him grow,
Unshipping his shoulder bones

Like human, everyday wings   5
That he has not ever used,
Releasing his hair from his brain,
A kingfisher's crest, confused

By the God-tilted light of Heaven.
His deep, window-watching smile   10
Comes closely upon us in waves,
And spreads, and now we are

At last within it, dancing.
Slowly we turn and shine
Upon what is holding us,   15
As under our feet he soars,

Struck dumb as the angel of Eden,
In wide, eye-opening rings.
Yet the hand on my shoulder fears
To feel my own wingblades spring,   20

To feel me sink slowly away
In my hair turned loose like a thought
Of a fisherbird dying in flight.
If I opened my arms, I could hear

Every shell in the sea find the word   25
It has tried to put into my mouth.
Broad flight would become of my dancing,
And I would obsess the whole sea,

But I keep rising and singing
With my last breath. Upon my back,   30
With his hand on my unborn wing,
A man rests easy as sunlight

Who has kept himself free of the forms
Of the deaf, down-soaring dead,
And me laid out and alive   35
For nothing at all, in his arms.

Mindoro, 1944

1960

Six boys have slung a coffin by the ropes
Above the dog-eye-colored land
And town of San José
Of hot dog-fur and tin,
And they, and all of it, are growing in-   5
ward, in the motion of the sun
Unbearably shimmering to uncoil.
Many have been killed, and they are lying down.
Light falls, man falls: together.
Sun rises from earth alone.   10

The bottled brightness of heat
Holds queerly a spade's scratched flame.
There is a log, a trembling barge
In air, and it is hard to hollow or to load.
Its wood-grain sews a sheet among their hands.   15
Each eye is equal in the mighty head
Of military gold. Behind their wheels,
The trucks are lifting roads from where they lie.
Wheels fall, man falls: together.
Dust rises from earth alone.   20

In the balance walking breathless in their palms
He must not seem to move or be aware.
He leans, he feels he leans
Slowly from fist to fist again around.
He does not know how much or where   25
He swings, nor yet how much
Of him is stalled between, afloat inside
The muscles of their arms. He feels it shake.
He feels it pant, a pack of dogs, with life.
Beast falls, man falls: together.   30
Birth rises from earth alone.

He strains to remember when.
May it be now he rises from his place
Like flame along the down of burning string,
Inwinding, as he glows among his knots,   35
Six tall sway-headed forms? And this be his?
"Who, among you come, has not yet seen
Mutilation in full flight slain?"
He asks. Truthfully they are still.
Truth falls, man falls: together.   40
Thought rises from earth alone.

He is! He is outside!
He glitters sandily all about the spade!
He dances like dust in the pit
In all their good arms at once!   45
Blind as he is, as a ball of paper on fire,
He knows he must do nothing with the world!
Nothing! And see it blazing, there! He cries,
And laughs in it. He clings with their hands to the ropes.
His heart stops all around him, in the sun.   50
He picks up everything and loves.
Sun falls, man falls: together.
Light rises from earth alone.

————————

Autumn

1960

I see the tree think it will turn
Brown, and tomorrow at dawn
It will change as it thinks it will change,

But faster, bringing in orange,
And smoking and king-killing gold.   5
The fire of death shall change colors,

But before its rich images die,
Some green will be thought of in glory.
The dead shall withhold it until

The sleep of the world take on   10
The air of awaiting an angel
To descend into Hell, and to blow

With his once-a-year breath upon grass roots,
And deliver the year from its thinking
To the mindless one color of life.   15

Listening to Foxhounds
1960

When in that gold
Of fires, quietly sitting
With the men whose brothers are hounds,

You hear the first tone
Of a dog on scent, you look from face   5
To face, to see whose will light up.

When that light comes
Inside the dark light of the fire,
You know which chosen man has heard

A thing like his own dead   10
Speak out in a marvelous, helpless voice
That he has been straining to hear.

Miles away in the dark,
His enchanted dog can sense
How his features glow like a savior's,   15

And begins to hunt
In a frenzy of desperate pride.
Among us, no one's eyes give off a light

For the red fox
Playing in and out of his scent,   20
Leaping stones, doubling back over water.

Who runs with the fox
Must sit here like his own image,
Giving nothing of himself

To the sensitive flames,   25
With no human joy rising up,
Coming out of his face to be seen.

And it is hard,
When the fox leaps into his burrow,
To keep that singing down,   30

To sit with the fire
Drawn into one's secret features,
And all eyes turning around

From the dark wood
Until they come, amazed, upon   35
A face that does not shine

Back from itself,
That holds its own light and takes more,
Like the face of the dead, sitting still,

Giving no sign,   40
Making no outcry, no matter
Who may be straining to hear.

Antipolis

1960

Through the town-making stones I step lightly.
Each thing in the market place looks
Clear through me, not able to help it.
Squid lounging in death in their barrel
See me staring through life down among them.   5
They deepen the depth of their gaze.
The eyes of the dead hold me brightly.
I take all their looks into mine
And lift them up

Alive, and carry them out through the door   10
The Greeks made to give on the sea.
The world opens wide and turns blue.
My heart shines in me like sunlight.
I scramble up sill after sill,
Past windows where women are washing   15
My strange, heavy, foreigner's clothes.
My voice in amazement dwindles
To that of a child,

And with it I call to my son,
Who reads Greek somewhere below me.   20
He answers; a dead tongue sings.
I leap to the bread-colored rampart,
And stroll there, sweating and staring
Down into the powder-blue ocean
With dozens of dead, round, all-seeing eyes   25
In my head, which have seen ships sink
Through this water

And gods rise, wearing their sails.
A hundred feet over the ocean,
My hands dead white with the flour   30
Of the market, knowing and saying
The same timeless thought as the sun,

Which thinks of itself in its glory
As Pericles' head on a coin,
I hear in my voice two children,   35
My son and my soul,

Sing to each other through ages.
In the windows, men with their women
Among my dark garments burn cleanly.
Because I am drunk on the rampart,   40
My son reads Homer more deeply,
And the blue sea has caught me alive
In my own glance, the look of some daring,
Unbelieved, believing and dancing
Most loving creature.   45

A View of Fujiyama after the War
1960

Wind, and all the midges in the air,
On wings you cannot see, awake
Where they must have been sleeping in flight.
I breathe, and twenty miles away

Snow streams from the mountain top   5
And all other mountains are nothing.
The ground of the enemy's country
Shakes; my bones settle back where they stand.

Through the bloom of gnats in the sun,
Shaken less than my heart by the tremor,   10
The blossom of a cherry tree appears.
The mountain returns my last breath,

And my hair blows, weightless as snow.
When it is still, when it is as still as this,

It could be a country where no one   15
Ever has died but of love.

I take the snow's breath and I speak it.
What I say has the form of a flame
Going all through the gnats like their spirit,
And for a swarming moment they become,   20

Almost, my own drunk face in the air
Against the one mountain in Heaven.
It is better to wait here quietly,
Not for my face to take flight,

But for someone to come from the dead   25
Other side of the war to this place:
Who thinks of this ground as his home,
Who thinks no one else can be here,

And that no one can see him pass
His hand through a visage of insects,   30
His hand through the cone of the mountain
To pluck the flower. But will he feel

His sobbing be dug like a wellspring
Or a deep water grow from his lids
To light, and break up the mountain   35
Which sends his last breath from its summit

As it dances together again?
Can he know that to live at the heart
Of his saved, shaken life, is to stand
Overcome by the enemy's peace?   40

Inside the River

1960

Dark, deeply. A red.
All levels moving
A given surface.
Break this. Step down.
Follow your right   5
Foot nakedly in
To another body.
Put on the river
Like a fleeing coat,
A garment of motion,   10
Tremendous, immortal.
Find a still root

To hold you in it.
Let flowing create
A new, inner being: 15
As the source in the mountain
Gives water in pulses,
These can be felt at
The heart of the current.
And here it is only   20
One wandering step
Forth, to the sea.
Your freed hair floating
Out of your brain,

Wait for a coming   25
And swimming idea.
Live like the dead
In their flying feeling.
Loom as a ghost
When life pours through it.   30
Crouch in the secret
Released underground
With the earth of the fields

All around you, gone
Into purposeful grains   35
That stream like dust

In a holy hallway.
Weight more changed
Than that of one
Now being born,   40
Let go the root.
Move with the world
As the deep dead move,
Opposed to nothing.
Release. Enter the sea   45
Like a winding wind.
No. Rise. Draw breath.
Sing. See no one.

———————

The Magus
1960

It is time for the others to come.
This child is no more than a god.

No cars are moving this night.
The lights in the houses go out.

I put these out with the rest.   5
From his crib, the child begins

To shine, letting forth one ray
Through the twelve simple bars of his bed

Down into the trees, where two
Long-lost other men shall be drawn   10

Slowly up to the brink of the house,
Slowly in through the breath on the window.

But how did I get in this room?
Is this my son, or another's?

Where is the woman to tell me   15
How my face is lit up by his body?

It is time for the others to come.
An event more miraculous yet

Is the thing I am shining to tell you.
This child is no more than a child.   20

1961–1967

Armor

1961–1962

When this is the thing you put on
The world is pieced slowly together
In the power of the crab and the insect.
The make of the eyeball changes
As over your mouth you draw down   5
A bird's bill made for a man.

As your weight upon earth is redoubled
There is no way of standing alone
More, or no way of being
More with the bound, shining dead.   10
You have put on what you should wear,
Not into the rattling of battle,

But into a silence where nothing
Threatens but Place itself: the shade
Of the forest, the strange, crowned   15
Motionless sunlight of Heaven,
With the redbird blinking and shooting
Across the nailed beam of the eyepiece.

In that light, in the wood, in armor,
I look in myself for the being   20
I was in a life before life
In a glade more silent than breathing,
Where I took off my body of metal
Like a brother whose features I knew

By the feel of their strength on my face   25
And whose limbs by the shining of mine.

In a vision I fasten him there,
The bright locust shell of my strength
Like a hanged man waiting in Heaven,
And then steal off to my life.   30

In my home, a night nearer death,
I wake with no shield on my breastbone,
Breathing deep through my sides like an insect,
My closed hand falling and rising
Where it lies like the dead on my heart.   35
I cannot remember my brother;

Before I was born he went from me
Ablaze with the meaning of typhoid.
In a fever I see him turn slowly
Under the strange, perfect branches   40
Where somehow I left him to wait
That I might be naked on earth,

His crowned face dazzlingly closed,
His curving limbs giving off
Pure energy into the leaves.   45
When I give up my hold on my breath
I long to dress deeply at last
In the gold of my waiting brother

Who shall wake and shine on my limbs
As I walk, made whole, into Heaven.   50
I shall not remember his face
Or my dazed, eternal one
Until I have opened my hand
And touched the grave glow of his breast

To stop the gaunt turning of metal: 55
Until I have let the still sun
Down into the stare of the eyepiece
And raised its bird's beak to confront
What man is within to live with me
When I begin living forever.   60

The Change

1961

Blue, unstirrable, dreaming,
The hammerhead goes by the boat,
Passing me slowly in looking.

He has singled me out from the others;
He has put his blue gaze in my brain.   5
The strength of creation sees through me:

The world is yet blind as beginning.
The shark's brutal form never changes.
No millions of years shall yet turn him

From himself to a man in love,   10
Yet I feel that impossible man
Hover near, emerging from darkness,

Like a creature of light from the ocean.
He is what I would make of myself
In ten millions years, if I could,   15

And arise from my brute of a body
To a thing the world never thought of
In a place as apparent as Heaven.

I name the blue shark in the water,
And the heart of my brain has spoken   20
To me, like an unknown brother,

Gently of ends and beginnings,
Gently of sources and outcomes,
Impossible, brighter than sunlight.

Hunting Civil War Relics
at Nimblewill Creek

1961

As he moves the mine detector
A few inches over the ground,
Making it vitally float
Among the ferns and weeds,
I come into this war   5
Slowly, with my one brother,
Watching his face grow deep
Between the earphones,
For I can tell
If we enter the buried battle   10
Of Nimblewill
Only by his expression.

Softly he wanders, parting
The grass with a dreaming hand.
No dead cry yet takes root   15
In his clapped ears
Or can be seen in his smile.
But underfoot I feel
The dead regroup,
The burst metals all in place,   20
The battle lines be drawn
Anew to include us
In Nimblewill,
And I carry the shovel and pick

More as if they were   25
Bright weapons that I bore.
A bird's cry breaks
In two, and into three parts.
We cross the creek; the cry
Shifts into another,   30
Nearer, bird, and is
Like the shout of a shadow—

Lived-with, appallingly close—
Or the soul, pronouncing
"Nimblewill":   35
Three tones; your being changes.

We climb the bank;
A faint light glows
On my brother's mouth.
I listen, as two birds fight   40
For a single voice, but he
Must be hearing the grave,
In pieces, all singing
To his clamped head,
For he smiles as if   45
He rose from the dead within
Green Nimblewill
And stood in his grandson's shape.

No shot from the buried war
Shall kill me now,   50
For the dead have waited here
A hundred years to create
Only the look on the face
Of my one brother,
Who stands among them, offering   55
A metal dish
Afloat in the trembling weeds,
With a long-buried light on his lips
At Nimblewill
And the dead outsinging two birds.   60

I choke the handle
Of the pick, and fall to my knees
To dig wherever he points,
To bring up mess tin or bullet,
To go underground   65
Still singing, myself,
Without a sound,
Like a man who renounces war,

Or one who shall lift up the past,
Not breathing "Father,"   70
At Nimblewill,
But saying, "Fathers! Fathers!"

————————

Via Appia
1961

Going through me, the Roman sun
Leaves the seeds of wings in my shoulders.
Two women are shining also.

We are watching the Roman stone
We sit on, float through the grass.   5
Beneath it a soldier is lying.

Moment by moment his lungs
With flowers are filling more deeply,
And his shield, with the lichen of rust.

If we were to step from his grave   10
We would fall through this earth as through water.
We would lie in the full weight of armor,

In the ponderous death of all Rome.
Yet now I am thinking of children,
Of the two ways to go after death.   15

With the blond, heavy girl, I can shed
This very sun down through the years
On my grandchildren's coarse, blinding hair;

With the dark, other one, I could twist
Black, vine-scented curls on their foreheads.   20
I choose the bright woman, and touch her.

I see that she looks more deeply
Into death, to watch life rise.
She could crack this stone with a smile.

Yet I think of the dark woman's children,   25
All spirit, and great-eyed with singing
In another world, waiting to come.

When I turn the blind sides of myself,
Like armor or gold water flashing,
And come back from death as another,   30

Unremembered, descending the sun,
Or drifting my dust through the smile
Of the stone love breaks like a wafer,

I shall come for my chorus of children
Kept from life by those that I shall   35
Have known in my present body.

Dark choir behind the huge light,
Thin voices with flowers for lungs,
I almost hear . . .
          I hear you.

————————

The Twin Falls

1961

They fall through my life and surround me
Where I stand on a stone held between them,
And help them sing down the lifting

Of leaves in the springtime valley.
If I move my bare arms, the wings   5
Of water shake and are whiter.

I dance on the unshaken stone
And the rock rises up in my voice
As water the shape of my shoulders

Falls past without passing or moving.　　　　　　10
Lifting up the blind spirit of bedrock,
My voice falls in waves on the green

Held up in a storm to receive it,
Where trees with their roots in my standing
Are singing it back to surround me　　　　　　15

And telling me how my light body
Falls through the still years of my life
On great, other wings than its own.

———————

The Summons

1961

For something out of sight,
I cup a grass-blade in my hands,
Tasting the root, and blow.
I speak to the wind, and it lives.
No hunter has taught me this call;　　　　　　5
It comes out of childhood and playgrounds.
I hang my longbow on a branch.
The wind at my feet extends

Quickly out, across the lake,
Containing the sound I have made　　　　　　10
The water below me becomes
Bright ploughland in its body.
I breathe on my thumbs, and am blowing

A horn that encircles the forest.
Across the lake, a tree   15
Now thrums in tremendous cadence.

Beneath it, some being stumbles,
And answers me slowly and greatly
With a tongue as rasping as sawgrass.
I lower my hands, and I listen   20
To the beast that shall die of its love.
I sound my green trumpet again,
And the whole wood sings in my palms.
The vast trees are tuned to my bowstring

And the deep-rooted voice I have summoned.   25
I have carried it here from a playground
Where I rolled in the grass with my brothers.
Nothing moves, but something intends to.
The water that puffed like a wing
Is one flattened blaze through the branches.   30
Something falls from the bank, and is swimming.
My voice turns around me like foliage,

And I pluck my longbow off the limb
Where it shines with a musical light,
And crouch within death, awaiting   35
The beast in the water, in love
With the palest and gentlest of children,
Whom the years have turned deadly with knowledge:
Who summons him forth, and now
Pulls wide the great, thoughtful arrow.   40

Fog Envelops the Animals

1961

Fog envelops the animals.
Not one can be seen, and they live.
At my knees, a cloud wears slowly
Up out of the buried earth.
In a white suit I stand waiting.   5

Soundlessly whiteness is eating
My visible self alive.
I shall enter this world like the dead,
Floating through tree trunks on currents
And streams of untouchable pureness   10

That shine without thinking of light.
My hands burn away at my sides
In the pale, risen ghosts of deep rivers.
In my hood peaked like a flame,
I feel my own long-hidden,   15

Long-sought invisibility
Come forth from my solid body.
I stand with all beasts in a cloud.
Of them I am deadly aware,
And they not of me, in this life.   20

Only my front teeth are showing
As the dry fog mounts to my lips
In a motion long buried in water,
And now, one by one, my teeth
Like rows of candles go out.   25

In the spirit of flame, my hood
Holds the face of my soul without burning,
And I drift forward
Through the hearts of the curdling oak trees,
Borne by the river of Heaven.   30

My arrows, keener than snowflakes,
Are with me whenever I touch them.
Above my head, the trees exchange their arms
In the purest fear upon earth.
Silence. Whiteness. Hunting.   35

———————

Facing Africa

1961

These are stone jetties,
And, in the close part of the night,
Connected to my feet by long
Warm, dangling shadows
On the buttressed water,   5
Boats are at rest.

Beyond, the harbor mouth opens
Much as you might believe
A human mouth would open
To say that all things are a darkness.   10
I sit believing this
As the boats beneath me dissolve

And shake with a haunted effort
To come into being again,
And my son nods at my side,   15
Looking out also
Into dark, through the painted
Living shadows of dead-still hulls

Toward where we imagine Africa
To bloom late at night   20
Like a lamp of sand held up,
A top-heavy hourglass, perhaps,

With its heaped, eternal grains
Falling, falling

Into the lower, green part   25
Which gives off quick, leafy flashes
Like glimpses of lightning.
We strain to encounter that image
Halfway from its shore to ours:
To understand   30

The undermined glowing of sand
Lifted at midnight
Somewhere far out above water,
The effortless flicker of trees
Where a rumor of beasts moves slowly   35
Like wave upon wave.

What life have we entered by this?
Here, where our bodies are,
With a green and gold light on his face,
My staring child's hand is in mine,   40
And in the stone
Fear like a dancing of peoples.

————————

In the Tree House at Night
1961

And now the green household is dark.
The half-moon completely is shining
On the earth-lighted tops of the trees.
To be dead, a house must be still.
The floor and the walls wave me slowly;   5
I am deep in them over my head.
The needles and pine cones about me

Are full of small birds at their roundest,
Their fists without mercy gripping
Hard down through the tree to the roots   10
To sing back at light when they feel it.
We lie here like angels in bodies,
My brothers and I, one dead,
The other asleep from much living,

In mid-air huddled beside me.   15
Dark climbed to us here as we climbed
Up the nails I have hammered all day
Through the sprained, comic rungs of the ladder
Of broom handles, crate slats, and laths
Foot by foot up the trunk to the branches   20
Where we came out at last over lakes

Of leaves, of fields disencumbered of earth
That move with the moves of the spirit.
Each nail that sustains us I set here;
Each nail in the house is now steadied   25
By my dead brother's huge, freckled hand.
Through the years, he has pointed his hammer
Up into these limbs, and told us

That we must ascend, and all lie here.
Step after step he has brought me,   30
Embracing the trunk as his body,
Shaking its limbs with my heartbeat,
Till the pine cones danced without wind
And fell from the branches like apples.
In the arm-slender forks of our dwelling   35

I breathe my live brother's light hair.
The blanket around us becomes
As solid as stone, and it sways.
With all my heart, I close
The blue, timeless eye of my mind.   40
Wind springs, as my dead brother smiles
And touches the tree at the root;

A shudder of joy runs up
The trunk; the needles tingle;
One bird uncontrollably cries. 45
The wind changes round, and I stir
Within another's life. Whose life?
Who is dead? Whose presence is living?
When may I fall strangely to earth,

Who am nailed to this branch by a spirit? 50
Can two bodies make up a third?
To sing, must I feel the world's light?
My green, graceful bones fill the air
With sleeping birds. Alone, alone
And with them I move gently. 55
I move at the heart of the world.

————

The Lifeguard

1961

In a stable of boats I lie still,
From all sleeping children hidden.
The leap of a fish from its shadow
Makes the whole lake instantly tremble.
With my foot on the water, I feel 5
The moon outside

Take on the utmost of its power.
I rise and go out through the boats.
I set my broad sole upon silver,
On the skin of the sky, on the moonlight, 10
Stepping outward from earth onto water
In quest of the miracle

This village of children believed
That I could perform as I dived

For one who had sunk from my sight. 15
I saw his cropped haircut go under.
I leapt, and my steep body flashed
Once, in the sun.

Dark drew all the light from my eyes.
Like a man who explores his death 20
By the pull of his slow-moving shoulders,
I hung head down in the cold,
Wide-eyed, contained, and alone
Among the weeds,

And my fingertips turned into stone 25
From clutching immovable blackness.
Time after time I leapt upward
Exploding in breath, and fell back
From the change in the children's faces
At my defeat. 30

Beneath them I swam to the boathouse
With only my life in my arms
To wait for the lake to shine back
At the risen moon with such power
That my steps on the light of the ripples 35
Might be sustained.

Beneath me is nothing but brightness
Like the ghost of a snowfield in summer.
As I move toward the center of the lake,
Which is also the center of the moon, 40
I am thinking of how l may be
The savior of one

Who has already died in my care.
The dark trees fade from around me.
The moon's dust hovers together. 45
I call softly out, and the child's
Voice answers through blinding water.
Patiently, slowly,

He rises, dilating to break
The surface of stone with his forehead.   50
He is one I do not remember
Having ever seen in his life.
The ground I stand on is trembling
Upon his smile.

I wash the black mud from my hands.   55
On a light given off by the grave
I kneel in the quick of the moon
At the heart of a distant forest
And hold in my arms a child
Of water, water, water.   60

———

The Salt Marsh

1961

Once you have let the first blade
Spring back behind you
To the way it has always been,
You no longer know where you are.
All you can see are the tall   5
Stalks of sawgrass, not sawing,
But each of them holding its tip
Exactly at the level where your hair

Begins to grow from your forehead.
Wherever you come to is   10
The same as before,
With the same blades of oversized grass,
And wherever you stop, the one
Blade just in front of you leans,
That one only, and touches you   15
At the place where your hair begins

To grow; at that predestined touch
Your spine tingles crystally, like salt,
And the image of a crane occurs,
Each flap of its wings creating   20
Its feathers anew, this time whiter,
As the sun destroys all points
Of the compass, refusing to move
From its chosen noon.

Where is the place you have come from   25
With your buried steps full of new roots?
You cannot leap up to look out,
Yet you do not sink,
But seem to grow, and the sound,
The oldest of sounds, is your breath   30
Sighing like acres.
If you stand as you are for long,

Green panic may finally give
Way to another sensation,
For when the embodying wind   35
Rises, the grasses begin to weave
A little, then all together,
Not bending enough for you
To see your way clear of the swaying,
But moving just the same,   40

And nothing prevents your bending
With them, helping their wave
Upon wave upon wave upon wave
By not opposing,
By willing your supple inclusion   45
Among fields without promise of harvest,
In their marvelous, spiritual walking
Everywhere, anywhere.

In the Lupanar at Pompeii
1961

There are tracks which belong to wheels
Long since turned to air and time.
Those are the powerful chariots
I follow down cobblestones,
Not being dragged, exactly,   5
But not of my own will, either,
Going past the flower sellers'
And the cindery produce market
And the rich man's home, and the house
Of the man who kept a dog   10
Set in mosaic.

As tourist, but mostly as lecher,
I seek out the dwelling of women
Who all expect me, still, because
They expect anybody who comes.   15
I am ready to pay, and I do,
And then go in among them
Where on the dark walls of their home
They hold their eternal postures,
Doing badly drawn, exacting,   20
Too-willing, wide-eyed things
With dry-eyed art.

I sit down in one of the rooms
Where it happened again and again.
I could be in prison, or dead,   25
Cast down for my sins in a cell
Still filled with a terrible motion
Like the heaving and sighing of earth
To be free of the heat it restrains.
I feel in my heart how the heart   30
Of the mountain broke, and the women
Fled onto the damp of the walls
And shaped their embraces

To include whoever would come here
After the stone-cutting chariots.   35
I think of the marvel of lust
Which can always, at any moment,
Become more than it believed,
And almost always is less:
I think of its possible passing   40
Beyond, into tender awareness,
Into helplessness, weeping, and death:
It must be like the first
Soft floating of ash,

When, in the world's frankest hands,   45
Someone lay with his body shaken
Free of the self: that amazement—
For we who must try to explain
Ourselves in the house of this flesh
Never can tell the quick heat   50
Of our own from another's breathing,
Nor yet from the floating of feathers
That form in our lungs when the mountain
Settles like odd, warm snow against
Our willing limbs.   55

We never can really tell
Whether nature condemns us or loves us
As we lie here dying of breath
And the painted, unchanging women,
Believing the desperate dead   60
Where they stripped to the skin of the soul
And whispered to us, as to
Their panting, observing selves:
"Passion. Before we die
Let us hope for no longer   65
But truly know it."

The Movement of Fish

1961

No water is still, on top.
Without wind, even, it is full
Of a chill, superficial agitation.
It is easy to forget,
Or not to know at all   5

That fish do not move
By means of this rippling
Along the outside of water, or
By anything touching on air.
Where they are, it is still,   10

Under a wooden bridge,
Under the poised oar
Of a boat, while the rower leans
And blows his mistaken breath
To make the surface shake,   15

Or yells at it, or sings,
Half believing the brilliant scan
Of ripples will carry the fish away
On his voice like a buried wind.
Or it may be that a fish   20

Is simply lying under
The ocean-broad sun
Which comes down onto him
Like a tremendous, suffusing
Open shadow   25

Of gold, where nothing is,
Sinking into the water,
Becoming dark around
His body. Where he is now
Could be gold mixed   30

With absolute blackness.
The surface at mid-sea shivers,
But he does not feel it
Like a breath, or like anything.
Yet suddenly his frame shakes,   35

Convulses the whole ocean
Under the trivial, quivering
Surface, and he is
Hundreds of feet away,
Still picking up speed, still shooting   40

Through half-gold,
Going nowhere. Nothing sees him.
One must think of this to understand
The instinct of fear and trembling,
And, of its one movement, the depth.   45

In the Mountain Tent
1961

I am hearing the shape of the rain
Take the shape of the tent and believe it,
Laying down all around where I lie
A profound, unspeakable law.
I obey, and am free-falling slowly   5

Through the thought-out leaves of the wood
Into the minds of animals.
I am there in the shining of water
Like dark, like light, out of Heaven.

I am there like the dead, or the beast   10
Itself, which thinks of a poem—
Green, plausible, living, and holy—

And cannot speak, but hears,
Called forth from the waiting of things,

A vast, proper, reinforced crying   15
With the sifted, harmonious pause,
The sustained intake of all breath
Before the first word of the Bible.

At midnight water dawns
Upon the held skulls of the foxes   20
And weasels and tousled hares
On the eastern side of the mountain.
Their light is the image I make

As I wait as if recently killed,
Receptive, fragile, half-smiling,   25
My brow watermarked with the mark
On the wing of a moth

And the tent taking shape on my body
Like ill-fitting, Heavenly clothes.
From holes in the ground comes my voice   30
In the God-silenced tongue of the beasts.
"I shall rise from the dead," I am saying.

———————

The Heaven of Animals
1961

Here they are. The soft eyes open.
If they have lived in a wood
It is a wood.
If they have lived on plains
It is grass rolling   5
Under their feet forever.

Having no souls, they have come,
Anyway, beyond their knowing.
Their instincts wholly bloom
And they rise.   10
The soft eyes open.

To match them, the landscape flowers,
Outdoing, desperately
Outdoing what is required:
The richest wood,   15
The deepest field.

For some of these,
It could not be the place
It is, without blood.
These hunt, as they have done,   20
But with claws and teeth grown perfect,

More deadly than they can believe.
They stalk more silently,
And crouch on the limbs of trees,
And their descent   25
Upon the bright backs of their prey

May take years
In a sovereign floating of joy.
And those that are hunted
Know this as their life,   30
Their reward: to walk

Under such trees in full knowledge
Of what is in glory above them,
And to feel no fear,
But acceptance, compliance.   35
Fulfilling themselves without pain

At the cycle's center,
They tremble, they walk

Under the tree,
They fall, they are torn,   40
They rise, they walk again.

———————

For the Nightly Ascent of the
Hunter Orion over a Forest Clearing
1961

Now secretness dies of the open.
Yet all around, all over, night
Things are waking fast,
Waking with all their power.
Who can arise   5

From his dilating shadow
When one foot is longing to tiptoe
And the other to take the live
Stand of a tree that belongs here?
As the owl's gaze   10

Most slowly begins to create
Its sight from the death of the sun,
As the mouse feels the whole wood turn
The gold of the owl's new eyes,
And the fox moves   15

Out of the ground where he sleeps,
No man can stand upright
And drag his body forth
Through an open space in the foliage
Unless he rises   20

As does the hunter Orion,
Thinking to cross a blue hollow

Through the dangers of twilight,
Feeling that he must run
And that he will   25

Take root forever and stand,
Does both at once, and neither,
Grows blind, and then sees everything,
Steps and becomes a man
Of stars instead,   30

Who from invisibility
Has come, arranged in the light
Of himself, revealed tremendously
In his fabulous, rigid, eternal
Unlooked-for role.   35

———————

Under Oaks

1962

In a hushed, tremendous descent
Like the banishment of iron and glass
From heaven to earth in confusion
The rain falls,

And the tree, in every leaf,   5
Huddles, to be nearer your head.
Instinctively you bow
As in a church
Flung down on you in panic from a cloud.
Perhaps it is here the lightning comes   10
To think of the sky's imprint
And the chosen tree.
At this thought you lift your head
And touch this tree yourself.

From your finger leaps no fire   15
Or holy mark,

But into you, out of the earth,
Flows enormous pride and daring
And the huge and joyous denial

Of the lightning   20
That has chosen, and stood alone
In a cloud of water, thinking
Of heaven emblazoned in wood, and said
Not now, not yet.

———————

Adam in Winter
1962

This road is a river, white
Of its slow-frozen light.
Not treading on earth, I walk
The turnpike of a dream,
Pursuing the buried stream   5
That fell beneath the snow.
I feel its waters grow
Thick ice to bear me up,
    But now I have knelt down.

But now I have knelt down   10
As if I swam out of the sky,
Or fell with tremendous force
Of gentleness, like snow,
Toward a thing I know.
Last night I turned and found   15
I lay with a rifled wound.
That bone completes me; I
    Must kneel with the gentle snow.

Some hand has entered the snow
To rummage me where I lay.   20
My rib has been plucked away
And taken to Heaven, or
Flung down on the icy floor.
A voice said, "Follow the river."
I have followed; now I hover   25
Near something the flakes half-hide
   That has come from my sleeping side.

It has come from my sleeping side,
Some being that could not be
Made of anything other than me: 30
Whose curve my heart fits in.
I lift the light bone in my palm
And feel my whole body grow warm.
Exhaling my soul out, bare,
My lungs take shape in the air.   35
   My rib moves in my hand.

My rib moves in my hand,
And all my other ribs move.
I whisper the warning of love.
A great image stirs in my breath,   40
Denying the body of death.
She stands in the shape of my lungs.
My heart beats like her wings,
Yet breath fades from my sight.
   My mouth no longer sheds light.   45

My mouth no longer sheds light,
Though I laugh with a magical sound
That heals my amazing wound.
All things grow warm in this place.
The green river trembles its ice.   50
She comes to me weeping, as if
She came to return my life,
Though purity dies, and I feel
   The ice turn sick at my heel.

The Hospital Window

1962

I have just come down from my father.
Higher and higher he lies
Above me in a blue light
Shed by a tinted window.
I drop through six white floors   5
And then step out onto pavement.

Still feeling my father ascend,
I start to cross the firm street,
My shoulder blades shining with all
The glass the huge building can raise.   10
Now I must turn round and face it,
And know his one pane from the others.

Each window possesses the sun
As though it burned there on a wick.
I wave, like a man catching fire.   15
All the deep-dyed windowpanes flash,
And, behind them, all the white rooms
They turn to the color of Heaven.

Ceremoniously, gravely, and weakly,
Dozens of pale hands are waving   20
Back, from inside their flames.
Yet one pure pane among these
Is the bright, erased blankness of nothing.
I know that my father is there,

In the shape of his death still living.   25
The traffic increases around me
Like a madness called down on my head.
The horns blast at me like shotguns,
And drivers lean out, driven crazy—
But now my propped-up father   30

Lifts his arm out of stillness at last.
The light from the window strikes me
And I turn as blue as a soul,
As the moment when I was born.
I am not afraid for my father—   35
Look! He is grinning; he is not

Afraid for my life, either,
As the wild engines stand at my knees
Shredding their gears and roaring,
And I hold each car in its place   40
For miles, inciting its horn
To blow down the walls of the world

That the dying may float without fear
In the bold blue gaze of my father.
Slowly I move to the sidewalk   45
With my pin-tingling hand half dead
At the end of my bloodless arm.
I carry it off in amazement,

High, still higher, still waving,
My recognized face fully mortal,   50
Yet not; not at all, in the pale,
Drained, otherworldly, stricken,
Created hue of stained glass.
I have just come down from my father.

————

A Dog Sleeping on My Feet
1962

Being his resting place,
I do not even tense
The muscles of a leg

Or I would seem to be changing.
Instead, I turn the page   5
Of the notebook, carefully not

Remembering what I have written,
For now, with my feet beneath him
Dying like embers,
The poem is beginning to move   10
Up through my pine-prickling legs
Out of the night wood,

Taking hold of the pen by my fingers.
Before me the fox floats lightly,
On fire with his holy scent.   15
All, all are running.
Marvelous is the pursuit,
Like a dazzle of nails through the ankles,

Like a twisting shout through the trees
Sent after the flying fox   20
Through the holes of logs, over streams
Stock-still with the pressure of moonlight.
My killed legs,
My legs of a dead thing, follow,

Quick as pins, through the forest,   25
And all rushes on into dark
And ends on the brightness of paper.
When my hand, which speaks in a daze
The hypnotized language of beasts,
Shall falter, and fail   30

Back into the human tongue,
And the dog gets up and goes out
To wander the dawning yard,
I shall crawl to my human bed
And lie there smiling at sunrise,   35
With the scent of the fox

Burning my brain like an incense,
Floating out of the night wood,
Coming home to my wife and my sons
From the dream of an animal,   40
Assembling the self I must wake to,
Sleeping to grow back my legs.

—————

After the Night Hunt
1962

Along the dark bank of the river
The moon through the laurel strikes
With the best inner parts of itself.
Where the ground is bright, it is water.
Part of the moon is its blackness.   5
It is still, that the river may flow.
I look for the light at its darkest
And step there mile after mile
    And do not fall away.

Snakes slip wholly into the moon   10
As into the source of their lives;
Bent fish leap out of it quickly
And shine before they return,
And birds hold branches as though
Borne somewhere safely by sleep   15
As the river would bear them,
Small shadows, tottering hugely,
    And not to fall away.

At last the lake opens my eyes
As it opens the moon from the forest   20
Like a great, shining book on its table.
I stand by my dew-heavy blanket

Looking over the vast, trembling script
And joy slides out of my breast
Winding back in a curve through the woods 25
Where I walked in the dark steps of moonlight
  And did not fall away.

I stand in my own coming sleep,
A tall spirit ready to wind
Like a ball of bright thread the wild river 30
All night around the still form
That shall lie exposed in the open,
Sustained at the heart of the danger
I have passed in the thickets this night
Which shall keep me safe till I wake 35
  And rise, and fall away.

———

The Gamecocks

1962

As I think of pine needles
My boyhood hangs on and destroys me;
My beard draws inward,
Into the roots of my face,
And cannot get out again, 5
And I grow hard and small
And secret, with the same
Doomed shock of lightheaded hair

That I had long years before
To climb between the pine trees. 10
I begin to rise through the valley
Through the hemmed night whiteness of fog
Up to the rows of cracked cages
My father built when my hair

Fell down on my vision as though   15
Someone had pitched hay on my head.

They are resting there
On their unmerciful feet
In the wet dark, their murderous brains
Shivering, and so white-hot they see,   20
Through the film of their eyelids, the sun
Race against time to be born,
The light come through the fog
Before it can burn.

My father's life was spent   25
Binding onto their crabbed, scaly ankles
The bent iron heels of their pride
Before he lay down in the green
Of the river pasture and thrust
A stone straight up from his breast   30
To say his name. And now,
With my youth rising slowly and groping

From pine bole to bole like the blind,
A cock cries out for blood.
Lying under that cry, the dawn   35
Knows it must come to this place.
My hair like a mighty crown
Expands and becomes the mist
That burns away in the sun,
And I am a lean, bald man   40

Standing between the white coops
As all of them lift up their voices
To pull the sun over the pines,
To pull my fierce-eyed father
From the low river mist of his grave.   45
But the listening dead lie stillest
When nearest their moment of rising,
When their dazed, aging sons lift hands

To their own faces now like their fathers',
Feeling beards as useless as pinestraw,   50
And the earthbound eagles close
Their untended feet on the roosts,
Drawing more power from earth
To raise the sun, but not
The dead, though almost those also,   55
Who yet may appear, some morning,

In my father's house
Of cages, where all night his legions have held
The great, crooked, summoning cry
Building in their long throats   60
As they stared, burning the film
Of death from their auburn eyes,
With lost, inconceivable challenge
Into the coming sun.

The Owl King
1962

I. The Call

Through the trees, with the moon underfoot,
More soft than I can, I call.
I hear the king of the owls sing
Where he moves with my son in the gloom.
My tongue floats off in the darkness.   5
I feel the deep dead turn
My blind child round toward my calling,
Through the trees, with the moon underfoot,

In a sound I cannot remember.
It whispers like straw in my ear,   10
And shakes like a stone under water.

My bones stand on tiptoe inside it.
Which part of the sound did I utter?
Is it song, or is half of it whistling?
What spirit has swallowed my tongue?   15
Or is it a sound I remember?

And yet it is coming back,
Having gone, adrift on its spirit,
Down, over and under the river,
And stood in a ring in a meadow   20
Round a child with a bird gravely dancing.
I hear the king of the owls sing.
I did not awaken that sound,
And yet it is coming back,

In touching every tree upon the hill   25
The breath falls out of my voice,
And yet the singing keeps on
The owls are dancing, fastened by their toes
Upon the pines. Come, son, and find me here,
In love with the sound of my voice.   30
Come calling the same soft song,
And touching every tree upon the hill.

II. THE OWL KING

I swore to myself I would see
When all but my seeing had failed.
Every light was too feeble to show   35
My world as I knew it must be.
At the top of the staring night
I sat on the oak in my shape
With my claws growing deep into wood
And my sight going slowly out   40
Inch by inch, as into a stone,
Disclosing the rabbits running
Beneath my bent, growing throne,
And the foxes lighting their hair,
And the serpent taking the shape   45

Of the stream of life as it slept.
When I thought of the floating sound
In which my wings would outspread,
I felt the hooked tufts on my head
Enlarge, and dream like a crown,   50
And my voice unplaceable grow
Like a feathery sigh;
I could not place it myself.
For years I humped on the tree
Whose leaves held the sun and the moon.   55
At last I opened my eyes
In the sun, and saw nothing there.
That night I parted my lids
Once more, and saw dark burn
Greater than sunlight or moonlight,   60
For it burned from deep within me.
The still wood glowed like a brain.
I prised up my claws, and spread
My huge, ashen wings from my body,
For I heard what I listened to hear.   65
Someone spoke to me out of the distance
In a voice like my own, but softer.
I rose like the moon from the branch.

Through trees at his light touch trembling
The blind child drifted to meet me,   70
His blue eyes shining like mine.
In a ragged clearing he stopped,
And I circled, beating above him,
Then fell to the ground and hopped
Forward, taking his hand in my claw.   75
Every tree's life lived in his fingers.
Gravely we trod with each other
As beasts at their own wedding, dance.
Through the forest, the questioning voice
Of his father came to us there,   80
As though the one voice of us both,
Its high, frightened sound becoming
A perfect, irrelevant music

In which we profoundly moved,
I in the innermost shining   85
Of my blazing, invented eyes,
And he in the total of dark.
Each night, now, high on the oak,
With his father calling like music,
He sits with me here on the bough,   90
His eyes inch by inch going forward
Through stone dark, burning and picking
The creatures out one by one,
Each waiting alive in its own
Peculiar light to be found: 95
The mouse in its bundle of terror,
The fox in the flame of its hair,
And the snake in the form of all life.
Each night he returns to his bed,
To the voice of his singing father,   100
To dream of the owl king sitting
Alone in the crown of my will.
In my ruling passion, he rests.
All dark shall come to light.

III. THE BLIND CHILD'S STORY

I am playing going down   105
In my weight lightly,
Down, down the hill.
No one calls me
Out of the air.
The heat is falling   110
On the backs of my hands
And holding coldness.
They say it shines two ways.
The darkness is great
And luminous in my eyes.   115
Down I am quickly going;
A leaf falls on me,
It must be a leaf I hear it
Be thin against me, and now

The ground is level,   120
It moves it is not ground,
My feet flow cold
And wet, and water rushes
Past as I climb out.
I am there, on the other side.   125
I own the entire world.

It closes a little; the sky
Must be cold, must be giving off
Creatures that stand here.
I say they shine one way   130
Trees they are trees around me,
Leaves branches and bark;
I can touch them all; I move
From one to another—someone said
I seem to be blessing them.   135
I am blessing them
Slowly, one after another
Deeper into the wood.

The dark is changing,
Its living is packed in closer   140
Overhead—more trees and leaves—
Tremendous. It touches
Something touches my hand,
Smelling it, a cold nose
Of breath, an ear of silk   145
Is gone. It is here I begin
To call to something unearthly.
Something is here, something before
Me sitting above me
In the wood in a crown,   150
Its eyes newborn in its head
From the death of the sun.
I can hear it rising on wings.
I hear that fluttering
Cease, and become   155
Pure soundless dancing

Like leaves not leaves;
Now down out of air
It lumbers to meet me,
Stepping oddly on earth,   160
Awkwardly, royally.
My father is calling

Through the touched trees;
All distance is weeping and singing.
In my hand I feel   165
A talon, a grandfather's claw
Bone cold and straining
To keep from breaking my skin.
I know this step, I know it,
And we are deep inside.   170
My father's voice is over
And under us, sighing.
Nothing is strange where we are.
The huge bird bows and returns,
For I, too, have done the same   175
As he leads me, rustling,
A pile of leaves in my hands;
The dry feathers shuffle like cards
On his dusty shoulders,
Not touching a tree,   180
Not brushing the side of a leaf
Or a point of grass.

We stop and stand like bushes.
But my father's music comes
In, goes on, comes in,   185
Into the wood,
Into the ceased dance.
And now the hard beak whispers
Softly, and we climb
Some steps of bark   190
Living and climbing with us
Into the leaves.
I sit among leaves,

And the whole branch hums
With the owl's full, weightless power   195
As he closes his feet on the wood.
My own feet dangle
And tingle down;
My head is pointing
Deep into moonlight,   200
Deep into branches and leaves,
Directing my blackness there,
The personal dark of my sight,
And now it is turning a color.
My eyes are blue at last.   205

Something within the place
I look is piled and coiled.
It lifts its head from itself.
Its form is lit, and gives back
What my eyes are giving it freely.   210
I learn from the master of sight
What to do when the sun is dead,
How to make the great darkness work
As it wants of itself to work.
I feel the tree where we sit   215
Grow under me, and live.
I may have been here for years;
In the coil, the heaped-up creature
May have taken that long to lift
His head, to break his tongue   220
From his thin lips,
But he is there. I shut my eyes
And my eyes are gold,
As gold as an owl's,
As gold as a king's.   225
I open them. Farther off,
Beyond the swaying serpent,
A creature is burning itself
In a smoke of hair through the bushes.
The fox moves; a small thing   230
Being caught, cries out,

And I understand
How beings and sounds go together;
I understand
The voice of my singing father.   235
I shall be king of the wood.

Our double throne shall grow
Forever, until I see
The self of every substance
As it crouches, hidden and free.   240
The owl's face runs with tears
As I take him in my arms
In the glow of original light
Of Heaven. I go down
In my weight lightly down   245
The tree, and now
Through the soul of the wood
I walk in consuming glory
Past the snake, the fox, and the mouse:
I see as the owl king sees,   250
By going in deeper than darkness.
The wood comes back in a light
It did not know it withheld,
And I can tell
By its breathing glow   255
Each tree on which I laid
My hands when I was blind.

I cross the cold-footed flowing,
The creek, a religious fire
Streaming my ankles away,   260
And climb through the slanted meadow.
My father cannot remember
That he ever lived in this house.
To himself he bays like a hound,
Entranced by the endless beauty   265
Of his grief-stricken singing and calling.
He is singing simply to moonlight,
Like a dog howling,

And it is holy song
Out of his mouth.   270
Father, I am coming,
I am here on my own;
I move as you sing,
As if it were Heaven.
It is Heaven. I am walking   275
To you and seeing
Where I walk home.
What I have touched, I see
With the dark of my blue eyes.
Far off, the owl king   280
Sings like my father, growing
In power. Father, I touch
Your face. I have not seen
My own, but it is yours.
I come, I advance,   285
I believe everything, I am here.

———————

The Rib

1962

Something has left itself scattered
Under a bush in the evening,
Not recalling what lay down at first
To make its claimed body for years
Disappear into air,   5

Or lay with its small bones desiring
To come slowly forth into twilight
Where the moon begins to raise up
A dead tree now at my side.
I pick up a rib   10

And something like what must be
The bite small animals die of
Encircles myself and the tree,
Coming round again, coming closer,
A breath forming teeth,   15

Warming the bones of my wrist.
That my radiant palm is unopened,
That my breast is still whole
When I feel it seized on and thrown down
By the madness of hunting   20

Is a miracle, like the dead moon
Creating black trees with stone fire.
Can it be that the wounds of beasts,
The hurts they inherit no words for,
Are like the mouths   25

Of holy beings we think of,
So strongly do they breathe upon us
Their bloodletting silence?
A rib in my right side speaks
To me more softly   30

Than Eve—the bidden, unfreeable shape
Of my own unfinished desire
For life, for death and the Other—
So that the wound in the air
And its giver   35

Far off in the brush, all teeth,
Hear me answer the patient world
Of love in my side imprisoned
As I rise, going moonward toward better
And better sleep.   40

To His Children in Darkness

1962

You hear my step
Come close, and stop.
I shut the door.
By the two-deck bed
And its breathing sheets   5
Houselight is killed
From off my breast.
I am unseen,
But sensed, but known,
And now begin   10

To be what I
Can never be,
But what I am
Within your dream:
A god or beast   15
Come true at last.
To one, I have
Like leaves grown here,
And furl my wings
As poplars sigh,   20

And slowly let
On him a breath
Drawn in a cloud,
In which he sees
Angelic hosts   25
Like blowing trees
Send me to earth
To root among
The secret soil
Of his dark room.   30

The other hears
A creature shed

Throughout the maze
The same long breath
As he conceives   35
That he no more
Desires to live
In blazing sun,
Nor shake to death
The animal   40

Of his own head.
I know what lies
Behind all words,
Like a beast, mismade,
Which finds its brain   45
Can sing alone
Without a sound
At what he is
And cannot change,
Or like a god   50

Which slowly breathes
Eternal life
Upon a soul
In deepest sleep.
My heart's one move   55
Comes now, and now.
A god strikes root
On touching earth.
A beast can hold
The thought of self   60

Between his horns
Until it shines.
That you may feel
What I must be
And cannot know   65
By standing here,
My sons, I bring

These beings home
Into your room.
They are. I am. 70

A Screened Porch in the Country

1962

All of them are sitting
Inside a lamp of coarse wire
And being in all directions
Shed upon darkness,
Their bodies softening to shadow, until 5
They come to rest out in the yard
In a kind of blurred golden country
In which they more deeply lie
Than if they were being created
Of Heavenly light. 10

Where they are floating beyond
Themselves, in peace,
Where they have laid down
Their souls and not known it,
The smallest creatures, 15
As every night they do,
Come to the edge of them
And sing, if they can,
Or, if they can't, simply shine
Their eyes back, sitting on haunches, 20

Pulsating and thinking of music.
Occasionally, something weightless
Touches the screen
With its body, dies,
Or is unmurmuringly hurt, 25

But mainly nothing happens
Except that a family continues
To be laid down
In the midst of its nightly creatures,
Not one of which openly comes   30

Into the golden shadow
Where the people are lying,
Emitted by their own house
So humanly that they become
More than human, and enter the place   35
Of small, blindly singing things,
Seeming to rejoice
Perpetually, without effort,
Without knowing why
Or how they do it.   40

————

The Dream Flood
1962

I ask and receive
The secret of falling unharmed
Forty nights from the darkness of Heaven,
Coming down in sheets and in atoms
Until I descend to the moon   5

Where it lies on the ground
And finds in my surface the shining
It knew it must have in the end.
No longer increasing, I stand
Taking sunlight transmitted by stone,   10

And then begin over fields
To expand like a mind seeking truth,

Piling fathoms of brightness in valleys,
Letting no hilltop break through me.
As I rise, the moon rises also   15

As the reborn look of creation
In the animals' eyes,
In the eyes of horses in stables
Who feel their warm heaviness swarm
Out of their mouths like their souls;   20

Their bodies in cell blocks of wood
Hang like a dust that has taken
Their shapes without knowing of horses.
When the straight sun strikes them at last
Their grains congeal as they must   25

And nail their scuffed hoofs to the earth.
I withdraw, in feeling the cloud
Of Heaven call dazzlingly to me
To drop off my horses and forests,
To leave a vague mist in the valleys   30

And the hilltops steaming.
O grasses and fence wire of glory
That have burned like a coral with depth,
Understand that I have stood shining
About loved and abandoned women: 35

For acres around their thin beds
Which lifted like mesmerized tables
And danced in mid-air of their rooms
Like the chairs that blind children dance with,
So that each, hanging deep in her morning   40

Rose-colored bath, shall implore
Those impotent waters, and sunlight
Straining in vain
With her lost, dead weight:
"Lift. I am dreaming. Lift."   45

Snow on a Southern State
1962

Alongside the train I labor
To change wholly into my spirit,
As the place of my birth falls upward

Into the snow,
And my pale, sealed face looks in   5
From the world where it ripples and sails,
Sliding through culverts,

Plunging through tunnels while flakes
Await my long, streaming return
As they wait for this country to rise   10

And become something else in mid-air.
With a just-opened clicking, I come
Forth into fresh, buried meadows
Of muffled night light

Where people still sit on their porches   15
Screened in for eternal summer,
Watching the snow

Like grated shadow sift
Impossibly to them.
Through the window I tell them dumbly   20
That the snow is like

A man, stretched out upon landscape
And a spotless berth,
Who is only passing through

Their country, who means no harm: 25
Who stares in distrust at his ghost
Also flying, feet first, through the distance.
Numbly, the lips of his spirit

Move, and a fur-bearing steeple looms up
Through the heart of his mirrored breast.   30
The small town where he was born

Assembles around it,
The neon trying, but obviously unreal,
The parked cars clumsily letting
Pureness, a blinding burden,   35

Come slowly upon them.
All are still, all are still,
For the breath-holding window and I

Only must move through the silence,
Bearing my huge, prone ghost   40
Up, out, and now flying over
The vapor-lamp-glowing high school

Into the coming fields
Like a thing we cannot put down.
Yet the glass gives out of my image   45

And the laid clicking dies, as the land
All around me shines with the power
Of renewing my youth
By changing the place where I lived it.

There is nothing here, now, to watch   50
The bedclothes whirl into flakes.
What should be warm in these blankets

Has powdered down into its own
Steel-blue and feathery visions
Of weddings opposed by the world: 55
Is hovering over

A dead cotton field, which awaits
Its touch as awaiting completion:
Is building the pinewoods again

For this one night of their lives: 60
With the equilibrium
Of bones, is falling, falling,
Falling into the river.

Fence Wire
1962

Too tight, it is running over
Too much of this ground to be still
Or to do anything but tremble
And disappear left and right
As far as the eye can see   5

Over hills, through woods,
Down roads, to arrive at last
Again where it connects,
Coming back from the other side
Of animals, defining their earthly estate   10

As the grass becomes snow
While they are standing and dreaming
Of grass and snow.
The winter hawk that sits upon its post,
Feeling the airy current of the wires,   15

Turns into a robin, sees that this is wrong,
Then into a boy, and into a man who holds
His palm on the top tense strand
With the whole farm feeding slowly
And nervously into his hand.   20

If the wire were cut anywhere
All his blood would fall to the ground
And leave him standing and staring

With a face as white as a Hereford's.
From years of surrounding grain,   25

Cows, horses, machinery trying to turn
To rust, the humming arrives each second,
A sound that arranges these acres
And holds them highstrung and enthralled.
Because of the light, chilled hand   30

On the top thread tuned to an E
Like the low string of a guitar,
The dead corn is more
Balanced in death than it was,
The animals more aware   35

Within the huge human embrace
Held up and borne out of sight
Upon short, unbreakable poles
Wherethrough the ruled land intones
Like a psalm: properly,   40

With its eyes closed,
Whether on the side of the animals
Or not, whether disappearing
Right, left, through trees or down roads,
Whether outside, around, or in.   45

———————

The Step
1962

Often, when the almighty screen
Of the theatre broadens, broadens out upon darkness
Beyond the width of my mind,

Revealing a mountain pass
Or flights of sea birds and waves, I get up quickly
And walk away before

The story begins, believing
That what I have seen may be reached by foot: that I
May clear the last rock

Or rise from a coastal marsh
To find them all standing there: the trees, the streams
Where the soul can say

This is what I was promised
When I found in Heaven my opening vision of earth
And wished to descend

Beholding, beholding.
No; in this city, though I have my best foot
Forward as always,

I have trodden no hill
Down until I stood upon the air, or risen slowly
On knees of cypress

From the silver of quicksand
Or seen what is here to be seen upon earth
Only in time by me.

And yet my foot,
The forward one, the one about to strike paydirt,
Falls with joy,

Always, remembering
That, were it real enough to carry me there,
I could set it anywhere:

In my child's room,
On the graves of my mother and brother and father,
Or on this street

And the mountains would open,
And the seas, with a life-giving view of incredible birds,   35
And the waters of marshes

Would quicken and breathe,
And the skies and stones and stars of the holy world
Would become as I think

I first beheld them   40
When they were promised, so that I stepped and fell
Into my narrowing gaze,

Who should have lain,
Forever, with my huge, growing vision intact,
Never sleeping or blinking,   45

But watching speechlessly,
Lost in belief, invisible, projecting, protecting
The idea of earth.

————

A Letter
1962

Looking out of the dark of the town
At midnight, looking down
Into water under the lighthouse:
Abstractedly, timelessly looking
For something beneath the jetty,   5
Waiting for the dazed, silent flash,

Like the painless explosion that kills one,
To come from above and slide over
And empty the surface for miles—
The useless, imperial sweep   10

Of utter light—you see
A thicket of little fish

Below the squared stone of your window,
Catching, as it passes,
The blue afterthought of the blaze.   15
Shone almost into full being,
Inlaid in frail gold in their floor,
Their collected vision sways

Like dust among them;
You can see the essential spark   20
Of sight, of intuition,
Travel from eye to eye.
The next leg of light that comes round
Shows nothing where they have been,

But words light up in the head   25
To take their deep place in the darkness,
Arcing quickly from image to image
Like mica catching the sun:
The words of a love letter,
Of a letter to a long-dead father,   30

To an unborn son, to a woman
Long another man's wife, to her children,
To anyone out of reach, not born,
Or dead, who lives again,
Is born, is young, is the same: 35
Anyone who can wait no longer

Beneath the huge blackness of time
Which lies concealing, concealing
What must gleam forth in the end,
Glimpsed, unchanging, and gone   40
When memory stands without sleep
And gets its strange spark from the world.

Springer Mountain [a]

1962

I have on four black sweaters
And over all of them closely
A sheep-herder's wool-hooded coat.
Nobody knows where I am
With my blue teeth under the dawn   5
In the pitch-black dark of my clothes
Crouching far down below sunlight
That will come at its own strange pace
Down the west side of Springer Mountain.
I believe it will bring the deer   10
Also down, keeping step and still dreaming,
Without their knowing why.
The rage to shed blood rises
And streams deeply into my breath

And almost becomes a white crown   15
That moves backward over my head.
Every unseen thing in the dark
Stands waiting to shine, and so shining.
The shiver of arrows in flight
Reaches mine where they slant in my quiver.   20
They try to rattle like antlers.
My insteps, arched by the sticks
Of walking, stone blind, to this place,
Become flat again in the stillness.
The cold puts a ring through my nose,   25
And my hair, matted down in the hood,
Becomes someone else's hair,
Or as it will be in the grave,
Uncombed, uncurbed forever.
In the dark my hands grow smaller   30
And now feel too small for the bow
As the fretted whistling of blackbirds
Begins, taking it from the top
In dead branches brimming

With near-visibility and change.   35
My white crown blooms and blooms
Out of my wool-warmed blood;
My eyesight slowly is falling
Into my brow leaf by leaf
Down the steep side of Springer Mountain.   40
I stand, the dark nearly shaken

Unwillingly off me, and grope
Upward through my last breath
Staring like young iron in my face.
On my back the faggot of arrows   45
Rattles and scratches its feathers.
The human silence is broken.
I rise and step beyond.
I go up over logs slowly
On my painfully reborn legs,   50
My ears putting out vast hearing
Among the invisible animals,
For I have seen the thin sun
Explore the high limbs of trees
That have climbed as I do to receive it;   55
I see the branches still held,
Kept formed all night as they were
By the thought of predictable light.
My heated head blowing white,
My heart made dangerously whole   60
By new beats found on this slope,
I advance, and a tree just above me
Goes inward, into fresh gold,
Slowly more standing full
Of itself, as the sun stands   65
On everything where I now am
As quietly as a hillside, just after
Its leaves, each in its right movement
Of falling, have fallen upon it.

There is no deer anywhere   70
Though my breast has passed forward

Into gold also without knowing.
I sit down and wait as in darkness.
My deep-frozen features
Break, releasing more light.   75
The sweat goes dead at the roots

Of my hair, for just inside
The light, the deer, one deer,
Is descending as though he were being
Created anew at each step.   80
Now he stands; the sun
Waits for his horns to move.
I may be the image between them,
In his just-wakened antlers hanging
Like a man in a rotten tree   85
Nailed until light comes:
A thing risen out of his brain
He has dreamed in the dark,
Stamping like a horse, which then
Lifted into his horns and stood   90
Like my cold breath, making a light,
And I am released and younger
At forty, than I ever have been.
I take aim, and feel come into the bow
A god's lonely tension and delight.   95
My hood's wings open on my head
And I believe I shall be,
At last, a naked man in the cold,
Released to the odd, vital things
In the woods alone possible to men   100
And possible only when alone.
Nearly loving, I show myself
And am ready to do a thing
Never thought of, but here to be done.
I cannot explain death or hunting,   105
Either, or what is called forth
When the steeped, brimming bow shall make
A humming, as of a name.
I hang my longbow on a branch.

The deer leaps away and then stops.   110
The sun comes into my mouth
And I step forward, stepping out

Of my shadow, pulling over
My head one dark heavy sweater
After another, my dungarees,   115
Boots, socks, all of all of it.
The sweat on my brow comes to life
In a fever like madness
And my breast passes onward and onward
Into gold, into shining skin.   120
I shake nearly out of the world,
Naked, putting forth unbearable light,
Not self-conscious, but silently
Raving into the dim changed white
Of my breath, more delicate   125
For coming from nakedness outward.
I think, beginning with laurel,
Like a beast loving
With the whole god bone of his horns.
The secret of human existence   130
Is excess and delight beyond logic
And secret and foolish joy,
Ritual compelled without reason,
Inexplicable action, wild laughter.
He is moving. I am moving with him   135

Around trees, inside and out
Of rotten stumps and groves
Of laurel and slash pine,
Through the tiny twigs and thorn
Thickets, unprotected and sure   140
Of the dead as of the living.
I rejoice everywhere I move.
I am here without weapons;
To be here is greatly enough
With the gold of my breast unwrapped,   145
Shatteringly shining and freezing,

My crazed laughter whiter than linen,
My all-seeing eyes scratched out
And in again, and perhaps
Bleeding good useless blood also   150
Thirty yards from the uninjured buck,
Imitating the steps of four legs
As well as I can with two,
My brain on fire with trying
To grow horns, exultant that it cannot,   155
For thirty seconds moving in the dance
As I most want to be and am,
As I never have been or will be.
He is gone below, and I limp back
And look for my clothes in the world,   160
Grinning, shaking my head

In amazement to last out my life.
I put on the warm-bodied wool,
My four sweaters inside out,
My bootlaces dangling and tripping,   165
And pick my bow off the limb
Where it trembles like a leaf
Nearly fallen, nock an arrow,
But leave my head free of the hood
And the roof of my mouth full of sunlight   170
And go down the unwinding deer track
In my warm tricked clothes
With the quick subtle grasp of the thorn
All through my burning legs,
No longer foolish or beyond   175
My life, but within it more greatly and strangely,
To hunt, in the shadow of Springer Mountain.

At the Home for Unwed Mothers

1962

Gradually it is
From all sides coming,
Out of the effortless sky,
Out of all water and earth,
Out of whatever is there.   5
She settles, closely keeping,
In a lath-and-canvas chair,
The only secret of time,
Silent, alone, growing
In greenness with it.   10

There is nothing so well
This summer hidden
As the hovering child's
Blind thinking it is Joy
Where its mother rests,   15
Half shadow, half stone,
Aware that the father could be
One out of many,
But then being sure,
Almost, that he is the one   20

She hates and loves with the same
Expanding helplessness.
He is smiling; he is far
Away, he does not know,
He does not care,   25
God-like, indifferent,
Unreachably smiling
Like the child's dazzled thought
That it is the process of love:
Like the child's great idea   30

Of her great joy.
And there are times

She feels, against her will,
Her whole body smile
With the unborn,   35
With the guiltless smile
Of the possible father,
Far away, untouched,
And she sets her face
In her most impossible frown,   40

But changing goes on, goes on,
And she can only be
Unhappy all summer,
Trying her best to believe
That the one she hates   45
And loves is the only father
Of the child, who moves
At night in the pure blindness
Of absolute being and joy,
Believing it must be hers,   50

Until at last she rises,
Undoing her face
From the frown of death,
And stands in the window
In the full moon   55
Mild upon pregnant women,
And smiles as she will,
Smiles gradually,
Smiles on all sides,
Smiles on whatever is there.   60

A Sound through the Floor

1962

How was this raised
Through the still house,
Beginning at low
Tide in north Europe,
A wind out of Flanders   5
Or a stranger country
Drawn in, and then
Released in the kitchen
To ripple the stairway,
To pulse in the room   10
Where I with my toys
Lay gathered in fever,
Hotter than firebrick?
For now there was nothing
To do but be in it: 15
In the sound of all voices
Rising together
Unbroken, unbroken
Beyond every word,
Now spindling down   20
To a needle's throbbing,
Now marshy and broad,
More deeply in being
Upon me in glory,
With a tongue in it woken   25
Rippling and flowing,
Changingly buried
Alive in mid-air
And all air rising
To where I lay   30
Illumined with scarlet.
It was my mother,
And then it was I
Becoming exultant
As her breath poured   35

From Flanders up
The swaybacked stair
Triumphantly bearing
A thing at its center
That chuckled at language   40
And granted it hope
Of slow resurrection:
The sound of an army
Believing in flutes
Or seawinds and sailors   45
In shells beyond diving.
Nothing has ever
Been so much living
Or so believing
Or as lonely as that,   50
So much of a cry
Not knowing it was
As that wide sound
Spindling and falling
Away to Europe   55
And then coming back
Up the sprained steps
To fill my sickroom
With a wind involving
All voices together   60
Outsinging their words,
And I upon it
Rose out of illness
Like a creature of breath
Called into its name: 65
So strangely, so truly
Called out of my dying
Or into a Heaven
Brighter than fever—
At my wooden men, lay   70
Looking, astounded,
And all, and I as well,
Burning, entirely whole,
Entirely still within joy.

On Discovering That My Hand Shakes

1962

If I could believe it is
A hidden terror
That fills my fingers with a new
Shattered and reverent feeling,
I might understand my flesh,   5
But it is not.
In awed recognition
I see you, for the first time,
Boyish knuckles
Brown in the light sun,   10
Tremble like my grandfather's,

Giving to all that I hold
A personal, intimate,
Superfluous, granted motion,
A momentary life.   15
An odd, trapped look comes over
The face of whoever is with me
As I shake hands
Or strike a match.
Others, more than I, can feel it,   20
For it is not like the movement
Of my own hand, at all—

Something else instructs it
In the mild, slight
Move of uncompromised being.   25
It is so steadily
Trembling without fear,
No fear at all,
But with so helpless an impulse
That death trembles with it also.   30
More direct, I am yet more subtle,
And I smile more than I am used to,
Possessing, now, what is required

To lay on the sleeping heads
Of children, to bring   35
To mad dogs a masterly calm,
To halt armies, turn rivers,
Or feed a bedraggled crowd:
The touch, fully mortal,
Benign, predestined,   40
Filled with incomparable patience,
With which completely to bless,
Or, in the stillness of miracle,
To raise the dead.

————————

At Darien Bridge

1962

The sea here used to look
As if many convicts had built it,

Standing deep in their ankle chains,
Ankle-deep in the water, to smite

The land and break it down to salt.   5
I was in this bog as a child

When they were all working all day
To drive the pilings down

I thought I saw the still sun
Strike the side of a hammer in flight

And from it a sea bird be born
To take off over the marshes.   10

As the gray climbs the side of my head
And cuts my brain off from the world,

I walk and wish mainly for birds,
For the one bird no one has looked for

To spring again from a flash   15
Of metal, perhaps from the scratched

Wedding band on my ring finger.
Recalling the chains of their feet,

I stand and look out over grasses
At the bridge they built, long abandoned,   20

Breaking down into water at last,
And long, like them, for freedom

Or death, or to believe again
That they worked on the ocean to give it

The unchanging, hopeless look   25
Out of which all miracles leap.

———————

In the Marble Quarry
1962

Beginning to dangle beneath
The wind that blows from the undermined wood,
    I feel the great pulley grind,

The thread I cling to lengthen
And let me soaring and spinning down into marble,   5
    Hooked and weightlessly happy

Where the squared sun shines
Back equally from all four sides, out of stone
    And years of dazzling labor,

To land at last among men   10
Who cut with power saws a Parian whiteness
    And, chewing slow tobacco,

    Their eyebrows like frost,
Shunt house-sized blocks and lash them to cables
    And send them heavenward   15

    Into small-town banks,
Into the columns and statues of government buildings,
    But mostly graves.

    I mount my monument and rise
Slowly and spinningly from the white-gloved men   20
    Toward the hewn sky

    Out of the basement of light,
Sadly, lifted through time's blinding layers
    On perhaps my tombstone

    In which the original shape   25
Michelangelo believed was in every rock upon earth
    Is heavily stirring,

    Surprised to be an angel,
To be waked in North Georgia by the ponderous play
    Of men with ten-ton blocks   30

    But no more surprised than I
To feel sadness fall off as though I myself
    Were rising from stone

    Held by a thread in midair,
Badly cut, local-looking, and totally uninspired,   35
    Not a masterwork

    Or even worth seeing at all
But the spirit of this place just the same,
    Felt here as joy.

The Dusk of Horses

1962

Right under their noses, the green
Of the field is paling away
Because of something fallen from the sky.

They see this, and put down
Their long heads deeper in grass   5
That only just escapes reflecting them

As the dream of a millpond would.
The color green flees over the grass
Like an insect, following the red sun over

The next hill. The grass is white.   10
There is no cloud so dark and white at once;
There is no pool at dawn that deepens

Their faces and thirsts as this does.
Now they are feeding on solid
Cloud, and, one by one,   15

With nails as silent as stars among the wood
Hewed down years ago and now rotten,
The stalls are put up around them.

Now if they lean, they come
On wood on any side. Not touching it, they sleep.   20
No beast ever lived who understood

What happened among the sun's fields,
Or cared why the color of grass
Fled over the hill while he stumbled,

Led by the halter to sleep   25
On his four taxed, worthy legs.
Each thinks he awakens where

The sun is black on the rooftop,
That the green is dancing in the next pasture,
And that the way to sleep 30

In a cloud, or in a risen lake,
Is to walk as though he were still
In the drained field standing, head down,

To pretend to sleep when led,
And thus to go under the ancient white 35
Of the meadow, as green goes

And whiteness comes up through his face
Holding stars and rotten rafters,
Quiet, fragrant, and relieved.

————————

The Beholders
1962

Far away under us, they are mowing on the green steps
Of the valley, taking long, unending swings
Among the ripe wheat.
It is something about them growing,
Growing smaller, that makes us look up and see 5
That what has come over them is a storm.

It is a blue-black storm the shape of this valley,
And includes, perhaps, in its darkness,
Three men in the air
Taking long, limber swings, cutting water. 10
Swaths start to fall and, on earth,
The men come closer together as they mow.

Now in the last stand of wheat they bend.
From above, we watch over them like gods,
Our chins on our hands,   15
Our great eyes staring, our throats dry
And aching to cry down on their heads
Some curse or blessing,

Some word we have never known, but we feel
That when the right time arrives, and more stillness,   20
Lightning will leap
From our mouths in reasonless justice
As they arc their scythes more slowly, taking care
Not to look up.

As darkness increases there comes   25
A dancing into each of their swings,
A dancing like men in a cloud.
We two are coming together
Also, along the wall.
No lightning yet falls from us   30

Where their long hooks catch on the last of the sun
And the color of the wheat passes upward,
Drawn off like standing water
Into the cloud, turning green;
The field becomes whiter and darker,   35
And fire in us gathers and gathers

Not to call down death to touch brightly
The only metal for miles
In the hands of judged, innocent men,
But for our use only, who in the first sheaves of rain   40
Sit thunderstruck, having now the power to speak
With deadly intent of love.

The Poisoned Man

1962

When the rattlesnake bit, I lay
In a dream of the country, and dreamed
Day after day of the river,

Where I sat with a jackknife and quickly
Opened my sole to the water.   5
Blood shed for the sake of one's life

Takes on the hid shape of the channel,
Disappearing under logs and through boulders.
The freezing river poured on

And, as it took hold of my blood,   10
Leapt up round the rocks and boiled over.
I felt that my heart's blood could flow

Unendingly out of the mountain,
Splitting bedrock apart upon redness,
And the current of life at my instep   15

Give deathlessly as a spring.
Some leaves fell from trees and whirled under.
I saw my struck bloodstream assume,

Inside the cold path of the river,
The inmost routes of a serpent   20
Through grass, through branches and leaves.

When I rose, the live oaks were ashen
And the wild grass was dead without flame.
Through the blasted cornfield I hobbled,

My foot tied up in my shirt,   25
And met my old wife in the garden,
Where she reached for a withering apple.

I lay in the country and dreamed
Of the substance and course of the river
While the different colors of fever   30

Like quilt patches flickered upon me.
At last I arose, with the poison
Gone out of the seam of the scar,

And brought my wife eastward and weeping,
Through the copper fields springing alive   35
With the promise of harvest for no one.

————

The Crows

1962

A strange man falling apart,
Stuffed into his clothes, is waiting,
Not quite a ghost,
But more like a crucified hobo
In the tall corn field   5
Where the wind is waving the grain
Around the horizon and then

In again to the center where he is.
His stillness makes the corn
More like a sea than it should be.   10
He is thinking of what to do
When the crows come
To him from the leaves of the forest,
The most intelligent of birds.

He is waiting to split their tongues   15
And release their malevolent truth,
For, unlike parrots, they
May well know what they are saying.

The wind stirs his trouser legs
But it is no natural movement;   20
It is like the stirring of a thing

That rigidly remembers its body,
And still, for one more day,
Must wear its cast-off clothes.
Above him the dark birds circle.   25
When they are no longer afraid
Of him, they will alight,
First on the ground, then

On his arms and shoulders and head
And peck at his blind, buttoned eyes.   30
Covered with them, he will wait
Until the most nightlike shall sit
On his right hand. Then he will seize it.
This evening, somewhere, the crow
Will awake to the power of speech   35

And try his new voice upon branches,
One half of his tongue conversing
With birds, and the other with men
Who sit in dim rooms like statues
Pondering the beauty of the dead,   40
Who long for demons floating
In shadow on the floor.

Then he will lift from the boughs
Of the gaunt fir tree and fly there,
His chill, practiced one word falling   45
Through the dark upon innocent homes
Until at drear midnight he comes
To the pale, right window, and,
Like someone gently rapping, taps.

Wall and Cloud

1962

The white cloud bearing to me the darkness of my mind
  Is coming in from the sea, a hundred feet out
    Where it is darkening the water and passing from it.
      Now it sails upon land, leaving the ocean brighter.
        Where we live, the wind is also timed, and set   5
      To come as the blood stands still.

To help what shall happen to me, I walk down the hill
  Where a useless brown wall moves through a stand of pines.
    I put my hand on its stone and feel the shade fall
      Up the other side and the sun cease shining there.   10
        Now I no longer have to help hold up the light;
          The cloud descends like the shadow of my brain.

As all grows dark around it, I can see what is in my mind
  Magically freed to glow of itself and its meaning.
    For example, I see my love, whose blond hair changes to black   15
      As she comes through a gate in the wall, bearing flowers
        Milked of their color and just before getting it back.
        The wind arrives upon us when it should.

Slowly we fill up with light, and the flowers take on
  The painful red of their life, and hurt to look at   20
    As the sun shines freshly into our brains, and the wall
      Casts from the other side a new shadow that cannot climb
        After us walking upward to the house, that stilly sharpens
          Into more and more reality, set deep in the light of the world.

A Poem about Bird-Catching by
One Who Has Never Caught a Bird
1962

Name their traps, you feel them flutter.
Say aloud the things that are supposed to catch them
    And you have a new sense of confinement:
        Nets, springes, lime.

Now, with these, move into the forest   5
Whose smaller branches, come from large still ones, shake
    With their senseless, precarious hopping.
        Bend twigs, and take

Their light lives into your hands.
But what, practically speaking, does one do with the lime?   10
    Do they eat it, or stick in it,
        Beating, all the time,

Their wings to fly, and not rising?
Are they buried, like murderers in quicklime, in the air?
    Does it burn them into submission?   15
        But as you ask, your snare

Begins to hide its meaning, and to work.
One simply leaves the first trap pondering slyly here,
    Perhaps, and goes deeper into the wood
        To set another.   20

How remember the places you have left them?
It may be that birds more gloriously sing than they know how
    When caught, surpassing the limits of music
        As blinded ones do,

And you may come back to your traps   25
By means of a singing more perfect and bodiless than angels',
    Where choir after choir through the leaves
        Swells and swells.

O I have set my engines, and at dusk,
With a net on a long pole, have run tensely back and forth   30
   Through dimness, where birds could see
      Only a small sort

Of linked, knitted, puckering cloud
Come over them out of the darkening leaves and failing light
   Amid the cold blinks of fireflies   35
      And swerved too late

To fall anywhere but in my hands
As all the trapped birds in the wood more wildly sang to name
   Another among their elect,
      White with lime,   40

Shining, and in the thin jails
Of string. Tell me what I must do with these I have
   Knocked down, but more with those which are
      Still as the grave:

Which imprisonment makes sit quietly   45
Hour after hour on my hands: which are not good to eat
   Or to sell: which are common as leaves,
      O Lord, and wait

For nothing at all: those which shocked
The pole I held most sickeningly of all, and fell   50
   To thinking silently of my bones
      And will not tell.

My weighted hands keep fluttering
When I pick up immovable birds and try to turn them loose.
   Just thinking about it, I can't sit still   55
      In my doomed house.

Walking the Fire Line
1963

Dead on one side
Or the other, I walk where fire gave out
Of its marvelous insanity, and sank

Underfoot in the wood
And died in the rain in the dark.   5
At odd times the natural border

Between life and death
Shows clearly; when you reach it, do not
Cross it back and forth, or favor

One side or the other   10
Or become dead black or bright green.
Stay on the line like a child

Stays on a crack
In the pavement until it gets home
And wing-walk between smoky rocks   15

And white, between ashes
And weeds. In sleep, you say, when the fire
Rises again from the earth where you balanced

And stands like the wall
Of an eternal city founded on this ground,   20
I come back and painlessly pass

From the living to the dead
And back again through the flame
And know in a flash how the rain chooses

To stop it just here   25
In the dark, and why a man dies when he does
And wanders into burnt blackness

Going past the flower
Still living an inch from its death,
Saved when the dark water fell.   30

Some night the walker
Shall rise to walk the fire line
Like a miracle man, knowing wholly

Not only how death
Stops and life begins and thrives   35
Just here, but why, but why.

———————

The Courtship
1963

Though lumber was scarce, we found it,
    Trading with rations of whiskey,
    And began to build on the clifftop
    Not a tent with a floor, but a house
Above the quiet island which had changed   5
    To peace one night while we slept:
    A three-room house with a view,
    A porch, two rugs, and a kitchen.
        All ends in gentleness.

    It was not a place to bring girls   10
    We would marry, but we liked
    To think of bringing others:
    Perhaps those, in the flesh,
    Cut out of polished magazines
And smiling like a harem from our walls.   15
    Each fluttered on her four nails
As we cut windows near her in the wind.
        All ends in gentleness.

The live slats under our camp chairs
Rocked, as we drank tea, becalmed   20
Our missions done, seeing the earth
No longer from aircraft, but a porch
We had built for idling upon.
In shorts and unmartial attire
We kept the high house for officers   25
And gentlemen, and dozed for weeks.
All ends in gentleness.

Yet strange claims settled upon us
For this was becoming home.
Each thought for the first time of children   30
By an unknown woman he should love
Enough to go back to war for,
Who kept this house by unlikeness
To the slick girls who trembled and chattered
All day and night on our walls.   35
All ends in gentleness.

Before we moved out, our girls,
Their immortal skin in tatters,
Flaked strangely away, still smiling,
And while we awaited that day   40
A captain went down the cliff
On a rope, each dangerous evening,
To bring back blue, foreign flowers
For no one, to place on the table.
All ends in gentleness.

Paestum

1963

One cloud in the sky comes from Greece.
The sun, set at noon, moves toward it
And is ready to change into rain.

Around a lemon tree throwing
A still shadow easily drawn
From the depths of Italian rock,
All things drop off their names
And softly stand in the warm   5
Speechless ruin of their being, and pride.
A wave falls, back of some trees.
Sound blooms as from a seed;
The human face wears for an instant
A white flash, vital and mortal,   10

Like the star on a horse's brow.
A man puts cautiously down
The useless, blue-eyed floating of his soul
Over the ruins, around
The eternal youth of well-water.   15
Down a road a thousand years old
Growing dazedly through the oats,
Awe comes into the city
As into a dead artist's home,
Where the stone and the unpicked lemon   20

Give the same hand-burning power
As to the curved palm
Of a genius sculpting.
Brightness goes under the fields
Travelling like shadow   25
Through the well-stones and brier-roots;
Dead crickets come back to life;
Snakes under the cloud live more

In their curves to move. Rain falls
With the instant, conclusive chill   30

Of a gnat flying into the eye.
Crows fall to the temple roof;
An American feels with his shoulders
Their new flightless weight be born
And the joy of the architect   35
Increase, as more birds land.
He remembers standing in briers
Ten minutes ago, in the sun,
As cast among tiny star-points
That cramped and created his body   40

By their sail-shapes' sensitive clinging,
Making him stand like a statue
With its face coming out of the stone
From the thousand shrewd, perilous scars
Left by the artist on marble.   45
The chipped columns brace in the rain-rays
For the crucial first instant of shining.
At the far edge of cloud, the sun
Arrives at its first thread of light.
Unpacking them slowly, it lays   50

Itself at the door of the temple.
Shining comes in from the woods,
Down the road at a walking pace
Like a thing that he owns and gets back.
Crows open their wings and rise   55
Without wind, by the force of new light.
Every woman alive in the ruins
Becomes a virgin again.
His nose, broken badly in childhood,
And the brier's coiled scratch on his wrist   60

Begin to hurt like each other.
A wave of water breaks inward

And a wave of grain lifts it up
And bears it toward him,
A crest he must catch like a swimmer, 65
Just as it breaks, to rise
Up the stairs of the temple.
The image of a knife bronze-glitters
With the primal, unshielded light
Of a bald man's brain 70

As he climbs to the place of sacrifice
Where the animals died for the gods
And cried through the human singing.
Crows set their wings to glide
In with him through the portals 75
But rise without will to the roof.
The shimmering skin of his head
Sheds a hero's blond shade on the ground.
He stares at the drops on his wrist
As at animal blood 80

That has power over Apollo.
His smile is brought slowly out
Of his unchanging skull by the sun;
He feels its doomed fixity turn
Uncertain and strange in the space 85
Where a wave shall break into light,
A crow feather whirl upon stone
And the brow-stars of horses shall flicker,
Gone bodiless, in the dark green
Middle limbs of the pine wood 90

Seeking human and stone broken faces:
Where a wave shall catch the noon sun
In a low, falling window and break it
And a statue shall break its nose off
Revealing a genius's smile 95
And the great fleet of thorns in the weeds
Shall sail for Piraeus

Bearing a man shaped by nettles
Like a masterpiece made by a bush
In the sculptor's absence: 100

Where the sails shall set course
By the star on a stallion's brow
And bear him, upright, in a track
Like the ram's horn etched on his wrist,
Inward, all night in an aching   105
Impossibly creative position
With a crow on his shoulder,
With his arms and his nose breaking off,
Till he wakes at the heart of Greece,
Steps down, is whole there, and stands.   110

Under Buzzards
1963

From too far under, you have seen

Them sail, with outer wing-feathers
Spread on the air like hands
Always open to flight's trembling gesture,
Gently seeking to clasp the whole world,   5
Far off, their power is slight.

But when one of them soars level:

When you are walking a ridge
He is flying beside in a trance,
The head, too, is there, fanatical,   10
Pulled to earth by its dowsing blood,
Full of intuitive knowledge
Of the dead, where they have hidden

Among bushes, wedged as they fell

In foetal positions in rocks   15
Or lying in fields in the sun,
Their hands opened slowly.
Now another one comes into being
Down the western shade of the ridge,
Controlling that side of the valley,   20

Taking hold of all of its air.

Now more throng in: another
From the north, and three
More from the morning sun
Where a mist of blue land is rising   25
To be the Cohutta Range.
Brothers, are we the dead

On an outing, middle-aged, bald,

Red-headed with over-exertion?
Shall we fall among stones,   30
Clutching our outdone hearts,
And feel the hills futilely try
To hide us from our called birds?
If we are theirs, why that

Is nothing: look level and closely   35

At what seeks us, shaping these ridges:
Between the long fingers of feathers
Drawing all the secret of balance
And ultimate meaning from air
And grave and valley and cloud   40
And dead and live body alike

Is a real king's never-wrong head.

Kudzu

1963

Japan invades. Far Eastern vines
Run from the clay banks they are

Supposed to keep from eroding,
Up telephone poles,
Which rear, half out of leafage,   5
As though they would shriek,
Like things smothered by their own
Green, mindless, unkillable ghosts.
In Georgia, the legend says
That you must close your windows   10

At night to keep it out of the house.
The glass is tinged with green, even so,

As the tendrils crawl over the fields.
The night the kudzu has
Your pasture, you sleep like the dead.   15
Silence has grown Oriental
And you cannot step upon ground:
Your leg plunges somewhere
It should not, it never should be,
Disappears, and waits to be struck   20

Anywhere between sole and kneecap:
For when the kudzu comes,

The snakes do, and weave themselves
Among its lengthening vines,
Their spade heads resting on leaves,   25
Growing also, in earthly power
And the huge circumstance of concealment.
One by one the cows stumble in,
Drooling a hot green froth,
And die, seeing the wood of their stalls   30

Strain to break into leaf.
In your closed house, with the vine

Tapping your window like lightning,
You remember what tactics to use.
In the wrong yellow fog-light of dawn   35
You herd them in, the hogs,
Head down in their hairy fat,
The meaty troops, to the pasture.
The leaves of the kudzu quake
With the serpents' fear, inside   40

The meadow ringed with men
Holding sticks, on the country roads.

The hogs disappear in the leaves.
The sound is intense, subhuman,
Nearly human with purposive rage.   45
There is no terror
Sound from the snakes.
No one can see the desperate, futile
Striking under the leaf heads.
Now and then, the flash of a long   50

Living vine, a cold belly,
Leaps up, torn apart, then falls

Under the tussling surface.
You have won, and wait for frost,
When, at the merest touch   55
Of cold, the kudzu turns
Black, withers inward and dies,
Leaving a mass of brown strings
Like the wires of a gigantic switchboard.
You open your windows,   60

With the lightning restored to the sky
And no leaves rising to bury

You alive inside your frail house,
And you think, in the opened cold,
Of the surface of things and its terrors,   65
And of the mistaken, mortal
Arrogance of the snakes
As the vines, growing insanely, sent
Great powers into their bodies
And the freedom to strike without warning: 70

From them, though they killed
Your cattle, such energy also flowed

To you from the knee-high meadow
(It was as though you had
A green sword twined among   75
The veins of your growing right arm—
Such strength as you would not believe
If you stood alone in a proper
Shaved field among your safe cows—):
Came in through your closed   80

Leafy windows and almighty sleep
And prospered, till rooted out.

———————

The Scarred Girl
1963

All glass may yet be whole
She thinks, it may be put together
From the deep inner flashing of her face.
One moment the windshield held

The countryside, the green   5
Level fields and the animals,
And these must be restored
To what they were when her brow

Broke into them for nothing, and began
Its sparkling under the gauze.   10
Though the still, small war for her beauty
Is stitched out of sight and lost,

It is not this field that she thinks of.
It is that her face, buried
And held up inside the slow scars,   15
Knows how the bright, fractured world

Burns and pulls and weeps
To come together again.
The green meadow lying in fragments
Under the splintered sunlight,   20

The cattle broken in pieces
By her useless, painful intrusion
Know that her visage contains
The process and hurt of their healing,

The hidden wounds that can   25
Restore anything, bringing the glass
Of the world together once more,
All as it was when she struck,

All except her. The shattered field
Where they dragged the telescoped car   30
Off to be pounded to scrap
Waits for her to get up,

For her calm, unimagined face
To emerge from the yards of its wrapping,
Red, raw, mixed-looking but entire,   35
A new face, an old life,

To confront the pale glass it has dreamed
Made whole and backed with wise silver,
Held in other hands brittle with dread,
A doctor's, a lip-biting nurse's,   40

Who do not see what she sees
Behind her odd face in the mirror:
The pastures of earth and of heaven
Restored and undamaged, the cattle

Risen out of their jagged graves   45
To walk in the seamless sunlight
And a newborn countenance
Put upon everything,

Her beauty gone, but to hover
Near for the rest of her life,   50
And good no nearer, but plainly
In sight, and the only way.

———

Drinking from a Helmet
1963

I

I climbed out, tired of waiting
For my foxhole to turn in the earth
On its side or its back for a grave,
And got in line
Somewhere in the roaring of dust.   5
Every tree on the island was nowhere,
Blasted away.

II

In the middle of combat, a graveyard
Was advancing after the troops
With laths and balls of string;   10

Grass already tinged it with order.
Between the new graves and the foxholes
A green water-truck stalled out.
I moved up on it, behind
The hill that cut off the firing.   15

III

My turn, and I shoved forward
A helmet I picked from the ground,
Not daring to take mine off
Where somebody else may have come
Loose from the steel of his head.   20

IV

Keeping the foxhole doubled
In my body and begging
For water, safety, and air,
I drew water out of the truckside
As if dreaming the helmet full.   25
In my hands, the sun
Came on in a feathery light.

V

In midair, water trimming
To my skinny dog-faced look
Showed my life's first all-out beard   30
Growing wildly, escaping from childhood,
Like the beards of the dead, all now
Underfoot beginning to grow.
Selected ripples wove through it,
Knocked loose with a touch from all sides   35
Of a brain killed early that morning,
Most likely, and now
In its absence holding
My sealed, sunny image from harm,

Weighing down my hands,   40
Shipping at the edges,
Too heavy on one side, then the other.

VI

I drank, with the timing of rust.
A vast military wedding
Somewhere advanced one step.   45

VII

All around, equipment drifting in light,
Men drinking like cattle and bushes,
Cans, leather, canvas and rifles,
Grass pouring down from the sun
And up from the ground.   50
Grass: and the summer advances
Invisibly into the tropics.
Wind, and the summer shivers
Through many men standing or lying
In the GI gardener's hand   55
Spreading and turning green
All over the hill.

VIII

At the middle of water
Bright circles dawned inward and outward
Like oak rings surviving the tree   60
As its soul, or like
The concentric gold spirit of time.
I kept trembling forward through something
Just born of me.

IX

My nearly dead power to pray   65
Like an army increased and assembled,

As when, in a harvest of sparks,
The helmet leapt from the furnace
And clamped itself
On the heads of a billion men.   70
Some words directed to Heaven
Went through all the strings of the graveyard
Like a message that someone sneaked in,
Tapping a telegraph key
At dead of night, then running   75
For his life.

X

I swayed, as if kissed in the brain.
Above the shelled palm-stumps I saw
How the tops of huge trees might be moved
In a place in my own country   80
I never had seen in my life.
In the closed dazzle of my mouth
I fought with a word in the water
To call on the dead to strain
Their muscles to get up and go there.   85
I felt the difference between
Sweat and tears when they rise,
Both trying to melt the brow down.

XI

On even the first day of death
The dead cannot rise up,   90
But their last thought hovers somewhere
For whoever finds it.
My uninjured face floated strangely
In the rings of a bodiless tree
Among them, also, a final   95
Idea lived, waiting
As in Ariel's limbed, growing jail.

XII

I stood as though I possessed
A cool, trembling man
Exactly my size, swallowed whole.   100
Leather swung at his waist
Web-cord, buckles, and metal,
Crouching over the dead
Where they waited for all their hands
To be connected like grass-roots.   105

XIII

In the brown half-life of my beard
The hair stood up
Like the awed hair lifting the back
Of a dog that has eaten a swan.
Now light like this   110
Staring into my face
Was the first thing around me at birth.
Be no more killed, it said.

XIV

The wind in the grass
Moved gently in secret flocks,   115
Then spread to be
Nothing, just where they were.
In delight's
Whole shining condition and risk,
I could see how my body might come   120
To be imagined by something
That thought of it only for joy.

XV

Fresh sweat and unbearable tears
Drawn up by my feet from the field
Between my eyebrows became   125
One thing at last.

And I could cry without hiding.
The world dissolved into gold;
I could have stepped up into air.
I drank and finished   130
Like tasting of Heaven,
Which is simply of,
At seventeen years,
Not dying wherever you are.

XVI

Enough   135
Shining, I picked up my carbine and said.
I threw my old helmet down
And put the wet one on
Warmed water ran over my face
My last thought changed, and I knew   140
I inherited one of the dead.

XVII

I saw tremendous trees
That would grow on the sun if they could,
Towering. I saw a fence
And two boys facing each other,   145
Quietly talking,
Looking in at the gigantic redwoods,
The rings in the trunks turning slowly
To raise up stupendous green.
They went away, one turning   150
The wheels of a blue bicycle,
The smaller one curled catercornered
In the handlebar basket.

XVIII

I would survive and go there,
Stepping off the train in a helmet   155
That held a man's last thought,

Which showed him his older brother
Showing him trees.
I would ride through all
California upon two wheels   160
Until I came to the white
Dirt road where they had been,
Hoping to meet his blond brother,
And to walk with him into the wood
Until we were lost,   165
Then take off the helmet
And tell him where I had stood,
What poured, what spilled, what swallowed:

XIX

And tell him I was the man.

———————

The Being
1963

I

It is there, above him, beyond, behind,

Distant, and near where he lies in his sleep
Bound down as for warranted torture.
Through his eyelids he sees it

Drop off its wings or its clothes.   5
He groans, and breaks almost from

Or into another sleep.
Something fills the bed he has been
Able only to half-fill.

He turns and buries his head.   10

II

Moving down his back,
Back up his back,
Is an infinite, unworldly frankness,
Showing him what an entire

Possession nakedness is.   15
Something over him

Is praying.
              It reaches down under
His eyelids and gently lifts them.
He expects to look straight into eyes   20
And to see thereby through the roof.

III

Darkness. The windowpane stirs.
His lids close again, and the room

Begins to breathe on him
As through the eyeholes of a mask.   25

The praying of prayer
Is not in the words but the breath.

It sees him and touches him
All over, from everywhere.
It lifts him from the mattress   30
To be able to flow around him

In the heat from a coal bed burning
Far under the earth
He enters—enters with . . .

What? His tongue? A word?   35
His own breath? Some part of his body?

All.

                    None.

He lies laughing silently
In the dark of utter delight.   40

IV

It glides, glides
Lightly over him, over his chest and legs.
All breath is called suddenly back

Out of laughter and weeping at once.
His face liquefies and freezes   45

Like a mask. He goes rigid
And breaks into sweat from his heart
All over his body

In something's hands.

V

He sleeps, and the windowpane   50
Ceases to flutter.
Frost crawls down off it
And backs into only
The bottom two corners of glass.

VI

He stirs, with the sun held at him   55
Out of late-winter dawn, and blazing
Levelly into his face.
He blazes back with his eyes closed,
Given, also, renewed

Fertility, to raise   60
Dead plants and half-dead beasts

Out of their thawing holes,

And children up,
From mortal women or angels,
As true to themselves as he   65

Is only in visited darkness
For one night out of the year,

And as he is now, seeing straight
Through the roof   wide   wider

Wide awake.   70

———————

Why in London the Blind Are Saviors
1963

On every side, street lamps are burning deeply
Back into themselves, not able
To throw what they have to throw.
They are centered around
A lost man's face   5
In the total white darkness of fog
Pressed against something
Hard, and listening hard.
Through the wall, through several walls,

A kind of tapping comes,   10
Taking all the time in the world

To be carefully, sanely gone.
Were the fog to lift
It would show bent, formal couples
Two by two through the pavements go,   15
Stepping by slow speculation
And magic, with one face of each
Pair turning upward in awe
As if promised sight by the sun.

Instead, a man has been found   20

By his mild, contemplative savior,
A native of these parts
To whom all sights are as one,
The fog the same as the sunlight,
All dark and all brightness the same,   25
To whom the walls must say yes
As his cane confirms the long streets
And the stranger regains his lit room
That burns behind doors like a vision.

But the fog does not lift, and he   30

Having useless and cloud-bound sight
Can touch but cannot feel
What the cobbles he stands on intend.
An angled stone turning a corner
Is touched, and does not touch back.   35
Leaving the hand out in limbo,
An invisible beggar's hand,
One must wait at the heart of the white-out
Until a white tapping assures

Each brick that it still stands   40

Where it has been counselled to stand,
The hand of a foreigner learns
How deep are the secrets of stone,

The other palm covers a pair
Of the world's most purposeless eyes,   45
The lamps choke on their light,
And a voice says over and over
To any lost soul in the city:
"I have come. Take my arm.

I know where I am. I am blind."   50

———————

A Folk Singer of the Thirties
1963

On a bed of gravel moving
Over the other gravel
Roadbed between the rails, I lay
As in my apartment now.
I felt the engine enter   5
A tunnel a half-mile away
And settled deeper
Into the stones of my sleep
Drifting through North Dakota.
I pulled thcm ovcr mc   10
For warmth, though it was summer,
And in the dark we pulled

Into the freight yards of Bismarck.
In the gravel car buried
To my nose in sledge-hammered stones,   15
My guitar beside me straining
Its breast beneath the rock,
I lay in the buzzing yards
And crimson hands swinging lights
Saw my closed eyes burn   20
Open and shine in their lanterns.

The yard bulls pulled me out,
Raining a rockslide of pebbles.
Bashed in the head, I lay

On the ground   25
As in my apartment now.
I spat out my teeth
Like corn, as they jerked me upright
To be an example for
The boys who would ride the freights   30
Looking for work, or for
Their American lives.
Four held me stretching against
The chalked red boards,
Spreading my hands and feet,   35
And nailed me to the boxcar
With twenty-penny nails.
I hung there open-mouthed
As though I had no more weight
Or voice. The train moved out.   40

Through the landscape I edged
And drifted, my head on my breast
As in my clean sheets now,
And went flying sideways through
The country, the rivers falling   45
Away beneath my safe
Immovable feet,
Close to me as they fell
Down under the boiling trestles,
And the fields and woods   50
Unfolded. Sometimes, behind me,
Going into the curves,
Cattle cried in unison,
Singing of stockyards
Where their tilted blood   55
Would be calmed and spilled.
I heard them until I sailed
Into the dark of the woods,

Flying always into the moonlight
And out again into rain   60
That filled my mouth
With a great life-giving word,
And into the many lights
The towns hung up for Christmas
Sales, the berries and tinsel,   65
And then out again
Into the countryside.
Everyone I passed

Could never believe what they saw,
But gave me one look   70
They would never forget, as I stood
In my overalls, stretched on the nails,
And went by, or stood
In the steaming night yards,
Waiting to couple on,   75
Overhanging the cattle coming
Into the cars from the night-lights.
The worst pain was when
We shuddered away from the platforms.
I lifted my head and croaked   80
Like a crow, and the nails
Vibrated with something like music
Endlessly clicking with movement
And the powerful, simple curves.
I learned where the oil lay   85
Under the fields,
Where the water ran
With the most industrial power,
Where the best corn would grow
And what manure to use   90
On any field that I saw.
If riches were there,
Whatever it was would light up
Like a bonfire seen through an eyelid
And begin to be words   95
That would go with the sound of the rails.

Ghostly bridges sprang up across rivers,
Mills towered where they would be,
Slums tottered, and buildings longed
To bear up their offices.   100
I hung for years
And in the end knew it all
Through pain: the land,
The future of profits and commerce
And also humility   105
Without which none of it mattered.
In the stockyards east of Chicago

One evening, the orphans assembled
Like choir boys
And drew the nails from my hands   110
And from my accustomed feet
I stumbled with them to their homes
In Hooverville

And began to speak
In a chapel of galvanized tin   115
Of what one wishes for
When streaming alone into woods
And out into sunlight and moonlight
And when having a station lamp bulb
In one eye and not the other   120
And under the bites
Of snowflakes and clouds of flies
And the squandered dust of the prairies
That will not settle back
Beneath the crops.   125
In my head the farms
And industrial sites were burning
To produce.
One night, I addressed the A.A.,
Almost singing,   130
And in the fiery,
Unconsummated desire

For drink that rose around me
From those mild-mannered men,
I mentioned a place for a shoe store   135
That I had seen near the yards
As a blackened hulk with potential.
A man rose up,
Took a drink from a secret bottle,
And hurried out of the room.   140
A year later to the day
He knelt at my feet
In a silver suit of raw silk.
I sang to industrial groups
With a pearl-inlaid guitar   145

And plucked the breast-straining strings
With a nail that had stood through my hand.
I could not keep silent
About the powers of water,
Or where the coal beds lay quaking,   150
Or where electrical force
Should stalk in its roofless halls
Alone through the night wood,
Where the bridges should leap,
Striving with all their might   155
To connect with the other shore
To carry the salesmen.
I gave all I knew
To the owners, and they went to work.
I waked, not buried in pebbles   160

Behind the tank car,
But in the glimmering steeple
That sprang as I said it would
And lifted the young married couples,
Clutching their credit cards,   165
Boldly into and out of
Their American lives.
I said to myself that the poor

Would always be poor until
The towers I knew of should rise   170
And the oil be tapped:
That I had literally sung
My sick country up from its deathbed,
But nothing would do,
No logical right holds the truth.   175
In the sealed rooms I think of this,
Recording the nursery songs
In a checkered and tailored shirt,

As a guest on TV shows
And in my apartment now: 180
This is all a thing I began
To believe, to change, and to sell
When I opened my mouth to the rich.

———

Bums, on Waking
1963

Bums, on waking,
Do not always find themselves
In gutters with water running over their legs
And the pillow of the curbstone
Turning hard as sleep drains from it.   5
Mostly, they do not know

But hope for where they shall come to.
The opening of the eye is precious,

And the shape of the body also,
Lying as it has fallen,   10
Disdainfully crumpling earthward
Out of alcohol.

Drunken under their eyelids
Like children sleeping toward Christmas,

They wait for the light to shine   15
Wherever it may decide.

Often it brings them staring
Through glass in the rich part of town,
Where the forms of humanized wax
Are arrested in midstride   20
With their heads turned, and dressed
By force. This is ordinary, and has come

To be disappointing.
They expect and hope for

Something totally other: 25
That while they staggered last night
For hours, they got clear,
Somehow, of the city; that they
Have burst through a hedge, and are lying
In a trampled rose garden,   30

Pillowed on a bulldog's side,
A watchdog's, whose breathing

Is like the earth's, unforced—
Or that they may, once a year
(Any dawn now), awaken   35
In church, not on the coffin boards
Of a back pew, or on furnace-room rags,
But on the steps of the altar

Where candles are opening their eyes
With all-seeing light   40

And the green stained glass of the windows
Falls on them like sanctified leaves.
Who else has quite the same

Commitment to not being sure
What he shall behold, come from sleep—   45
A child, a policeman, an effigy?

Who else has died and thus risen?
Never knowing how they have got there,

They might just as well have walked
On water, through walls, out of graves,   50
Through potter's fields and through barns,
Through slums where their stony pillows
Refused to harden, because of
Their hope for this morning's first light,

With water moving over their legs   55
More like living cover than it is.

––––––––––

Goodbye to Serpents
1963

Through rain falling on us no faster
Than it runs down the wall we go through,
My son and I shed Paris like a skin
And slip into a cage to say goodbye.
Through a hole in the wall   5
Of the Jardin des Plantes
We come to go round

The animals for the last time;
Tomorrow we set out for home.
For some reason it is the snakes   10
To which we seem to owe
The longest farewell of our lives.
These have no bars, but drift
On an island held still by a moat,

Unobstructedly gazing out.   15
My son will not move from watching
Them through the dust of cold water,
And neither will I, when I realize
That this is my farewell
To Europe also. I begin to look   20
More intently than I ever have.

In the moat one is easily swimming
Like the essence of swimming itself,
Pure line and confident curve
Requiring no arms or legs.   25
In a tree, a bush, there is one
Whose body is living there motionless,
Emotionless, with drops running down,

His slack tail holding a small
Growing gem that will not fall.   30
I can see one's eyes in the brush,
As fixed as a portrait's,
Gazing into, discovering, forgetting
The heart of all rainfall and sorrow.
He licks at the air,   35

Tasting the carded water
Changed by the leaves of his home.
The rain stops in midair before him
Mesmerized as a bird—
A harmony of drops in which I see   40
Towers and churches, domes,
Capitals, streets like the shining

Paths of the Jardin des Plantes,
All old, all cold with my gaze
In glittering, unearthly fascination.   45
I say, "Yes! So I have seen them!
But I have brought also the human,
The presence of self and of love."
Yet it is not so. My son shifts

Uneasily back and away, bored now,   50
A tourist to the bitter end,
And I know I have not been moved
Enough by the things I have moved through,
And I have seen what I have seen

Unchanged, hypnotized, and perceptive: 55
The jewelled branches,
The chandeliers, the windows
Made for looking through only when weeping,
The continent hazy with grief,
The water in the air without support   60
Sustained in the serpent's eye.

Horses and Prisoners
1963

In the war where many men fell
Wind blew in a ring, and was grass.
Many horses fell also to rifles
On a track in the Philippine Islands
And divided their still, wiry meat   5
To be eaten by prisoners.
I sat at the finish line
At the end of the war

Knowing that I would live.
Long grass went around me, half wind,   10
Where I rode the rail of the infield
And the dead horses travelled in waves
On past the finishing post.
Dead wind lay down in live grass,
The flowers, pounding like hooves,   15
Stood up in the sun and were still,

And my mind, like a fence on fire,
Went around those unknown men:
Those who tore from the red, light bones
The intensified meat of hunger   20
And then lay down open-eyed
In a raw, straining dream of new life.
Joy entered the truth and flowed over
As the wind rose out of the grass

Leaping with red and white flowers: 25
Joy in the bone-strewn infield
Where clouds of barbed wire contained
Men who ran in a vision of greenness,
Sustained by the death of beasts,
On the tips of the sensitive grass blades,   30
Each footstep putting forth petals,
Their bones light and strong as the wind.

From the fence I dropped off and waded
Knee-deep in the billowing homestretch
And picked up the red of one flower.   35
It beat in my hand like my heart,
Filled with the pulse of the air,
And I felt my long thighbones yearn
To leap with the trained, racing dead.
When beasts are fallen in wars   40

For food, men seeking a reason to live
Stand mired in the on-going grass
And sway there, sweating and thinking,
With fire coming out of their brains
Like the thought of food and life   45
Of prisoners. When death moves close
In the night, I think I can kill it:
Let a man let his mind burn and change him

To one who was prisoner here
As he sings in his sleep in his home,   50

His mane streaming over the pillows,
The white threads of time
Mixed with the hair of his temples,
His grave-grass risen without him:
Now, in the green of that sleep,   55
Let him start the air of the island

From the tangled gate of jute string
That hangs from the battered grandstand
Where hope comes from animal blood
And the hooves of ghosts become flowers   60
That a captive may run as in Heaven:
Let him strip the dead shirt from his chest
And, sighing like all saved men,
Take his nude child in his arms.

———————

Blowgun and Rattlesnake
1963

I

Some fires are heard most truly
Among dry rocks
On the sunward side of a hill.
The sound that comes from the leaves there
Is the lifted burning   5
Away of an angry tail.

II

There is a long dazzling pipe
That can be brought to bear.
The sun's intensest point
Tilts up and back down it   10
Like the bubble in a carpenter's level.

A skin diver's mouthpiece
Fits the inside expression of the lips;
A plastic cone fits cleanly
The inside expression of the pipe,   15
And, taped to the cone,
Is a knitting needle
Or a section of coat hanger
Sharpened on pavement.

III

The snake's watching head must be seen,   20
Going back and back until
It can recoil no more.
Gradually you can tell
Where the rings emerge from the bush
Without moving, and camouflage—   25
The diamond-dust-cut back—
Loses its secrecy.
You will never see the tail,
Dissolving louder and louder.

IV

Hold the sun still on the pipe   30
And build your breath like a basement.
Sight down into the head,
Into one eye if you can.
Hold the eye, mythical stone
Of the bird-charmer,   35
The thing that birds believe
Is the sun come near them,
Bringing, bringing.

V

He very likely expects
Almost anything,   40
But not, surely, this:

The sun like a bubble trued,
A man, unnaturally still,
Exploding in sunlight,
A coat hanger, sharpened by scraping   45
On a suburban driveway,
Aimed from the lungs.

VI

Put down your aluminum tube,
One end to the ground, like a dazzling
Staff towering over your head.   50
Lean on it, and watch
As though the tumultuous bush
Were thrashing with unspoken fire
About to break out, and you
A shepherd and prophet   55
Whose pasture is desert.

VII

His death has looped him into
Each intimate branch of the bush.
The head dangles clear, and through it
Is the intimate force of your breath,   60
Black, red, and still,
Shed twelve feet away.

VIII

Cut the rattle loose, and scrub
The long one drop of blood
From the unbent shaft.   65
Insert the needle back
Into your last breath
That feels as if it would sing
And blow these rocks into sand
And that sand up into storms   70

And whirlwinds with voices
Giving commandments.

IX

Go up the hill, keeping always
The sun balanced on your shoulders.
Listen. Listen,   75
All the time preparing,
Inside your face, the smile
To fit the mouthpiece
Unseen: some constricted
Expression inside a smile: 80
That of a man who wishes
Only utmost and holy reply
To reach him
From red rock and greasewood,
Ready once more   85
To dam himself up with his lips,
To put himself into a tube
Like a desert scroll—
A last word lasting forever
In the brain of serpents—   90
And then on a shimmering hillside
To explode, and listen again
For something else.

————

In the Child's Night
1963

On distant sides of the bed
We lie together in the winter house
Trying to go away.

Something thinks, "You must be made for it,
And tune your quiet body like a fish   5
To the stars of the Milky Way

To pass into the star-sea, into sleep,
By means of the heart of the current,
The holy secret of flowing."

Yet levels of depth are wrestling   10
And rising from us; we are still.
The quilt pattern—a child's pink whale—

Has surfaced through ice at midnight
And now is dancing upon
The dead cold and middle of the air   15

On my son's feet:
His short legs are trampling the bedclothes
Into the darkness above us

Where the chill of consciousness broods
Like a thing of absolute evil.   20
I rise to do freezing battle

With my bare hands
I enter the faraway other
Side of the struggling bed

And turn him to face me.   25
The stitched beast falls, and we
Are sewn warmly into a sea-shroud

It begins to haul through the dark.
Holding my son's
Best kicking foot in my hand,   30

I begin to move with the moon
As it must have felt when it went
From the sea to dwell in the sky,

As we near the vast beginning,
The unborn stars of the wellhead,   35
The secret of the game.

———

Cherrylog Road
1963

Off Highway 106
At Cherrylog Road I entered
The '34 Ford without wheels,
Smothered in kudzu,
With a seat pulled out to run   5
Corn whiskey down from the hills,

And then from the other side
Crept into an Essex
With a rumble seat of red leather
And then out again, aboard   10
A blue Chevrolet, releasing
The rust from its other color,

Reared up on three building blocks.
None had the same body heat;
I changed with them inward, toward   15
The weedy heart of the junkyard,
For I knew that Doris Holbrook
Would escape from her father at noon

And would come from the farm
To seek parts owned by the sun   20
Among the abandoned chassis,
Sitting in each in turn
As I did, leaning forward
As in a wild stock-car race

In the parking lot of the dead.   25
Time after time, I climbed in
And out the other side, like
An envoy or movie star
Met at the station by crickets.
A radiator cap raised its head,   30

Become a real toad or a kingsnake
As I neared the hub of the yard,
Passing through many states,
Many lives, to reach
Some grandmother's long Pierce-Arrow   35
Sending platters of blindness forth

From its nickel hubcaps
And spilling its tender upholstery
On sleepy roaches,
The glass panel in between   40
Lady and colored driver
Not all the way broken out,

The back-seat phone
Still on its hook.
I got in as though to exclaim,   45
"Let us go to the orphan asylum,
John; I have some old toys
For children who say their prayers."

I popped with sweat as I thought
I heard Doris Holbrook scrape   50
Like a mouse in the southern-state sun
That was eating the paint in blisters
From a hundred car tops and hoods.
She was tapping like code,

Loosening the screws,   55
Carrying off headlights,
Sparkplugs, bumpers,

Cracked mirrors and gear-knobs,
Getting ready, already,
To go back with something to show   60

Other than her lips' new trembling
I would hold to me soon, soon,
Where I sat in the ripped back seat
Talking over the interphone,
Praying for Doris Holbrook   65
To come from her father's farm

And to get back there
With no trace of me on her face
To be seen by her red-haired father
Who would change, in the squalling barn,   70
Her back's pale skin with a strop,
Then lay for me

In a bootlegger's roasting car
With a string-triggered 12-gauge shotgun
To blast the breath from the air.   75
Not cut by the jagged windshields,
Through the acres of wrecks she came
With a wrench in her hand,

Through dust where the blacksnake dies
Of boredom, and the beetle knows   80
The compost has no more life.
Someone outside would have seen
The oldest car's door inexplicably
Close from within:

I held her and held her and held her,   85
Convoyed at terrific speed
By the stalled, dreaming traffic around us,
So the blacksnake, stiff
With inaction, curved back
Into life, and hunted the mouse   90

With deadly overexcitement,
The beetles reclaimed their field
As we clung, glued together,
With the hooks of the seat springs
Working through to catch us red-handed   95
Amidst the gray, breathless batting

That burst from the seat at our backs.
We left by separate doors
Into the changed, other bodies
Of cars, she down Cherrylog Road   100
And I to my motorcycle
Parked like the soul of the junkyard

Restored, a bicycle fleshed
With power, and tore off
Up Highway 106, continually   105
Drunk on the wind in my mouth,
Wringing the handlebar for speed,
Wild to be wreckage forever.

Breath
1963

Breath is on my face when the cloudy sun
    Is on my neck.
By it, the dangers of water are carefully
    Kept; kept back:

This is done with your father again   5
    In memory, it says.
Let me kneel on the boards of the rowboat,
    Father, where it sways

Among the fins and shovel heads
        Of surfaced sharks   10
And remember how I saw come shaping up
        Through lightening darks

Of the bay another thing that rose
        From the depths on air
And opened the green of its skull to breathe   15
        What we breathed there.

A porpoise circled around where I
        Lay in your hands
And felt my fear apportioned to the sharks,
        Which fell to sands   20

Two hundred feet down within cold.
        Looking over the side,
I saw that beak rise up beneath my face
        And a hole in the head

Open greenly, and then show living pink,   25
        And breath come out
In a mild, unhurried, unfathomable sigh
        That raised the boat

And left us all but singing in midair.
        Have you not seen,   30
Father, in Heaven, the eye of earthly things
        Open and breathe green,

Bestowing comfort on the mortal soul
        In deadly doubt,
Sustaining the spirit moving on the waters   35
        In hopeless light?

We arched and plunged with that beast to land.
        Amazing, that unsealed lung
Come up from the dark; that breath, controlled,
        Greater than song,   40

That huge body raised from the sea
    Secretly smiling
And shaped by the air it had carried
    Through the stark sailing

And changeless ignorance of brutes,   45
    So that a dream
Began in my closed head, of the curves and rolling
    Powers of seraphim,

That lift the good man's coffin on their breath
    And bear it up,   50
A rowboat, from the sons' depleting grief
    That will not stop:

Those that hide within time till the time
    Is wholly right,
Then come to us slowly, out of nowhere and anywhere risen,   55
    Breathlessly bright.

The Driver

1963

At the end of the war I arose
From my bed in the tent and walked
Where the island fell through white stones
Until it became the green sea.
Into light that dazzled my brain   5
Like the new thought of peace, I walked
Until I was swimming and singing.

Over the foundered landing craft
That took the island, I floated,
And then like a thistle came   10
On the deep wind of water to rest

Far out, my long legs of shadow down-
pointing to ground where my soul
Could take root and spring as it must.

Below me a rusted halftrack   15
Moved in the depths with the movement
One sees a thing take through tears
Of joy, or terrible sorrow,
A thing which in quietness lies
Beyond both. Slowly I sank   20
And slid into the driver's shattered seat.

Driving through the country of the drowned
On a sealed, secret-keeping breath,
Ten feet under water, I sat still,
Getting used to the burning stare   25
Of the wide-eyed dead after battle.
I saw, through the sensitive roof—
The uneasy, lyrical skin that lies

Between death and life, trembling always—
An airplane come over, perfectly   30
Soundless, but could not tell
Why I lived, or why I was sitting,
With my lungs being shaped like two bells,
At the wheel of a craft in a wave
Of attack that broke upon coral.   35

"I become pure spirit," I tried
To say, in a bright smoke of bubbles,
But I was becoming no more
Than haunted, for to be so
Is to sink out of sight, and to lose   40
The power of speech in the presence
Of the dead, with the eyes turning green,

And to leap at last for the sky
Very nearly too late, where another
Leapt and could not break into   45

His breath, where it lay, in battle
As in peace, available, secret,
Dazzling and huge, filled with sunlight,
For thousands of miles on the water.

————

The Ice Skin
1963

All things that go deep enough
Into rain and cold
Take on, before they break down,
A shining in every part.
The necks of slender trees   5
Reel under it, too much crowned,
Like princes dressing as kings,

And the redwoods let sink their branches
Like arms that try to hold buckets
Filling slowly with diamonds   10

Until a cannon goes off
Somewhere inside the still trunk
And a limb breaks, just before midnight,
Plunging houses into the darkness
And hands into cupboards, all seeking   15
Candles, and finding each other.
There is this skin

Always waiting in cold-enough air.
I have seen aircraft, in war,
Squatting on runways,   20

Dazed with their own enclosed,
Coming-forth, intensified color
As though seen by a child in a poem.

I have felt growing over
Me in the heated death rooms   25
Of uncles, the ice
Skin, that which the dying

Lose, and we others,
In their thawing presence, take on.
I have felt the heroic glaze   30

Also, in hospital waiting
Rooms: that masterly shining
And the slow weight that makes you sit
Like an emperor, fallen, becoming
His monument, with the stiff thorns   35
Of fear upside down on the brow,
An overturned kingdom:

Through the window of ice
I have stared at my son in his cage,
Just born, just born.   40

I touched the frost of my eyebrows
To the cold he turned to
Blindly, but sensing a thing.
Neither glass nor the jagged
Helm on my forehead would melt.   45
My son now stands with his head
At my shoulder. I

Stand, stooping more, but the same,
Not knowing whether
I will break before I can feel,   50

Before I can give up my powers,
Or whether the ice light
In my eyes will ever snap off
Before I die. I am still,
And my son, doing what he was taught,   55
Listening hard for a buried cannon,
Stands also, calm as glass.

The Leap

1964

The only thing I have of Jane MacNaughton
Is one instant of a dancing-class dance.
She was the fastest runner in the seventh grade,
My scrapbook says, even when boys were beginning
To be as big as the girls,   5
But I do not have her running in my mind,
Though Frances Lane is there, Agnes Fraser,
Fat Betty Lou Black in the boys-against-girls
Relays we ran at recess: she must have run

Like the other girls, with her skirts tucked up   10
So they would be like bloomers,
But I cannot tell; that part of her is gone.
What I do have is when she came,
With the hem of her skirt where it should be
For a young lady, into the annual dance   15
Of the dancing class we all hated, and with a light
Grave leap, jumped up and touched the end
Of one of the paper-ring decorations

To see if she could reach it. She could,
And reached me now as well, hanging in my mind   20
From a brown chain of brittle paper, thin
And muscular, wide-mouthed, eager to prove
Whatever it proves when you leap
In a new dress, a new womanhood, among the boys
Whom you easily left in the dust   25
Of the passionless playground. If I said I saw
In the paper where Jane MacNaughton Hill,

Mother of four, leapt to her death from a window
Of a downtown hotel, and that her body crushed-in
The top of a parked taxi, and that I held   30
Without trembling a picture of her lying cradled
In that papery steel as though lying in the grass,

One shoe idly off, arms folded across her breast,
I would not believe myself. I would say
The convenient thing, that it was a bad dream   35
Of maturity, to see that eternal process

Most obsessively wrong with the world
Come out of her light, earth-spurning feet
Grown heavy: would say that in the dusty heels
Of the playground some boy who did not depend   40
On speed of foot, caught and betrayed her.
Jane, stay where you are in my first mind:
It was odd in that school, at that dance.
I and the other slow-footed yokels sat in corners
Cutting rings out of drawing paper   45

Before you leapt in your new dress
And touched the end of something I began,
Above the couples struggling on the floor,
New men and women clutching at each other
And prancing foolishly as bears: hold on   50
To that ring I made for you, Jane—
My feet are nailed to the ground
By dust I swallowed thirty years ago—
While I examine my hands.

————

Mary Sheffield
1964

Forever at war news   I am
thinking there   nearly naked
low green of water   hard overflowed forms

water sits running   quietly carving
red rocks forcing white from the current   5

parts of midstream   join
I sit with one hand   joining
the other hand shyly   fine sand under

still feet   and Mary Sheffield
singing   passed-through   10

sustained in the   poured forms of live oaks
taking root   in the last tracks
of left and right foot   river flowing

into my mind   nearly naked
the last day but one   before world war.   15

When the slight wind dies
each leaf still has   two places
such music   touched alive

guitar strings   sounds   join
In the stone's shoal   of swimming   20

the best twigs I have   the best
sailing leaves   in memory
pass   threading through

all things spread sail   sounds gather
on blunt stone   streaming white   25

E minor   gently running
I sit with one hand   in the strange life
of the other   watching water throng

on one stone   loving Mary Sheffield
for her chord changes   river always   30

before war   I sit down and
anywhere   water flows   the breastplate of time
rusts off me   sounds   green forms   low voice

new music   long   long
past.   35

Fox Blood

1964

Blood blister over my thumb-moon
Rising, under clear still plastic
Still rising strongly, on the rise
Of unleashed dog-sounds: sound broke,
Log opened. Moon rose   5

Clear bright. Dark homeland
Peeled backward, scrambling its vines.
Stream showed, scent paled
In the spray of mountain-cold water.
The smell dogs followed   10

In the bush-thorns hung like a scarf,
The silver sharp creek
Cut; off yonder, fox feet
Went printing into the dark: *there,*
In the other wood,   15

The uncornered animal's, running
Is half floating off
Upon instinct. Sails spread, fox wings
Lift him alive over gullies,
Hair tips all over him lightly   20

Touched with the moon's red silver,
Back-hearing around
The stream of his body the tongue of hounds
Feather him. In his own animal sun
Made of human moonlight,   25

He flies like a bolt running home,
Whose passage kills the current in the river,
Whose track through the cornfield shakes
The symmetry from the rows.
Once shot, he dives through a bush   30

And disappears into air.
That is the bush my hand
Went deeply through as I followed.
Like a wild hammer blazed my right thumb
In the flashlight and moonlight   35

And dried to one drop
Of fox blood I nail-polished in,
That lopsided animal sun
Over the nearly buried
Or rising human half-moon,   40

My glassed skin halfmooning wrongly.
Between them, the logging road, the stopped
Stream, the disappearance into
The one bush's common, foreseen
Superhuman door: 45

All this where I nailed it,
With my wife's nailbrush, on my finger,
To keep, not under, but over
My thumb, a hammering day-and-night sign
Of that country.   50

———————

For the Linden Moth
1964

Here comes a noon dream through the eyelids
Bearing out of the sun a deep wood
Where tens, where thousands of small creatures
Are hanged by the neck to await
Their wings. From every hardwood limb,   5
Let down on invisible threads

As if in sacks, they struggle, contending with
Themselves, and sentenced justly
To writhe until glorified.
In sun-sleep I hear them chewing,   10

My swarmed-over leaf-lids riddled
With irreparable hotpoints like stars.

If I am asked upon waking
If there is a sound at the heart
Of the forest if no one hears it,   15
I say yes, it is like the gnawing

Of the larvae of the linden moth
Destroying the hickory leaves.

Struggling to change in midair,
On their monofilament threads,   20
To their other and better selves.
I say, too—being unsilenceable

Upon the subject—that hanged men die
Of hunger, not able to eat

The leaves of the gallows tree,   25
Writhing, waiting for wings
On which to soar up around
That blasted and emptied trunk,
Sun-dreaming that they have swallowed
Whole blazing-green forests alive   30

To ascend in a cloud of night-moths
Whose jaws resurrection has stopped,
Who leave their silken ropes slipped,
Unstrung on the let-in air

Wherethrough wings for all creatures have come   35
Too late and just in time.

The Rafters
1964

My father never finished
The ceiling, but light would stop

At the eight-foot level, knowing
How far it could go and be light.
Pure darkness held up the roof   5
And pine rafters wandered through that.
My sister and my dead brother,

Not dead then, would climb
Into them after supper,

Taking off from the sprained brass bedstead   10
Into great wheels and flowers
Of spider webs; gray sucked-dry moths,
Hanging head-down, saw us coming
As the lamp went away at the speed

Of light, standing finally firm   15
Deep down in the living room,

A small star not giving up
Until we fell, and the four
Shining balls of the bedstead snapped
Their scratched lights off around us.   20
We knew all the dirt on those beams,

Scrambling forward just after the mice
(A mouse we dislodged fell all

One afternoon through the four-legged void
To arrive just in time for dinner   25
In the rice-and-potato soup.)
With the dark staying good around us,
We sometimes went all the way up

To the top of the narrowing roof,
To the odd inner peak of our life,   30

Where we could hear, very low,
The night wind come to a point.
That was the place we went
When strangers came, all of us shy
Out of our country minds: 35

When my father had city men in
To look at gamecocks, we

Took off, straight up from the bed-bars
Flaring with tarnish and brass
And crossed, with a knowing shudder,   40
The not-finished ceiling of light,
And hid there, watching my father

Pour corn liquor out of glass bell-jars.
All during my childhood, no stranger

Ever looked up and saw anything—   45
A pale, moth-gray, heel-hanging
Sucked dry small vivid face—
But all felt that something was there,
And kept looking up, as the wind

Drew down to a point overhead.   50
The most loved thing I still hear

My father say from his seat
In the low, self-sealing light,
From the distant one star of our house,
Is "Sure; they used to be mine,   55
But now they just haunt the place."

Winter Trout

1964

In the concrete cells of the hatchery
He nourished a dream of living
Under the ice, the long preparations
For the strange heat of feeling slowly

Roofs melt to a rhythmic green, 5
But now, in the first cold of freedom,
Riding motionless under the road
Of ice, shaping the heart

Of the buried stream with his tail,
He knows that his powers come 10
From the fire and stillness of freezing.
With the small tremors of his form

The banks shift imperceptibly,
Shift back, tremble, settle,
Shift, all within utter stillness. 15
I keep in my quiver now

An arrow whose head is half-missing.
It is useless, but I will not change
The pulled, broken tooth of its head
For I have walked upon banks 20

Shaken with the watchfulness of trout
Like walking barefoot in sleep
On the swaying tips of a grainfield,
On the long, just-bending stems,

Almost weightless, able to leap 25
Great distances, yet not leaping
Because each step on that ground
Gave a new sense of limitless hope.

Under the ice the trout rode,
Trembling, in the mastered heart   30
Of the creek, with what he could do.
I set myself up as a statue

With a bow, my red woolen back
Climbed slowly by thoughtful brambles
And dead beggar-lice, to shoot   35
At an angle down through the shadow

Of ice, and spear the trout
With a shot like Ulysses'
Through the ax heads, with the great weapon.
I shot, and the trout did not move   40

But was gone, and the banks
Went rigid under my feet
As the arrow floated away
Under the paving of ice.

I froze my right hand to retrieve it   45
As a blessing or warning,
As a sign of the penalties
For breaking into closed worlds

Where the wary controllers lie
At the heart of their power,   50
A pure void of shadowy purpose
Where the gods live, attuning the world,

Laying plans for the first green
They ever have lived, to melt
The ice from their great crowns.   55
Their secret enemies break

Like statues, as the king rises slowly,
Keeping only the thinnest film

Of his element—imagination—
Before his eyes as he lifts   60

Into spring, with the wood upside down
Balanced perfectly in all its leaves
And roots as he deeply has
All winter made provision for,

The surface full of gold flakes   65
Of the raw undersides of leaves,
And the thing seen right,
For once, that winter bought.

————————

Chenille

1964

There are two facing peacocks
     Or a ship flapping
On its own white tufted sail
At roadside, near a mill;

Flamingoes also are hanging   5
     By their bills on bedspreads
And an occasional mallard.
These you can buy anywhere.
They are made by machine
From a sanctioned, unholy pattern   10
Rigid with industry.
They hoard the smell of oil

And hum like looms all night
     Into your pores, reweaving
Your body from bobbins.   15
There is only one quiet

Place—in a scuppernong arbor—
    Where animals as they
Would be, are born into sleep-cloth:
A middle-aged man's grandmother   20
Sits in the summer green light
Of leaves, gone toothless
For eating grapes better,
And pulls the animals through

With a darning needle: 25
    Deer, rabbits and birds,
Red whales and unicorns,
Winged elephants, crowned ants:

Beasts that cannot be thought of
    By the wholly sane   30
Rise up in the rough, blurred
Flowers of fuzzy cloth
In only their timeless outlines
Like the beasts of Heaven:
Those sketched out badly, divinely   35
By stars not wholly sane.

Love, I have slept in that house.
    There it was winter.
The tattered moonfields crept
Through the trellis, and fell   40

In vine-tangled shade on my face
    Like thrown-away knitting
Before cloud came and dimmed
Those scars from off me.
My fingernails chilled   45
To the bone. I called
For another body to be
With me, and warm us both.

A unicorn neighed; I folded
    His neck in my arms   50
And was safe, as he lay down.
All night, from thickening Heaven,

Someone up there kept throwing
    Bedspreads upon me.
Softly I called, and they came: 55
The ox and the basilisk,
The griffin, the phoenix, the lion—
Light-bodied, only the essence,
The tufted, creative starfields
Behind the assembling clouds—   60

The snake from the apple tree came
    To save me from freezing,
And at last the lung-winged ship
On its own sail scented with potash

Fell sighing upon us all.   65
    The last two nails
Of cold died out in my nostrils
Under the dance-weight of beasts.
I lay, breathing like thread,
An inspired outline of myself,   70
As rain began greatly to fall,
And closed the door of the Ark.

On the Coosawattee
1964

I. By Canoe through the Fir Forest

Into the slain tons of needles,
On something like time and dark knowledge
That cannot be told, we are riding
Over white stones forward through fir trees,
To follow whatever the river   5
Through the clasping of roots follows deeply.

As we go inward, more trunks
Climb from the edge of the water
And turn on the banks and stand growing.
The nerves in the patches of tree-light   10
On the ripples can feel no death,
But shake like the wings of angels

With light hard-pressed to keep up
Though it is in place on each feather.
Heavy woods in one movement around us   15
Flow back along either side
Bringing in more essential curves;
Small stones in their thousands turn corners

Under water and bear us on
Through the glittering, surfacing wingbeats   20
Cast from above. As we pass over,
As we pass through each hover of gold,
We lift up our blades from the water
And the blades of our shoulders,

Our rowing muscles, our wings,   25
Are still and tremble, undying,
Drifting deeper into the forest.
Each light comes into our life

Past the man in front's changed hair
Then along the wing-balancing floor   30

And then onto me and one eye
And into my mouth for an instant.
The stones beneath us grow rounder
As I taste the fretted light fall
Through living needles to be here   35
Like a word I can feed on forever

Or believe like a vision I have
Or want to conceive out of greenness.
While the world fades, it is *becoming*.
As the trees shut away all seeing,   40
In my mouth I mix it with sunlight.
Here, in the dark, it is *being*.

II. Below Ellijay

Coming into Ellijay on the green
Idling freeway of the broad river   45
From the hill farms and pine woods,
We saw first the little stores
That backed down the red clay banks,
The blue flash of bottleglass
And the rippled tin heat-haze of sheds   50

Where country mechanics were flying.
A poultry-processing plant
Smoked in the late morning air;
The bridge we rode under clattered
As we wound back out into fields.   55
But the water that held us had changed;
The town had slowed it and used it;

The wind had died in the tool sheds.
When we looked overboard, we knew.
Each thing was mistakenly feathered,   60
Muffled thickly in cast-off whiteness:

Each log was bedraggled in plumage
And accepting more feathers from water;
Each boulder under the green

Was becoming a lewd, setting hen   65
Moultingly under us brooding
In the sick, buried wind of the river,
Wavering, dying, increasing
From the plucked refuse of the plant,
And beside us uselessly floated—   70
Following, dipping, returning,

Turning frankly around to eye us,
To eye something else, to eye
Us again—a skinned chicken head,
Its gaze unperturbed and abiding.   75
All morning we floated on feathers
Among the drawn heads which appeared
Everywhere, from under the logs

Of feathers, from upstream behind us,
Lounging back to us from ahead,   80
Until we believed ourselves doomed
And the planet corrupted forever,
With stones turned to pullets, not struggling
But into more monstrousness shed,
Our canoe trailing more and more feathers   85

And the eye of the devil upon us
Closing drunkenly in from all sides,
And could have been on the Styx
In the blaze of noon, till we felt
The quickening pulse of the rapids   90
And entered upon it like men
Who sense that the world can be cleansed

Among rocks pallid only with water,
And plunged there like the unborn
Who see earthly streams without taint   95

Flow beneath them, while their wing feathers
Slough off behind them in Heaven
As they dress in the blinding clothes
Of nakedness for their fall.

III. THE INUNDATION

Down there is a stone that holds my deepest sleep   100
And buries it deeper and deeper
Under the green, skinny lake
That is going back into the Georgia hills
And climbing them day and night
Behind the new dam.   105

And there is another stone, that boiled with white,
Where Braselton and I clung and fought
With our own canoe
That flung us in the rapids we had ridden
So that it might turn and take on   110
A ton of mountain water

And swing and bear down through the flying cloud
Of foam upon our violent rock
And pin us there.
With our backs to the wall of that boulder,   115
We yelled and kept it off us as we could,
Broke both paddles,

Then wedged it with the paddle stumps up over
The rock till the hull split, and it leapt and fell
Into the afterfall.   120
In life preservers we whirled ourselves away
And floated aimlessly down into calm water,
Turning like objects,

Then crawled upon shore and were found in the afternoon
By Lucas Gentry and his hunting dog, asleep   125
On a vast, gentle stone.

At a touch we woke, and followed the strange woods boy
Up the bluff, and looked down on the roaring river's
Last day in its bed.

And now I cannot sleep at all, until I think   130
Of the Coosa, out of a clear blue sky
Overswelling its banks,
Its great stones falling through it into dark,
Its creeks becoming inlets, where water
Skiers already poise.   135

Over me it rises, too, but breathable, like cloud,
A green and silver cloud above which quiet
Lucas Gentry stands.
His dog whines, as the last rock of the wild river
Goes under, its white water lapses green,   140
And the leaping stone

Where we almost died takes on the settled repose
Of that other where we lay down and met
Our profoundest sleep
Rising from it to us, as the battered sides   145
Of the canoe gave deeper and deeper shade,
And Lucas Gentry,

Who may have been the accepting spirit of the place
Come to call us to higher ground,
Bent to raise   150
Us from the sleep of the yet-to-be-drowned,
There, with the black dream of the dead canoe
Over our faces.

Springer Mountain [b]
1964

Four sweaters are woven upon me,
All black, all sweating and waiting,
And a sheepherder's coat's wool hood,
Buttoned strainingly, holds my eyes
With their sight deepfrozen outside them   5
From their gaze toward a single tree.
I am here where I never have been,
In the limbs of my warmest clothes,
Waiting for light to crawl, weakly
From leaf to dead leaf onto leaf   10
Down the western side of the mountain.
Deer sleeping in light far above me

Have already woken, and moved,
In step with the sun moving strangely
Down toward the dark knit of my thicket   15
Where my breath takes shape on the air
Like a white helmet come from the lungs.
The one tree I hope for goes inward
And reaches the limbs of its gold.
My eyesight hangs partly between   20
Two twigs on the upslanting ground,
Then steps like a god from the dead
Wet of a half-rotted oak log
Steeply into the full of my brow.
My thighbones groaningly break   25

Upward, releasing my body
To climb, and to find among humus
New insteps made of snapped sticks.
On my back the faggot of arrows
Rattles and scratches its feathers.   30

I go up over logs slowly
On my painfully reborn legs,

My ears putting out vast hearing
Among the invisible animals,

Passing under thin branches held still,   35
Kept formed all night as they were
By the thought of predictable light.
The sun comes openly in
To my mouth, and is blown out white,

But no deer is anywhere near me.   40
I sit down and wait as in darkness.

The sweat goes dead at the roots

Of my hair: a deer is created
Descending, then standing and looking.
The sun stands and waits for his horns   45

To move. I may be there, also,
Between them, in head bones uplifted
Like a man in an animal tree
Nailed until light comes:
A dream of the unfeared hunter   50
Who has formed in his brain in the dark
And rose with light into his horns,
Naked, and I have turned younger

At forty than I ever have been.
I hang my longbow on a branch.   55
The buck leaps away and then stops,
And I step forward, stepping out

Of my shadow and pulling over
My head one dark heavy sweater
After another, my dungarees falling   60
Till they can be kicked away,
Boots, socks, all that is on me
Off. The world catches fire.
I put an unbearable light

Into breath skinned alive of its garments: 65
I think, beginning with laurel,
Like a beast loving
With the whole god bone of his horns:
The green of excess is upon me
Like deer in fir thickets in winter   70
Stamping and dreaming of men
Who will kneel with them naked to break
The ice from streams with their faces
And drink from the lifespring of beasts.
He is moving. I am with him   75

Down the shuddering hillside moving
Through trees and around, inside
And out of stumps and groves
Of laurel and slash pine,
Through hip-searing branches and thorn   80
Brakes, unprotected and sure,
Winding down to the waters of life
Where they stand petrified in a creek bed
Yet melt and flow from the hills
At the touch of an animal visage,   85

Rejoicing wherever I come to
With the gold of my breast unwrapped,
My crazed laughter pure as good church-cloth,
My brain dazed and pointed with trying
To grow horns, glad that it cannot,   90
For a few steps deep in the dance
Of what I most am and should be
And can be only once in this life.
He is gone below, and I limp
To look for my clothes in the world,   95

A middle-aged, softening man
Grinning and shaking his head
In amazement to last him forever.
I put on the warm-bodied wool,

The four sweaters inside out,   100
The bootlaces dangling and tripping,
Then pick my tense bow off the limb
And turn with the unwinding hooftracks,
In my good, tricked clothes,
To hunt, under Springer Mountain,   105
Deer for the first and last time.

Approaching Prayer
1964

A moment tries to come in
Through the windows, when one must go
Beyond what there is in the room,

But it must come straight down.
Lord, it is time,   5

And I must get up and start
To circle through my father's empty house
Looking for things to put on
Or to strip myself of
So that I can fall to my knees   10
And produce a word I can't say
Until all my reason is slain.

Here is the gray sweater
My father wore in the cold,
The snapped threads growing all over it   15
Like his gray body hair.
The spurs of his gamecocks glimmer
Also, in my light, dry hand.
And here is the head of a boar
I once helped to kill with two arrows: 20

Two things of my father's
Wild, Bible-reading life
And my own best and stillest moment
In a hog's head waiting for glory.

All these I set up in the attic,   25
The boar's head, gaffs, and the sweater
On a chair, and gaze in the dark
Up into the boar's painted gullet.

Nothing. Perhaps I should feel more foolish,
Even, than this.   30
I put on the ravelled nerves

And gray hairs of my tall father
In the dry grave growing like fleece,
Strap his bird spurs to my heels
And kneel down under the skylight.   35
I put on the hollow hog's head
Gazing straight up
With star points in the glass eyes
That would blind anything that looked in

And cause it to utter words.   40
The night sky fills with a light

Of hunting: with leaves
And sweat and the panting of dogs

Where one tries hard to draw breath,
A single breath, and hold it.   45
I draw the breath of life
For the dead hog:
I catch it from the still air,
Hold it in the boar's rigid mouth,
And see   50

   A young aging man with a bow
   And a green arrow pulled to his cheek

Standing deep in a mountain creek bed,
Stiller than trees or stones,
Waiting and staring 55

Beasts, angels,
I am nearly that motionless now

There is a frantic leaping at my sides
Of dogs coming out of the water

The moon and the stars do not move 60

I bare my teeth, and my mouth
Opens, a foot long, popping with tushes

A word goes through my closed lips

I gore a dog, he falls, falls back
Still snapping, turns away and dies 65
While swimming. I feel each hair on my back
Stand up through the eye of a needle

Where the hair was
On my head stands up
As if it were there 70

The man is still; he is stiller: still

Yes.

Something comes out of him
Like a shaft of sunlight or starlight.
I go forward toward him 75

(Beasts, angels)

With light standing through me,
Covered with dogs, but the water
Tilts to the sound of the bowstring

The planets attune all their orbits   80

    The sound from his fingers,
    Like a plucked word, quickly pierces
    Me again, the trees try to dance
    Clumsily out of the wood

I have said something else   85

    And underneath, underwater,
    In the creek bed are dancing
    The sleepy pebbles

The universe is creaking like boards
Thumping with heartbeats   90
And bonebeats

    And every image of death
    In my head turns red with blood.
    The man of blood does not move

My father is pale on my body   95

    The dogs of blood
    Hang to my ears,
    The shadowy bones of the limbs
    The sun lays on the water
    Mass darkly together   100

Moonlight, moonlight

    The sun mounts my hackles
    And I fall; I roll
    In the water;
    My tongue spills blood   105
    Bound for the ocean;
    It moves away, and I see
    The trees strain and part, see him
    Look upward

Inside the hair helmet   110
I look upward out of the total
Stillness of killing with arrows.
I have seen the hog see me kill him
And I was as still as I hoped.
I am that still now, and now.   115
My father's sweater
Swarms over me in the dark.
I see nothing, but for a second

Something goes through me
Like an accident, a negligent glance,   120
Like the explosion of a star
Six billion light years off
Whose light gives out

Just as it goes straight through me.
The boar's blood is sailing through rivers   125
Bearing the living image
Of my most murderous stillness.
It picks up speed
And my heart pounds.
The chicken-blood rust at my heels   130
Freshens, as though near a death wound
Or flight. I nearly lift
From the floor, from my father's grave
Crawling over my chest,

And then get up   135
In the way I usually do.
I take off the head of the hog
And the gaffs and the panting sweater
And go down the dusty stairs
And never come back.   140

I don't know quite what has happened
Or that anything has,

Hoping only that
The irrelevancies one thinks of
When trying to pray   145
Are the prayer,

And that I have got by my own
Means to the hovering place
Where I can say with any
Other than the desert fathers—   150
Those who saw angels come,
Their body glow shining on bushes
And sheep's wool and animal eyes,
To answer what questions men asked
In Heaven's tongue,   155
Using images of earth
Almightily:

    PROPHECIES, FIRE IN THE SINFUL TOWERS,
    WASTE AND FRUITION IN THE LAND,
    CORN, LOCUSTS AND ASHES,   160
    THE LION'S SKULL PULSING WITH HONEY,
    THE BLOOD OF THE FIRST-BORN,
    A GIRL MADE PREGNANT WITH A GLANCE
    LIKE AN EXPLODING STAR
    AND A CHILD BORN OF UTTER LIGHT—   165

Where I can say only, and truly,
That my stillness was violent enough,
That my brain had blood enough,
That my right hand was steady enough,
That the warmth of my father's wool grave   170
Imparted love enough
And the keen heels of feathery slaughter
Provided lift enough,
That reason was dead enough
For something important to be: 175

That, if not heard,
It may have been somehow said.

Reincarnation (I)

1964

Still, passed through the spokes of an old wheel, on and around
The hub's furry rust in the weeds and shadows of the riverbank,
This one is feeling his life as a man move slowly away.
Fallen from that estate, he has gone down on his knees
And beyond, disappearing into the egg buried under the sand   5

And wakened to the low world being born, consisting now
Of the wheel on its side not turning, but leaning to rot away
In the sun a few feet farther off than it is for any man.
The roots bulge quietly under the earth beneath him;
With his tongue he can hear them in their concerted effort   10

To raise something, anything, out of the dark of the ground.
He has come by gliding, by inserting the head between stems.
Everything follows that as naturally as the creation
Of the world, leaving behind arms and legs, leaving behind
The intervals between tracks, leaving one long wavering step   15

In sand and none in grass: he moves through, moving nothing,
And the grass stands as never entered. It is in the new
Life of resurrection that one can come in one's own time
To a place like a rotting wheel, the white paint flaking from it,
Rust slowly emerging, and coil halfway through it, stopped   20

By a just administration of light and dark over the diamonds
Of the body. Here, also naturally growing, is a flat leaf
To rest the new head upon. The stem bends but knows the weight
And does not touch the ground, holding the snub, patterned face
Swaying with the roots of things. Inside the jaws, saliva   25

Has turned ice cold, drawn from bird eggs and thunderstruck rodents,
Dusty pine needles, blunt stones, horse dung, leaf mold,
But mainly, now, from waiting—all the time a symbol of evil—
Not for food, but for the first man to walk by the gentle river:
Minute by minute the head becomes more poisonous and poised.   30

Here in the wheel is the place to wait, with the eyes unclosable,
Unanswerable, the tongue occasionally listening, this time
No place in the body desiring to burn the tail away or to warn,
But only to pass on, handless, what yet may be transferred
In a sudden giving-withdrawing move, like a county judge striking a match.   35

———————

The Second Sleep
1964

Curled, too much curled, he was sleeping

In a chair too small for him, a restless chair
That held no place for his arms;

In his sleep he grew legs to replace them

As his father liftingly strained   5
And carried him to the next room.

All the time he settled away

A gentle man looked upon him
And then walked out of the house

And started his evergreen car.   10

Terrific impact, none his,
Killed him three blocks to the north.

In his second sleep the boy heard

The reared-up tearing of metal
Where a glassed-in face leapt and broke,   15

But to him it was something else,

An animal clash, a shock of resolving antlers,
And slept on, deeper and deeper

Into the mating season.

The next room filled with women; his nostrils   20
Flared, his eyes grew wide

And shot with blood under eyelids.

Brow lowered in strife, he stamped
In the laurel thicket, a herd of does

Trembling around him. Into the rhododendron   25

His rival faded like rain.
He stared around wildly, head down.

In the undying green, they woke him.

———————

The Firebombing
1964

Denke daran, dass nach den grossen Zerstörungen
Jedermann beweisen wird, dass er unschuldig war.

Günter Eich

Or hast thou an arm like God?

The Book of Job

Homeowners unite.

All families lie together, though some are burned alive.
The others try to feel
For them. Some can, it is often said.

Starve and take off   5

Twenty years in the suburbs, and the palm trees willingly leap
Into the flashlights,
And there is beneath them also
A booted crackling of snailshells and coral sticks.
There are cowl flaps and the tilt cross of propellers,   10
The shovel-marked clouds' far sides against the moon,
The enemy filling up the hills
With ceremonial graves. At my somewhere among these,

Snap, a bulb is tricked on in the cockpit

And some technical-minded stranger with my hands   15
Is sitting in a glass treasure-hole of blue light,
Having potential fire under the undeodorized arms
Of his wings, on thin bomb-shackles,
The "tear-drop-shaped" 300-gallon drop-tanks
Filled with napalm and gasoline.   20

Thinking forward ten minutes
From that, there is also the burst straight out
Of the overcast into the moon; there is now
The moon-metal-shine of propellers, the quarter-
moonstone, aimed at the waves,   25
Stopped on the cumulus.

There is then this re-entry
Into cloud, for the engines to ponder their sound.
In white dark the aircraft shrinks; Japan

Dilates around it like a thought.   30
Coming out, the one who is here is over
Land, passing over the all-night grainflelds,
In dark paint over
The woods with one silver side,
Rice-water calm at all levels   35
Of the terraced hill.

                    Enemy rivers and trees
Sliding off me like snakeskin,
Strips of vapor spooled from the wingtips
Going   invisible   passing   over   on   40
Over   bridges   roads for nightwalkers
Sunday night in the enemy's country   absolute
Calm   the moon's face   coming   slowly
About
            the inland sea   45
Slants   is woven with wire thread
Levels out   holds together like a quilt
Off the starboard wing   cloud flickers
At my glassed-off forehead   the moon's now and again
Uninterrupted face going forward   50
Over the waves in a glide-path
Lost into land.

Going: going with it

Combat booze by my side in a cratered canteen,
Bourbon frighteningly mixed   55
With GI pineapple juice,
Dogs trembling under me for hundreds of miles, on many
Islands, sleep-smelling that ungodly mixture
Of napalm and high-octane fuel,
Good bourbon and GI juice.   60

Rivers circling behind me around
Come to the fore, and bring
A town with everyone darkened.
Five thousand people are sleeping off
An all-day American drone.   65
Twenty years in the suburbs have not shown me
Which ones were hit and which not.

Haul on the wheel   racking slowly
The aircraft blackly around
In a dark dream   that   that is   70
That is like flying inside someone's head

Think of this   think of this

I did not think of my house
But think of my house now

Where the lawn mower rests on its laurels   75
Where the diet exists
For my own good   where I try to drop
Twenty years, eating figs in the pantry
Blinded by each and all
Of the eye-catching cans that gladly have caught my wife's eye   80
Until I cannot say
Where the screwdriver is   where the children
Get off the bus   where the new
Scoutmaster lives   where the fly
Hones his front legs   where the hammock folds   85
Its erotic daydreams   where the Sunday
School text for the day has been put   where the fire
Wood is   where the payments
For everything under the sun
Pile peacefully up,   90

But in this half-paid-for pantry
Among the red lids that screw off
With an easy half-twist to the left
And the long drawers crammed with dim spoons,
I still have charge—secret charge—   95
Of the fire developed to cling
To everything: to golf carts and fingernail
Scissors as yet unborn   tennis shoes
Grocery baskets   toy fire engines
New Buicks stalled by the half-moon   100
Shining at midnight on crossroads   green paint
Of jolly garden tools   red Christmas ribbons:

Not atoms, these, but glue inspired
By love of country to burn,
The apotheosis of gelatin.   105

Behind me having risen the Southern Cross
Set up by chaplains in the Ryukyus—
Orion, Scorpio, the immortal silver
Like the myths of king-
insects at swarming time—   110
One mosquito, dead drunk
On altitude, drones on, far under the engines,
And bites between
The oxygen mask and the eye.
The enemy-colored skin of families   115
Determines to hold its color
In sleep, as my hand turns whiter
Than ever, clutching the toggle—
The ship shakes   bucks
Fire hangs   not yet fire   120
In the air above Beppu
For I am fulfilling

An "anti-morale" raid upon it.
All leashes of dogs
Break under the first bomb, around those   125
In bed, or late in the public baths: around those
Who inch forward on their hands
Into medicinal waters.
Their heads come up with a roar
Of Chicago fire: 130
Come up with the carp pond showing
The bathhouse upside down,
Standing stiller to show it more
As I sail artistically over
The resort town followed by farms,   135
Singing and twisting
All the handles in heaven   kicking
The small cattle off their feet
In a red costly blast
Flinging jelly over the walls   140
As in a chemical war-
fare field demonstration.
With fire of mine like a cat

Holding onto another man's walls,
My hat should crawl on my head   145
In streetcars, thinking of it,
The fat on my body should pale.

Gun down
The engines, the eight blades sighing
For the moment when the roofs will connect   150
Their flames, and make a town burning with all
American fire.
                    Reflections of houses catch;
Fire shuttles from pond to pond
In every direction, till hundreds flash with one death.   155
With this in the dark of the mind,
Death will not be what it should;
Will not, even now, even when
My exhaled face in the mirror
Of bars, dilates in a cloud like Japan.   160
The death of children is ponds
Shutter-flashing; responding mirrors; it climbs
The terraces of hills
Smaller and smaller, a mote of red dust
At a hundred feet; at a hundred and one it goes out.   165
That is what should have got in
To my eye

And shown the insides of houses, the low tables
Catch fire from the floor mats,
Blaze up in gas around their heads   170
Like a dream of suddenly growing
Too intense for war. Ah, under one's dark arms
Something strange-scented falls—when those on earth
Die, there is not even sound;
One is cool and enthralled in the cockpit,   175
Turned blue by the power of beauty,
In a pale treasure-hole of soft light
Deep in aesthetic contemplation,
Seeing the ponds catch fire
And cast it through ring after ring   180

Of land: O death in the middle
Of acres of inch-deep water!   Useless

Firing   small arms
Speckles   from the river
Bank   one ninety-millimeter   185
Misses   far down   wrong petals   gone

It is this detachment,
The honored aesthetic evil,
The greatest sense of power in one's life,
That must be shed in bars, or by whatever   190
Means, by starvation
Visions in well-stocked pantries:
The moment when the moon sails in between
The tail-booms   the rudders nod   I swing
Over   directly over the heart   195
The *heart* of the fire. A mosquito burns out on my cheek
With the cold of my face   there are the eyes
In blue light   bar light
All masked but them   the moon
Crossing from left to right   in the streams below   200
Oriental fish form quickly
In the chemical shine,
In their eyes one tiny seed
Of deranged, Old Testament light.

Letting go   letting go   205
The plane rises gently   dark forms
Glide off me   long water   pales
In safe zones   a new cry enters
The voice box of chained family dogs

We buck   leap over something   210
Not there   settle back
Leave it   leave it clinging and crying
It consumes them in a hot
Body-flash, old age or menopause
Of children, clings and burns   215

                                    eating through
And when a reed mat catches fire
From me, it explodes through field after field
Bearing its sleeper   another

Bomb finds a home   220
And clings to it like a child. And so

Goodbye to the grassy mountains
To cloud streaming from the night engines
Flags   pennons   curved silks
Of air   myself streaming also   225
My body covered
With flags, the air of flags
Between the engines.
Forever I do sleep in that position,
Forever in a turn   230
For home that breaks out streaming banners
From my wingtips,
Wholly in position to admire.

O then I knock it off
And turn for home over the black complex thread worked through   235
The silver night-sea,
Following the huge, moon-washed steppingstones
Of the Ryukyus south,
The nightgrass of mountains billowing softly
In my rising heat.   240
                        Turn and tread down
The yellow stones of the islands
To where Okinawa burns,
Pure gold, on the radar screen,
Beholding, beneath, the actual island form   245
In the vast water-silver poured just above solid ground,
An inch of water extending for thousands of miles
Above flat ploughland. Say "down," and it is done.

All this, and I am still hungry,
Still twenty years overweight, still unable   250

To get down there or see
What really happened.
                                        But it may be that I could not,
If I tried, say to any
Who lived there, deep in my flames: say, in cold   255
Grinning sweat, as to another
Of these homeowners who are always curving
Near me down the different-grassed street: say
As though to the neighbor
I borrowed the hedge-clippers from   260
On the darker-grassed side of the two,
Come in, my house is yours, come in
If you can, if you
Can pass this unfired door. It is that I can imagine
At the threshold nothing   265
With its ears crackling off
Like powdery leaves,
Nothing with children of ashes, nothing not
Amiable, gentle, well-meaning,
A little nervous for no   270
Reason   a little worried   a little too loud
Or too easygoing   nothing I haven't lived with
For twenty years, still nothing not as
American as I am, and proud of it.

Absolution? Sentence? No matter;   275
The thing itself is in that.

Them, Crying

1964

In the well-fed cage-sound of diesels,
Here, in the cab's boxed wind,
He is called to by something beyond
His life. In the sun's long haul

Of light, each week at this place,   5
He sings to the truck's eight wheels

But at night it is worse than useless:
The great building shoots and holds

Its rays, and he hears, through the engine,
Through the killed words of his own song,   10
Them: them crying. Unmarried, unchildlike,
Half-bearded and foul-mouthed, he feels
His hands lean away to the right
And bear the truck spiraling down

To the four streets going around   15
And around and around the hospital.

He sits, and the voices are louder,
An awakening, part-song sound
Calling anyone out of the life
He thought he led: a sound less than twelve   20
Years old, which wakes to the less-than-nothing
Of a bent glass straw in a glass

With small sleepless bubbles stuck to it:
Which feels a new mouth sewn shut

In a small body's back or its side   25
And would free some angelic voice
From the black crimped thread,
The snipped cat-whiskers of a wound—
A sound that can find no way
To attack the huge, orderly flowers.   30

At one-thirty he is drawn in,
Drawn in, drawn in and in,

Listening, through dozens of Bakelite floors
And walls, brogan-stepping along
Through green-tiled nightlighted rooms   35

Where implements bake in glass cases,
Through halls full of cloudy test tubes,
Up and down self-service elevators

That open both sides at once,
Through closets of lubricants,   40

Through a black beehive of typed labels,
Through intimate theatres
Scrubbed down with Lysol and salt,
Through a sordid district of pails,
Until, on the third floor rear   45
Of the donated Southeast Wing,

He comes on a man holding wrongly
A doll with feigning-closed eyes,

And a fat woman, hat in her lap,
Has crashed through a chairback to sleep.   50
Unbelonging, he circles their circle;
Then, as though a stitch broke
In his stomach, he wheels and goes through
The double-frosted warning-marked door.

Twelve parents at bay intone   55
In the brain waves that wash around heroes:

    Come, stripped to your T-shirt sleeves,
    Your coveralls, blue jeans, or chains,
    Your helmets or thickening haircuts,
    Your white coats, your rock-pounding foreheads,   60
    For our children lie there beyond us
    In the still, foreign city of pain

    Singing backward into the world
    To those never seen before,

    Old cool-handed doctors and young ones,   65
    Capped girls bearing vessels of glucose,

Ginger ward boys, pan handlers, technicians,
Thieves, nightwalkers, truckers, and drunkards
Who must hear, not listening, them:
Them, crying: for they rise only unto   70

Those few who transcend themselves,
The superhuman tenderness of strangers.

———————

The Escape
1964

From my great-grandmother on,
My family lies at Fairmount
In a small rigid house of Tate marble.
A Civil War general, a small one,
Rises into the air,   5
Always fifty feet away,
And there are always flowers
Surrounding him as he lifts
His sword and calls back over his shoulder
To his troops, none of which lie   10
Under the decent plots and polished stones
Of the civilian dead. Once I saw,
Or said I did, a lily wrapped
Around his tense hand and sword hilt.
An enormous glass-fronted hospital   15
Rises across the street, the traffic
Roars equally from all four sides,
And often, from a textile mill,
A teen-age girl wanders by,
Her head in a singing cloth   20
Still humming with bobbins and looms.
In summer, the hospital orderlies eat
Their lunches on the lawn
From wet-spotted brown paper bags,

While behind them the portioned glass   25
Of the hospital blindingly fits
The noon sun together:
A tremendous vertical blaze
From which one piece—off-center, northwest—
Is gone, where a window is open.   30
I have escaped from Fairmount
Through that square hole in the light,
Having found where that piece of the sun's
Stupendous puzzle resides. It is
Lying in the woods, in a small, unfenced   35
County graveyard in Alabama.
It is on an open book
Of cardboard and paper, a simulated Bible,
All white, like a giant bride's,
The only real pages the ones   40
The book opens to; light
From the trees is falling squarely
On the few large, hand-written words.
On a hunting trip I walked through
That place, far from all relatives   45
And wars, from bobbins and lilies and trucks.
Because of what I had seen,

I walked through the evergreen gates
Of the forest ranger's station,
And out to my car, and drove   50
To the county seat, and bought
My own secret grave-plot there
For thirty-seven dollars and a half.
A young deer, a spike buck, stood
Among the graves, slowly puzzling out   55
The not-quite-edible words
Of the book lying under
A panel of the sun forever
Missing from the noonlight of Fairmount.
I remember that, and sleep   60
Easier, seeing the animal head
Nuzzling the fragment of Scripture,

Browsing, before the first blotting rain
On the fragile book
Of the new dead, on words I take care,   65
Even in sleep, not to read,
Hoping for Genesis.

———————

Faces Seen Once
1964

Faces seen once are seen

To fade from around one feature,
Leaving a chin, a scar, an expression

Forever in the air beneath a streetlight,
Glancing in boredom from the window   5
Of a bus in a country town,
Showing teeth for a moment only,
All of which die out of mind, except
One silver one.

Who had the dog-bitten ear?   10
The granulated lids? The birthmark?

Faces seen once change always

Into and out of each other:
An eye you saw in Toulon
Is gazing at you down a tin drainpipe   15
You played with as a dull child
In Robertstown, Georgia.
There it is April; the one eye

Concentrates, the rusty pipe

Is trembling; behind the eye   20
Is a pine tree blurring with tears:

You and someone's blue eye
Transforming your boyhood are weeping
For an only son drowned in warm water
With the French fleet off Senegal.   25
Soon after, the cancer-clamped face
Of your great-grandfather relaxes,

Smiles again with the lips of a newsboy.
Faces seen once make up

One face being organized   30

And changed and known less all the time,
Unsexed, amorphous, growing in necessity
As you deepen in age.
The brow wrinkles, a blind, all-knowing
Questioning look comes over it,   35
And every face in the street begins

To partake of the look in the eyes,

Every nose is part of that nose
And changes the nose; every innocence and every

Unspoken-of guilt goes into it,   40
Into the face of the one
Encountered, unknowable person who waits
For you all over the world,
In coffee shops, filling stations, bars,
In mills and orphan asylums,   45

In hospitals, prisons, at parties,
Yearning to be one thing.

At your death, they—it is there,

And the features congeal,
Having taken the last visage in,   50
Over you, pretesting its smile,
The skin the indwelling no
Color of all colors mingled,
The eyes asking all there is.

Composed, your own face trembles near   55

Joining that other, knowing
That finally something must break

Or speak. A silver tooth gleams;
You mumble, whispering "You
Are human, are what I have witnessed.   60
You are all faces seen once."
Through the bent, staring, unstable dark
Of a drainpipe, Unity hears you—

A God-roar of hearing—say only
"You are an angel's too-realized   65

Unbearable memoryless face."

———————

Angina
1964

That one who is the dreamer lies mostly in her left arm,
Where the pain shows first,
Tuned in on the inmost heart,
Never escaping. On the blue, bodied mound of chenille,
That limb lies still.   5
Death in the heart must be calm,

Must not look suddenly, but catch the windowframed squirrel
In a mild blue corner
Of an eye staring straight at the ceiling
And hold him there.   10
Cornered also, the oak tree moves
All the ruffled green way toward itself

Around the squirrel thinking of the sun
As small boys and girls tiptoe in
Overawed by their own existence,   15
For courtly doctors long dead
Have told her that to bear children
Was to die, and they are the healthy issue

Of four of those. Oh, beside that room the oak leaves
Burn out their green in an instant, renew it all   20
From the roots when the wind stops.
All afternoon she dreams of letters
To disc jockeys, requesting the "old songs,"
The songs of the nineties, when she married, and caught

With her first child rheumatic fever.   25
Existence is family: sometime,
Inadequate ghosts round the bed,
But mostly voices, low voices of serious drunkards
Coming in with the night light on
And the pink radio turned down;   30

She hears them ruin themselves
On the rain-weeping wires, the bearing-everything poles,
Then dozes, not knowing sleeping from dying—
It is day. Limbs stiffen when the heart beats
Wrongly. Her left arm tingles,   35
The squirrel's eye blazes up, the telephone rings,

Her children and her children's children fail
In school, marriage, abstinence, business.
But when I think of love

With the best of myself—that odd power—   40
I think of riding, by chairlift,
Up a staircase burning with dust

In the afternoon sun slanted also
Like stairs without steps
To a room where an old woman lies   45
Who can stand on her own two feet
Only six strange hours every month:
Where such a still one lies smiling

And takes her appalling risks
In absolute calm, helped only by the most   50
Helplessly bad music in the world, where death,
A chastened, respectful presence
Forced by years of excessive quiet
To be stiller than wallpaper roses,

Waits, twined in the roses, saying slowly   55
To itself as sprier and sprier
Generations of disc jockeys chatter,
I must be still and not worry,
Not worry, not worry, to hold
My peace, my poor place, my own.   60

———————

Pursuit from Under
1964

Often, in these blue meadows,
I hear what passes for the bark of seals

And on August week ends the cold of a personal ice age
Comes up through my bare feet
Which are trying to walk like a boy's again   5

So that nothing on earth can have changed
On the ground where I was raised.

The dark grass here is like
The pads of mukluks going on and on

Because I once burned kerosene to read   10
Myself near the North Pole
In the journal of Arctic explorers
Found, years after death, preserved
In a tent, part of whose canvas they had eaten

Before the last entry.   15
All over my father's land

The seal holes sigh like an organ,
And one entry carries more terror
Than the blank page that signified death
In 1912, on the icecap.   20
It says that, under the ice,

The killer whale darts and distorts,
Cut down by the flawing glass

To a weasel's shadow,
And when, through his ceiling, he sees   25
Anything darker than snow
He falls away
To gather more and more force

From the iron depths of cold water,
His shadow dwindling   30

Almost to nothing at all, then charges
Straight up, looms up at the ice and smashes
Into it with his forehead
To splinter the roof, to isolate seal or man
On a drifting piece of the floe   35

Which he can overturn.
If you run, he will follow you

Under the frozen pane,
Turning as you do, zigzagging,
And at the most uncertain of your ground   40
Will shatter through, and lean,
And breathe frankly in your face

An enormous breath smelling of fish.
With the stale lungs staining your air

You know the unsaid recognition   45
Of which the explorers died:
They had been given an image
Of how the downed dead pursue us.
They knew, as they starved to death,

That not only in the snow   50
But in the family field

The small shadow moves,
And under bare feet in the summer:
That somewhere the turf will heave,
And the outraged breath of the dead,   55
So long held, will form

Unbreathably around the living.
The cows low oddly here

As I pass, a small bidden shape
Going with me, trembling like foxfire   60
Under my heels and their hooves.
I shall write this by kerosene,
Pitch a tent in the pasture, and starve.

The War Wound

1964

It wounded well—one time and
A half: once with instant blood and again
Reinfecting blackly, years later. Now all
    Is calm at the heel of my hand

    Where I grabbed, in a bellied-   5
in airplane, and caught the dark glass
Offered once in a lifetime by
    The brittle tachometer.

    Moons by the thousands
Have risen in all that time; I hold   10
The healed half-moon of that night.
    I tell it to shine as still

    As it can in the temperate flesh
That never since has balled into a fist,
To hover on nylon guitar strings   15
    Like the folk-moon itself;

    I tell it to burn like a poison
When my two children threaten themselves,
Wall-walking, or off the deep end
    Of a county swimming pool,   20

    And with thousands of moons
Coming over me year after year,
I lie with it well under cover,
    The war of the millions,

    Through glass ground under   25
Heel twenty-one years ago
Concentrating its light on my hand,
    Small, but with world-fury.

Reincarnation (II)

1964

> the white thing was so white, its wings so wide,
> and in those for ever exiled waters
>
> *Melville*

> As apparitional as sails that cross
> Some page of figures to be filed away
>
> *Hart Crane*

One can do   one begins to   one can only

Circle   eyes wide with fearing the spirit

Of weight   as though to be born   to awaken to what one is
Were to be carried   passed out
With enormous cushions of air under the arms   5
Straight up   the head growing stranger
And released between wings near an iceberg

It is too much to ask   to ask
For   under the white mild sun
On that huge frozen point to move   10

As one is so easily doing

Boring into it with one's new
Born excessive eye   after a long
Half-sleeping self-doubting voyage   until
The unbased mountain falters   15
Turns over like a whale   one screams for the first time

With a wordless voice   swings over
The berg's last treasured bubble
Straightens   wings trembling   RIDING!
Rises into a new South   20

Sensitive current   checks each wing
It is living there
                            and starts out.

There is then this night
Crawling slowly in under one wing   25
This night of all nights
Aloft   a night five thousand feet up
Where he soars among the as-yet-unnamed
The billion unmentionable stars
Each in its right relation   30
To his course   he shivers   changes his heading
Slightly   feels the heavenly bodies
Shake   alter   line up in the right conjunction
For mating   for the plunge
Toward the egg   he soars   borne toward his offspring   35

By the Dragon balanced exactly
Against the Lion   the sense of the galaxies
Right from moment to moment
Drawing slowly for him a Great
Circle   all the stars in the sky   40
Embued with the miracle of
The single human Christmas one
Conjoining to stand now over
A rocky island ten thousand
Miles of water away.   45
                            With a cold new heart
With celestial feathered crutches
A "new start" like a Freudian dream
Of a new start   he hurtles as if motionless
All the air in the upper world   50
Splitting apart on his lips.

Sleep   *wingless*—NO!
The stars appear, rimmed with red
Space under his breastbone maintains
Itself   he sighs like a man   55
Between his cambered wings

Letting down now   curving around
Into the wind   slowly toward
Any wave   that—
That one.   He folds his wings and moves   60
With the mid-Pacific
Carried for miles in no particular direction
On a single wave   a wandering hill
Surging softly along in a powerful
Long-lost phosphorous seethe   folded in those wings   65
Those ultimate wings   home is like   home is
A folding of wings   Mother
Something whispers   one eye opens   a star shifts
Does not fall   from the eyes of the Swan   he dreams

He sees the Southern Cross   70
Painfully over the horizon   drawing itself
Together   inching
Higher each night of the world   thorn
Points   tilted   he watches   not to be taken in
By the False Cross   as in   in   75
Another life   not taken

Knowing the true south rises
In a better make of cross   smaller   compact
And where its lights must appear.
Just after midnight he rises   80
And goes for it   joy with him
Springing out of the water
Disguised as wind   he checks each feather
As the stars burn out   waiting
Taking his course on faith until   85
The east begins
To pulse with unstoppable light.
Now darkness and dawn melt exactly
Together on one indifferent rill
Which sinks and is   90
Another   he lives

In renewed light, utterly alone!
In five days there is one ship
Dragging its small chewed off-white
Of ship-water   one candle in a too-human cabin   95
One vessel moving embedded
In its blue endurable country

Water warms   thereafter it is not
That the sea begins to tinge
Like a vast, laid smoke   100
But that he closes his eyes and feels himself
Turning whiter and whiter   upheld

At his whitest it is

Midnight   the equator   the center of the world
He sneaks across   afire   105
With himself   the stars change all their figures
Reach toward him   closer
And now begin to flow
Into his cracked-open mouth   down his throat
A string of lights   emblems   patterns of fire   all   110
Directions   myths   Hydras
Centaurs   Wolves   Virgins
Eating them all   eating
The void   possessing
Music   order   repose   115
Hovering   moving on his armbones   crawling
On warm air   covering the whole ocean   the sea deadens
He dulls   new constellations pale off
Him   unmapped roads open out of his breast
Beyond the sick feeling   120
Of those whose arms drag at treasures   it is like

Roosting   like holding one's arms out
In a clean nightshirt   a good dream   it is all
Instinct   he thinks   I have been born
This way.   125

                    Goes on
His small head holding
It all   the continents firmly fixed
By his gaze   five new ships turned
Rusty by his rich shadow.   130
His seamless shoulders of dawn-gold
Open   he opens
Them wider   an inch wider and he would

Trees   voices   white garments   meadows
Fail   under him again are   135
Mullet believing their freedom
Is to go anywhere they like in their collected shape
The form of an unthrown net
With no net anywhere near them.
Of these he eats.   140
                         Taking off again
He rocks forward three more days
Twenty-four hours a day
Balancing without thinking—
In doubt, he opens his bill   145
And vastness adjusts him
He trims his shoulders and planes   up

Up   stalls

In midocean   falls off
Comes down in a long, unbeheld   150
Curve that draws him deep into
                              evening

Incredible pasture.

The Cross is up.   Looking in through its four panes
He sees something   a clean desk-top   155
Papers shuffled   hears
Something   a bird word
A too-human word   a word

That should have been somewhere spoken
That now can be frankly said   160
With long stiff lips into
The center of the Southern Cross
A word enabling one to fly

Out the window of office buildings
Lifts up on wings of its own   165
To say itself over and over   sails on
Under the unowned stars   sails as if walking
Out the window
That is what I said
That is what I should   that is   170

Dawn.   Panic   one moment of thinking
Himself in the hell of thumbs   once more   a man
Disguised in these wings   alone   No   again
He thinks   I am here   I have been born
This way   raised up from   raised up in   175
Myself   my soul
Undivided at last   thrown slowly forward
Toward an unmanned island.

Day overcomes   night comes over
Day with day already   180

Coming behind it   the sun halved in the east
The moon pressing feathers together.
Who thinks his bones are light
Enough, should try it   it is for everyone
He thinks   the world is for everything born—   185
I always had
These wings   buried deep in my back:
There is a wing-growing motion
Half-alive in every creature.

Comes down   skims for fifty miles   190
All afternoon lies skimming

His white shadow burning his breast
The flying-fish darting before him
In and out of the ash-film glaze

On "because it is there"   into almighty cloud   195

In rain crying hoarsely
No place to go except
Forward into water in the eyes
Tons of water falling on the back
For hours   no sight   no insight   200
Beating up   trying
To rise above it   not knowing which way
Is up   no stars   crying
Home   fire   windows   for God
Sake   beating down   up   up-down   205
No help   streaming   another
Death   vertigo   falling
Upward   mother   God   country
Then seizing one grain of water in his mouth
Glides forward   heavy with cloud   210
Enveloped   gigantic   blazing with St. Elmo's
Fire   alone at the heart
Of rain   pure bird   heaving up   going

Up from that
                    and from that   215

Finally breaking

Out   where the sun is violently shining

On the useless enormous ploughland
Of cloud   then up
From just above it   up   220
Reducing the clouds more and more
To the color of their own defeat
The beauty of history   forgotten bird-

kingdoms packed in batting
The soft country   the endless fields   225
Raining away beneath him   to be dead
In one life is to enter
Another   to break out   to rise above   the clouds
Fail   pull back their rain

Dissolve.   All the basic blue beneath   230
Comes back, tattering through. He cries out
As at sight of home   a last human face
In a mirror dazzles   he reaches
Glides off on one wing   stretching himself wider
Floats into night   dark follows   235
At his pace
                    the stars' threads all connect
On him   and, each in its place, the islands
Rise   small form of beaches

Treeless   tons of guano   eggshells   240
Of generations
                    down
                                circling

Mistrusting

The land   coming in   245
Wings ultra-sensitive
To solids   the ground not reflecting his breast
Feet tentatively out
Creaking   close   closer
Earth blurring   tilt back and brace   250
Against the wind   closest   touch

Sprawl.   In ridiculous wings, he flounders,
He waddles   he goes to sleep
In a stillness of body not otherwise to be found
Upheld for one night   255
With his wings closed   the stiff land failing to rock him.

Here mating   the new life
Shall not be lost   wings tangle
Over the beaches   over the pale
Sketches of coral reefs   treading the air   260
The father moving almost
At once out the vast blue door
He feels it swing open
The island fall off him   the sun

Rise in the shape of an egg   enormous   265
Over the islands
                    passing out
Over the cliffs   scudding
Fifteen feet from the poor skinned sod
Dazing with purity the eyes of turtles   270
Lizards   then feeling the world at once
Sheerly restore the sea   the island not
Glanced back at   where the egg
Fills with almighty feathers
The dead rise, wrapped in their wings   275
The last thread of white
Is drawn from the foot of the cliffs
As the great sea takes itself back
From around the island

And he sails out   heads north   280
His eyes already on icebergs
Ten thousand miles off   already feeling
The shiver of the equator as it crosses
His body at its absolute
Midnight whiteness   285
                    and death also
Stands waiting   years away
In midair   beats
Balanced on starpoints
Latitude and longitude correct   290
Oriented by instinct   by stars
By the sun in one eye the moon
In the other   bird-death

Hovers for years on its wings
With a time-sense that cannot fail   295
Waits to change
Him again   circles   abides   no feather
Falling   conceived by stars and the void
Is born perpetually
In midair   where it shall be   300
Where it is.

———————

The Common Grave
1964

I

Some sit and stare
In an unknown direction, though most lie still,
Knowing that every season
Must be wintered.

II

The mover of mists and streams   5
Is usually in the weeds
By twilight, taking slowly
A dark dedicated field-shape.

III

Of all those who are under,
Many are looking over   10
Their shoulder, although it is only one leap
To beyond-reason gold, only one
Breath to the sun's great city.
All ages of mankind unite
Where it is dark enough.   15

IV

The midstrides of out-of-shape runners,
The discarded strokes of bad swimmers,
Open-mouthed at the wrong time—
All these are hooked wrongly together.
A rumor runs through them like roots: 20
They must try even harder
To bring into their vast,
Indiscriminate embrace
All of humanity.

V

In someone's hand an acorn   25
Pulses, thinking
It is only one leap,
Only one.

VI

In the field by twilight are
The faller in leaves through October,   30
The white-headed flyer in thistles
Finding out secret currents of air,
The raiser of mists from the creekbed,
A fish extending his body
Through all the curves of the river,   35
The incredible moon in the voice box
Of dogs on All Souls' Night.

VII

All creatures tumbled together
Get back in their wildest arms
No single thing but each other,   40
Hear only sounds like train sounds,
Cattle sounds, earth-shakers.

VIII

The mover of all things struggles
In the green-crowded, green-crowned nightmare
Of a great king packed in an acorn.   45
A train bends round a curve
Like a fish. An oak tree breaks
Out and shoves for the moonlight,
Bearing leaves which shall murmur for years,
Dumfoundedly, like mouths opened all at once   50
At just the wrong time to be heard,
      Others, others.

Children Reading
1964

As the afternoon sun moves over them, as the leaves fall,
Their lips move; the light they read in
Both is and is not this light; another thing glows
Equally from the sun and the page, and from the minds
Of the readers, compounding a vision that rises   5
From all the lights they have looked on
In their vivid few years, few days.

The lips move on, as if inventing the words
And saying them for some absent presence, for someone who must
Eventually hear; it is as if they were saying   10
That all things which must be imagined
Come from what we know; the Bible itself has grasses
That grow in this yard, and the desert is made
From the stones of this driveway.

The secret syllables tell how the helm must be put   15
Over, to bear the hero past harm, and somewhere on a sea
As dark as Coca-Cola, Ulysses changes, hearing on the wind
The soundless tongues under the hackberry bush of home

Enchant the air, and feels again the homeward longing
The sirens sing into the ear of time.
There are children,   20

Creating the world from words, the words from the world
They believe. They can tell you about it, for their intensity
Has felt it all, the lift of water, the taste of the food
Of the gods, so that heroes searching for home are at home
With them, and the ghost as well, moving its silent lips   25
With futile love near its living kin, the ghost
Like a wind-blown sheet,

A perilous breathing of gauze. These hear, and stand at night
In moonlit, toy-filled rooms, taking tribute from the deepest
Sleep of the race: children, still moving their mouths   30
Inside their dreams, still finding the world
And saying it soundlessly, their own lives coming true,
Certain and strange, as the day's reading swarms on the page,
Certain and strange in each word.

———————

Sled Burial, Dream Ceremony
1965

While the south rains, the north
Is snowing, and the dead southerner
Is taken there. He lies with the top of his casket
Open, his hair combed, the particles in the air
Changing to other things. The train stops   5

In a small furry village, and men in flap-eared caps
And others with women's scarves tied around their heads
And business hats over those, unload him,
And one of them reaches inside the coffin and places
The southerner's hand at the center   10

Of his dead breast. They load him onto a sled,
An old-fashioned sled with high-curled runners,
Drawn by horses with bells, and begin
To walk out of town, past dull red barns
Inching closer to the road as it snows   15

Harder, past an army of gunny-sacked bushes,
Past horses with flakes in the hollows of their sway-backs,
Past round faces drawn by children
On kitchen windows, all shedding basic-shaped tears.
The coffin top still is wide open;   20

His dead eyes stare through his lids,
Not fooled that the snow is cotton. The woods fall
Slowly off all of them, until they are walking
Between rigid little houses of ice-fishers
On a plain which is a great plain of water   25

Until the last rabbit track fails, and they are
At the center. They take axes, shovels, mattocks,
Dig the snow away, and saw the ice in the form
Of his coffin, lifting the slab like a door
Without hinges. The snow creaks under the sled   30

As they unload him like hay, holding his weight by ropes.
Sensing an unwanted freedom, a fish
Slides by, under the hole leading up through the snow
To nothing, and is gone. The coffin's shadow
Is white, and they stand there, gunny-sacked bushes,   35

Summoned from village sleep into someone else's dream
Of death, and let him down, still seeing the flakes in the air
At the place they are born of pure shadow
Like his dead eyelids, rocking for a moment like a boat
On utter foreignness, before he fills and sails down.   40

The Shark's Parlor

1965

Memory: I can take my head and strike it on a wall   on Cumberland Island
Where the night tide came crawling under the stairs   came up the first
Two or three steps   and the cottage stood on poles all night
With the sea sprawled under it   as we dreamed of the great fin circling
Under the bedroom floor. In daylight there was my first brassy taste of beer   5
And Payton Ford and I came back from the Glynn County slaughterhouse
With a bucket of entrails and blood. We tied one end of a hawser
To a spindling porch pillar and rowed straight out of the house
Three hundred yards into the vast front yard of windless blue water
The rope outslithering its coil   the two-gallon jug stoppered and sealed   10
With wax   and a ten-foot chain leader   a drop-forged shark hook nestling.
We cast our blood on the waters   the land blood easily passing
For sea blood   and we sat in it for a moment with the stain spreading
Out from the boat   sat in a new radiance   in the pond of blood in the sea
Waiting for fins   waiting to spill our guts also in the glowing water.   15
We dumped the bucket, and baited the hook with a run-over collie pup. The jug
Bobbed, trying to shake off the sun as a dog would shake off the sea.
We rowed to the house   feeling the same water lift the boat a new way,
All the time seeing where we lived rise and dip with the oars.
We tied up and sat down in rocking chairs, one eye or the other responding   20
To the blue-eye wink of the jug. Payton got us a beer and we sat

All morning sat there with blood on our minds   the red mark out
In the harbor slowly failing us   then   the house groaned   the rope
Sprang out of the water   splinters flew   we leapt from our chairs
And grabbed the rope   hauled   did nothing   the house coming subtly   25
Apart   all around us   underfoot   boards beginning to sparkle like sand
With the glinting of the bright hidden parts of ten-year-old nails
Pulling out   the tarred poles we slept propped-up on   leaning to sea
As in land wind   crabs scuttling from under the floor   as we took turns about
Two more porch pillars   and looked out and saw   something, a fish-flash   30
An almighty fin in trouble   a moiling of secret forces   a false start
Of water   a round wave growing: in the whole of Cumberland Sound the one ripple.
Payton took off without a word   I could not hold him either

But clung to the rope anyway: it was the whole house bending
Its nails that held whatever it was   coming in a little and like a fool   35
I took up the slack on my wrist. The rope drew gently   jerked   I lifted
Clean off the porch and hit the water   the same water it was in
I felt in blue blazing terror at the bottom of the stairs and scrambled
Back up looking desperately into the human house as deeply as I could
Stopping my gaze before it went out the wire screen of the back door   40
Stopped it on the thistled rattan   the rugs I lay on and read
On my mother's sewing basket with next winter's socks spilling from it
The flimsy vacation furniture   a bucktoothed picture of myself.
Payton came back with three men from a filling station   and glanced at me
Dripping water   inexplicable   then we all grabbed hold like a tug-of-war.   45

We were gaining a little   from us a cry went up   from everywhere
People came running. Behind us the house filled with men and boys.
On the third step from the sea I took my place   looking down the rope
Going into the ocean, humming and shaking off drops. A houseful
Of people put their backs into it   going up the steps from me   50
Into the living room   through the kitchen   down the back stairs
Up and over a hill of sand   across the dust road   and onto a raised field
Of dunes   we were gaining   the rope in my hands began to be wet
With deeper water   all other haulers retreated through the house
But Payton and I on the stairs   drawing hand over hand on our blood   55
Drawing into existence by the nose   a huge body   becoming
A hammerhead   rolling in beery shallows   and I began to let up
But the rope still strained behind me   the town had gone
Pulling-mad in our house: far away in a field of sand they struggled
They had turned their backs on the sea   bent double   some on their knees   60
The rope over their shoulders like a bag of gold   they strove for the ideal
Esso station across the scorched meadow   with the distant fish coming up
The front stairs   the sagging boards   still coming in   up   taking
Another step   toward the empty house   where the rope stood straining
By itself through the rooms   in the middle of the air. "Pass the word,"   65
Payton said, and I screamed it: "Let up, good God, let up!" to no one there.
The shark flopped on the porch, grating with salt-sand   driving back in
The nails he had pulled out   coughing chunks of his formless blood.
The screen door banged and tore off   he scrambled on his tail   slid
Curved   did a thing from another world   and was out of his element and in   70

Our vacation paradise   cutting all four legs from under the dinner table
With one deep-water move   he unwove the rugs in a moment, throwing pints
Of blood over everything we owned   knocked the buck teeth out of my picture
His odd head full of crushed jelly-glass splinters and radio tubes   thrashing
Among the pages of fan magazines   all the movie stars drenched in sea-blood.   75
Each time we thought he was dead   he struggled back and smashed
One more thing   in all coming back to die   three or four more times after death.
At last we got him out   log-rolling him   greasing his sandpaper skin
With lard to slide him   pulling on his chained lips as the tide came
Tumbled him down the steps as the first night wave went under the floor.   80
He drifted off   head back   belly white as the moon. What could I do but buy
That house   for the one black mark still there   against death   a forehead-
toucher in the room he circles beneath   and has been invited to wreck?
Blood hard as iron on the wall   black with time   still bloodlike
Can be touched whenever the brow is drunk enough: all changes: Memory: 85
Something like three-dimensional dancing in the limbs   with age
Feeling more in two worlds than one   in all worlds the growing encounters.

———————

The Night Pool
1965

There is this other element that shines
At night near human dwellings, glows like wool
From the sides of itself, far down:

From the deep end of heated water
I am moving toward her, first swimming,   5
Then touching my light feet to the floor,

Rising like steam from the surface
To take her in my arms, beneath the one window
Still giving off unsleeping light.

There is this other element, it being late   10
Enough, and in it I lift her, and can carry
Her over any threshold in the world,

Into any of these houses, apartments,
Her shoulders streaming, or above them
Into the mythical palaces. Her body lies   15

In my arms like a child's, not drowned,
Not drowned, and I float with her off
My feet. We are here; we move differently,

Sustained, closer together, not weighing
On ourselves or on each other, not near fish   20
Or anything but light, the one human light

From above that we lie in, breathing
Its precious abandoned gold. We rise out
Into our frozen land-bodies, and her lips

Turn blue, sealed against me. What I can do   25
In the unforgivable cold, in the least
Sustaining of all brute worlds, is to say

Nothing, not ask forgiveness, but only
Give her all that in my condition
I own, wrap her in many towels.   30

———————

Gamecock

1965

Fear, jealousy and murder are the same
When they put on their long reddish feathers,
Their shawl neck and moccasin head

In a tree bearing levels of women.
There is yet no thread   5

Of light, and his scabbed feet tighten,
Holding sleep as though it were lockjaw,
His feathers damp, his eyes crazed
And cracked like the eyes
Of a chicken head cut off or wrung-necked   10

While he waits for the sun's only cry
All night building up in his throat
To leap out and turn the day red,
To tumble his hens from the pine tree,
And then will go down, his hackles   15

Up, looking everywhere for the other
Cock who could not be there,
Head ruffed and sullenly stepping
As upon his best human-curved steel;
He is like any fierce   20

Old man in a terminal ward:
There is the same look of waiting
That the sun prepares itself for;
The enraged, surviving-
another-day blood,   25

And from him at dawn comes the same
Cry that the world cannot stop.
In all the great building's blue windows
The sun gains strength; on all floors, women
Awaken—wives, nurses, sisters and daughters—   30

And he lies back, his eyes filmed, unappeased,
As all of them, clucking, pillow-patting,
Come to help his best savagery blaze, doomed, dead-
game, demanding, unreasonably
Battling to the death for what is his.   35

The Head-Aim

1965

Sick of your arms,
You must follow an endless track

Into the world that crawls,
That gets up on four legs
When the moon rises from a bed of grass,   5
The night one vast and vivid
Tangle of scents.

You must throw your arms
Like broken sticks into the alder creek

And learn to aim the head.   10
There is nothing you can pick up
With fingers any more, nothing
But the new head choked with long teeth,
The jaws, on fire with rabies,

Lifting out of the weeds.   15
This is the whole secret of being

Inhuman: to aim the head as you should,
And to hold back in the body
What the mouth might otherwise speak:
Immortal poems—those matters of life and death—   20
When the lips curl back

And the eyes prepare to sink
Also, in the jerking fur of the other.

Fox, marten, weasel,
No one can give you hands.   25
Let the eyes see death say it all
Straight into your oncoming face, the head
Not fail, not tell.

The Fiend

1965

He has only to pass by a tree   moodily walking   head down
A worried accountant   not with it   and he is swarming
He is gliding up the underside light of leaves   upfloating
In a seersucker suit   passing window after window of her building.
He finds her at last, chewing gum   talking on the telephone.   5
The wind sways him softly   comfortably sighing   she must bathe
Or sleep.   She gets up, and he follows her along the branch
Into another room.   She stands there for a moment   and the teddy bear
On the bed feels its guts spin as she takes it by the leg and tosses
It off.   She touches one button at her throat, and rigor mortis   10
Slithers into his pockets, making everything there—keys, pen
And secret love—stand up. He brings from those depths the knife
And flicks it open   it glints on the moon one time   carries
Through the dead walls   making a wormy static on the TV screen.
He parts the swarm of gnats that live excitedly at this perilous level   15
Parts the rarified light high windows give out into inhabited trees
Opens his lower body to the moon. This night the apartments are sinking

To ground level   burying their sleepers in the soil   burying all floors
But the one where a sullen shopgirl gets ready to take a shower,
Her hair in rigid curlers, and the rest.   When she gives up   20
Her aqua terry-cloth robe the wind quits in mid-tree   the birds
Freeze to their perches round his head   a purely human light
Comes out of a one-man oak   around her an energy field   she stands
Rooted   not turning to anything else   then begins to move like a saint
Her stressed nipples rising like things about to crawl off her   as he gets   25
A hold on himself.   With that clasp she changes   senses   something

Some breath through the fragile walls   some all-seeing eye
Of God   some touch that enfolds her body   some hand come up out of roots
That carries her as she moves   swaying   at this rare height. She wraps
The curtain around her and streams.   The room fades.   Then coming   30
Forth magnificently   the window blurred from within   she moves in a cloud
Chamber   the tree in the oak currents sailing   in clear air keeping pace

With her white breathless closet—he sees her mistily part her lips
As if singing to him   come up from river-fog   almost hears her as if
She sang alone in a cloud   its warmed light streaming into his branches   35
Out through the gauze glass of the window.   She takes off her bathing cap
The tree with him ascending   himself and the birds all moving
In darkness together   sleep crumbling the bark in their claws.
By this time he holds in his awkward, subtle limbs the limbs

Of a hundred understanding trees. He has learned what a plant is like   40
When it moves near a human habitation   moving closer the later it is
Unfurling its leaves near bedrooms   still keeping its wilderness life
Twigs covering his body with only one way out   for his eyes into inner light
Of a chosen window   living with them night after night   watching
Watching with them at times their favorite TV shows   learning—   45
Though now and then he hears a faint sound: gunshot, bombing,
Building-fall—how to read lips: the lips of laconic cowboys
Bank robbers   old and young doctors tense-faced   gesturing savagely
In wards and corridors   like reading the lips of the dead

The lips of men interrupting the program at the wrong time   50
To sell you a good used car on the Night Owl Show   men silently reporting
The news out the window.   But the living as well, three-dimensioned,
Silent as the small gray dead, must sleep at last   must save their lives
By taking off their clothes. It is his beholding that saves them:
God help the dweller in windowless basements   the one obsessed   55
With drawing curtains this night. At three o'clock in the morning
He descends   a medium-sized shadow   while that one sleeps and turns
In her high bed in loss   as he goes limb by limb   quietly down
The trunk with one lighted side. Ground upon which he could not explain
His presence he walks with toes uncurled from branches, his bird-movements   60
Dying hard. At the sidewalk he changes   gains weight   a solid citizen

Once more.   At apartments there is less danger from dogs, but he has
For those a super-quiet hand   a hand to calm sparrows and rivers,
And watchdogs in half-tended bushes lie with him watching their women
Undress   the dog's honest eyes and the man's the same pure beast's   65
Comprehending the same essentials. Not one of these beheld would ever give
Him a second look   but he gives them all a first look that goes

On and on   conferring immortality while it lasts   while the suburb's leaves
Hold still enough   while whatever dog he has with him holds its breath
Yet seems to thick-pant   impatient as he with the indifferent men   70
Drifting in and out of the rooms   or staying on, too tired to move
Reading the sports page   dozing   plainly unworthy   for what women want
Dwells in bushes and trees: what they want is to look outward,

To look with the light streaming into the April limbs   to stand straighter
While their husbands' lips dry out   feeling that something is there   75
That could dwell in no earthly house: that in poplar trees or beneath
The warped roundabout of the clothesline   in the sordid disorder
Of communal backyards   some being is there in the shrubs
Sitting comfortably on a child's striped rubber ball filled with rainwater
Muffling his glasses with a small studious hand against a sudden   80
Flash of houselight from within   or flash from himself   a needle's eye
Uncontrollable   blaze of uncompromised being. Ah, the lingerie
Hung in the bathroom! The domestic motions of single girls living together
A plump girl girding her loins against her moon-summoned blood:
In that moon he stands   the only male lit by it, covered with leaf-shapes.   85
He coughs, and the smallest root responds   and in his lust he is set
By the wind in motion. That movement can restore the green eyes
Of middle age   looking   renewed   through the qualified light
Not quite reaching him where he stands again on the usual branch
Of his oldest love   his tie not loosened   a plastic shield   90
In his breast pocket full of pencils and ballpoint pens given him by salesmen
His hat correctly placed to shade his eyes   a natural gambler's tilt
And in summer wears an eyeshade   a straw hat Caribbean style.
In some guise or other he is near them when they are weeping without sound
When the teen-age son has quit school   when the girl has broken up   95
With the basketball star   when the banker walks out on his wife.
He sees mothers counsel desperately with pulsing girls face down
On beds full of overstuffed beasts   sees men dress as women
In ante-bellum costumes with bonnets   sees doctors come, looking oddly
Like himself   though inside the houses   worming a medical arm   100
Up under the cringing covers   sees children put angrily to bed
Sees one told an invisible fairy story   with lips moving silently as his
Are also moving   the book's few pages bright. It will take years
But at last he will shed his leaves   burn his roots   give up

Invisibility   will step out   will make himself known to the one   105
He cannot see loosen her blouse   take off luxuriously   with lips
Compressed against her mouth-stain   her dress   her stockings
Her magic underwear.   To that one he will come   up frustrated pines
Down alleys   through window blinds   blind windows   kitchen doors
On summer evenings. It will be something small that sets him off: 110
Perhaps a pair of lace pants on a clothesline   gradually losing
Water to the sun   filling out in the warm light with a well-rounded
Feminine wind as he watches   having spent so many sleepless nights
Because of her   because of her hand on a shade always coming down
In his face   not leaving even a shadow stripped naked upon the brown paper   115
Waiting for her now in a green outdated car with a final declaration
Of love   pretending to read   and when she comes and takes down
Her pants, he will casually follow her in   like a door-to-door salesman
The godlike movement of trees stiffening with him   the light
Of a hundred favored windows   gone wrong somewhere in his glasses   120
Where his knocked-off panama hat was   in his painfully vanishing hair.

———————

Dust

1965

Lying at home
Anywhere   it can change not only the color
But the shape of the finger that runs along it   leaving a trail
That disappears from the earth; nothing can follow
Where that hand has walked and withdrawn.   5
And I have lain in bed at home and watched

Through a haze
Of afternoon liquor   the sun come down through it
Dropping off at the window sill from which the dust has risen
With no voice   the voices of children   to spin   10
In a stunned silence   the individual motes
All with a shape apiece   wool fragments

Small segments
Of rope tricks   spirochetes boring into the very
Body of light   and if you move your hand through their air   15
They dip   weave   then assume in the altered brightness
The places they have had, and all
Their wandering. Wherever it is,

It rises;
The place stands up and whirls   as in valleys   20
Of Arizona   where the world-armies of dust gather in sleeping
Hordes. I have seen them walking
Nearly out of the world   on a crazed foot
Spinning the ground beneath them

Into chaos.   25
These are dust devils, and in that sunny room
With the shape of their motes unmassed   not given a desert
I have closed my eyes and changed them into forms
Of fire   the dying's vision
Of incandescent worms: 30

For moment
After moment have lain as though whirling
Toward myself from the grains of the earth   in a cone
Of sunlight   massing my forces
To live in time   drawn into a shape   35
Of dust   and in that place

A woman
Came from my spinning side. There we lay
And stared at the ceiling of our house   at the extra motes
That danced about the raising of our hands   40
Unable to get in-
to a human form at this time

But ready
For children we might raise and call our own,
Teach to sing   to sweep the sills   to lift their hands   45

And make the dust dance in the air
Like bodies: ready:
Ready, always, for the next.

————————

Buckdancer's Choice
1965

So I would hear out those lungs,
The air split into nine levels,
Some gift of tongues of the whistler

In the invalid's bed: my mother,
Warbling all day to herself   5
The thousand variations of one song;

It is called Buckdancer's Choice.
For years, they have all been dying
Out, the classic buck-and-wing men

Of traveling minstrel shows;   10
With them also an old woman
Was dying of breathless angina,

Yet still found breath enough
To whistle up in my head
A sight like a one-man band,   15

Freed black, with cymbals at heel,
An ex-slave who thrivingly danced
To the ring of his own clashing light

Through the thousand variations of one song
All day to my mother's prone music,   20
The invalid's warbler's note,

While I crept close to the wall
Sock-footed, to hear the sounds alter,
Her tongue like a mockingbird's break

Through stratum after stratum of a tone   25
Proclaiming what choices there are
For the last dancers of their kind,

For ill women and for all slaves
Of death, and children enchanted at walls
With a brass-beating glow underfoot,   30

Not dancing but nearly risen
Through barnlike, theatrelike houses
On the wings of the buck and wing.

———————

The Celebration
1965

All wheels; a man breathed fire,
Exhaling like a blowtorch down the road
And burnt the stripper's gown
Above her moving-barely feet.
A condemned train climbed from the earth   5
Up stilted nightlights zooming in a track.
I ambled along in that crowd

Between the gambling wheels
At carnival time with the others
Where the dodgem cars shuddered, sparking   10
On grillwire, each in his vehicle half
In control, half helplessly power-mad
As he was in the traffic that brought him.
No one blazed at me; then I saw

My mother and my father, he leaning   15
On a dog-chewed cane, she wrapped to the nose
In the fur of exhausted weasels.
I believed them buried miles back
In the country, in the faint sleep
Of the old, and had not thought to be   20
On this of all nights compelled

To follow where they led, not losing
Sight, with my heart enlarging whenever
I saw his crippled Stetson bob, saw her
With the teddy bear won on the waning   25
Whip of his right arm. They laughed;
She clung to him; then suddenly
The Wheel of wheels was turning

The colored night around.
They climbed aboard. My God, they rose   30
Above me, stopped themselves and swayed
Fifty feet up; he pointed
With his toothed cane, and took in
The whole Midway till they dropped,
Came down, went from me, came and went   35

Faster and faster, going up backward,
Cresting, out-topping, falling roundly.
From the crowd I watched them,
Their gold teeth flashing,
Until my eyes blurred with their riding   40
Lights, and I turned from the standing
To the moving mob, and went on:

Stepped upon sparking shocks
Of recognition when I saw my feet
Among the others, knowing them given,   45
Understanding the whirling impulse
From which I had been born,
The great gift of shaken lights,
The being wholly lifted with another,

All this having all and nothing   50
To do with. Believers, I have seen
The wheel in the middle of the air
Where old age rises and laughs,
And on Lakewood Midway became
In five strides a kind of loving,   55
A mortal, a dutiful son.

————

The Aura
1965

He used to wake to him
With a sense of music coming
Along with a body in movement.
It swayed with the motion of a hip
Rolling into the bathroom,   5
And, lying in bed in the winter dark

Of fathers, he heard rock-and-roll
Closed off while water ran through it,
Then the door opening, music
Opening, strolling down the hall,   10
Bad music moving all over
The house, electric guitars that followed

Some body around. It was his son,
With his portable radio always
At his belt, leaning over, adjusting the dial   15
For disc jockeys. That would be
The Skimmers, and that the Last
Survivors, moaning afar in the kitchen,

Who moved when the living moved.
He could hear him coming   20

From far away, every dawn,
And now the sound still coming
From everywhere is grief,
Unstoppable. At the beginning

Of his teens, his last year   25
Of bicycles, the wild
Music, traveling through the suburbs
From junior high, was broken on the road.
But it leapt everywhere
Into odd places: from every angle   30

It does not cease to be heard, the aura
Surrounding his son. He cannot hear it early
In the morning, unless he turns on his radio
By the bed, or leaves it on all night,
But in supermarkets it comes   35
Forth from the walls; it glances

From plate glass in department stores,
And he moves within his boy's
Chosen sounds: in cars, theatres,
In filling stations, in beer joints   40
Where he sits as though in the next phase
His son would have lived, hearing voices

Giving prizes for naming of tunes, those stations
Never off the air. He sits still
Wherever he is, as though caught   45
With music on him, or as if he were
About to be given it somewhere
In the region of the stomach:

That sound is the same, and yet not—
There is too much steadiness in it: none   50
Is carried rightly, none wavers
With the motion of adolescent walking, none

Lumbers as it should. Still, it is there
In trios of girls, in fake folk singers

From Brooklyn, and he enters, anywhere,   55
His son's life without the waking-
to-it, the irreplaceable motion
Of a body. Bongoes. Steel
Guitars. A precious cheapness
He would have grown out of. Something. Music.   60

———————

Mangham
1965

Somewhere between bells the right angles staggered
And Mangham poised, sensing thunder,
Something crooked in the straight lines of his brain.
Chalk dust rose from his shoulders, lost more
Weight, settled upward. The blackboard altered   5
Its screech, and the teeth of the children were set
On edge.

Above our doped heads the ceiling whitened
As the part in Mr. Mangham's hair
Lost its way; a gray lock fell;   10
Behind him as he turned, the Law
Of Cosines. He pressed the middle of his brow
With a handkerchief, looking at all of us
As he stepped

Quickly out of the room. In the center   15
Of the high school a sound arose from us,
A hive sound, amazing, increasing. I tore up my note
To Serena Hill, and leaned and spoke
Boldly to her in person. At the threshold

Mr. Mangham appeared with a handkerchief   20
Full of lumps;

He had raided the lunchroom icebox, and held
A knotted cloth full of soupy cubes
Dripping down his gray face: held it
Left-handed, lifted his good   25
Right arm. The signs appeared again,
The blackboard filled
With crazy proofs,

Lines wavering on the powdery blackness,
The dark night of the adolescent mind,   30
Conceiving drunken constellations,
Equilateral triangles, others of thirty-
sixty-ninety degrees, traced by a seismograph,
All figures melting from the ice-
colors of his chalk.   35

It should be in a tent in the desert
That I remember Mangham's last day
In that class, for his cracked voice was speaking
Of perfection, sphere-music,
Through the stroke that blazed in his mind   40
As our hive toned down
And Pythagoras howled

For more ice: it should be in contemplative sand
Or in a corner that I ought to sit
On a high stool, Mangham's age now,   45
On my head a conical hat, a dunce cap
Covered with moons and stars and jagged bands
Of brain-lightning, the ceiling above me
White with the chalk motes

Of stars from my shoulders, the night blazoned   50
With the angles of galaxies forming
To a silent music's accords,

Proving once and for all that I have no head
For figures, but knowing that that did not stop
Mangham for one freezing minute   55
Of his death

From explaining for my own good, from the good
Side of his face, while the other
Mixed unfelt sweat and ice water, what I never
Could get to save my soul: those things that, once   60
Established, cannot be changed by angels,
Devils, lightning, ice or indifference:
Identities! Identities!

———————

Sustainment

1965

Here at the level of leaves supposedly for good
Stopped dead on the ground,
From the safety of picturesque height she was suddenly
Falling into the creek, the path
That held her become a flight of dirt. She   5
And the horse screamed all together, and went down.

Not knowing her, but knowing who she was
Before the creek bank gave
Way and the hooves broke through into creek-shaped air,
I come walking past all the remaining leaves   10
At the edge, knowing the snow of dirt
Down the bank has long since stopped,

Seeing the gap in the ledge above the stream
Still hold the print
Of a horse's head-down side, aware that I can stoop   15
With my love, who is with me, and feel

The earth of that blurred impression
Where it is cold with time and many unmeaningful rains.

Love, this wood can support our passion, though leaves
Are not enough death   20
To balance what we must act out. Let me double down
My autumn raincoat near the summer pit
Where the unknowable woman was riding proudly
The high crest of June, her pink shirt open-throated,

Her four hooves knocking deeply on the earth, the water   25
Unconsciously holding
Its flow in the pressure of sunlight, a snail
Glinting like a molar at the brink,
And felt it all give way in one clear scream
Lifted out the horse through her lipsticked mouth,   30

And then, ripping the path clean out of the woods,
Landslid down fifty feet,
Snapping high-grade leather, past any help in the world
As the horse turned over her, in a long changed shape
Loomed once, crossed the sun and the upper trees   35
Like a myth with a hold on her feet, and fell on her

With all his intended mass. Know, love, that we
Shall rise from here
Where she did not, lying now where we have come
Beneath the scrambling animal weight   40
Of lust, but that we may sense also
What it involves to change in one half-breath

From a thing half-beast—that huge-striding joy
Between the thighs—
To the wholly human in time   45
To die, here at this height
Near the vague body-print of a being that struggled
Up, all animal, leaving the human clothes

In their sodden bundle, and wandered the lane of water
Upstream and home, 50
His bridle dragging, his saddle
Maniacally wrenched, stopping often to drink
Entirely, his eyes receiving bright pebbles,
His head in his own image where it flowed.

———————

Deer among Cattle
1965

Here and there in the searing beam
Of my hand going through the night meadow
They all are grazing

With pins of human light in their eyes.
A wild one also is eating 5
The human grass,

Slender, graceful, domesticated
By darkness, among the bred-
for-slaughter,

Having bounded their paralyzed fence 10
And inclined his branched forehead onto
Their green frosted table,

The only live thing in this flashlight
Who can leave whenever he wishes,
Turn grass into forest, 15

Foreclose inhuman brightness from his eyes
But stands here still, unperturbed,
In their wide-open country,

The sparks from my hand in his pupils
Unmatched anywhere among cattle,   20

Grazing with them the night of the hammer
As one of their own who shall rise.

———————

Slave Quarters

1965

In the great place the great house is gone from   in the sun
Room, near the kitchen of air   I look across at low walls
Of slave quarters, and feel my imagining loins

Rise with the madness of Owners
To take off the Master's white clothes   5
And slide all the way into moonlight
Two hundred years old with this moon.
Let me go,

Ablaze with my old me-
scent, in moonlight made by the mind   10
From the dusk sun, in the yard where my dogs would smell
For once what I totally am,
Flaming up in their brains as the Master
They but dimly had sensed through my clothes:
Let me stand as though moving   15

At midnight, now at the instant of sundown
When the wind turns

From sea wind to land, and the marsh grass
Hovers, changing direction:
                                        there was this house   20
That fell before I got out. I can pull

It over me where I stand, up from the earth,
Back out of the shells
Of the sea:

                become with the change of this air   25
A coastal islander, proud of his grounds,

His dogs, his spinet
From Savannah, his pale daughters,
His war with the sawgrass, pushed back into
The sea it crawled from. Nearer dark, unseen,   30
I can begin to dance
Inside my gabardine suit
As though I had left my silk nightshirt

In the hall of mahogany, and crept
To slave quarters to live out   35
The secret legend of Owners. Ah, stand up,
Blond loins, another
Love is possible! My thin wife would be sleeping
Or would not mention my absence:

                        the moonlight   40

On these rocks can be picked like cotton
By a crazed Owner dancing-mad
With the secret repossession of his body

Phosphorescent and mindless, shedding
Blond-headed shadow on the sand,   45
Hounds pressing in their sleep
Around him, smelling his footblood
On the strange ground that lies between skins
With the roof blowing off slave quarters
To let the moon in burning   50
The years away
In just that corner where crabgrass proves it lives
Outside of time.
Who seeks the other color of his body,
His loins giving off a frail light   55

On the dark lively shipwreck of grass   sees
Water live where
The half-moon touches,
The moon made whole in one wave
Very far from the silent piano   the copy of Walter Scott   60
Closed on its thin-papered battles
Where his daughter practiced, decorum preventing the one
Bead of sweat in all that lace   collected at her throat
From breaking and humanly running
Over Mozart's unmortal keys—   65

                          I come past
A sand crab pacing sideways   his eyes out
On stalks   the bug-eyed vision of fiddler
Crabs sneaking a light on the run
From the split moon   holding in it a white man stepping   70
Down the road of clamshells and cotton   his eyes out
On stems   the tops of the sugar
Cane soaring   the sawgrass walking:
                                              I come past
The stale pools left   75
Over from high tide—where the crab in the night sand
Is basting himself with his claws   moving ripples outward
Feasting on brightness
                          and above
A gull also crabs slowly,   80
Tacks, jibes   then turning the corner
Of wind, receives himself like a brother
As he glides down upon his reflection:

My body has a color not yet freed:
In that ruined house let me throw   85
Obsessive gentility off;
Let Africa rise upon me like a man
Whose instincts are delivered from their chains
Where they lay close-packed and wide-eyed
In muslin sheets   90
As though in the miserly holding
Of too many breaths by one ship.   Now

Worked in silver   their work lies all
Around me   the fields dissolving
Into the sea   and   not on a horse   95
I stoop to the soil   working
Gathering   moving to the rhythm of a music
That has crossed the ocean in chains

In the grass the great singing void of slave

Labor about me   the moonlight bringing   100
Sweat out of my back as though   the sun
Changed skins upon me   some other
Man moving near me on horseback   whom I look in the eyes
Once a day:

                    there in that corner   105

Her bed turned to grass. Unsheltered by these walls
The outside fields form slowly
Anew, in a kind of barrelling blowing,
Bend in all the right places   as faintly Michael rows
The boat ashore   his spiritual lungs   110
Entirely filling the sail.   How take on the guilt

Of slavers? How shudder like one who made
Money from buying a people
To work as ghosts
In this blowing solitude?   115
I only stand here upon shells   dressed poorly
For nakedness   poorly
For the dark wrecked hovel of rebirth

Picking my way in thought
To the black room   120
Where starlight blows off the roof
And the great beasts that died with the minds
Of the first slaves, stand at the door, asking
For death, asking to be
Forgotten: the sadness of elephants   125

The visionary pain in the heads
Of incredibly poisonous snakes
Lion   wildebeest   giraffe   all purchased also
When one wished only
Labor   130
      those beasts becoming
For the white man the animals of Eden
Emblems of sexual treasure   all beasts attending
Me now   my dreamed dogs snarling at the shades
Of eland and cheetah   135
On the dispossessed ground where I dance
In my clothes beyond movement:

In nine months she would lie
With a knife between her teeth to cut the pain
Of bearing   140
A child who belongs in no world   my hair in that boy
Turned black   my skin
Darkened by half   his, lightened
By that half exactly   the beasts of Africa reduced
To cave shadows flickering on his brow   145
As I think of him: a child would rise from that place
With half my skin.   He could for an instant
Of every day   when the wind turns   look
Me in the eyes.   What do you feel when passing

Your blood beyond death   150
To another in secret: into
Another who takes your features   and adds
A misplaced Africa to them,
Changing them forever
As they must live? What happens   155
To you, when such a one bears
You after your death into rings
Of battling light   a heavyweight champion
Through the swirling glass of four doors,
In epauletted coats   into places   160
Where you learn to wait
On tables   into sitting in all-night cages

Of parking lots   into raising
A sun-sided spade in a gang
Of men on a tar road working   165
Until the crickets give up?
What happens when the sun goes down

And the white man's loins still stir
In a house of air   still draw him toward
Slave quarters? When Michael's voice is heard   170
Bending the sail like grass,
The real moon begins to come
Apart on the water
And two hundred years are turned back
On with the headlights of a car?   175
When you learn that there is no hatred
Like love in the eyes
Of a wholly owned face? When you think of what
It would be like   what it has been
What it is to look once a day   180
Into an only
Son's brown, waiting, wholly possessed
Amazing eyes, and not
Acknowledge, but own?

———————

Hedge Life
1965

At morning we all look out
As our dwelling lightens; we have been somewhere.
With dew our porous home
Is dense, wound up like a spring,

Which is solid as motherlode   5
At night. Those who live in these apartments

Exist for the feeling of growth
As thick as it can get, but filled with

Concealment. When lightning
Strikes us, we are safe; there is nothing to strike, no bole 10
For all-fire's shattered right arm.
We are small creatures, surviving

On the one breath that grows
In our lungs in the complex green, reassured in the dawn
silver heavy as wool. We wait 15
With crowded excitement

For our house to spring
Slowly out of night-wet to the sun; beneath us,
The moon hacked to pieces on the ground.
None but we are curled 20

Here, rising another inch,
Knowing that what held us solid in the moon is still
With us, where the outside flowers flash
In bits, creatures travel

Beyond us, like rain, 25
The great sun floats in a fringed bag, all stones quiver
With the wind that moves us.
We trade laughters silently

Back and forth, and feel,
As we dreamed we did last night, our noses safe in our fur, 30
That what is happening to us in our dwelling
Is true: That on either side

As we sleep, as we wake, as we rise
Like springs, the house is winding away across the fields,
Stopped only momentarily by roads, 35
King-walking hill after hill.

Coming Back to America

1965

We descended the first night from Europe   riding the ship's sling
Into the basement.   Forty floors of home weighed on us.   We broke through
To a room, and fell to drinking madly with all those boozing, reading
The Gideon Bible in a dazzle of homecoming scripture   Assyrian armies
The scythes of chariots blazing like the windows of the city   all cast   5
Into our eyes in all-night squinting barbaric rays of violent unavoidable glory.
There were a "million dollars in ice cubes" outside our metal door;
The dead water clattered down hour after hour as we fought with salesmen
For the little blocks that would make whole our long savage drinks.
I took a swaying shower, and we packed the whole bathroom of towels into   10
Our dusty luggage, battling paid-for opulence with whatever weapon
Came to hand.   We slept; I woke up early, knowing that I was suffering
But not why. My breath would not stir, nor the room's.   I sweated
Ice in the closeness   my head hurt with the Sleep of a Thousand Lights
That the green baize drapes could not darken.   I got up, bearing   15
Everything   found my sharp Roman shoes   went out   following signs
That said SWIMMING POOL.   Flashing bulbs on a red-eyed panel, I passed
Through ceiling after ceiling of sleeping salesmen and whores, and came out
On the roof.   The pool water trembled with the few in their rooms
Still making love.   This was air.   A skinny girl lifeguard worked   20
At her nails; the dawn shone on her right leg in a healthy, twisted flame.
It made me squint   slick and lacquered with scars   with the wild smoky city
Around it   the great breath to be drawn above sleepers   the hazy
Morning towers.   We sat and talked   she said a five-car wreck
Of taxis in Bensonhurst had knocked her out and taken her kneecap   25
But nothing else.   I pondered this   the sun shook off a last heavy
Hotel   and she leapt and was in the fragile green pool as though
I were still sleeping it off eleven floors under her: she turned in a water
Ballet by herself   graceful   unredeemable   her tough face exactly
As beautiful and integral as the sun come out of the city.   Vulnerable,   30
Hurt in my country's murderous speed, she moved   and I would have taken
Her in my arms in water throbbing with the passion of travelling men,
Unkillable, both of us, at forty stories in the morning   and could have
Flown with her   our weightlessness preserved by the magic pool drawn from
Under the streets   out of that pond   passing over the meaningless   35

Guardrail   feeling the whole air pulse like water sleepless with desperate
Love-making   lifting us out of sleep into the city summer dawn
Of hundreds of feet of gray space spinning with pigeons now under
Us   among new panels of sun in the buildings blasting light silently
Back and forth across streets between them: could have moved with her   40
In all this   over the floods of glare raised up in sheets   the gauze
Distances where warehouses strove to become   over the ship I had ridden
Home in   riding gently   whitely   beneath.   Ah, lift us, green
City water, as we turn the harbor around with our legs   lazily changing
The plan of the city with motions like thistles   like the majestic swirl   45
Of soot   the winged seed of pigeons   and so would have held her
As I held my head   a-stammer with light   defending it against the terrible
Morning sun of drinkers   in that pain, exalting in the blind notion
Of cradling her somewhere above ships and buses   in the air like a water
Ballet   dancing deep among the dawn buildings in a purely private   50
Embrace of impossibility   a love that could not have been guessed:
Woman   being   idea   temple dancer   tough girl from Bensonhurst
With a knee rebuilt out of sunlight   returned-to amazement   O claspable
Symbol   the unforeseen on home ground   The thing that sustains us forever
In other places!   55

———————

The Birthday Dream
1965

At the worst place in the hills above the city
Late at night I was driving   cutting through
The overbalancing slums. There was no soul or body
In the streets. I turned right   then left somewhere
Near the top, dead-ending into a wall. A car   5
Pulled out and blocked me. Four men detached from it.
I got out too. It was Saturday night   the thrill
Of trouble shimmered on the concrete. One shadow
Had a bottle of wine. I stood and said, say, Buddy,
Give me a drink of that wine   not at all fearing   10
Shaking   as on anything but dream bones   dream

Feet I would have. He said, We're looking for somebody
To beat up. It won't be me, I said   and took him
By the arm with one hand and tossed him into the air.
Snow fell from the clearness in time for there   15
To be a snowbank for him to fall into elbow-first.
He got up, holding the wine. This guy is too big,
He said, he is too big for us; get the Professor.
Four of us stood together as the wind blew and the snow
Disappeared   and watched the lights of the city   20
Shine   some others appearing   among them   some
Going out   and watched the lava-flow of headlights off
In the valley. Like a gunshot in the building next to us
A light went out   and down came a middle-aged man
With a hairy chest; his gold-trimmed track shorts had   25
YMCA Instructor on them   and I knew it was time
For the arm game. We stretched out on our stomachs
On top of the dead-end wall. On one side was the drop
We had all been looking into   and the other side sank
Away with my car   with the men: two darks lifted   30
Us toward the moon. We put our elbows on the wall
And clasped palms. Something had placed gold-rimmed
Glasses of wine beside us   apartment lights hung in them
Loosely   and we lay nose to nose at the beginning
Of that ceremony; I saw the distant traffic cross him   35
From eye to eye. Slowly I started to push   and he
To push. My body grew as it lay   forced against his
But nothing moved. I could feel the blood vessels
In my brow distend   extend   grow over the wall like vines
And in my neck   swell like a trumpet player's: I gritted   40
Into his impassive face   where the far lights moved   this is
What I want   this is what I came for. The city pulsed
And trembled in my arm   shook with my effort   for miles
In every direction   and from far below in the dark
I heard the voices of men raised up in a cry of wild   45
Encouragement   of terror   joy   as I strained to push
His locked hand down. I could not move him   did not want
To move him   would not yield. The world strove with my body
To overcome   the highways shuddered   writhed   came apart
At the centerline   far below us a silent train went by   50

A warning light⠀⠀and slowly from the embodying air was loaded
With thousands of ghostly new cars⠀⠀in tiered racks
The light like pale wine in their tinted windshields.
The culture swarmed around me like my blood⠀⠀transfigured
By force. I put my head down and pushed with all my life⠀⠀⠀⠀55
And writing sprang under my forehead⠀⠀onto the concrete:
Graffiti scratched with a nail⠀⠀a boot heel⠀⠀an ice pick
A tire iron⠀⠀a scrap of metal from a stolen car⠀⠀saying
You are here⠀⠀⠀⠀⠀⠀⠀⠀⠀⠀⠀⠀⠀⠀⠀⠀⠀and I woke
Entangled with my wife, who labored⠀⠀pled⠀⠀screamed⠀⠀⠀⠀60
To bring me forth. The room was full of mildness. I was forty.

False Youth
Summer
1965

I have had my time⠀⠀dressed up as something else,
Have thrown time off my track by my disguise.
This can happen when one puts on a hunter's cap,
An unearned cowboy hat⠀⠀a buckskin coat⠀⠀or something
From outer space, that a child you have got has got⠀⠀⠀⠀5
For Christmas. It is oddest and best in the uniform
Of your country⠀⠀long laid in boxes and now let out
To hold the self-betrayed form in the intolerant shape
Of its youth.⠀⠀I have had my time doing such,

Sitting with Phyllis Huntley as though I were my own⠀⠀⠀⠀10
Son surrounded by wisteria⠀⠀hearing mosquitoes without
The irritation middle age puts on their wings: have sat
By a big vine going round the rotten, imperial pillars
Of southern Mississippi. All family sounds drew back

Through the house in time to leave us hanging⠀⠀⠀⠀15
By rusty chains. In the dark, dressed up in my militant youth,
I might have just come down from the black sky⠀⠀alive

With an ancient war   dead with twenty million   twenty
Years ago   when my belt cried aloud for more holes
And I soft-saluted every changing shape   that saluted me,   20
And many that did not: every tree   pole   every bush
Of wisteria   as I came down from the air toward some girl

Or other. Decked out in something strange my country
Dreamed up   I have had my time in that swing,
The double chair that moves at the edge of dark   25
Where the years stand just out of range of house-
light, their hands folded at their fat waists, respectful
As figures at a funeral. And from out of the air an enormous
Grin came down, to remake my face   as I thought of children
Of mine almost her age   and a mosquito droned like an immortal   30
Engine. I have had my time of moving back and forth
With Phyllis Huntley   and of the movement of her small hand
Inside mine, as she told me how she learned to work
An electric computer in less than two afternoons of her job
At the air base. The uniform tightened as I sat   35
Debating with a family man away from home. I would not listen
To him, for what these boys want is to taste a little life
Before they die: that is when their wings begin to shine
Most brilliantly from their breasts into the darkness
And the beery breath of a fierce boy demands of the fat man   40
He's dying of   more air   more air   through the tight belt
Of time   more life   more now   than when death was faced
Less slowly   more now than then   more now.

––––––––

Seeking the Chosen
1965

It is good, when leaving a place
Forever, to crawl in it
A little. So many times in that yard
I had been hit on the head

By an acorn, my brain was full   5
Of trees that struck me like lightning
Out of one almighty oak.
When I left that house I went down on my knees

And fell with the acorns
Rotting in the grass   10
To try to find out which of us would get
Up again from the ground
And go through the trouble of rebirth.
Nuts pelted my bestial form
All afternoon, some dying   15
In flight, some dying of my skull

And back and shoulderblades
But all day I went on all fours
Up and down and around the same path
I followed when mowing the lawn,   20
Moving like a hog among the shells
Of powerless acorns, looking for the few
Trees that would come of the deluge
Of hulls: what few of the living

From the dead lying everywhere   25
Unchanged. That was farewell,
And I imagine now two things that touch the top
Of my head with thought, unexpected as lightning
Out of leaves. One is that the yard is
Choked with trees, and that I would smother   30
On chlorophyll before I could
Knee-walk to the house. The other is that

This lawn is still crawlable, but that a single
Shoot I found with a split of green
And one pigtail of a root I was lucky   35
Enough to hold in my hand and put back
To clutch again the essential of earth
Where it was meant to be held,
Took hold, that it now would hold
Me, that I could still achieve it, still rise.   40

Adultery

1966

We have all been in rooms
We cannot die in, and they are odd places, and sad.
Often Indians are standing eagle-armed on hills

In the sunrise   open wide to the Great Spirit
Or gliding in canoes   or cattle are browsing on the walls   5
Far away   gazing down with the eyes of our children

Not far away   or there are men driving
The last railspike, which has turned
Gold in their hands. Gigantic forepleasure lives

Among such scenes, and we are alone with it   10
At last. There is always some weeping
Between us   and someone is always checking

A wrist watch by the bed to see how much
Longer we have left. Nothing can come
Of this   nothing can come   15

Of us: of me with my grim techniques
Or you who have sealed your womb
With a ring of convulsive rubber:

Although we come together,
Nothing will come of us. But we would not give   20
It up, for death is beaten

By praying Indians   by distant cows   historical
Hammers   by hazardous meetings that bridge
A continent. One could never die here

Never die   never die   25
While crying. My lover, my dear one
I will see you next week

When I'm in town. I will call you
If I can. Please get hold of   please don't
Oh God, Please don't any more I can't bear. . . Listen: 30

We have done it again   we are
Still living. Sit up and smile,
God bless you. Guilt is magical.

———————

False Youth
Winter
1966

Through an ice storm in Nashville I took a student home,
Sliding off the road twice or three times; for this
She asked me in. She was a living-in-the-city
Country girl   who on her glazed porch broke off
An icicle, and bit through its blank bone: brought me   5
Into another life   in the shining-skinned clapboard house
Surrounded by a world where creatures could not stand,
Where people broke hip after hip. At the door my feet
Took hold, and at the fire I sat down with her blind
Grandmother. All over the double room were things   10
That would never freeze, but would have taken well
To ice: long tassels hanging from lamps   curtains
Of beads   a shawl on the mantel   all endless things
To touch   untangle   all things intended to be
Inexhaustible to hands. She sat there, fondling   15

What was in reach   staring into the fire with me
Never batting a lid. I talked to her easily   eagerly
Of my childhood   my mother whistling in her heartsick bed
My father grooming his gamecocks. She rocked, fingering
The lace on the arm of the chair   changing its pattern   20
Like a game of chess. Before I left, she turned and raised
Her hands, and asked me to bend down. An icicle stiffened
In my stomach   as she drew on my one lock of hair
Feeling the individual rare strands   not pulling any
Out. I closed my eyes as she put her fingertips lightly   25
On them   and saw, behind sight   something in me   fire
Swirl in a great shape like a fingerprint   like none other
In the history of the earth   looping   holding its wild lines
Of human force. Her forefinger   then her keen nail
Went all the way along the deep middle line of my brow   30
Not guessing but knowing   quivering   deepening
Whatever I showed by it. She said, you must laugh a lot
Or be in the sun, and I began to laugh quietly against
The truth, so she might feel what the line she followed
Did then. Her hands fell   and she said to herself, My God,   35
To have a growing boy. You cannot fool the blind, I knew
As I battled for air   standing   laughing a lot as she
Said I must do   squinting also as in the brightest sun
In Georgia   to make good   to make good the line in my head.
She lifted her face like a swimmer; the fire swarmed   40
On my false, created visage   as she rocked and took up
The tassel of a lamp. Some kind of song may have passed
Between our closed mouths as I headed   into the ice.
My face froze with the vast world of time   in a smile
That has never left me since my thirty-eighth year   45
When I skated like an out-of-shape bear to my Chevrolet
And spun my wheels on glass: that time when age was caught
In a thaw in a ravelling room   when I conceived of my finger
Print as a shape of fire   and of youth as a lifetime search
For the blind.   50

The Bee

1966

to the football coaches of
Clemson College, 1942

One dot
Grainily shifting   we at roadside and
The smallest wings coming   along the rail fence out
Of the woods   one dot   of all that green. It now
Becomes flesh-crawling   then the quite still   5
Of stinging. I must live faster for my terrified
Small son   it is on him. Has come. Clings.

Old wingback, come
To life. If your knee action is high
Enough, the fat may fall in time   God damn   10
You, Dickey, *dig*   this is your last time to cut
And run   but you must give it everything you have
Left, for screaming near your screaming child is the sheer
Murder of California traffic: some bee hangs driving

Your child   15
Blindly onto the highway. Get there however
Is still possible. Long live what I badly did
At Clemson   and all of my clumsiest drives
For the ball   all of my trying to turn
The corner downfield   and my spindling explosions   20
Through the five-hole over tackle. O backfield

Coach Shag Norton,
Tell me as you never yet have told me
To get the lead out   scream whatever will get
The slow-motion of middle age off me   I cannot   25
Make it this way   I will have to leave
My feet   they are gone   I have him where
He lives   and down we go singing with screams into

The dirt,
Son-screams of fathers   screams of dead coaches turning   30
To approval   and from between us the bee rises screaming
With flight   grainily shifting   riding the rail fence
Back into the woods   traffic blasting past us
Unchanged, nothing heard through the air-
conditioning glass   we lying at roadside full   35

Of the forearm prints
Of roadrocks   strawberries on our elbows as from
Scrimmage with the varsity   now we can get
Up   stand   turn away from the highway   look straight
Into trees. See, there is nothing coming out   no   40
Smallest wing   no shift of a flight-grain   nothing
Nothing. Let us go in, son, and listen

For some tobacco-
mumbling voice in the branches   to say "That's
a little better," to our lives still hanging   45
By a hair. There is nothing to stop us   we can go
Deep   deeper   into elms, and listen to traffic die
Roaring, like a football crowd from which we have
Vanished. Dead coaches live in the air, son   live

In the ear   50
Like fathers, and *urge*   and *urge*. They want you better
Than you are. When needed, they rise and curse you   they scream
When something must be saved. Here, under this tree,
We can sit down. You can sleep, and I can try
To give back what I have earned by keeping us   55
Alive, and safe from bees: the smile of some kind

Of savior—
Of touchdowns, of fumbles, battles,
Lives. Let me sit here with you, son,
As on the bench, while the first string takes back   60
Over, far away   and say with my silentest tongue, with the man-
creating bruises of my arms   with a live leaf a quick
Dead hand on my shoulder, "Coach Norton, I am your boy."

For the Last Wolverine
1966

They will soon be down

To one, but he still will be
For a little while   still will be stopping

The flakes in the air with a look,
Surrounding himself with the silence   5
Of whitening snarls. Let him eat
The last red meal of the condemned

To extinction, tearing the guts

From an elk. Yet that is not enough
For me. I would have him eat   10

The heart, and, from it, have an idea
Stream into his gnawing head
That he no longer has a thing
To lose, and so can walk

Out into the open, in the full   15

Pale of the sub-Arctic sun
Where a single spruce tree is dying

Higher and higher. Let him climb it
With all his meanness and strength.
Lord, we have come to the end   20
Of this kind of vision of heaven,

As the sky breaks open

Its fans around him and shimmers
And into its northern gates he rises

Snarling   complete   in the joy of a weasel   25
With an elk's horned heart in his stomach
Looking straight into the eternal
Blue, where he hauls his kind. I would have it all

My way: at the top of that tree I place

The New World's last eagle   30
Hunched in mangy feathers   giving

Up on the theory of flight.
Dear God of the wildness of poetry, let them mate
To the death in the rotten branches,
Let the tree sway and burst into flame   35

And mingle them, crackling with feathers,

In crownfire. Let something come
Of it   something gigantic   legendary

Rise beyond reason over hills
Of ice   SCREAMING   that it cannot die,   40
That it has come back, this time
On wings, and will spare no earthly thing:

That it will hover, made purely of northern

Lights, at dusk   and fall
On men building roads: will perch   45

On the moose's horn like a falcon
Riding into battle   into holy war against
Screaming railroad crews: will pull
Whole traplines like fibres from the snow

In the long-jawed night of fur trappers.   50

But, small, filthy, unwinged,
You will soon be crouching

Alone, with maybe some dim racial notion
Of being the last, but none of how much
Your unnoticed going will mean: 55
How much the timid poem needs

The mindless explosion of your rage,

The glutton's internal fire   the elk's
Heart in the belly, sprouting wings,

The pact of the "blind swallowing   60
Thing," with himself, to eat
The world, and not to be driven off it
Until it is gone, even if it takes

Forever. I take you as you are

And make of you what I will,   65
Skunk-bear, carcajou, bloodthirsty

Non-survivor.
            Lord, let me die   but not die
Out.

———————

Encounter in the Cage Country
1966

What I was would not work
For them all, for I had not caught
The lion's eye. I was walking down

The cellblock in green glasses   and came
At last to the place where someone was hiding   5
His spots in his black hide.

Unchangeably they were there,
Driven in as by eyes
Like mine, his darkness ablaze   •

In the stinking sun of the beast house.   10
Among the crowd, he found me
Out   and dropped his bloody snack

And came to the perilous edge
Of the cage, where the great bars tremble
Like wire. All Sunday ambling stopped,   15

The curved cells tightened around
Us all   as we saw he was watching only
Me. I knew the stage was set, and I began

To perform   first saunt'ring   then stalking
Back and forth like a sentry   faked   20
As if to run   and at one brilliant move

I made as though drawing a gun from my hip-
bone, the bite-sized children broke
Up changing their concept of laughter,

But none of this changed his eyes, or changed   25
My green glasses. Alert, attentive,
He waited for what I could give him:

My moves   my throat   my wildest love,
The eyes behind my eyes. Instead, I left
Him, though he followed me right to the end   30

Of concrete. I wiped my face, and lifted off
My glasses. Light blasted the world of shade
Back under every park bush   the crowd

Quailed from me   I was inside and out
Of myself   and something was given a life-   35
mission to say to me hungrily over

And over and over   *your moves are exactly right*
For a few things in this world: we know you
When you come, Green Eyes, Green Eyes.

————

The Sheep Child

1966

Farm boys wild to couple
With anything   with soft-wooded trees
With mounds of earth   mounds
Of pinestraw   will keep themselves off
Animals by legends of their own: 5
In the hay-tunnel dark
And dung of barns, they will
Say   I have heard tell

That in a museum in Atlanta
Way back in a corner somewhere   10
There's this thing that's only half
Sheep   like a woolly baby
Pickled in alcohol   because
Those things can't live   his eyes
Are open   but you can't stand to look   15
I heard from somebody who . . .

But this is now almost all
Gone. The boys have taken
Their own true wives in the city,
The sheep are safe in the west hill   20
Pasture   but we who were born there
Still are not sure. Are we,
Because we remember, remembered
In the terrible dust of museums?

Merely with his eyes, the sheep-child may   25

Be saying   saying

I am here, in my father's house.
I who am half of your world, came deeply
To my mother in the long grass
Of the west pasture, where she stood like moonlight   30
Listening for foxes. It was something like love
From another world that seized her
From behind, and she gave, not lifting her head
Out of dew, without ever looking, her best
Self to that great need. Turned loose, she dipped her face   35
Farther into the chill of the earth, and in a sound
Of sobbing   of something stumbling
Away, began, as she must do,
To carry me. I woke, dying,

In the summer sun of the hillside, with my eyes   40
Far more than human. I saw for a blazing moment
The great grassy world from both sides,
Man and beast in the round of their need,
And the hill wind stirred in my wool,
My hoof and my hand clasped each other,   45
I ate my one meal
Of milk, and died
Staring. From dark grass I came straight

To my father's house, whose dust
Whirls up in the halls for no reason   50
When no one comes   piling deep in a hellish mild corner,
And, through my immortal waters,
I meet the sun's grains eye
To eye, and they fail at my closet of glass.
Dead, I am most surely living   55
In the minds of farm boys: I am he who drives
Them like wolves from the hound bitch and calf
And from the chaste ewe in the wind.
They go into woods   into bean fields   they go
Deep into their known right hands. Dreaming of me,   60
They groan   they wait   they suffer
Themselves, they marry, they raise their kind.

Turning Away
Variations on Estrangement
1966

I

Something for a long time has gone wrong,
Got in between this you and that one other
And now   here   you must turn away.

Beyond! Beyond! Another life moves

In numbing clarity begins   5
By looking out the simple-minded window,
The face untimely relieved
Of living the expression of its love.

II

Shy, sad, adolescent   separated-out
The gaze stands alone in the meadow   10
Like a king starting out on a journey
Away from all things that he knows.
It stands there   there

With the ghost's will to see and not tell
What it sees with its nerveless vision   15
Of sorrow, its queen-killing glare:
The apple tree in the wind
Paling with noon sleep,
Light pouring down from the day-moon
White-hot inside the sun's mildness,   20

The eyes clamped by an ordinary meadow
As by the latest masterpiece
Under the sun.

III

For the face a studded look slowly
Arrives from a gulley of chickweed
Like a beard, come from something
Unwanted, that the face cannot help all its life.
Hair curls inside the jaws
Unstoppable   mindless   turns white
Turns straight   chokes
Helplessly, in more and more dangerous
Iron-masked silence.

25

30

IV

A deadly, dramatic compression
Is made of the normal brow. Because of it
The presence of the hand upon the sill
Calms and does not shake the thing beheld.
Every stone within sight stands ready
To give you its secret
Of impassivity, its unquestionable
Silence: you wear
Its reason for existence where you stand

35

40

So still   the tongue grows solid also
Holding back the rock speech.

V

A hooked shape threads
Through your nostrils, and you have
Caesar's eagle look, and nothing
For it to do,
Even though, on the golden
Imperial helmet, little doors close over
Your face, and your head is covered
With military flowers.

45

50

VI

Turning away,
You foresee the same fields you watch.
They are there an instant
Before they are ready: a stream being slowly suspended   55
Between its weeds, running where it once was,
Keeping its choir-sounds going
All like crowned boys
But now among grasses that are
An enormous green bright growing No   60
That frees forever.

VII

The mutual scar on the hand of man
And woman, earned in the kitchen,
Comes forth   rises for you to brush
Off like a cutworm   65
As the weed with wings explodes
In air, laying in front of you down
Cheap flowers by hundreds of thousands
And you try to get by heart
The words written after the end   70

Of every marriage manual, back
To the beginning, saying
Change; form again; flee.

VIII

Despair and exultation
Lie down together and thrash   75
In the hot grass, no blade moving,
A stark freedom primes your new loins:
Turning away, you can breed
With the farthest women

And the farthest also in time: breed   80
Through bees, like flowers and bushes:
Breed Greeks, Egyptians and Romans   hoplites
Peasants   caged kings   clairvoyant bastards:
The earth's whole history blazes
To become this light   85
For you are released to all others,

All places and times of all women,
And for their children hunger
Also: for those who could be half
You, half someone unmet,   90
Someone dead, immortal, or coming.

Near you, some being suddenly
Also free, is weeping her body away.

IX

The watched fields shake   shake
Half blind with scrutiny.   95
All working together, grasshoppers
Push on a stem apiece
And the breathless meadow begins
To sway   dissolve   revolve:

Faintness   but the brain rights   100
Itself with a sigh in the skull
And sees again nothing
But intensified grass. Listen:
When this much is wrong, one can fix one's head

In peacetime   turning away   105
From an old peaceful love
To a helmet of silent war
Against the universe   and see
What to do with it all: see with the eyes
Of a very great general   110

Roads ditches trees
Which have sunk their roots to provide
Not shade but covering-fire.

X

Somewhere in this guarded encampment
The soul stands stealthily up   115
To desert: stands up like the sex
About to run   running
Through pinewoods   creeks   changes of light   night
And day   the wide universe streaming over it
As it stands there panting   over-sensitized   120
Filled with blood from the feet

Heartbeating   surviving   in the last

Place   in cloud river meadowgrass or grave   waiting
For bird beast or plant to tell it
How to use itself   whom to meet   what to do   125
Which way to go to join
The most ineffectual army   the defiant, trembling
Corps of the unattached.

XI

Fear passes
Into sweat hidden openly   130
In the instant new lines of the brow. The field
Deepens in peace, as though, even
Before battle, it were rich-
ening with a generation's
Thousand best, quietest men   135
In long grass bending east
To west. Turning away, seeing fearful
Ordinary ground, boys' eyes manlike go,
The middle-aged man's like a desperate
Boy's, the old man's like a new angel's   140

Beholding the river in all
White places   rushing
At and burning its boulders
Quietly   the current laid
In threads   as, idly, a conqueror's horse,   145

Ox-headed, is born of the shape of a cloud
That was an unnoticed
Deep-hanging bed.
Water waves in the air,
A slant, branded darkness   150
From a distant field full of horses
Uprisen into a cloud
That is their oversoul.

XII

Under the great drifting stallion
With his foreleg bloatedly cocked, the armed   155
Men who could spring from your teeth
Double their strength in your jaws:

XIII

So many battles
Fought in cow pastures   fought back
And forth over anybody's farm   160
With men or only
With wounded eyes—
Fought in the near yellow crops
And the same crops blue farther off.

XIV

Dead armies' breath like a sunflower   165
Stirs, where the loved-too-long
Lie with a whimper of scythes.
Coming to them, the seeds

Of distant plants either die
Or burn out when they touch 170
Ground, or are born in this place.
Rain is born rain: let tons of repossessed
Water walk to us!

XV

You may have swallowed a thistle
Or the first drop of rain; 175
You have been open-mouthed.
Now speak of battles that bring

To light no blood, but strew the meadows
With inner lives:
Speak now with the thistle's sharpness 180
Piercing   floating   descending
In flowers all over the field
With a dog-noise low in the calyx.

XVI

Like a hound, you can smell the earth change
As your cloud comes over the sun 185
Like a called horse.
The long field summons its armies
From every underground
Direction. Prepare to fight
The past   flee   lie down, 190
Heartbeat a noise in your head
Like knocking the rungs from a ladder:
So many things stand wide
Open! Distance is helplessly deep
On all sides   and you can enter, alone, 195
Anything   anything can go
On wherever it wishes   anywhere in the world or in time
But here and now.

XVII

Turning away, the eyes do not mist over
Despite the alien sobbing in the room.   200
Withhold! Withhold! Stand by this window
         As on guard
Duty   rehearsing what you will answer
      If questioned   stand

General   deserter   freed slave belovèd of all,   205
     Giving off behind your back
      Ridiculous energy   stand

    Like a proof of character learned
   From Caesar's *Wars*   from novels
       Read in the dark,   210
     Thinking of your life as a thing
        That can be learned,
As those earnest young heroes learned theirs,
      Later, much later on.

The Flash
1966

Something far off   buried deep and free
In the country   can always strike you dead
Center of the brain. There is never anything

It could be   but you go dazzled
Dazzled   and all the air in that   5
Direction swarms   waits
For that day-lightning
For hoe blade   buckle   bifocal
To reach you. Whatever it does

Again is worth waiting for   10
Worth stopping the car   worth standing alone
For   and arranging the body

For light to score off you
In its own way, and send
Across the wheat   the broad silent   15

Blue valley, your long-awaited,
Blinding, blood-brotherly
Beyond-speech answer.

———————

Sun

1967

O Lord, it was all night
Consuming me   skin crawling tighter than any
Skin of my teeth. Bleary with ointments, dazzling
Through the dark house   man red as iron   glowing
Blazing up anew with each bad   5
Breath from the bellowing curtains

I had held the sun longer
Than it could stay   and in the dark it turned
My face on, infra-red: there were cracks circling
My eyes where I had squinted   10
Up from stone-blind sand, and seen
Eternal fire   coronas   huge

Vertical banners of flame
Leap scrollingly from the sun and tatter
To nothing in blue-veined space   15
On the smoked-crimson glass of my lids.

When the sun fell, I slit my eyeskins
In the dazed ruddy muddle of twilight

And in the mirror saw whiteness
Run from my eyes like tears   going upward   20
And sideways   slanting   as well as falling,
All in straight lines like rays
Shining   and behind me, careful not
To touch without giving me a chance

To brace myself   a smeared   25
Suffering woman came merging her flame-shaken
Body halo with mine   her nose still clownish
With oxides: walked to me sweating
Blood, and turned around. I peeled off
Her bathing suit like her skin   her colors   30

Wincing   she silently biting
Her tongue off   her back crisscrossed with stripes
Where winter had caught her and whipped her.
We stumbled together, and in the double heat
The last of my blond hair blazed up,   35
Burned off me forever   as we dived

For the cool of the bed
In agony even at holding hands   the blisters
On our shoulders shifting   crackling
Releasing boiling water on the sheets. *O Lord*   40
Who can turn out the sun, turn out that neighbor's
One bulb on his badminton court

For we are dying
Of light   searing each other   not able
To stop   to get away   she screaming O Lord   45
Apollo or *Water, Water*   as the moonlight drove
Us down on the tangled grid
Where in the end we lay

Suffering equally   in the sun
Backlashed from the moon's brutal stone   50
And meeting itself where we had stored it up
All afternoon in pain   in the gentlest touch
As we lay, O Lord,
In Hell, in love.

————

Falling
1967

A 29-year-old stewardess fell . . . to her death tonight when she was
swept through an emergency door that suddenly sprang open. . . .
The body . . . was found . . . three hours after the accident.

New York Times

The states when they black out and lie there rolling   when they turn
To something transcontinental   move by   drawing moonlight out of the great
One-sided stone hung off the starboard wingtip   some sleeper next to
An engine is groaning for coffee   and there is faintly coming in
Somewhere the vast beast-whistle of space. In the galley with its racks   5
Of trays   she rummages for a blanket   and moves in her slim tailored
Uniform to pin it over the cry at the top of the door. As though she blew

The door down with a silent blast from her lungs   frozen   she is black
Out finding herself   with the plane nowhere and her body taking by the throat
The undying cry of the void   falling   living   beginning to be something   10
That no one has ever been and lived through   screaming without enough air
Still neat   lipsticked   stockinged   girdled by regulation   her hat
Still on   her arms and legs in no world   and yet spaced also strangely
With utter placid rightness on thin air   taking her time   she holds it
In many places   and now, still thousands of feet from her death   she seems   15
To slow   she develops interest   she turns in her maneuverable body

To watch it. She is hung high up in the overwhelming middle of things   in her
Self   in low body-whistling wrapped intensely   in all her dark dance-weight

Coming down from a marvellous leap   with the delaying, dumfounding ease
Of a dream of being drawn   like endless moonlight to the harvest soil   20
Of a central state of one's country   with a great gradual warmth coming
Over her   floating   finding more and more breath in what she has been using
For breath   as the levels become more human   seeing clouds placed honestly
Below her left and right   riding slowly toward them   she clasps it all
To her and can hang her hands and feet in it in peculiar ways   and   25
Her eyes opened wide by wind, can open her mouth as wide   wider and suck
All the heat from the cornfields   can go down on her back with a feeling
Of stupendous pillows stacked under her   and can turn   turn as to someone
In bed   smile, understood in darkness   can go away   slant   slide
Off tumbling   into the emblem of a bird with its wings half-spread   30
Or whirl madly on herself   in endless gymnastics in the growing warmth
Of wheatfields rising toward the harvest moon   There is time to live
In superhuman health   seeing mortal unreachable lights far down seeing
An ultimate highway with one late priceless car probing it   arriving
In a square town   and off her starboard arm the glitter of water catches   35
The moon by its one shaken side   scaled, roaming silver   My God it is good
And evil   lying in one after another of all the positions for love
Making   dancing   sleeping   and now cloud wisps at her no
Raincoat   no matter   all small towns brokenly brighter from inside
Cloud   she walks over them like rain   bursts out to behold a Greyhound   40
Bus shooting light through its sides   it is the signal to go straight
Down like a glorious diver   then feet first   her skirt stripped beautifully
Up   her face in fear-scented cloths   her legs deliriously bare   then
Arms out   she slow-rolls over   steadies out   waits for something great
To take control of her   trembles near feathers   planes head-down   45
The quick movements of bird-necks turning her head   gold eyes   the insight-
eyesight of owls blazing into the hencoops   a taste for chicken overwhelming
Her   the long-range vision of hawks enlarging all human lights of cars
Freight trains   looped bridges   enlarging the moon racing slowly
Through all the curves of a river   all the darks of the midwest blazing   50
From above. A rabbit in a bush turns white   the smothering chickens
Huddle   for over them there is still time for something to live
With the streaming half-idea of a long stoop   a hurtling   a fall
That is controlled   that plummets as it wills   turns gravity
Into a new condition, showing its other side like a moon   shining   55
New Powers   there is still time to live on a breath made of nothing
But the whole night   time for her to remember to arrange her skirt

Like a diagram of a bat   tightly it guides her   she has this flying-skin
Made of garments   and there are also those sky-divers on TV   sailing
In sunlight   smiling under their goggles   swapping batons back and forth   60
And He who jumped without a chute and was handed one by a diving
Buddy. She looks for her grinning companion   white teeth   nowhere
She is screaming   singing hymns   her thin human wings spread out
From her neat shoulders   the air beast-crooning to her   warbling
And she can no longer behold the huge partial form of the world   now   65
She is watching her country lose its evoked master shape   watching it lose
And gain   get back its houses and people   watching it bring up
Its local lights   single homes   lamps on barn roofs   if she fell
Into water she might live   like a diver   cleaving   perfect   plunge

Into another   heavy silver   unbreathable   slowing   saving   70
Element: there is water   there is time to perfect all the fine
Points of diving   feet together   toes pointed   hands shaped right
To insert her into water like a needle   to come out healthily dripping
And be handed a Coca-Cola   there they are   there are the waters
Of life   the moon packed and coiled in a reservoir   so let me begin   75
To plane across the night air of Kansas   opening my eyes superhumanly
Bright   to the dammed moon   opening the natural wings of my jacket
By Don Loper   moving like a hunting owl toward the glitter of water
One cannot just *fall   just tumble screaming all that time   one must* use
It   she is now through with all   through all   clouds   damp   hair   80
Straightened   the last wisp of fog pulled apart on her face like wool   revealing
New darks   new progressions of headlights along dirt roads   from chaos

And night   a gradual warming   a new-made, inevitable world of one's own
Country   a great stone of light in its waiting waters   hold   hold out
For water: who knows when what correct young woman must take up her body   85
And fly   and head for the moon-crazed inner eye of midwest imprisoned
Water   stored up for her for years   the arms of her jacket slipping
Air up her sleeves to go   all over her? What final things can be said
Of one who starts out sheerly in her body in the high middle of night
Air   to track down water like a rabbit where it lies like life itself   90
Off to the right in Kansas? She goes toward   the blazing-bare lake
Her skirts neat   her hands and face warmed more and more by the air
Rising from pastures of beans   and under her   under chenille bedspreads
The farm girls are feeling the goddess in them struggle and rise brooding

On the scratch-shining posts of the bed   dreaming of female signs   95
Of the moon   male blood like iron   of what is really said by the moan
Of airliners passing over them at dead of midwest midnight   passing
Over brush fires   burning out in silence on little hills   and will wake
To see the woman they should be   struggling on the rooftree to become
Stars.   For her the ground is closer   water is nearer   she passes   100
It   then banks   turns   her sleeves fluttering differently as she rolls
Out to face the east, where the sun shall come up from wheatfields she must
Do something with water   fly to it   fall in it   drink it   rise
From it   but there is none left upon earth   the clouds have drunk it back
The plants have sucked it down   there are standing toward her only   105
The common fields of death   she comes back from flying to falling
Returns to a powerful cry   the silent scream with which she blew down
The coupled door of the airliner   nearly   nearly losing hold
Of what she has done   remembers   remembers the shape at the heart
Of cloud   fashionably swirling   remembers she still has time to die   110
Beyond explanation. Let her now take off her hat in summer air the contour
Of cornfields   and have enough time to kick off her one remaining
Shoe with the toes   of the other foot   to unhook her stockings
With calm fingers, noting how fatally easy it is to undress in midair
Near death   when the body will assume without effort any position   115
Except the one that will sustain it   enable it to rise   live
Not die   nine farms hover close   widen   eight of them separate, leaving
One in the middle   then the fields of that farm do the same   there is no
Way to back off   from her chosen ground   but she sheds the jacket
With its silver sad impotent wings   sheds the bat's guiding tailpiece   120
Of her skirt   the lightning-charged clinging of her blouse   the intimate
Inner flying-garment of her slip in which she rides like the holy ghost
Of a virgin   sheds the long windsocks of her stockings   absurd
Brassiere   then feels the girdle required by regulations squirming
Off her: no longer monobuttocked   she feels the girdle flutter   shake   125
In her hand   and float   upward   her clothes rising off her ascending
Into cloud   and fights away from her head the last sharp dangerous shoe
Like a dumb bird   and now will drop in   SOON   now will drop

In like this   the greatest thing that ever came to Kansas   down from all
Heights   all levels of American breath   layered in the lungs from the frail   130
Chill of space to the loam where extinction slumbers in corn tassels thickly

And breathes like rich farmers counting: will come among them after
Her last superhuman act   the last slow careful passing of her hands
All over her unharmed body   desired by every sleeper in his dream:
Boys finding for the first time their loins filled with heart's blood   135
Widowed farmers whose hands float under light covers to find themselves
Arisen at sunrise   the splendid position of blood unearthly drawn
Toward clouds   all feel something   pass over them as she passes
Her palms over *her* long legs   *her* small breasts   and deeply between
Her thighs   her hair shot loose from all pins   streaming in the wind   140
Of her body   let her come openly   trying at the last second to land
On her back   This is it   THIS

                                 All those who find her impressed
In the soft loam   gone down   driven well into the image of her body
The furrows for miles flowing in upon her where she lies very deep   145
In her mortal outline   in the earth as it is in cloud   can tell nothing
But that she is there   inexplicable   unquestionable   and remember
That something broke in them as well   and began to live and die more
When they walked for no reason into their fields to where the whole earth
Caught her   interrupted her maiden flight   told her how to lie   she cannot   150
Turn   go away   cannot move   cannot slide off it and assume another
Position   no sky-diver with any grin could save her   hold her in his arms
Plummet with her   unfold above her his wedding silks   she can no longer
Mark the rain with whirling women that take the place of a dead wife
Or the goddess in Norwegian farm girls   or all the back-breaking whores   155
Of Wichita. All the known air above her is not giving up quite one
Breath   it is all gone   and yet not dead   not anywhere else
Quite   lying still in the field on her back   sensing the smells
Of incessant growth try to lift her   a little sight left in the corner
Of one eye   fading   seeing something wave   lies believing   160
That she could have made it   at the best part of her brief goddess
State   to water   gone in headfirst   come out smiling   invulnerable
Girl in a bathing-suit ad   but she is lying like a sunbather at the last
Of moonlight   half-buried in her impact on the earth   not far
From a railroad trestle   a water tank   she could see if she could   165
Raise her head from her modest hole   with her clothes beginning
To come down all over Kansas   into bushes   on the dewy sixth green
Of a golf course   one shoe   her girdle coming down fantastically
On a clothesline, where it belongs   her blouse on a lightning rod:

Lies in the fields   in *this* field   on her broken back as though on   170
A cloud she cannot drop through   while farmers sleepwalk without
Their women from houses   a walk like falling toward the far waters
Of life   in moonlight   toward the dreamed eternal meaning of their farms
Toward the flowering of the harvest in their hands   that tragic cost
Feels herself go   go toward   go outward   breathes at last fully   175
Not   and tries   less   once   tries   tries   AH, GOD—

———————

Snakebite

1967

I am the one

And there is no way not
To be me   not to have been flagged

Down from underneath where back
Drop ten deadly and   5
Dead pine logs   here and where
They have fallen. Now come

To surprise:

Surprise at the dosage   at the shot
In the foot   at the ground   10

Where I walk   at what
It can do and the ways
Of giving: at dry fish scales
That can float away

In a long dusty arm   15

Now getting itself   frankly lost
Swimming against the current

Of pinestraw   winging wider a stump
And a stone. Here is where
I am the one chosen: 20
Something has licked my heel

     Like a surgeon

And I have a problem with
My right foot and my life.

It is hard to think of dying   25
But not of killing: hold the good
Foot ready to put on his head
Except that it leaves me only

     On a stage of pine logs

Something like an actor   so   30
Let me sit down and draw

My tiny sword   unfold it
Where the dead sharpen needles
By the million. It is the role
I have been cast in;   35

     It calls for blood.

Act it out before the wind
Blows: unspilt blood

Will kill you. Open
The new-footed tingling. Cut.   40
Cut deep, as a brother would.
Cut to save it. Me.

Power and Light

1967

. . . only connect . . .

E. M. Forster

I may even be
A man, I tell my wife: all day I climb myself
Bowlegged up those damned poles   rooster-heeled in all
Kinds of weather   and what is there when I get
Home? Yes, woman trailing ground-oil   5
Like a snail, home is where I climb down,
And this is the house I pass through on my way

To power and light.
Going into the basement is slow, but the built-on smell of home
Beneath home gets better with age   the ground fermenting   10
And spilling through the barrel-cracks of plaster   the dark
Lying on the floor, ready for use   as I crack
The seal on the bottle   like I tell you it takes
A man to pour whiskey in the dark   and CLOSE THE DOOR between

The children and me.   15
The heads of nails drift deeper through their boards
And disappear. Years in the family dark have made me good
At this   nothing else is so good   pure fires of the Self
Rise crooning in lively blackness   and the silence around them,
Like the silence inside a mouth, squirms with colors,   20
The marvellous worms of the eye float out into the real

World   sunspots
Dancing as though existence were
One huge closed eye   and I feel the wires running
Like the life-force along the limed rafters   and all connections   25
With poles   with the tarred naked belly-buckled black
Trees I hook to my heels   with the shrill phone calls leaping
Long distance   long distances through my hands   all connections

Even the one
With my wife, turn good   turn better than good   turn good   30
Not quite, but in the deep sway of underground   among the roots
That bend like branches   all things connect   and stream
Toward light and speech   tingle   rock like a powerline in wind,
Like a man working, drunk on pine-moves   the sun in the socket
Of his shoulder   and on his neck dancing like dice-dots,   35

And I laugh
Like my own fate watching over me night and day   at home
Underground   or flung up on towers walking
Over mountains   my charged hair standing on end   crossing
The sickled, slaughtered alleys of timber   40
Where the lines loop and crackle on their gallows.
Far under the grass of my grave, I drink like a man

The night before
Resurrection Day. My watch glows with the time to rise
And shine. Never think I don't know my profession   45
Will lift me: why, all over hell the lights burn in your eyes,
People are calling each other   weeping with a hundred thousand
Volts   making deals   pleading   laughing like fate,
Far off, invulnerable   or with the right word pierced

To the heart   50
By wires I held, shooting off their ghostly mouths,
In my gloves. The house spins   I strap crampons to my shoes
To climb the basement stairs, sinking my heels in the tree-
life of the boards. Thorns! Thorns! I am bursting
Into the kitchen, into the sad way-station   55
Of my home, holding a double handful of wires

Spitting like sparklers
On the Fourth of July. Woman, I know the secret of sitting
In light   of eating a limp piece of bread   under
The red-veined eyeball of a bulb. It is all in how you are   60
Grounded. To bread I can see, I say, as it disappears and agrees
With me   the dark is drunk   and I am a man
Who turns on. I am a man.

Dark Ones

1967

We in all lights are coming
Home   transfixed and carried away
From where we work:
                        when the sun moves down
The railroad tracks, and dies a little way   5
Off in the weeds, lights we have made come on
And carry us: this is how
We are coming, O all
Our dark ones, our darlings.

Now we float down from aircraft   10

From trains   now at our car
Lights the doors

                        of our home
Garage spring open   we enter and fall
Down in our souls to pray for light   15
To fail: fail pleasantly with gin,
With problems of children   but fail   fade
Back into our tinted walls:

Let the airports carry it all night

Let the highways support it on their poles   20
Shining on beer cans
                                rolling drunk in the weeds
After their one fearful bounce:
Lord, let those lights give up
On us: office lights, cast like shade   25
On fire, from their banks of blue sticks:
A light like the mange, on papers,
On the heads emerging from scratch pads,

Those crammed, volcanic faces
Dreadful to see.   30
                              All those are creatures
Of light. Let them leave me   let all
Human switches be finally snapped
Off at once   let me go with my dark
Darling, into myself: O let there be   35
Someone in it with me:

Let us move everything

Off us, and lie touching
With all we have.
                              O creature   40
Of darkness, let us lie stretched out
Without shadow or weight.
Fasten your hand where my heart
Would burst, if I moved
From your side. You are   45

Who holds. Hold then   hold my heart

Down from bursting
Into light: hold it still and at rest
In the center of walls
That cannot get their colors   50
Back without light: O Glory, there is nothing
Yet at the sill   no grain or thread
Of sun   no light as the heart

Beats, feeding from your hand.

Bread

1967

Old boys, the cracked boards spread before
You, bread and spam   fruit cocktail   powder
Of eggs. I who had not risen, but just come down
From the night sky   knew always this was nothing
Like home   for under the table I was cut deep   5
    In the shoes

To make them like sandals no stateside store
Even sold   and my shirtsleeves were ragged as
Though chopped off by propellers in the dark.
It was all our squadron, old boys: it was thus   10
I sat with you on your first morning
    On the earth,

Old boys newly risen from a B-25 sinking slowly
Into the swamps of Ceram. Patrick said
We got out   we got out on the wings   15
And lived there   we spread our weight
Thin as we could   arms and legs spread, we lay
    Down night and day,

We lived on the wings. When one of us got to one
Knee to spear a frog   to catch a snake   20
To eat, we lost another inch. O that water,
He said. O that water. Old boys, when you first
Rose, I sat with you in the mess-tent
    On solid ground,

At the unsinkable feast, and looked at the bread   25
Given to lizard-eaters. They set it down
And it glowed from under   your tongues
Fluttered   you reached   the scales fell
From your eyes   all of us weightless from living
    On wings so long   30

No one could escape   no one could sink or swim
Or fly. I looked at your yellow eyeballs
Come up   evolved   drawn out of the world's slime
Amphibious eyes   and Patrick said Bread
Is good   I sat you in my own last war   35
          Poem   I closed my eyes

I ate the food I ne'er had eat.

———————

May Day Sermon to the Women of Gilmer County, Georgia, by a Woman Preacher Leaving the Baptist Church
1967

Each year at this time I shall be telling you of the Lord
—Fog, gamecock, snake and neighbor—giving men all the help they need
To drag their daughters into barns. Children, I shall be showing you
The fox hide stretched on the door   like a flying squirrel   fly
Open   to show you the dark where the one pole of light is paid out   5
In spring by the loft, and in it the croker sacks sprawling and shuttling
Themselves into place as it comes   comes   through spiders dead
Drunk on their threads   the hogs' fat bristling   the milk
Snake in the rafters unbending through gnats to touch the last place
Alive on the sun with his tongue   I shall be flickering from my mouth   10
Oil   grease cans   lard cans   nubbins   cobs   night
Coming   floating   each May with night coming I cannot help
Telling you how he hauls her to the centerpole   how the tractor moves
Over as he sets his feet and hauls   hauls   ravels her arms and hair
In stump chains: Telling: telling of Jehovah come and gone   15
Down on His belly   descending   creek-curving   blowing His legs

Like candles, out   putting North Georgia copper on His head
To crawl in under the door in dust red enough to breathe
The breath of Adam into: Children, be brought where she screams and begs

To the sacks of corn and coal   to nails   to the swelling ticks   20
On the near side of mules, for the Lord's own man has found the limp
Rubber that lies in the gulley   the penis-skin like a serpent
Under the weaving willow.
                                        Listen: often a girl in the country,
Mostly sweating   mostly in spring, deep enough in the holy Bible   25
Belt, will feel her hair rise up   arms rise, and this not any wish

Of hers, and clothes like lint shredding off her   abominations
In the sight of the Lord: will hear the Book speak like a father
Gone mad: each year at this time will hear the utmost sound
Of herself, as her lungs cut, one after one, every long track   30
Spiders have coaxed from their guts   stunned spiders fall
Into Pandemonium   fall   fall   and begin to dance like a girl
On the red clay floor of Hell   she screaming   her father screaming
Scripture CHAPter and verse   beating it into her with a weeping
Willow branch   the animals stomping   she prancing and climbing   35
Her hair   beasts shifting from foot to foot about the stormed
Steel of the anvil   the tractor gaslessly straining   believing
It must pull up a stump   pull   pull down the walls of the barn
Like Dagon's temple   set the Ark of the Lord in its place   change all
Things for good, by pain. Each year at this time you will be looking up   40
Gnats in the air   they boil   recombine   go mad with striving
To form the face of her lover, as when he lay at Nickajack Creek
With her by his motorcycle   looming   face trembling with exhaust
Fumes   humming insanely—each May you hear her father scream like God
And King James as he flails   cuds richen   bulls chew themselves whitefaced   45
Deeper into their feed bags, and he cries something the Lord   cries
Words! Words! Ah, when they leap   when they are let out of the Bible's
Black box   they whistle   they grab the nearest girl and do her hair up
For her lover in root-breaking chains   and she knows she was born to hang
In the middle of Gilmer County   to dance, on May Day, with holy   50
Words all around her   with beasts with insects   O children NOW
In five bags of chicken-feed the torsos of prophets form   writhe
Die out as her freckled flesh   as flesh and the Devil twist and turn
Her body to love   cram her mouth with defiance   give her words
To battle with the Bible's in the air: she shrieks sweet Jesus and God   55
I'm glad   O my God-darling   O lover   O angel-stud   dear heart
Of life put it in me   *give*   you're killing   KILLING: each

Night each year at this time I shall be telling you of the snake-
doctor drifting from the loft, a dragonfly, where she is wringing
Out the tractor's muddy chains   where her cotton socks prance,   60
Where her shoes as though one ankle were broken, stand with night
Coming   and creatures drawn by the stars, out of their high holes
By moon-hunger driven   part the leaves   crawl out of Grimes Nose
And Brasstown Bald: on this night only I can tell how the weasel pauses
Each year in the middle of the road   looks up at the evening blue   65
Star   to hear her say again   O again YOU CAN BEAT ME TO DEATH
And I'll still be glad:
                        Sisters, it is time to show you rust
Smashing the lard cans more in   spring after spring   bullbats
Swifts   barn swallows   mule bits clashing on walls   mist turning   70
Up white out of warm creeks: all over, fog taking the soul from the body
Of water   gaining   rising up trees   sifting up through smoking green
Frenzied levels of gamecocks sleeping from the roots   stream-curves
Of mist: wherever on God's land is water, roads rise up the shape of rivers
Of no return: O sisters, it is time   you cannot sleep with Jehovah   75

Searching for what to be, on ground that has called Him from His Book:
Shall He be the pain in the willow, or the copperhead's kingly riding
In kudzu, growing with vines toward the cows   or the wild face working over
A virgin, swarming like gnats   or the grass of the west field, bending
East, to sweep into bags and turn brown   or shall He rise, white on white,   80
From Nickajack Creek as a road?   The barn creaks like an Ark   beasts
Smell everywhere the streams drawn out by their souls   the flood-
sigh of grass in the spring   they shall be saved   they know as she screams
Of sin   as the weasel stares   the hog strains toward the woods
That hold its primeval powers: 85
                         Often a girl in the country will find herself
Dancing with God in a mule's eye, twilight drifting in straws from the dark
Overhead of hay   cows working their sprained jaws sideways at the hour
Of night all things are called: when gnats in their own midst and fury
Of swarming-time, crowd into the barn   their sixty-year day consumed   90
In this sunset   die in a great face of light that swarms and screams
Of love.
        Each May you will crouch like a sawhorse to make yourself
More here   you will be cow chips   chickens croaking for her hands
That shook the corn over the ground   bouncing   kicked this way   95

And that, by the many beaks   and every last one of you will groan
Like nails barely holding   and your hair be full of the gray
Glints of stump chains.   Children, each year at this time you shall have
Back-pain, but also heaven   but also   also this lovely other life-
pain between the thighs: woman-child or woman in bed in Gilmer   100
County   smiling in sleep like blood-beast and Venus together
Dancing the road as I speak, get up   up in your socks and take
The pain you were born for: that rose through her body straight
Up from the earth like a plant, like the process that raised overhead
The limbs of the uninjured willow.   105
                                Children, it is true
That the kudzu advances, its copperheads drunk and tremendous
With hiding, toward the cows   and wild fences cannot hold the string
Beans as they overshoot their fields: that in May the weasel loves love
As much as blood   that in the dusk bottoms young deer stand half   110
In existence, munching cornshucks   true that when the wind blows
Right   Nickajack releases its mist   the willow-leaves stiffen once
More   altogether   you can hear   each year at this time you can hear
No   Now, no   Now   Yes   Again   More   O   O my God
I love it   love you   don't leave   don't   don't stop O GLORY   115
Be:
                        More dark   more coming   fox-fire crawls over the okra-
patch   as through it a real fox creeps to claim his father's fur
Flying on doornails   the quartermoon on the outhouse begins to shine
With the quartermoonlight of this night   as she falls and rises,   120
Chained to a sapling like a tractor   WHIPPED for the wind in the willow
Tree   WHIPPED for Bathsheba and David   WHIPPED for the woman taken
Anywhere   anytime   WHIPPED for the virgin sighing   bleeding
From her body   for the sap and green of the year   for her own good
And evil: 125
            Sisters, who is your lover? Has he done nothing but come
And go?   Has your father nailed his cast skin to the wall as evidence
Of sin?   Is it flying like a serpent in the darkness   dripping pure radiant
        venom
Of manhood?
                            Yes, but *he* is unreeling in hills between his long legs   130
The concrete of the highway   his face in the moon beginning
To burn   twitch   dance like an overhead swarm   he feels a nail
Beat through his loins far away   he rises in pain and delight, as spirit

Enters his sex   sways   forms   rises with the forced, choked, red
Blood of her red-headed image, in the red-dust, Adam-colored clay   135
Whirling and leaping   creating   calling: O on the dim, gray man-
track of cement flowing into his mouth   each year he turns the moon back
Around on his handlebars   her image going all over him like the wind
Blasting up his sleeves. He turns off the highway, and
                                       Ah, children,   140
There is now something élse to hear: there is now this madness of engine
Noise in the bushes   past reason   ungodly   squealing   reverting
Like a hog turned loose in the woods   Yes, as he passes the first
Trees of God's land   game-hens overhead   and the farm is ON
Him   everything is more   *more*   MORE as he enters the black   145
Bible's white swirling ground   O daughters   his heartbeat great
With trees   some blue leaves coming   NOW   and right away fire
In the right eye   Lord   more   MORE   O Glory   land
Of Glory: ground-branches hard to get through   coops where fryers huddle
To death, as the star-beast dances and scratches at their home-boards,   150
His rubber stiffens on its nails: Sisters, understand about men and sheaths:

About nakedness: understand how butterflies, amazed, pass out
Of their natal silks   how the tight snake takes a great breath   bursts
Through himself and leaves himself behind   how a man casts finally
Off everything that shields him from another   beholds his loins   155
Shine with his children forever   burn with the very juice
Of resurrection: such shining is how the spring creek comes
Forth from its sunken rocks   it is how the trout foams and turns on
Himself   heads upstream, breathing mist like water, for the cold
Mountain of his birth   flowing   sliding in and through the ego-   160
maniacal sleep of gamecocks   shooting past a man with one new blind
Side   who feels his skinned penis rise like a fish through the dark
Woods, in a strange lifted-loving form   a snake about to burst
Through itself on May Day   and leave behind on the ground   still
Still   the shape of a fooled thing's body: 165
                                   he comes on,   comes
Through the laurel, wiped out on his right by an eye-twig   now he
Is crossing the cow track   his hat in his hand going on before
His face   then up   slowly over   over like the Carolina moon
Coming into Georgia   feels the farm close its Bible and ground-   170
fog over him   his dark side blazing   something whipping

By, beyond sight: each year at this time I shall be letting you
Know when she cannot stand   when the chains fall back on
To the tractor   when you should get up   when neither she nor the pole
Has any more sap   and her striped arms and red hair must keep her   175
From falling   when she feels God's willow laid on her, at last,
With no more pressure than hay, and she has finished crying to her lover's
Shifting face   and his hand when he gave it   placed it, unconsumed,
In her young burning bush.   Each year by dark she has learned

That home is to hang in   home is where your father cuts the baby   180
Fat from your flanks for the Lord, as you scream for the viny foreskin
Of the motorcycle rider. Children, by dark   by now, when he drops
The dying branch and lets her down   when the red clay flats
Of her feet hit the earth   all things have heard—fog, gamecock
Snake and lover—and we listen: Listen, children, for the fog to lift   185
The form of sluggish creeks into the air: each spring, each creek
On the Lord's land flows in two   O sisters, lovers, flows in two
Places: where it was, and in the low branches of pines where chickens
Sleep in mist   and that is where you will find roads floating free
Of the earth   winding   leading unbrokenly out of the farm of God   190
The father:
                    Each year at this time she is coming from the barn   she
Falls once, hair hurting her back   stumbles walking naked
With dignity   walks with no help to the house   lies face down
In her room, burning   tuning in   hearing in the spun rust-   195
groan of bedsprings, his engine root and thunder like a pig,
Knowing who it is   must be   knowing that the face of gnats will wake
In the woods, as a man: there is nothing else this time of night
But her dream of having wheels between her legs: tires, man,
Everything she can hold, pulsing together   her father walking   200
Reading   intoning   calling   his legs blown out by the ground-
fogging creeks of his land: Listen   listen like females each year
In May   O glory   to the sound   the sound of your man gone wild
With love in the woods   let your nipples rise   and leave your feet
To hear: This is when moths flutter in from the open, and Hell   205
Fire of the oil lamp shrivels them   and it is said
To her: said like the Lord's voice trying to find a way
Outside the Bible   O sisters   O women and children who will be
Women of Gilmer County   you farm girls and Ellijay cotton mill

Girls, get up   each May Day   up in your socks   it is the father   210
Sound   going on about God   making, a hundred feet down,
The well beat its bucket like a gong: she goes to the kitchen,
Stands with the inside grain of pinewood whirling on her like a cloud
Of wire   picks up a useful object   two   they are not themselves
Tonight   each hones itself as the moon does   new by phases   215
Of fog   floating unchanged into the house   coming atom
By atom   sheepswool   different smokes   breathed like the Word
Of nothing, round her seated father. Often a girl in the country,
Mostly in spring   mostly bleeding   deep enough in the holy Bible
Belt   will feel her arms rise up   up   and this not any wish   220
Of hers   will stand, waiting for word.   O daughters, he is rambling
In Obadiah   the pride of thine heart hath deceived thee, thou
That dwelleth in the clefts of the rock, whose habitation is high
That saith in his heart   O daughters   who shall bring me down
To the ground?   And she comes down   putting her back into   225
The hatchet   often   often   he is brought down   laid out
Lashing   smoking   sucking wind: Children, each year at this time
A girl will tend to take an ice pick in both hands   a lone pine
Needle   will hover   hover: Children, each year at this time
Things happen quickly   and it is easy for a needle to pass   230
Through the eye of a man bound for Heaven   she leaves it   naked goes
Without further sin through the house   floating in and out of all
Four rooms   comes onto the porch on cloud-feet   steps down and out
And around to the barn   pain changing   her old screams hanging
By the hair around her: Children, in May, often a girl in the country   235
Will find herself lifting wood   her arms like hair rising up
To undo locks   raise latches   set gates aside   turn all things
Loose   shoo them out   shove   pull   O hogs are leaping ten
Million years back through fog   cows walking worriedly   passing out
Of the Ark   from stalls where God's voice cursed and mumbled   240
At milking time   moving   moving   disappearing   drifting
In cloud   cows in the alders already lowing far off   no one
Can find them each year: she comes back to the house and grabs double
Handfuls of clothes
                    and her lover, with his one eye of amazing grace   245
Of sight, sees her coming as she was born   swirling   developing
Toward him   she hears him grunt   she hears him creaking
His saddle   dead-engined   she conjures one foot whole from the ground-

fog to climb him behind   he stands up   stomps   catches   roars
Blasts the leaves from a blinding twig   wheels   they blaze up   250
Together   she breathing to match him   her hands on his warm belly
His hard blood renewing like a snake   O now   now as he twists
His wrist, and takes off with their bodies:
                                        each May you will hear it
Said that the sun came as always   the sun of next day burned   255
Them off with the mist: that when the river fell back on its bed
Of water   they fell from life   from limbs   they went with it
To Hell   three-eyed   in love, their legs around an engine, her arms
Around him.   But now, except for each year at this time, their sound
Has died: except when the creek-bed thicks its mist   gives up   260
The white of its flow to the air   comes off   lifts into the pinepoles
Of May Day   comes back as you come awake in your socks and crotchhair
On new-mooned nights of spring   I speak   you listen and the pines fill
With motorcycle sound as they rise, stoned out of their minds on the white
Lightning of fog   singing   the saddlebags full of her clothes   265
Flying   snagging   shoes hurling away   stockings grabbed-off
Unwinding and furling on twigs: all we know   all we could follow
Them by was her underwear   was stocking after stocking where it tore
Away, and a long slip stretched on a thorn   all these few gave
Out. Children, you know it: that place was where they took   270
Off into the air   died   disappeared   entered my mouth   your mind
Each year   each pale, curved breath   each year as she holds him
Closer wherever he hurtles   taking her   taking her   she going forever
Where he goes   with the highways of rivers   through one-eyed
Twigs   through clouds of chickens   and grass with them bends   275
Double   the animals lift their heads   peanuts and beans exchange
Shells in joy   joy like the speed of the body and rock-bottom
Joy: joy by which the creek bed appeared to bear them out of the Bible
's farm   through pine-clouds of gamecocks where no earthly track
Is, but those risen out of warm currents   streams born to hang   280
In the pines of Nickajack Creek: tonight her hands are under
His crackling jacket   the pain in her back enough to go through
Them both her buttocks blazing in the sheepskin saddle: tell those
Who look for them   who follow by rayon stockings   who look on human
Highways   on tracks of cement and gravel   black weeping roads   285
Of tar: tell them that she and her rider have taken no dirt
Nor any paved road   no path for cattle   no county trunk or trail

Or any track upon earth, but have roared like a hog on May Day
Through pines and willows: that when he met the insane vine
Of the scuppernong   he tilted his handlebars back and took   290
The road that rises in the cold mountain spring from warm creeks:
O women in your rayon from Lindale, I shall be telling you to go
To Hell   by cloud   down where the chicken walk is running
To weeds   and anyone can show you where the tire marks gave out
And her last stocking was cast   and you stand as still as a weasel   295
Under Venus   before you dance   dance yourself blue with blood-
joy looking into the limbs   looking up into where they rode
Through cocks tightening roots with their sleep-claws. Children,
They are gone: gone as the owl rises, when God takes the stone
Blind sun off its eyes, and it sees   sees hurtle in the utter dark   300
Gold of its sight, a boy and a girl buried deep in the cloud
Of their speed   drunk, children   drunk with pain and the throttle
Wide open, in love   with a mindless sound   with her red hair
In the wind streaming gladly for them both   more than gladly
As the barn settles under the weight of its pain   the stalls fill once   305
More with trampling like Exodus   the snake doctor gone the rats beginning
On the last beans   and all the chicks she fed, each year at this time
Burst from their eggs as she passes:
                                         Children, it is true that mice
No longer bunch on the rafters, but wade the fields like the moon,   310
Shifting in patches   ravenous   the horse floats, smoking with flies,
To the water-trough   coming back less often   learning to make
Do with the flowing drink of deer   the mountain standing   cold
Flowing into his mouth   grass underfoot   dew   horse or what
ever he is now   moves back into trees where the bull walks   315
With a male light spread between his horns   some say screams like a girl
And her father yelling together:
                                         Ah, this night in the dark laurel
Green of the quartermoon I shall be telling you that the creek's last
Ascension is the same   is made of water and air   heat and cold   320
This year as before: telling you not to believe every scream you hear
Is the Bible's: it may be you or me   it may be her sinful barn-
howling for the serpent, as her father whips her, using the tried
And true rhythms of the Lord.   Sisters, an old man at times like this
Moon, is always being found   yes found with an ice-pick on his mind,   325
A willow limb in his hand.   By now, the night-moths have come

Have taken his Bible and read it   have flown, dissolved, having found
Nothing in it for them.   I shall be telling you at each moon   each
Year at this time, Venus rises   the weasel goes mad at the death
In the egg, of the chicks she fed for him by hand: mad in the middle   330
Of human space he dances   blue-eyed   dances with Venus rising
Like blood-lust over the road   O tell your daughters   tell them
That the creek's ghost can still   O still can carry double
Weight of true lovers   any time   any night as the wild turkeys claw
Into the old pines of gamecocks   and with a cow's tongue, the Bible calls   335
For its own, and is not heard   and even God's unsettled great white father-
head with its ear to the ground, cannot hear   know   cannot pick
Up where they are   where her red hair is streaming through the white
Hairs of His centerless breast: with the moon   He cries with the cow all
Its life penned up with Noah in the barn   talk of original   340
Sin as the milk spurts   talk of women   talk of judgment and flood
And the promised land:

                            Telling on May Day, children: telling
That the animals are saved without rain   that they are long gone
From here   gone with the sun   gone with the woman taken   345
In speed   gone with the one-eyed mechanic   that the barn falls in
Like Jericho at the bull's voice   at the weasel's dance   at the hog's
Primeval squeal   the uncut hay walks when the wind prophesies in the west
Pasture   the animals move   roam, with kudzu creating all the earth
East of the hayfield: Listen: each year at this time the county speaks   350
With its beasts and sinners   with its blood: the county speaks of nothing
Else each year at this time: speaks as beasts speak to themselves
Of holiness learned in the barn: Listen   O daughters   turn   turn
In your sleep   rise with your backs on fire   in spring   in your socks
Into the arms of your lovers: every last one of you, listen one-eyed   355
With your man   in hiding   in fog where the animals walk through
The white breast of the Lord   muttering   walk with nothing
To do but be   in the spring laurel in the mist and self-sharpened
Moon   walk through the resurrected creeks   through the Lord
At their own pace   the cow shuts its mouth and the Bible is still   360
Still open at anything   we are gone   the barn wanders over the earth.

The Christmas Towns

1967

So much of life is spent driving,
So much in small towns
In the dusk, where one stops,
Puts a dime in a parking meter,
And saunters, invisible, among   5
These particular strangers.
There are some times when this is

At Christmas, in a town in south Alabama,

And, hanging over the streets
On wires, are green bunting, many old   10
Decorations, some plastic new ones as well,
Brittle, well-meaning, and wrong.
The sun at the end of the main street
Is dull red, and puts a bright red
On all the faces seen once.   15

One wishes to stroll all the way

Into the sun, but the town will not last,
Though down by the railroad station
The gaiety does not diminish.
You are in one of the Christmas towns   20
With the store-haunting clean country children,
Enchanted by the colors that come out
Of town-hall attics and fire departments and soar

Over their heads once a year:

Strangers may also know them, who spend,   25
For space and time to be here—
To walk under flowering rags,
A warm winter sun in their eyes—

Only ten silver cents in a lifetime.
This buys a lot on this day: 30
Warmth for both hands outside

The pockets, a forehead crimson

With the first dark, a silence in oneself
Amongst the countrified noise,
A feeling of having bathed in secret   35
Inside one's clothes: an hour
To be unnoticed and ghostlike,
Clear-eyed, damp-haired and smiling
And awestruck by the legends of the race.

1968–1973

Victory

1968

By September 3rd I had made my bundle
Of boards and a bag of nails. America, I was high
On Okinawa, with the fleet lying on its back
Under me, whispering "I can't help it"
                  and all ships firing up fire   5
Fighting liquids   sucking seawater, hoses climbing and coloring
The air, for Victory. I was clear-seeing
The morning   far-seeing backward
And forward from the cliff. I turned on the ground
And dug in, my nails and bag of magic   10
Boards from the tent-floor trembling to be
A throne. I was ready to sail
The island toward life
After death, left hand following right into the snail
shelled ground, then knocking down and nailing down my chair like a box   15
seat in the worldwide window of peace   and sat and lay down my arms
On the stomped grains of ammo-crates heavy with the soles
Of buddies who had helped me wreck the tent
In peace-joy, and of others long buried
At sea. The island rocked with the spectrum   20
Bombardment of the fleet   and there I was
For sure   saved and plucked naked to my shirt
And lids. I raised my head to the sun.
What I saw was two birthdays

Back, in the jungle, before I sailed high on the rainbow   25
Waters of victory   before the sun
Of armistice morning burned into my chest
The great V of Allied Conquest. Now it was not here
With the ships sucking up fire

Water and spraying it wild   30
Through every color, or where, unthreatened, my navel burned
Burned like an entry-wound. Lord, I deepened
Memory, and lay in the light high and wide
Open, murmuring "I can't help it" as I went
South in my mind   35
                                        Yes Mother
                   there were two fine hands
Driving the jeep: mine, much better than before, for you had sent
Whiskey. What could I do but make the graveyards soar! O you coming
Allied Victory, I rambled in the night of two birthdays   40
Ago, the battle of Buna stoned
In moonlight   stone-dead left and right   going nowhere
Near friend or foe, but turned off into the thickest
Dark. O yes, Mother, let me tell you: the vines split and locked:
About where you'd never know me is   45
Where I stalled
                        and sat bolt up-
right in the moonlit bucket
Seat throne of war
                                cascading the bottle to drink   50
To victory, and to what I would do, when the time came,
With my body. The world leapt like the world
Driving nails, and the moon burned with the light it had when it split

From the earth. I slept and it was foretold
That I would live. My head came true   55
In a great smile. I reached for the bottle. It was dying and the moon
Writhed closer to be free; it could answer
My smile of foreknowledge. I forgot the mosquitoes that were going
Mad on my blood, of biting me once too often on the bites
Of bites. Had the Form in the moon come from the dead soldier   60
Of your bottle, Mother? Let down in blocked
Out light, a snakehead hung, its eyes putting into mine
Visions of a victory at sea. New Guinea froze. Midair was steady

Between. Snake-eyes needle-eyed   its
Lips halving its head   65
Stayed shut. I held up the last drop

In the bottle, and invited him
To sin   to celebrate
The Allied victory to come. He pulled back a little over
The evil of the thing I meant   70
To stand for brotherhood. Nightshining his scales on Detroit
Glass, he stayed on and on
My mind. I found out the angel
Of peace is limbless and the day will come
I said, when no difference is between   75
My skin and the great fleets
Delirious with survival. Mother, I was drunk enough on your birthday
Present, not to die there. I backed the jeep out
Of the Buna weeds
                        and, finally, where the sun struck   80
The side of the hill, there I was

                                        back from the dark side
Of the mind, burning like a prism over the conquering Catherine
Wheel of the fleet. But ah, I turned

        I sank I lay back dead   85
Drunk on a cold table   I had closed my eyes
And gone north   and lay to change
Colors all night. Out of the Nothing of occupation
Duty, I must have asked for the snake: I asked or the enemy told
Or my snakeskin told   90
Itself to be. Before I knew it in Yokohama, it was at my throat
Beginning with its tail, cutting through the world
wide Victory sign   moving under
My armpit like a sailor's, scale
By scale. Carbon-arc-light spat in the faces of the four   95
Men who bent over me, for the future lay brilliantly in
The needles of the enemy. Naked I lay on their zinc
Table, murmuring "I can't help it."
He coiled around me, yet

Headless   I turned with him side   100
To side, as the peaceful enemy
Designed   a spectrum of scales O yes

Mother I was in the tattoo parlor to this day
Not knowing how I got there as he grew,
Red scales sucking up color   blue   105
White with my skin running out of the world
Wide sun. Frothing with pinpricks, filling with ink
I lay and it lay
Now over my heart   limbless I fell and moved like moonlight
On the needles   moving to hang my head   110
In a drunk boy's face, and watch him while he dreamed
Of victory at sea. I retched but choked
It back, for he had crossed my breast, and I knew that many-
colored snakeskin was living with my heart   our hearts
Beat as one   port-of-call red   Yokohama blue   115
O yes and now he lay low

On my belly, and gathered together the rainbow
Ships of Buckner Bay. I slumbered deep and he crossed the small
Of my back   increased
His patchwork hold on my hip   passed through the V between   120
My legs, and came
Around once more   all but the head   then I was turning   the snake
Coiled round my right thigh and crossed
Me with light hands   I felt myself opened
Just enough, where the serpent staggered on his last   125
Colors   needles gasping for air   jack-hammering
My right haunch burned by the hundreds
Of holes, as the snake shone on me complete   escaping
Forever   surviving   crushing   going home
To the bowels of the living,   130
His master, and the new prince of peace.

The Lord in the Air

1968

... If the spectator could ... make a friend & companion of one of these
Images of wonder ... then would he meet the Lord in the air & ... be happy.

Blake

Shook down   shook up on these trees they have come
From moment to this moment floating on   in   and this
   Moment changes now not with the light for my son
   Has come   has come out with one crow floating
   Off a limb   back on and off   off a limb in other   5
   Sunlight turning and making him call himself

   Blacker   then settles back   back into the other
   Moment. They hunch and face in. O yes they are all in
    These very trees of the son-faced and fenced-
    in backyard   waiting for my boy and the Lord   10
   In the air. O parents great things can be released
From your left-handed son's left hand! They don't know

   It, but he has them all in his palm, and now puts them
   All in his mouth. Out by the blue swoon of the pool
   He lifts the wood whistle to his blond lips. A scratch-   15
    long sound rises out of him   the trees flap and fall
   Back, and ah there are crows dealt out all over inside
The light   they mix and mingle   dive   swerve throughout

    Themselves   calling   self-shuffling   saying
With my boy's other tongue   sailing   meeting the Lord   20
Of their stolen voice in the air   and more incoming from miles
   Away are here   they wheel in blast after blast
   In the child's lungs, as he speaks to them in the only
Word they understand   the *one*   the syllable that means

Everything to them   he has them cold: their several   25
        Accents   they cry with him they know more than all
    They have known   fear grief good danger love and marriage
        With the Lord in the air. The pool trembles   my boy falls
            From his voice   falls in stitches to the concrete   one
            More word he says   not intended   never heard   he gives   30

        Them a tone never struck in the egg   in the million years
        Of their voice   the whole sky laughs with crows   they creak
        And croak with hilarity   black winged belly-laughs they tell
                Each other   the great joke of flight   sound living
    Deep in the sun and waiting   a sound more or less   or more   35
    Like warning, like marriage. O Chris come in, drop off now

    Black birds from your tongue of wood, back into our neighbor
Trees   into other dimensions, their added-to moment and light
    Plays over the pool in lovely silence like new   surely like new
            Power over birds and beasts: something that has come in   40
            From all over   come out but not for betrayal, or to call
        Up death or desire, but only to give   give what was never.

———

The Eye-Beaters
1968

for Mary Bookwalter

A man visits
a Home for
Children in
Indiana,
some of whom
have gone
blind there.

Come something   come blood sunlight   come and they break
Through the child-wall, taking heart from the two left feet
Of your sound: are groping for the Visitor in the tall corn
Green of Indiana. You may be the light, for they have seen it coming
From people: have seen it on cricket and brick have seen it   5
Seen it fade   seen slowly the edge of things fail   all corn
Green fail   heard fields grind   press with insects and go round
To the back of the head. They are blind. Listen   listen well

A therapist explains why the children strike their eyes.

To your walking that gathers the blind in bonds   gathers these
Who have fought with themselves   have blacked their eyes wide   10
Open, toddling like dolls and like penguins   soft-knotted down,
Protected, arms bound to their sides in gauze, but dark is not
To be stood in that way: they holler   howl till they can shred
Their gentle ropes   whirl and come loose. They *know* they should see
But *what,* now? When their fists smash their eyeballs, they behold no   15
Stranger giving light from his palms. What they glimpse has flared
In mankind from the beginning. In the asylum, children turn to go
    back
Into the race: turn their heads without comment into the black magic
Migraine of caves. Smudge-eyed, wide-eyed, gouged, horned, caved-
in, they are silent: it is for you to guess what they hold back inside   20
The brown and hazel   inside the failed green   the vacant blue-

The Visitor begins to invent a fiction to save his mind.

eyed floating of the soul. Was that lightning   was that a heart-
struck leap   somewhere before birth? Why do you eat the green
    summer
Air like smoky meat? Ah, Stranger, you do not visit this place,
You live or die in it   you brain-scream you beat your eyes to see   25
The junebug take off backwards   spin   connect his body-sound
To what he is in the air. But under the fist, on the hand-stomped bone,
A bison leaps out of rock   fades   a long-haired nine-year-old clubs
Her eye, imploding with vision   dark   bright again   again again
A beast, before her arms are tied. Can it be? Lord, when they slug   30
Their blue cheeks blacker, can it be that they do not see the wings
And green of insects   or the therapist suffering kindly   but a tribal
    light old

He tries to see what they see then they beat their eyes.

Enough to be seen without sight? There, quiet children stand
    watching
A man striped and heavy with pigment, lift his hand with color
    coming
From him. Bestial, working like God, he moves on stone he is
    drawing   35
A half-cloud of beasts on the wall. They crane closer, helping,
    beating
Harder, light blazing inward from their fists   and see   see leap
From the shocked head-nerves, great herds of deer on the hacked
    glory plain

1968–1973　:　415

Of the cave wall: antelope   elk: blind children strike for the middle
Of the brain, where the race is young. Stranger, they stand here   40
And fill your mind with beasts: ibex   quagga   rhinoceros of wool-
gathering smoke: cave bear   aurochs   mammoth: beings that appear
Only in the memory of caves   the niches filled, not with Virgins,
But with the squat shapes of the Mother. In glimmers of mid-brain
    pain
The forms of animals are struck like water from the stone   where
    hunger   45
And rage   where the Visitor's helplessness and terror   all
Move on the walls and create.
                                                (Look up: the sun is taking its stand on four
        o'clock of Indiana time, painfully blazing   fist of a ball of fire
God struck from His one eye).   50
                                                No; you see only dead beasts playing
In the bloody handprint on the stone where God gropes like a man
Like a child, for animals   where the artist hunts and slashes, glowing
Like entrail-blood, tracking the wounded game across the limestone
As it is conceived. The spoor leads   his hand changes   grows   55
Hair like a bison   horns like an elk   unshapes   in a deer-leap
    emerges
From the spear-pitted rock, becoming what it can make unrolling
Not sparing itself clenching re-forming rising   beating
For light.

His Reason   *Ah, you think it, Stranger: you'd like that you try hard*   60
argues   *To think it, to think for them. But what you see, in the half-inner sight*
with his   *Of squinting, are only fields   only children whose hands are tied away*
invention.   *From them for their own good   children waiting to smash their dead*
                  Eyes, live faces, to see nothing. As before, they come to you smiling,
                  Using their strange body-English. *But why is it* this *they have made up*   65
                  In your mind? Why painting and hunting? Why animals showing how
                      God
                  Is subject to the pictures in the cave   their clotted colors like blood
                  On His hands as the wild horse burns   as the running buck turns red
                  From His palm, while children twist in their white ropes, eyes wide,
                  Their heads in the dark meat of bruises?   70
                                                And now, blind hunters,

Swaying in concert like corn   sweet-faced   tribe-swaying at the
     red wall,
Of the blind like a cooking-fire   shoulder-moving, moaning as the
     cave-
artist moaned when he drew the bull-elk to the heart   come ring
Me round. I will undo you. Come, and your hands will be free to fly   75
Straight into your faces, and shake the human vision to its roots
Flint-chipping sparks spring up: I can see   feel   see another elk
Ignite with his own becoming: it is time.
                                        Yes, indeed, I know it is not
So   I am trying to make it   make something   make them make me   80
Re-invent the vision of the race   knowing the blind must see
By magic or nothing. Therapists, I admit it; it helps me to think
That they can give themselves, like God from their scabby fists,
     the original
Images of mankind: that when they beat their eyes, I witness how
I survive, in my sun-blinded mind: that the beasts are calling to God   85
And man for art, when the blind open wide and strike their incurable
     eyes
In Indiana. *And yet, O Stranger, those beasts and mother-figures are all*
Made up by you. They are your therapy. There is nothing inside their dark,
Nothing behind their eyes but the nerve that kills the sun above the corn
Field   no hunt no meat no pain-struck spark no vision   no pre-history   90
For the blind   nothing but blackness forever   nothing but a new bruise
Risen upon the old.

                         They have gone away; the doors have shut

The children
retire, but he   on you
hears them   And your makeshift salvation. Yet your head still keeps what you
behind their   would put in theirs
wall.   If you were God. Bring down your lids like a cave, and try to see   95
By the race alone. Collective memory stirs   herd-breathes   stamps
In snow-smoke, as the cave takes hold. You are artist and beast and
The picture of the beast: you are a ring of men and the stampeded
     bones
Tumbling into the meat-pit. A child screams out in fury, but where,
In the time of man? O brother, quiver and sweat: It is true that no
     thing   100

Anyone can do is good enough for them: not Braille not data

Processing   not "learning TV repair" not music   no, and not not
    being

"A burden": none of these, but only vision: what they see must be
    crucial

To the human race. It is so; to let you live with yourself after seeing

Them, they must be thought to see by what has caused   is causing
    us all   105

To survive. In the late sun of the asylum, you know nothing else will
    do

You; the rest is mere light. In the palm of the hand the color red is
    calling

For blood   the forest-fire roars on the cook-stone, smoke-smothered
    and lightning-

born   and the race hangs on meat and illusion   hangs on nothing

But a magical art. Stranger, you may as well take your own life   110

Blood   brain-blood, as vision. Yes; that hammering on the door is
    not

Your heart, or the great pulse of insects; it is blind children beating

Their eyes to throw a picture on the wall. Once more you hear a child
    yell

In pure killing fury   pure triumph pure acceptance   as his hands
    burst

Their bonds. It is happening. Half-broken light flickers with agony   115

Like a head   throwing up the beast-paint the wall cannot shake

For a million years.

      Hold on to your fantasy; it is all that can save

*A man with good eyes in this place. Hold on, though doctors keep
    telling*

You to back off   to be what you came as   back off from the actual   120

*Wall of their screaming room, as green comes all around you with its
    ears*

Of corn, its local, all-insect hum, given junebugs and flies wherever

They are, in midair. No;

      by God. There is no help for this but madness,

Perversity. Think that somewhere under their pummeled lids they
    gather   125

At the wall of art-crazed beasts, and the sun blazing into the blackout
Of the cave, dies of vision. A spell sways in. It is time for the night
Hunt, and the wild meat of survival. The wall glimmers that God
    and man
Never forgot. I have put history out. An innocent eye, it is closed
Off, outside in the sun. Wind moans like an artist. The tribal
    children lie   130
On their rocks in their animal skins   seeing in spurts of eye-beating
Dream, the deer, still wet with creation, open its image to the heart's

He leaves
the Home.   Blood, as I step forward, as I move through the beast-paint of the
    stone,
Taken over, submitting, brain-weeping. Light me a torch with what
    we have preserved
Of lightning. Cloud bellows in my hand. God man hunter artist
    father   135
Be with me. My prey is rock-trembling, calling. Beast, get in
My way. Your body opens onto the plain. Deer, take me into your life-
lined form. I merge, I pass beyond in secret   in perversity and the
    sheer
Despair of invention   my double-clear bifocals off   my reason
    gone
Like eyes. Therapist, farewell at the living end. Give me my spear.   140

Knock
1969

Sharing   what sharing   quickly who
Is outside   in   both you together here
And unseen out   let the bed huddle and jump

Naked in the quick dead middle
Of the night, making what is to be   5
There   you being broken by something

Open where the door thins out
Making frames of the room's early-
warning wood   is the code still

The same can the five fingers   10
Of the hand still show against
Anything? Have they come for us?

———————

The Place

1969

We are nerve-blowing now. Unspeaking and whiteness around. Warm wind
Was never here. Snow has no move. So this
Has placed us. Dark is with it nearly, for this last of day-
Shaking of shores.

Night is down on us; hold me with all your fur.   5
These waters have put every grain of their ice
Into our red hand-marrow. Statue-faced, let us breathe
On each other   let us breathe the ice

Sweeping into the air, for it has crossed to
Within us, rigidly airborne, impassable from crossing   10
Miles of lake-freeze in our
Overwhelming direction. They hang true lovers with thread-

steel through the nose. It hurts straight up and down
Inside us. This is where we come, and we are cross-
eyed with love and every tooth   15
root aches. Lover, this is where:

I can tell you here.

Madness

1969

*(Time: Spring. Place: Virginia. A domestic dog wanders from the house, is
bitten by a rabid female fox, runs mad himself, and has to be hunted down,
killed, and beheaded.)*

Lay in the house mostly living
With children when they called   mostly
Under the table begging for scraps lay with the head
On a family foot
Or stretched out on a side,   5
Firesided. Had no running
Running, ever.
Would lie relaxed, eyes dim

With appreciation, licking the pure contentment
Of long   long notched   10
Black lips. Would lap up milk like a cat and swim clear
In brown grateful eyes. That was then, before the Spring
Lay down and out
Under a tree, not far but a little far and out
Of sight of the house.   15
Rain had sown thick and gone

From the house where the living
Was done, where scraps fell and fire banked full
On one sleeping side of the spirit
Of the household   20
and it was best
To get up and wander
Out, out of sight. Help me was shouted
To the world of females   anyone will do
To the smoking leaves.   25

Love could be smelt. All things burned deep
In eyes that were dim from looking
At the undersides of tables   patient with being the god
Of small children. In Spring it is better with no
Doors which the god   30
Of households must beg at   no locks where the wind blows
The world's furry women
About in heat. And there

She lay, firesided, bushy-assed, her head
On the ground wide open, slopping soap: 35
Come   come close
She said like a god's
Wild mistress said come
On boy, I'm what you come

Out here in the bushes for. She burned alive   40
In her smell, and the eyes she looked at burned
With gratitude, thrown a point-eared scrap
Of the world's women, hot-tailed and hunted: she bit down
Hard on a great yell
To the house being eaten alive   45
By April's leaves. Bawled; they came and found.
The children cried

Helping tote to the full moon
Of the kitchen "I carried the head"   O full of eyes
Heads kept coming across, and friends and family   50
Hurt   hurt
The spirit of the household, on the kitchen
Table being thick-sewed   they saying it was barbed
Wire looked like
It got him, and he had no business running   55

Off like that. Black lips curled as they bathed off
Blood, bathed blood. Staggered up under
The table making loud
A low-born sound, and went feeling

For the outer limits   60
Of the woods   felt them break and take in
The world   the frame turn loose and the house
Not mean what it said it was. Lay down and out
Of sight and could not get up
The head, lying on God's foot firesided   65
Fireheaded   formed a thought
Of Spring   of trees in wildfire
Of the mind speeded up   and put all thirst

Into the leaves. They grew
Unlimited. Soap boiled   70
Between black lips: the house
Spirit jumped up beyond   began to run   shot
Through the yard and bit down
On the youngest child. And when it sprang down
And out across the pasture, the grains of its footprints leapt   75
Free, where horses that shied from its low

New sound were gathered, and men swung themselves
Up to learn what Spring
Had a new way to tell, by bringing up
And out the speed of the fields. A long horn blew   80
Firesided   the mad head sang
Along the furrows   bouncing and echoing from earth
To earth through the body
Turning   doubling back
Through the weather of love running wild and the horses full   85

Of strangers coming after. Fence wire fell and rose
Flaming with messages as the spirit ran
Ran with house-hair
Burr-picking madly   and after came

Men   horses   spirits   90
Of households leaping crazily beyond
Their limits, dragging their bodies by the foaming throat through grass
And beggar-lice and by the red dust

Road where men blazed and roared
With their shoulders   blew it down and apart where it ran   95
And lay down on the earth of God's
One foot and the foot beneath the table kicked
The white mouth shut: this was something

In Spring in mild brown eyes   as strangers
Cut off the head and carried and held it   100
Up, blazing with consequence   blazing
With freedom saying   bringing
Help   help   madness   help.

Living There

1969

The Keeper
Is silent   is living in the air not
Breathable, of time. It is gray
Winter in the woods where he lives.
They've been cut down; you can see through   5
What he is keeping   what used to be a room
In a house with one side turned
To trees. There are no woods now, only other
Houses. Old Self like a younger brother, like a son, we'd come rambling
Out of the house in wagons, turn off the back   10
Driveway and bump at full bump-speed down
Through the woods, the branches flickering
With us, with the whole thing of home
A blur, gone rolling in leaves. But people are always coming

To know woods   to know rooms in houses   15
That've been torn down. Where we live, you and I,
My youth and my middle
Age   where we live with our family, miles away

From home, from my old home,
        I have rooms 20
I keep, but this old one, the one where I grew
        Up, is in the air
        Of winter it is over
Other houses like a ghost. The house lives only
        In my head while I look and the sun sinks 25
Through the floors that were here: the floors
Of time. Brother, it is a long way to the real

House I keep. Those rooms are growing
        Intolerable in minds I made
        Up, though all seems calm when I walk 30
Into them as though I belonged there. Sleepers are stirring   an arm
  lies
        Over a face, and the lights are burning
        In the fish tank. It is not like this,
But it will be. One day those forms will rise
        And leave   and age 35
And come back   and that house will flame like this
        In the Keeper's head
        With the last sun; it will be gone,
        And someone will not be able
        To believe there is only nothing 40

Where his room was, next to his father's
Blue-eyed   blue-eyed   the fixer   the wagon-master
        Blazing in death
        With life: will not be able to look
        Into windows of the room where he saw, 45
        For the first time, his own blood.
        That room fills only with dying
Solar flame   with only the backyard wind
        Only the lack
Of trees, of the screech-owl my mother always thought 50
Was a hurt dog. And tell me for the Lord God
    's sake, where are all our old

Dogs?
      Home?
             Which way is that?   55
     Is it this vacant lot? These woven fences?
          Or is it hundreds

    Of miles away, where I am the Keeper
      Of rooms turning night and day
   Into memory? Is it the place I now live   60
     And die in   the place I manage
   In? Is it with those people who never knew
These people, except for me? Those people sleeping
      Eating my food   loading
Their minds with love   their rooms with what they love   65
    And must lose, and cannot forget? Those fish
Tanks   those James Bond posters   those telescopes
     And microscopes and the hidden pictures
  Of naked girls? Who are they? And will they come foolishly
        Back to stare at nothing   70
But sunset, where the blood flowed and the wagon wheel grew whole
  in the hands
Of the bald-headed father? Will they look into those rooms where now
They sleep, and see nothing but moonlight   nothing but everything
          Far and long
     Gone, long gone? Why does the Keeper go blind   75
    With sunset? The mad, weeping Keeper who can't keep
  A God-damned thing   who knows he can't keep everything
     Or anything alive: none of his rooms, his people
       His past, his youth, himself
      But cannot let them die? Yes, I keep   80
Some of those people, not in wagons but in the all-night glimmer
     Of fish   in the secret glimmer
    Of unfolding girls. I think I know—
  I know them well. I call them, for a little while, sons.

Blood

1969

In a cold night
Of somebody. Is there other
Breath? What did I say?
Or do?

Mercy.   5
MERCY!

There is nothing,
But did I do it? I did something.
Merciful, merciful
O God, what? And   10

Am I still drunk?
Not enough O

Is there any light O where
Do you *touch* this room?
O father   15

Of Heaven my head cannot
Lift but my hand maybe—
Nobody is breathing   what weapon
was it? Light smashes

Down there is nothing but   20
Blood blood all over

Me and blood. Her hair is smeared.
My God what has got loose
In here at last? Who *is*

This girl? She is   25
Some other town some far
From home: knife

Razor, fingernails O she has been opened
Somewhere and yet

She sighs she turns in the slaughtered sheets   30
To me in the blood of her children.
Where in what month?

In the cold in the blood
Of life, she turns
To me, and my weapon   35
Will never recover its blood.
Who is

This woman? No matter; she is safe.
She is safe with me.

————

Diabetes
1969

I. Sugar

One night I thirsted like a prince
Then like a king
Then like an empire   like a world
On fire. I rose and flowed away and fell
Once more to sleep. In an hour I was back   5
In the kingdom   staggering, my belly going round with self-
made night-water, wondering what
The hell. Months of having a tongue
Of flame convinced me: I had better not go
On this way. The doctor was young   10

And nice. He said, I must tell you,
My friend, that it is needles moderation
And exercise. You don't want to look forward
To gangrene and kidney

Failure   boils blindness infection skin trouble falling   15
Teeth coma and death.
                              O.K.
                                   In sleep my mouth went dry
With my answer   and in it burned the sands
Of time with new fury. Sleep could give me no water   20
But my own. Gangrene in white
Was in my wife's hand at breakfast
Heaped like a mountain. Moderation, moderation,
My friend, and exercise. Each time the barbell
Rose   each time a foot fell   25
Jogging, it counted itself
One death   two death   three death and resurrection
For a little while. Not bad! I always knew it would have to be somewhere around
The house: the real
Symbol of Time I could eat   30
And live with, coming true when I opened my mouth:
True in the coffee and the child's birthday
Cake   helping sickness be fire-
tongued, sleepless and water-
logged   but not bad, sweet sand   35
Of time, my friend, an everyday—
A livable death at last.

II. Under Buzzards

for Robert Penn Warren

Heavy summer. Heavy. Companion, if we climb our mortal bodies
High with great effort, we shall find ourselves
Flying with the life   40

Of the birds of death. We have come up
Under buzzards   they face us

Slowly   slowly circling   and as we watch them they turn us
Around, and you and I spin
Slowly, slowly rounding   45
Out the hill. We are level
Exactly on this moment; exactly on the same bird-

plane with those deaths. They are the salvation of our sense
Of glorious movement. Brother, it is right for us to face
Them every which way, and come to ourselves and come   50
From every direction
There is. Whirl and stand fast!
Whence cometh death, O Lord?
On the downwind, riding fire,

Of Hogback Ridge.   55
But listen: what is dead here?
They are not falling but waiting   but waiting
Riding, and they may know
The rotten, nervous sweetness of my blood.

Somewhere riding the updraft   60
Of a far forest fire, they sensed the city sugar
The doctors found in time.
My eyes are green as lettuce with my diet,
My weight is down,

One pocket nailed with needles and injections, the other dragging   65
With sugar cubes to balance me in life
And hold my blood
Level, level. Tell me, black riders, does this do any good?
Tell me what I need to know about my time
In the world. O out of the fiery   70

Furnace of pine-woods, in the sap-smoke and crownfire of needles,
Say when I'll die. When will the sugar rise boiling

Against me, and my brain be sweetened
to death?
                    In heavy summer, like this day.   75
All right! Physicians, witness! I will shoot my veins
        Full of insulin. Let the needle burn
            In. From your terrible heads
The flight-blood drains   and you are falling back
            Back to the body-raising   80

    Fire.
        Heavy summer. Heavy. My blood is clear
    For a time. Is it too clear? Heat waves are rising
    Without birds. But something is gone from me,
        Friend. This is too sensible. Really it is better   85
    To know when to die   better for my blood
    To stream with the death-wish of birds.
        You know, I had just as soon crush
            This doomed syringe
Between two mountain rocks, and bury this needle in needles   90

    Of trees. Companion, open that beer.
    How the body works   how hard it works
        For its medical books is not
        Everything: everything is how
    Much glory is in it: heavy summer is right   95

    For a long drink of beer. Red sugar of my eyeballs
        Feels them turn blindly
        In the fire   rising   turning   turning
        Back to Hogback Ridge, and it is all
Delicious, brother: my body is turning   is flashing unbalanced   100
    Sweetness everywhere, and I am calling my birds.

Venom

1969

for William Haast

Forever, it comes from the head. *Where does it end?*
In life-blood. All over it, in fact, like thrown
Off and thrown-again light. There is little help
For it, but there is some.

The priest of poison: where is he? Who is   5
His latest snake? How does he work?

He has taken it all, brother, and his body lies
With its hand in ice, in a lung

Of iron
                but at last he rises, his heart changing   10
What the snake thought. Tooth-marks all over
Him are chattering of life, not death, not
What God gave them. He shimmers

With healing. He will lie down again
With him the snake has entered.   15
His blood will flow the length
Of the veins of both. They will clasp arms and double-dream

Of the snake in the low long smothering
Sun. Look down! They stretch out giving
And taking. Clouds of family beat the windows   20
Of doctors with their breath. Here lies

The man made good by a hundred
Bites. It is not God but a human
Body they pray to: Turn the poison
Round turn it back on itself O turn it   25

Good: better than life they whisper:
Turn it, they hammer whitely:
Turn it, turn it,
Brother.

———————

The Cancer Match
1969

Lord, you've sent both
And may have come yourself. I will sit down, bearing up under
The death of light very well, and we will all
Have a drink. Two or three, maybe.
I see now the delights   5

Of being let "come home"
From the hospital.
Night!
I don't have all the time
In the world, but I have all night.   10
I have space for me and my house,
And I have cancer and whiskey

In a lovely relation.
They are squared off, here on my ground. They are fighting,
Or are they dancing? I have been told   and told   15
That medicine has no hope, or anything
More to give,

But they have no idea
What hope is, or how it comes. You take these two things:
This bourbon and this thing growing. Why,   20
They are like boys! They bow
To each other

Like judo masters,
One of them jumping for joy, and I watch them struggle
All around the room, inside and out   25
Of the house, as they battle
Near the mailbox

And superbly
For the street-lights! Internally, I rise like my old self
To watch: and remember, ladies and gentlemen,   30
We are looking at this match
From the standpoint

Of tonight
Alone. Swarm over him, my joy, my laughter, my Basic Life
Force! Let your bright sword-arm stream   35
Into that turgid hulk, the worst
Of me, growing:

Get 'im, O Self
Like a belovèd son! One more time! Tonight we are going
Good   better and better   we are going   40
To win, and not only win but win
Big, win big.

———————

Pine

1969

—successive apprehensions—

I

Low-cloudly it whistles, changing heads
On you. How hard to hold and shape head-round.
So any hard hold
Now loses; form breathes near. Close to forest-form

By ear, so landscape is eyelessly   5
Sighing through needle-eyes. O drawn off
The deep end, step right up
And be where. It could be a net
Spreading field: mid-whistling crossed with an edge and a life
Guarding sound. Overhead assign the bright and dark   10
Heels distance-running from all   overdrawing the only sound
Of this sound   sound of a life-mass
Drawn in long lines in the air   unbroken   brother-saving
Sound merely soft
And loudly soft just in time   then nothing and then   15
Soft   soft   and a little caring-for   sift-softening
And soared-to. O ankle-wings lightening and fleeing
Brothers sending back for you
To join the air and live right: O justice-scales leaning toward mercy
Wherever. Justice is exciting in the wind   20
As escape continuing   as an ax hurling
Toward sound and shock. Nothing so just as wind
In its place in low cloud
Of its tree-voice stopped and on-going   footless flight
Sound like brothers coming on as   25
All-comers coming and fleeing
From ear-you and pine, and all pine.

II

What mainly for the brow-hair
Has been blowing, dimensions and glows in:
Air the most like   30
Transfusion expands and only
There it is fresh
From overhead, steep-brewing and heavy from deep
Down upcoming new
To the lungs like a lean cave swimming—   35
Throat-light and iron
Warm spray on the inside face
Cutting often and cooling-out and brow
Opening and haunting freshly. So have you changed to this

You like a sea-wall   40
Tarred as a stump and blowing
Your skull like clover   lung-swimming in rosin
Dwelling
by breath
breath: 45
Whose head like a cave opens living
With eddies   needle-sapped out
Of its mind by this face-lifting
Face like a tree-beast
Listening, resetting the man-broken nose   50
bones on wine
Currents, as taste goes wild
And wells up   recalls   recovers and calls
For its own, for pure spirit
Food: windfalls and wavers out again   55
From nothing, in green sinus-packs.

III

More and more, through slow breaks
In the wind   no a different no this
Wind, another life of you rises,
A saliva-gland burns like a tree.   60
You are what you eat
and what will flutter
Like food if you turn completely
To your mouth, and stand wide open?
A wafer of bark, another   65
Needle, bitter rain by the mouthful coming.
Hunger swirls and slowly down
Showers   and are your children
What you eat? What green of horror
And manna in the next eye   70
To come from you? And will he whistle
From head to foot?

Bitter rain by the mouthful coming.

IV

More hands on the terrible rough.
More pain but more than all   75
Is lodged in the leg-insides. More holding,
Though, more swaying. Rise and ride
Like this and wear and ride
Away with a passionate faceful
Of ply and points. The whole thing turns   80
On earth, throwing off a dark
Flood of four ways
Of being here blind and bending
Blacked-out and framed
Suspended and found alive in the rough palm-   85
And thigh-fires of friction, embracing in the beyond
It all, where,
Opening one by one, you still can open
One thing more. A final form
And color at last comes out   90
Of you alone putting it all
Together like nothing
Here like almighty

V

Glory.

————————

Messages
1969

to and from my sons

I. Butterflies

Over and around   grass banked and packed short and holding back
Water, we have been

Playing, my son, in pure abandon,
And we still are. We play, and play inside our play and play
Inside of that, where butterflies are increasing   5
The deeper we get
And lake-water ceases to strain. Ah, to play in a great field of light
With your son, both men, both
Young and old! Ah, it was then, Chris,

As now! You lay down on the earth   10
Dam, and I rambled forth and did not look and found
And found like a blueprint of animal
Life, the whole skeleton of a cow. O son, left
In pure abandon, I sat down inside the bones in the light
Of pine trees, studying the tiny holes   15
In the head, and where the ants
Could not get through, the nerves had left
Their messages. I sat in the unmoving hearse
Flying, carried by cow-bones in pure
Abandon, back to you. I picked up the head   20
And inside the nose-place were packets
And whole undealt decks
Of thin bones, like shaved playing cards.
I won the horns. They twisted loose from the forehead
And would not twist back   as I gambled and rocked   25
With the skull in my lap,
The cow not straining to live. In that car I rode
Far off
          and in
                    and in   30
While you were sleeping off the light
Of the world.
                    And when I came
From the bone dust in pure abandon, I found you lying on the earth
Dam, slanted in the grass that held back   35
The water, your hands behind your head,
Gazing through your eyelids into the universal
Light, and the butterflies were going

. . . Here

                                            here   40

     here
     here

                                    from here

madly over

                             to   45

here

                                   here.

    They went over you   here   and through you
      Here   no   yes and tattered apart,
        Beat out over water and back   50
        To earth, and over my oldest
      Son asleep: their ragged, brave wings
   Pulsed on the blue flowers   shook like the inmost
      Play   and blazed all over and around
        Where you slept holding back   55
  Water without strain.
                    That is all, but like all joy
On earth and water,
         In bones and in wings and in light,

It is a gamble. It is play, son, now   60
As then. I put the horns beside you in the grass
And turned back to my handsprings and my leaps.

II. Giving a Son to the Sea

Gentle blondness and the moray eel go at the same time
On in my mind as you grow, who fired at me at the age
    Of six, a Christmas toy for child   65
    Spies: a bullet with a Special Secret
Message Compartment. My hands undid the bullet meant
    For my heart, and it read aloud
    "I love you." That message hits me most
When I watch you swim, that being your only talent.   70
The sea obsesses you, and your room is full of it:

    Your room is full
    Of flippers and snorkels and books
    On spearfishing.
             O the depths,   75
My gentle son. Out of that room and into the real
    Wonder and weightless horror
    Of water into the shifts of vastness
You will probably go, for someone must lead
    Mankind, your father and your sons,   80
    Down there to live, or we all die
    Of crowding. Many of you
    Will die, in the cold roll
    Of the bottom currents, and the life lost
More totally than anywhere, there in the dark   85
Of no breath at all.
           And I must let you go, out of your gentle
    Childhood into your own man suspended
    In its body, slowly waving its feet
Deeper and deeper, while the dark grows, the cold   90
    Grows careless, the sun is put
    Out by the weight of the planet
As it sinks to the bottom. Maybe you will find us there

An agonizing new life, much like the life
Of the drowned, where we will farm eat sleep and bear children   95
Who dream of birds.
                              Switch on your sea-lamp, then,
And go downward, son, with your only message
Echoing. Your message to the world, remember,
                              Came to your father   100
At Christmas like a bullet. When the great fish roll
With you, herded deep in the deepest dance,
When the shark cuts through your invisible
Trail, I will send back
That message, though nothing that lives   105
Underwater will ever receive it.
That does not matter, my gentle blond
Son. That does not matter.

––––––––––

In the Pocket
1969

—NFL—

Going backward
All of me and some
Of my friends are forming a shell   my arm is looking
Everywhere and some are breaking
In   breaking down   5
And out   breaking
Across, and one is going deep   deeper
Than my arm. Where is Number One hooking
Into the violent green alive
With linebackers? I cannot find him he cannot beat   10
His man   I fall back more
Into the pocket   it is raging and breaking
Number Two has disappeared into the chalk

Of the sideline   Number Three is cutting with half
A step of grace   my friends are crumbling   15
Around me the wrong color
Is looming   hands are coming
Up and over between
My arm and Number Three: throw it hit him in the middle
Of his enemies   hit move scramble   20
Before death and the ground
Come up   LEAP STAND KILL DIE STRIKE

Now.

————————

Looking for the Buckhead Boys
1969

Some of the time, going home, I go
Blind and can't find it.
The house I lived in growing up and out
The doors of high school is torn
Down and cleared   5
Away for further development, but that does not stop me.
First in the heart
Of my blind spot are
The Buckhead Boys. If I can find them, even one,
I'm home. And if I can find him   catch him in or around   10
Buckhead, I'll never die: it's likely my youth will walk
Inside me like a king.

First of all, going home, I must go
To Wender and Roberts' Drug Store, for driving through I saw it
Shining   renewed   renewed   15
In chromium, but still there.
It's one of the places the Buckhead Boys used to be, before
Beer turned teen-ager.
Tommy Nichols

Is not there. The Drug Store is full of women   20
Made of cosmetics. Tommy Nichols has never been
In such a place: he was the Number Two Man on the Mile
Relay Team in his day.
                                        What day?
My day. Where was I?   25
                        Number Three, and there are some sunlit pictures
In the Book of the Dead to prove it: the 1939
North Fulton High School Annual. Go down,
                        Go down

To Tyree's Pool Hall, for there was more   30
Concentration of the spirit
Of the Buckhead Boys
In there, than anywhere else in the world.
                                        Do I want some shoes
To walk all over Buckhead like a king   35
Nobody knows? Well, I can get them at Tyree's;
It's a shoe store now. I could tell you where every spittoon
Ought to be standing. Charlie Gates used to say one of these days
I'm gonna get myself the reputation of being
The bravest man in Buckhead. I'm going in Tyree's toilet   40
And pull down my pants and take a shit.
                                        Maybe
Charlie's the key: the man who would say that would never leave
Buckhead. Where is he? Maybe I ought to look up
Some Old Merchants. Why didn't I think of that   45
Before?
                Lord, Lord! Like a king!

Hardware. Hardware and Hardware Merchants
Never die, and they have everything on hand
There is to know. Somewhere in the wood-screws Mr. Hamby may have 50
My Prodigal's Crown on sale. He showed up
For every football game at home
Or away, in the hills of North Georgia. There he is, as old
As ever.
                Mr. Hamby, remember me?   55
                        God A'Mighty! Ain't you the one

Who fumbled the punt and lost the Russell game?
                                        That's right.
                    How're them butter fingers?
                                        Still butter, I say,   60
Still fumbling. But what about the rest of the team? What about Charlie
    Gates?
                    He the boy that got lime in his eye from the goal line
When y'all played Gainesville?
                                        Right.
                                        I don't know. Seems to me I see . . .   65

            See? See? What does Charlie Gates see in his eye burning
            With the goal line? Does he see a middle-aged man from the Book
                Of the Dead looking for him in magic shoes
            From Tyree's disappeared pool hall?
                                        Mr. Hamby, Mr. Hamby,   70
            Where? Where is Mont Black?
                                        Paralyzed. Doctors can't do nothing.
                    Where is Dick Shea?
                                        Assistant Sales Manager
Of Kraft Cheese.   75
            How about Punchy Henderson?
                                        Died of a heart attack
                    Watching high school football
                    In South Carolina.
                                        Old Punchy, the last   80
            Of the windsprinters, and now for no reason the first
                Of the heart attacks.
                                        Harmon Quigley?
                    He's up at County Work Farm
            Sixteen. Doing all right up there; be out next year.   85

            Didn't anybody get to be a doctor
Or lawyer?
                    Sure. Bobby Laster's a chiropractor. He's right out here
                    At Bolton; got a real good business.
            Jack Siple?   90
                    Moved away.

Gordon Hamm?

                                            Dead

In the war.

                O the Book   95
         Of the Dead, and the dead bright sun on the page
            Where the team stands ready to explode
      In all directions with Time. Did you say you see Charlie
              Gates every now and then?

                                    Seems to me.   100

Where?

        He may be out yonder at the Gulf Station between here and
           Sandy Springs.

                Let me go pull my car out
                Of the parking lot in back
Of Wender and Roberts'. Do I need gas? No; let me drive around the block   105
              Let me drive around Buckhead
         A few dozen times   turning   turning in my foreign
         Car till the town spins   whirls till the chrome vanishes
          From Wender and Roberts'   the spittoons are remade
    From the sun itself   the dead pages flutter the hearts rise up, that lie   110
           In the ground, and Bobby Laster's backbreaking fingers
          Pick up a cue-stick   Tommy Nichols and I rack the balls
             And Charlie Gates walks into Tyree's un-
                 imaginable toilet.

                              I go north   115
              Now, and I can use fifty

Cents' worth of gas.

                    It is Gulf. I pull in and praise the Lord Charlie
              Gates comes out. His blue shirt dazzles
          Like a baton-pass. He squints he looks at me   120
   Through the goal line. Charlie, Charlie, we have won away from
                 We have won at home
         In the last minute. Can you see me? You say
              What I say: where in God
       Almighty have you been all this time? I don't know,   125
     Charlie. I don't know. But I've come to tell you a secret

That has to be put into code. Understand what I mean when I say
To the one man who came back alive
From the Book of the Dead   to the bravest man
In Buckhead   to the lime-eyed ghost   130
Blue-wavering in the fumes
Of good Gulf gas, "Fill 'er up."
With wine? Light? Heart-attack blood? The contents of Tyree's toilet?
The beer
Of teen-age sons? No; just
"Fill 'er up. Fill 'er up, Charlie."   135

Root-light, or the Lawyer's Daughter
1969

That any just to long for
The rest of my life, would come, diving like a lifetime
Explosion in the juices
Of palmettoes flowing
Red in the St. Mary's River as it sets in the east   5
Georgia from Florida off, makes whatever child
I was lie still, dividing
Swampy states   watching
The lawyer's daughter shocked
With silver   and I wished for all holds   10
On her like root-light. She came flying
Down from Eugene Talmadge
Bridge, just to long for as I burst with never
Rising never
Having seen her except where she worked   15
For J. C. Penney in Folkston. Her regular hours
Took fire, and God's burning bush of the morning
Sermon was put on her; I had never seen it where
It has to be. If you asked me how to find the Image
Of Woman to last   20
All your life, I'd say go lie

Down underwater for nothing
Under a bridge and hold Georgia
And Florida from getting at each other   hold
Like walls of wine. Be eight years old from Folkston ten 25
From Kingsland twelve miles in the clean palmetto color
Just as it blasts
Down with a body   red and silver buck
Naked with bubbles on Sunday   root
light explodes 30
Head-down, and there she is.

———————

Drums Where I Live
1969

So that sleeping and waking
Drum, drum, every day the first part of the sun,
Its upper rim
And rhythm, I live here. I and my family pass, in the new house,
Into the great light mumbling one 5
Two three four, marching in place like boys
Laid out, all voices of the living and the dead
To come and hovering
Between brought in
to cadence.   It is not 10
A heart, but many men.   Someone said it is
Comfort, comforting to hear them.   Not every
Sun-up, neighbor: now and then I wish I had a chance
To take my chances
With silence. More and more 15
They seem to be waiting
For the day   more and more as my son sighs all over the house
Intercom.   I know, I know: he is counting
His years.   When we rise, the drums
Have stopped. But I know from the jungle of childhood 20
Movies what that means. There is nothing in the grenades'

Coming-closer bursts to worry
Anyone; they are Expanding
The Range.   It is only in the morning
Paper that a trainee hangs himself   25
On the obstacle course.   And it is nothing but nerves
That make something human, a cry,
Float like a needle on the sunlight
From the stockade.   But every night I sleep assured
That the drums are going   30
To reach me at dawn like light
Where I live, and my heart, my blood and my family will assemble
Four barely-livable counts.   Dismissed,
Personnel.   The sun is clear
Of Basic Training.   This time, this   35
Is my war and where in God's
Name did it start?   In peace, two, three, four:
In peace peace peace peace

One two

In sleep.   40

————————

Mercy
1969

Ah, this night   this night mortality wails out
Over Saint Joseph's   this night and every   over Mercy   Mercy
Mercy Manor. Who can be dressed right for the long cry?
Who can have his tie knotted to suit the cinder Doctors'
Parking Lot? O yes I'm walking   and we go   I go   5
In   into a whorehouse
And convent rolled
Into   into something   into the slant streets of slum
Atlanta. I've brought the House Mother

A bottle of gin. She goes for ice   10
Rattling the kitchen somewhere over   under
The long cry. Fay hasn't come in
Yet; she's scrubbing
For Doctor Evans. Television bulks as the girls pass
In, rising   15
Up the stairs, and one says to me, What
Say, Good Looking. Something wails like a held-down saint
In Saint Joseph's. The kids, the Mother   the House
Mother says, all act like babies these days. Some of them are, I say
In a low scream. Not all, she says, not all.   20
You ever been a nurse?
I ask. No; my husband was in wholesale furniture.
Passed away last year of a kidney
Disease; they couldn't do anything for him
At all: he said you go and work   25
With those girls who've been so good
To me. And here I am, Good
Looking. Fay ought to be
Here in a little while.
The girls that went up are coming   30
Down, turning the leaves
Of the sign-out book. You waiting for Fay? Yes.
She'll be a little while. O.K.
More ice, to ice-pack
The gin. The last door opens.   35
It is Fay. This night mortality wails out. Who died,
My love? Whom could you not do anything for? Is that some stranger's
Blood on your thigh? O love I know you by the lysol smell you give
Vaseline. Died   died
On the table.   40
She'll just be a minute. These are good girls, the Mother
Says. Fay's a good girl. She's been married; her aunt's
Keeping the kids. I reckon you know that, though. I do,
And I say outside
Of time, there must be some way she can strip   45
Blood off   somebody's blood   strip and comb down and out
That long dark hair. She's overhead

Naked she's streaming
In the long cry   she has her face in her hands
In the shower, thinking of children   50
Her children in and out
Of Saint Joseph's   she is drying   my eyes burn
Like a towel   and perfume and disinfectant battle
In her armpits   she is stamping
On the ceiling to get her shoes to fit: Lord, Lord, where are you,   55
Fay? O yes, you big cow-bodied
Love O yes you have changed
To black   you are in deep
Dark and your pale face rages
With fatigue. Mother   Mother   House   60
Mother of Mercy
Manor, you can have the rest
Of the gin. The cinders of the parking lot are blazing all around
Saint Joseph's; the doctors are leaving. Turn out the light as you go up
To your husband's furniture, and come   65
Here to me, you big
Bosomed hard handed hard
Working worker for Life, you. I'll give you something
Good   something like a long cry
Out over the ashes of cars   something like a scream through
hundreds of bright   70
Bolted-down windows. O take me into
Your black. Without caring, care
For me. Hold my head in your wide scrubbed
Hands bring up
My lips. I wail like all   75
Saint Joseph's   like mortality
This night   and I nearly am dead
In love   Collapsed on the street   struck down
By my heart, with the wail
Coming to me, borne in ambulances voice   80
By voice into Saint Joseph's   nearly dead
On arrival   on the table beyond
All help: She would bend
Over me like this   sink down

With me in her white dress   85
Changing to black   we sink
Down flickering
Like television   like Arthur Godfrey's face
Coming on   huge   happy.
About us   happy   90
About everything   O bring up
My lips   hold them down don't let them cry
With the cry   close   closer   eyeball to eyeball
In my arms, O queen of death
Alive, and with me at the end.   95

———————

Haunting the Maneuvers
1969

Prepared for death and unprepared
For war, there was Louisiana   there was Eisenhower a Lieutenant
Colonel and there was I
As an Invasion Force.   The Defenders were attacking
And I was in the pinestraw   5
Advancing   inching through the aircraft of the Home
Force.   Sacks of flour were bursting
All over the trees. Now if one of them damned things hits you in the head
It's gonna kill you just as sure as if
It was a real bomb   10
So watch it.   Yes Sir.   I was watching
It.   One sack came tumbling after
Me no matter
What.   Not in the head,   though,
I thought thank God at least   15
Not dead.
But I was dead.   The sergeant said go sit
Over there: you are the first man killed.   It's KP for you
For the whole rest of the war.   This war,

Anyway.   Yes Sir.   The Defenders had struck   20
The first blow: I was plastered.   I thought why this
Is easy: there's not a drop
Of blood there's only death
White on me; I can live
Through.   25
                    I lived through in the Hell
Of latrine duty, but mostly on KP, on metal
Trays that dovetailed to each other, stacked by the ton in the field
Kitchens. I moved them all at one time
Or other, and the Defenders   30
Ate   ate and went back to killing
My buddies with blanks and bread. But when I slept on that well
Defended ground   the pinestraw stirred   each needle pointed up
Into the dark like a compass, and white   whiter
Than my skin, edible, human-eyed through the pines,   35
Issued a great mass
Laugh   a great lecture-laugh by the chaplain's one
Dirty joke, I rose
Over the unprepared boys   over the war
Games the war   40
Within a war   over the trucks with mystical signs
On them that said TANK   over World War One
Enfield rifles filled with dud rounds   self-rising
Through the branches   driven up like a small cloud
Of the enemy's food   at the same time bread   45

And bomb, swanned out like a diver, I came
From my death over both sleeping armies,
Over Eisenhower dreaming of invasion.   Where are you,
My enemy?   My body won't work any more
For you: I stare down like stars   50
Of yeast: you will have to catch me,
And eat me.   Where are you, invading
Friends?   Who else is dead?   O those who are in this
With me, I can see nothing
But what is coming   can say   55
Nothing but what the first-killed

Working hard all day for his vision
Of war says best: the age-old Why
In God's name Why
In Louisiana, Boys   O Why
In Hell are we doing this?

60

————

Apollo
1969, 1970

I. For the First Manned Moon Orbit

So long
So long as the void
Is hysterical, bolted out, you float on nothing

But procedure alone,

Eating, sleeping like a man
Deprived of the weight of his own
And all humanity in the name
Of a new life
and through this, making new
Time slowly, the moon comes.
Its mountains bulge
They crack they hold together
Closer   spreading   smashed crust
Of uncanny rock   ash-glowing   alchemicalizing the sun
With peace: with the peace of a country
Bombed-out by the universe.
You lean back from the great light-
shattered face   the pale blaze
Of God-stone coming

5

10

15

Close   too close, and the dead seas turn
The craters hover   turn

20

Their dark side to kill
The radio, and the one voice
Of earth.
You and your computers have brought out   25
The silence of mountains the animal
Eye has not seen since the earth split.
Since God first found geometry
Would move   move
In mysterious ways. You hang   30

Mysteriously, pulling the moon-dark pulling,
And solitude breaks down
Like an electrical system: it is something

Else: nothing is something
Something I am trying   35
To say O God

Almighty! To come back! To complete the curve   to come back
Singing with procedure   back through the last dark
Of the moon, past the dim ritual
Random stones of oblivion, and through the blinding edge   40
Of moonlight into the sun

And behold

The blue planet steeped in its dream

Of reality, its calculated vision shaking with
The only love.   45

II. The Moon Ground

You look as though
You know me, though the world we came from is striking
You in the forehead like Apollo. Buddy,
We have brought the gods. We know what it is to shine
Far off, with earth. We alone   50
Of all men, could take off
Our shoes and fly. One-sixth of ourselves, we have gathered,
Both of us, under another one
Of us overhead. He is reading the dials he is understanding
Time, to save our lives. You and I are in earth   55
light and deep moon
shadow on magic ground
Of the dead new world, and we do not but we could
Leap over each other, like children in the universal playground
of stones   60
but we must not play
At being here: we must look
We must look for it: the stones are going to tell us
Not the why but the how of all things. Brother, your gold face flashes
On me. It is the earth. I hear your deep voice rumbling from the body   65
Of its huge clothes   Why did we come here
It does not say, but the ground looms, and the secret
Of time is lying
Within amazing reach. It is everywhere

We walk, our glass heads shimmering with absolute heat   70
And cold. We leap slowly
Along it. We will take back the very stones
Of Time, and build it where we live. Or in the cloud
striped blue of home, will the secret crumble
In our hands with air? Will the moon-plague kill our children   75
In their beds? The Human Planet trembles in its black
Sky with what we do   I can see it hanging in the god-gold only
Brother of your face. We are this world: we are
The only men. What hope is there at home
In the azure of breath, or here with the stone   80
Dead secret? My massive clothes bubble around me
Crackling with static and Gray's
Elegy helplessly coming
From my heart, and I say I think something
From high school I remember Now   85
Fades the glimmering landscape on the sight, and all the air
A solemn stillness holds. Earth glimmers
And in its air-color a solemn stillness holds
It. O brother! Earth-faced god! APOLLO! My eyes blind
With unreachable tears   my breath goes all over   90
Me and cannot escape. We are here to do one
Thing only, and that is rock by rock to carry the moon to take it
Back. Our clothes embrace we cannot touch we cannot
Kneel. We stare into the moon
dust, the earth-blazing ground. We laugh, with the beautiful craze   95
Of static. We bend, we pick up stones.

––––––––––––

Camden Town

1970

—Army Air Corps, Flight Training, 1943—

With this you trim it. Do it right and the thing'll fly
Itself. Now get up there and get those lazy-
eights down. A check-ride's coming at you

Next week.
       I took off in the Stearman like stealing two hundred and twenty
         horses   5
Of escape from the Air Corps.
                        The cold turned purple with the open
          Cockpit, and the water behind me being
     The East, dimmed out.   I put the nose on the white sun
       And trimmed the ship.   The altimeter made me   10
   At six thousand feet.   We were stable: myself, the plane,
          The earth everywhere
         Small in its things with cold
       But vast beneath.   The needles on the panel
     All locked together, and a banner like World War One   15
  Tore at my head, streaming from my helmet in the wind.
       I drew it down: down under the instruments
    Down where the rudder pedals made small corrections
    Better than my feet   down where I could ride on faith
       And trim, the aircraft slightly cocked   20
      But holding the West by a needle.   I was in
  Death's baby machine, that led to the fighters and bombers,
      But training, here in the lone purple,
  For something else.   I pulled down my helmet-flaps and droned
         With fight-sleep.   Near death   25
      My watch stopped.   I knew it, for I felt the Cadet
    Barracks of Camden die like time, and "There's a war on"
   Die, and no one could groan from the dark of the bottom
       Bunk to his haggard instructor, I tried
       I tried to do what you said   I tried   tried   30
  No;   never.   No one ever lived to prove he thought he saw
  An aircraft with no pilot showing: I would have to become
  A legend, curled up out of sight with all the Western World
Coming at me under the floor-mat, minute after minute, cold azures,
        Small trains and warbound highways,   35
  All entering flight-sleep.   Nothing mattered but to rest in the winter
         Sun beginning to go
  Down early.   My hands in my armpits, I lay with my sheep-lined head
        Next to the small air-moves
    Of the rudder pedals, dreaming of letting go   letting go   40

The cold   the war   the Cadet Program and my peanut-faced
Instructor and his maps.   No maps   no world   no love
But this.   Nothing can fail when you go below
The instruments.   Wait till the moon.   Then.   Then.
But no.   When the waters of Camden Town died, then so   45
Did I, for good.   I got up bitterly, bitter to be
Controlling, re-entering the fast colds
Of my scarf, and put my hands and feet where the plane was made
For them.   My goggles blazed with darkness as I turned,
And the compass was wrenched from its dream   50
Of all the West.   From luxurious
Death in uncaring I swung
East, and the deaths and nightmares
And training of many.

———————

Exchanges

1970

—Phi Beta Kappa Poem, Harvard, 1970—

Being in the form of a dead-living dialogue with Joseph Trumbull Stickney (1874–1904).
Stickney's words are in italics.

Under the cliff, green powered in from the open,
Changed   and she
And I crouched at the edge
Five hundred feet above the ocean's suicide in a horizon
And bubble of oil.   Smog and sweet love!   We had the music for the whale-   5
death of the world. About us the environment crumbled
In yellow light. There was no forth-
coming of wave-silver, but silver would flash now
And then through, turning side-on in many mullet
To the sun to die, as I tuned   10
The wild guitar. This won't get any worse

Until tomorrow, I said
Of Los Angeles, gazing out through "moderate eye
damage"   twisting the pegs   and under the strings

—The gray crane spanned his level, gracious flight   15

Knowing better than to come
To rest on anything, or touch
Zuma Point here and now.

—O sea

Of California, thou Pacific,   20
For which the multitude of mortals bound
Go trembling headlong and with terrific
Outcry are drowned:
Day-moon meant more
Far from us   dazing the oil-slick with the untouched remainder   25
Of the universe   spreading   contracting
Catching fish at the living end
In their last eye   the guitar rang moon and murder
And Appalachian love, and sent them shimmering from the cliff

—The burning season shone   30
On the vast feather-shapes of the open
Sea tranquilized by off-
shore drilling
where gulls flapped in black
Gold   black   35
Magic of corporations—

—So here did mix the land's breath and the sea's:
Among the beautiful murders
Showering down ballad
After ballad on the rainbows of forever lost   40
Petroleum that blew its caps and turned on
All living things, we sang and prayed for purity, scattered everywhere
Among the stones
Of other worlds   and asked the moon to stay off us

As far as it always had, and especially far   45
From L.A.   I playing from childhood also
Like the Georgia mountains   the wind out of Malibu whipped her
Long hair into "Wildwood Flower"   her blue eye   —*whose eye*
Was somewhat strangely more than blue
Closed   50
                    —*and if we lived*
We were the cresting of a tide wherein
An endless motion rose exemplified.
                                        In

            —*The gentle ecstasy of earth*   ·   55
        And ruination, we lay on the threatened grass
Of cliffs, she tangled in my strings, her dark hair tuned
            To me, the mountains humming back
            Into resolution, in the great low-crying key
            Of A.   60

        —*I saw the moon and heard her sing.*
        I saw her sing and heard the moon.

            O vibrating mountains and bronze
        Strings, O oil-slicks in the moderately damaged eye
                And the sides of fish flashing out   65
One more time   birds black with corporations, turn me over to those

    —*Maddened with hunger for another world:*
                                        She lies in Glendale,
        In Forest Lawn.
                                        O astronauts,   70
                Poets, all those
Of the line of wizards and saviors, spend your lives
            And billions of dollars to show me
                The small true world
                Of death, the place we sang to   75
        From Zuma.   I read and imagine everything
            I can of the gray airless ground
        Of the moon   sphere cracked and bombarded
        By negation   pure death, where death has not

Yet come 80
   —where yet no god appears
        Who knows?
There might be some unknown
Consolation in knowing California
  Is not the deadest world of all 85
Until tomorrow: might be some satisfaction
  Gone spatial some hope
Like absolute zero, when the earth can become

   —The last of earthly things
  Carelessly blooming in immensity 90
      and live men ride
Fleeing outward
  —a white flame tapering at the core of space their hatches
  —Firm-barred against the fearful universe until
   In the easy-leaping country 95
 Of death, beings—*still armored in their visionary gold*
Do human deeds.
   What deeds?
    Will Los Angeles rise from the Sea
  Of Tranquillity, on a great bubble 100
  Of capped breath and oil? Not yet;
  The first men will see that desolation
  Unimproved, before the freeways
  Link it to Earth. Ah, to leap or lie
   On some universal ruin 105
Not ruined by us! To be able to say—*Am I dead*
  That I'm so far?
    But where I stand,
Here, under the moon, the moon
 —Breaks desperate magic on the world I know, 110

On Glendale. *—All through the shadows crying grows, until*
 The wailing is like grass upon the ground.
      It is I
Howling like a dog for the moon, for Zuma Point no matter what
 The eye-damage howling to bring her back note 115

By note like a childhood mountain
In the key of A   or, lacking that, howling
For anything   for the ultimate death   pure death
For the blaze of the outer dark   for escape
From L.A. smoldering and eye-   120
burning along the freeways   from rubber-smoke
And exhaust streaming *into the endless shadow*
Of my memory.   —Let me grind alone
And turn my knuckles in the granite
Of the moon   125
                        where underfoot the stones
—*wild with mysterious truth*
                                lie in their universal
            Positions, in a place of no breath
And one machine   130
                    and for these reasons and many
            Another I was quartered and drawn
To Cape Canaveral, with my tangled dream of Los Angeles
And death and the moon, my dead girl still tuned to me
    In my tangled guitar.   The environment crumbled   135
            In red light, and raised up by dawn
Almighty buildings.
                        —*I felt a time like tremor in my limbs.*
        I wished to be bound that morning
    For the true dead land, the land made to sustain   140
        No life at all, giving out the unruined light
That shines on the fish slicks of Zuma.
                        —*Are we the people of the end?*
                                Before us all
            The sun burst   145

From a machine   timed   slowly   tilting   leaning
Upward   drawn moonward inch by inch   faster
    Faster   a great composite roar battered
        Like a board at the very bone
        Marrow, and in the hardshell case   150
    I sat on, the strings vibrated not with
Mountains   but made the shapeless and very

1968–1973   :   463

Music of the universal

    Abyss

              —and all the air   155

Was marvelous and sorrowful

                        as we beheld,

Exploding with solitude   blasting into the eyes and body,

    Rising   rising in dreadful machine-

pain as we prayed   as the newsmen fell to their knees   as the quality

    of life   160

        And death changed forever

For better or worse

        —Apollo springing naked to the light.

        Nothing for me

      Was solved.   I wandered the beach   165

         Mumbling to a dead poet

    In the key of A, looking for the rainbow

         Of oil, and the doomed

  Among the fish.

             —Let us speak softly of living.   170

The Angel
1970

At the edge of dusk, at the hour

When daylight sings under its breath,

When neither day nor night

Has power over the other,

At the hour one knows no more   5

The god one was by chance,

At the hour when one hesitates

To believe one is self-betrayed,

—In the shadow of my shadow, an angel,

The most beautiful ever beheld,   10

An angel of utter whiteness,
—Angel of snow, of winter—
Came suddenly to murmur
My name, in the shadow that I was.
It was the time of twilight   15
When fear comes on, and one hesitates
To believe that one was, once
He who wished to outlive us.

It was that solitude
Of the day singing under its breath,   20
That moment, that silence
Where, on one side, daylight is lost,
And on the other, darkness waits.
But when the angel had said my name
It was no longer night or day;   25
All things had changed their colors
And came from another world
—From a world where one has no look,
Where the hand is no longer a hand,
Where shadow no longer seeks shadow   30
To become what it was.

The angel had folded its wings
To look like everyone else;
It held them under its arms
Or they would have flown away.   35
It put its steps into mine,
And its steps were of silence,
Of the silence of a snowy day,
Though this was an evening in spring.
The lovely white angel in my shadow   40
Under its footsteps left shining
Only a long trail of white shadows.

It had said my name. There was
A star which came into the sky,
And then another, still another,   45
And then so many one could not see

The sky, but a huge thicket of stars
Who most beautiful formed
All the letters of my name.
And now it was totally night,   50
And I walked with my eyes closed
And my hand in the hand of my angel.

All the silence was of snow,
Like a snow in springtime,
All the night was a silence   55
And the silence was in me
And was only my own silence,
When my angel of silence,
My angel of snow and winter,
Left my shadow for his   60
And spread out his wings and took me
Into their clearness of light
And bore me so far from the sky
That I thought I had died of myself.

Then, suddenly, I saw appear   65
All those who wore my face
And who no longer looked like me,
Those whom I never had been,
Those whom I had hoped for in myself,
Those I had waited for elsewhere,   70
Those who had sought me in vain
And had not recognized me,
Those who always wear the mask
Of unforeseeable meetings,
Those of pure chance, of first love   75
Those that one holds to one's heart,
And of whom the heart can know nothing.
Those of whose love one can die
When love is that kind of wound,
That absence, that solitude,   80
A great cry into solitude
Which one is alone in hearing.
They were there, all my faces

That I had not suffered or been.
They were all my likenesses   85
But I did not know them.

A voice sought in mine
All the voices of those faces,
And I heard their voices singing
In the songs that the white angel   90
Sang, in the sky's black depths.
And I heard all those voices
In those I had caused to fall silent
Without knowing, without hearing them,
One evening of my adolescence   95
When I thought I held in myself
All those by whom I was loved.
All those to whom I was promised
Without knowing, of the heart of nothing,
At the heart of rejoicing oblivion   100
Where neither night nor day is
—An evening of my adolescence
At the hour when day and night
Do not know that there is a sharing
More difficult than confession,   105
When one is bewildered by mystery
—When my mystery summoned together
So many faces on mine,
So many unseeing faces
To whom I was not permitted   110
To give their flesh and their sight
Then, the angel reappeared
And said to me: "Regret nothing
When you have nothing to regret!
Who gave you the right to live?   115
You have never had such a right
Since it is conceded to no one,
Since it is bought only
With the lead of false coin.
We should accept undergoing   120
Everything that we must suffer

To deprive our existence of breath.
You have never had the right to live.
You have not had time to choose,
Since, to live, one first must choose.   125
You have not chosen your ghost,
Or your double, or your witness;
You have not chosen your suffering,
You have not chosen that child
Who decided your destiny   130
(He was upright, against a tree,
And watched, between the branches,
The roads that led into Heaven
As the night made more of them);
You have not chosen your love,   135
Or even the shadow of love
—You have not even chosen yourself
From among those of whom you desired
Your endless fulfillment.
But the one that deep in yourself   140
You breathe, the invisible one that I see,
The one that makes my wings beat
In the exact wind of your heart,
The one that guards over the silence
To which you should be devoted,   145
At the heart of white, utter limbo,
At the heart of all-hallowed limbo
The one that you could not conquer:
Will you tell me, heart against heart,
What your remorse has made of him?"   150
And the angel beat his wings
And fled as one dies,
Repeating my name most softly
Where my body was multiplied
In a kingdom of clouds   155
And there was no other star
Than mine, in the heaven of my name.

And now, when the hour comes back
When Heaven sings under its breath,

When neither daylight nor dark   160
Has power over the other,
When my own mystery confounds me,
I feel pass over my face
The shadow of so many likenesses,
Of so many lost profiles,   165
That I no longer know who I am:
This exile who gazes at me
With all the eyes he has given me
Which can no longer open,
Or the stranger that I look upon   170
With a look that is not mine
And reveals to me nothing at all
But a shade where my shadow is lost.

Kamikaze

1971

And I shudder
        and come to my senses—Look!

His elbows dug into the green table,
a former kamikaze pilot—a dead man, Japanese,
truly—is talking about Raskolnikov.   5
At a "Symposium on the Novel," he's forty-five,
an old man. He's like
polite sobbing . . .
        he's like a scream
strangled by a necktie. And through us   10
and somewhere past us,
through shimose flak and the shade of Lazo,
like the yellow shine of Hiroshima,
reeling,
        his face flies past.   15
But in his throat you can't tell

whether it's a lump of tears
or a cough-lump, or what.
                              The Emperor wanted him to grow up
humble, his death already assigned . . .   20
                              a kamikaze.
Sure, it's great to swim along
hands and bouquets, to be slapped on the back by the military
there, at the parade. Sure,
it's fine to be a "hero of the people." But hero   25
in the name of *what?*
                              With a few buddies,
this one shucked off his hero-status
and said he'd just as soon stay
alive.   30
        That took more guts than exploding
for a god-damned lie!
                              I'm supposed to be hell-for-leather
myself,
            but what of my life and death, really?   35
What *do* I think, sinful and mortal,
among sinful, mortal people?
                              We're all assigned our deaths . . .
We're kamikazes. The "divine wind" . . .
the wind of death whistles in our ears: 40
every footfall on this bomb-cratered planet
is a step toward death.
                              So what if I get busted-up and crushed
but not because a dictator says so? I'll pull the control column
up by the roots   45
            firewall the throttle
on collision course, and go out
like the last battering ram.

                    But sons, daughters,
descendants,   50
            though my body sifts down in ashes, I'd like,
from the scraps of my plane, something good to explode
through to you.
            How strange it is, though,

to seem to yourself always dying   55
                                        in the sky for not

anything! To turn out to be lied-to
And still living in the face of your death-
assignment, and to be evil
as well! Yes, a living evil   60
long since supposed to be gone!

————————

Pitching and Rolling

1971

Here we go! We're RE-E-ELING!
                        The glass-framed instructions
                                        rip off their nails.—
A Spidola record player bashes you in the head
                        with Doris Day.—   5
Borscht, lazing in the galley,
                        takes off straight up, splashing madly—
A bay leaf from the borscht,
                        stuck to the ceiling, steams.
Reel on! buddy!   10
      Sure; you'd like to catch hold of a bush or some grass with your hands!
The cabin boy staggers.
                        The helmsman staggers.
                                        The boatswain staggers.
                                                I'm staggering—   15
The waves like wolfhounds—
                        You're just the same, Twentieth Century,
right-left
                left-right
                                up-down   20
                                        down-up—
Reeling!
        All instructions shatter—
                        all the portraits smash to hell!

Faces are death   white drawn   wasted   25
                              under the stern, a rat-like screech
And all over the place it's dense with kasha
                              with downwind screams
nothing but pitching and rolling, staggering, curving
with the taste of sick stomach in your mouth.   30
        Reeling!
                        A barrel jumps down the deck
throwing itself at people.
Hey, old buddies, we're in for it now
                              but keep it cool anyway.   35
Crawl out of your cabins, otherwise
                              it's *kaput* for us all.
Reeling . . .
            But the eyes of the harpooner
                              a ringtailed roarer   40
are strained, and his forelock's standing straight up.
He makes a soundless sign to the sailors
                              and steals sideways
with a rope
            to the flipped out barrel   45
and pitches himself like a cat
                        splitting open the crowd,
For he knows, you bastard pitch and roll, things can get rough—
He's learned by heart, right through his skin, his red head,
He's had it beat down through his skull: 50
Either you jump on the barrel
                or it'll jump all over you!
We're reeling!
            But the barrel's still, it's no longer running wild . . .
We're reeling!   55
            Clear weather won't run off from us . . .
Reeling!
        We may be seasick, darkness in front of our eyes—
But we'll out-reel you
                        bad trip   60
                anyway . . .

Assignation

1971

No, no! Believe me!
               I've come to the wrong place!
I've made a god-awful mistake! Even the glass
In my hand's an accident
                 and so's the gauze glance   5
Of the woman who runs the joint.
                     "Let's dance, huh?
You're pale . . .
           Didn't get enough sleep?"
And I feel like there's no place   10
To hide, but say, anyway, in a rush
"I'll go get dressed . . .
             No, no . . . it's just
That I ended up out of bounds . . ."
And later, trailing me as I leave: 15
             "This is where booze gets you . . .
What do you mean, 'not here'? *Right* here! Right here every time!
You bug everybody, and you're so satisfied
With yourself about it. Zhenichka,
You've got a problem."   20
             I shove the frost of my hands
Down my pockets, and the streets around are snow,
Deep snow.   I dive into a cab.   Buddy, kick this thing! Behind the Falcon
There's a room.   They're supposed to be waiting for me there.
She opens the door   25
         but what the hell's wrong with her?
Why the crazy look?
            "It's almost five o'clock.
You sure you couldn't come a little later?
Well, forget it.   Come on in.   Where else could you go now?"   30
Shall I explode
        with a laugh
           or maybe with tears?
I tell you I was scribbling doggerel
              but I got lost someplace.   35

I hide from the eyes. Wavering I move backwards:
"No, no! Believe me! I've come to the wrong place!"
Once again the night

          once again snow
and somebody's insolent song   40
and somebody's clean, pure laughter.
I could do with a cigarette.
In the blizzard Pushkin's demons flash past
And their contemptuous, bucktoothed grin
Scares me to death.   45
                    And the kiosks
And the drugstores
                and the social security offices
Scare me just as much . . .
                    No, no!   Believe me!   I've ended up   50
In the wrong place again . . .
                    It's *horrible* to live
And even more horrible
                  not to live . . .
                            Ach, this being homeless   55
Like the Wandering Jew. . . Lord!   Now I've gotten myself
Into the wrong century
                  wrong epoch
                      geologic era
                              wrong number   60
The wrong place again
              I'm wrong
                    I've got it wrong . . .
I go, slouching my shoulders like I'd do
if I'd lost some bet,   65
              and Ah, I know it. . . everybody knows it . . .
I can't pay off.

[In aircraft, the newest,
inexorable models]

1971

In aircraft, the newest, inexorable models,
I was zooming up like passion,
Flying from hope to hope,
Killing this one, then that one.

But hope was in the middle,   5
Beyond this flinging and the take-off markers,
Like a seal on a chip of ice
With its sad muzzle lifted.

I pressed my lip to my lip   10
On the bitter sweetness of flight
Candy, but got scared quick, bursting with a double-love
Like an empty aerogram.

Tenderness called me like the void
Into the rustling of fallen-off clothes,   15
But the touch of any hope plunged me
Again into hopelessness.

I sped back and forth in a sick panic,
With a hard-hit mask of a face,
With a mind split two ways,   20
Both ways false.

Look: once through the whirling of the earth
I saw from a taxi window
That a center-split pine
Moaned by the road like a lyre.   25

So you see it wasn't *that* crazy
That, a flying Wandering Jew, I
Involved the sky—right?—I said
The sky, in my private life.

And the straight routes of the flights slice through   30
The downpours, now here, now there—you almost want to cut them,
Like the strings of a groaning lyre
Between two hopeless hopes.

———————

Doing the Twist on Nails
1971

When you throw your dancing shoes out, back over your shoulder,
And lose yourself, you find yourself twisting on the stage,
                    dancing,
                      dancing,
                        dancing—   5
let that pink boy whip you around—I can tell you:
Life doesn't dance this way—
        That way dances death.
Thighs
        shoulders   10
                breasts:
                    they're all in it!
Inside you, dead drunk,
                wheezes of air are dancing
Somebody else's ring   15
            dances on your hand,
And your face by itself
            doesn't dance at all
Flying, lifelessly, above all the body's life
Like a mask taken off your dead head.   20
And this stage—
           is only one part of that cross
On which they once
           crucified Jesus;
The nails shot through to the other side, and you began   25
To dance on them,
           sticking out.

                                    And you dance
On the nails
              nails   30
On sandals red as rust
                     on the thorn-points of tears: Listen,
Because I once loved you, tiresomely, gloomily,
I also hammered the crooks of my nails
                                    into this page.   35
Ah, bestial, beastly music,
                     do you keep on getting stronger?
No one can see the blood
                     ooze from your foot-soles—
To wash the steps with clean water,   40
I'd rather you'd do it, Mary Magdalene,
                                    not Jesus.
I'll wash all their days, their yesterdays, not like a brother would
For a sister,
              but like a sister for a sister.   45
I'll kneel down and pick up your feet
And hold them quietly, and with kisses try to do something
About their wounds.

———————

[I dreamed I already loved you]
1971

I dreamed I already loved you.
I dreamed I already killed you.

But you rose again; another form,
A girl on the little ball of the earth,
Naive simplicity, curve-necked   5
On that early canvas of Picasso,
And prayed to me with your ribs
"Love me," as though you said, "Don't push me off."

I'm that played out, grown-up acrobat,
Hunchbacked with senseless muscles,   10
Who knows that advice is a lie,
That sooner or later there's falling.

I'm too scared to say I love you
Because I'd be saying I'll kill you.

For in the depths of a face I can see through   15
I see the faces—can't count them—
Which, right on the spot, or maybe
Not right away, I tortured to death.

You're pale from the mortal balance. You say
"I know everything; I was all of them.   20
I know you've already loved me.
I know you've already killed me.
But I won't spin the globe backwards
We're on: Love again, and then kill again."

Lord, you're young. Stop your globe.   25
I'm tired of killing. I'm not a damn thing but old.

You move the earth beneath your little feet,
You fall, "Love me."
It's only in those eyes—so similar—you say
"This time don't kill me."   30

[Poetry gives off smoke]
1971

But only the divine word . . .
Pushkin

Poetry gives off smoke
but it doesn't die out.
It acts kind of crazy, flutteringly,
when it chooses us.
     This fellow's no fool,   5
sucking tranquillizers,
toting in a little briefcase
a boiled beet-root.
      Right now he'd like a mousse
or baba au rhum,   10
    but the Muse—
       some kind of Muse!—
grabs him
   by the scruff of the neck!
Thoughts drill a hole in his forehead,   15
and he's mislaid the spoon—
and he's a giant! Socrates, for the Lord's sake . . .
in an Oblomov dust-jacket. O.K. . . .
he's no Apollo—
      he's puny and ugly,   20
skinny: he's like a golden mushroom,
unsteady . . .
   transparent.
But suddenly some sort of whistling
is in his ears, and then . . .   25
      a period!
And like a slugger's hook
      across the chops of the ages,
a line!
    And there   30
    an insane little bird

falls off its feet,
        a crazy rag-picker,
              drunk,
a kind of society clown. But something gives her the word   35
and—
      like branches in winter,
God rings from within, and her eyelids turn
to marble.
        And here's a bum   40
             a shaman,
really—
      from among the lunatics!
Pour him champagne,
         bring him   45
women, not rum cakes!
          Suddenly an order from within
will come through sternly, and he's the instant
voice of the people, damned near
Savonarola!   50
Poetry acts kind of strange, it flutters
when it chooses us.
And it has no mercy, either,
afterwards. It stamps "Pure Souls"
on us . . . but who's the judge?   55
         Yes,
for the horse-blinkered multitudes we're "decadents,"
but for our*selves,* we ourselves are . . . are . . .
well, yes! Redemption!

In the Wax Museum at Hamburg

1971

Full of blocky majesty,
arrogant, dock-tailed,
German princes glower

at the Russian communist.
                              All the presidents,   5
chancellors
                    in their different kinds of gut-
meanness look darkly out
                              each his own kind,
his caste, and all their crooked   10
vulgarity is in that.
                    These are the wounders
of life. They warped it,
                              suffocated it, and so
they're immortalized here—   15
                              or, no,
they're waxed.
                    In the midst of these grown fat
these greasy fools, and emaciated, malicious monsters
how did you fall,   20
                    Schiller?
How about you,
                    Mozart?
You should have landed
                              in luminous meadows;   25
Should have come down among
                              deep-woods flowers.
But you're here—
                    my old buddies,
Enemies—   30
                    the whole damned lot. The enemies' looks are trying
To kill me, but it's not so bad,
This not being liked
                              by Bismarck, and surely not
By Hitler.   35
                    I keep looking, and gradually I see,
Among them like fatal ghosts,
                              the shaped, candle-stick figures
Of enemies
                    still living. Yes. Still living.   40
There's one
                    premier,

There's another one, and *he's*
No shining example
          and he's not either.   45
But maybe they *are*
          examples: yes,
but of the mean, the cruel,
the phony . . .
I'd like to get them here *themselves,*   50
Into the wax museum
          by the scruff of the neck,
By the seat of the britches!
          It'd be great
To arrange 'em according to their crimes—   55
And let 'em be buried in wax
          as ugly as *they* are!
I tell you, the wax museum is wild
For more bums and bastards!
          Me,   60
I'm sick and tired of 'em! Sons-of-bitches
Have been lying to us too damned long!
It's time to drown 'em alive—
Right! In wax!
          Let wax plaster their mouths   65
Shut, let it stop their hands
          where they are
          and let them stand
Still
   still   70
      very still
And dead
      like good little children
          very still
          very   75
Obedient.
      Right here and now I'm coming out with my program
For revolution! I call on
EVERYONE! Drag 'em from their platform,
And while you're doing it, laugh and whistle   80

As loud as you can!
                    Go *get* 'em,
People! Let's have a little more
Pure rage!

                    It's time to pull down all this trash   85
From their easy chairs
                    like pulling nails and being crazy
About pulling nails!
                    It's time, under hot bright lights,
To drag down out of their balconies   90
This collection of stupid faces
Like carp from scummy green pools.
It's time, it's really time at last
To get rid of junk like this!
                    Into the wax museum   95
Of liars
          with these priests of a lousy temple!
People!
        SAY IT!
                    Don't clam up!   100
                              Into the wax museum
With all heads of state
Who're headless!
                    And if somebody lies, even
if he does it in a new way,   105
                    then
Stuff his gullet with wax!
                    Into the wax museum!
There's still a lot of bullshit around,
And plenty of liars . . . Hey,   110
BEES! Get off your ass!
Wax, little brothers! We need it!

Idol

1971

Down in the pine needles
in the snowstorm-stogged ravine
an Evenki idol stands
fixing his eyes on the *taiga*.

Aggressively squinting,   5
he watched until the time came
when Evenki women started
hauling presents to him.

They brought him mukluks and parkas,
they brought him honey and fur,   10
figuring that he'd pray
but mainly think for them all.

In the dark assurance
that he'd understand,
they'd smear his mouth   15
with warm deer blood.

But what could he do, the phony
little god,
with his fierce, wooden
whittled-down soul?   20

Now he's looking through the branches,
abandoned and dead.
No one believes in him;
no one prays to him.

Did I just dream this up? At night   25
In his ravine, far off yonder,
he sets his eyes
on fire, overgrown with moss,

And listening to the snowstorm
blast down, licks   30
his lips. Lord, I know it.
He wants blood.

————

Old Bookkeeper

1971

I don't have any pain. None at all.
Really, I don't estimate anything
unnecessary. Cramming a pillow under the seat
of my pants, I sit down in black oversleeves.

Here the same signatures and stamps   5
are. On the table papers rustle,
rustle, tired out, and so sadly
rustle, saying I'll be sixty. Soon.

Ah, the Chief—he's young! Powerful!
Today like always, shaved just so . . .   10
Fiddling with rosaries made out of
papcr clips, talking to mc about football.

Ah, the Chief! . . . he's clean *enough*,
and not so *much* of a son-of-a-bitch,
but I can see everything he's trying to hide   15
under that slick shine, his face.

Ah, the Chief—How easy he is
on himself! He wears those signet rings!
Only he don't walk so straight
in his beautiful new suede shoes!   20

I'll leave this little office. I'll smile,
not knowing why, at spring,

and get on the train that goes out
to Mytischchi, and everywhere farther away.

I'll get off where four ugly women   25
Live by the river. They're old, too.
One of them's gotten so tired that
any day I'll ask her to marry me.

And when I go back to my closet   30
in stillness that reminds me of "Prima,"
from the big wormy chest of drawers
I'll take out one snapshot.

There, hands propped on clumsy hipbones,
looking straight into History   35
at its worst, I stand, a civil guardsman,
not young, in the great year '41.

I'll hear the rumble of planes,
shots and wild songs in the wind,
and my lips will whisper something,   40
but I can't make it out, myself.

———————

At the Military Registration and Enlistment Center

1971

To the low cradle-song of the rails,
like a bone-tired oiler of expresses,
Zima Station slept on and on.
And the steeple on the District Soviet slept,
and a drunk slept in the cunette   5
and the watchman by the Grain Storage Center.

Like a Zima man, no Muscovite,
I walked and walked, breathing the smoke from my tobacco,
through the rustle of leaves and through somebody's dreams.
The rain touched the snare of the tin roofs . . .   10
And suddenly I heard a woman:
"Ah, if only there wasn't a war."

The moon slipped through piles of straw,
through little porches, shutters, slatted fences,
and, stopped right in my latest tracks,   15
sensing something of the future, I saw—
beheld, maybe—like a sad shade of the night,
a woman: one.

She was listening to something hidden in everything
that was dozing off. Her age; well, she was getting on   20
with it: fifty, at least; maybe more.
She was running along the handrails
with her palm, in a special way, a widow's way,
under the weathered-out signboard on the building:
"The Zima Military Registration and Enlistment Office."   25
Most likely she was coming from work
when something overran her, pushed her like a wave
to those handrails . . . in her the war came back
to life:
            a war without flags, without bands,   30
a war that had taken her breadwinner.
                                    And here,
leaning on the handrails
—the same ones, the same as before—
she sent a prayer down the tracks after her husband,   35
and then walked on, heavy with child
and with a right hand whose strength had gone
touched you, handrails, again, and in her left
like death, she held
a Notice: the Notice of all   40
Notices.
            Ah, if only there wasn't a war!
(His hands held an accordion)

If only there wasn't . . .
   (and a spoon stuck in his right boot)   45
      . . . a war, if only there wasn't . .
   (a crumb of tobacco on his lip)
      . . . a war . . .
   (He was loud when he was drunk a little,—
   "Now don't you worry about Leshka!   50
   Not a damn thing's going to happen."—
   but in his eyes, a deep pain,
   looking out.)
   Ah, if only there wasn't a war!

————

The Heat in Rome

1971

Monks,
      all soutanes left to the devil,
Dive into those Roman fountains!
           All right,
Signor premier-ministro,   5
Into the Po with you! Right down,
Presto-presto! *You!* Get on down
Under it!
      And like burros
             and like mules   10
To the water, ambassadors!
         To the water, ambassadors' wives!
Millionaire,
      holler in sheer confusion,
"Mister, can you spare me some shade?"   15
            Get together for once—big shots
With the simple people!
        O you common sweat!
*Every*thing's sweat-soaked—
        feelings too.   20

Newspapers are sticky underwear:
The Madonna cries . . .
                              A miracle!
                                        Miracle!
But don't you believe it—   25
                    sweat's pouring off her.
Over forty Centigrade . . .
                         the thermometer explodes;
Mercury dances dead-drunk in the dust
Like little world-globes   30
That the countries have all slipped off.
Everything melts to pieces, ravels—
Everything's gotten so soft—
                              even the State.
Gouge off   35
              the temple-marble
And munch it like chewing gum.
                         And the bronze-coated kings,
heroes,
              gods   40
                    are as miserable as
They'll ever be, as if made of plasticine:
Poke 'em with your finger;
                         they'll fall down.
On the Piazza dell' Indipendenza   45
I drown, more helpless than a baby,
                              up to my chest
In melted asphalt.
                 Hey! Anybody!
                              ANYbody!   50
No, damn it—
              Nobody answers.
                              Living independently . . . ?
You could call it
Drowning independently!   55
                         And over it all
A bare-ass poet drones out
                         prophetic lines:
"The cows in the pastures've all rotted,

The Milky Way has curdled in the sky,   60
Peoples and vegetables give off all
Kinds of stinks! Awful currents of air!
SALVATION! It's in peeling off! A mass striptease!
Friends!
                    Romans!   65
                              Don't turn yourselves into corpses!
Don't be afraid of beauty! It's *virginal!*
Only cop-outs wear clothes!
                              Rip off your jockey shorts! Your panties!"
Ladies gasp, "I've *got* to have it! OZONE! Some *Ozone,* for God's sake!"   70
They've announced,
                    giving wings to the tailors,
that the fashionable thing to wear *this* season
Is the dress of the naked king.
                              "Ha HA! All History tells you   75
It's been the *real* fashion
                    for *thousands* of years!"
"O dear deputy of ours, you never take one step
                              into the villages,
but the villages have gotten gut-poor . . .   80
Where is everything you promised?"
"*I* promised?
          Ah yes! Ah yes indeed!—
I forgot . . . but you'll forgive me! It's just this *heat!*"
"Why're you so limp, Baby?   85
                    Can we straighten you out with wine?
Let's lie in the ice-box . . .
                    maybe things'll work out in there . . ."
Deputies before their constituents
                              impotents before their wives   90
Killers before prosecutors
                    lawyers before killers
All justify themselves, good-naturedly as anything:
"There's no *air!* It's stuffy!
                    Stuffy, and hot from lies. RUSSIA!   95
Lend us some of that damned
SNOW!" But rumors're all over—pure gibberish!—that there's no snow
In Russia!

And new rumors
Are flying   100
        circling Rome
That there are no icebergs
At the Poles
                that books are turning green
With mold in the libraries   105
                                that in the museums the colors are dripping
From the pictures.
                                And the weakening City of Night doesn't sleep.
You've got to decide something
Right *now!* Make up your mind, even if those who never drew breath   110
Say, "There's no air to breathe."
                                Lord! From the skin of the world—
Dirty grease!
                If only somebody could *ventilate*
The earth! All planes   115
                missiles
                                destroyers
All submachine guns
                rifles
                                and, with 'em,   120
The false coin of the orator's tongue
                                the bronze brows of heads
Of state who've lost out . . . melt 'em! MELT 'em!
                                                Melt 'em
To make fans!   125
        Fans! Ah, fans!
Fans.
        Maybe it'd help *some* . . .

False Youth

Autumn
Clothes of the Age
1971

for Susan Tuckerman Dickey

Three red foxes on my head, come down
There last Christmas from Brooks Brothers
As a joke, I wander down Harden Street
In Columbia, South Carolina, fur-haired and bald,
Looking for impulse in camera stores and redneck greeting cards.   5
A pole is spinning
Colors I have little use for, but I go in
Anyway, and take off my fox hat and jacket
They have not seen from behind yet.   The barber does what he can
With what I have left, and I hear the end man say, as my own   10
Hair-cutter turns my face
To the floor, Jesus, if there's anything I hate
It's a middle-aged hippie.   Well, so do I, I swallow
Back: so do I   so do I
And to hell.   I get up, and somebody else says   15
When're you gonna put on that hat,
Buddy?   Right now.   Another says softly,
Goodbye, Fox.   I arm my denim jacket
On and walk to the door, stopping for the murmur of chairs,
And there it is   20
              hand-stitched by the needles of the mother
Of my grandson   eagle riding on his claws with a banner
Outstretched as the wings of my shoulders,
Coming after me with his flag
Disintegrating, his one eye raveling   25
Out, filthy strings flying
From the white feathers, one wing nearly gone:
Blind eagle but flying
Where I walk, where I stop with my fox
Head at the glass to let the row of chairs spell it out   30
And get a lifetime look at my bird's

One word, raggedly blazing with extinction and soaring loose
In red threads burning up white until I am shot in the back
Through my wings   or ripped apart
For rags: 35

Poetry.

——————

For the Death of Lombardi
1971

I never played for you.   You'd have thrown
Me off the team on my best day—
No guts, maybe   not enough speed,
Yet running in my mind
As Paul Hornung, I made it here   5
With the others, sprinting down railroad tracks,
Hurdling bushes and backyard Cyclone
Fences, through city after city, to stand, at last, around you
Exhausted,   exalted, pale
As though you'd said "Nice going":   pale   10
As a hospital wall.   You are holding us
Millions together: those who played for you, and those who entered the bodies
Of Bart Starr, Donny Anderson, Ray Nitschke, Jerry Kramer
Through the snowing tube on Sunday afternoon,
Warm, playing painlessly   15
In the snows of Green Bay Stadium, some of us drunk
On much-advertised beer   some old   some in other
Hospitals—most, middle-aged
And at home.   Here you summon us, lying under
The surgical snows.   Coach, look up: we are here: 20
We are held in this room
Like cancer.
The Crab has you, and to him
And to us you whisper
Drive, *Drive.*   Jerry Kramer's face floats near—real, pale—   25

We others dream ourselves
Around you, and far away in the mountains, driving hard
Through the drifts, Marshall of the Vikings, plunging   burning
Twenty-dollar bills to stay alive, says, still
Alive, "I wouldn't be here   30
If it weren't for the lessons of football." Vince, they've told us:
When the surgeons got themselves
Together and cut loose
Two feet of your large intestine, the Crab whirled up   whirled out
Of the lost gut and caught you again   35
Higher up.   Everyone's helpless
But cancer.   Around your bed the knocked-out teeth like hail-pebbles
Rattle down   miles of adhesive tape from hands and ankles
Writhe in the room like vines   gallons of sweat blaze in buckets
In the corners   the blue and yellow of bruises   40
Make one vast sunset around you.   No one understands you.
Coach, don't you know that some of us were ruined
For life?   Everybody can't win.   What of almost all
Of us, Vince?   We lost.   And our greatest loss was that we could not survive
Football. Paul Hornung has withdrawn   45
From me, and I am middle-aged and gray, like these others.
What holds us here? It is that you are dying by the code you made us
What we are by.   Yes, Coach, it is true: love-hate is stronger
Than either love or hate.   Into the weekly, inescapable dance
Of speed, deception, and pain   50
You led us, and brought us here weeping,
But as men.   Or, you who created us as George
Patton created armies, did you discover the worst
In us: aggression   meanness   deception   delight in giving
Pain to others, for money?   Did you make of us, indeed,   55
Figments   over-specialized, brutal ghosts
Who could have been real
Men in a better sense?   Have you driven us mad
Over nothing?   Does your death set us free?

Too late.   We stand here among   60
Discarded TV commercials:
Among beer-cans and razor-blades and hair-tonic bottles,
Stinking with male deodorants: we stand here

Among teeth and filthy miles
Of unwound tapes, novocaine needles, contracts, champagne   65
Mixed with shower-water, unraveling elastic, bloody faceguards,
And the Crab, in his new, high position
Works soundlessly.   In dying
You give us no choice, Coach,
Either.   We've got to believe there's such a thing   70
As winning.   The Sunday spirit-screen
Comes on   the bruise-colors brighten   deepen
On the wall   the last tooth spits itself free
Of a line-backer's aging head   knee-cartilage cracks,
A boy wraps his face in a red jersey and crams it into   75
A rusty locker to sob, and we're with you
We're with you all the way
You're going forever, Vince.

————

The Rain Guitar

1972

—England, 1962—

The water-grass under had never waved
But one way.   It showed me that flow is forever
Sealed from rain in a weir.   For some reason having
To do with Winchester, I was sitting on my guitar case
Watching nothing but eelgrass trying to go downstream with all
    the right motions   5
But one. I had on a sweater, and my threads were opening
Like mouths with rain. It mattered to me not at all
That a bridge was stumping
With a man, or that he came near and cast a fish
    thread into the weir.   I had no line and no feeling.   10
I had nothing to do with fish
But my eyes on the grass they hid in, waving with the one move of trying
To be somewhere else. With what I had, what could I do?

I got out my guitar, that somebody told me was supposed to improve
        With moisture—or was it when it dried out?—and hit the lowest   15
            And loudest chord.   The drops that were falling just then
                Hammered like Georgia railroad track
                With E.   The man went into a kind of fishing
                Turn.   Play it, he said through his pipe.   There
        I went, fast as I could with cold fingers.   The strings shook   20
With drops.   A buck dance settled on the weir.   Where was the city
                Cathedral in all this?
            Out of sight, but somewhere around.
                Play a little more
        Of that, he said, and cast.   Music-wood shone,   25
            Getting worse or better faster than it liked:
                Improvement or disintegration
                Supposed to take years, fell on it
                By the gallon. It darkened and rang
        Like chimes. My sweater collapsed, and the rain reached   30
My underwear. I picked, the guitar showered, and he cast to the mountain
                Music.   His wood leg tapped
            On the cobbles.   Memories of many men
                Hung, rain-faced, improving, sealed-off
        In the weir.   I found myself playing Australian   35
Versions of British marching songs.   Mouths opened all over me; I sang,
                His legs beat and marched
                Like companions.   I was Air Force,
                I said.   So was I; I picked
        This up in Burma, he said, tapping his gone leg   40
            With his fly rod, as Burma and the South
                west Pacific and North Georgia reeled,
            Rapped, cast, chimed, darkened and drew down
                Cathedral water, and improved.

Reunioning Dialogue

1973

—New York, 1972, St. Moritz bar—

Two men meet, by accident or design, in a New York bar almost thirty years after the event they talk about. They were formerly a two-man crew attached to a night-fighter squadron in the Philippines during World War II, and neither has ever been able to ascertain what happened on a particular mission. What happened took place just after the squadron had received, as its official aircraft, the Northrop P-61 Black Widow, the first U.S. plane made specifically for night-fighter and night-intruder work, complete with automatic pilot, new "scan" radar—the Hughes SCR 720—binoculars for the pilot, and many other features not to be found in the A-20's and B-25's hitherto used by such squadrons in the Pacific. The poem is concerned with what they say about that night, and is dedicated to Jack Egginton and Ed Traverse, who lived it.

Didn't we double!

Sure, when we used to lie out under the wing
Double-teaming the Nips near our own hole
In the ground   opening an eye

For the Southern Cross, and we'd see something cut the stars   5

Out into some kind of shape, the shape of a new Widow

Black Widow
and all over the perimeter the ninety millimeters would open

Up on Heaven   the sirens would go off
And we'd know better than not to dive   10
for the palm logs,
The foxhole filled with fear-slime, and lie there,
Brains beating like wings
our new wings from Northrop,
The enemy looking for the aircraft   15
We slept under.
Well, we knew what we wanted,

Didn't we?
                    To get out from under our own wings,
To let them lift us   20
                      together
                              lift us out of the sleep
With a hole in it, and slot back fresh windows and climb in the
     squared-off   cool
         Of the Cross.
                        Angels, Observer!   25
                                Nine thousand angels,
         Pilot! The altitude of the Heavenly Host

     In the Philippines is that completely air-conditioned
Nine thousand feet!
                        I couldn't wait to fool with the automatic
                      pilot,   30
     And I went absolutely crazy over Howard Hughes' last word
     In radar!
                      Remember?
                            We were pulling convoy cover.
By my figures we were seven hundred miles south of base, my eyes
     brilliant sweeps   35
Of electronic yellow, watching the spinner painting-in the fleet,
     The arranged, lingering images of the huge fortunes
     Of war   *the great distances and secret relationships*
Between tankers and troopships   *and on my screen, God's small,*
     brilliant chess-set
                      Of world war, as we sat   40
        Circling
                  relaxing in all the original freshness
          Of the Cross, comfortable and light
      And deadly: night-cool of nine thousand angels
      Over the fleet.   45
                      You called back with clear, new
     Electricity: *Hey, Buddy, how're you liking this?*
     What a war!   *I said.*   *The scope just pulses away*
Like a little old yellow heart.   *The convoy comes in, the convoy goes out*
               And comes right back in for you and me   50
              And Uncle Sam.

It was easy,

Right?   Milk run?   Why, by God, we *flew* on milk!

I cut-in the automatic pilot and leaned back

In the cool of those southern stars, and could have spent the rest of my life   55

Watching the gyros jiggle the wheel

With little moves like an invisible man   like a ghost

Was flying us.   The next thing I knew the intercom busted in

With YOU   I looked down and out

I looked the radar down   60

To the depths of its empty yellow heart.   I didn't have a ship

To my name.

And I said where in Hell

Are we?   Jesus God, I was afraid of my watch   afraid to look

Afraid the son of a bitch had stopped.   But no,   65

Four hours had gone to Hell

Somewhere in the South Pacific.   Our engines were sucking wind,

Running on fumes, and I started calling everything that had a code

Name south of our island.   Nothing.   But I thought of the

five boys

From our squadron   all volleyball players   70

With no heads, and all but one

Island south of us was Japanese   I thought I could hear the sword swish,

But it was a wisp arriving

In my earphones   an American spirit crackling

That we were over Cebu.   They had one strip and no lights,   75

Lumps and holes in the runway and the moon

Almost gone.   I said to the Seabees get me a couple of things

That burn;   I'll try to come down between 'em.

—Can you hold out for fifteen minutes?—

Just about.   80

They doubled.   Two pairs of lights came running.

Together   then split   stopped and gave us five thousand devilish feet

Of blackness laid out maybe on the ground. I said hold on,

Buddy;   this may just be it.   We drifted in   full

Flaps   nose-high   easing   easing   cleared the first lighted jeep   85

Hit and

Bounced   came down again hit a hole
And double-bounced   the great new night-
gathering binoculars came unshipped and banged me in the head
As I fought for hot, heavy ground,   90
Trying to go straight for the rest of my life
For the other jeep,
Doing anything and everything to slaughter
The speed, and finally down
Got down to the speed of a jeep   down   95
Down and turned off into the bushes that'd been pouring
By   pouring with sweat and killed
The engine.   Man, was I shaking!   I couldn't even undo the hatch.
You pounded at me
From underneath.   I'm all right, I said, drawing in the stuffed heat of life,   100
Of my life. I climbed down, rattling the new black
California bolts of the wings.

Buddy, would you sit there and tell me,
How we got over Cebu?   Why, it was the wrong goddamned *island!*
Why didn't you give me a course   105
Correction?   Our million dollar Black Widow bird like to've carried us off
And killed us!   How come you didn't say a thing
For four hours?
                    I'm sorry, Pilot, but that Southern Cross
                    Had the most delicious lungs   110
            For me.   We'd jumped out of our hole
    On wings   the heat was off   and weight, and I could breathe
        At last.   I was asleep.
                                Well, for the Lord's sake,
                Observer   Navigator   Miracle   115
                Map-reader   second half of the best
        Two-man crew in night-fighters, as we sit here
            In Central Park, where on earth in that war
        Have we *been?*
                    I don't know.   I told you I was asleep.   120

Well, Old Buddy, the ghosts had us
For sure, then.   Ghosts and angels.   Nobody else.
I guess   in Central Park   I can tell you, too, after all
These years.   So was I.

———————

Remnant Water

1973

Here in the thrust-green

Grass-wind and thin surface now nearly
Again and again for the instant   .

Each other   hair-lined backwater barely there and it
Utterly: 5
                        this that was deep flashing—
Tiny grid-like waves   wire-touched water—
No more, and comes what is left

Of the gone depths duly arriving
Into the weeds belly-up: 10
                              one carp now knowing grass
And also thorn-shucks and seeds
Can outstay him:
                        next to the slain lake the inlet
Trembles   seine-pressure in something of the last   15
Rippling   grass in the slow-burning

Slow-browning dance learned from green;
A hundred acres of canceled water come down
To death-mud shaking
Its one pool   stomach-pool   holding the dead one diving up   20
Busting his gut in weeds   in scum-gruel glowing with belly-white
Unhooked   around him all grass in a bristling sail taking off back-
blowing.   Here in the dry hood I am watching

Alone, in my tribal sweat   my people gone my fish rolling
Beneath me   and I die   25
Waiting   will wait out
The blank judgment given only
In ruination's suck-holing acre   wait and make the sound surrounding NO

Laugh primally: be
Like an open-gut flash   an open under-   30
water eye with the thumb
pressure to brain the winter-wool head of me,
Spinning my guts with my fish in the old place,
Suffering its consequences, dying,
Living up to it.   35

———————

The Zodiac
1976

This poem is based on another of the same title.
It was written by Hendrik Marsman, who was killed by a torpedo in the North Atlantic in 1940.
It is in no sense a translation, for the liberties I have taken with Marsman's original poem are such that the poem I publish here, with the exception of a few lines, is completely my own.
Its twelve sections are the story of a drunken and perhaps dying Dutch poet who returns to his home in Amsterdam after years of travel and tries desperately to relate himself, by means of stars, to the universe.

—homage to Hendrik Marsman, lost at sea, 1940—

I
The Man I'm telling you about brought himself back alive
A couple of years ago.   He's here,
Making no trouble
over the broker's peaceful
Open-bay office at the corner of two canals   5

That square off and starfish into four streets
    Stumbling like mine-tunnels all over town.

  To the right, his window leaps and blinds
                     and sees
The bridges shrivel on contact with low cloud   10
                  leaning to reach out
  Of his rent-range
           and get to feudal doors:
    Big-rich houses whose thick basement-stones
      Turn water into cement inch by inch   15
    As the tide grovels down.
                When that tide turns
Hé turns left   his eyes back-swivel into his head
    In hangover-pain like the flu   the flu
   Dizzy with tree-tops   20
         all dead, but the eye going
Barely getting   but getting you're damn right but still
   Getting them.
            Trees, all right.   No leaves.   All right,
Trees, stand   25
     and deliver. They stand and deliver
Not much: stand
Wobble-rooted, in the crumbling docks.
             So what?

The town square below, deserted as a Siberian crater, lies in the middle   30
Of his white-writing darkness   stroboscoped   red-stopped by the stammering
   mess
   Of the city's unbombed neon, sent through rivers and many cities
        By fourth-class mail from Hell.

All right, since you want to, look:

   Somebody's lugged a priest's failed prison-cell   35
   Swaybacked up the broker's cut-rate stairs. He rents it on credit.
No picture
    nothing but a bed and desk
  And empty paper.

A flower couldn't make it in this place.   40
It couldn't live, or couldn't get here at all.
                    No flower could get up these steps,
                    It'd wither at the hollowness
Of these foot-stomping

                    failed creative-man's boards—   45
                    There's nothing to bring love or death

            Or creative boredom through the walls.
                                                Walls,

            Ah walls.   They're the whole place.   And any time,
        The easting and westing city in the windows   50
        Plainly are not true
                            without a drink.   But the *walls*—
        Weightless   ridiculous   bare
            Are there just enough to be dreadful
Whether they're spinning or not.   They're there to go round him   55

    And keep the floor turning with the earth.
He moves among stars.
                    Sure.   We all do, but he is star-*crazed*, mad

    With *Einfühlung,* with connecting and joining things that lay their meanings

            Over billions of light years   60
                            eons of time—Ah,

        Years of light: billions of them: they are pictures

        Of some sort of meaning.   He thinks the secret

        Can be read. But human faces swim through
    Cancer   Scorpio   Leo   through all the stupefying design,   65

And all he can add to it or make of it, living or dead:
                    An eye lash-flicker, a responsive
                                    light-year light
            From the pit of the stomach, and a young face comes on,

Trying for the pit of his poem   70
                                   strange   remembered
Comes on faintly, like the faint, structural light
Of Alnilam, without which Orion

          Would have no center   the Hunter
Could not hunt, in the winter clouds.   75
                                        The face comes on

Glowing with billions of miles   burning like nebulae,
          Like the horse-head nebula in Orion—

          She was always a little horse-faced,
At least in profile   she is some strange tint   80
Of second-order blue: intensity   she is eternal
As long as *he* lives—the stars and his balls meet
And she shows herself as any face does
          That *is* eternal, raying in and out
Of the body of a man: in profile   sketched-in by stars   85
          Better than the ones God set turning

          Around us forever.
                               The trees night-pale
Out.   Vacuum.
                    Absolute living-space-white.   Only one way beyond   90

The room.
          The Zodiac.
      ˊ
                    He must solve it   must believe it   learn to read it
                    No, wallow in it

As poetry.   95
                    He's drunk.   Other drunks, it's alligators
          Or rats, their scales and eyes
Turning the cold moon molten on the floor.—   With him, it's his party-time army

          Of soldier ants; they march over
          His writing hand, heading for the Amazon Basin.   100
          He can take *them* . . .

He bristles   itches like a sawdust-pile

But something's more important than flesh-crawling
To gain an image
               line by line: they give him an idea. Suppose— 105

     Well, let's just suppose I . . .

    No ants.   No idea.   Maybe they'll come back
    All wildly drunk, and dance
    Into the writing.   It's worth a try.

   Hot damn, here they come! He knows them, name for name   110
   As they surround his fingers, and carry the maze
   Onto the paper: they're named for generals.
                                He thinks
   That way: of history, with his skin
                    with everything   115

He has, including delirium tremens
              staring straight

Into the lamp.   You are a strange creature,

Light,
    he says to light.   Maybe one day I'll get something   120
Bigger than ants   maybe something from the sea.
    Keep knocking back the *aquavit.* By the way, my man, get that *aqua!*
There's a time acoming when the life of the sea   when

    The stars and their creatures get together.

Light   125
    is another way. This is when the sun drifts in
    Like it does in any window, but this sun is coming
From the east part of town.   Shit, I don't know where I am
    This desk is rolling like the sea
               Come home   come to my home—   130

I'll never make it to land.   I am alone:

I am my brother:

I look at my own decoration
               Outside of the page:
                              three rods: they're turning modernly—   135
     A mobile he's got up
Above the bed, from splintered bottle-bits and coat-hangers:

You know they are, there really *are*
               Small, smashed greens revolving
In a room.   140
               It all hangs together, and *you* made it:
               Its axis is spinning
Through the Zodiac.
                         He flicks it and sets the model
               For a universe of green, see-through stars   145
Going faster.   The white walls stagger
          With lights:
     He has to hold onto the chair: the room is pitching and rolling—
          He's sick   seasick with his own stars,
                    seasick and airsick   sick   150

With the Zodiac.

Even drunk
     Even in the white, whiskey-struck, splintered star of a bottle-room dancing,
               He knows he's not fooling himself   he knows

               Not a damn thing of stars   of God   of space   155

Of time   love night death sex fire numbers signs words,

Not much of poetry.   But by God, we've got a *universe*

Here

          Those designs of time are saying *some*thing
          Or maybe something or *other*.   160

1968–1973 : 507

Night—

Night tells us.   It's coming—

Venus shades it and breaks it.   Will the animals come back
Gently, creatively open,

Like they were?   165
     Yes.

The great, burning Beings   melt into place
A few billion-lighted inept beasts

Of God—

    What else is there?   What other signs.   what other symbols   170

   Are *any*thing beside these?   If the thing hasn't been said
This way,   then God can't say it.

        Unknown.   Unknown.
   His mobile made of human shattering-art
    Is idling through space, and also oddly, indifferently,   175
Supremely, through beauty as well.   Yes,

   Sideways through beauty.   He swirls in his man-made universe,

His room, his liquor, both the new bottle and the old
    Fragmented godlike one.
He never gets tired.   Through his green, moving speckles,   180

He looks sideways, out and up   and there it is:
   The perpetual Eden of space
        there when you want it.

What animal's getting outlined?
    All space is being bolted   185
  Together: eternal blackness

studded with creatures.

Stars.

    Beasts.   Nothing left but the void

           Deep-hammering its creatures with light-years.   190

Years made of light.

        Only light.

        Yes.

But what about the damned *room?*

God-beast-stars   wine-bottle constellations   jack-off dreams   195

    And silence. That's about it.

        They're all one-eyed—

The Lion   the Scorpion   the others coming—

    Their one-eyed eyesight billions of years

In the making, making and mixing with the liquor-bottle green   200

Splintered shadows   *art*-shadows, for God's sake:

    Look, stupid, get your nose out of the sky for once.

There're things that are *close* to you, too. Look at *them!*

        Don't cringe: look right out over town.

Real birds. There they are in their curves, moving in their great element   205

      That causes our planet to be blue and causes us all

        To breathe. Ah, long ghostly drift

    Of wings.

          Well, son of a bitch.

              He sits and writes,   210

    And the paper begins to run

           with signs.

      But he can't get rid of himself enough

    To write poetry. He keeps thinking Goddamn

      I've misused myself   I've fucked up   I haven't worked—   215

I've traveled and screwed too much,

        but   but by dawn, now   NOW

    Something   coming   through-coming   down-coming   up

To me   ME!
                His hand reaches, dazzling with drink   half alive,   220
            for the half-dead vision.   That room and its page come in and
                                                       out
Of being.   You talk about *looking:*   would you look at *that*
Electric page!   What the hell did I say?   Did *I* say that?
           You bastard, you. Why didn't you know that before?   225
        Where the hell have you been with your *head?*
You and the paper should have known it, you and the ink: you write

                    Everybody writes

With blackness. Night. Why has it taken you all this time?
                 All this travel, all those lives   230
              You've fucked up? All those books read
          Not deep enough? It's staring you right in the face   The
                              secret—
        Is whiteness.   You can do *anything* with that.   But no—
           The secret is that on whiteness you can release   235
           The blackness,
                 The night sky.   Whiteness is death   is dying
     For human words to raise it from purity   from the grave
        Of too much light.   Words must come to it
     Words from *any*where   from   from   240
Swamps   mountains   mud   shit   hospitals   wars   travels   from

       Stars

From the Zodiac.
            You son of a bitch, you! Don't try to get away from yourself!
I won't have it! You know God-damned well I mean you! And you too,   245
     Pythagoras!   Put down that guitar, lyre, whatever it is!
You've driven me nuts enough with your music of the spheres!
     But I'll bet you know what to know:

     Where God once stood in the stadium
Of European history, and battled mankind in the blue air   250
     Of manmade curses, under the exploding flags

Of dawn,   I'd put something else now:

    I'd put something overhead   something new: a new beast

    For the Zodiac.   I'd say to myself like a man

                    Bartending for God,   255
                        What'll it be?
    Great! The stars are mine, and so is
                    The imagination to work them—
                                    To create.
          Christ, would you tell me why my head   260
    Keeps thinking up these nit-witted, useless images?

                  Whiskey helps.
    But it does.   It does.   And now I'm working
        With *constellations*!   What'll it *be*, Heaven? What new creature
    Would you *like* up there? Listen, you universal son-of-a-bitch   265
    You're talking to a poet now, so don't give me a lot of shit.
        My old man was a God-damned astronomer
    Of sorts
            —and didn't he say the whole sky's *invented?*
                Well, I am now in*vent*ing. You've *got* a Crab: 270
    Especially tonight.   I love to eat them: They scare me to death!
            My head is smashed with *aquavit,*
    And I've got a damn good Lobster in it   for   for
            The Zodiac   I'll send it right up.
                          And   listen now   275
I want *big* stars: some red   some white   also blue-white dwarves—
    I want *everybody* to see my lobster! This'll be a *healing* lobster:
    Not Cancer.   People will pray to him.   He'll have a good effect
On Time.
            Now what I want to do is stretch him out   280

    Jesus, Christ, I'm drunk
                I said stretch   stretch
Him out is what I said   stretch him out for millions
    Of light years.   His eye   his eye

    I'll make blue-white, so that the thing   285

Will cut and go deep and heal.   God, the *claws* that son-of-a-bitch

        Is going to get from You! The clock-spire is telling me
To lie
        for glory.   This is a poet talking to You
Like you talked to yourself, when you made all this up   while you conceived   290

          The Zodiac. From every tower in Europe:
       From my lifework and stupid travels and loneliness
          And drunkenness, I'm changing the heavens
      In my head. Get up there, baby, and dance on your claws:
          On the claws God's going to give you.   295
                I'm just before throwing up
      All over myself.   I've failed again.   My lobster can't make it
        To Heaven.   He's right here in town.   It must be the DTs.

       You know, old lyre-picking buddy,
You in your whirling triangles, your terror of looking into a glass   300
        Beside a light, your waking from ancient new-math,
To say, "Wretches, leave those beans alone," and "Do not eat the heart,"
         You know   you know you've given me
       Triangular eyes. You know that from the black death,
                of the forest of beast-   305
       Symbols, the stars are beaten down by drunks
Into the page.
         By GOD the poem is *in* there   out there
       Somewhere   the lines that will change
       Everything, like your squares and square roots   310
         Creating the heavenly music.
               It's somewhere,
Old great crazy thinker
           ah
              farther down   315

In the abyss.   It takes triangular eyes
       To see Heaven.   I got 'em from you.
              All right,
I've got what I want, for now, at least.

                    The paper staggers   320
From black to white to black, then to a kind of throbbing gold
               And blue, like the missal he read as a boy. It's like something
                              He dreamed of finding
          In a cave, where the wellspring of creative blood
     Bubbles without death.   325
                         Where the hell *is* the light
     Of the universe?   Gone out and around
          The world.   Oh my God

     You've got to look up
                         again: You've   *got* to do it   you're
                              committed   330
To it   look up   UP   you failed son of a bitch up MORE

               There it is
     Your favorite constellation
                    the hurdling-deep Hunter

                         Orion   335

With dim Alnilam sputtering in the middle.
                              Well, but   quiet   why?
               Why that one?   Why do you even remember
          The name?   The star's no good: not pretty,
     Not a good navigational aid.   340
               Ah, but secret.

                    Ah, but central.

Let me explain it to you: that strange, overlooked, barely existing star

          Is essential to the belt
Of the great, great Hunter.   345
                    Look.
                         Just look.   The sword hangs down
The dog star travels on   on like European Christian soldiers going on

Before.

                The whole thing's hacked out   350
            Like cuneiform.   All right, so Orion's not in
                The Zodiac.   We'll *put* him in, along with some other things.
            He should never've been blackballed, even by Pythagoras.
                All right, friend, my friend myself, feel friendly
            Toward yourself.   It's possible, you know.   One more *aquavit*   355
                And you'll be entitled to breathe.
                                        He breathes
            Breathes deeply.
                            You know, like me, he says to the sideways
            Of the mobile,   360
                        the stars are gasping
                    For understanding.   They've *had* Ptolemy,
                    They've *had* Babylon
                            but now they want Hubble
        They want Fred Hoyle and the steady-state.   365
                            But what they really want   need
                            Is a poet   and

    I'm going to have to be it.

        And all the time I'm sitting here the astronomers are singing

                Dies Irae, to the Day of Judgment's horn.   370

                                                WHEN?

            In all this immensity, all this telescope-country,
                Why the microscopic searching
                            Of the useless human heart?

                    Why not die,   375
                                and breathe Heaven,
    But not to have to *look* at it, not kill yourself trying to read it?

    Except that there's relief   except
                            that there are birds.

    There's one, a real *creature,* out there in a human city.   380

He's never seen a star
In his life, and if he has,

       It didn't register.   There's no star-sound   star-silence
Around him.   He's in my main, starved winter tree,
He's the best thing I've got to my west.   385
                       When I look west I know
Everything's not over yet. I can always come back to earth.

But I want to come back with the secret
                       with the poem
That links up my balls and the strange, silent words   390
     Of God   his scrambled zoo   and my own words
                           and includes the earth

    Among the symbols.
               Listen: you're talking to yourself
    About Time: about clocks   spires   wheels: there are times   395

          There is Time
    Which the time-bell can't hold back
                    but gives
                        GIVES

Gives like vomit or diarrhea   but when it comes it is   400
          The sound of new metal.

Well, all right.   Slowly the city drags and strays about in
                  Its wheedling darkness.

          He looks up
    From his paper-scrap   his overworked script   and,   405

       Work-beast-white, he wanders to the window,
    Getting himself brain-ready ready for the pale-cell-game
       He plays with the outside, when he turns his eyes down
       Into trees, into human life,
                    into the human-hair gray,   410
       Man's aging-hair-gray

Impenetrably thin   catching-up-with-and-passing the
                              never-all-there,
          Going-toward-blackness   thornless
          Thicket of twilight.   415

                              Words.

          How?

                              II

          A clock smash-bongs.   Stun.   Stun.
A spire's hiding out in the sound   tower-sound and now
          Floating over him and living on the nerve   420

Of the instant, vibrating like a hangover:

          Time.

He waits.   God, I'm going to ask you one question:
          What do *wheels* and *machinery* have to do with Time?

With stars?   You know damn well I've never been able to master   425
          A watch-maker's laugh.
                              Overhead in the midst of Nothing,
Is the very clock for a drunk man.   For the Lord also?
Is it some kind of *compass?*   Is direction involved, maybe,
          Or is it nothing but the valve-grinding   430
Human noise of duration?   Do the wheels shift gears?
          If they do, then Time shifts gears.

                              —No; no:

Don't use that idea.
                    It's simple enough, this town clock,   435
                    The whole time-thing: after all
There's only this rosette of a great golden stylized asshole:

In human towns   in this one   in all of them—Ha! this is *our* symbol
        of eternity?
               Well, it's not good enough.

        Night.   Walking.   Time.   440
                    Nothing.
He goes on without anywhere to go. This is what you call Europe.
        Right?   The clock strokes pass
            Through him, aching like tooth-nerves, and he thinks

Our lives have been told, as long as we've had them,   445
                         that the Father
            Must be torn apart in the son.
                          Why?
                          He swings up

             Through his eyes, and God   450
Whirls slowly in men's numbers   in the gilded Gothic
Of thorn-spiked Time.   What the hell: Can't eternity *stand* itself?
        Men caught that great wild creature minute
            By shitty minute and smashed it down
        Into a rickety music box.   455
                Stun.   Stun.   Stun.
        The new hour's here.   He stares, aging, at new Time.

I know God-damned well it's not what they say it is:
        Clock-hands   heart-rhythm   moon-pulses   blood-flow
            of women—

No.   460
        It's just an uncreated vertigo
        Busted up by events.   Probably—now get this—
        The thing most like it is Cancer   both in and out

Of the Zodiac: everywhere existing in some form:
        In the stars   in works of art   in your belly,   465
        In the terrified breast of a woman,
        In your fate, or another's:
                      the thing that eats.

If Cancer dies overhead,
It dies everywhere.   Now try *that* one out, you and your ideas   470

     For poems.   Every poet wants
     To change those stars around.
                      Look: those right *there:*

     Those above the clock.
                   Religion, Europe, death, and the stars: 475
I'm holding them all in my balls, right now.
And the old *aquavit* is mixing them up—they're getting to know—
     They're *crazy* about each other!
     Where God stood once in the stadium
Of European history, and battled mankind in the blue air   480
     For domination, under the exploding Olympic-style flags
     Of dawn, I'd put something *else* now:
                     something overhead.

     God, at your best, you're my old—

You really *are* the water of life!   Look: here's what I'm going to do   485

     For you. I'm going to swirl the constellation Cancer
Around like rice in a bucket, and out of that'll come a new beast

For the Zodiac!
     I say right now, under the crashing clock, like a man
Bartending for God,   490
     What'll it be?
Do you want me to decide?   The stars are mine as well as yours,
     And don't forget it   and Christ
Would you tell me why my head keeps thinking
     Up these half-assed, useless images?   495
                     Whiskey helps.
But it does.   It does.   Swirl on, sky! Now, I'm working
With constellations.   What'll it be, Heaven? What new earthly creature

Would you like up there? Listen, you universal son of a bitch
I've heard it all   I've said it all—   500

You're talking to poet now, so don't give me a lot of shit.
                    You've got to remember that my old man
Was an astronomer, of sorts, and didn't he say the whole night sky's
                    invented?
Well, I am now *inventing*. You've *got* a crab.   Right?   505

        How about a *Lobster* up there? With a snap of two right fingers
            Cancer will whirl like an anthill   people will rise
Singing from their beds and take their wheaten children in their arms,

            Who thought their parents were departing
        For the hammer-clawed stars of death. They'll live   510

And live. A *Lobster!* What an idea!   An idea God never had.   Listen, My God,
        That thing'll be great!   He's coming into my head—
            Is he inside or out?   No, I can *see* him!
        The DT's aren't failing me: The light of Time shines on him
                He's huge   he's a religious fanatic   515
        He's gone wild because he can't go to Heaven
            He's waving his feelers   his saw-hands
            He's praying to the town clock   to minutes   millennia
        He's praying the dial's stations of the Cross   he sees me
                Imagination and dissipation both fire at me   520
        Point-blank   O God, no   NO   I was playing   I didn't mean it
        I'll never write it, I swear   CLAWS   claws   CLAWS

                He's going to kill me.

                        III

    Hallucination fading.   Underseas are tired of crawling
            In a beast   waving claws for a drunk   525
        Under man's dim, round Time.   Weird ring
                Of city-time.   Well, now:
                                    night hits a long stride.
            There's the last tower-tone.   You might know it.
Bronze.   530
        He feels it. The thing hurts. Time hurts. Jesus does it.
                        Man,

God-damn it,
                    you're one *too!*   Man   MAN   listen to me
                    Like God listened when he went mad   535
Over drunk lobsters.   This is Time, and more than that,
Time in Europe
                                        Son of a bitch.
                         His life is shot   my life is shot.
              It's also shit.   He knows it.   Where's it all gone off to?   540
The gods are in pieces
                         All over Europe.
                                        But, by God, not *God*—

He sees himself standing up—

    Dawn-rights.   How the hell did he ever get home?   545
         What home?   You call this white sty a *home?*
    Yes, but *look* . . .
                         The vision's thorn-blue
                                        between a slope
And the hot sky.   550
                         And now his travels begin to swarm
    All over him. He falls into clichés
    Right and left, from his windows! That remembered Greek blue
    Is *fantastic!*   That's all: no words
    But the ones anybody'd use: the one from humanity's garbage-can   555
Of language.
                    A poet has got to do better. . . *That* blue
                    Jesus, look at *that* in your memory!
    There   *there*   *that* blue   that *blue*
    Over some Demetrian island   something that's an island   560
              More or less, with its present hour smoking

    Over it . . . It's worth it all   worth it and lifted
    Into memory
                    he's lifted   he rises on the great, historical strength
    Of columns.   Look, you son of a bitch, I know what peace is,   565
    He says to his morning drink.   Peace, PEACE, you asshole . . .
    Look at me, mirror.   My *eyes* are full of it, of the pale blue fumes
    Of Mediterranean distance.   Isn't that *enough?*   The fresh stuff?

The old stuff . . .
                    —but, damn it, forgetting keeps moving in   closer.   570

          It's that thing you might call death.
                                        The walled, infinite
Peaceful-sea-beast-blue   moves in   in   it has a face

Bewildered, all-competent   everlasting   sure it will lie forever

Lie in the depths in distance-smoke: he's been there   575
          Among the columns:
                              among Europe. He can't tell Europe
From his own death, from his monstrous, peaceful   fierce
          Timelessness. It follows like the images
          Of day-sleep.   580
                         Water-pressure   smoke   crabs
Lobsters.
          All RIGHT, reader, that's enough.   Let him go:

Let him go back to traveling   let him go on   in   onward   backward . . .

Ah, to hell with it: he can't quit.   585
                         Neither can you, reader.
He travels   he rises up
                    you with him, hovering on his shoulders,
                    A gas-fume reader   a gull a sleep and a smoke
          Of distance   a ruined column, riding him,   590
          His trapezius muscles in your deadly   your DT lobster's
          Your loving claws:
                         god-*damn*   it, he *can't* quit,
          But—*listen* to me—how can he *rise*
                         When he's *digging?* Digging through the smoke   595
          Of distance, throwing columns around to find   throwing
          To find   throwing distance   swaying   swaying into his head . . .
          He's drunk again.   Maybe that's all.   Maybe there's nothing maybe
          There's a mystery   mystery nearly got-to
          Now   NOW   600
                    No.
                    I can't get it.   Ah,

But now he can think about his grave.   It's not so bad;
It will be better than this.   There's something there for him—
    At least it'll be in Europe, and he won't be sick   605
    For the impossible: with other-world nostalgia,
    With the countries of the earth.   Holland is good enough
    To die in.   That's the place to lay down
    His screwed-up body-meat   That's it.
                           This is it.   610

It's that thing you might call home.

IV

He moves.
        While he's going
He sees the moon white-out. But it maintains itself
    Barely, in   some kind of thing   615

    Vibrating faintly with existence,   inside a crown
    Of desperate trees.   Image of Spring,

Old Buddy. But where in this neon,
Where in *hell* am I *going?* Well, it looks like I've come to some kind of

    Lit-up ravine—   620

Well, what on God's earth *is* it?   I can barely make out
    A black church.   Now come on now: are you sure?

I can't cross it.   It moves across me
    Like an all-mighty stone.   But is it *universal?*
    The thing's been lifted from the beginning   625
        Into this night-black—
                 Into the Zodiac.

Without   that hugely mortal beast   animal   multi-animal animal
    There'd be no present time:
    Without the clock-dome, no city here,   630
    Without the axis and the poet's image   God's image

No turning stars   no Zodiac   without God's conceiving

Of Heaven as beast-infested   of Heaven in terms of beasts
    There'd be no calendar   dates   seasons
No Babylon   those abstractions that blitzed their numbers   635
    Into the Colosseum's crazy gates   and down
                                 down
    Into the woven beads that make the rosary
      Live   sing and swirl like stars

    Of creatures.   640

        Well, enough.   He loafs around
The square.   He might be a cock-sucker
Looking for trade.   He's got a platform   a springboard
For himself . . .
        Nobody sees him;   645
            nobody cares.

He thinks he's sending night-letters
To Mars, and yet he's looking straight
Into the Milky Way   right now he's liking the hang of it—
Now he's with Venus   he's getting a hard-on   650
      My God, look at that love-star   hammock-swaying
Moving like an ass   moving the sky along.

V

Dark.

Bed-dark.   The night can get at him here   and it comes,
Tide after tide   and his nightmares rise and fall off him   655
      On the dry waves of the moon

    Thinking:
    The faster I sleep
    The faster the universe sleeps.
             And the deeper I breathe   660

The higher the night can climb
                              and the higher the singing will be.
          Bird, maybe?   *Night*ingale?   Ridiculous
                                        but over me
They're all one-eyed: the animals of light are in profile;   665
They're flat: God can't draw in depth
                When He uses constellations: the stars are beyond Him,
                Beyond his skill;   He can't handle them right.
                      A child could do better.
At the moment I'm passing truly   670
                        into sleep, a single star goes out

In each beast.
                    Right.
                        The eye.
                              The eye, but can it be   675
That from the creative movement of the first light
On the face of the waters   from Time   from Genesis

The orbiting story   the insane mathematics   the ellipsis
Of history: the whole thing: time art life death stars
Love blood till the last fire explodes into dark   680
The last image   the candlestick the book and the lamb's fleece
Flame in delight at the longed-for end of it all
          Will flame in one human eye?   Right or left?   Well, old soul,
          What is it?
What does it mean, poet?   Is all this nothing but the clock-stunned light 685
Of my mind, or a kind of river-reflection of my basic sleep
Breaking down   sleeping down into reprisal-fear of God:
          The Zodiac standing over, pouring into
              The dreams that are killing me?

                              VI

Dreams, crossing the body, in and out and around   crossing   690
                Whatever is left of me. What does that include?   Images:

Monsters.   Nothing else.   Monsters of stars.
The moon dies like a beast.   Not a stone beast or a statue:

A *beast.*   But it can't fall   it's in a gully of clouds,
A shameless place, like the rest of nature is.   695

At this idea, one part of his brain goes soft
As cloud, so the Lobster can come.

Soft brain, but the spirit turns to fire
Pure cosmic tetanus. The sponge of his brain drinks it up:
          In the place where the thing is   seethes   700

The sweat of thought breaks out.
                            It crowns him like a fungus:
Idea of love.
        Love?
             Yes, but who'll put a washrag on him?   705
       It wouldn't matter: his whole skull's   broken out with it.
           There's no sponge, no rag—

           Poet's lockjaw; he can't speak: there's nothing

Nothing for his mouth.

VII

O flesh, that takes on any dirt   710
      At all
            I can't get you back in shape—
It'd be better to go on being
What I was   at one time or another: a plant
In the dead-black flaming flowing   715
Round flume of Time.

Words fade before his eyes
Like water-vapor, and the seed he thinks he's got available to give
          Some woman, fades back
          Deep into his balls, like a solar   720
          Phenomenon, like cloud
          Crossing the Goat—

He comes back, and some weird change comes on:
Our man may be getting double-sexed
       Or something worse 725
            or better—
                 but either way
His children are already murdered: they'll never *be* until the Goat
    Shines blindingly, and Time ends. Then, no,
       Either. Nothing will ever be. 730

       He says from his terrible star-sleep,
       Don't shack up with the intellect:
       Don't put your prick in a cold womb.
       Nothing but walking snakes would come of *that*—

       But if you conceive with meat 735

       Alone,
           that child, too, is doomed.
      Look.   The moon has whited-out the script
          Your hand drove into the paper.

       This poetry that's draining your bones 740
          Of marrow has no more life
       Than the gray grass of public parks.

Leave it, and get out.   Go back to the life of a man.
    Leave the stars.   They're not saying what you think.
God is a rotten artist: he can't draw 745
With stars worth a shit   He can't say what He should
      To men   He can't say   speak   with   with
Stars what you want Him to
               Ah, but the key *image*
Tonight   *tonight* 750
         is the gully   gullies:

Clouds make them, and other Realities
    Are revealed in Heaven, as clouds drift across,
Mysterious   sperm-colored:
            Yes. 755

There, the world is original, and the Zodiac shines anew
    After every night-cloud.   New
With a nameless tiredness   a depth
    Of field I can't read   an oblivion with no bottom

        To it, ever, or never.   760

                                VIII

    Sun.   Hand-steadying brightness   Time
To city-drift leg after leg, looking Peace
    In its empty eyes as things are beginning
            Already to go twelve hours
    Toward the other side of the clock, the old twilight   765
            When God's crazy beasts will come back.
            Death is twenty-eight years old
    Today.   Somewhere in between sunrise
        And dusk he'll be bumming around.
                                    Now he walks over water   770
        He's on a bridge. He feels truly rejected
                                    but as he passes,
            Vacancy puts on his head
        The claw-hammer hair of terror.
                            He moves along the slain canal   775
    Snoring in its bronze
Between docks.
            The fish, too,
        Are afraid of the sun
Under the half-stacked greens of the rotten bridge,   780
And light falls with the ultimate marigold horror:

    Innocence.
            The fish fin-flutter   able
Unable to hide their secrets any longer: what they know of Heaven
    As stars come down   come effortlessly down   down   785
Through water.   The trees are motionless, helping their leaves hold back

    Breath   life-death-breath—BACK: it's not time—

From the transparent rippling
          European story they've been told to tell
  Themselves when everybody's dead   790
                    they glitter the water.

      They shake with dawn-fear.

                            IX

Again, his stepping stops him.   No reason.   Just does.
He's right here.   Then he's drawn wavering into the fort
                    Where the old house stands   795
On the vine-stalking hill.   The town moat gets with the dawn,
          The morning loses time
Under the elm-heavy night, and in lost time   drift the swans
                    On-down, asleep.
          He roams all the way round, one finger tracing   800
A house-size circle on the wall.   The stone trembles   scrambles—
          Comes clear: here was his room

          Here his mother twisted pain to death
              In her left breast—
                    Above that wrung one window on the battle-tower   805
His father hauled, each night the Beasts had their one-eyes,
His telescope across the galleried desert-might of Heaven.
                    Far, far beneath the body
Of his boy   the cellar filled with rats. Their scrambling made his poor,
   rich youth
Shake all night, every night. His face and neck were like sponges   810
              Squeezed, slick with the green slime
              That gave the book-backs on his shelves
              Leprosy itself, and broke them out like relief-maps.
              The garden, he thinks, was here,
          Bald   a few sparse elephant-head hairs   815

      Where as a kid he'd ambled grumbling like a ghost
              In tulip shadow,
              The light humid cool

Of the family maze.

     The garden where he hid the body—   820
His own—somewhere under the grape-roof—well,

Let him cry, and wipe his face on dead leaves
    Over the little bitch who filled, with *his* hand,
His diary with dreadful verses.

Why didn't he *do* it? That thing that scared him limp   825
    In daylight, that he did all night with himself?
    He should have screwed her or killed her
And he did—both—a hundred times. So would you.
    Sure, sure. He always put it off. Nothing would happen.
Too late anyway.   Too shy.   She'd pass right by him in the street,   830
    Still, even if she saw him, joking with that asshole
    She married, who'd once been a school-god to him.

    Over.   All that's left of her is the dark of a home

She never visited.   There's no one in it; the man outside—myself—
    Is understanding he's in the business   835
        Of doublecrossing his dreams.

The grave of youth?   HA!   *I told you:*   there's nobody *in* it!

    Why the hell did he come out here?

He lays his forehead on the salt stone-grains of the wall,
Then puts an ivy-leaf between. He turns his cheek.   840

    Outrage. Bare moon-stone. His ear's there
    And the rock prepares.   It stills   stills
    With his mother's voice. He grinds his hearing
    Into the masonry   it is   it is   it says
"Never come back here.   845
        Don't wander around your own youth.
    Time is too painful here. Nothing stays with you
But what you remember." The memory-animal crouched

Head-down   a huge lizard   in these vines, sleeping like winter,
Wrapped in dead leaves, lifts its eyes and pulls its lips back   850

            Only at reunion.

         He looks toward the window
         Behind whose frozen glass he'd fucked
         The first body he could get hold of.

         Leaving skin, he tears himself off the wall.   855

Goodbye?
        You're goddamned right, goodbye: this is *the* goodbye.

        "You must leave here in every way," she'd said.
        "When you feel the past draw you by the small intestine

        You've got to go somewhere else.   Anywhere.   860
Somewhere no footstep has scrambled.   Go for the empty road."

        "There's not any road," he says to the ivy
Massing with darkness behind him   "that doesn't have tracks,
        Most of them men's.   They've always been there."
             He sees his mother, laid-out in space,   865
             Point to the moon. "That thing," she says,
        "Puts man-tracks out like candles."
                He gets all the way away

            At last winding a little more
        Than the garden path can wind.   He struggles in weeds,   870
             Cursing, passing along
            The piss-smell standing with the stable,
            And reads on the first and last door,
               Where his father's live
            Starry letters had stood, a new   875

Designation   of somebody once human and here,
          Now also moved away, dead, forgotten too,

         His long name harder than time.

X

Tenderness, ache on me,   and lay your neck
On the slight shoulder-breathing of my arm . . .   880
There's nobody to be tender with—
This man has given up
On anything stronger than he is.

He's traveled everywhere
But no place has ever done any good.   885
What does his soul matter, saved like a Caesar-headed goldpiece,
When the world's dying?

He goes to the window,
Hating everything, worn out, looking into the shook heart
Of the city.   890

Yet the stairwell hammers lightly
Alive: a young step, nimble as foxfire,
And the vital shimmer of a real face
Backs-off the white of the room.
He closes his eyes, for the voice.   895
"My head is paralyzed with longing—"

He is quiet, but his arm is with her   around
Her belly and tailbone.
His heart broods: he knows that nothing,
Even love, can kill off his lonesomeness.   900

Twilight passes, then night.

Their bodies are found by the dawn, their souls
Fallen from them, left in the night
Of patterns   the night that's just finished
Overwhelming the earth.   905

Fading   fading   faded . . .

They lie like the expanding universe.

Too much light.   Too much love.

XI

A big room, a high one;
His first time in somebody else's.   910
Past the window, wind and rain
Paper-chasing each other to death,

And in the half-light, one of Kandinsky's paintings,
Squeezes art's blood out of the wallpaper.
Rolls over and over   915
Joyfully, rapid-fire.   The lamp seeps on;
He thaws, forge-red like the stove,
Going blue with room-smoke—
And he shakes free of two years of wandering
Like melting-off European snows.   920

He tells.

He polar-bears through the room.
When he turns, a great grin breaks out.
The bottle pops its cork, and talk rushes over   rushes into
Cheese and gin   women   politics—   925
All changed   all the same . . .
Getting darker,
And by God, there's the *fish* market, gleaming its billion scales
Upward to him through the window.
More lights go on.   930
Where was he this time last year? He sees it:
Sees himself for a second at the Tetuan Friday Market,
And the *chalif,* through a double shine of trumpets,
Go into the tiny mosque.   It's all in pictures
In his friend's drunk-book.   He feels his last year, and his back   935
To the foreign wall. He turns page after page
Of the world   the post-cards he's sent,

Eagerly, desperately, looking for himself,
Tired, yellow with jaundice as an old portrait,
                                  and something—   940
    That's it.   He's just heard an accordion:
        Two squeezed-lung, last-ditch
            First-ditch Dutch chords

    And he's back home

XII

        A day like that.   But afterwards the fire   945
    Comes straight down through the roof, white-lightning nightfall,
    A face-up flash. Poetry. Triangular eyesight. It draws his
    fingers together at the edge
    Around a pencil.   He crouches bestially,
            The darkness stretched out on the waters   950
        Pulls back, humming Genesis. From wave-stars lifts
            A single island wild with sunlight,
        The white sheet of paper in the room.

    He's far out and far in, his hands in a field of snow.
        He's making a black horizon with all the moves   955
        Of his defeated body. The virgin sheet becomes
    More and more his, more and more another mistake,

But now, *now*
        Oh God you rocky landscape   give me,   Give
Me drop by drop   960
            desert water at least.
        I want now to write about deserts

    And in the dark the sand begins to cry
    For living water that not a sun or star
Can kill, and for the splay camel-prints that bring men,   965
    And the ocean with its enormous crooning, begs

    For haunted sailors   for refugees putting back

Flesh on their ever-tumbling bones
    To man that fleet,
                            for in its ships   970
        Only, the sea becomes the sea.

    Oh my own soul, put me in a solar boat.
        Come into one of these hands
        Bringing quietness and the rare belief
    That I can steer this strange craft to the morning   975
Land that sleeps   in the universe on all horizons
        And give this home-come man who listens in his room

        To the rush and flare of his father
        Drawn at the speed of light to Heaven
Through the wrong end of his telescope, expanding the universe,   980
        The instrument the tuning-fork—
    He'll flick it with his bandless wedding-finger—
        Which at a touch reveals the form
        Of the time-loaded European music
            That poetry has never really found,   985
        Undecipherable as God's bad, Heavenly sketches,
    Involving fortress and flower, vine and wine and bone,

    And shall vibrate through the western world
So long as the hand can hold its island
        Of blazing paper, and bleed for its images: 990
        Make what it can of what is:

        So long as the spirit hurls on space
        The star-beasts of intellect and madness.

1977–1997

The Strength of Fields

1977

. . . a separation from the world, a penetration to some source of power and a life-
enhancing return . . .

Van Gennep, *Rites de Passage*

Moth-force a small town always has,

Given the night.
What field-forms can be,
Outlying the small civic light-decisions over
A man walking near home? 5
Men are not where he is
Exactly now, but they are around him   around him like the strength

Of fields.   The solar system floats on
Above him in town-moths.
Tell me, train-sound, 10
With all your long-lost grief,
what I can give.
Dear Lord of all the fields
what am I going to *do?*
Street-lights, blue-force and frail 15
As the homes of men, tell me how to do it   how
To withdraw   how to penetrate and find the source
Of the power you always had
light as a moth, and rising
With the level and moonlit expansion 20
Of the fields around, and the sleep of hoping men.

You?   I?   What difference is there?   We can all be saved

By a secret blooming. Now as I walk
The   night   and you walk with me   we know simplicity
Is close to the source that sleeping men   25
Search for in their home-deep beds.

We know that the sun is away   we know that the sun can be conquered
By moths, in blue home-town air.
The stars splinter, pointed and wild. The dead lie under
The pastures.   They look on and help.   Tell me, freight-train,   30
When there is no one else
To hear.   Tell me in a voice the sea
Would have, if it had not a better one: as it lifts,
Hundreds of miles away, its fumbling, deep-structured roar
Like the profound, unstoppable craving   35
Of nations for their wish.
Hunger, time and the moon:

The moon lying on the brain
as on the excited sea   as on
The strength of fields.   Lord, let me shake   40
With purpose.   Wild hope can always spring
From tended strength.   Everything is in that.
That and nothing but kindness.   More kindness, dear Lord
Of the renewing green.
That is where it all has to start: 45
With the simplest things.   More kindness will do nothing less
Than save every sleeping one
And night-walking one

Of us.
My life belongs to the world. I will do what I can.   50

The Voyage of the Needle

1978

The child comes sometimes with his mother's needle
And draws a bath with his hand.   These are your fifty years
        Of fingers, cast down among
        The hard-driven echoes of tile
In the thresholding sound of run water.   Here the sun divides light   5
      From the Venetian sector of the dark
Where you sink through both,
                  and warmly, more slowly than being
Smoothed and stretched, your bodying barge-ripples die.
        A gauze of thin paper upholds   10
      The needle, then soaks like an eyelid
        And falls, uncontrolling, away.
                The hung metal voyages alone,
   Like the trembling north-nerve of a compass,
On surface tension, that magic, like a mother's spell   15
Cast in sharp seed in your childhood, in scientific trickery rooted
And flowering in elation. It is her brimming otherworld
That rides on the needle's frail lake, on death's precarious membrane,
      Navigating through all level latitudes,
          Containing a human body   20
       She gave, and saved to bear, by a spell
From physics, this fragile cargo.   "Mother," you say,
      "I am lying in a transference
       Of joy and glory: come to me
   From underground, from under the perilous balance   25
      Of a thicket of thorns.   I lie
As unmoving. Bring the needle to breathless harbor
       Somewhere on my body, that I may rise
        And tell. My sex is too deep,
My eyes too high for your touch. O let it reach me at the lips'   30
      Water-level, the thorns burst
    Into rain on your wooded grave, the needle plunge
Through the skin of charmed water and die, that I may speak at last
       With up-bearing magic
     Of this household, weightless as love."   35

Mexican Valley

1978

—homage and invention, Octavio Paz—

The day works on
               works out its transparent body.   With fire, the bodiless hammer,
Light knocks me flat.
          Then lifts me.   Hooked on-
to the central flame-stone, I am nothing but a pause between   5
Two vibrations
          of pressureless glow: Heaven
And trees. Tlaloc help me
        I am pure space:
One of the principal future-lost battlefields   10
Of light. Through my body, I see my other bodies

Flocking and dancing   fighting each other
With solar joy.   Every stone leaps inward, while the sun tears out my eyes
And my Heaven-knifed, stone-drunken heart.
              Yes,   15
But behind my gone sight is a spiral of wings.
          Now   *now*
My winged eyes are fetched-back and singing: yes singing like buzzards
         From the black-feathered crown-shifts of air
       That have always wished to be singing   20
               over this valley.
And I lean over my song
      Within trees, God knows where,
            in Mexico
No matter what they say, it is not bad here.   No, it is good: 25
It is better than anything the astronomers can dream up
With their sweaty computers.   I've shaved my chest off to be
      Slowly-nearer and now without junk-hair
That is not really me   instantaneously nearer
      Soft universal power!   It is warm, it is maybe even a little   30
Too hot, but glorious, here at the center   all the center there is
Before history . . . I send you a searing Yes

From the thousand cross-glittering black-holes of obsidian:
             I am like the *theory* of a blade
      That closes rather than opens   *closes:*   35
      That sends something back
Other than blood.   Among leaves, I have torn out the heart of the sun
                   The long-lost Mexican sun.

———————

Undersea Fragment in Colons
1979

—Vicente Aleixandre—

Swordfish, I know you are tired: tired out with the sharpness of your face:
      Exhausted with the impossibility of ever
Piercing the shade: with feeling the tunnel-breathing streamline of your flesh
      Enter and depart   depart
                              spirit-level after level of Death   5
                   Tamped flat, and laid
Where there is no hillside grave.
                              Take this as it settles, then: word
   That behind your incomparable weapon chokes and builds,
      Blocked and balanced in your sides   10
        Instinct with meridians: word: the x-mark of certain world-numbers
          Blood-brothering   rising blade-headed
To an element as basic as the water
                         unraveling in layers from around you:
             Strata trapped and stitched   15
By your face like tapestry
                   thinning   exploding
      The depth-imploded isinglass eye
                              west of Greenwich and shocked   20
Into latitude   into the sea-birds' winged sea   tonnage of shifting silence now
                   Freed to the unleashed Time
      And timing of coordinates: all solid-light:

Pierceable sun   its flash-folded counterpart beneath   25
        By the billion: word: in one leap the layers,

        The slant ladder of soundlessness: word: world: sea:
            Flight partaking of tunnels   fins, of quills and airfoils:
                Word: unwitnessed numbers   nailed noon   enchanted three
                    minutes
Of the sun's best effort of height   this space   time   this   30
        Hang-period   meridian passage:
                    Sing.

                            ———————

When

1979

—Pierre Reverdy—

A prisoner in this space perpetually narrow
With my left-over hands left on my eyelids
With none of the words that reason can bring itself

To invent
            I play the hell-game   5
That dances on the horizon.   Space in darkness makes it better,

And it may be there are people passing through me—
There may even be a song
                    of some kind

        The cloud fills itself full of hovering holes   10

        The needle loses itself
        In clothes-covered sharpness

        The thunder stops short—

A few more minutes
                    I start to shake: 15
It's too late   too late ever to act   to act at all:

This is the thing as it will be.
All around, chains are gritting on each other
Like blackboard chalk   every tree
In the world is going to fall.   20

The window opens to summer.

———————

Low Voice, Out Loud

1979

—Léon-Paul Fargue—

A good many times I've come down among you.
I've brought down my mountains, and washed them, just as a cloud would
    have done
But you   YOU   cannot even begin to guess the *space*
Of the great shadows that've just gone past us.   5
                                            But, look:
I come out of you!
                    I was your hands   your life-work
Your bleeding eyes   your red cubby-hole!   And that guitar:

To you, one touch of E minor is suicide!   10

I need you.
                I have lifted the anchor.
                                For the thousandth time
I have smelled your shoes.
                        There I have done it, close to you and me: 15
I have lifted the anchor.

                    Whoever loves well
Punishes well.   But don't go
Against my rhythm.
                    It is by you that the man   in this case myself   20
Limits himself to being   his own being
A man: Identity blind, deaf
And indivisible!
                    I am tired of existing
As an animal of intelligence—   25

Don't try to name what is nameless.

Nothing   Everything.   Nothing.
                    Rest easy, love. It is best:
Let us go back into the immense and soft-handed, double

Fire-bringing ignorance.   30

————————

Purgation [first version]
1979

—*Po Chü-yi*—

Beyond the eye, grasses go over the long fields.
Every season it happens, as though I—no; I and you,
Dear friend—decreed it. It is what we would like to have,

And it is there.
                    It is the season for wildfire,   5
And it will come, but will never quite get every one
Of the grasses.   There is some green left, this year as last,

For us.   Once more they are tall
In the April wind.   They make the old road *be*

The road, where you and I go toward the old, beetle-eaten   10
City gate.   Oh, fire, come *on!*   I trust you.

My ancient human friend, you are dead, as we both know.
But I remember, and I feel the grass and the fire
Get together in April   with you and me, and that
Is what I want   both age-gazing living and dead   15

        both sighing like grass and fire.

———

The Ax-God
Sea-Pursuit
1979

—after Alfred Jarry—

On the horizon, through the steam of exhausted blast-furnaces   fog   Yes
Pure Chance blows, as though it were really itself   blows
Not very well, and moans and shakes bells.

These are the sounds that invented salt.   But, listen,
Waves, we are among the arced demons you are hiding   5

In the visiting green gullies of your mountains.
Where the shoreline clamps a lost quivering over all
Of us, a huge and shadow-cast shape looms over muck.
We crawl round his feet, loose as lizards,

While, like a filthy Caesar on his chariot,   10
Or on a marble, leg-crossing plinth,
Carving a whale-boat from a tree-trunk, he . . .

Well, in that branching boat, he'll run
Us down, league for league   down   down to
The last of the sea's center-speeding   15

Center-spreading and ropeless knots.   Green   blue   white
Time space distance: starting from the shore

His arms of unhealable, veined copper   over us
Raise to Heaven a breathing blue ax.

———————

Nameless

1979

—near Eugenio Montale—

Sure. All the time I come up on the evil
                              of just living:

It's been the strangled creek that still tries
To bubble like water   it's been the death-rattling leaf
Dried out for no reason   5
                    and the tripped-sprawling horse.

As for anything good: you find it for me
And I'll look at it.   All I can come up with
Is an enclosure: the religion-faking sun-blasted rack
Of divine Indifference.   As I say, Sure: 10

It's the statue in its somnolescence
Of primitive, hectored stone.   It's noon

And cloud   and the falcon in circles,
Who planes, as high as he can get,

                    For nothing.   15

Math

1979

—*Lautréamont*—

Numbers who can't ever hear me

                          I'll say it anyway

All the way from my age-old school.   You're still in my heart,

       And I can feel you go through there

Like a clean sea-wave.   I breathed-in, instinctively,   5

From the one-two, one-two counts

       Of the soft-rocking cradle

       As drinking from a universal spring

                          older than the sun:

Numbers. There is this wave of matched, watched numbers   10

In my school-soul.   Sometimes it is like smoke: I can't get through it.

Sometimes I believe that you've put   put in place of my heart

Inhuman logic.   Coldness

                  beyond bearing.   And yet . . . because of you

My intelligence has grown far beyond me   15

                      from the frozen, radiant center

Of that ravishing clarity you give: give to those

Who most truly love you   and can find you: *Listen,* ever-deaf numbers.

                           Hail! *I* hail you

           Arithmetic!   Algebra!   Geometry!   20

       Triangle gone luminous!

Judas

1979

—Georg Heym, resurrected from under the ice—

Mark.   Hair, one strand of it, can curl
Over your forehead like a branding-iron.
And meaningless winds   and many voices can be whispering
Like creek-flow, staying and going by.

But he runs close to His side like a mongrel,   5
And in the sick mud he picks up everything said
To him, and weighs it in his quivering hands.
                                             It is dead.

Ah, most gently in the swaying dusk,
The Lord walked down   10
Over the white fields.   Ear by ear, green by green,
Yellow by yellow, the corn-ears, the stalks, the sheer *growing*
Glorified. His feet were as small as houseflies, as they were perpetually being

Sent-down step by step
                          From the golden hysteria of Heaven.   15

———————

Small Song

1979

—from the Hungarian of Attila Jozsef,
head crushed between two boxcars—

I'm laughing, but being very quiet about it.
I've got my pipe and my knife:
I am quiet, and laughing like hell.

All hail, Wind!   Let my song fall in jigsaw fragments!

Nobody is my friend except the one who can say   5
"I take pleasure in his misery."

I am of shadow and of sun   of the sun
            Returning always,

And I laugh, silently.

———————

Poem [b]
1979

—from the Finnish of Saima Harmaja—

O death, so dear to me,
Do you remember when someone loved you?

Let all our blood-kin come back, into
Your soft, embalmed half-shadow.

Look.   I'm making no gestures.   5
I like and don't like
Your diligent work.   I try not to pay attention.
Other troubles I can stand.   Not yours.

Free my soul
            and open your blinding jail.   10

O my sweet, owned death,
Lift the used-up one,
The soul half-opened as a wound
                        and let him fly.

A Saying of Farewell
1979

—homage, Nordahl Grieg—

You've dressed yourself so white for it!   And you poise
As on the edge of an undersea cliff, for departure.
We two are the only ones who know that this lost instant
      Is not lost, but is the end
          Of life.   5

"It's as though we were dying, this calm twilight."
  No;   only you.   I hang on watch,
High up in Time.   Step off and fall as the wind rolls the earth

Over you like a wave. I am left on duty with the heart
      Going out over everything, no sleep   10

      In sight   braced,   monster-eyed,
    Outstaring the shaken powder of fatigue   mist—
      By your clothes and mine white-bled

    Raging with discovery like a prow
      Into the oncoming Never.   15

———————

For the Running of the
New York City Marathon
1979

If you would run

If you would quicken the city with your pelting,
    Then line up, be counted, and change

Your body into time, and with me through the boxed maze flee
        On soft hooves, saying   all saying in flock-breath   5
        Take me there.
                                I am against you
            And with you: I am second
Wind and native muscle in the streets   my image lost and discovered
            Among yours: lost and found in the endless panes   10
        Of a many-gestured bald-headed woman, caught between
    One set of clothes and tomorrow's: naked, pleading in her wax
            For the right, silent words to praise
            The herd-hammering pulse of our sneakers,
            And the time gone by when we paced   15
        River-sided, close-packed in our jostled beginning,
            O my multitudes.
                            We are streaming from the many to the one
        At a time, our ghosts chopped-up by the windows
Of merchants;   the mirroring store-fronts let us, this one day,   20
            Wear on our heads feet and backs
    What we would wish.   This day I have taken in my stride
        Swank jogging-suits rayed with bright emblems
    Too good for me: have worn in blood-sweating weather
    Blizzard-blind parkas and mukluks, a lightning-struck hairpiece   25
        Or two, and the plumes of displayed Zulu chieftains.

Through the colors of day I move as one must move
                His shadow somewhere on
Farther into the dark.   Any hour now   any minute
                Attend the last rites   30
        Of pure plod-balance! Smoke of the sacrificial
Olympic lamb in the Deli!   O swooping and hairline-hanging
        Civic-minded placement of bridges! Hallelujas of bars!
        Teach those who have trained in the sunrise
            On junk-food and pop, how to rest   how to rise   35
    From the timed city's never-die dead.   Through the spattering echo
    Of Vulcanized hundreds, being given the finish-line hot-foot,
            I am lolloping through to the end,
    By man-dressing mannequins clad   by flashes of sun on squared rivers
    As we breast our own breathless arrival: as we home in,   40
            Ahead of me   me   and behind me

All winning over the squirrel-wheel's outlasted stillness, on the unearthly pull and fall
        Of our half-baked soles, all agony-
            smiles and all winning—

        All winning, one after one.   45

———————

Purgation (second version)
1980

—homage, Po Chü-yi—

Before and after the eye, grasses go over the long fields.
    Every season they walk on
                        by us, as though I—no; I and you,
        Dear friend—decreed it. One time or another
They are here. Grass   season . . . yet we are no longer the best   5
        Of us.
            Lie stiller, closer; in the April I love

    For its juices, there is too much green for your grave.
        I feel that the Spring should ignite with what is
Unnatural as we; ours, but God-suspected. It should come in one furious
    step, and leave   10
Some—a little—green for us; never quite get every one of the hummocks
    tremoring vaguely
        Tall in the passed-through air. They'd make the old road *be*
    The road for old men, where you and I used to wander toward
        The beetle-eaten city gate, as the year leaned into us.
            Oh fire, come *on!* I trust you!   15

    My ancient human friend, you are dead, as we both know.

    But I remember, and I call for something serious, uncalled-for
By anyone else, to sweep, to *use*

the dryness we've caused to become us! Like the
    grasshopper

I speak, nearly covered with dust, from the footprint   and ask   20
Not for the line-squall lightning:
            the cloud's faking veins—Yes! I catch myself:
    No; not the ripped cloud's open touch   the fireball hay
        Of August
              but for flame too old to live   25
      Or die, to travel like a wide wild contrary
    Single-minded brow over the year's right growing
  In April
    over us   *for us*   as we sway stubbornly near death
          From both sides   age-gazing   30

Both sighing like grass and fire.

————

The Surround
1980

Imagining Herself as the Environment,
She Speaks to James Wright at Sundown

Still-down on all sides
             from all over:
Dusk: seizure, quell, and hyper-glow.
  I cannot make, and cannot stop
  The old-stone footprints quickening   5
    To live feet, for here I must
Stand, and almost pass, where the sun burns
Down in pine-cone smouldering   needle-nervèd with flame-threads;
    The sound of the last ax

Fails, and yet will be almost everywhere   10
Till midnight: here
                         and still half-coming.
Pray, beginning sleeper, and let your mind dissolve me as I
Straighten, upright from the overflow crouch: pray with all
Your heart-muscle,   15
The longing-muscle only, as the bird in its hunting sorrows
Bides in good falling—gone
The gather-voices, and more the alone ones.
Pray with the soul-straining of echo

Of the lost ax, that the footprints of all   20
Predators, moving like old-stone, like
Clean leaves, grey and sensitive as willows',
Will have left their intensified beauty
And alertness around you, when you wake,
And that the blood and waste of them   25
Will be gone, or not known.   Become
All stark soul and overreach   the ax in the air
Now come, now still half-way
                         and the echo, possessing the tree
Struck to the heart-ring.   At last, let there be   30
No ax encircling you, no claw, no life-giving death
Of anything, but the moon broad-lying and peerless,

The living strive of it, the breaking and coming together,
Its long-smelted, half-holy strike
On water.   Rest in soft flame   gentle threads of pine-cone   35
Fire: fire from a still-growing source
Upright around you.   Stay with me
And without me, hearing
Your hearing come back in a circle.   After midnight no ax
Shall be harmful to your wholeness,   40
No blood-loss give life.   You are in your rings, and growing
In darkness.   I quell and thicken
Away.   I am

The surround, and you are your own.

The Eagle's Mile

1980

for Justice William Douglas

The Emmet's Inch & Eagle's Mile
Blake

Unwarned, catch into this
With everything you have:
the trout streaming with all its quick
In the strong curve   all things on all sides
In motion   the soul strenuous   5
And still
in time-flow as in water blowing
Fresh and for a long time

Downhill   something like air it is
Also and it is dawn   10

There in merciless look-down
As though an eagle or Adam
In lightning, or both, were watching uncontrollably
For meat, among the leaves. Douglas, with you
The soul tries it one-eyed, half your sight left hanging in a river   15
In England, long before you died,

And now thát one, that and the new one
Struck from death's instant—
Lightning's: like mankind on impulse blind-
siding God—true-up together and ride   20
On silence, enraptured surveillance,

The eagle's mile. Catch into this, and broaden

Into and over

The mountain rivers, over the leaf-tunnel path:

Appalachia, where the trail lies always hidden   25

Like prey, through the trembling south-north of the forest
Continent, from Springer Mountain to Maine,
And you may walk

Using not surpassing

The trout's hoisted stand-off with the channel,   30
Or power-hang the same in the shattered nerves
Of lightning: like Adam find yourself splintering out
Somewhere on the eagle's mile, on peerless, barbaric distance
Clairvoyant with hunger,

Or can begin   can be   begin to be   35
What out-gentles, and may evade:
This second of the second year
Of death, it would be best for the living
If it were your impulse to step out of grass-bed sleep

As valuably   as cautiously   40

As a spike-buck, head humming with the first male split
Of the brain-bone, as it tunes to the forked twigs
Of the long trail

Where Douglas you once walked in a white shirt as a man
In the early fall, fire-breathing with oak-leaves,   45
Your patched tunnel-gaze exactly right
For the buried track,
the England-curved water strong
Far-off with your other sight, both fresh-waters marbling together

Supporting not surpassing   50

What flows   what balances

In it. Douglas, power-hang in it all now, for all
The whole thing is worth: catch without warning

Somewhere in the North Georgia creek like ghost-muscle tensing
        Forever, or on the high grass-bed   55
Yellow of dawn, catch like a man stamp-printed by God-
        shock, blue as the very foot
      Of fire. Catch into the hunted
Horns of the buck, and thus into the deepest hearing—
        Nerveless, all bone, bone-tuned   60
  To leaves and twigs—with the grass drying wildly
When you woke   where you stood with all blades rising
  Behind you, and stepped out
                         possessing the trail,
    The racked bramble on either side shining   65
     Like a hornet, your death drawing life
  From growth
          from flow, as in the gill-cleansing turn
     Of the creek
           or from the fountain-twist   70
     Of flight, that rounds you
     Off, and shies you downwind
     Side-faced, all-seeing with hunger,

    And over this, steep and straight-up
        In the eagle's mile   75
 Let Adam, far from the closed smoke of mills
       And blue as the foot
Of every flame, true-up with blind-side outflash
      The once-more instantly
   Wild world: over Brasstown Bald   80

   Splinter uncontrollably whole.

Scion
1980

I. With Rose, at Cemetery

          Kin: quiet grasses.   Above,
Lace: white logic   fretted cloud-cloth.
                              In steady-state insolence
          I bring up a family
Look: a look like sword-grass, that will leave on anything human   5
     A swirl-cut, the unfurling touch of a world-wound
          Given straight out
Of my forehead, and having all the work and tide-
pull of the dead, from their oblong, thrilling frame-tension
          Filled here with sunlight.   10

          God give me them,
     God gave them me, with a hedgerow grip on a rose
And black brows: in over-sifted, high-concentrate cloth
     And a high-fashion nudity, that shall come
Of it, when the time comes.   15
                         Now at any good time
Of this struck eleven o'clock, I can look forth on you
     Or anyone, as though you were being grazed
          Forever by a final tense of threads,
     The inmost brimming feather-hone of light.   20

     The dead work into a rose
          By back-breaking leisure, head-up,
          Grave-dirt exploding like powder
Into sunlit lace, and I lie and look back through their labor
          Upon their dark dazzle of needles,   25
          Their mineral buckets and ore-boats
Like millwheels, pinnacling, restoring lightly
          All over me from the green mines
          And black-holes of the family plot.
                              I am one of them   30

For as long as we all shall die
And be counted.   I am the one this late morning
Pulled-through alive: the one frame-humming, conveying the tension,
Black-browed from the black-holes
Of family peace.   My uncle's brows are still   35
As they were, growing out in mine,

                    and I rest with good gut-
feel in the hand-loomed bright-out,
In the dead's between-stitches breathing,
And am watchful as to what I do   40
With the swirl-cut of my straight look,
And of whom among the living it shall fix
With trembling, with unanswerable logic,
With green depth and short deadly grasses,

With my dead full-time and work-singing.   45

II. In Lace and Whalebone

Bull-headed, big-busted,
Distrustful and mystical: my summoned kind of looks
As I stand here going back
And back, from mother to mother: I am totally them in the eyebrows,
Breasts, breath and butt: 50
           You, never-met Grandmother of the fields
Of death, who laid this frail dress
Most freshly down, I stand now in your closed bones,
Sucked-in, in your magic tackle, taking whatever,

From the stark freedom under the land,   55
From under the sea, from the bones of the deepest beast,
Shaped now entirely by me, by whatever
Breath I draw.   I smell of clear
Hope-surfeited cedar: ghost-smell and forest-smell
Laid down in dim vital boughs   60
And risen in lace
        and a feeling of nakedness is broadening
                  world-wide out
From me ring on ring—a refining of open-work skin—to go

With you, and I have added   65
Bad temper, high cheek-bones and exultation:
            fill out these ribs

For something ripped-up and boiled-down,
        Plundered and rendered, come over me
From a blanched ruck of thorned, bungled blubber,   70
    From rolling ovens raking-down their fires

For animal oil, to light room after room
In peculiar glister, from a slim sculpt of blown-hollow crystal:
            Intent and soft-fingered
Precipitous light, each touch to the wick like drawing   75
First blood in a great hounded ring

                                    the hand blunted and gone
Fathomless, in rose and ash, and cannot throw
        The huddled burn out of its palm:

It is all in the one breath, as in the hush   80
    Of the hand: the gull stripped downwind, sheering off
To come back slow,

                    the squandered fat-trash boiling in the wake,
The weird mammalian bleating of bled creatures,

A thrall of ships: 85
                    lyric hanging of rope
(The snarled and sure entanglement of space),
    Jarred, hissing squalls, tumultuous yaw-cries
Of butchery, stressed waves that part, close, re-open
    Then seethe and graze: I hold-in my lungs   90
And hand, and try-out the blood-bones of my mothers,
And I tell you they are volcanic, full of exhorted hoverings:
                                                This animal:

        This animal: I stand and think

Its feed   its feel   its whole lifetime on one air: 95
        In lightning-strikes I watch it leap
And welter   blue wide-eyes   lung-blood up-misting under

Stamped splits of astounding concentration,
But soundless,
                        the crammed wake blazing with fat   100
And phosphor,
                        the moon stoning down, Venus rising,

            And we can hold, woman on woman,
This dusk if no other
                        and we will now, all of us combining,   105
            Open one hand.
                                    Blood into light.

Is possible: lamp, lace and tackle   paired bones of the deep
            Rapture
                surviving   reviving, and wearing well   110
            For this sundown, and not any other,
                In the one depth

            Without levels, deepening for us.

——————————

From Time
1981

Deborah for Years at the Piano

My hands that were not born completely
Matched   that struck at a hurt wire upward
            Somewhere on the uncentered plain
Without cause: my hands that could not befriend
            Themselves, though openly fielded: 5
            That never came out

            Intercepting: that could get nothing back
Of a diamonded pay-off, the whole long-promised

Harmonic blaze of boredom never coming—

                                                  now flock   10

In a slow change like limitless gazing:

From back-handed, disheartening cliff-sound, are now

A new, level anvilling of tones,

Spread crown, an evening sprinkle of height,

Perfected wandering.   Here is   15

The whole body cousinly: are

Heartenings, charged with invented time,

A chord with lawn-broadness,

Lean clarities.

                    With a fresh, gangling resonance   20

Truing handsomely, I draw on left-handed space

For a brave ballast shelving and bracing, and from it,

                                      then, the light

Prowling lift-off, the treble's strewn search and

                                  wide-angle glitter.

How much of the body was wasted

Before I drew up here!   Who would have thought how much music   25

The forearms had in them!   How much of Schumann and Bach

In the shoulders, and the draining of the calves!

I sit, as everlasting,

In the overleaf and memory-make of tedium,

The past freely with me   both hands   30

Full in the overlook, the dead at their work-bench altars

Half-approving

                time-releasing.

Deborah Burning a Doll
Made of House-Wood

1981

I know, I know it was necessary for us to have things of this kind,
which acquiesced in everything

Rainer Maria Rilke

I set you level,
Your eyes like the twin beasts of a wall.

As a child I believed I had grown you,
And I hummed as I mixed the blind nails
Of this house with the light wood of Heaven—   5
The rootless trees there—falling in love
With carpenters—their painted, pure clothes, their flawless
Bagginess, their God-balanced bubbles, their levels.
I am leaving: I have freed the shelves

So that you may burn cleanly, in sheer degrees   10
Of domestic ascent, unfolding
Boards one after the other, like a fireman
His rungs out of Hell
or some holocaust
whelmed and climbing: 15

You only now, alone in the stepped, stripped closet, staring
Out onto me, with the guaranteed kiss
Off-flaking, involvedly smiling,
Cradling and throning,
With the eyes of a wall and two creatures: 20

Ungainly   unbroken   hungering
For me, braving and bearing:
Themed, intolerable, born and unborn child
Of this house—of table and floorboard and cupboard,
Of stranger and hammering virgin—   25

At the flash-point of makeup I shadow
My own eyes with house-paint, learning
From yours, and the shelves of Heaven-wood

          take fire from the roots

      Of earth, dust bodies into smoke   30
The planks of your pulverized high-chair,
    Paint blazes on the eyelids

  Of the living in all colors, bestowing the power to see
         Pure loss, and see it
With infinite force, with sun-force: 35

                you gesture
   Limply, with unspeakable aliveness,
    Through the kindling of a child's
Squared mess of an indoor wood-yard

             and I level   40
 Stay level
       and kneel and disappear slowly

Into Time, as you, with sun-center force, take up the house
  In Hell-roaring steps, a Heaven-beaming holocaust
    Of slats   45
    and burn   burn off

    Just once, for good.

Deborah, Moon, Mirror, Right Hand Rising

1981

Rising behind me
And coming into my right hand

Is the wide-open collisionless color of the whole night
Ringed-in, pure surface.　　All pores cold with cream,
I have reached the bright reception of my palm, the full　　　　　5
Steady of the oval,

Afterglowing in the hang-time of my image,
　　　　　　　　　　　　　　　　mowed down
　　　　Inside by the moon coming up
In my face, in the blocked-back shimmer of the sun　　　　　10
　　　　Cutting glass in secret, into

　　　　New Being angled with thresholds.
　　　　Woman of the child

　　　　I was, I am shone-through now
In circles, as though the moon in my hand were falling　　　　　15

　　　　Concentrically, on the spirit of a tree
　　　　With no tree thought of, but with

High-concentrate quiet, and the curving essence of God-ruined God-willed
God-moved slow stone.　　I am shining for the first time　　at last
　　　　All-told.　　The glass now no more than half　　　　　20

　　　　An enemy, I leave it
For the moon to move through, as it moves in strong rings
Through me, leaving something in the air between
　　　　　　　　　　　　　　　　the moon and sun

　　　　That is not the mirror:　　　　　25

　　　　A woman's live playing of the universe
　　　　As inner light, stands clear,
　　　　And is, where I last was.

Veer-Voices
Two Sisters under Crows
1981

Sometimes are living those who have been seen
        Together   those farthest leaning
            With some dark birds and fielded
Below them   countercrying and hawing in savage openness
        For every reason.   Such are as we, to come out   5
            And under and balance-cruise,

    Cross-slanting and making long, raw, exhaustless
        Secret-ballot assertions   feeding and self-
                supporting our surround

    By all angles of outcry; it seems to lift and steady us   10
            To the ground.   If I were to say to you
                From a stand-off of corn-rows—
                Say to you just as I entered
                Their shifting, bi-lingual rasping,
                    The crows' vector-cloud   15
            And parable, my sister, this is where we eat

            The last of our dawn-dust hanging
        Stranded and steady behind us   shall say
    We should have known we would end up in full
            Health here   end up pilfering   20

            A crossroads and passing out
        One kind of voice in skinned speeches
    All over the place   leaning and flying
            Passing into
                            flying in and out   25
    Of each other
                        with nothing to tell of
        But the angles of light-sensitive dust
            Between fences leaded with dew,

30

You might say back,

Come with me
Into the high-tension carry
Of these fences: come in a double stand-down
From the night-mass of families—
Rooms of world-wearying order, our stifled folk—   35
And bring them forth with us,
Stalk-standing, space-burning, to call
All over, to hear
These wires—thumb-echo of the harp
Pronged with herding whispers, cross-handed   40
Fingered—and all
Of us would be then

Veer-crying and straining like wire
Redoubling its prongs, and could contrive to praise
Sufficiently, and counterpraise   45
Barbed wire and these crows:
Their spirit-shifting splits
Of tongue, their cry of unfathomable hordes.

————

Heraldic
Deborah and Horse in Morning Forest
1981

and indeed a floating flag is like wind visible and what weeds are in a current;
it gives it thew and fires it and bloods it in

Gerard Manley Hopkins

It could be that nothing you could do
Could keep you from stepping out and blooding-in
An all-out blinding heraldry for this:
A blurred momentum-flag

That must be seen sleep-weathered and six-leggèd,   5
Brindling and throwing off limbo-light

Of barns

And the Lord shall say that the stasis of the wood
Shall be struck full in the vitals where it stands
And move on, everywhere,   10
As fast as any can ride.   This,

And reality at the same time shall strike
Home to the sun completely
By surprise, as twigs from all sprung angles to the eyeball,
And the forest jackstraw and craze   15
Instantaneously with speed and connivance

As these two headbrass themselves and head
At last for what they have seen through sleep
Cleared of nails: the wildly hidden log prowling upward
Toward their promised leap,   20
Toward their brute and searching terror and control.
Nothing for them both
But the great fallen tree's shaggy straining
For hazard, its plunge of years ago
Still trembling in the vines that bind it down.   25
Nothing for them

But chance and forge-green hurtling: but the strangulation
Of undergrowing twine-snarls breaking off
Wherever they charge and come on
Like a deafening of tunnels laid open   30
In flaying and slot-glancing sunlight:
Beast-work of all outright challenge,
Gigantic strides shaping her sex,
Lift up through the bodiless battering
Of the sun on the power-browed forest: 35

You witnesses, come waking profoundly:

Put the headbrass into the wind
Of their   speed and the nursing glow of her hands
On the sown reins: Plan to leave earth
And a hoofmark in midair   40
Leave, in the heavenly muscle
Of whole cloth vibrantly, in the forge-green
Sun-hammering potential of the dead.

Hang it, and earn it.

————

Springhouse, Menses, Held Apple, House and Beyond

1981

Nothing but one life: all stands:
I go out with my main ear in each stone

End-stopping a creek: territorially

Listen, and beyond the live seepage of rock
Is a window cleanly blinded with an orchard.   5
Everything the world has made
This day, through sheen and rock
Can pierce   through stone and glass
And air, I hear.
                           My hand inertially rounding,   10
I love far in and far from me:
The stalled tightening of distant fruit, the wasp's delaying
Uncontested spasm at the pane.

Sealed and sweeping depth
Is part of me now, and I ride it, gone bright inside in the dark 15
Of the raised, rounded quarry and its cool;

I am reined-in and thriving with the wasp:
I meet now vibrantly with him
And unbearably at the broad window:
When he gives up the glass, I shall rise and walk out through all the walls 20

Of my father's house   holding, but not at bay,
High-energy cloth where I scotched it
Like iron between my legs
                              and go

Whole-hearted and undoctored toward the hillside 25
Beaming its distances, the fruit in my hand
Encompassing, crackling with vitality
Like a burning basket
                    the day-moon stronger
In me than on me   outdoing what is left of the wasp's 30
Smattering and hard-nosed abandon
And pick up his rifling thread
Where it lays out my wandering for me
Center-boring through fields of ray-flowers:
I help it   I ride it   I invent it 35
To death and follow down   shameless with energy

From the closed river flowering,
Upgathered and delighted in the hive's
High-risk and conglomerate frenzy:

One life 40
brought to bear
On what I require:

A stone house, a father, a window,
The wasp's holocaust of location,
The bees' winnowed over-stressed time-zone, 45
Far orchards blazing with slant.

The Lyric Beasts

1981

—Dancer to Audience—

What works for me

As in your flatland stillness you grow,
Not ashen witnesses,
But eye-bones, eye-muscle fields of hovering
With me,   5
        is this: is with me:
Is a body out-believing existence:

The shining of perfection, the myth-chill.

I hold what I have,
Hold hard, and wait for my travel   10
To time-bind, and be raised
High enough in closed flight, high enough in low candle-
        power to burn barns and set
All rafters free:
                to reach and rarefy the lyric beasts.   15

Some distance
Down, unfurl   sit loosed and hawking
At me, as I am hurled and buried
Out of you in midair,
In hounded flame-outs stalling and renewing,   20
Pale with chasm-sweat, through Chaos
Set going by imaginative laws,
One flawless seizure bringing on another,
The search-and-destroy of creatures in the void.

In your ashen ditch of witness   25
Take off your bags of shot, and be with me
As one, like a rising curtain,
        materializing, enchanted with unnecessary being,

Emblem-eyed, degenerate with symbols,
Work-beasts of lightness, icy with void-sweat,   30
For, in bitter, over-valued radiation,
One form may live from another, and may follow

The grain of closed flight, as through board.
In the loft of the ice-bound
Soft-heeled foot, we shall leave nothing   35
To chance, enfabled, driven-up
Toward death in some foregone position—the dead-lift,
The go-devil fury—knowing that flight is only
One of the floating latencies of muscle:
An infinite elongation.   40
                        Come from your hovering ashes;
Join and defy me
To out-live you   out-die   outflesh   out-spirit

At the eerie, demonic torpor of the crest,
Young outriders of the Absolute,   45
Swan   flower   phoenix,
Controlled, illusory fire is best
For us.   Rise and on faith

Follow.   It is better that I should be;
Be what I am not, and I am.   50

————

Tapestry and Sail

1981

—She Imagines Herself a Figure Upon Them—

A wrong look into heavy stone
And twilight, wove my body,
And I was snowing with the withering hiss of thread.
My head was last, and with it came

An eyesight needle-pointing like a thorn-bush.   5
I came to pass
                    slant-lit, Heaven-keeping with the rest
Of the museum, causing History to hang clear of earth
With me in it, carded and blazing.   Rigidly I swayed

Among those morningless strings, like stained glass   10
        Avertedly yearning: here a tree   a Lord
            There a falcon on fist   an eagle
            Worried into cloud, strained up
On gagging filaments   there a compacted antelope
        With such apparent motion stitched to death   15
            That God would pluck His image
        Clean of feathers if I leapt   or breathed
Over the smothered plain:
                    the Past, hung up like beast-hides,
            Half-eaten, half-stolen   20
        Not enough.
                    Well, I was not for it:
        I stubborned in that lost wall
Of over-worked dust, and came away
                            in high wind,   25
        Rattling and flaring
    On the lodge-pole craze and flutter of the sail,
        Confounding, slatting and flocking,
On-going with manhandled drift, wide-open in the lightning's

Re-emphasizing split, the sea's holy no-win roar.   30
        I took the right pose coming off
    The air, and of a wild and ghostly battering
Was born, and signed-on
                        and now steady down
To movement, to the cloth's relationless flurries,   35
Sparring for recovery   feather-battling   lulling,
    Tautening and resolving, dwelling slowly.

The Olympian

1982

—False Youth: Spring—

Los Angeles back-yarding in its blue-eyed waters
Of empty swim, by my tract-house of packaged hard-candy
I lay in wait with the sun
And celebrity beer
                for the Olympian,   5
Now my oldest boy's junior
High school algebra teacher, who had brought back the black-magic gold
Of the East, down the fast lane,
Freewaying, superhuman with rubberized home-stretch,
        The four hundred meters from Tokyo   10
To Balboa Boulevard, leaving in his wake
All over the earth, the Others, the nation-motley doom-striped ones,
        Those heart-eating sprinters, those Losers.
        With Olympia Beer I was warming

        Warming up with the best chill waters   15
        Of the West Coast, cascading never-ending
Down out of Washington State. Now is your moment of truth
With me at last, O Champion! for I had laid a course as strange
To him as to me. Steeplechase! I had always leapt into water
        Feet first, and could get out   20
Faster than in.   I was ready for the Big One:
        For the Water Jump in the corner
Of the lax, purfled pool, under the cemented palm
        Where at night the shrewd rat climbed
And rustled and ruled the brown fronds over the underlit   25
        Blue oval, surveying Sepulveda,
        And in its color and kind, suffered
World recognition.
                With a slide-rule in his shirt-pocket,
        His bullet-proof glasses drawing   30
Into points—competitive points—and fish-eye-lensing,
        Crossflashing on my hogged, haggard grassplot

Of slapped-down, laid-back Sepulveda, just after he'd Won It All,
He came lankily, finely drawn
Onto my turf, where all the time I had been laying   35
For him, building my energy-starches,
My hilarious, pizza-fed fury. My career of fat
Lay in the speed-trap, in the buckets and tools of the game-plan,
The snarls of purified rope. Then dawned the strict gods of Sparta,
The free gods of Athens! O lungs of Pheidippides collapsing in a square   40
Of the delivered city! O hot, just-hurdlable gates
Of deck-chairs! Lounges! A measured universe
Of exhilarating laws! Here I had come   there I'd gone
Laying it down   confusing, staggering
The fast lane and the slow, on and over   45
And over recliners, sun-cots, cleaning-poles and beach-balls,
Foiled cans of rusty rat-poison   bowing, split casks
Of diatomaceous earth   corks spaced-out like California
On blue-and-white dacron cords   lost-and-found swim-fins
Unmatched and pigeon-toed   half-hearted air   50
In blazing rings   doughnuts and play rafts   dragons and elephants
Blown-up by mouth, now sighing most of life
Away   the lawful No-Running signs
Turned to the wall. And all the time, all the time,
Under the brown-browed, rose-ash glower   55
Of the smog-bank, the crows, long gone
Gray with the risen freeways, were thronging and hawing
To be Doves of Peace   to be turned
Loose, displaying and escaping, over the jolted crowds
Of Unimart, the rammed Victory Stand,   60
                              and in the rose-ash
Of early dusk, we called our wives, gray as crows
In their golf-hats, to the secret Olympics, laid down in my laws
Within laws, where world champions, now mad with the moon
Of moonlighting, sold running shoes. This so, we insisted   65
On commercials, those all-comers'
Career-dreams of athletes: "We are brought to you by the Bringers of the Flame,
The double-dry double martini," those women said. "Get set!
Get set! You're being born
Again, in spite of everything!" James Bond and my smallest boy   70
Blazed with one cap-pistol together. We hove like whales from the line.

Twice around

We were going for, cursing and cruising like ghosts, over dog-food bowls,
Over sprinklers passed-out from their spin-off
Of rainbows and I was losing   75
But not badly, and even gained a little, coming out
Of the water-jump and over the jump-rope, and out of him or maybe
Me   surely me   burst a mindless deep
Belching blindsiding laugh down the backstretch
Of earth-kegs and dirty cleansing-tools that skinned the dust   80
From the under-blue, and for one unsettling moment left it
Blazing and mattering. I blazed I felt great I was a great
Plaster stadium-god   lagging   lolloping   hanging
In there with the best: was running pale and heavy
With cement-dust   from two wives running   85
Then coming around   coming back
Down the slow lane   lurching   lorry-swaying:
Now toward two wives making up for   —making
The gelatin-murmur of crowds, I pounded, wet and laboring,
And then, half a pool   90
Behind, went into the bell-lap.
I was holding my own
Back there, as we rounded
Past the stands   he a long first and I
A world-class second and counting   95
On my finish or something   Yes! My finish to come
From the home turf like an ascension   all-seeing
World-recognized   poison-proof   smoke-proof   time-proof
Out of the pool, a rat's climb grappling
Half-a-lap half-a-lap   still alive   100
In mid-stride, louring, lumbering, crow-hopping
Behind the athlete's unhurried
Slack, unearthly footling lope:
I stepped low and heavy
Over the last light rope, smashed water with my sole   105
Flat   climbed, lurched, legged it and duck-footed
For home   a good not shameful
Second   this was all right and everything

But no! My weave   my plan   the run
Of my knots had caught up with him   caught   110
Him where he lived
                    —in his feet—
                                    and he was down
In styrofoam, and on a bloated blessèd doughnut-ring
Of rubber rolled: the finish-line leapt   exploded   115
Into Reality, shot-through with deathless flame, crossed with white paper:
Swam illicitly, aboundingly
Like wind-aided glory. With courage to do credit
To any rat, I cornered and turned
It on. He came back instantly, but instantly was not soon   120
Enough, for I charged past like a slow freight
All over the earth, and had got it
And gone   long gone   and burst

Through the living tissue: breasted and blanked
The Tape and can feel it   125

Bannering, still, on my chest
Like wing-span, that once was toilet-paper, torn epically
Where the true Olympian slurred
His foot and fell, and I felt my lungs collapsing in a square
Of the City, like Pheidippides dying of the sheer   130
Good of my news.
                    Far off, still rising at rose dusk
And night, free under the low-browed smoke, and grayer
Than any fake peace-bird,
Like a called crow I answer   135
Myself utterly, with a whole laugh—that body-language one-world
One word of joy—straight into the ruining tons
Of smoke that trash my head and doom it
And keep it recognized
                                    in the age   140
And condition of my kind, and hear also, maybe not entirely
From myself, the Olympian's laugh
Coming from somewhere
Behind, blindsidedly, getting the point

At last, sighing like ghosts and like rubber, for fat 145
And luck, all over the earth, where that day and any and every
Day after it, devil hindmost and Goddamn it

To glory, I lumbered for gold.

————

Deborah in Mountain Sound
Bell, Glacier, Rose
1982

Averaging-sound

Of space-thinning   space-harvesting metal—

Obsessional, the outstaying
Life-longing intervals, wherein,

Reasonless as cloud, the male's one luminosity 5
is frozen

In a great winding winter-lust around her.
Any man must feel
In him, the glacier's rammed carry
Of upheaval, 10
change,

A lockjaw concentration on his loins
Now glowing, inch-dreaming under the oval

Of the bell interruptedly cloven:
With one glance, one instant 15

Crystallization

Of an eyelash she is set, the mason's rose

Of ice-sculpture in her fist,

Her image flash-frozen, unmerited
And radiant in the making-fluid of men.   20

————————

Ray-Flowers I

1982

—Deborah as Winged Seed, Descending with Others—

As when we all fell all day

Consenting

Sight-softening   space-massing
Time-thickening   time-floating more

Light   5

Unparalleled   aimlessness of
Mortality-haze   all noon, all afternoon

I was dawning and hanging

Sown

Into it with other   harmonic distances   10
Sunflowers   dandelions   thistles

Consenting

Holy spirits of drift   slow-thriving
I had taken   a gentle hold on
The other field   multitudinous gravity   15

Consenting

suspended

Around us   paced, mazing
Choral hush and blaze   Having come
I now from unshakable ground   20
Offer free passage descending
Through the worked, lopped glory-call of crows: Come down
Come down as I inhale

And stand, and show you where.   Come:
Muffle   splinter   increase   fill   25
Down, and mist,
Lucent, stung with thaw,
Through the psychic mob-sound of bees: fall
                      fall to
Fall through their ranging brim   30

Consenting

Super-nerved with weightlessness:

All girls of cloud and ego in your time,
Smoked-out of millennial air-space,
Empowered with blurr, lie down   35
With bindweed force   with angelic clutter and stillness

As I hold out and for you unfold
This feather—frond of a bird
Elsewhere—:   pale-off and grow
Akin to it, down-haired, like the near side of smoke,   40

A young smoke of common spring sunlight:
                      vivid drowse

And curvature   instinct and huge
With vanishing-power, into
The whole mingling oversouling loom   45
Of this generation
settling
hovering
mixing
My year and yours   50
just here, last year
Or next
or now, no matter when

Or where we fall, or fell.

————

Ray-Flowers II

1982

What could have slow-thrown me so vastly,
So far, among surfing, softly-
built distances,
Somewhere in a sweeping, unobstructed
Holding-pattern of lightness?   Is this how I helped to cause   5
Whole fields of cast presence to stand
With wider and wider natures in this light?

Smoking well-heads of blossom,
Anti-matter and easement, we huddle down
Unfolding, and balance-bloom is final   10
This year, over the unstirring plow.
Reprisal-furies of softness,
Sisters   spring-rising girls,

Pooled, eddying girls, sated and triumphant
On chance, now resting   15
Somewhere on the general brink, by gaunt fountains—

Annealing and equalling
Spirits of land, now,
                                solidify and tremble
As a caused meadow,   20
                                the place of
This season only   but this instant
Total, seething and fronting
All the way to the hills,

The near hills, thinning with overreach.   25

————————

Doorstep, Lightning, Waif-Dreaming
1982

Who can tell who was born of what?
I go sitting on the doorsteps of unknowns
And ask, and hear nothing
From the rhythmical ghosts of those others,
Or from myself while I am there, but only   5
The solid shifts of drumming made of heart.
I come always softly,
My head full of lingering off-prints

Of lightning—vital, engendering blank,
The interim spraddling crack   the crowning rollback   10
Whited-out *ex nihilo*
                                and I am as good as appearing
The other time.   I come of a root-system of fire, as it fires
Point-blank at this hearthstone and doorstep: there is
A tingling of light-sensitive hairs   15
Between me: my clothes flicker
And glow with it, under the bracketing split
Of sky, the fasting, saint-hinting glimmer,
The shifting blasts of echo, relocating,
And of an orphaning blaze   20

I have been stressed, and born, and stamped
Alive on this doorstep.   I believe it between cloud
And echo, and my own chosen-and-sifted footstep
    Arriving,
                engendered, endangered, loving,   25

        Dangerous, seeking ground.

                ————

Deborah in Ancient Lingerie,
in Thin Oak over Creek
1982

    Having found out this morning I was born
            Born to be hung
    Low down in the braced weave of plants

            I can do.   I can cling
            Beginning to be the all   5
    Of the strain of trail-blazing a circle
            Over water, I can do
                        tanager
glimmer
            glimmer and shoot   10
    Red like a bolt I can do.   and any but completely
            Buck-naked diving I can do
    In my album bloomers:
                        a live twig flimmering back
Across the eyeball   15
            on the way up, and make it strike and spark
            Tears and no brain-
    sweat but a close-out of wings over down-
            driven midstreaming rocks

I can do: a praying enlargement   20
Of shadow I can do, and run it up a tree:
An unparalleled cutting of the sense

Of time from around me, I can do—a salamander's circular nightmare
Of renewal by fire, I can make
Of common sunlight, by climbing: 25
                a slant into air from a burrow
      I can do: reversal
    Of every day sunburn
            I can do, and turn to a ghost:
    The golden Great Chain of Being   30
I can throw in and do
          The health-sweat of baby-fat freckles
  I can do
      gently, just over you:
             balance-beam disdain   35

    Like heron-veins over the forest
    When my spirit is branching, when I
    Catch it and don't spend it, I can do:
    All kinds of caused shade
  I can do, and unparalleled being   40
          I can do, snake-screaming,
   Withering, foster-parenting for animals
    I can do
      very gently from just about
  Right over you, I can do   45
      at no great height I can do
           and bear
And counter-balance and do
    and half-sway and do
        and sway   50
           and outsway and do.

The Lode

1982

—Deborah's Rain-Longing—

Flash-points deadening and twining
With wall:
                    rain, and its nailed smoke—
Cobbled, snailing surfaces,
Jammed drops at the dead-level stroke   gravity's slow   5
      Secretional slashes on this house—
Lost laterals, rinses . . .
                     my pared thumb
Just come from my mouth,
                 half-slaked, half-eaten,   10

I haze outward, stamped and sidling
Through splinters of shatter-proof water, glass of

Metal-sweat, as on death-cell plumbing,
     My small bush rallying surely
On time, near the free-standing snail-tracks—   15

     Trial passion   cunning

Blanked resins stranded like fields
In twires of steep matchless erosion . . .

Hard-pressed to do what I can
    For myself, I am intent   20
    On selecting which position
  Is most mine, most unusual in delight
In this studied water   in this whole suspended gentleness
  Seething with impulse.   There is one place
  Come from me, to feather me, and capable   25
  Of sparking like glory-touched steel-wool

When all sucked-up sun-water is falling
Potently, modestly, like this   and
I am in it in every position

It carries, and taking every chance   30
With myself   every off-chance of slow-release being,

Within doors   within glass
In the grit-smell of casters and ladles   the new-mown pane
Unmorselling.
Teach me   35

And learn me, wanderer: every man-jack rain-soaked and vital
To the bone, without me good as dead:
Be somewhere within the outside   within
My naked breath.   Keep warming,
Deep weak forestry.   40

Rainfall, give me my chance.

Deborah and Deirdre as Drunk Bridesmaids
Foot-Racing at Daybreak
1982

Dawn dust.   We were right.   Haze of open damp
In levels beaded and barrelling   sleep mingling with speed and straining

Of no heat-shadow   nowhere to be left
Behind   time-sparks over the grass   sunrise

From blade to blade splaying in muscle-light   5
Gone to tracks tattering and shimmering

All over   beggar-lice   brierbrambles
Picked off in consuming abandon

By these long clothes: open-browed on the blood-road,
Dawn mist just crossing us backward   10

Into passionate burn-off—pokeweed   oakenshaw
No end to the entrance—

Footloose in creature-glow   we rose
With us we were right

In there, with our hats in our hands   15
Together we blew the night roadblock

Plunging and reaching   flinging, redoubling
Flat-out in sprung dust and not dying, yet dying

Of devil and sawtooth of laughter—
Where can we belong   how can we   20

Eye-witness except in this rambling
And beginning through shadblow and firebush

In level-out and stride-out and sing-out,
Good draggle and time-sparks?   Look up: look out

From the overdrive-side of free-floating—   25
O next blaze of Liberation Fence-rails

O flat stretch of wood-lot and hazel
And all that wide-open dust,

That winging of hedgerows and stump-blasting
Freshness, what's headlong to us now?   30

Summons

1982

Through the flexing swamp
Have someone be nearing

Through the free blurr of sleep
With strong naked night-lights
Have someone be nearing   5

Sought for crimes against death
Snow-blanked and fog-footed
By the ritual meadow
Have someone be nearing

With a primitive flourish   10
In simplicity floating
Raw with space and insurgence
In a proud shaggy jacket
Have someone be nearing

With a walking-horse sureness   15
But walking in flashes
In lamp-rust and harvest
From a shanty-like chapel
With a glimmer like jazz
Have someone be nearing   20

From a massacre fleeing
No others forsaking
With untested invention
And jackhammer insistence
In a bright misty onslaught   25
In warmth past the telling
Have someone be nearing

With no visions of profit
But tingling with bridge-bulbs

In a stud's brimming harness   30
With delivery-room patience
Taking straw from around me
With a crowding like swimmers
With unparalleled rhythm
    Have someone be nearing   35

With primal instructions
With emergency grappling
With centrifuge fury
Through artillery panic
By his mother just pardoned   40
Like a stark mossy stallion
With great room for improvement
Through a glad slant of orchards
    Have someone be nearing

With no power of waiting   45
With no single ambition
With a hamstring heat-healing
Like a tall sprinting wonder
With upbringing well-hidden
With a ring from a pine-trunk   50
Through the ice-dreams of sunstroke
With half of my first child
With invention unending
    Have someone be nearing

      unending   55

      invention

      go for it

      unending

Lakes of Värmland

1982

—with André Frénaud—

Under the terrible north-light north-sea
Light blue: severe smile of a warrior who sleeps in chain-mail
Like a child: sleeps for the many, in water turned to brass
By the dumped cannon of Charles the Twelfth—
                                          leave them at their level,   5
                    O Sweden, like the ultimate weapons,
          Like the last war-dead
                              steeped in the angles of your just light—

A single pine tree standing for my heart, I wish to gather near them
            Anything that grows; myrtle, this stuff could be,   10

                Or bilberry; whatever.

————————

Form

1982

—with André Frénaud—

I

Pull out the pissed-on clinkers,
Rake down the ashes of my bed, and come in

And let's do it, as cold as we can get,

Calving into the void like glaciers
Into the green Northern Sea. Give me a cliff-shudder   5

When you're finishing, before you split off
Unheard, almost booming: cliff-shudder   child-shudder

That ends it. We have been here before, as you know.

II

We have been here again, humped-up and splintering
  Like ice-junk: here it has happened   10
But we missed it, and dead birds from many migrations
 Float eye-up between us,
        between bergs, Carrara-piles

Where we chopped and hacked, shattering glass, searching jaggedly
  For the radiant nude ice-sculpture   15
 That never showed   never shaped itself free

  Of us   was never anything
But chip-chaff and gentian-blue zero
        and, as before,
  The glorious being we froze together   20
To bring forth, that we chiseled toward closer and closer,
  Whinging and ringing, weeping

 For discovery: that together we have annihilated
  But not found, is now no more

  Than our two hostile cadavers, together.   25

Heads

1982

—with Lucien Becker—

I

There is no longer any reason to confuse
My breath with the room's. Sleep empties the pillow;
The world looks into various windows
Where human beings are unfinished,

Like blueprints; no substance has come.   5
Meadow-saffron dries, tenses. Morning pulverizes it
With a single vague foot, heavy as with
All the sleepless eyelids that there are.

The wellsprings are gray as the sky;
The smoky wind, a wind for headless people,   10
Flees with the thousands of voices
That solitude waits for, like tide-slack.

Above the roofs everything is empty;
Light cannot get all the way up
To where it was, stalled in dim lamp-bulbs   15
And bottles drunk dry to hold it down.

II

Beyond the sill the day has started and quit.
The sheet has cut off my head; my mirror's
Still deep with the whole night,
And the road has made great progress   20

Into the wall. A fly goes all around
In a big balance. I used to lie here, darling,

With unimproved light: I took it from your brow
To mine, a glimmer over well-springs,

Not zoned, not floor-planned for death.
But a building you can see through is rising:
They are settling and dressing the stones
That pain from everywhere, so long as human,

Fastens onto like clothespins. Lie still, though;
We're not hanging. You are always covered
By your smooth forehead and your eyelids;
You are grazed by no tissued humming

Of razor wire, or by the shadows that come out
Framing, scraping, hosing-down sides of glass,
And leave for a specified time
The sides of their heads against banks.

————————

Poem [c]

1982

*—through a French poet, Roland Bouhéret,
and my running father—*

For having left the birds that left me
Better streaks on my eyes than they can make
On any sky alive:
for having broken loose new stars
By opening to the storm a deaf window

At the moment the summer park closed:
for having rubbed out,
From cliffs not dangerous enough, or cold enough
For you,
the name of the dead,

I hear the sound of fresh steps seeding toward me,
Steps I could take.

Gene,

Dead in the full of July
Ten years ago, I have learned all the tracks   15
Of the stars of that month: they give me more body-authority
Than a beast-birth in straw.   Believe me I have kept

The old river that ran like something from a crock,
Through the cow-battered weeds: that runs over us
As baptismal water always;   20
I believe I could be walking there

Like high valleys crossing,
In the long laconic open-striding fullness

Of your muscular death.   In whole air your form
Takes up with me best, giving more than it could   25
In the hospital's mirror-blanked room
Where you leaned toward the grim parks under you

Before they closed,
and out of the rattling rails
Of your cocked bed, talked about mowing, nothing   30
But mowing, of all weird, unearthly
Earthly things: like a shower of grassblades
Talked, tilted and talked,
and shivered, down past you, the gaunt
Traffic-islands into green; from that time on, I saw them   35
As blocked fields, part of elsewhere.

But we are advancing
By steps that grew back to my door,
And if I set your long name in the wind
And it comes back spelling out   40
The name of a far port-of-call,
the place we never got to,

That is all right.
And yet, with the ashy river
Running like a soul where I'm headed,   45
Even with the names of harbors that swarmed all over me
When I hit the open, when I paced myself exactly
With the current—these and the birds, the old cows,

Have stubborned here
stalled   no matter how I increase   50
My leg-beat, or stretch and find myself
Calling out in mid-stride.   You are motionless, you are in the middle
Of elsewhere, breathing the herd-breath
Of the dead—singled and in-line breathing

Among so many—looking in the same direction   55
As the rest of them, your long legs covered with burrs
And bent weeds, splinters of grassblades:
Squared-off, power-bodied, pollen-lidded

You are: green-leggèd, but nailed there.

———————

Attempted Departure
1982

—with André du Bouchet—

I come back

hoping to leave

From these planks; for farewell and for lift-off I am lighting
Four walls of a fire, here. Blank plaster comes alive
On me in square gold: my shadow goes giddy with dimension, dropping off   5
The outflanked pious hunger of the flat;
The damn thing can come at me now

Like death, from anywhere

                              but while I stand
                No side protected, at home, play-penned   10
With holocaust
                  the slashes disappear from this flayed back, like
My step on the rammed road,

                              the only thing fleeing.

                         ————————

Crystal
1983

              Press of a thorn, quick
              Illogic of pain. Earth cold,
              Immensity of winter, sky close—
                                  lightning:
              Universe flicked by a finger   5
              Where an open untended wound
              Branched like a fire-map the day
                  Before this; at evening

        Was a lily, guarded and tall. Crystal, I take your thorn,
              Whirling among the other veils,   10

              Shaking with naturalness

              That could talk but does not;
              That keeps two bloodless roses
              Apart with a knife, at the instant
              The single flake piercing my hand   15

        Shatters, turns outward to range-drift.

For a Time and Place
1983

—A South Carolina Inauguration of Richard Riley as Governor—

May we be able to begin with ourselves
Underfoot and rising,
Peering through leaves we have basketed, through tendrils hanging
Like bait, through flowers,
Through lifted grave-soil: peering   5
Past the short tree that stands
In place for us, sawed-off unbendable: a thing
Pile-driven down
And flowering from the impact—such weaving
Consuming delicacy in the leaves, out of such   10
Up-wedged and pineappled bark! We look alive
Through those petals in the censer-swung pots: through
That swinging soil, and the split leaves fountaining out
Of the mauled tree, to the east horizon vibrant
With whole-earth hold-down, past a single sail pillowing   15
From there on out.

We peer also from the flat
Slant sand, west from estuary-glitter,
From the reed-beds bending inland
At dawn as we do, to the high-ground hard-hurdling   20
Power of the down-mountain torrent: at a blue-ridged glance
From the ocean, we see all we have
Is unified as a quilt: the long leaves of the short tree,
The tough churchly feathers, dance rice-like this side of
The far-out wave-break's lounging   25
Curved insolent long sparking thorn, and
The gull's involving balance, his sweeping-through shuttle-run
Downwind; his tapestry-move
Is laid on our shoulders, where the unspilled dead
Are riding, wild with flowers, collision-colors   30
At the hairline, tended, sufficient, dead-level with us
From now on out.

What visions to us from all this lived
Humidity? What insights from the blue haze alone? From kudzu?
From snake-vine? From the native dog-sized deer   35
From island to island floating, their head-bones
Eternal and formal,
Collisionless? We are standing mainly on blends
Of sand, red-rooted, in dark
Near-fever air, and there is a certain weaving   40
At our backs, like a gull's over-the-shoulder
Peel-off downwind. Assuming those wings, we keep gazing
From goat-grass to the high
Shifts, splits, and barreling
Alcohol of the rocks, all the way from minnows flashing whole   45
The bright brittle shallows, waiting for our momentum
From here on out.

It is true, we like our air warm
And wild, and the bark of our trees
Overlapping backward and upward   50
Stoutly, the shocks of tough leaves counter-
balancing, with a flicker of lostness. Beside the dead,
The straw-sucking marsh, we have stood where every blade
Of eelgrass thrilled like a hand-line
For the huge bass hanging in the shade   55
Of the sunken bush, and have heard the unstuffed moss
Hiss like a laundry-iron. This point between
The baskets and the tree is where we best
Are, and would be: our soil, our soul,
Our sail, our black horizon simmering like a mainspring,   60
Our rocky water falling like a mountain
Ledge-to-ledge naturally headlong,
Unstoppable, and our momentum
In place, overcoming, coming over us
And from us   65
from now on out.

Craters

1983

—with Michel Leiris—

Roots out of the ground and ongoing
The way wé are, some of them—

Spokes   earth-slats   a raft made of humped planks
Slung down and that's right: wired together
By the horizon: it's what *these* roads   5
Are growing through: fatal roads,
No encounters, the hacked grass burning with battle-song—

Then when we get *our* voices together,
When we mix in that savage way, in the gully of throats
Where the fog piles up, and we turn our long cadences loose   10
Over the grooved pasture, the running fence of song

Will flap and mount straight up for miles

Very high, all staring stridulation,
Softer than beer-hops:

       one of the days when the wind breathes slackly,   15
Making the lightest perches tremble
Like hostile stems interlacing,
As in the heart a lock of blond hair knots on itself
Suicidally, insolubly
       someone will plough-out a door,   20
A staircase will dig itself down, its haunted spiral

Will blacken and come out

Where the ashes of those who were once turned to Pompeian lava
Will abandon their smouldering silkworks,
Their velvet slags, and take on the courtliness   25
Of ghosts: then, then the sky will be gone from us

Forever, we wretched ones who can love nothing
But light.
                    Such will the craters tell you—any crater
Will tell you, dry-heaving and crouching: 30
                              will tell us we've stumbled
    Onto one:
              we're in one, dry-heaving and crouching.

————

Farmers
A Fragment
1983

—with André Frénaud—

There are not many meteors over the flat country

Of the old; not one metaphor between the ploughblade
    And the dirt
                  not much for the spirit: not enough
        To raise the eyes past the horizon-line   5
Even to the Lord, even with neck-muscles like a bull's
For the up-toss. The modest face has no fear

    Of following a center-split swaying track
              Through grain and straw
        To the grave, or of the honor of work   10
With muck and animals, as a man born reconciled
              With his dead kin:

When love gives him back the rough red of his face he dares

To true-up the seasons of life with the raggedness of earth,
    With the underground stream as it turns its water   15
    Into the free stand of the well: a language takes hold

And keeps on, barely making it, made
By pain: the pain that's had him ever since school,
At the same time the indivisible common good
Being shared among the family   20
Came clear to him: he disappears into fog

He reappears he forces out his voice

Over the field   he extends his figures

With a dead-right clumsiness,
And the blazon that changes every year   25
Its yellow and green squares, announces at each moment
What must be said: the justice that the power of man installs
In exhausted fresh-air coupling with the earth:
                                        Slogger—

                    Figure of glory   30

Less and more than real, fooled always
By the unforseeable: so nailed by your steps
Into the same steps   so marked by wisdom calamitously come by,
And always uncertain, valiantly balancing,
So stripped, so hog-poor still, after a long day   35
In the immemorial, that I cannot say to you
Where you will hear me,
Farmer, there will be no end to your knowing

The pastures drawn breathless by the furrow,
The fields, heartsick, unquenchable   arid   40
                                        avid,
The forgivable slowness, the whispered prophecies of weather:
Winter   spring, the season that always comes through
For you, and never enough,

But only dies, turning out   45
In its fragile green, its rich greens,
To be nothing but the great stain of blankness

Changing again—

Gravedigger

On Sunday, you come back Monday to the laying-out   50
In squares, of your infinite land
                    the furs of snow do not reach us
When they should
             the moon has troubled the sown seed . . .

———

To Be Done in Winter
1984

in memoriam, T.C.

What you hold,
Don't drink it all. Throw what you have left of it
Out, and stand. Where the drink went away
Rejoice that your fingers are burning
Like hammered snow.   5

He makes no sound: the cold flurries, and he comes all the way
Back into life; in the mind
There is no decay. Imagine him
As to behold him, for if you fail
To remember, he lies without   10
What his body was.
                 His short shadow
Is on you.   Bring him in, now, with tools
And elements. Behold him

With your arms: encircle him,   15
Bring him in with the forge and the crystal,

With the spark-pounding cold.

————————

World
1984

One sea.   The present hour.   One moon
        Hangs, beaming Time
Into the void.
                        Any light in the west
Is fragile.   That orange one, too, with the others.   5

As for the east road, there are no limits,
        So everything on it is flying
        Toward the core: magnet-flying.
        All around, clouds whirl

Like the foam of an ocean gone, at last,   10
        Beyond its will: gone total.

        Listen: among the all-out joys
        Of that blue, beyond mortal men,
        Another ocean stirs that might
Not be blood, water that is not an anvil.   15
Watch for something, this one time in your life,
        To rise from sea-flats
        On gentle, half torn-away wings.

        There, no man exists.
        At the edge where you must cross   20
        Gold falters and comes, but never

Gets into the right bones: never once
Into your wrists—
                    instead
Fire surges like an arm, for the place   25
Where crimson must blanch.

Boundless, boundless air. Your voice would have nothing to do
If you could black-out and produce it.   Death slips away, as though
It would be finite,
Bracing bare walls. It is time for some man   30
To scream out his forest heart,
His hilarious blood, his stone sadness. Listen:
There is only one death:
Only one way to picture
A death: covered by the sky come in   35
From far off, and crumbling, a man

Dries out where he has been backed
Against a wall.   See him for good; a man drying

Toward invisibility.

———————

Earth

1984

Always as it holds us in one place, the earth
Grows as it moves, exhaling
Its rooted joy. I stand in tracks
Where nothing starves. Vegetation, green blush,
You and I sail today   5
Through newly infinite
Space on this surfeited hillside. Complacency has its own force

Leafed-out with renewal. I cannot be anything
But alive, in a place as far

From the blank and the stark, as this.   10

———————

Sea
1984

Who told you that the sea said something,
Something toward the beaches?
Let it spread more, belligerent with light,
Saying one thing, resounding,

Up front for all of us!   5

———————

Air
1985

Air, much greater than the sea—
More basic, more human than the sea: all thát air
Is calm:
            unpeopled, wearing the high lucidity

Of vigil. Maybe one day the mere surface   5
Of the earth will feel you. But the air
You can never keep doesn't know
When it lived in your chest:

Mindless, nerveless, breathless,
The air glitters   10
All the outside, and keeps carrying

You from within.

————————

Cobra

1985

Cobra, nothing but eyes,
A land-mass lying down
Around itself, among dry leaves. Near you, all hearts
Loop, square-knot; tie-off.

Cobra on crystal, sterile-skinned,   5
Hissing like a file   astringent

Silky—
          Cousin to vertigo
The cobra slithers, gazing at its other sky,
Its scales overlaid;   10
A whole skin dealt to it

Like a hand of cards. In this proximity
Everything, body to body,
Is between frozen thighs, or between breasts
Heaped like shaved ice. Virgin, hissing freshly   15
As a knife, look closer:
Below both of you the land convulses
As it appears. Hold ground—

Belated, exorbitant ground.

Spring-Shock
1986

All bubbles travelling

In tubes, and being lights: up down and around
They were: blue, red and every man uncaught

And guilty. Prison-paleness
Over the street between strobes   5
Unfailingly. But no light
On top of anything moving, until
The last, one:
          one. Whoever it was switched it

Dead when he saw me. Winter; not dreamlike but a dream and cars   10
Of that. I took my stand where they were called
By absent law to stop, obstructedly raging

And I could not get in. All their windows
Were sealed and throbbing
With strobe, red and blue, red and blue   15

And go. One pulled out of the flight
Of others; pulled up and may have had back-road
Dust on it   red dust in a last shot
Of blue. A man in a cowboy hat rolled down

The window on my side. His voice   20
Was home-born Southern; Oklahoma, Texas,
Could have been. Manhandling my overcoat, I slid
Ín there with him. Central Park South, I said,
A war-safety zone; the St. Moritz.

He turned up   25

One of the streets with no lights. Into the seat
I settled; black buildings thickened
Around us, high tenements flattening
Into squares; warehouses now,
They were; maybe docks. I watched. No birds.   30
No trash-cans. The car died

Between two alley walls

And froze, and a voice at last, still
Out of Oklahoma, said "I want your money."
                                 We were present   35
In silence. A brought-on up-backward thock

Took place, and on the fresh blade
A light alive in the hand
New-born with spring-shock. It was mine
At sixty. "I want your car," I said.   40

Two Women

1987

—Cumberland Island—

I

Alone here. Beach, drum out
What you want to say: a dolphin,
Sockets, sword-flats. Seething landscape of hilts, no limits are set

In you. Sand, sand,
Hear me out: Hear me out with wind   5
Going over, past
All sound but sand. Listen,

Clean vastness, I am alone here.

I should be, for I have
No mark.   10
            Woman, because I don't love you,
            Draw back the first

    Of your feet, for the other will fall
    After it, and keep on coming. Hold back

    A little, your printed pursuit, your   15

    Unstemming impurity.

                        II

        Early light: light less
    Than other light. Sandal without power
        To mark sand. Softly,
Her hair downward-burning, she walks here, her foot-touch   20

        The place itself,

    Like sand-grains, unintended,

        Born infinite.

            ————————

Daybreak
1987

—Pawley's Jetty—

You sit here on solid sand banks trying to figure
    What the difference is when you see
    The sun and at the same time see the ocean
Has no choice: none, but to advance more or less
        As it does: 5
                waves

Which were, a moment ago, actual
Bodiless sounds that could have been airborne,
Now bring you nothing but face-off

After face-off, with only gravitational sprawls   10
Laid in amongst them. To those crests
Dying hard, you have nothing to say:
                                                    you cannot help it

If you emerge; it is not your fault. You show: you stare

Into the cancelling gullies, saved only by dreaming a future   15
Of walking forward, in which you can always go flat

Flat down where the shallows have fallen
Clear: where water is shucked of all wave-law:
                    Lies running: runs

In skylight, gradually cleaning, and you gaze straight into   20

The whole trembling forehead of yourself
Under you, and at your feet find your body

No different from cloud, among the other
See-through images, as you are flawingly
Thought of,   25
                    but purely, somewhere,

Somewhere in all thought.

Vessels

1987

—the Waccamaw Road—

When the sound of forest leaves is like the sleep-talk
Of half-brothers; when it trembles   shorts itself out
Between branches, and is like light that does not cost
    Itself any light, let me turn: turn right thén,

    Right as it happens and say: I crave wandering   5
        And giving: I crave

      My own blood, that makes the body
        Of the lover in my arms give up
On the great sparking vault of her form,
                        when I think instead   10
      Of my real brother, who talks like no leaf
      Or no half,
          and of the road he will be on
        As my body drops off
      And the step he takes from me   15
Comes kicking,
        and he feels the starry head that has hovered

  Above him all his life

        come down on his, like mine

    Exactly,   20

    or near enough.

Meadow Bridge
1987

There might be working some kind of throwaway

Meditation on Being, just
From what I am looking at
Right here. I can't tell, myself. But it may already have happened
When I batted my eye—   5
           a new fix

Of sun lined out, squaring off: a fresh
Steel bridge,
        exactly true
To a crosscut of starkness   10
And silver.
      Tell me: why do I want
To put over it, the right hand drawing

Inexhaustibly drawing
        out of the left, a vibration   15

Of threads? This also, beholders,
    Is a fact: gauze
Burns off,
    keeps coming: the bridge breaks through anything
I can pull from my hand. No matter how I brim, there is   20

No softening.

Field, what hope?

Tomb Stone

1987

This place named you,
And what business I have here
Is what I think it is
And only that. I must ask you, though, not to fall

Any farther,   5
                        and to forgive me
For coming here, as I keep doing,
                                    as I have done
        For a while in a vertical body
    That breathes the rectangular solitude   10

Risen over you. I want time to tell the others
    Not to come, for I understand

        Now, that deep enough
        In death, the earth becomes
    Absolute earth. Hold all there is: hold on   15
        And forgive, while I tell thém as I tell
    Myself where I stand: Don't let a breast

        Echo, because of a foot.

        Pass, human step.

Eagles

1987

If I told you I used to know the circular truth

Of the void,
                    that I have been all over it building
        My height
                            receiving overlook   5

    And that my feathers were not
Of feather-make, but broke from a desire to drink
    The rain before it falls
                        or as it is falling:

If I were to tell you that the rise of any free bird   10
            Is better

                the larger the bird is,

    And that I found myself one of these
    Without surprise, you would understand

That this makes of air a thing that would be liberty   15
        Enough for any world but this one,
        And could see how I should have gone

        Up and out of all

                    áll of it

            On feathers glinting   20

    Multitudinously as rain, as silica-sparks around
    One form with wings, as it is hammered loose
            From rock, at dead
        Of classic light: that is, at dead

                Of light.   25

Believe, too,
While you're at it, that the flight of eagles has
For use, long muscles steeped only
In escape,
                    and moves through   30
Clouds that will open to nothing

But ít, where the bird leaves behind
All sympathy: leaves
The man who, for twenty lines
Of a new poem, thought he would not be shut   35
From those wings: believed

He could be going. I speak to you from where

I was shook off: I say again, shook
Like thís, the words I had
When I could not spread: 40

When thát bird rose

Without my shoulders: Leave my unstretched weight,
My sympathy grovelling
In weeds and nothing, and go
                        up from the human down-   45
beat in my hand. Go up without anything

Of me in your wings, but remember me in your feet

As you fold them. The higher rock ís
The more it lives. Where you take hold, Í will take

Thát stand in my mind, rock bird alive with the spirit-   50
    life of height,
                    on my down-thousands
        Of fathoms, classic

Claw-stone, everything under.

The Little More

1987

JBTD

I

But the little more: the little more
This boy will be, is hard
For me to talk of
But harder for him. Manhood is only a little more,
A little more time, a little more everything than he   5

Has on him now. He would know, if he could go forward
From where he puts down his ball,
His top, his willow spear,
           that he will face into the air
Where the others his age will be breaking, or be   10
About to break,
           and he will watch them grow pale
With the warnings of doctors,
And all their balloons, and parents and the other
           Dead will be floating   15

Away from them, over the mountains.
           I would tell him

     This is where the quiet

Valley comes in, and the red creek
Where he will row with no other,   20
The water around each blade
Explosive, ablaze with his only initials,
     Joy set in the bending void
Between the oars
           and swung,   25
As the last balloon disappears, needing
Color no more. Yes! This is when the far mountain

Will come to him, under his feet
Of its own wish
                when he steps up   30

From water, and in the wind he will start
To hear the enormous resonance
Children cannot make out: of his own gigantic
Continuous stride over all ferocious rocks

That can be known.   35

II

From the ones who have grown all they can
Come and stop softly, boy,
On the strong side of the road

That the other side does not see. Then move.
Put your feet where you look,   40
                    and not

Where you look, and none of your tracks
Will pass off, but wander, and for you

Be fresh places, free and aggressive.

Boy who will always be glanced-at   45
                   and then fixed

In warm gazes, already the past knows
It cannot invent you again,

For the glitter on top of the current
Is not the current.   50
           No, but what dances on it is
More beautiful than what takes its time
Beneath, running on a single unreleased
Eternal breath, rammed

With carry, its all-out dream and dread   55

Surging bull-breasted,
Head-down, unblocked.

———————

Gila Bend
1987

Where aerial gunnery was, you think at first a cadaver

On foot might get through

Forty years after. Shots of space pelter back

Off the dead bullets; walking, you should brand, brand
    The ground but you don't: you leave   5

    Not a thing moving on a sand mountain
    Smashed flat by something that didn't know
    What else to do.
                This silver small-stone heat
    No man can cross; no man could get   10

    To his feet, even to rise face-out

Full-force from the grave, where the sun is down on him

Alone, harder than resurrection

Is úp: down harder

             harder   15

Much harder than that.

The Six

1987

When you think strong enough, you get something
You don't mean
And you dó: something prized-out,
Splintered, like a rock quarry going
Through you and over you   5
Like love, and past and on

Like love: whatever arms, legs, head,

Breastbone, whatever feet and hands you love most,
Most want to live
And die with, are given out as flying   10
Related rock; are charged
With the life that lives
By means of stone. The body of your lover tries to form and be

Those six stones. For some reason

They are hurtling, and if you meet them head-on   15
You will know something nobody means

But her. She is moving at the speed of light

Some place else, and though she passes
Through you like rock-salt, she is still six
And not one.   20

But neither is the rain
Single, blotting number and stone
With vibrancy; neither is the rain, I tell you,
Man riddled with rocks
And lust: 25

The rain putting out
Your wretched, sympathetic

Stone-jawed poetic head, its allotted
Fresh bodies falling as you stand

In amongst, falling and more   30
Than falling   falling more

Falling   now falling

More than now.

———————

Weeds
1988

Stars and grass
Have between them a connection I'd like to make
More of—find some way to bring them

To one level any way I can,
And put many weeds in amongst. O woman, now that I'm thinking,   5
Be in there somewhere! Until now, of the things I made up
Only the weeds are any good: Between them,

Nondescript and tough, I peer,
The backs of my hands

At the sides of my face, parting the stringy stalks.   10
Tangible, distant woman, here the earth waits for you
With what it does not need
To guess: with what it truly has
In its hands. Through pigweed and sawgrass

Move; move sharply; move ín   15
Through anything,
                    and hurt, if you have to. Don't come down;

Come forward. A man loves you.

The One

1988

No barometer but yellow
Forecast of wide fields that they give out
Themselves, giving out they stand
In total freedom,

And will stand and day is down all of it   5

On an ear of corn. One. The color one:
One, nearly transparent
With existence. The tree at the fence must be kept

Outside, between winds; let it wait. Its movement,

     Any movement, is not   10

In the distillation. Block it there. Let everything bring it
To an all-time stop just short of new
     Wind   just short
   Of its leaves;

         its other leaves.   15

     One.

     Inside.

     Yellow.

   All others not.

     One.   20

     One.

The Three

1988

I alone, solemn land
           clear, clean land,

See your change, just as you give up part
Of your reality:
        a scythe-sighing flight of low birds   5
Now being gone:
          I, oversouling for an instant

With them,
       I alone
See you as more than you would have   10

Bé seen, yourself:
          grassland,
Dark grassland, with three birds higher
Than those that have left.
           They are úp there   15
With great power:
       so high they take this evening for good
Into their force-lines. I alone move

Where the other birds were, the low ones,
    Still swaying in the unreal direction   20
    Flocking with them. They are gone

And will always be gone; even where they believe
    They were is disappearing. But thése three
    Have the height to power-line all

Land: land thís clear. Any three birds hanging high enough   25
      From you trace the same paths
    As strong horses circling
        for a man alone, born level-eyed

As a pasture, but like the land
Tilting, looking up.   30

This may be it, too.

————————

Basics
1988

I. Level

Who has told you what discoveries
There are, along the stressed blank
Of a median line? From it, nothing

Can finally fall. Like a spellbinder's pass
A tense placid principle continues   5

Over it, and when you follow you have the drift,

The balance of many compass needles
Verging to the pole. *Bring down your arms, voyager,*

And the soul goes out
Surrounding, humming   10
                          standing by means

Of the match-up in long arm-bones

Dropped:
            held out and drawn back   back ín

Out of the open   15
                compass-quivering and verging
At your sides, as median movement

Lays itself bare: a closed vein of bisected marble, where

Along the hairline stem
Of the continuum, you progress, trembling   20
With the plumb-bob quiver of mid-earth,
                                        with others in joy
Moving also, in line,

Equalling, armlessing.

II. SIMPLEX

Comes a single thread   25
                    monofilament coming

Strengthening   engrossing and slitting
Into the fine-spun life

To come, foretold in whatever
Ecstasy there's been, but never suspected, never included   30
In what was believed. The balance of the spiral
Had been waiting, and could take

What was given it: the single upthrust through
The hanging acid, the helix spun and spellbound

By the God-set of chemistry, the twine much deeper   35
Than any two bodies imagined
They could die for: insinuate, woven
Single strand, third serpent
Of the medical wood, circling the staff of life

Into the very body   40

Of the future, deadly
But family, having known from the beginning

Of the sun, what will take it on.

Heat makes this, heat makes any
Word: human lungs,   45
Human lips. Not like eternity, which, naked, every time
Will call on lightning
To say it all: No after
Or before. We try for that

And fail. Our voice   50
Fails, but for an instant
Is like the other; breath alone
That came as though humanly panting
From far back, in unspeakably beautiful

Empty space   55

And struck: at just this moment
Found the word "golden."

———————

Night Bird

1988

Some beating in there

That has bunched, and backed
Up in it out of moonlight, and now
Is somewhere around. You are sure that like a curving grave

It must be able to fall   5
                    and rise
                                and fall and that's
Right, and rise
                    on your left hand
                                or other   10

Or behind your back on one hand

You don't have and suddenly there is no limit

To what a man can get out of
His failure to see:
                              this gleam   15

Of air down the nape of the neck, and in it everything
    There is of flight
                    and nothing else,
                                    and it is

    All right and all over you   20
    From around
                    as you are carried

    In yourself and there is no way
    To nothing-but-walk—

    No way and a bidden flurry   25
    And a half-you of air.

————————

Sleepers

1988

There is a sound you can make, as if someone asked you
    To sing between oar strokes, or as though
    Your birth-cry came back, and you put it into sails
    Over water,
                    or without vocal cords, like a torso,   5
    Said what it meant, regardless. That is the voice
        For sleepers; find it—
    Use it and you can join them, that assault-force

Without a muscle, fighting for space

To lift in planned rows over graveyards   10
Like full battalions. Not one can give you the location
Of his stump-stillness, or even one

Of his edges; none knows where his body will end,
Or what it is stamped with
This moment: agate,   15

Nova-burst   earthworm
Owl feather.
Sound off, sleepers,
Headless singers. One.
One, two: Sound off.   20
Not knowing where your tombs
Already lie, assemble, sail through

The lifted spaces, unburied.

———————

Snow Thickets
1988

Helplessly besieging: it is dim,

Unity wavering

Wavering on us, the land in canceling flak. From inside, you and I
Are watching gravity come down

In monotonous awe   5
each flake a part

Of it, or not. With no blinking, we do
As the snow does

eyes burning   thorns hooding   our tongues

Being born: we watch, under the bush   10

Being bound, those all-whites yearning
For anvil-points, for contact,
                      still holding
The airborne embattlement:

Offered and cutthroat   lost   15
Very great winning hand

Down-dealt to the upthrust.

Expanses
1988

Enjoyable clouds, and a man comes;

It's true, he's alive, but from this distance
No one could tell he is breathing.
You want to be sure he knows, though,
Not to confuse the sea   5
With any kind of heart: never to mix blood with something

As free as foam. The color white is wing, water, cloud;
It is best as sail.

Sail.

Drawn always off, off the sea   10
To the chopped soft road, your look
Goes willingly yonder, to and through
The far friendly mountain

                                    then

Back over earth level-jawed   shoulder-energy widening   15
          From water, everywhere there is land,

               Brother: boundless,
     Earthbound, trouble-free, and all you want—

          Joy like short grass.

                    ————————

Moon Flock
1988

          No, don't ask me to give you
     What happened in my head when the dark felt
     It should change: when the black ploughblade
     Went through and dissolved. That was bad enough,

          But if you want to understand   5

Frustration, look up while the moon, which is nothing

          But a wild white world,

     Struggles overhead: fights to grow wings
          For its creatures but cannot get
Creatures to have them. It is known: nothing can be put   10

          Up on a wind with no air;
          No wing can lift from stones
Lighter than earth-stones, where a man could leap

          Leap till he's nearly forever

          Overhead: overhead floating.   15

No wings,
In all that lightness. You want to understand:

All right. You don't have to look up, but can look straight

Straight

Straight out   out over the night sea   20
As it comes in. Do that.
Do it and think of your death, too, as a white world

Struggling for wings. Then
All the water your eyesight will hold
While it can, will not be lost   25

And neither will the moon
As it strains and does nothing
But quiver
          when the whole earth places you
Underfoot   30
          as though suspended
For good. You deserve it. Yóu should be

That moon flock; and not, as you will be,
A moveless man floating in the earth

As though overhead, where it is not   35
Possible to wave your arms
At something, or at nothing: at a white world

Or at your mother, or at the ocean
In shock, that I told you about, all insanity
And necessity when it sees you, and is right at you   40

Coming
          hair-tearing

Hair-tearing and coming.

Daughter

1989

Hospital, and the fathers' room, where light
Won't look you in the eye. No emergency
But birth. I sit with the friend, and listen

To the unwounded clock. Indirectly glowing, he is grayer,
    Unshaven as I. We are both old men   5
      Or nearly. He is innocent. Yet:
    What fathers are waiting to be born
    But myself, whom the friend watches
With blessed directness? No other man but a worker

    With an injured eyeball; his face had been there   10
When part of an engine flew up.
                       A tall nurse blotted with ink
    And blood goes through. Something written
On her? Blood of my wife? A doctor with a blanket
Comes round a blind corner. "Who gets this little girl?"   15
      I peer into wool: a creature
Somewhat strangely more than red. Dipped in fire.

No one speaks. The friend does not stir; he is innocent
      Again: the child is between
Me and the man with one eye. We battle in the air,   20
    Three-eyed, over the new-born. The doctor says,
"All right, now. Which one of you had a breech baby?"
    All around I look: look at the possible
Wounded father. He may be losing: he opens his bad eye.
    I half-close one of mine, hoping to win   25
Or help. Breech baby. I don't know. I tell my name.
    Taking the doctor by his arms
Around her, the child of fire moves off. I would give one eye for her

    Already. If she's not mine I'll steal her.
The doctor comes back. The friend stirs; both our beards   30

Quicken: the doctor is standing
Over me, saying, "This one's yours."
                              It is done: I set my feet
In Heavenly power, and get up. In place of plastic, manned rubber
                And wrong light, I say wordlessly   35
Roll, real God. Roll through us. I shake hands

    With the one-eyed man. He has not gained
A child, but may get back his eye; I hope it will return
    By summer starlight.
                              The child almost setting   40
Its wool on fire, I hold it in the first and last power
    It came from: that goes on all the time
    There is, shunting the glacier, whirling
    Whole forests from their tops, moving

    Lava, the flowing stone: moving the hand   45
        Of anyone, ever. Child of fire,

Look up. Look up as I lean and mumble you are part
Of flowing stone: understand: you are part of the wave,
            Of the glacier's irrevocable
Millennial inch.   50
                "This is the one," the friend repeats
    In his end-of-it daze, his beard gone
Nearly silver, now, with honor, in the all-night night
        Of early morning. Godfather, I say

    To him: not father of God, but assistant   55
Father to this one. All forests are moving, all waves,
        All lava and ice. I lean. I touch

    One finger. Real God, roll.

            Roll.

Circuit

1990

Beaches; it is true: they go on   ón
And on, but as they ram and pack, foreseeing

Around a curve, always   slow-going headlong

For the circle
                         swerving from water   5
But not really, their minds on a perfect connection, no matter
How long it takes. You can't be
On them without making the choice
To meet yourself no matter

        How long. Don't be afraid;   10
        It will come   will hit you

Straight out of the wind, on wings or not,
        Where you have blanked yourself

Still with your feet. It may be raining

        In twilight, a sensitive stripping   15
Of arrow feathers, a lost trajectory struck
Stock-stilling through them,
                            or where you cannot tell
        If the earth is green or red,

Basically, or if the rock with your feet on it   20

Has floated over the water. As for where you are standing

Nów, there are none of those things; there are only
        In one shallow spray-pool   thís one

Strong horses circling. Stretch and tell me, Lord;
  Let the place talk.   25

    This may just be it.

————————

To the Butterflies
1990

—homage, Central America—

Open windows; we always have them, háve
  To have them. We widen

Them all, and butterflies come in, and come

To rest on our mirrors, breathing with their wings

    Almost like light,   5
  Or better, almost like flight,

  And then leave. Others come,
Háve to come, and some of the time this happens
  We are singing, trying hard,

    But it comes out a croak   10
  From dryness, and when we move it is like
    Moving muscles of powder, but
  Really no muscles are on us; they are all gone
    Into sweat. Every light the hand turns on
  Hurts the eyes, and there is nowhere on earth   15
    That the heels of the feet
Are so hot, and they cannot be cooled.
                          I love to know nothing

    Of the sun; I love to feel

That I float, forgotten,   20
                    with two warm rivers
That cannot touch me, on a stream come down
            Between them from a mountain
            Of frozen rain. We all have wanted,

            Too long, not to have our tears,   25
            Our salt-showing tears, dry before anyone
                  Can see them, dry
                  Before we can feel them,
            Or find out what they really have
            To do with grief. To say that I am not true   30
                  To fever is to say I am not
            Loyal to my green country,
                              not true, not real
                  Myself,
                        so I say it in secret   35

            In steam: Forgive me, butterflies:
                  I know you have to have
            All this heat for your colors,
                              but you are breathless, too,
                  In spite of your breathing   40

            Wings and God help me I must say it before I melt
                  Into the sugar-sick ground:
                              If we could do it

            Without dimming the butterflies, we should find some way
                  To get on the good side of North: Yes North and enough   45

                  Cold: Yes cold

            And snow! I've heard of it! Flakes lilting onto us!

                  Life light on the common grave

            Shapeless with swelter! Every tongue of us out
                  To be new to that taste! Mountains of rain   50

Gone into feather-fall
Floating us out of it! But not dimming   not fading
The butterflies
or the hats and handkerchiefs.
Let the wings on our mirrors   55

In whatever falls

Keep breathing   Keep burning

and us, Lord, please—

And us in the dresses and shirts.

———————

Show Us the Sea
1990

—an opening fragment—

Real God, roll
roll as a result
Of a whole thing: ocean:
This: wide altar-shudder of miles

Given twelve new dead-level powers   5
Of glass, in borrowed binoculars, set into

The hand-held eyes of this man

And no other, his second son coming to his head

Like Armageddon, with the last wave. Real God,
Through both hands and my head, in depth-bright distance, roll   10
In raw free sharpness

Of sight, and let my son come,
Exploding with proximity, and with him bring voices
Faintly around him, the sounds not matching
The size of their magnified bodies. No harm;   I am invisible   15

With sand.   The sea, only, is on-coming
Face-on, with my boy's
Impact incandescent on my head
                                                as he strikes

A hero's improbable stance: flesh that would be bronze,   20
Be stone, the form of stone, struck from within

The stone. Statue, yes: creature lured into being
By gestures it has chosen in its sleep.

———————

The Drift-Spell

1993

—a fragment—

When you come off the beach, son, when you leave the sea

I shall appear, without your knowing.
As you learn why and where
We are going, with no words we shall willow

Through naked tourists,   5
Passive nothing bodies stogged in sand
From where I watched you glory in your body
And gloried with you but are leaving
To move across the highway

And into woods: shall pass through, on   10
Into the open, walking in step

And out of step, into the churchyard, going where she is:
Where she lies on a silk pillow
Under moss the color of her eyes, and like them
Full of the drift-spell. Moss, son, is the grey part of silver,   15
Moving as though found in air

By other air, the half-alive, the half-life
Of tree-breath: precious, perilous, marking time

Over her. Your mother is here, son, with the others, amongst
The tree-hanging, wandering dead, the stomach-sway   20
Of swaying moss. These dead and no others are around us,
Not falling, not dying, not one of them sick, in the mild

Wilderness of the cemetery. It may be an owl
Will fly. No; there is only one, descended
Ascended into rock. It is part of your mother: it was   25

It is her bird, now
New on the upright of the grave
Graven, and will be here as long as stone

Will hold an image. Without words, we shall know
That we have her forever: are learning to the full   30
What we have: death, and the day's light,

The three of us in love. Moss,
Your mother's eyes, and an owl in stone.

Love, and the day's light?

No, she is honest with us   35
Anywhere, son. Death and the day's light

With us here, full of the drift-spell.

Last Hours

1994

for Tom

Not Stonewall

Not Longstreet

    commanders of your endless enlistment on both

Sides of the Civil War

        but mostly South   5

I have come to tell you, Tom,

That Longstreet has failed and, as well, Melville,
    Who feared him,   has failed,   even though he said

Longstreet moves through the hauntedness:

        Tom, Tom,   10

He does not know what has come: Longstreet does not know

How salvation for the doomed arrives
    A hundred and thirty years later: salvation for the Civil War

Fanatic, the cancer-dying brother. Take it where you find it
    Where it comes to you from everywhere   15

And anywhere, Brother. Man, I do love you past

The long-lost limits of love, but Longstreet will not do

Any longer. I know it   I have lived it: you have put your life,

Your mind, your blood, into researching the projectiles

    Of that war,   20

        but you are dying, now, Tom, and nothing will do

Any longer, of the bullet-stripped trees
        Of Malvern Hill. Where should we go? The nurse

    And the rest of us? Where? What should we do?

    Tom, your teeth minute by minute   25
    Grow longer with cancer. Your tongue is white

        With suffering: Your face is an all-out skull.
        I have never seen you like this.
I see you now, Brother, floundering, sweating to struggle free

    Of the Civil War that has no more use. I have tried,   30

        I have held to history for a while
        Because you did, because it meant so much

To you. Watching you die, I have come to know, one more time,

        Stonewall will not help: he has no ambushing
        Military power over the dying. Munitions, projectiles   35
        Cannot be part of death this time, although

You could have directed their fire.

                                    The nurse has left

The white room, again, to family. Who will help? Your daughter

        Settles into a paperback.   Ah, Tom, expert   40
        In logistics, troop movement: your only girl settles,

Settles near and goes right by

The dead war you loved. Will your life
            Of devotion help you: life given utterly

To a lost cause? Brother, I can show you: this is my last shot.   45
            As I stand by your bed I am wearing
            A Confederate belt buckle you unearthed
            By map and shovel, by entrenching tool, from the red

    Rain-sodden battle of Antietam

                                                    and handed to me   50

        And hand it still, and cinch it
            To your brother's gut

        Now and from now on out. Does it help? No.

    Brother, I understand: your pain is great. No planned retreat

From it: Longstreet cannot come up, fall back, or come through   55

        The hauntedness. Your daughter sinks into reading

        And starts her voice. No more munitions,
    No more projectiles, Tom. The South cannot win; but here,

        Here in the paperback

    Is something else. In your daughter's hand for some reason   60
            Known only to women is the step-by-step

    Chronicle of Theodore Bundy. I repeat: Longstreet has failed
            To help your life,

    Your death. The stranger is beside you. It is Bundy moving

        As Longstreet moved, but now through the hauntedness   65

        Of Florida State. The deliberate stranger has come

In time: has come to be here

In the white room. The teeth shoot from your gums
With pain: more pain: but now you are engaged
    Beyond the artillery: beyond where you were   70

At Chancellorsville. This time,

Old campaigner, I tell you, I tell you and again
    Your brother does not know

Where salvation comes from. Take it where you find it

    On your deathbed, Tom: where it comes to you   75

From anywhere. Longstreet has dissolved

Into the hauntedness. Follow now: follow
The other murderer. Listen: there is one more girl

    Walking innocently home: home
To the sorority house. She is your daughter reading   80

    To you: she is the final
Unprotected girl.   Watch.   Wait.   Follow.   Follow

    The murderer, for he has caught the interest

Of your brain's last blood. Last: the last of it.
        Crouch in the last hedge   85
    Of Tallahassee: hover
Over the reading girl: she is part
    Of your death, glad to be so.   Almost dead now,

Brother, you suspend yourself over her, the one girl
    Of your loins, in some form yet unknown,   90
Bound to the killer. Disembodied from your pain, you swim

In air, in the last delight, as Longstreet hovered
Through the hauntedness, your daughter the last
Victim, as she reads to you those chronicles
Of stalking. And while you stalk, stalk   95

In midair, Brother, take this: your blood kin's last word

Of love: follow not me
But the murderer. He will kill
The pain, in the one good act

Long after his execution. Follow. He is helping. Go with him,   100

Brother; he will cross you over

Better than I can, will get you there

No matter what.   Follow.

Follow on.

———————

Breaking the Field
1994

for the punt returners

A high one coming.   Nosing down it is turning
              Over to make itself come down harder
And faster to me
              near me.
                    Shift   stutter-step   back   right   5
    Right   Got it.
                                    now
Look everywhere at once: left right and up the middle:
    Nothing but wrong colors.   In the midst

One good block out of nowhere.   Chaos   field breaking—   10

    Closing jerseys, all wrong.   Not many friends
      But the right ones.   The chaos must be better:
        Let's break it more, friends.
                Look everywhere
      One last time. Closing colors, but in amongst   15

Green shows like a grasshopper: through everything, green
    Of the broken field.   Men down all over   Space closing, but
      Beyond friends and enemies, green.   Green daylight:

    Left.   Left.   Green still showing

      A little.   Go there.   20

———————

Conch
1996

Cry of something

Forgot and empowered   intact both dead and alive:

    Gland-cry   clear, clean,
    Discreet, undiminished, hovered-in

By you, infinitely encircling what the shudder-   5
    dark under the mullet-field's spread
    Inch of undercover in the sun

Says: inexhaustibly lost sound

    Of the shell, it speaks
      Only itself,   10
    Delaying, unmarvelling, unmoralizing:

<pre>
                Limitless last word
            Released from spiraling.
                                        There is no
        Whole truth, but this is what we have,   15

                And it goes on
        Beyond impact, beyond reach, beyond recall,
                Not passing

                As I catch myself
        Catching myself listening to the conch   20
        Without the shell: the one voice, now,

        For my son coming naked from the ocean,
            Myself created new-human

            By limit, father-rooted in sand.
</pre>

———————

The Confederate Line at Ogeechee Creek

1997

<pre>
Falling back from Millen, we saw obstructions
Parallel: backwater, copper-scaled stump-chains
Uncoiling, uniting: harrow of murderous rust,
Ditches, breastworks heart-beating, a last stand

Of pine, sawhorses, clotheslines, millstones,   5
Bushes tense with the hoarded standstill
Of briars. Here we took one step back, and now
None back. Slash-pines balance and lean

Into the line. Every underground breath
Breaks its own hold, and will speak   10
</pre>

Not only by granite.
                    Backwater stirs. Hawks
Hover like needles, trembling and trembling

Into certainty, all beaks and hooks
Set North. Tecumseh, not this time.   15

———————

Entering Scott's Night
1997

—F. Scott Fitzgerald, 1896–1940—

Interweaving
                    of histories:
A torso enchanted into thread. Time spun inside-
out, and worn so. A sweater only, but, as another time,
          Another life shaped it.   5
                              Am I my other,
          Yet, in double-time stitches? No;
      Not quite; not in the looking glass. It will be so

When I step outside, this night: this night when the past
          Has not passed. There   10
                              here, in the paper-lit garden,
      A dark-glowing field of folk, the dead, the celebrants
      Making company as Scott would have them,
          Who brought their time

      Through time. Wearing the inner skin   15
      Of a sweater, ghost garment, I am with them,
Some flying from the thing they feared, and some
          Seeking the object of another's fear.
On fountain-shifted ground, among straight bricks
          Woven serpentine into walls,   20

In leaves and loom-light and time,
In the grass-lamp glow

Of hedges, all are still,
And a hooded spark from lanterns
Travels from glass to glass, from eye to eye   25
Like intuition. It is Scott's,
Moving in two times, among us
As we stand fountain-raining, imperilled
In celebrant stillness, with the shadow of a woman

On serpent-stone totally dancing.   30

Poems of
Uncertain Date

The Baggage King

There in New Guinea, by the grounded metal
And the birds' free flight,
Under their cries, far under:
Under them at the level of the ocean
We came from the rusted freighter   5

With a thousand bags, duffel,
Kit-bags, B-4's, A-3's,
Barracks bags, handbags,
Kits, "personal bags," musette bags,
Parachutes, kith and kin,   10
And were left, there,
The recruits,
The never-failing replacements

As the ship drew out in darkness to the sea.
There the trucks came,   15
Or were supposed to come
Out of combat,
Moaning like the wounded,
Like the enemy and friend
Of life, to take us to the tents   20
Where the boys who came a week earlier

Lay in a cold sweat,
Or their ghosts lay, sweating
In a small tepid fog from the ground.
This was done, but I could not find   25
My bag, my flying gear, my books,
And so would not leave
The mountain of baggage.

When the last truck deserted, groaning
Through the great, besieging mud,   30
I saw the mound of baggage
Begin to sink through the clay
Like the hill of a dead king
Beleaguered by mosquitoes and flies
Losing their way in the dark.   35
Not knowing what this thing was

That at last I climbed aboard, clambering over
The musette bags which crunched
Like eggs, the long case
Where the guitar was straining its breast   40
Up the long, crumbling slope of baggage
I sat in trashy triumph at the top,
Knowing my own equipment, my own link
With the past was buried beneath me, or lost,

And not caring, not at all,   45
But only knowing that I was there,
Drenched in sweat, my shirt open down to my balls,
Nineteen years old, commanding the beach
Where life and death had striven, but safe
At the top of the heap, in the dark   50
Where no lights came through
From the water, and nothing yet struck.

———

Patience
In the Mill
CA. 1957

Through a place in the roof the sun came down
Where in a hail of light Mike Cole sat up,
His menial harness broken on his arms.

It shed a circle upon him,
As if he certainly were blessed, to be filling the cockpit with blood   5
Blushed eagerly from his face,
And laid on the sunburst of dials with glowing hands.
He could not look, but did,
And saw a smear, like egg, on the ragged panel wiped.
It was his other eye, which last had looked   10
In seeing his engine die from a vibrant disk
To four great innocent sails.

Through his own incredible sternness
Of pain, he heard the sirens flare
On the gunned dust of the strip,   15
And motes from the stacks of sugar whirled
And unsupported slept upon the air, beside his props
Like petals carved from off the basined floor.

A tooth lodged in his throat.
He did not speak of it, but a loft of children   20
In the light he had let in
Were standing and piping. He could not sing with them,
And almost wept,
                but like a child, forgot,

And wandered, lost, among their faces,   25
Opening the bags, tasting the slanted sugar as he would.

————

The Liberator Explodes

There, in the order of traffic
Of aircraft. Where one of them once
Was moving, in a clumsy hover,
It is like a blow through the sky
That does not move.   5

Why would you watch it
Before it becomes of fire?
There are many arranged on the air.
This one you might be watching,
Held in a fear   10

That contains no fear, but boredom, or fascination,
As it turns on the final approach.
Or you might be watching another
That does not fall.
If it is this one, you see   15
For an instant, nothing special. It is hanging down
As it would, the big wheels not spinning,
And now are fire:

One shot, a great one,
By accident takes place where the plane is: 20
The plane was. All of it is gone
Save the part that goes in on one wing,
There, off the end of the runway.

Then comes the shape
Of a silence made of an army   25
In one breath all watching wildly.
Things move out, and toward
Where it must have come down

There, off the end of the runway,
Still alive with a little of fire.   30
Here is the purest of fact
That took place like the purest of symbols.
The mind fires over and over

An aircraft that has blown away distance,
But cannot fetch that fact,   35
Or remember or know or imagine
What the faces of those must have felt
There in the brief shot of light,

And so must lie down again, and again,
Below the ground moved by palm-leaves   40
Of the mind of that time, and let that fade,
And lie in the luck of salvation
In the cities,
In the suburbs of time, until

There cracks across the simplest of the mind's   45
Eyes, that purchase of terror on the air,
The burst of light within flame,
Magnificent, final, and you behold your own
Unmirrored face freely explode,
And face, beyond faces,   50
Your brother of parallel fire.

———————

The Place of the Skull

—1945—

I used to get up, in the tent,
In the canvas sewn over the stroke
And shimmer of the inside of an orange,
And from my banged canteen the cup
Tip full of a curve of water, and pour it out on my head.   5
The air would be breathless; the others would

Be breathing it, all asleep.
Across the downed gilt of the canvas, the shadow of a fly
In the outside world would go
Like a bullet, saying, "Maze."   10
I would dry my hands, and pick up the poetry books

And walk through the area, out,
Over the rise with the crumbled machine-gun pit,
In the licked, light, chalky dazzle

Kicking the laces of my shoes along, 15
Until sea blue from under my belt

Trembled up, as down
To a bench in the stillest side
Of height, I came, to meet my holy masters in the Word
Above the gauze- and powder-burning bay. 20

I would sit all morning and read
In the sun, the page coming off my eye
More quivered-in than all the blue danced-up
By the miles of centerless waves, that spread to say
If I reached off the book, my hand would die 25

In the sea, of fire, with Shelley and with Crane,
And never touch the ships that anchored there.
The Spirit moving on the face of print
Left out the nights, when past the honest sleepers of the fleet

I rose in starry harness on the air, 30
And in my rubber mouth, from out the slender breeze
Of oxygen, I made a song of what I meant to kill
Before I poured my hanging head
From a can of water, and sat
Again above the bay, which loved the Word, and caught 35

My country's ships in such a full
And furious holocaust of soul,
The lines of ashen text marked off the graves
Where all my men, who sailed the ships, must die
For lack of Good, that I drew off the page. 40
I bit the silent tongue

Of men and angels, reading on
In the sound of engines run-up on the strip,
A grizzle of fly-wings, saying,
"Who asks for Truth at a time like this 45

Is shut from pity, and will slay his own
Whose vision kills the meaning of his view:

Only the larger war, with God,
Half-knows such seeming peace."

———————

Obstructions

Things placed there

First a cornfield
Where you wandered, drunk on your own afterbirth,
Weaving and crying.
The ears on the stalks were blackened   5
Two clouds went over the sun
Like lop-ears, and when they passed, you could see
That the rows of corn each made
A little road; down one
Of these you stumbled, and where you came out   10
A deer was eating the rotten shucks

Beyond that

Men, boys almost men,
Stood before a goal,
And you dressed in plastic and leather,   15
Carrying something in your arm,
And fled into the midst
Into the grunting midst of them.
They opened like rows of corn,
And you plunged through   20

Into a motel

In Fresno, California
Where a girl with a face you'd forget
Lay tangled in sheets.
In the early morning you rose,   25
In the gray, still light,
And tumbled into the swimming pool
Whose waters lapped and tingled
With the mighty rhythm of cottages
Where the pilots lay with their girls   30

Drunk on that water

You crawled barefooted over
A rusted aircraft engine,
A Pratt and Whitney
Pulled out of the ocean and junked,   35
Crusted with barnacles,
The cylinders fused into the block
From too much water-injection.
Past that it was moonlight

Shining over the island,   40

The graves out of sight
Every which way you could swivel.
Naked, you got ready, and set out
With a canteen of bourbon
And grapefruit juice,   45
Through the graves that opened in fans
Of infinite, knee-high perspectives,
Shifting like spokes of the wheel
That turned Okinawa through sea-foam.

Various ships took you away   50

To schools, to peacetime France,
And at last into the lap
Of students, each looking at you
With the stone question

In the heads of Greek statues   55
Who ask where their arms
And legs and the tips of their noses
Have gone. Your two sons took you

Under the arms, out through

The students, aging themselves,   60
And brought you to a broad field,
Green turning paler with dusk.
You pulled a cane from a bush
And sat there, looking at nothing
But how it all whitens and darkens,   65
Bourbon and beer still fasting,
Still tasting of ghosts, who all like it.

————————

Canebrake

1950s

    Morning; it shows
Its suppleness, and the massed green bones of strength.
Beyond, the river rises
Like a serpent touched at the tip of the tail,
And sprung, thereby, in a flurry of feathers to the eyes.   5

The road is still, and does itself no good,
As you kick its ruts into the little field.
From your feet, far out above
Your head, is a silence made of sounds.
Is it the pencil leaves   10
Of the stalks, you hear, or the river sprouting, unseen?

Making not the shadow of a thing
Beyond the naked stems, the sun
Casts a game of jackstraws on ground.

It might be better if,   15
Feeling it hopelessly exposed, you put your hand
On one of the light, slim, jointed tubes.
Thus, in a dream some years from now, you may have entered

The sway of the sprinkled leaves on top,
And seen the serpent lift his blinding head   20
Out of the side of the river,
The hot green wind come forth,
Come in and thatch a staler roof
To the roof of your drying mouth.
Insect-like, among the grassy posts,   25
You still may learn which gradual sound

Is the river's, and which the fending of leaves.
Here is another place that moves within
If motionless. Stand, swaying a little, here,

Your hand a support of classic, columned   30
Yet untameable air, and feel for the needle's
Word to be split, in peace, on the tongue of the serpent
An army of angry children would stomp to death,
Afraid it would speak, as it will.

The Wish to Be Buried Where
One Has Made Love

1950s

At dawn, in one move, a trout
Drew his body out the length of the river;

The sun smote the rocks into view.
We walked with the earthless footsteps

Of children about to be born.   5
We lay on the rocks, strangely flaming;

The trees from across the river
Came, in their next shadows, slowly;

A wind sprang out of their leaves
And broke, as I touched the guitar.   10

At dusk the boulders arose
Until they stood shafting in moonlight.

A curved muscle shook in the river,
As I stung the last note from the string,

And we lay, looking up through the stones   15
As through time, and saw there

A fish like a new current swimming,
A reflexing tree on the water.

We lie here, responding forever.

———————

The Wheelchair Drunk

1950s

I never had arms before
Those five martinis swooped into my room,
And I can tell you now that the thing I am in will dance,

Dancing not against but with
The bricks of the building, and whatever   5
Holds the glazed floors still while the elevator drops through.

Those doors I double-burst
And jolt down the footless stairs
Looking anywhere for a bar. Who brought that chilled pitcher

To the foot of my throne now stares   10
Open-mouthed out the window as I reel
The spokes forward faster than they ever intended

And unwind myself,
A horseless sulky, an old-fashioned ashcan,
Top-heavily happy, spinning my wheels in the sun   15

With light chopped to bits around
My center of gravity. This is where I bump
Down off the sidewalk, crossing a street where drivers

Blanch at the thought
Of running me down, even though they have   20
The light and the law on their side—and now must find

A driveway somewhere
To come in off the street and join
Wire carts full of soap-flakes and babies. I have forgotten

Why I can't rise and walk,   25
Stand on the lawns, push my self-starting chair
Out under a truck and let them smash-stop each other,

Holding up delivery
Of the U.S. mail, Grandma Foster's Pies,
Clothing store dummies, toilet seats or rose-dozens,   30

But it's certain I can't,
And so must go as I am, in my dressing gown,
Toward the dark neon alive in the middle of morning,

Unrolling an endless rail
On either side of me out of my powerful palms.   35
But it will be hard, hard to get through those two blocks:

I desire to hear
At every crossroads all the unhandled other
Wheels scream helplessly dead, for suddenly I love nothing

So much as to whirl   40
In the middle of traffic, holding up like a thief
Of delight those bread-trucks, those frustrated bridge-players:

To sit here like money
Lost and found in the perilous streets, and spin
Myself on a magical dime, getting better and brighter and better.   45

————————

The Mission

1950s

—*1944*—

    After the first long mission north
We flew, one hot night in the Philippines,
Before the sun came up
Mike Hall and I went down to San Jose,
And stood his jeep beside   5
A doorway of a pulsing thread of light,
And broke the thread, and went inside
A blacked-out house where a family sat

He knew. They flashed their steel-rimmed spectacles,
Their gold-capped teeth on Mike,   10
Called him MacArthur's little flying boy,
And brought the *tuba* out, a sweet-potato wine.
The oldest girl lit a candle;
I took a jelly-jar to drink,

And she and I went up the stairs, her gentle shape coming out   15
Of the eye of fire, and set
Upon my drying forehead as I climbed

Up under the roof, half-tin, half-leaves,
Where a blowing window opened forth
Its frame in stars, beyond the village.   20
A ghostly race-track far below
Into sight began to fade, in the valley's dawn.
I felt the roaring smile I'd held
Between the shimmering engine-disks, die out

And sink beneath my face, and sleep,   25
As my mind on the race-track wandered in the wind,
And into beautiful running, wake.
Hearing the little horses charge
For the far turn, I ran and ran
To catch them all before they surely died   30
Of outdone hearts.
Holding a fragile, calloused hand,
Hearing Mike and the still girl's family
Laugh, downstairs, and her sick brother,
Loved by me, unknown,   35
Sigh in the straw

Next room, I ran
With the marvellous horses,
Eyes and breath like theirs,
And a heart I could not trust for long: 40
Not leading, but in good position, there,
Home-stretched on the island-turned wheel.

The Coral Flight
1950s

In the hurricane wind
We crept into the aircraft, anchored
By their wings to the coral floor.
In the long roaring night we cramped
On the metal floor, along   5

The walls. I sat in the gunner's compartment
On an ammunition-box, leaning my head
On the bull-headed bulwark.
A flashlight burned in the craft.
In the wind, I was amazed   10

That we seemed to be airborne
In infinite flight, though anchored
To the sand-bagged stone of the island.
There was no pilot, though
One of us sat   15

In the pilot's seat, dishing up meat
From a tin can. At midnight,
The aircraft broke from its moorings,
And shuddered to the side, in a dance
of tons, actually flapping its wings,   20

And finally came to a halt
With its wing-tip ground down to pieces
By the side of a sea-creature's cliff.
As we hung there,
The flashlight gone out without glory,   25

I believed we yet more securely
Flew, and winged
Through a gigantic dream of the war
Where we fought no certified enemy,
But the obstinate world itself.   30

On into the gray dawn we shuddered,
Gnashing against the stout coral,
Until, at the end, I sat up,
With sand dust deep in my eyes,
And saw where we were,   35

Not landed, but beached,
Absolutely wrecked,
The engines, the tail, the wing,
Everything, but come through
The shuddering of death,   40

Having, some of us, actually dozed,
But none of us not having dreamed
That we were in flight, as never
Before, all the way out of earth,
Somehow still at war,   45
But a war that meant something
To the soul, at every
Floored mile we had flown in the dark.

———

The Valley

1950s

—*1945*—

   Steady, the simple pleasures
Of silence, of sea-blue sound
Coming up the valley from the beach.
They made us be things inside them,
Where slowly we sat on our porch,   5
Full of the large view of war.

The site they had given us to clean
And live upon, once laid of dust and every undug grave,
Had dazed us till we shone. When first we topped
And saw forth from the rise, Mike Hall had said,   10
"Good Jesus, what a place to live."
And what a place for many to have died.

The sun began to open. We tore apart some boxes and made floors
The last two months of war
We lived in the long-legged huts we nailed   15
With their porches out over the valley.
Peace came, and the sound of terror died
In the wind the length of the leaves
We sewed in strips and laced above our heads.
All day and night the roof was whispering,   20
"It is all too good, too good."

Where is the thing that shoved coffins
Through the bright orange sun of the Philippines?
Where are the aircraft, tinning with rain on the strip?
And Appleby dead, torn apart and still   25
Kicking in dusty grass? And Lalley, his head cut loose?
And Ward, shot dead through the roof of a mill?

What was it all, thus come to, but our good?
In air we sat, and the stakes went down   30
Far under us, into earth.
Like the British, we drank tea. The box-tops of the porch
Hummed with a sand of termites, at our feet.
At night, rot leapt into the wind
And, humming still, began to pray for the hut   35

To fall, as once we prayed
For all us young replacements to go home.
I think of the valley, now, as Life:
Broad with great peace, such blueness everywhere
One looked or breathed or sang,   40

And death filled with relief,
And think of most

The insect treasures, mounting from what there is
Missing, in everything.

———————

The Contest

1950s

—Amputee Ward, Okinawa, 1945—

    What is it has mounted?
Hollowness whirled by the waist, it is.
In the blood cave, wind is falling,
Falling short.
Right and left are melted into one.   5
He doubles his hands.
He has closed them.

There on the page of the magazine
Where he knows
Her honest: where he knows her   10
As she is: as she is holding
The cold door of a Frigidaire
Burning with porcelain sweat,

Is a game of drawing.
You go between dotted, numbered points   15
Enclosing Shape;
These are stars. Around his leg
Riding in space as silently as the earth,
Led from star to star by the hand
He feels their outline come to be.   20
The place of the island is bright

Upon the wind.
Head-down he follows, with his pencil.

As the last of marks would be made,
To Win (for *You: anyone:* a child!)   25
Joining one side of his thigh to the other,
Lining the island frailly out of water,
He thinks of her standing there coldly swinging
His body in through the door,
His face like a dancer's, deep in birth.   30

The pencil runs, runs on,
Runs down. His brain rustles: his lungs reverse
The vital haze of breath into a sound
Of asking. What would he win,
If he won? Where does it say that?   35
What does it say? *That his eye of a man*
Is blinded. His eye of an angel opens.
It is that, again, of sleep.

Beholding: it is all beholding.
At her hand, where the Winner's Money flutters,   40
And the island ripples
Its station in the sea up through the tent,
The frozen, mass-dazzling
Page of Heaven turns, and swings
Its eggs and fruit and crawling   45
Rain in streaks across his face,

And in his eye-lidded mask
He sleeps, somewhere between
His bed, and the broad, unloosable shot
Of distance. Then like a room he is waking   50
Behind the window clearness of his leg
Planted against the sun.
                              He and the girl go slow

With one another, round one another,
Flesh-tinted, in the bright ad,   55

And it is night. The moon, from its milk-teeth,
Sings into the dance they are making.
The shell-dusts of beaches quiver
Beneath his thigh, and there the air is pawing.

There is this he. Which? Now slowly alive   60
In the clearing of print with the money,
The girl, and the bright door crazed with cold.
But listen! It all has that greatness of hover!
The hover of muscle in sleep

That the bones cross, dropping,   65
Dropping: and there
The wool-spinning breath of a flock, but touched
To be broaded upon itself like fields, maintained
Of an inside dancing

Against no motion of otherness.   70
He scrawls on, writing in for the Rules of the Contest
His lips not shucked with grief,
He floats like a shadow upon his mouth,
And now the running statue of his blood
Is tranquil in the missing of its stride.   75

From the earth's one side he has been cut,
And there she stands, in his last step.
He goes there, dreaming with the whites of his eyes.

Among the trees between, the surgeon stops,
Playing a country tune upon his saw,   80
Sun like a chicken's foot
About him tensed and timed.
Under him, a prone man is singing in unison
With the water-bending notes of the metal.
A mown plot of lancets lies   85
All-strewn and shivering with his face.

She moves from beside the ice-box, goes round
Their toothless song four times,

While they cut down his leg and throw it off
To the island dogs. *He weeps, she is gone.*   90
Then the branches bubble with lights;
The wind breathes hoarsely down his throat.
The veins of marble open

Beneath his back. A shadow opens out above his foot.
His voice spreads through the towels of his blood.   95
Will she not come

Again; will she not come?
With his hands down under him, he feels
Through the slab being lost among the leaves,
The floor of a church come up and stop.   100
He struggles to stand, the roof of his mouth
A shape of flame. Mosaic scatters his heels.
What step? She whispers.

"In Sleep, Death's Masque, God dances."
The heron-footed whirlpool at his waist   105
Gently: gently again
Corrodes into rain; his vanished pores, in a steep
Drowsing of motes, make a placeless water of light
Come still. There, in the swung sensation
Of a wound, she dazzles,   110
Dazzles the pool of urine in his loins.
In the faceted house of the tent, he lies,

Trying to hold on, yet moved
Inevitably from sleep.
Here, in the hoist of leather,   115

The swamp of gauze, the spittle-slick of rubber,
What can he do but close his eyes? What else,
In peace without shade?
Beside the sea—the farthest sound of brothers
Headlong loading lumber—   120
He shakes clean of his beard and starts to cry.

There on the page is drawn
A Polar Bear, in the place where the leg
Was starred and shining on itself, and now is gone.
Yet the paper keeps giving her off,   125
And the ice-box, and the Rules, and the money.
By God, by God
(And the night's moon, when it comes,
Stopped sheer at beauty, all around itself, by the sea),

He will cut her out. Just *her!*   130
A medic brings him scissors, and he grins.
The page turns, out in his breath; she slips and slips
The whiteness from her sides,
Trembling, becoming,
And her body is given unto him.   135
His heart stops all around him, in the sun.
He picks up everything and loves.

————————

Invitation au Voyage

1950s

  Rest on the bright decks
Among the others, all of them seeming your family.
When your eyes go out past the ship,
Often you can see
An immense ragged angel,   5
The sun, come on you from the water where you sit.

Your head is suddenly luminous,
And all there is
Trembles to you, through the circling
And weaving gulls, in and out   10
Of the great wild shape on the sea.

Night come, leave everyone,
And lean by yourself on the rail,
Where the god has turned
To silver, and thin   15
As a cross-cut saw on the little waves.
I shall be

Believing in the wide-spread, pale-blue dark,
And a man, there, close to himself,
Looking far over and hearing   20
Not gulls, but the sound of feathers.

————

Hart Crane

1950s

   Sight, from the ocean dazzling,
Moved, within somewhere the rim
Of the actual wheel of glittering.
A gull before me shaped
Off, one wing down, then righted roundingly.   5

My looking out
Concealed it all.
I could not understand what he had meant,
Nor the surgical boil of the wake
Through which, a moment of the sea,   10

He piled and fell, a long slow presence of the pounding heart,
As the sea through a vastness of levels turned
Black, all over,

And breath, on a kind of saying, closed.
It could not matter, through the sunlight he was in;   15
No quiet of gull or froth could help,

But somewhere in the falling
Passion, his legs rebelled, and kicked
Most piteously; his arms fought off
Unstrikeable water, and the heart utterly gave out   20

In the man not yet all dead.
If one, along this unrelated beach,
Ran, as he could, and shouted with everything
He found inside himself, and did his best
To tear his body's life from him by every shred,   25

He would know that one must run
Or fall from a thing to be truly in it,
The hands in wind or water gone wildly for no hold,
The feet, there sprinting or terribly thrashing to say
Awarded, awarded, awarded.   30

————————

The Archers

1950s

The boys are sighting with their muscles
Down the long crested shafts of the arrows.
Their forearms and somnolent eyelids
Are infinitely precious in the sun,
And the bold, cocked fingers of their right hands   5
Are tingling like springs,
As their beast's gaze, gone miraculously down
The feather-spinning roads of the arrows,
Refines the small treasure of the target
Beyond price, beyond aim, beyond the world,   10
Beyond the deep, surrounded gold of the center
Inflicted by this second only.

Walter Armistead

Remember: not making
Memory climb the mind, as he
The half-dead rustling-still of summer tree,
But come, amazed with love, to stand, this hour dissolved

Upon him years away,   5
The axe lashed to his wrist.
Upright and braced in my head
Two hundred yards from me, as then,

He sets the tingling arches of his feet
On two great boughs, and swings.   10
I hear the dead limbs fall, and,
At every stroke, like Time to cut him down,

An axe within the wood knock back.
Those were the years we thought of being men,
And we must labor for it, hauling ourselves up ropes,   15
Running long hours in the woods,

Swinging our mauls and axes till we shook,
And afterwards, our muscles stunned with blood,
Coming back to the summer of the house, and the room
Where, in a harp of light, the great harp leant.   20

Then he would play
Parts of the missing music
Of the dead limbs on the lawn. It was a thing
I since have made him say: would not have thought of, then,

Hearing the sad rippled humming-forth, and forth.   25
Remember, remember
(How many years since his death
Exploded in air, whose body the earth never reached?)

Not so much the knocking of the axe
Inside the trunk, the answering one,   30
Or the stricken tree that cut the sun
Apart, and strewed it powerfully, shook, upon his head,

But the loom of rain he held between his hands,
The strings, the winter of the leaves.

————————

For Richard Wilbur

1950s

    In such a tremendous window
Seated, the whole rich dark came through,

And the Arno most, we watched and talked

And the traffic roared through the vital ruins of Florence
Beneath, on a narrow street;   5
The river trembled in golden paints.

I thought that either you or I,
Or both, could rise from the mossy casement,
And from a standing start
Could clear the whole wild shaken street   10
To the river, where light felt for its shape.

It was a thing to think of: we could do it.
But here in the aftermath,
In the other heart of traffic, I sit
In the opening American night, and, through you, remember   15
That the great wild thing is not seeing
All the way in to the center,
But holding yourself at the edge,
Alive, where one can get a look.

Drifting

POST-1960

for Al Braselton

I

It is worth it to get
Down there under the seats, stretched believingly out
    With your feet together,

Thinking of nothing but the smell of bait and the sky
    And the bow coming   5
To a point and the stern squared off until doomsday;

    It is good to go for hours
With the wind down the lake in some unhindered direction
    And feel the stem of one weed

Rise somewhere unseen, near land, and stop you dead.   10
    It is also good to sense
The wind die, and the boat move gravely, without it,

    Back onto the depths,
And to sail, positioned for burial, broadly smiling,
    Until the center is reached,   15

The bones form a teeming new order, the boat does not
    Sail, but spins, not going
Down, too light for the maelstrom's grand passion,

    And the embodied hull
Sheds perfect rings outward, messageless, always received,   20
    For there is time.

Once in a lifetime a man must empty his pockets
    On the bank of a river,
Take out two monogrammed handkerchiefs and tie them

    To the oars stuck in the sand: 25
These mark the edge of the known; he will sail from here
    On the grains of the mountain,

Ground fine, on the sea's winding, unappeasable call
    Sent through his blood-curves,
On thousand-pound boulders that sensitize the water   30

    Like a skin, like banner-cloth,
And scrape with the weight and authority of the dead
    On the floor of the human house,

And in his relaxed biceps will comprehend how the snake's
    Body is one with the heart   35
Of the current, and how his abandoned oars must stand

    Signifying a triumph,
So that he can roll, in a long mind-motion, the river
    Up like a bolt of cloth,

Snipping it off at the sea, and store it on land   40
    In a camphored clothes closet
In its huge red impure length of blazing mud and movement,

    Bronze suns, dim clouds
Of rocks, and all the surprising flashes of things that never
    Cease to stream,   45

And thus, a rare hand dropped off the balancing chair side
    As on a snake's back,
Feeling the world go unopposedly where it will, may sit

In an uncontrollable
And wholly justified dance of pure acceptance   50
On the grains of the mountain,

Drifting round and round a great foaming banner, unfurled
On all four walls
While two named handkerchiefs flutter at his surpassed frontier.

————————

For Robert Bhain Campbell

POST-1960

Unwandering, I can move
One hand, then both,
But not the hand to write what you can hear.
Young poet asleep within cancer,
I feel you changing with   5
I feel you changing my language.

Here is the place where I sit,
In-breathing the childhood sea,
But still a city man moves here
As under traffic bridges.   10
For him, there is no death so far,
So out and down, as yours

Here in the sail-set sundown,
As though God were moved by His wind,
A man like a ghost may walk.   15
I have no picture, or memory,
But a tall sick man, and some words.

I like him; I love him,
I shall soon sit cold in an office,
Hearing the sea swing, the dead man step: 20

The sun at sunset in the mind
Never fails, never fails.

There is Berryman's poem, where you were a bird.
And I, an unsocial man,
Live working for some kind of living   25
In a job where there is no light. But
I can summon, can summon,
And your face in my mind is hid
By a beard I read you once grew.

Listen: the people in their parks   30
Think nothing, think of nothing.
But not for them I remember
Or invent or wish for memory
With a man from poems reconstructed.
But not so well, Bhain Campbell.   35
But not in your own flesh,
Young poet asleep within cancer.
I open your book again. If it were gone,
Where could I get another?
It is the place   40
That with yourself you have made, you say,

Deeper than the falling of the sun,
You say, you are saying.
And all and steadily deep
From that ultimate place where you speak, and I   45
In my office death-wish, must hear.

———————

A Morning
1960s (?)

A dog surroundingly howls.
Painfully he is changing
His voice from a voice for the moon

To the voice he has for the sun.
I stoop, and my hands are shining;
I have picked up a piece of the sea

To feel how a tall girl has swum
Yesterday in it too deeply,
And, below the light, has become

More naked than Eve in the garden.
I drop her strange body on cobbles.
My hands are shining with fever,

And I understand
The long, changing word of the dog
With the moon dying out in his voice,

And the pain when the sun came up
For the first time on angel-shut gates,
In its rays set closer than teeth.

5

10

15

Lazarus to the Assembled
1960s (?)

It is you who have made light crawl
And become the hot, caved-in brightness
Where I lie without shadow or weight
Inside the whole weight of the hill,
Now, thinking, "Alive. Alive shortly.
I cannot stay here with this."
   As the stone rolled away

I heard you frightenedly speak
As though you had hidden the dead.
I can, you cannot know
That this cannot be done.
I move; you try to be still,

5

10

But now I begin to feel
Your movement set in, like a forest

By a miracle touched at the roots.   15
My life, coming back, runs through
Body after body among you,
And as far as the heart of the city.
In the dark of a jar in the market
Clear water as helplessly shakes.   20
By stirrings such as these I return.

I am the dead new-born.
From the mouth of the cave, the sun
Comes into my mouth,
And I can devour all light.   25
The water in wells
Is ringing like cymbals.
The doors of the houses fly open.

"Bring out your dead," I cry,
And how this must be done   30
You can, I cannot know.
Instead, I lie here feasting
On your habitual dust
Of sunlight. Slowly I bend
And sit upright like a man   35

Who does a hard exercise
That must be good for him.
How long have I been gone?
My failed face shines and stares.
The hill falls off me, and I   40
Step out, beholding my people
Who have waited in blinding clothes.

As the stone rolled away
Your movement set in like a forest.
By stirrings such as these I return.   45
The doors of the houses fly open

And I stand upright like a man
You can, I cannot know
  Who has waited in blinding clothes.

You move; I try to be still,   50
By a miracle touched at the roots.
And now I begin to feel
Body after body born among you.
I cannot stay here with this!
The sun comes into my mouth.   55
"Bring out your dead," I cry.

––––––––––

The Sprinter at Forty
1960s (?)

Knowing that nothing is in it,
I walk late at night out and down
Toward the glimmering mail box
Where it sits among houses whose windows
Throw light without trouble or searching.   5
Under the street lamp I pause

With my hand on the dew of my name
Hammered strongly in metal and urgent,
And find that my body is shaking
Out the old, longest muscles of its thighs.   10
As light after light in the houses
Snaps out all around me for acres,

I receive the wish to live more
Which nothing but motion can answer.
I touch down my fingers to pavement   15
And rise, and begin to run
Up the curved, crucial lane of the asphalt
Passing under the street lamps

And between the dark houses where men,
Grown suddenly light with amazement,   20
Cry out for their youth among nightmares
Of debt, and turn to their women.
Like a choir, something rises about me
And I try for the finish until

I am doing all I can do.   25
I tell you, sleepers, a thing
You know without having to move
From the shook, nailed blocks of your beds:
That wide-open running at forty
Is best done alone after midnight,   30

Seeing your shadow run with you
Maned with locked light under lamps
Where it sharpens and fades and renews,
Where gold after gold takes it up
Like the members of a relay team   35
Passing hope from hand into hand,

You know that youth occurs
In bursts, many times in a life,
And fades, and strains and comes.
Such a shade is now covering ground.   40
I see my thin hair shine
Again and again, and the earth

Between your houses be changed
And charged with successive golds
As I stomp there. The fat on my body leaps   45
In joy, and the past has exactly returned
From the dead, at dead of night,
In violent motion, sliding on cement.

Poems for Children

Tucky the Hunter

1978

He shot the two-horned rhino with his double-barreled gun,
He shot the dusty python for sleeping in the sun.
He shot the bullish elephant, the king of pachyderms,
He shot the bristling cougar, and fed him to the worms.
He shot the grinning crocodile in the Ganges thick and brown,   5
While he gobbled up a newsboy in the middle of the town.
Alaska knew his courage whenever he came back,
For he'd shot the gruesome grizzly, and the bumbling Kodiak.
He shot the mountainous King-Kong, whom everybody knows;
He was holding up a kicking girl, and pulling off her clothes.   10
He shot the bearded Barbary goat, as it sat looking wise,
And, creeping into Eden, shot the Bird of Paradise.
With his knife hung from his studded belt his double-barreled gun,
Tucky the Hunter hunted on, through the suburbs of the sun.
Where flamingos put the moon out, then lay down in the weeds,   15
And night sprayed burning egrets on the ever-swinging reeds,
Where the moon charged like a red-eyed bull, then plunged into the sea,
Tucky hunted EVERYTHING—but I hope not YOU and ME!
He shot the snapping wolverine, just as it sallied forth;
His great gun bammed, and that was IT for the Demon of the North.   20
He shot the one-eyed Yonghy, and then he bagged the Bo,
Then finished off the triple of the Yonghy-Bonghy-Bo.
He shot the native boomalong, with its eye of night-shade blue;
And the yellow Malay monkey for doing nasties in the zoo.
At Samarkand the whirling stars all whistle wild and pale,   25
And so they do off Durban, where Tucky shot the whale.
He shot the smiling Devil, in flames of blow-torch blue;
The angels came out dancing, and Tucky shot them too.
Like clay pipes in a gallery, he shot the trembling stars,
He shot the burly Bintarong—but he NEVER shot at cars!   30

And he shot everything there was, but they weren't really DEAD!
All summer, winter, spring and fall he shot them in his bed.
For a pop-gun has strange powers, and the animals know this:
It wounds with simple love alone, with the tension of a kiss.
And when the pop-gun fires, a loving life for the bold   35
Is born in the heart of a hunter, a hunter five years old.
The animals would rise and wait in tree-top and in den
And watch the West-red sun go down so Tuck could hunt again.
When the real sun sank as the earth rolled, Tuck's OWN moon and HIS sun
Came out, and HE'D set out, with his knife and double gun.   40
One night he started all alone for the coast of Palawan;
And shot the gristly Tiger-Shark and the ever-dying swan.
He shot the scented meadow-lark; he slew it for its song,
And put the song in his pocket as he hunted right along,
And when his mother came for him, before the break of light,   45
She wondered where he'd got that song, so mournful and so right.
She wondered where he'd got that song, that sounded like noon-flight;
She wondered where he'd got it, in the middle of the night.
And the beasts all rose up singing, as she took Tuck in her arms,
And everything was banished that comes from night's alarms.   50
The animals and fish were there, and birds flew through the room;
There was nothing but Creation in night's suburban gloom.
And the beasts were glad to be there, that fell to Tucky's gun;
They were glad to be a part of that great nocturnal fun.
And they were grave and stately, but laughing with delight,   55
As Susan raised up Tucky in the middle of the night.
The hunt was almost over; for Tuck was growing up,
And he'd never have any more to drink from inspiration's cup.
But while he was a little child, for a time that wouldn't last long,
He held within his pocket the meadow-lark's light song.   60
And the animals rose up singing when Susan held him near
All the beasts that Tucky shot were seen both dear and clear:
And his mother, Susan, then most strangely began to sing
The song of the single meadow-lark, and the song of the Cobra King:
She sang of strange night-wonders, meant just for mother and son: 65
She sang as only a mother can sing to her one and only one,
And the animals sang with her; they sang of all the stars:
They sang on the streets of the suburbs of Venus and of Mars:

They sang in mystic double-tongue, the tongue of man and beast,
They sang of Far West buffalo, and the jungles of the East,   70
And Susan lay down singing, very far from night's alarms.
His mother lay down singing in Tucky's valiant arms.

———————

Bronwen, the Traw, and the Shape-Shifter
1986

Book One

Blue rocks and an ocean-wide river
And a house that sat out on a ledge:
With her mother and father and flowers
Bronwen lived at the morning-glow edge.

From the window she'd look out at daybreak   5
Deep into the brimming blue haze
That, while her blue eyes stood watching,
Burned away in the river's far blaze.

Her mother'd look up from her planting
In her light-blowing dahlia blouse   10
As Bronwen came over the flagstones
In her sunflower hat from the house.

She would kneel in the brown of the garden
With the pines and their jack-strawing straw
And dig round the roses and tulips   15
With the tingling three prongs of her traw.

The traw was a kind of a trowel
But her dad made it curve like a claw,
And cut out with tin-snips the fingers
Of the world's only really real traw.   20

The fat worms knew she meant business,
As, with ointment of zinc on her nose,
She dug for the magical color
That comes up through the stem of the rose.

But when sun passed the bee-wingèd greenhouse   25
Growing big and red, less and less bright,
She would lift up her eyes from the rose bed
And look round, in the less and less light.

The grass would grow dark, and the flowers,
And the sun disappear in a field   30
Off yonder where roads came together
And the light in the river was sealed,

And the All-Dark would rise from the hedges
On its single dim monsterous foot,
And walk in thick steps from the orchard   35
And through the high bedrooms like soot.

Bronwen knew that the All-Dark would find her
As it did in its path every night;
It would come as though coming behind her
And blank everything else out of sight.   40

For the All-Dark was more than the evening,
And wasn't the worst thing of all,
For the All-Dark turned loose the Shape-Shifter,
And stood and looked in from the hall.

Where the cracks of her blue door went lightless   45
The All-Dark took charge of the wall;
It hung like the wrong side of brightness,
And was nothing, and more than the wall.

It lies like a great bed of nothing,
It stands on the floor and the chair,   50
It rides the strange square of the window,
And is everything there that is there.

It builds itself high like a cliffside,
It layers itself like a cake,
In children's dim rooms like a half-world   55
It stands all around till they wake.

But that's not the worst of the All-Dark,
Though its silence is part of the worst;
The worst is the Shapes that come from it,
And the last is as bad as the first.   60

It turns loose a thing from its middle,
A cloud-shape with fingers of coal
That drops a black rain on the bedspread
And makes a deep noise like a hole.

In the fall when the window is rattling,   65
It's the shape a dark air-shape would have
If it turned itself topsy-turvy
And blew from a terrible cave.

From its side grows a red hand of fire
With its fingers more dreadful to see   70
Than the spiked slow leaves of the fly-trap
When they close round the wings of the bee.

It hums like a shell or a kite string
Or a well bucket hit with a brook
If the bucket were round as the darkness   75
And the well were as deep as the room.

Book Two

In the ring of the All-Dark lay Bronwen
With the pane on one side, and the moon
With the four Shape-Shifters emerging
And making their moves one by one.   80

But a light knock came on the window
A knock like the tail of a kite,

A sound not made by the All-Dark
Or by any wrong shape of the night.

No other knock came on the glass-dark   85
But Bronwen looked out toward the rap
That a leaf might have made in its falling
And the stem turned around with a tap.

A shadow stood up looking inward,
And was there, not trying to pass,   90
A shape like the shape of a mitten
That changed the whole life of the glass.

The fur of its shade ruffled softly
As it held the far side of the chill.
Who would let such a soft thing stay warmless?   95
Bronwen lifted the sash from the sill.

In glided a spread-open squirrel
With its eyes not taken from her.
It looked like the ones of her garden,
But it sat, and then folded its fur.   100

It came down to rest on her bed-foot
But she couldn't feel it at all,
For she couldn't imagine or make up
Anything so light, graceful and small.

At the window more squirrels were shadowed;   105
They sailed in, but with never one wing,
And the one on her bedspread said nothing,
But in a leaf's voice started to sing.

"Are you Bronwen of the Blue Cliffs,
Of the garden and the sun?   110
Are you Bronwen of your parents
And their one and only one?

"Are you Bronwen of the roses,
And the crow's split-level caw?
Are you Bronwen of the fountain?   115
Are you Bronwen of the traw?"

                                                          .

I am Bronwen Bronwen Bronwen,
I am Bronwen of the hose
I am Bronwen of the sprinkler
I am Bronwen of the rose.   120

I am Bronwen Bronwen Bronwen
I am Bronwen most of all,
I am Bronwen when I do and when I don't.
I am Bronwen of the blue eyes
I am Bronwen of the cliffs   125
I am Bronwen when I will and when I won't.

I am Bronwen Bronwen Bronwen
I am Bronwen all the time
I am Bronwen with three freckles on my nose
I am Bronwen of the rabbit   130
I am Bronwen of the wren
I am Bronwen from my pigtails to my toes.

I am Bronwen Bronwen Bronwen
I am Bronwen once again.
When you see me you are glad at what you saw.   135
I am Bronwen of the fountain
Of the river rose once more
I am Bronwen of the blue eyes and the traw.

"You must come with us in moonlight,
You must glide with us and cross   140
The wide grey star-bright river
In a shawl of riding-moss."

.

But you are only squirrels
No matter how you try;
You are only mitten-squirrels,   145
And you can't even fly!

"We can't fly like hawks and eagles,
We can't go where condors go,
But on silver nights of autumn
We glide down and down like snow.   150

"We are flying squirrels only
But we float like thistledown.
We ride like every wind there is
Where every wind has flown.

"We must take you to our country,   155
We must lift you like a ghost.
You must take a magic weapon,
The thing you love the most.

"It can't be big and scary,
It must have its own right name: 160
The most loved and the most you use,
For these are both the same.

"You must wear a hat that makes you
The Bronwen of the sun,
And that turns you around like a flower   165
To light the All-Darkening One."

I'll go if you will take me
Bronwen said, *and I will cross*
With my traw the wide grey river
In a shawl of moon and moss.   170

In a net of threads they set her,
In a room gone more than still;
In light tree-wool they lifted
And launched out from the sill.

The river grew in greyness   175
As the cliff fell from them where
They rode on simple air alone
That was there and there and there.

Through the moss she watched the stars stay,
Amazing where they stood;   180
In moss she traveled free and clear
Through a wild and rootless wood.

For gliding is not walking
And is better than them all;
When you ride with flying squirrels   185
You cannot ever fall.

So Bronwen lay back watching
The stars move through the threads;
All children should have such delight
When they look out from their beds.   190

They should see the gentle ruffling fur
Of squirrels at their ease
Upholding them in gentle air
In the swaying strings of trees.

Book Three

They sank to the far Earth so gently   195
That there was no change in the air;
They touched the low leap of a hilltop
And came to rest cradling, just there.

It was the softest green country
That a moss-bed in flight ever felt;   200
If there'd've been more softness, even,
It would have had reason to melt.

The squirrel who'd sat on her bed-foot
In her home on the high steady stone

Brought a kingly great squirrel to meet her   205
And she took his gold paw in her own.

"We have brought you far over the water
Because we are living in fear.
You may think this the gentlest of countries
But a one-footed terror lives here.   210

"Its name is the great-spreading All-Dark
And it falls on us here in the East
Where the sun rolls away to the westward
And leaves us to each secret beast.

"The weasels can find us, and night hawks,   215
From the snakes we go rigid with fright,
And we fall to the owls and the wildcats
And all things that can see without light.

"We have heard that you have in your garden
A tool like a marvelous claw   220
That can take on our own kind of magic."
Bronwen said, *It's all true. It's my traw.*

But how did you hear that I had it?
And I SURELY don't know how to fight!
"The hat on your blond head turns sunward   225
And against all the force of the night."

But how did you know I was living
Where the rock rises up from the rock?
And how did you know just which window,
And just how to knock, and not knock?   230

"The sea gull told us, the robin,
And the wren and the red butterfly;
All the wings that come over the river
And do their best things in the sky."

I'll do what you asked me to come for   235
Bronwen said, *but where must I go?*
"First to the bright turning fountain
Where the waters rise up as they flow.

"Then you'll fight in the Rocky Arena,
The All-Dark's main cave and his lair.   240
It's like a great hole and a quarry,
And the Shape-Shifter lives with him there."

In a clearing the fountain was turning
And the squirrels placed Bronwen inside.
She stood still as the live drops went round her   245
Like a ring she could center with pride.

She gazed through the high rounding water
And the shapes that danced there like the moon
Were angels and horses and dolphins
That went and came back as they spun.   250

And sometimes they danced all together
So the horse and the dolphin were one
And you could not tell running from swimming
Or how this bright mystery was done.

She held up the traw to the sparkle,   255
To the bend of the high looping lines,
And three drops fell misting together
On the traw, and its three tingling tines.

A sea gull sent one, and a llama;
The tines of the traw took their glow;   260
From the horse and the dolphin, the other
As they leapt in the flash and the flow.

The shape of the angel so flickered
That you couldn't be sure it was there:

It was quick, it was gone, it was coming,   265
The thinnest light-shape in the air,

But a spark would flash out like a feather
Or like something some deep hand had stirred,
Its movement so quick and so fleeting
It could come from no earth-wingèd bird.   270

And the squirrels then lifted out Bronnie
From the fountain that turned like a wheel
With the three touched tines of her weapon
That now had a quickened new feel.

"Are you game for the rocks and the darkness?"   275
The King of the Squirrels said then.
Yes I am, and for the Shape-Shifter,
Bronwen said, *just show where and say when.*

"Where the blackness is blacker than any,
Like a great open mouth, like a jaw,   280
You must do what you can with your gumption
And your sunflower hat and your traw."

She was there, in the stone-blinded silence,
And listened, and heard nothing stir;
But a sound like a low-brimming whisper   285
Rose then, and came toward her.

In a second she was high in a whirlwind,
She was upside down, turning like straw,
But her hat stayed in place, although cockeyed,
And she held to her fountainous traw.   290

Touch the root, touch the root, she kept saying:
If I can just tumble and find
Where the foot whirls alone on the wild ground
I can cut all the strength from the wind.

And she swanned herself out like a diver   295
Spinning down through that buffeting hall
And touched the crazed foot of the air-beast
And the wind fell off, and let fall.

Bronwen picked herself up from the gravel,
From sharp stony soil of that bed;   300
She had got only strawberried elbows
But one tine of the traw had gone dead.

All the stone now glowed like a foundry
Like the claw-hammered steel of a forge;
Smoke poured from the jaws of the rock-face   305
And filled all the grim of the gorge.

Fire leapt out for Bronwen and found her;
She gasped, and she started to choke
As the animal-flame went around her
And tears came to her from the smoke.   310

Touch the blue, touch the blue, she said gamely,
For I broke the wind's strength at the root,
And she leaned and struck down with her prong-tool
The torch-purple fan of the foot.

The fire lost its circle and passion   315
And the smoke lost its black lungs for good;
There were only ashes and embers
In the ring where smudged Bronnie stood.

I have only one tine from the fountain,
Bronwen thought, and looked down; it was true—   320
The water had blessed the three fingers;
She had one, but she still needed two.

The All-Dark gives no time for waiting;
When it fails it comes right back again.

A great tidal wave sprang for Bronnie   325
That the rocks had held somewhere within.

Her feet were swept out from under
And she hung in the curve of a wave;
The bottom-sand swirled up around her
Like the grains in a dust-devil's cave.   330

The foot of this thing moves too swiftly,
Bronwen thought, as she struggled for breath,
I can't do what I did with the others
For this foot is more deadly than death.

I must somehow get up to the topside   335
To save what I'm trying to save;
I must reap the wild white of the water,
For a wave with no crest is no wave.

With her dog-paddle strokes and her hat down
On her ears like an umbrella-flower,   340
Bronwen frog-leggèd up the green smash-wall
And reached the white line of its power.

Along this she sped like a sunfish;
Like the triple-toothed blade of a saw
As the crest of the wave was reaped helpless   345
Was the last rushing tine of her traw.

The wave sank down into sand-dust;
Like a shell, dripping Bronwen rolled there
With her traw bent, flattened, and corkscrewed
And the water gone safe as the air.   350

BOOK FOUR

But beneath her two feet there then opened
The endless deep black of the earth;
Though Bronwen stood fast, she knew surely
That this was death's go-for-broke birth.

"Come back, leap back, gutsy Bronwen,   355
For your traw has gone dead in your hand;
You cannot fight the mad suck-hole
That can take the whole life of the land."

No, I'll stand once again, said blond Bronwen,
I'll stand with my traw and my hat;   360
I'll stand, for the world's frightened children;
If it's that, it'll have to be that.

Bronwen felt herself going under
As beneath a black bodiless tongue;
She was swallowed without any warning   365
And down useless darkness was flung.

Her traw almost left her forever
As she sank in this most deadly calm;
But the handle she'd taken for granted
Was a new living blaze in her palm,   370

For something had touched it in passing
When the horses and dolphins had dashed
And the fountain had spun like a river
And the light drops had misted and flashed.

A heat came into her fingers   375
As, from the dazzled dead tines,
The handle turned round and was with her
Like a lightning-struck crest of dry pines.

What had touched it was father or feather,
Or what had just thought it was there;   380
It was angel or bird mixed with water,
Or a one-lifetime trick of the air,

But the flash from the quick of the fountain
Found the mud at the glut of its suck
And the earth healed entirely around her   385
And some was just guts, and some luck,

For she rose in the lightening stone-space
Now like a rock garden she knew,
And Bronwen had beaten the dark back
With her eyes of bluebonnet blue.   390

The King of the Squirrels came to her
Where she stood with her beaten-up traw
And took her light hand laced with scratches
In the royal gold gold of his paw.

"You have beaten the All-Dark forever: 395
All his height and his breadth and his length,
For, huge as he is, he is nothing:
The Shifter was all of his strength.

"The snake and the weasel drew from him,
From his earth, water, fire, and air;   400
Against these our efforts were futile;
We could never find someone who'd dare

"To face the Four Forms in the open;
We were many, but weaker than few;
Now the All-Dark will keep the Shades hidden   405
And will sleep as the rest of us do."

You're welcome, said Bronwen, and curtsied,
What a hard-working night THIS has been!
I can't say "There was nothing to it,"
And I sure wouldn't do it again!   410

"To get you back over the river
We'll have to use muscle and wit
For you live on a cliff-top already
And we'll need to get higher than it.

"We have a steep mountain, and from it   415
A single pine tree rises high;
It's the best that we've got, and the nearest
This country can get to the sky.

"So you and my best-gliding squirrels
Must climb to the top branches there   420
So we can create our own angle
And invent the right downslope of air."

At home, Bronwen said, *there's a cupboard,*
Very tall, where they keep my pink cup.
I learned to climb anything that way,   425
Anything in the world that goes up.

I love to go higher and higher;
Dad says that when I make my moves
I can get up on anything standing:
Bookcases, broom-closets and stoves.   430

So don't fret about me and your hilltop
And the climb to the top of your tree,
For a trunk and some limbs on a mountain
Will be less than a chair-back to me.

So she and the King's twenty squirrels   435
Climbed and clung where the top branches shook
And the green peace was boundless, and living,
And was everywhere Bronwen could look.

A fresh net of moss came together;
Bronwen lay in its fragrant new weave   440
And the Squirrels, grasping all its light edges,
Spread the fur of their light sides, to leave.

Let me have one more look, cried Bronwen,
Though her eyelids were wearing her out;
The whole land took over her memory,   445
And they were the same, just about.

From the twigs that were smallest and highest
Where Bron in the whole country slept
The squirrels took aim upon distance
And lifted their sleeper, and leapt.   450

They slid from the top of the country
Where Bronwen had won what she'd won,
Her sunflower hat pulled down over
Her eyes, to keep out the sun.

One or two grey glimpses of river   455
Where sunrise burned vivid and pale
Were all that Bronwen remembered
Of her journey home, and one sail

Like a butterfly-pinch on the water
Where she dreamt in her squirrel-borne loom   460
And the blue cliffs rose high and brought to her
The flowered blue walls of her room.

Her mother and father'd not missed her,
For she was the same as she'd been,
As she came down the stairs to the flagstones   465
And was part of the same morning scene.

But the earth of the garden was kinder;
Underfoot it could never give way;
It held up the tulips and dahlias
Just enough, and the roses would stay   470

Where they wished to, in no earthly danger
Because Bron had been where she'd been,
And the sheaf of the rainbowing sprinkler
Turned round like the fountain she'd seen

The breeze stirred the stems and the flowers,   475
The best that could happen to air;
You'd not think that a one-footed demon,
Turned loose, had ever spun there.

On the hearth the embers glowed deeply;
Bronwen gazed with their warmth on her face,   480
Or sometimes read, or played checkers
With every red disc in its place.

She liked the red checkers better;
She built kings at the enemy's back,
And she and the flames played together   485
Against the always-beat black.

And then, when the last embers shifted,
And All-Quiet came to the walls
Bronwen climbed up the stairs to her bedroom
And turned out the lights in the halls.   490

With all children safe from the Shifter
And the traw's dented glow on the shelf
Bronwen slept like lilies and dahlias
And the All-Dark slept in itself.

Apparatus Criticus

Abbreviations

Achievement   *The Achievement of James Dickey: A Comprehensive Selection of His Poems*. Edited with an introduction by Laurence Lieberman. Glenview, Ill.: Scott, Foresman, 1968.

Arnett   David L. Arnett, "An Interview with James Dickey." *Contemporary Literature* 16 (Summer 1975) 286–300. Partially reprinted in Baughman, 71–83.

Babel   *Babel to Byzantium: Poets & Poetry Now*. New York: Farrar, Straus & Giroux, 1968.

Baughman   *The Voiced Connections of James Dickey: Interviews and Conversations*. Edited by Ronald Baughman. Columbia: University of South Carolina Press, 1989.

Bird of Paper   *A Bird of Paper: Poems of Vicente Aleixandre*. Translated from the Spanish by Willis Barnstone and David Garrison. Athens: Ohio University Press, 1982.

Boleman-Herring   Elizabeth Boleman-Herring, "James Dickey: An Interview." *James Dickey Newsletter* 12 (Spring 1996): 13–18.

Broughton   *The Writer's Mind: Interviews with American Authors*. Vol. 2. Edited by Irv Broughton. Fayetteville: University of Arkansas Press, 1990.

Buckdancer   *Buckdancer's Choice*. Middletown, Conn.: Wesleyan University Press, 1965.

Central Motion   *The Central Motion: Poems 1968–1979*. Middletown, Conn.: Wesleyan University Press, 1983.

Christensen   Paul Christensen, "Ritual Magic: An Interview with James Dickey." *Lone Star Review* 3 (July/August 1981): 3–4. Reprinted in *Night Hurdling*, 219–29.

"Comments"   "Comments to Accompany *Poems 1957–1967*." *Barat Review* 3 (January 1968): 9–15.

Compton   Thorne Compton, "Imagination at Full Stretch: An Interview with James Dickey." *James Dickey Newsletter* 20 (Fall 2003): 31–42.

Dickey Reader   *The James Dickey Reader*. Edited by Henry Hart. New York: Simon & Schuster, 1999.

Drowning	*Drowning with Others.* Middletown, Conn.: Wesleyan University Press, 1962.
Eagle	*The Eagle's Mile.* Hanover, N.H.: Wesleyan University Press / University Press of New England, 1990.
Early Motion	*The Early Motion: Drowning with Others and Helmets.* Middletown, Conn.: Wesleyan University Press, 1981.
Eclipse	"An Interview with James Dickey." *Eclipse* (San Fernando Valley State College, California State University at Northridge), no. 5 (1965–66): 5–20. Reprinted in Baughman, 12–27.
Enemy	*The Enemy from Eden.* Illustrated by Ron Sauter. Northridge, Calif.: Lord John Press, 1978.
"Eye of the Fire"	"The Eye of the Fire." *Oxford American* 39 (May/June 2001): 58–65
Eye-Beaters	*The Eye-Beaters, Blood, Victory, Madness, Buckhead and Mercy.* Garden City, N.Y.: Doubleday, 1970.
Falling	*Falling, May Day Sermon, and Other Poems.* Middleton, Conn.: Wesleyan University Press, 1981.
False	*False Youth: Four Seasons.* Dallas: Pressworks Publishing Inc., 1983.
Four Poems	*Four Poems.* Winston-Salem, N.C.: Privately printed by Palaemon Press, 1979.
Friedmann	Peggy Friedmann and Betty Bedell, "A Conversation with James Dickey." *Kalliope* 1 (February 1979): 30–35. Reprinted in Baughman, 169–72.
God's Images	*God's Images: The Bible, A New Vision,* with Marvin Hayes. Birmingham: Oxmoor House, 1977.
Greiner	Donald J. Greiner, "Making the Truth: James Dickey's Last Major Interview." *James Dickey Newsletter* 23 (Fall 2006): 1–26.
Hart	Henry Hart, *James Dickey: The World as a Lie.* New York: Picador USA, 2000.
Helmets	*Helmets.* Middletown, Conn.: Wesleyan University Press, 1964.
Head-Deep	*Head-Deep in Strange Sounds: Free-Flight Improvisations from the UnEnglish.* Winston-Salem, N.C.: Palaemon Press, 1979.
Heyen	William Heyen and Peter Marchant, "A Conversation with James Dickey." *Southern Review,* n.s. 9 (January 1973): 135–56.
History	*History of the 418th Night Fighter Squadron.* Edited by Stanley E. Logan, David O. Sullivan, and Millie Sullivan. Santa Fe: S. E. Logan Books, 2001.
Intervisions	*Intervisions: Poems and Photographs.* With Sharon Anglin Kuhne. Foreword by Betty Adcock. Penland, N.C.: Visualternatives, 1983.
Into the Stone	*Into the Stone and Other Poems* in *Poets of Today VII.* Edited by John Hall Wheelock. New York: Scribners, 1960.
Logue	John Logue, "James Dickey Describes His Life and Works as He 'Moves toward Hercules.'" *Southern Living* 6 (February 1971): 44–49, 60, 65. Reprinted in Baughman, 50–70.

Mademoiselle interview	"The Poet Tries to Make a Kind of Order: A 'Self-Interview' with James Dickey." *Mademoiselle* 71 (September 1970): 142–43, 209–10, 212.
Night	*Night Hurdling: Poems, Essays, Conversations, Commencements, and Afterwords.* Columbia & Bloomfield Hills: Bruccoli Clark, 1983.
NYQ interview	William Packard, "Craft Interview with James Dickey." *New York Quarterly* 10 (Spring 1972): 16–35.
One Voice 1	*The One Voice of James Dickey: His Letters and Life, 1942–1969.* Edited by Gordon Van Ness. Columbia: University of Missouri Press, 2003.
One Voice 2	*The One Voice of James Dickey: His Letters and Life, 1970–1997.* Edited by Gordon Van Ness. Columbia: University of Missouri Press, 2005.
Playboy interview	Geoffrey Norman, "Playboy Interview: James Dickey." *Playboy* 20 (November 1973): 81–82, 86, 89, 92, 94, 212–16. Reprinted in Baughman, 109–32.
Poems 57–67	*Poems 1957–1967.* Middletown, Conn.: Wesleyan University Press, 1967.
Poems	*Poems.* Melbourne, Australia: Sun Books, 1968.
Puella	*Puella.* Garden City, N.Y.: Doubleday, 1982.
Puella (Pyracantha)	*Puella.* Tempe, Ariz.: Pyracantha Press, 1985.
Roberts	Francis Roberts, "James Dickey: An Interview." *Per/Se* 3 (Spring 1968) 8–12. Reprinted in Baughman, 41–49.
Scion	*Scion,* with illustrations by Timothy Engelland. Deerfield, Mass.: Deerfield Press / Dublin: Gallery Press, 1980.
Selected	*James Dickey: The Selected Poems.* Edited by Robert Kirschten. Hanover, N.H. & London: University Press of New England, 1998.
Self	*Self-Interviews.* Recorded and edited by Barbara and James Reiss. Garden City, N.Y.: Doubleday, 1970. Reprinted, Baton Rouge: Louisiana State University, 1984.
Sorties	*Sorties: Journals and New Essays.* Garden City, N.Y.: Doubleday, 1971.
Stolen Apples	Yevgeny Yevtushenko, *Stolen Apples with English Adaptations by James Dickey, Geoffrey Dutton, Lawrence Ferlinghetti, Anthony Kahn, Stanley Kunitz, George Reavey, John Updike, Richard Wilbur.* Garden City, N.Y.: Doubleday, 1971.
Strength	*The Strength of Fields.* Garden City, N.Y.: Doubleday, 1979.
Striking	*Striking In: The Early Notebooks of James Dickey.* Edited with introductions by Gordon Van Ness. Columbia: University of Missouri Press, 1996.
Suarez	Ernest Suarez, "An Interview with James Dickey." *Contemporary Literature* 31 (Summer 1990): 117–32.
Summer	Christopher Dickey, *Summer of Deliverance.* New York: Simon & Schuster, 1998.
Teaching	*Teaching in America.* Proceedings of the 5th Annual Conference April 2–4, 1967. Washington D.C.: National Committee for Support of the Public Schools, 1967.

"Things Happen"	"Things Happen: An Interview with James Dickey." *Wisconsin Review* 2 (December 1966): 2, 4–6. Reprinted in Baughman, 28–36.
Two Poems	*Two Poems of the Air*. Portland, Ore.: Centicore Press, 1964.
Unmuzzled Ox interview	"Interview: James Dickey." *Unmuzzled Ox* 3, no. 2 (1975): 74–85. Reprinted in Baughman, 84–93.
Van Ness	Gordon Van Ness, "Living beyond Recall: An Interview with James Dickey." *James Dickey Newsletter* 3 (Spring 1987): 17–26. Reprinted in Baughman, 247–57.
Värmland	*Värmland: Poems Based on Other Poems*. Winston-Salem, N.C.: Palaemon Press, 1982.
Veteran	*Veteran Birth. The Gadfly Poems 1947–1949*. Illustrated by Robert Dance. Winston-Salem, N.C.: Palaemon Press, 1978.
Whole Motion	*The Whole Motion: Collected Poems 1945–1992*. Hanover, N.H. & London: Wesleyan University Press / University Press of New England, 1992.
Writer's Voice	*The Writer's Voice: Conversations with Contemporary Writers*. Conducted by John Graham. Edited by George Garrett. New York: William Morrow, 1973.

ANTHOLOGIES REPRINTING DICKEY POEMS

America in Literature: The South. Edited by Sara Marshall. New York: Scribners, 1979.

America in Poetry with Paintings, Drawings, Photographs, and Other Works of Art. Edited by Charles Sullivan. New York: Abradale Press, 1988.

American Literature: Tradition and Innovation. Vol. 2. Edited by Harrison T. Meserole. Lexington, Mass.: D.C. Heath, 1969.

American Poetry. Edited by Gay Wilson Allen, Walter B. Rideout, and James K. Robinson. New York: Harper & Row, 1965.

American Poetry 1965: Critical Quarterly Poetry Supplement 6 (1965).

American Religious Poems. Edited by Harold Bloom and Jesse Zuba. New York: Library of America, 2006.

American Sports Poems. Edited by R. R. Knudson and May Swenson. New York: Orchard Books, [1988].

The American Tradition in Literature. Edited by Sculley Bradley et al. 4th ed. Vol. 2. New York: Grosset & Dunlap, 1974.

America's 85 Greatest Living Authors Present This Is My Best in the Third Quarter of the Century. Edited by Whit Burnett. Garden City, N.Y.: Doubleday, 1970.

Anthology of American Literature II: Realism to the Present. Edited by George McMichael. New York: Macmillan, 1974.

The Appalachian Trail Reader. Edited by David Emblidge. New York: Oxford University Press, 1996.

Appreciating Poetry. Edited by Richard Sugg. Boston: Houghton Mifflin, 1975.

Articles of War: A Collection of American Poetry about World War II. Edited by Leon Stokesbury with an introduction by Paul Fussell. Fayetteville: University of Arkansas Press, 1990.

Beach Glass and Other Poems. Edited by Paul Molloy. New York: Four Winds Press, 1970.

Because I Fly: A Collection of Aviation Poetry. Edited by Helmut Reda. New York: McGraw-Hill, 2002.

Beginnings in Poetry: A Motley Book of Poems. Edited by William J. Martz. Chicago: Scott, Foresman, 1965.

Best Poems of 1960: The Borestone Mountain Poetry Awards 1961, a Compilation of Original Poetry Published in Magazines of the English-Speaking World in 1960. Vol. 13. Edited by Lionel Stevenson et al. Palo Alto, Calif.: Pacific Books, 1961.

Best Poems of 1961: The Borestone Mountain Poetry Awards 1962, a Compilation of Original Poetry Published in Magazines of the English-Speaking World in 1961. Vol. 14. Edited by Stevenson et al. Palo Alto, Calif.: Pacific Books, 1962.

Best Poems of 1962: The Borestone Mountain Poetry Awards 1963, a Compilation of Original Poetry Published in Magazines of the English-Speaking World in 1962. Vol. 15. Edited by Stevenson et al. Palo Alto, Calif.: Pacific Books, 1963.

Best Poems of 1963: The Borestone Mountain Poetry Awards 1964, a Compilation of Original Poetry Published in Magazines of the English-Speaking World in 1963. Vol. 16. Edited by Stevenson et al. Palo Alto, Calif.: Pacific Books, 1964.

Best Poems of 1964: The Borestone Mountain Poetry Awards 1965, a Compilation of Original Poetry Published in Magazines of the English-Speaking World in 1964. Vol. 17. Edited by Stevenson et al. Palo Alto, Calif.: Pacific Books, 1965.

Best Poems of 1965: The Borestone Mountain Poetry Awards 1966, a Compilation of Original Poetry Published in Magazines of the English-Speaking World in 1965. Vol. 18. Edited by Stevenson et al. Palo Alto, Calif.: Pacific Books, 1966.

Best Poems of 1966: The Borestone Mountain Poetry Awards 1967, a Compilation of Original Poetry Published in Magazines of the English-Speaking World in 1966. Vol. 19. Edited by Stevenson et al. Palo Alto, Calif.: Pacific Books, 1967.

Best Poems of 1970: The Borestone Mountain Poetry Awards 1971, a Compilation of Original Poetry Published in Magazines of the English-Speaking World in 1970. Vol. 23. Edited by Stevenson et al. Palo Alto, Calif.: Pacific Books, 1971.

The Body Electric: America's Best Poetry from the American Poetry Review. Edited by Stephen Berg, David Bonanno, and Arthur Vogelsang. New York & London: Norton, 2000.

Brother Songs: A Male Anthology of Poetry. Edited by Jim Perlman. Minneapolis: Holy Cow! Press [1979].

Campfire Legends. Edited by John Long. Merrillville, Ind.: ICS Books, 1993.

The College Anthology of British and American Poetry. 2nd ed. Edited by A. Kent Hieatt and William Park. Boston: Allyn & Bacon, 1972.

The Columbia Anthology of American Poetry. Edited by Jay Parini. New York: Columbia University Press, 1995.

Contemporary American Poetry. Edited by Donald Hall. Baltimore: Penguin Books [1963].

Contemporary American Poetry. Edited by A. Poulin, Jr. Boston: Houghton Mifflin, 1971.

The Contemporary American Poets: American Poetry since 1940. Edited by Mark Strand. New York: World, 1969.

Contemporary Poetry in America. Edited by Miller Williams. New York: Random House, 1973.

Contemporary Southern Poetry: An Anthology. Edited by Guy Owen and Mary C. Williams. Baton Rouge: Louisiana State University Press, 1979.

A Controversy of Poets: An Anthology of Contemporary American Poetry. Edited by Paris Leary and Robert Kelly. Garden City: Anchor Books, 1965.

Cosmos Club Poets through the Years: An Anthology. Washington, D.C.: Cosmos Club, 2000.

Decade: A Collection of Poems from the First Ten Years of the Wesleyan Poetry Program. Edited by Norman Holmes Pearson. Middletown, Conn.: Wesleyan University Press, 1969.

Deep Ecology. Edited by Michael Tobias. San Diego: Avant Books, 1985.

The Distinctive Voice: Twentieth-Century American Poetry. Edited by William J. Martz. Glenview, Ill.: Scott, Foresman, 1966.

Divided Light: Father and Son Poems, A Twentieth Century American Anthology. Edited by Jason Shinder. New York: Sheep Meadow Press, 1983.

Dog Music: Poetry about Dogs. Edited by Joseph Duemer and Jim Simmerman. New York: St. Martin's Press, 1996.

Doors into Poetry. 2nd ed. Edited by Chad Walsh. Englewood Cliffs, N.J.: Prentice-Hall, 1970.

Earth, Air, Fire, and Water: A Collection of over 125 Poems. Edited by Francis Monson McCullough. New York: Coward, McCann & Geoghegan, 1971.

Encounters: An Anthology from the First Ten Years of Encounter *Magazine.* Edited by Stephen Spender, Irving Kristol, and Melvin J. Lasky. New York: Basic Books, 1963.

The Enduring Voice: Concerns in Literature, Present and Past. Edited by Margaret Ganz and Julia Ebel. New York: Macmillan, 1972.

The Experience of Literature: A Reader with Commentaries. Edited by Lionel Trilling. Garden City, N.Y.: Doubleday, 1967.

Exploring Poetry. Edited by M.L. Rosenthal and A. J. M. Smith. 2nd ed. New York: Macmillan, 1973.

The Faber Book of Modern Verse. 3rd ed., rev. Edited by Michael Roberts. London: Faber & Faber, 1965.

50 Modern American and British Poets, 1920–1970. Edited by Louis Untermeyer. New York: David McKay, 1973.

Fine Frenzy: Enduring Themes in Poetry. Edited by Robert Baylor and Brenda Stokes. New York: McGraw-Hill, 1972.

Forgotten Language: Contemporary Poets and Nature. Edited by Christopher Merrill. Salt Lake City: Peregrine Smith Books, 1991.

From Three Sides: Reading for Writers. Edited by Joseph Maiolo and Jill Brantley. Englewood Cliffs, N.J.: Prentice-Hall, 1976.

Galaxy: Literary Modes and Genres. Edited by Mark Schorer. New York: Harcourt, Brace & World, 1967.

Gathered Waters: An Anthology of River Poems. Edited by Cort Conley. Cambridge, Idaho: Backeddy Books, 1985.

A Geography of Poets: An Anthology of the New Poetry. Edited by Edward Field. New York: Bantam, 1979.

Georgia Voices. Vol.3: Poetry. Edited by Hugh Ruppersburg. Athens & London: University of Georgia Press, 2000.

Getting into Poetry. Edited by Morris Sweetkind. Boston: Holbrook Press, 1972.

The Giant Book of Poetry. Edited by William H. Roetzheim. San Diego: Level Four Press, 2000.

The Great Ideas Today: 1968. Edited by Robert M. Hutchins and Mortimer J. Adler. Chicago: Encyclopedia Britannica, 1968.

Grooving the Symbol. Edited by Richard W. Lid. New York: Free Press, 1970.

The Harvard Book of Contemporary American Poetry. Edited by Helen Vendler. Cambridge, Mass.: Belknap Press, 1985.

Heath Introduction to Poetry. Edited by Joseph de Roche. Lexington, Mass.: D.C. Heath, 1975.

Hero's Way: Contemporary Poems in the Mythic Tradition. Edited by John Alexander Allen. Englewood Cliffs, N.J.: Prentice-Hall, 1971.

How Does a Poem Mean? Edited by John Ciardi. Boston: Houghton Mifflin, 1975.

Inside Outer Space: New Poems of the Space Age. Edited by Robert Vas Dias. Garden City, N.Y.: Doubleday, 1970.

An Introduction to Poetry. 2nd ed. Edited by Louis Simpson. New York: St. Martin's Press, 1972.

An Introduction to Poetry. 2nd ed. Edited by X. J. Kennedy. Boston: Little, Brown, 1971.

Invitation to Poetry. Edited by Janet M. Cotter. Cambridge, Mass.: Winthrop, 1974.

Kaleidoscope. Edited by M. Jerry Weiss. Perspectives on Man series. Menlo Park, Calif.: Cummings, 1970.

Lirică Americană Contemporană. Edited and translated by Virgil Teodorescu and Petronela Negoșanu. Bucharest: Albatros, 1980.

Literary Nashville. Edited by Patrick Allen. Athens, Ga.: Hill Street Press, 1999.

Literature: A Collection of Mythology and Folklore, Short Stories, Poetry and Drama. Edited by James Burl Hogins. 3rd ed. Chicago: Science Research Associates. 1984.

Literature in America: The Modern Age. Edited by Charles Caplan. New York: Free Press, 1971.

The Literature of America: Twentieth Century. Edited by Mark Schorer. New York: McGraw-Hill, 1970.

The Logic of Poetry. Edited by Richard Monaco and John Briggs. New York: McGraw-Hill, 1974.

Lombardi. Edited by John Wiebusch. Chicago: Follett, 1971.

Longman Anthology of Contemporary American Poetry. 2nd ed. Edited by Stuart Friebert and David Young. New York: Longman, 1989.

The Made Thing: An Anthology of Contemporary Southern Poetry. Edited by Leon Stokesbury. Fayetteville: University of Arkansas Press, 1987.

Making It New. Edited by JoAn E. Chace and William M. Chace. San Francisco: Canfield Press, 1973.

Man to Himself. Edited by M. Jerry Weiss. Menlo Park, Calif.: Cummings, 1970.

The Many Worlds of Poetry. Edited by Jacob Drachler and Virginia R. Terris. New York: Knopf, 1969.

Men-Talk: An Anthology of Male Experience Poetry. Edited by Elliot Fried and Barry Singer. Eugene, Ore.: Pacific House, 1985.

Mindscapes: Poems for the Real World. Edited by Richard Peck. New York: Delacorte Press, 1971.

The Modern Age: Literature. 2nd ed. Edited by Leonard Lief and James F. Light. New York: Holt, Rinehart & Winston, 1972.

Modern American Poetry. Edited by Louis Untermeyer. New and enlarged ed. New York: Harcourt, Brace & World, 1962.

Modern Poems: An Introduction to Poetry. Edited by Richard Ellmann and Robert O'Clair. New York: Norton, 1976.

More than a Game. Edited by John Wiebusch. Englewood Cliffs, N.J.: Prentice-Hall, 1974.

Motion: American Sports Poems. Edited by Noah Blaustein with a foreword by John Edgar Wideman. Iowa City: University of Iowa Press, 2001.

New Coasts and Strange Harbors: Discovering Poems. Edited by Helen Hill and Agnes Perkins. New York: Crowell, 1974.

The New Consciousness: An Anthology of the New Literature. Edited by Albert J. LaValley. Cambridge, Mass.: Winthrop, 1972.

The New Modern Poetry: British and American Poetry since World War II. Edited by M. L. Rosenthal. New York: Macmillan, 1967.

New Oxford Book of Modern Verse. Edited by Richard Ellmann. New York: Oxford University Press, 1976.

New Poets of England and America: Second Selection. Edited by Donald Hall and Robert Pack. New York: World, 1962.

New Southern Poets: Selected Poems from Southern Poetry Review. Edited by Guy Owen and Mary C. Williams. Chapel Hill: University of North Carolina Press, 1975.

New York: Poems. Edited by Howard Moss. New York: Avon, 1980.

The New York Times Book of Verse. Edited by Thomas Lask. New York: Macmillan, 1970.

The New Yorker Book of Poems. New York: Viking Press, 1969.

Norton Anthology of Modern Poetry. Edited by Richard Ellman and Robert O'Clair. New York: Norton, 1973.

The Norton Anthology of Poetry. Edited by Arthur Eastman, Alexander W. Allison, et al. New York: Norton, 1970.

Now Voices: The Poetry of the Present. Edited by Angelo Carli and Theodore Kilman. New York: Scribners, 1971.

Old Glory: American War Poems from the Revolutionary War to the War on Terrorism. Edited by Robert Hedin. New York: Persea Books, 2004.

On Doctoring: Stories, Poems, Essays. Edited by Richard Reynolds and John Stone. New York: Simon & Schuster, 1991.

One Hundred American Poems: Masterpieces of Lyric, Epic, and Ballad from Pre-Colonial Times to the Present. 2nd ed. Edited by Selden Rodman. New York: New American Library, 1972.

One Hundred American Poems of the Twentieth Century. Edited by Laurence Perrine and James M. Reid. New York: Harcourt, Brace & World, 1966.

100 Postwar Poems British and American. Edited by M. L. Rosenthal. New York: Macmillan, 1968.

Oxford Book of War Poetry. Edited by Jon Stallworthy. Oxford: Oxford University Press, 1984.

Pictures That Storm inside My Head: Poems for the Inner You. Edited by Richard Peck. New York: Avon, 1976.

The Pocket Book of Modern Verse: English and American Poetry of the Last Hundred Years from Walt Whitman to the Contemporaries. Edited by Oscar Williams. Revised by Hyman J. Soboiloff. New York: Washington Square Press, 1972.

The Poem: An Anthology. Edited by Stanley B. Greenfield and A. Kingsley Weatherhead. 2nd ed. New York: Appleton-Century-Crofts, 1972.

Poems from The Virginia Quarterly Review, *1925–1967.* Charlottesville: University Press of Virginia, 1969.

Poems of Our Moment. Edited by John Hollander. New York: Pegasus, 1968.

Poems on Poetry: The Mirror's Garland. Edited by Robert Wallace and James G. Taaffe. New York: Dutton, 1965.

Poetry: A Closer Look. Edited by James M. Reid, John Ciardi, and Laurence Perrine. New York: Harcourt, Brace & World, 1963.

Poetry: An Introductory Anthology. Edited by Hazard Adams. Boston: Little, Brown, 1968.

The Poetry *Anthology: 1912–1977: Sixty-Five Years of America's Most Distinguished Verse Magazine.* Edited by Daryl Hine and Joseph Parisi. Boston: Houghton Mifflin, 1978.

Poetry and Its Conventions: An Anthology of Contemporary American Poetry. Edited by Frederick R. Lapides and John T. Shawcross. New York: Free Press, 1972.

Poetry Past and Present. Edited by Frank Brady and Martin Price. New York: Harcourt Brace Jovanovich, 1974.

Poetry: Points of Departure. Edited by Henry Taylor. Cambridge, Mass.: Winthrop, 1974.

Poetry: Premeditated Art. Edited by Judson Jerome. Boston: Houghton Mifflin, 1968.

Poetry Southeast, 1950–1970. Edited by Frank Steele. Martin: Tennessee Poetry Journal, 1968.

Poetry: *The Golden Anniversary Issue.* Chicago: University of Chicago Press, 1967.

The Poetry of the Negro, 1746–1970. Rev. and updated ed. Edited by Langston Hughes and Arna Bontemps. Garden City, N.Y.: Doubleday, 1970.

Possibilities of Poetry: An Anthology of American Contemporaries. Edited by Richard Kostelanetz. New York: Dell, 1970.

Preferences. Introduction by Richard Howard and photographs by Thomas Victor. New York: Viking, 1974.

Reading Modern Poetry. Rev. ed. Edited by Paul Engle and Warren Carrier. Glenview, Ill.: Scott, Foresman, 1968.

Reading Poetry. 2nd ed. Edited by Fred B. Millet, Arthur W. Hoffman, and David R. Clark. New York: Harper & Row, 1968.

Reading, Writing, and Rhetoric. Edited by James Burl Hogins. 2nd ed. Chicago: Science Research Associates, 1977.

Shake the Kaleidoscope: A New Anthology of Modern Poetry. Edited by Milton Klonsky. New York: Pocket Books, 1973.

Singular Voices: American Poetry Today. Edited by Stephen Berg. New York: Avon Books, 1985.

Some Haystacks Don't Even Have Any Needle and Other Complete Modern Poems. Edited by Stephen Dunning, Edward Lueders, and Hugh Smith. New York: Lothrop, Lee & Shepard, 1969.

Sound and Sense: An Introduction to Poetry. Edited by Laurence Perrine. 3rd ed. New York: Harcourt, Brace & World, 1969; 4th ed., 1973.

Sounds and Silences: Poetry for Now. Edited by Richard Peck. New York: Delacorte, 1970; rev. ed., New York: Dell, 1990.

A Southern Album: Recollections of Some People and Places and Times Gone By. Edited by Irwin Glusker with a narrative by Willie Morris. Birmingham, Ala.: Oxmoor House, 1975.

Southern Christmas: Literary Classics of the Holidays. Edited by Judy Long and Thomas Payton. Athens, Ga.: Hill Street Press, 1998.

Southern Writing in the Sixties: Poetry. Edited by John William Corrington and Miller Williams. Baton Rouge: Louisiana State University Press, 1967.

Splash! Great Writing about Swimming. Edited by Laurel Blossom with a preface by George Plimpton. Hopewell, N.J.: Ecco Press, 1996.

Sports Poems. Edited by R. R. Knudson and P. K. Ebert. New York: Dell, 1971.

Strongly Spent: 50 Years of Poetry. Shenandoah 53 (Spring–Summer 2003).

Themes in American Literature. Edited by Charles Genthe and George Keithley. Lexington, Mass.: D.C. Heath, 1972.

Things Appalachian. Edited by William Plumley, Marjorie Warner, and Lorena Anderson. Charleston, W. Va.: MHC Publications, 1976.

Today's Poets: American and British Poetry since the 1930's. Edited by Chad Walsh. New York: Scribners, 1965.

To See the World Afresh. Edited by Lilian Moore and Judith Thurman. New York: Atheneum, 1974.

The Total Experience of Poetry: An Introductory Anthology. Edited by Ruth Thompson and Marvin Thompson. New York: Random House, 1970.

The Treasury of American Poetry. Edited by Nancy Sullivan. Garden City, N.Y.: Doubleday, 1978.

A Tricentennial Anthology of South Carolina Literature, 1670–1970. Edited by Richard James Calhoun and John Caldwell Guilds. Columbia: University of South Carolina Press, 1971.

Twentieth Century Poetry. Edited by Carol Marshall. New York: Houghton Mifflin, 1971.

Twentieth Century Poetry: American and British (1900–1970): An American-British Anthology. Edited by John Malcolm Brinnin and Bill Read. New York: McGraw-Hill, 1970.

Twentieth Century Treasury of Sports. Edited by Al Silverman and Brian Silverman. New York: Viking, 1992.

The Vintage Book of Contemporary American Poetry. Edited by J.D. McClatchy. 2nd ed. New York: Vintage, 2003.

Visions of America by the Poets of Our Time. Edited by David Kherdian. Illustrated by Nonny Hogrogian. New York: Macmillan, 1973.

The Voice That Is Great within Us: American Poetry of the Twentieth Century. Edited by Hayden Carruth. Toronto & New York: Bantam Books, 1970.

The Ways of the Poem. Revised ed. Edited by Josephine Miles. Englewood Cliffs, N.J.: Prentice-Hall, 1972.

The Wesleyan Tradition: Four Decades of American Poetry. Hanover, N.H.: University Press of New England, 1993.

What's in a Poem? Edited by John Rylander and Edith Rylander. Encino & Belmont, Calif.: Dickenson, 1972.

Where Is Vietnam? American Poets Respond: An Anthology of Contemporary Poems. Edited by Walter Lowenfels. Garden City, N.Y.: Doubleday: 1967.

Workshop: A Spontaneous Approach to Literature. Edited by Robert Crotty, Robert L. McRoberts, and Geoffrey Clark. Menlo Park, Calif.: Cummings, 1971.

The World on Wheels: Reading/Thinking/Writing about the Automobile in America. Edited by R. S. Baker and P. L. Van Osdol. Boston: Allyn & Bacon, 1972.

Arrangement of the Apparatus

This apparatus lists the pertinent publication information on each poem, beginning with its first appearance in print and the principal Dickey collections in which it was published. The entry for each poem also lists its reprintings in various anthologies.

Under "Notes" I have added biographical and historical information to elucidate the poems. Some of this information may be common knowledge now (Arthur Godfrey, Esso) but may not be later.

The last part of the entry on each poem lists variants among the printed texts and typescripts. Preferred readings are given first, followed by the authority or authorities in parentheses, and separated from lesser readings by a vertical bar (|). Editorial notes and comments are made in square brackets. Words separated by a solidus (/) indicate the division of one line into two. When a blank line has been inserted or deleted against the majority of the readings, only the exception is noted.

As Dickey himself asserted, "I really don't believe in Eliot's theory of autotelic art, in which the poem has nothing to do with the man who wrote it. . . . I think they're absolutely incapable of being dissociated from each other" (*Self-Interviews,* 24; see *Night Hurdling,* 311). By identifying points of history, geography, or biography, I intend no statement regarding the quality of the poem or whether the "events" of the poem did or did not happen in fact. Dickey himself was clear on this point: "Every poem—particularly those which make use of a figure designated in the poem as 'I'—is both an exploration and an invention of identity. . . . The poet . . . sits outside the poem, not so much putting his I-figure through an action, but attempting to find out what the I-figure will do, under the circumstances as they develop. . . . During the writing of the poem, the poet comes to feel that he is releasing into its proper field of response a portion of himself that he has never really understood" ("The Self as Agent," *Sorties,* 155; see also Christensen, 3). And again: "In my own work, you know, there seems to be almost no poem that I've written that is literally a factual representation of what actually occurred at a certain time and space, time-space continuum" (Heyen, 140).

Dickey was well aware of the limitations of an excessively informative introduction to a poem: "I once heard Howard Nemerov read. He said, 'The writing of the following poem came about when I was writing the following poem'" ("Comments," 11). As much as he admired Robert Penn Warren, Dickey produced *Self-Interviews* and talked about his own poems at length in many other venues because he intrinsically believed that Warren's (and the other New Critics') maintenance of the notion that the extent of the author's statement of his own intention in a given work is less rewarding than close literary analysis. Dickey did not wholly reject the intentional fallacy, nor did he reject deep analysis of his own poems by others, but he nonetheless thought that the poet's views on his own work should be, if not the last, then at least the first word in any discussion of the poems. "I'm not trying to impose an official interpretation on the poems; that would be the last thing I would want to do. As one reader of my verse and as the person who happened to create the poems, I offer the following remarks for whatever interest they have to people who want to look at the poems from my standpoint as well as their own" (*Self-Interviews*, 83).

The Poems
—*1947–1960*—

Christmas Shopping, 1947

First Publication: As Jim Dickey, *Gadfly* (Vanderbilt University) 3 (Winter 1947): 59.
Collected: *Veteran* [9].
Reprinted: *Southern Christmas*, 64.
Variants:
3–4: [blank line inserted] (*Veteran*)
8: witness (*Gadfly*) | sitness (*Veteran*, TS [typo])
14: [one line] (*Gadfly*) | [line divided] (*Veteran*, TS)
16: autumn (*Gadfly*) | autum (*Veteran* [typo])

Sea Island

First Publication: *Gadfly* (Vanderbilt University) 3 (Spring 1948): 104.
Collected: *Veteran* [10].
Variants:
5: Once (*Gadfly*) | One (*Veteran*, TS)

King Crab and Rattler

First Publication: *Gadfly* (Vanderbilt University) 3 (Spring 1948): 104–5.
Collected: *Veteran* [11].
Notes:
15: The term "therianthropic" means combining human and animal form (see, for example, "The Sheep Child").
Variants:
10–11: [blank line inserted] (*Veteran*)

Reflections in a Bloodstone Ring

First Publication: As Jim Dickey, *Coraddi: Annual Arts Forum Issue* (Woman's College of North Carolina, Greensboro) 52, no. 3 (1948): 23.

Amputee Ward: Okinawa, 1945

First Publication: As Jim Dickey, *Coraddi. Annual Arts Forum Issue.* (Woman's College of North Carolina Greensboro) 52, no. 3 (1948): 23.

NOTES: In July 1945 Dickey was stationed on Okinawa in the Ryukyu Islands, where horrendous fighting had taken place from April to late June (see "Victory"). He was horrified at the carnage (Van Ness, 21–22; Baughman, 252). From Okinawa he flew as navigator in the P-61 night bombing and strafing missions over Japan before and after the bombing of Hiroshima (August 6) and Nagasaki (August 9) until the Japanese surrender on September 2. For other poems set on Okinawa, see "The Coral Flight," "The Driver," "The Contest," and "The Work of Art." ("Amputee Ward" appears as a subheading in "The Contest" and "The Work of Art.")
VARIANTS:
5: furrowed [corrected] | farrowed (*Coraddi* [typo])
10: See Hart Crane, "The Broken Tower," line 31: "The angelus of wars"

Whittern and the Kite

FIRST PUBLICATION: *Gadfly* (Vanderbilt University) 4 (Summer 1949): 26.
COLLECTED: *Veteran* [13].
NOTES: Capt. Harold B. Whittern (1921–2000), of Delaware, Indiana, was a much-decorated pilot and operations officer in Dickey's squadron in Mindoro. By 1945 he had flown kites in Finschhafen, but became gaunt from malaria (Hart, 87) and returned to the States on July 7, 1945. Dickey wrote in the squadron history, "He was acclaimed the hottest and most fearless pilot in the outfit, as well as one of the squarest shooters in his dealing with members of the Squadron" (*History,* 96).
1: "Bird-of-Freedom" was the name for a large transport plane that evacuated soldiers from combat theaters—in contrast to Whittern's little kite.
2: The Japanese flag, known as *hinomaru* ("sun disc"), is a large blood-red circle on a field of white.
10: A "chutestack" is parachutists joined together vertically in descent.
15: The military theorist Carl von Clausewitz (1780–1831) was the author of *Vom Kriege* (On War, 1832), which grew from his observations on the French Revolution and the Napoleonic Wars.
VARIANTS:
3–4: [no blank line] (*Gadfly*) | [blank line inserted] (*Veteran*)

The Shark at the Window

FIRST PUBLICATION: *Sewanee Review* 59 (Spring 1951): 290–91.
REPRINTED: Broadside (Winston-Salem, N.C.: Palaemon Press, 1977).
NOTES: According to Dickey, "the poem was about my brother's wedding. . . . Maxine (who was working for American Airlines) and I went up for the wedding in Anderson, Indiana, and drove back. We got caught in a great fog and crept along for hours. . . . This was mixed up in my mind—and in the poem—with a trip that my brother and I had made to Florida where we stopped by Marineland and stood and stared in fascination at a huge shark through one of those portholes where you're level with the fish" (*Self,* 40); "I was fascinated by those huge creatures drifting by with that kind of blank look in their eyes. It's so blank that you're quite convinced they know a lot

more than you could ever know. And they know it in ways more useful than the things that you know are useful to you." (*Playboy* interview, 89; Baughman, 113). "I'd written it in college when I was in graduate school" [*sic*] (Logue, 60; Baughman, 63). Thomas Swift Dickey (1925–1987) married Patsy Hamilton (b. 1926), of Anderson, Indiana, on December 18, 1949. According to Monroe K. Spears, the poem was accepted by the *Sewanee Review* "in 1947 or 1948" but not published until 1951 ("James Dickey's Poetry," *Southern Review* 30 [Autumn 1994]: 752–53). For Dickey and sharks, see "The Shark's Parlor."

12–13: Caddis fly, also known as sedge fly or rail fly, is normally found in freshwater streams and are a favorite model for fly fishermen.

17: *Ephemera* is a genus of mayfly; see "May Day Sermon," lines 89–90.

26: Tartar horse: a small wild horse, also called "tarpan," now extinct.

42: Dickey used the large sea snail's shell late in life for the poem "Conch."

Of Holy War

FIRST PUBLICATION: As James L. Dickey, *Poetry* 79 (October 1951): 24.
REPRINTED: *Poetry* 121 (October 1972): 7.
NOTES: The reference is John Bunyan's *The Holy War* (1682).

4: Acre is the city on Haifa Bay in northern Israel that was the key passage to the Levant. Crusaders captured Acre from the Arabs in 1104 and made it the chief harbor for Palestine. Saladin recaptured it in 1187 but surrendered it to Richard the Lionheart in 1191. It was the last bastion of the Crusaders, falling a century later to the Muslim slave-warriors the Mamluks.

5: Caen, the richest medieval town in Normandy, was sacked and burned in 1346 by William the Conqueror and bombed heavily in 1944.

11: "embered," meaning strewn with embers.

The Child in Armor

FIRST PUBLICATION: As James L. Dickey, *Poetry* 82 (June 1953): 137.
COLLECTED: *Striking*, 259–60.
NOTES: The poet's son Christopher Swift Dickey (b. 1951) was two years old when this poem was published. He figures in "Utterance I," "The String," "Antipolis," "Hunting Civil War Relics on Nimblewill Creek," "To His Children in Darkness," "The Ice Skin," "The Aura," "Messages," "To the Butterflies," and possibly "The Drift-Spell."

The Anniversary

FIRST PUBLICATION: As James L. Dickey, *Poetry* 82 (June 1953): 138–39.
COLLECTED: *Striking*, 248–49.
NOTES: Intended for *Into the Stone* but cut by Wheelock; included in TS of *Into the Stone*. Dickey wrote Andrew Lytle on May 7, 1954, that he intended the poem to be "a kind of lament, and tried to give it the curious drive and exultation that comes to me when I associate longing and music (the guitar)." See further *Crux*, 67. At this early stage of Dickey's career, he was greatly influ-

enced by T. S. Eliot, who was instrumental in restoring the reputation of John Donne. The title of Dickey's poem recalls Donne's "The Anniversarie." The meter recalls John Skelton (1460–1529). Dickey described the poem as "grafting Lorca onto Skelton. . . . Strong rhythmic drive, rimes (Skelton), joie de vivre, strong visual and sensuous images (Lorca)" (*Striking*, 201).

30: Donne's alchemy motif is present (see "Love Alchemy" [1633] and "A Valediction Forbidden Mourning").

Utterance I

FIRST PUBLICATION: As James L. Dickey, *Soundings: Writings from the Rice Institute* (Houston, Tex.: Anson Jones Press, 1953): 114–15.

NOTES:. Dickey was stationed at the James Connally Air Force Base in Waco, Texas, when Maxine Dickey gave birth to Christopher Dickey in Nashville on August 31, 1951. "'Utterance I': I wanted to write a poem with some *believing* in it" (*Striking*, 107). On "Utterance" poems see "The Sprinter's Mother."

1–3: For an early version of these lines, see *Striking*, 186.

The Ground of Killing

FIRST PUBLICATION: *Sewanee Review* 62 (Autumn 1954): 623–64.

COLLECTED: *Striking*, 272–73.

NOTES: Intended for *Into the Stone,* but cut by Wheelock.

10–11: For the white bird, see "Reincarnation (II)."

VARIANTS:

13: waters think (*Sewanee Review*) | water thinks (*Striking*)

The Sprinter's Mother

FIRST PUBLICATION: *Shenandoah* 6 (Spring 1955): 17–18.

COLLECTED: *Striking*, 260–62.

NOTES: At this point in his career, Dickey was writing sequences of three or more poems (such as "Utterances"; see *Striking*, 185–86, 211): "It rounds out a kind of design I began with the [Angel of the] Maze: to write about the effects of death on people in different familial relationships: in the Maze an old man and his wife, in Father and Sons, that, and in this one a boy and his mother: a hard subject." See further *Crux*, 80. Nevertheless Dickey added two more "Sprinter" poems to form a three-poem sequence of the sprinter young ("The Sprinter's Mother"), in middle age ("The Sprinter at Forty"), and dead ("The Sprinter's Sleep"). Dickey's frustrating rivalry with his popular and athletic brother lies behind these poems. Dickey's mother, Maibelle Swift Dickey (see "Angina" and "Buckdancer's Choice"), was born in 1888 and did not die until June 10, 1977. "The Shenandoah people . . . more or less commissioned the poem" (*Crux*, 81). ("Father and Sons" was never published. Copies of the poem are in the libraries of Emory and Vanderbilt.) *Shenandoah*, the Washington and Lee University review, was edited in 1955 by Edward M. Hood. Runners figure importantly also in "For the Running of the New York City Marathon" and "The Olympian."

VARIANTS:

16: cocked murmuring (*Shenandoah*) | quick-limed cinders (*Striking*)

54: if taken back to (*Shenandoah*) | though retaken by (*Striking*)

58: cloud: (*Shenandoah*) | cloud; (*Striking*)

The Angel of the Maze

FIRST PUBLICATION: *Poetry* 86 (June 1955): 147–53.

COLLECTED: *Whole Motion*, 31–35.

NOTES: Discussed in *Crux*, 67. See "The Sprinter's Mother" (above) and *Striking*, 211–13 and 216–17, where Dickey's notes make it clear that the old man in the big house is intended to be his uncle and namesake, James Lafayette Dickey, Jr. (1875–1968), and the angel is the spirit of his recently deceased wife, the Catholic Katherine Cox McWhorter (1878–1953), whom he had married in 1895. "Uncle Jim" and his brothers had been left considerable property by their father, James L. Dickey, Sr. (1847–1910), who had made a fortune developing real estate in Fannin County, Georgia. In 1903 James Sr. bought a four-hundred-acre farm as a summer home in what is now the Tuxedo Park section of Atlanta. In 1904 he sold a significant parcel of land to the banker Robert Flournoy Maddox (1870–1965), who was elected mayor of Atlanta in 1909. Maddox built a mansion he called Woodhaven there and in 1963 sold it to the state of Georgia, which demolished the home and built the present governor's mansion on the site. (This account differs from Dickey's memory as recounted in Hart, 12). At James Sr.'s death, his property was subdivided and much was bought the next year by the Tuxedo Park Company. "Uncle Jim" sold fire insurance as president of the Dickey-Mangham Agency and lived in a mansion he called Arden, built in 1917 (line 27), on twenty-five acres at 456 West Paces Ferry Road in Atlanta, the site of this poem. He and his wife donated the land for St. Joseph's Hospital in Atlanta (see "Mercy").

81: Robert Falcon Scott (1868–1912), an officer of the British Royal Navy, acquired the status of a national hero by leading two expeditions to Antarctica, the successful "Discovery" in 1901–4 and the disastrous "Terra Nova" of 1910–13, in which he reached the South Pole (later than a team of Norwegians) but died of exhaustion and cold with his party on the journey back from the pole. See "Pursuit from Under."

162: Ervin John Dickey (1881–1970) was "Uncle Jim's" brother, who also sold fire insurance.

VARIANTS:

50: day (*Poetry*) | day, (*Whole Motion*)

The Confrontation of the Hero

FIRST PUBLICATION: As James L. Dickey, "The Confrontation of the Hero (April 1945)," *Sewanee Review* 63 (Summer 1955): 461–64.

COLLECTED: *Whole Motion*, 10–13.

NOTES: Intended for *Into the Stone*, but cut by Wheelock. In an undated letter to Andrew Lytle, Dickey described the poem as "a kind of personal farewell to the war, and to the use of myth. . . . using the myth of Perseus and the Medusa as a glass through which to see the war" (*Crux*, 82; see further, 82–84).

11: "'line astern' is the standard ground-strafing formation" (*Crux*, 83).

20: "the 'Ram' is Aries, whose 'house' the sun enters on March 21, in astrology" (*Crux*, 83).

76: "the Japanese fortified their ancestral tombs and machine-gunned from them" (*Crux*, 83).

89–91: "The snow of thistle blown by the enemy, which is as close as I could get to the 'all nature mourns' theme of the conventional elegy, and still keep an edge of irony, is also the Medusa's looking into the mirror of the shield" (*Crux*, 82).

Variants:

107: untroubled (*Sewanee Review,* TS) | peaceful (*Whole Motion*)

The Vigils

First Publication: *Beloit Poetry Journal* 6 (Fall 1955): 21–23.

The Flight

First Publication: *Beloit Poetry Journal* 6 (Summer 1956): 16–19.

Collected: *Striking,* 270–72.

Notes: See "Haunting the Maneuvers."

Variants:

12: begins (*Beloit*) | starts (*Striking*)

17: point (*Beloit*) | drop (*Striking*)

17: branching (*Beloit*) | spread (*Striking*)

18: falls down invisibly (*Beloit*) | downfalls (*Striking*)

20: slept (*Beloit*) | kept (*Striking*)

21: Divided undiscoverably, (*Beloit*) | The wings slant (*Striking*)

22: his (*Beloit*) | those (*Striking*)

25: Like the world-driven (*Beloit*) | As in the held (*Striking*)

37: massed, airy (*Beloit*) | air-mass (*Striking*)

56: Beaten with (*Beloit*) | Risen in (*Striking*)

64: animals (*Beloit*) | beasts (*Striking*)

64: flood (*Beloit*) | the open (*Striking*)

65: In the open depth of shadow (*Beloit*) | Shadow of death (*Striking*)

89: mediocrity (*Beloit*) | lines (*Striking*)

94: with the (*Beloit*) | the last (*Striking*)

94: round (*Beloit*) | around (*Striking*)

The Father's Body

First Publication: *Poetry* 89 (December 1956): 145–49.

Collected: *Striking,* 240–43.

Notes: Begun in France in 1955 (*Striking,* 234). "As a result of writing this poem and reading it at the insistence of a group of ladies at the University of Florida ['the Pen Women's Society or something to that effect'], I got into a certain amount of trouble which I resolved by simply walking out. . . . I left the University and went to New York to become a businessman of whatever kind it's possible to become at the age of thirty-three"(*Self*, 43; *One Voice 1*, 261). See also *Summer*, 79–80, *One Voice 1*, 146–47; Hart, 197–201. Though a typescript of this poem is included with the carbons of poems in *Into the Stone*, Wheelock cut it, and Dickey did not allow this poem to be reprinted until forty years after its original publication.

VARIANTS:

9: to back with (*Poetry*, TS) | with him from (*Striking*)

10: hovers out (*Poetry*, TS) | hovers-out (*Striking*)

32: As (*Poetry*, TS) | Like (*Striking*)

32: stiff, (*Poetry*, TS) | stiff (*Striking*)

43: keeps running (*Poetry*, TS) | running (*Striking*)

84: backward (*Poetry*, TS) | silver-backed (*Striking*)

84: silver (*Poetry*, TS) | blue (*Striking*)

85: blooms out (*Poetry*, TS) | blooms, (*Striking*)

97: eyes are (*Poetry*, TS) | eyes, (*Striking*)

The Swimmer

FIRST PUBLICATION: *Partisan Review* 24 (Spring 1957): 244–46.

COLLECTED: *Striking*, 243–45.

NOTES: Begun in France in late 1954 or early 1955 (*Striking*, 229). Intended for *Into the Stone*, but cut by Wheelock; very different poem in TS of *Into the Stone*.

VARIANTS:

5: graze formally among (*Partisan Review*) | form singly from (*Striking*)

51: new, (*Partisan Review*) | new (*Striking*)

51: up, (*Partisan Review*) | up (*Striking*

56: his (*Partisan Review*) | my (*Striking*)

62: Meshes emptily there, (*Partisan Review*) | Meshes there (*Striking*)

62: flowers. (*Partisan Review*) | flowers: (*Striking*)

66: And as the (*Partisan Review*) | The (*Striking*)

68: out, the (*Partisan Review*) | out. The (*Striking*)

79: face (*Partisan Review*) | man-face (*Striking*)

The First Morning of Cancer

FIRST PUBLICATION: *Poetry* 90 (May 1957): 97–102.

COLLECTED: *Striking*, 280–84.

NOTES: Begun in Atlanta in 1956 just after Dickey started his advertising career. Intended for *Into the Stone*, but cut by Wheelock. Dickey called it "an ambitious and kind of pretentious poem that I wrote when I really didn't know what I was doing. I'm glad I wrote it" (Arnett, 290; Baughman, 74). Discussed in *Self*, 46–47. For other poems involving cancer, see "The Hospital Window," "The Cancer Match," "For the Death of Lombardi," and "Last Hours."

124–27: compare "Lazarus to the Assembled," 43–45.

130–35: compare "Lazarus to the Assembled," 22–25.

Variants:

5: tongue drawn down (*Poetry,* TS) | tongue (*Striking*)

40: And now (*Poetry,* TS) | Now (*Striking*)

40: looked, and the (*Poetry,* TS) | looked. The (*Striking*)

48: window (*Poetry,* TS) | clearing window (*Striking*)

52: blue hulk (*Poetry,* TS) | singling blue (*Striking*)

53: Gazing (*Poetry,* TS) | To be gazing (*Striking*)

69: great hedge (*Poetry,* TS) | hedge (*Striking*)

76: back (*Poetry,* TS) | neck (*Striking*)

86: struck like flint (*Poetry,* TS) | struck, like flint, (*Striking*)

115: knitted shape (*Poetry,* TS) | two-shape (*Striking*)

115: two great ironing-boards, (*Poetry,* TS) | ironing-boards (*Striking*)

149: placed (*Poetry,* TS) | flickered (*Striking*)

To Be Edward Thomas

First Publication: *The Beloit Poetry Journal Chapbook,* no. 5 (Summer 1957): 10–15.

Collected: *Striking,* 275–79, as one of "Two Poems on Poets."

Notes: Phillip Edward Thomas (1878–1917) from a young age wrote prolifically on the natural world of his native England, but he was unfulfilled by his accomplishments in prose. In 1913 at the age of thirty-five, he met Robert Frost (1874–1963), who was spending sixteen months in England and had just had his first collection of poems published there. Frost encouraged Thomas to express his love of the pastoral landscape in poetry using the naturalistic expression that distinguished Frost's own verse. Most of Thomas's poetry was published posthumously, and an *editio maior, Collected Poems,* edited by R. George Thomas, appeared in 1978. Frost said of Edward Thomas: "His concern to the last was what it had always been, to touch earthly things and come as near them in words as words could come." Dickey was writing a poem about Frost, "whom I don't really care much for, and even less as a man, but I had a rather nice afternoon with him in Florida in 1955. We walked beside the ocean, and we . . . talked about how much the English poet Edward Thomas had meant to him. He said, 'He's the only human being that I ever truly loved.' I thought this was strange . . . " (Randall A. Smith, "James Dickey Interview, Part II: November 7, 1995," *James Dickey Newsletter* 21 [Fall 2004]: 39). Dickey would naturally be drawn to a man who found his poetic gifts rather late and was given only two years to develop them before being killed in war. That might have been Dickey's story.

4: Though Frost was thirty-nine when he met Thomas in 1913, he is referred to as "old" here and at lines 17, 21, and 44; when Dickey published this poem, Frost was eighty-three. As a schoolboy, Dickey had admired Frost greatly (Hart, 34), but in "Robert Frost, Man and Myth" (*Atlantic* 218 [November 1966]: 53–56; *Babel,* 200–209), a review of Lawrance Thompson's *Robert Frost: The Early Years* (1966), Dickey described the wholly artificial persona Frost created ("the Robert Frost Story") to disguise his quite unpleasant real self in order to become the public face of poetry for a generation, a characteristic of Dickey's own life and career. As to Frost's poetry, Dickey wrote, "He, as much as any American poet, brought convincingness of tone into poetry, and made of it a gauge against which all poetry would inevitably have to be tried."

10: Dickey's one-year job teaching at the University of Florida was cut short after protests about his reading of "The Father's Body" (see Hart, 196–203).

33: Thomas's "As the Team's Head Brass" "describes a team ploughing and lovers meeting in the country during World War I. It portrays war as both an interruption of the country life and a decayer of it. I don't know what 'head brass' is on a horse's head, what kind of accoutrement or equipment it is. . . . But the 'team's head brass' struck me as a phrase, and, in writing the poem about walking around with Robert Frost, I took that line or that image from Edward Thomas as one of the things that might have been instrumental in the solidification of the friendship between Frost and Thomas. And I felt like since I did feel that that might be so as we were walking along the beach at sundown, that I might have something of the same sort of splash of intuition that maybe they had, or maybe Thomas had, or maybe Thomas had because of Frost, or something like that, and then the phrase came to me: 'a horse-headed flash in the sun.' I thought, yeah, that's what I want to put right here in the poem" (Smith, "James Dickey Interview," 39–40). For "head brass" see "Heraldic," line 17.

42–43: Thomas and his wife, Helen, moved frequently from country cottage to country cottage because of their own economic instability.

72–75: Dickey may have been thinking of the St. Augustine lighthouse, the nearest lighthouse to Gainesville. It has black and white spiral stripes, a red lantern, and a light that flashes every thirty seconds.

94: Vimy Ridge is the site of the battle that pitted the Canadian Corps against the German Sixth Army on April 9–12, 1917. It was the first phase of the longer battle of Arras. Thomas was killed by a shell the morning of the first day.

105–6: Compare "In the Mountain Tent" and "The Heaven of Animals."

VARIANTS:

28: Saw-edged (*Beloit Chapbook*) | Cross-cut (*Striking*)

43: no (*Beloit Chapbook*) | no live (*Striking*)

43: nearest (*Beloit Chapbook*) | near (*Striking*)

50–52: said / Gravely his old and laboring breath away. / He bent upon (*Beloit Chapbook*) | bent / Upon (*Striking*)

58: Determined (*Beloit Chapbook*) | Singled (*Striking*)

67: of the (*Beloit Chapbook*) | of (*Striking*)

95: mowing (*Beloit Chapbook*) |moving (*Striking*)

97: hall (*Beloit Chapbook*) | tunnel (*Striking*)

141: to (*Beloit Chapbook*) | through (*Striking*)

141: in (*Beloit Chapbook*) | of (*Striking*)

143: bundle-bodied (*Beloit Chapbook*) | flag-draped (*Striking*)

144–47: flash: to be seen / As the dead see, in the living, the bright horse known in life / And come back from the sun / In a (*Beloit Chapbook*) | place but in / A horse-headed flash from the sun, / A (*Striking*)

149: Intimate invaluable (*Beloit Chapbook*) | Inviolable (*Striking*)

150: made (*Beloit Chapbook*) | found (*Striking*)

151: Alive with what human light? (*Beloit Chapbook*) | Swing to you in all-human light. (*Striking*)

The Work of Art

FIRST PUBLICATION: *Hudson Review* 10 (Autumn 1957): 400–402.

COLLECTED: With "The Contest" as "Two Versions of the Same Poem" in *Striking*, 267–69.

NOTES: Intended for *Into the Stone* but cut by Wheelock; included with TS of *Into the Stone*. Other poems set in Okinawa include "Amputee Ward: Okinawa, 1945" (which is a subheading in this poem), "The Coral Flight," "Victory," and "The Driver."

28: For this phrase see Jeremiah 46:14: "Stand fast, and prepare thee; for the sword shall devour round about thee."

77: "To the Queen," a toast.

VARIANTS:

23: grouped (*Hudson*, TS) | met to form (*Striking*)

58: burned in (*Hudson*, TS) | held by (*Striking*)

67: meditation (*Hudson*, TS) | mediation (*Striking*)

75: bodiless (*Hudson*, TS) | bodiness (*Striking*)

The Red Bow

FIRST PUBLICATION: *Sewanee Review* 65 (Autumn 1957): 627–34.

COLLECTED: *Striking*, 250–55.

NOTES:. Intended for *Into the Stone* but cut by Wheelock; included with TS of *Into the Stone*.

117: See "Poem [a]," line 2.

191: *The House of Earth* (1935) is the title of the collected "Oriental" novels of Pearl S. Buck (1892–1973).

VARIANTS:

1: well (*Sewanee Review*) | far (*Striking*)

4: up (*Sewanee Review*, TS) | their (*Striking*)

10: and (*Sewanee Review*, TS) | through (*Striking*)

22: blinding sensitivity (*Sewanee Review*, TS) | sensitivity (*Striking*)

26: advance the (*Sewanee Review*, TS) | advances (*Striking*)

27: built (*Sewanee Review*, TS) | hid (*Striking*)

71: Level (*Sewanee Review*, TS) | Straight down (*Striking*)

72: blinding wood (*Sewanee Review*, TS) | wood (*Striking*)

82: pulled (*Sewanee Review*, TS) | drew (*Striking*)

85: earth (*Sewanee Review*, TS) | air (*Striking*)

86: Off warmly (*Sewanee Review*, TS) | Off-centered (*Striking*)

87: There, where (*Sewanee Review*, TS) | Where (*Striking*)

102: Act (*Sewanee Review*, TS) | act (*Striking*)

129: something (TS, *Striking*) | sometthing (*Sewanee Review*)

132: floated shine (*Sewanee Review*, TS) | shine (*Striking*)

133: danced (*Sewanee Review*, TS) | rose (*Striking*)
134: singing above (*Sewanee Review*, TS) | above (*Striking*)
149: single (*Sewanee Review*, TS) | singled (*Striking*)
179: into (*Sewanee Review*, TS) | in (*Striking*)
180: As it (*Sewanee Review*, TS) | It (*Striking*)
180: vibrating shape, consumed (*Sewanee Review*, TS) | self-consuming shape (*Striking*)

The Sprinter's Sleep

FIRST PUBLICATION: *Yale Review* 47 (Autumn 1957): 72.
COLLECTED: *Into the Stone*, 71.
NOTES: "It came out of a real dream I had, which in turn came out of seven or eight years of run-
   ning on high-school, prep-school and college track teams" (*Crux*, 144). The working title was
   "The Vision of the Sprinter" (*Crux*, 84). Perhaps the germ of the poem is an entry in *Striking*,
   211: "'Sprinter': 'dead / Heat.'" This poem has an affinity with the film *Field of Dreams* (1989),
   from the novel *Shoeless Joe* (1982) by Ray Kinsella. Other poems involving running include
   "The Sprinter's Mother," "The Sprinter's Sleep," "For the Running of the New York City Mara-
   thon," and "The Olympian."

The Cypresses

FIRST PUBLICATION: *Quarterly Review of Literature* 9 (Winter 1958): 268–70.

Poem [a]

FIRST PUBLICATION: *Quarterly Review of Literature* 9 (Winter 1958): 270–71.
COLLECTED: *Into the Stone*, 69–70.
REPRINTED: *Quarterly Review of Literature* 19 (Spring–Summer 1974): 202–3.
NOTES: Included with the TS of *Into the Stone*. This is one of three poems originally titled "Poem"
and distinguished in this edition by the bracketed letters [a], [b], and [c].
2 and 50: See "The Red Bow," line 117.
22: On Dickey's "Uncle Jim," see "Angel of the Maze."

A Beginning Poet, Aged Sixty-Five

FIRST PUBLICATION: *Quarterly Review of Literature* 9 (Winter 1958) 272–73.
COLLECTED: *Striking*, 279–80.
NOTES: See "To Landrum Guy, Beginning to Write at Sixty."
48: The Fourth Horseman of the Apocalypse is Death mounted on a pale horse (Revelations
   6:1–8).
VARIANTS:
29–30: moon light (*Quarterly Review*) | moon-light (*Striking*)
31: waterfall's shuddering sound (*Quarterly Review*) | waterfall-shudder of silence (*Striking*)

Genesis

FIRST PUBLICATION: *Commentary* 25 (May 1958): 427.
COLLECTED: *Striking*, 249–50.
NOTES: Intended for *Into the Stone* but cut by Wheelock; included in TS of *Into the Stone*.
VARIANTS:
22: tuning-fork, and singing curvèdly (*Commentary*, TS) | thin tool, forkèdly singing (*Striking*)

Joel Cahill Dead

FIRST PUBLICATION: *Beloit Poetry Journal* 8 (Summer 1958): 18–19
REPRINTED: *Beloit Poetry Journal* 51 (Fall 2000–Winter 2001): 53–54.
NOTES: The germ of this poem appears in one of Dickey's notebooks from 1952 (Ken Autrey, "'Working the Notebook to Death': James Dickey's Journals," *James Dickey Newsletter* 6 [Spring 1990]: 23–24). In *Alnilam* Joel Cahill is a skilled trainee who apparently dies in a training accident while estranged from his father. According to Dickey, the poem "is actually a scene from a novel that I suppose I shall never finish, called <u>The Table of the Sun.</u> That actual Joel Cahill was a boy named Pike, who was in primary training with me in Hemmet, California, in 1942. He went against his flight-plan and flew over a forest fire, crashed, and was killed" (*Crux*, 139). On the veracity of Dickey's remembrance, see Hart, 676.

Dover: Believing in Kings

FIRST PUBLICATION: *Poetry* 92 (August 1958): 283–90.
COLLECTED: *Drowning*, 57–63; *Poems* 57–67, 87–93; *Early Motion*, 51–58; *Whole Motion*, 104–10.
NOTES: Dickey and his young family visited Dover, England, on September 1, 1954 (*Striking*, 100). "I thought it might be an extremely complex and interesting problem to write a relatively long poem using all the clichés about kings, about their being confined in dungeons and escaping, about the man in the iron mask, and so on" (*Self*, 100). Dickey's friend and fellow-poet James Wright (1927–1980; see "The Surround") advised Dickey during the composition of this poem, which won the Union League Civic and Arts Foundation Award from *Poetry* in 1958. The poem was intended for *Into the Stone* but was cut by Wheelock. On parricide, see "Approaching Prayer."
5: The Strait of Dover is the narrowest part of the English Channel (twenty-one miles). In 1950 Florence May Chadwick (1918–1995) broke the 1926 record of Gertrude Ederle (1905–2003) for swimming across the channel from Calais to Dover. In 1951 Chadwick became the first woman to swim the channel beginning from Dover. Photographs of her emerging from the sea at Dover—covered in grease to keep her warm—appeared in *Time* (September 24, 1954, 54) and other publications.
6: "ale of shallows" echoes a World War I poem, "The Vale of Shadows" (1915), by the American poet Clinton Scollard (1860–1932).
10: A typical Dickey chiasmus from this period.
57–70: The denouement of *King Lear* takes place at Dover, where the old king is to meet Gloucester. He is led there by his son and tries to commit suicide by leaping off a cliff (see line 148).

103–8: In Alexandre Dumas's *The Man in the Iron Mask* (1848), the musketeer Aramis kidnaps Louis XIV, imprisons him in the Bastille, and puts his twin brother, Philippe, on the throne. Louis is restored to the kingship, in part by d'Artagnan. Philippe, threatened with execution (see lines 106–9), is required to wear an iron mask (lines 104–6) on his way to prison. Aramis ultimately escapes France for Spain by sea (99–102).

113–15: Arthur pulls Excalibur from a stone in Malory's *Morte d'Arthur* (bk. 1, chaps. 5–6).

115: Lightborn (Anglicized "Lucifer") is the assassin hired by Mortimer Junior to kill Edward II; Lightborn does so by setting him up to his waist in water in the dungeon of Berkeley Castle (and is then himself killed) in Marlowe's *Edward II*, 5.4.

129–32: Aeneas carried his father, Anchises, on his back to escape Troy in *Aeneid* 2.707–8.

166: The regicide Oliver Cromwell was posthumously hanged (see lines 106–8) and Charles II had Cromwell's head set on a pike above Westminster, where it remained for more than twenty-five years.

178–79: "Every Man a King" speech by Sen. Huey P. Long (1893–1935) of Louisiana, February 23, 1934, in *The Senate 1789–1989: Classic Speeches, 1830–1993*, edited by Robert C. Byrd and Wendy Wolff (Washington, D.C.: U.S. Government Printing Office, 1994), 583–93.

201: *Timon of Athens* (4.3): "The moon's an arrant thief, / and her pale fire she snatches from her son."

202: "fishing flash": see "The Shark's Parlor," line 30.

207: Poseidon, god of water, would wear a green crown, but poets and athletes would wear green garlands of ivy, myrtle, or laurel.

VARIANTS:

11: sackcloth (*Drowning, Poems 57–67, Early Motion, Whole Motion*) | sack-cloth (*Poetry*)

30: Inside (*Drowning, Poems 57–67, Early Motion, Whole Motion*) | Beside (*Poetry*)

47: thumbprint (*Drowning, Poems 57–67, Early Motion, Whole Motion*) | thumb-print (*Poetry*)

59: shook (*Poems 57–67, Early Motion, Whole Motion*) | quivered (*Poetry, Drowning*)

69: images (*Poetry, Drowning, Poems 57–67*) | shadows (*Early Motion, Whole Motion*)

72: spooned out (*Drowning, Poems 57–67, Early Motion, Whole Motion*) | spooned-out (*Poetry*)

73: candle thread (*Drowning, Poems 57–67, Early Motion, Whole Motion*) | candle-thread (*Poetry*)

82: thing in flame (*Poetry, Drowning, Poems 57–67*) | things in flame (*Early Motion*) | things in the flame (*Whole Motion*)

87: shadow dancing stilly (*Poetry, Drowning*) | shadow, struck down (*Poems 57–67*) | shadow, laid stilly (*Early Motion, Whole Motion*)

87: me, (*Drowning, Poems 57–67, Early Motion, Whole Motion*) | me (*Poetry*)

90: candle shade (*Drowning, Poems 57–67, Early Motion, Whole Motion*) | candle-shade (*Poetry*)

104: panted (*Poetry, Drowning, Poems 57–67*) | breathed (*Early Motion, Whole Motion*)

108: pothooks (*Drowning, Poems 57–67, Early Motion, Whole Motion*) | pot-hooks (*Poetry*)

131: get (*Drowning, Poems 57–67, Early Motion, Whole Motion*) | bear (*Poetry*)

133: swanlike (*Drowning, Poems 57–67, Early Motion, Whole Motion*) | swan-like (*Poetry*)

134: scepter (*Drowning, Poems 57–67, Early Motion, Whole Motion*) | sceptre (*Poetry*)

135: goatlike (*Drowning, Poems 57–67, Early Motion, Whole Motion*) | goat-like (*Poetry*)

141: cloudlike (*Drowning, Poems 57–67, Early Motion, Whole Motion*) | cloud-like (*Poetry*)

148: cliff top (*Drowning, Poems 57–67, Early Motion, Whole Motion*) | clifftop (*Poetry*)

160: Surpassingly (*Poetry, Drowning, Poems 57–67*) | Surprisingly (*Early Motion, Whole Motion*)

165: prisons (*Poetry, Drowning, Poems 57–67*) | prison (*Early Motion, Whole Motion*)

175: legged (*Drowning, Poems 57–67, Early Motion, Whole Motion*) | leggèd (*Poetry*)

177: arising (*Poetry, Drowning, Poems 57–67*) | gotten-up (*Early Motion, Whole Motion*)

193: halfway (*Drowning, Poems 57–67, Early Motion, Whole Motion*) | half-way (*Poetry*)

201: hairspring (*Drowning, Poems 57–67, Early Motion, Whole Motion*) | hair-spring (*Poetry*)

217: blue jeans (*Drowning, Poems 57–67, Early Motion, Whole Motion*) | blue-jeans (*Poetry*)

220: seaside (*Drowning, Poems 57–67, Early Motion, Whole Motion*) | sea-side (*Poetry*)

220: sheep track (*Drowning, Poems 57–67, Early Motion, Whole Motion*) | sheep-track (*Poetry*)

The Falls

First Publication: *Impetus,* no. 3 (Winter 1959): 3–4.

Collected: *Striking,* 262–63.

Variants:

26: Risingly roaring (*Impetus*) | Rising soaringly (*Striking*)

34: lift (*Impetus*) | true (*Striking*)

37: To do nothing but rest in (*Impetus*) | I rest idly in the midmost of (*Striking*)

46: insupportable (*Impetus*) | unsupportable (*Striking*)

The Other

First Publication: *Yale Review* 48 (Spring 1959): 398–400.

Collected: *Into the Stone,* 72–74; *Poems 57–67,* 34; *Whole Motion,* 61–63.

Reprinted: *Poems of Our Moment,* 58–60.

Notes: "It is about the obsessive effort boys have to 'build themselves up' physically, along about their fifteenth year" (*Crux,* 144). Dickey claimed to work "most fruitfully in cases in which there was no clear-cut distinction between what was actually happening and what was happening in the mind of a character in the poem" (*Babel,* 287).

7: This "bronze" refers both to the statue of Apollo and to that of the bull in lines 53–56.

19: On Dickey's dead older brother, see "The String," "The Underground Stream," and "In the Tree House at Night."

21: Apollo as god of poetry and prophecy may here mean that the narrator has both a realization of the resurrective power of poetry and the vision to see where that poetry will take him.

24: A temple to Apollo was erected at Delphi, the site where the god slew the Python.

27: The "house" may refer to the temple to Pythian Apollo, where the Delphic oracle, claiming the voice of Apollo, brought forth prophecies (for a price) in the ancient world.

50: The "wing-bone" or scapula is shaped like an ancient lyre.

53–56: The picture is the tauroctony, or ritual slaying of a sacred bull, by Mithras as depicted in *Mithras Tauroctony,* a famous statue in the British Museum with a dog and serpent drinking the bull's blood and a scorpion attacking its testicles. The sacrifice heralds the coming of spring.

Variants:

9: ear-drums (TS, *Into the Stone, Poems 57–67, Whole Motion*) | eardrums (*Yale Review*)

The Vegetable King

First Publication: *Sewanee Review* 67 (Spring 1959): 278–80.
Collected: *Into the Stone*, 49–51; *Poems 57–67*, 23; *Whole Motion*, 53–55.

Notes: "In 'The Vegetable King,' I try to mythologize my family; this, I guess, is my answer to Eliot's use of the Osiris myth. It was one of the first poems in which I was able to use a myth in a way peculiar to me and at the same time make it something that could happen to anybody" (*Self*, 85). "Osiris" was a provisional title of this poem in a draft stage (Washington University Collection MSS box 12, F189). "It is really a human parable, and not so much indicative of growth, decay, and death of cultures as Eliot imagines" (*Crux*, 155). See also *Striking*, 89–91. The only full-length story of Osiris is given by Plutarch (*De Iside et Osiride*, edited by John Gwyn Griffiths [Cardiff: University of Wales Press, 1970]) and is discussed at length in J. G. Frazer's *The New Golden Bough* (New York: Criterion, 1959), sec. 242–72. The Egyptian king Osiris, having converted his people from cannibalism and given them laws, set out to teach agriculture to the rest of the world. Successful enough to be worshipped worldwide as a deity (hence "Vegetable King"), he was conspired against by his brother, Set, murdered by being sealed in a coffer and set afloat down the Nile ("the drowned god," line 30) on the seventeenth day of Athyr, roughly our November 13 (Frazer, sec. 257), the month of sowing in Egypt for the harvest in the spring. Osiris's sister Isis found his body in reeds downriver ("picturing grass / . . . in the unconsecrated grove," lines 11–12), but when she left it to find her son Horus, Set came upon the body by chance, cut it into fourteen pieces ("hacked apart in the growing cold / Of the year," lines 34–35), and scattered them along the Nile. Isis buried each part (except the genitals, which had been eaten by fish) where she found it (Plutarch, *De Iside et Osiride*, sec. 12–20). The sorrow of Osiris's two sisters was so great that the sun god, Ra, sent Anubis to put the body back together ("assembled / From the trembling, untroubled river," lines 35–36). Osiris thus became god of the Underworld, returning each year to ensure a bountiful harvest from March through May ("One night each April," line 6). He is regularly represented as a mummy (Fraser, sec. 246), as in "bloodless as a god" (line 38) and "mummied" (line 52). The term "Vegetable King" is applied by Louis Figuier in *The Vegetable World* (1857) to the baobab, in whose hollowed-out trunk poets are buried. This poem won the *Sewanee Review*'s Longview Foundation Award in 1960.

7: As the poem is set in April, the "musty sleeping-bag" may represent the mummy-form in which Osiris is portrayed, rather than the coffer in which he was killed late in the year.

21, 61: Dickey's regular expressions for the constellations of the zodiac.

54: The severed head of Osiris is buried in Abydos, the holiest site in Egypt (Fraser, sec.246).

63–64: According to Aristotle (*Metaphysics* 986a), the Pythagoreans considered "the whole universe to be a musical scale or number." Pythagoreans thought that the ten spheres of the solar system generated musical sounds, the nearer ones lower tones, the farther ones higher tones, all of which, because the spacing of the spheres corresponded to the Pythagorean musical ratios, produced a harmony among the spheres. Plato, in his *Timaeus* (35–36d) described the circles of heaven divided into musical ratios. See "The Zodiac."

Variants:

2: door (*Into the Stone, Poems 57–67, Whole Motion*) | door, (*Sewanee Review*, TS)

39: Who (*Into the Stone, Poems 57–67, Whole Motion*) | And (*Sewanee Review,* TS)

39: returns (*Into the Stone, Poems 57–67, Whole Motion*) | returned (*Sewanee Review,* TS)

The Jewel

FIRST PUBLICATION: *Saturday Review* 42 (June 6, 1959): 38.

COLLECTED: *Into the Stone,* 57–58; *Poems 57–67,* 28–29; *Whole Motion,* 57–58.

REPRINTED: *Achievement,* 24–25.

VARIANTS:

21: him, (TS, *Into the Stone, Poems 57–67, Whole Motion*) | him (*Saturday Review*)

The Game

FIRST PUBLICATION: *Poetry* 94 (July 1959): 211–12.

COLLECTED: *Into the Stone,* 47.

NOTES: At Vanderbilt in fall 1948, Dickey took a course in cultural anthropology for which he wrote a term paper on the Murngin tribe of northern Australia. Dickey incorporated elements of Murngin life, chiefly the communion with the dead at a sacred water hole into this poem, "The Signs," and "The Underground Stream" (see *One Voice 1,* 28).

22: See "Giving a Son to the Sea" (part of "Messages").

VARIANTS:

16: Into (*Into the Stone*) | Drawn into (*Poetry*) ["Drawn" added in Dickey's holograph to TS.]

The Landfall

FIRST PUBLICATION: *Poetry* 94 (July 1959): 213–15.

COLLECTED: *Into the Stone,* 91.

REPRINTED: Poetry *Anthology,* 359–61.

NOTES: Dickey placed this poem last in *Into the Stone.* "I wanted the tone and feeling at the end of the poem to be what I had to say to people: the thing I would leave them with" (*Crux,* 163).

13: "In spite of the fact that we have no such fleet as we should have, we have conquered for ourselves a place in the sun" (Kaiser Wilhelm II of Germany, "Speech to the North German Regatta Association, 1901, in C. Gauss, *The German Kaiser as Shown in His Public Utterances* [New York: Scribners, 1915]: 181). *A Place in the Sun* was also the title of the 1951 film version of Theodore Dreiser's novel *An American Tragedy* (1925).

VARIANTS:

10: Flame up (*Into the Stone*) | Burn out (*Poetry*)

10: burn out (*Into the Stone*) | come back (*Poetry*) [corrected to *Poetry* reading by Dickey's holograph in TS]

The Signs

FIRST PUBLICATION: *Poetry* 94 (July 1959): 215–18.

COLLECTED: *Into the Stone*, 39.

NOTES: Kevin Webster Dickey was born in the Crawford Long Hospital in Atlanta on August 18, 1958. He figures in "Reading Genesis to a Blind Child," "To His Children in Darkness," "The Bee," "Messages," "The Drift-Spell," and "Obstructions." On the Murngin elements, see notes for "The Game."

4: Janus, a mythical king who was deified after his death, is depicted with two faces looking in opposite directions and is said to have ruled his city in Rome (the Janiculum) in a period considered a golden age of peace, plenty, and honesty.

14: Achilles was killed by an arrow shot into his heel by Apollo or guided by Apollo from the bow of Paris. In the Underworld, Achilles is said to have married either Medea, Iphigenia, or Helen.

17–21: The next life described here is reminiscent of the Underworld of Virgil in book 6 of the *Aeneid*, with its setting beneath the earth, its population of humanlike shades, and its rivers, streams, and lakes; that the shades embody elements of the poet's guilt recalls Dante.

26: "Ether" (or "aether") was the upper region of space and the aura that surrounded divinities.

47: See "Cherrylog Road," line 108: "Wild to be wreckage forever."

52: In 1949 Hope Muntz published *The Golden Warrior* about King Harold and the Norman Conquest.

57: Apollo was the most beautiful of the gods.

VARIANTS:

24: blind: in love, in love. (*Into the Stone*) | blind with life. (*Poetry*) ["in love, in love" crossed out by Dickey on TS, "with life" written above line]

The Enclosure

FIRST PUBLICATION: *Poetry* 94 (July 1959): 218–20.

COLLECTED: *Into the Stone*, 55–56; *Poems 57–67*, 26–27; *Whole Motion*, 55–57.

NOTES: Discussed in *Self*, 91–92. For the fantasy of sovereign power over women of another race, see "Slave Quarters."

VARIANTS:

36: nipa (*Into the Stone*, *Poems 57–67*, *Whole Motion*) | napa (*Poetry*, TS) [Nipa is a large palm tree of the Philippines and Australia with long leaves used for thatching; napa is Chinese cabbage.]

The Performance

FIRST PUBLICATION: *Poetry* 94 (July 1959): 220–21.

COLLECTED: *Into the Stone*, 59–60; *Poems 57–67*, 30–31; *Self*, 95–96; *Whole Motion*, 58–59.

REPRINTED: *Achievement*, 25–27; *Articles of War*, 106–7; *Contemporary American Poetry* (Hall), 77–78; *Contemporary American Poets*, 63–64; *Contemporary Southern Poetry*, 77–78; *Exploring Poetry*, 455–56; *Modern Poems*, 377–78; *New Oxford Book of Modern Verse*, 856–57; *New Poets*, 211–12; *Norton Anthology of Modern Poetry*, 1030–31; *Poems*, 9–10; *Wesleyan Tradition*, 52–54; *Workshop*, 206–7.

NOTES: In this poem the poet "remembers Armstrong as a close friend who was an amateur gymnast, but who was a little bit weak in the arms. He was tall and thin. He couldn't perform very well the gymnastic movements that required the handstand. So when he didn't have anything else to do, he would get out in the squadron area and practice his handstand. . . . [The poet] comes up with the reminiscence on the basis of the failed handstand, which the poet imagines was perfected at the last moment, just before he was killed" (Greiner, 8); see also *Texas Review* 5 (Spring–Summer 1984) 78; *Night,* 279. 2nd Lt. Donald H. Armstrong (1921–1945), born in Pennsylvania, had left a failed marriage back home in Buffalo, New York, an experience that may have led to the headstrong behavior Dickey admired from afar. The depth of their friendship has been called into question (Hart, 97), but there is no reason to doubt Dickey's admiration for Armstrong, who was "always doing gymnastic tricks in the squadron area. He used to do flips and all kind of such things, and would work on his handstands. He was a tall fellow, and because his center of gravity was high, it was hard for him to do handstands" (*Self,* 93). Armstrong at 6'1" was tall and weighed 150 lbs. at the time of his enlistment in 1942. He had become a pilot while Dickey had failed to, but the taller and heavier Dickey could do handstands, which the weaker Armstrong could not (Hart, 99; Muldrow does handstands in *To the White Sea*). On the night of March 16, 1945, Armstrong and his radio officer, James J. Lally (1920–1945) of Massachusetts, were flying air cover for a convoy to Panay, about one hundred miles from where the 418th was based. On the return Armstrong buzzed an airfield in San Jose to see if it were held by the Japanese or by Philippine guerrillas. He crashed into a stand of coconut trees (Hart, 97). In his portion of *History* (68), Dickey reported that Armstrong and Lally "high-speed stalled close to the ground over the Jap strip at San Jose, Panay, and crashed northwest of the field. . . . Finally the [Filipino] guerrillas informed us that ARMSTRONG had been killed and LALLY, badly injured, was in the hands of the enemy" (see further, *Self,* 93). Two months after Armstrong's crash, there appeared on page 97 of the May 14, 1945, issue of *Life* a full-page photograph of an Australian pilot named Leonard Siffleet (1916–1943) blindfolded on his knees on a beach next to a grave and about to be beheaded by a Japanese soldier, Yasuno Chikao, wielding a two-handed *shin gunto* sword. The event had taken place two years earlier on October 24, 1943, on Aitae Beach in Papua, New Guinea, near where Lally was executed. Siffleet was tall and thin like Armstrong and was to be executed alone. The photograph, like the poem, freezes the moment of anticipation before the blow is struck. Subsequent investigation by squadron members 2nd Lt. Spencer M. Porter (b. 1921) and his radar officer Herbert Vaughn (b. 1923) uncovered that the Japanese had treated Lally's wounds and then beheaded him. Two months after learning this, Dickey undoubtedly read the account of Japanese sergeant Takeo Kawaii in *Stars and Stripes* (December 6, 1945) regarding the procedures and methods of beheading two Allied prisoners on Cebu Island, March 26, 1945, ten days after Armstrong and Lally went down. Kawaii described the executions as taking place in a schoolyard, which likely gave Dickey the setting for "Between Two Prisoners," published the year after "The Performance." Kawaii noted that the prisoners knelt beside a grave dug for them in the sand, perhaps the source of Armstrong's "inadequate grave" (line 24).

Armstrong and Lally's fate was the most haunting of Dickey's war experiences. At Vanderbilt he wrote an essay titled "Tacloban" (the Philippine city that was the 418th's next station), which expressed his admiration for Armstrong (Hart, 352), and in the 1950s he wrote a short story, "The

Eye of the Fire," in which a pilot is killed and his radar officer beheaded, and its protagonists napalm a Japanese schoolhouse in revenge (published posthumously in *Oxford American* 39 [June 2001]: 58–65). Dickey recalled the event (with Appleby representing Armstrong) in "The Valley," 25–26. Long after "The Performance" and "Between Two Prisoners," Dickey included a beheading of an American in *To the White Sea* (103–5). See also "Reunioning Dialogue," lines 69–72.

This poem was Dickey's favorite "in terms of the meaning it had" when he wrote it (Broughton, 184–85). See *Self*, 92–95; *Southern Review*, n.s., 9 (Winter 1973): 136–38; and *Texas Review* 5 (Spring–Summer 1984): 78; Baughman, 216. On Dickey's reworking of the actual event, see Hart, 99–100 and compare *Self*, 94: "The poem isn't about the facts of Armstrong's death, because the narrator is trying to imagine them"; and *Southern Review*, 140: "'The Performance' is based on what I remember of a pilot in my squadron . . . but the business of having a vision of him being beheaded and doing flips and things beside his grave is just something that I made up."
VARIANTS:
2: sun, (*Into the Stone, Poems 57–67, Whole Motion*) | sun (*Poetry*, TS)
5: side (*Into the Stone, Poems 57–67, Whole Motion*) | side, (*Poetry*, TS)
13: Dust fanned (TS, *Into the Stone Poems 57–67*) | Armed (*Poetry*)

The String

FIRST PUBLICATION: *Poetry* 94 (July 1959): 222–23.
COLLECTED: *Into the Stone*, 45–46; *Poems 57–67*, 21; *Whole Motion*, 51–53.
REPRINTED: *Achievement*, 23–24;
NOTES: Dickey's brother Eugene (1914–1921) died at the age of six "of what was then called 'brain fever,' but which was almost certainly meningitis" (*Crux*, 358). Dickey included him in the outline of his unpublished novel "The Romantic" (*Striking*, 166). See "The Other," "Armor," and "The Underground Stream," where the poet says, "and claim his own grave face / That mine might live in its place" (lines 52–53) ". . . the one whose death, in my father's mind, was the reason for his birth, had lain in his sickbed making string figures hour after hour" (*Summer*, 26). This poem is discussed in *Self* (88–89). On string figures in general, see Caroline Furness Jayne, *String Figures and How to Make Them: A Study of Cat's-Cradle in Many Lands* (New York: Dover, 1962).
15: Jacob's ladder is a familiar Osage Indian string figure also known as "Osage Diamonds" (Jayne, 24). "Jacob's Coffin" is not mentioned in the account of Joseph taking Jacob's body from Egypt to Canaan for burial in Genesis 50, but according to the Talmud (b. Sotah 13a), Jacob's coffin was laden with the crowns of his discordant family and the chief men of the Pharaoh, ultimately leading to the reconciliation of Joseph and Esau, who had been betrayed by his brother, Jacob.
24: Euclid of Alexandria (fl. 300 b.c.e.) was the founder of geometry. Dickey may have been thinking of Vachel Lindsay's poem "Euclid," which says: "Old Euclid drew a circle / On a sand-beach long ago. / He bounded and enclosed it / With angles thus and so." Early versions of "The String" read "Diogenes" here. Several Greek philosophers were named Diogenes, including Diogenes the Cynic (412–323 b.c.e.), Diogenes the Stoic (230–150 b.c.e.), or Diogenes the Epicurean (second century b.c.e.), but none was known for making diagrams in the sand.
41: On the "Cat's Cradle," see Jayne, xii–xv, 324.
49: "I have always felt a sense of guilt that my birth depended on my brother's death" (*Self*, 89).

Variants:

7, 14, 21, 28, 35, 42, 49: [lines indented] (*Poetry*) | [holograph note to indent] (TS)

24: Euclid's (*Whole Motion*) | Diogenes' (*Poetry*, TS, *Into the Stone, Poems 57–67*)

On the Hill below the Lighthouse

First Publication: As "Below the Lighthouse," *Poetry* 94 (July 1959): 223–25.

Collected: *Into the Stone*, 85–86, *Poems 57–67*, 43–44; *Whole Motion*, 66–67.

Reprinted: *New Poets*, 210–11; *Poems of Our Moment*, 55–56; *Poetry and Its Conventions*, 19–20.

Notes: Discussed in *Self*, 98.

21–25: The "bright arm" of light may be drawn from the lighthouse whose beam crossed over the Villa Lou Galidou, which Dickey and family rented in Cap d'Antibes in 1954: "We are about three-quarters of the way up the Hill, on top of which is the cap lighthouse" (*Crux*, 78). For a domestic lighthouse, see "To Be Edward Thomas," 72–75.

28: Chiasmus; for another see "Dover: Believing in Kings," 10.

Variants:

31, 35, 42: Coming back, coming back, going over. (*Into the Stone, Poems 57–67, Whole Motion*) | Going over, gone over, coming back. (*Poetry*)

Into the Stone

First Publication: *Poetry* 94 (July 1959): 225–26.

Collected: *Into the Stone*, 89–90; *Poems 57–67*, 47; *Whole Motion*, 69–70.

Reprinted: *Poems*, 13–14.

Notes: "For a long time I have been trying to do two things in poetry, both of which I have been told one should not do. The first is to get away, by whatever means, from the idea of a poem as objet d'art, which is a notion I have always hated, however much it has been drilled into me. The other is to be able to make statements, one after the other: This happens, this happens, then this happens. To go with all this, I have been trying to assert connections in nature where none exists: to make the world do what I say, rather than what it actually does. 'Stars shine and (therefore) wings grow'" (*Crux*, 162–63). "I began with an abstract theory about experience, and especially about love. . . . Eventually the poem becomes an assertion that not only the world of the person in love is changed by the new love relationship, but the whole universe is changed" (*Self*, 98). The "stone" may be the moon, as in line 2 and "Near Darien," line 12. The image of the title remained with Dickey to the end of his career: "To see beyond what any human, any man who has ever been born, could see. Like I tell you, out of the snowdrift, into the snowdrift, into the stone" (*To the White Sea,* 271).

Variants:

5: Of (*Poetry*, TS, *Into the Stone*) | If (*Poems 57–67, Whole Motion* [typo])

27: shaken (*Into the Stone, Poems 57–67, Whole Motion*)| shook (TS, *Poetry*)

27: sun (*Into the Stone, Poems 57–67, Whole Motion*) | bright sun (TS, *Poetry*)

Awaiting the Swimmer

FIRST PUBLICATION: *Kenyon Review* 21 (Autumn 1959): 609–10.
COLLECTED: *Into the Stone*, 81–82; *Poems 57–67*, 41–42; *Whole Motion*, 65–66.
REPRINTED: *Intervisions*, 20–23.
NOTES: "I thought I had found an interesting way to talk about cowardice: what it must be like for a man to be in love with a woman like a Hemingwayesque man, in that she's trying to prove something to herself physically; in this case, that she can swim across a river. But the man can't swim. . . . She's the strong-willed one; he's just an adjunct of her, and yet he has to take the male role in love-making. What would this do to their relationship?" (*Self*, 97).
VARIANTS:
23: move (*Into the Stone*, *Poems 57–67*, *Whole Motion*) | walk (*Kenyon*, TS)

Orpheus before Hades

FIRST PUBLICATION: *New Yorker* 35 (December 5, 1959): 52.
COLLECTED: *Into the Stone*, 83–84.
REPRINTED: *Hero's Way*, 95–96.
NOTES: This is the first of the sixty poems Dickey published in the *New Yorker*. The most famous of the Orpheus tales, his loss and failed recapture of Eurydice, is most memorably told by Virgil in *Georgics* 4.453–525, and Ovid in *Metamorphoses* 10.1–11.84, but the story also occurs in Plato's *Symposium*, and a fuller account in Apollodorus, *The Library*, 1.32, where Orpheus, after losing Eurydice, tried unsuccessfully to rescue her from Hades a second time and died. The figure of Orpheus watching Pluto's wife, Persephone, return in the spring of each year while Eurydice remains in the Underworld, reflects the ancient association of Eurydice and Persephone. See Günther Züntz, *Persephone: Three Essays on Religion and Thought in Magna Graecia* (Oxford: Clarendon Press, 1971). Dickey greatly admired *Sonnets to Orpheus* (1922) by Rainer Maria Rilke (1875–1926). See *Striking*, 58.
VARIANTS:
1: leaf (TS, *Into the Stone*) | leaf, (*New Yorker*)
1: branch, (TS, *Into the Stone*) | branch (*New Yorker*)
11: stand (TS, *Into the Stone*) | stand, (*New Yorker*)
11: field (TS, *Into the Stone*) | field, (*New Yorker*)
15: Spring (TS, *Into the Stone*) | spring (*New Yorker*)
17: fern; (TS, *Into the Stone*) | fern. (*New Yorker*)
22: sing (TS, *Into the Stone*) | sing, (*New Yorker*)
29: lyre (TS, *Into the Stone*) | lyre, (*New Yorker*)
30: snow-flake (TS, *Into the Stone*) | snowflake (*New Yorker*)
31: shining: (TS, *Into the Stone*) | shining, (*New Yorker*)
32: heartbreak (TS, *Into the Stone*) | heartbreak, (*New Yorker*)
34: where (*Into the Stone*) | that (*New Yorker*) [crossed out in Dickey's holograph in TS, "where" written above]

Reading Genesis to a Blind Child

FIRST PUBLICATION: *Wormwood Review* 1, no. 1 (1960) [15–17].

COLLECTED: *Whole Motion,* 40–42.

NOTES: On blindness see "Why in London the Blind Are Saviors"; "The Owl King"; "The Eye-Beaters"; "Night Bird"; *Striking,* 209; headnote to "Cahill Is Blind," *Esquire* 85 (February 1976): 67; and *Alnilam.*

12: Kevin, Dickey's "second-born son," was fully sighted from his birth in 1958 ("The Signs").

A Child's Room

FIRST PUBLICATION: *Quarterly Review of Literature* 10 (Winter 1960): 247–48.

NOTES: Submitted to *Atlantic* October 23, 1958 (*One Voice 1,* 286–87). In Virgil's *Georgics* 4, after Eurydice has died because of him (see "Orpheus before Hades"), Aristaeus visits his mother, who is spinning, the typical virtuous pastime of ancient wives and mothers.

The Wedding

FIRST PUBLICATION: *Quarterly Review of Literature* 10 (Winter 1960): 248–49.

COLLECTED: *Into the Stone,* 61–62; *Poems 57–67,* 32–33; *Whole Motion,* 59–60

NOTES: To cope with the tedium in Finschhafen, Papua, New Guinea, in January 1945, soldiers hammered Dutch coins into rings (Hart, 85). Dickey refers to this in "Eye of the Fire" (line 60) and in an unpublished novel of the 1950s, "The Romantic" (*Striking,* 165n55). He sent a ring that he had "pounded out of a silver dollar" to his brother Tom on March 2, 1945 (*One Voice 1,* 71).

48: Polycrates threw his ring into the sea to propitiate Nemesis (and later found it in a fish). Perhaps Dickey is also referring to the doges of Venice, who threw rings into the sea on Ascension Day to assert that the Adriatic should serve Venice as a wife served her husband.

VARIANTS:

3: lived-with (*Into the Stone, Poems 57 67, Whole Motion*) | lived with (*Quarterly Review,* TS)

31: wives (*Into the Stone, Poems 57–67, Whole Motion*) | wives, (*Quarterly Review,* TS)

Near Darien

FIRST PUBLICATION: *Quarterly Review of Literature* 10 (Winter 1960): 247.

COLLECTED: *Into the Stone,* 87–88; *Poems 57–67,* 45–46; *Whole Motion,* 68–69.

REPRINTED: *Quarterly Review of Literature* 19 (Spring–Summer 1974): 212–13.

NOTES: Darien is a popular vacation spot on the southeast coast of Georgia, north of St. Simons and the Sea Islands, where Dickey as son and father vacationed in the summers.

VARIANTS:

15: miles (TS, *Into the Stone, Poems 57–67, Whole Motion*) | miles, (*Quarterly Review*)

15: surface (TS, *Into the Stone, Poems 57–67, Whole Motion*) | surface, (*Quarterly Review*)

17: one flame (*Into the Stone, Poems 57–67, Whole Motion*) | flame (*Quarterly Review,* TS)

18: sun, (*Into the Stone, Poems 57–67, Whole Motion*) | sun; (*Quarterly Review*) | moon (TS)

24: woman (*Into the Stone, Poems 57–67, Whole Motion*) | woman, (*Quarterly Review,* TS)

25: takes its breath from my mouth, (*Into the Stone, Poems 57–67, Whole Motion*) | takes its breath from my mouth (*Quarterly Review*) | gets back its old flame (TS)

35: man and wife (*Into the Stone, Poems 57–67, Whole Motion*) | she and I (*Quarterly Review*) | my wife and I (TS)

38: vast, (*Into the Stone, Poems 57–67, Whole Motion*) | vast (*Quarterly Review,* TS)

The Scratch

First Publication: *Quarterly Review of Literature* 10 (Winter 1960): 251–53.

Collected: *Drowning,* 70–71; *Early Motion,* 66–67; *Whole Motion,* 114–15.

Reprinted: *American Poetry,* 1016–18; *Quarterly Review of Literature* 19 (Spring–Summer 1974): 213–15; *Quarterly Review of Literature: 50th Anniversary Anthology,* edited by T. and R. Weiss, 12, no. 32/33 (1993): 404–5.

Variants:

18: long-necked (*Drowning, Early Motion, Whole Motion*) | long-toothed (TS, *Quarterly Review*) ["toothed" changed to "necked" in Dickey's hand on TS]

25: wellspring (*Drowning, Early Motion, Whole Motion*) | well-spring (TS, *Quarterly Review*)

32: Who (*Drowning, Early Motion, Whole Motion*) | Whom (TS, *Quarterly Review*)

Uncle

First Publication: *Quarterly Review of Literature* 10 (Winter 1960): 253–54.

Collected: *Into the Stone,* 67–68.

Notes: On "Uncle Jim," see "The Angel of the Maze," line 13. "Uncle Jim," who suffered from arthritis and gout, used a cane for many years. His favorite had the head of a hound in honor of the hounds he kept and ran.

22: Ursa Major contains the asterism known as the Big Dipper, whose stars have proper motions in the direction of Sagittarius. Ursa Major moves from high in the sky in spring to low in autumn (as the "bear" prepares to hibernate). The constellation is identified with Callisto but also with Artemis, who lives in her own inviolable precinct far from men, is embodied in moonlight, and causes animals and trees to dance.

56: Gen. 1:22, 28; 9:1, 7; 35:11: "Be fertile and have increase." For the triple repetition at the end of a poem, see "The Lifeguard" and "Snow on a Southern State." For the three-sentence final line, see "Fog Envelops the Animals."

Variants:

15: down on (*Into the Stone*) | down (*Quarterly Review*)

The Island

First Publication: *Sewanee Review* 68 (Winter 1960): 89–90.

Collected: *Drowning,* 53–54; *Early Motion,* 48–49; *Whole Motion,* 101–3.

NOTES: With "The Underground Stream," one of Dickey's few uses of rhymed couplets, apart from his children's poems; see "The Scratch."

2–3: Rilke, "Sonnets to Orpheus," 2: 29.4–5, "what preys on you will / strengthen from such nourishment."

Sleeping Out at Easter

FIRST PUBLICATION: *Virginia Quarterly Review* 36 (Spring 1960): 218–19.

COLLECTED: *Into the Stone,* 37–38; *Poems 57–67,* 17; *Whole Motion,* 49–50.

REPRINTED: *Poems from* The Virginia Quarterly Review, 89–90; *Reading Modern Poetry,* 90–92; *Self,* 87–88.

NOTES: "In the spring I did sleep out in a sleeping bag in a little pine grove behind my suburban house when I was in the advertising business in Atlanta. But I didn't wake up feeling that I was Christ. That's something I made up" (*Self,* 85). Dickey claimed that with this poem, which he began "at the typewriter one afternoon in an American business office," he found "what I wanted: a strange incantatory sound, a simplicity that was direct without being thin, and a sense of imaginative urgency that I had never been able to get into verse before" (*Babel,* 284). The repetition of the first line as the last line of each stanza and all such lines collected as the final stanza, "so far as I know, I invented for the occasion" (*Babel,* 285). For a facsimile of the MS, see Janet Larsen McHughes, "From Manuscript to Performance Script: The Evolution of a Poem," *Literature in Performance* 2 (November 1981): 26–49; reprinted in *"Struggling for Wings": The Art of James Dickey,* edited by Robert Kirschsten (Columbia: University of South Carolina Press, 1997), 93–117.

VARIANTS:

36: child (TS, *Into the Stone, Poems 57–67, Whole Motion*) | son (*Virginia Quarterly Review*)

The Prodigal

FIRST PUBLICATION: *Poetry Northwest* 1 (Spring–Summer 1960): 10–13.

NOTES: Dickey experimented with constantly changing rhyme (and off-rhyme) schemes in these stanzas.

89–96: For Eugene Dickey and his fighting birds, see "The Gamecocks."

To Landrum Guy, Beginning to Write at Sixty

FIRST PUBLICATION: As "To a Beginning Poet, Aged Sixty," *Atlantic* 205 (May 1960): 69.

COLLECTED: *Drowning,* 87–88; *Early Motion,* 84–85; *Whole Motion,* 126–27.

REPRINTED: *Poems on Poetry,* 239–40.

NOTES: Landrum Guy (1902–1976) spent his working life as a researcher and fact checker for the "City Guide" reference series in various cities across the country. He retired to a two-room shack behind his brother's house in Decatur, Georgia, intending to spend the rest of his life reading. He enrolled in the Dickey poetry workshop offered under the auspices of Emory University's adult education program in 1961–62. The group, which also included future author Rosemary

Daniell (b. 1935), often met in Guy's residence, each paying Dickey five dollars and all the beer he could drink to read and talk about their poetry. See Daniell, *Fatal Flowers* (New York: Holt, 1980), 162–63, and Hart, 269–71. Dickey had a similar experience at San Fernando Valley State College with Helen Sorrells (b. 1908). See *Crux,* 345.

The title of the poem is similar to "A Beginning Poet, Aged Sixty-Five," but according to Dickey, "I don't even have a copy of the one that was published in the *Quarterly Review.* I don't remember what it was like. . . . there are two completely different approaches and ways of talking about the same guy and the same situation. . . . I know that one was collected when Richard Wilbur was my editor and told me to do the one that I did rather than the other one, so I did that one" (Arnett, 296–97; Baughman, 80).

VARIANTS:

2: listening, (TS, *Drowning, Early Motion, Whole Motion*) | listening (*Atlantic*)

23: More (TS, *Drowning, Early Motion, Whole Motion*) | More, (*Atlantic*)

The Underground Stream

FIRST PUBLICATION: *New Yorker* 36 (May 21, 1960): 42.

COLLECTED: *Into the Stone,* 43–44; *Poems 57–67,* 19–20; *Whole Motion,* 50–51.

REPRINTED: *Intervisions,* 40–43; *New Oxford Book of Modern Verse,* 855–56; *Poems of Our Moment,* 56–57.

NOTES: In 1960 Dickey was translating André Frénaud's "Les Paysans" (see "Farmers") and may have gotten the title for "The Underground Stream" from line 15 of his translation. On the Murngin influence of communing with the dead at a body of water, see notes to "The Game." On "no one being able to create (the image of) his own brother" see *Self,* 190.

27: first love: possibly a reference to Dickey's high-school sweetheart, Daisy Eastman, who committed suicide before she was thirty, according to Dickey, "by eating lawn fertilizer" (Hart, 42). There may also be a reminiscence of his high-school friend Mary Ann Robinson, whose suicide was the event recalled in "The Leap."

28: Thomas Campion (1567–1620), English composer of lyrics chiefly for the lute, as well as a poet and physician.

41: Dickey's brother Eugene died at the age of six, two years before James Dickey was born. "I have always felt a sense of guilt that my birth depended on my brother's death" (*Self,* 89). On his dead brother, see also "The String," "In the Tree House at Night," and "The Other" (*Striking,* 84). John Donne's "The Ecstasie," involves the spirits of two lovers, which have left their bodies, but in Dickey's poem the poet is isolated, not drawn into closer union with his beloved. This is one of Dickey's few poems in rhymed couplets.

VARIANTS:

14: smiling, (*Into the Stone, Poems 57–67, Whole Motion*) | smiling (*New Yorker*)

17: mile (*Into the Stone, Poems 57–67, Whole Motion*) | mile, (*New Yorker*)

18: Of (*Into the Stone, Poems 57–67, Whole Motion*) | On (*New Yorker*)

22: world, (*Into the Stone, Poems 57–67, Whole Motion*) | world (*New Yorker*)

42: cadaver, (*Into the Stone, Poems 57–67, Whole Motion*) | cadaver (*New Yorker*)

43: grow, (*Into the Stone, Poems 57–67, Whole Motion*) | grow (*New Yorker*)

46: stone, (*Into the Stone, Poems 57–67, Whole Motion*) |stone— (*New Yorker*)

Walking on Water

FIRST PUBLICATION: *New Yorker* 36 (June 18, 1960): 44.

COLLECTED: *Into the Stone*, 77–78; *Poems 57–67*, 39–40; *Whole Motion*, 64–65.

REPRINTED: *American Religious Poems*, 371–72; *Best Poems of 1960*, 41–42; *Intervisions*, 11–15; *New Poets*, 206–7; *Poems*, 11–12; *Poetry Pilot: The Newsletter of the American Academy of Poets* (Spring 1997).

NOTES: This poem is "based on the fact that I once saw a little boy who seemed to be standing on the water of Hampton River, in south Georgia. If a little boy stands on a big enough plank, his weight will make it sink under the water just enough to be invisible. . . . He would seem to be like a junior Christ. And the shark would follow like a dog, a dangerous brute in a world he never bargained for" (*Self*, 96–97). For Jesus walking on water, see Matthew 14:25. For Dickey and sharks, see "The Shark's Parlor."

32: Felicia Dorothea Hemans (1793–1835) wrote "The Boy Stood on the Burning Deck," the story of the young boy Casabianca at the Battle of the Nile (1798).

VARIANTS:

1: it (TS, *Into the Stone, Poems 57–67, Whole Motion*) | it— (*New Yorker*)

2: it, (TS, *Into the Stone, Poems 57–67, Whole Motion*) | it— (*New Yorker*)

3: clam-shell (TS, *Into the Stone, Poems 57–67, Whole Motion*) | clamshell (*New Yorker*)

11: sliding: (TS, *Into the Stone, Poems 57–67, Whole Motion*) | sliding— (*New Yorker*)

16: footprint, (TS, *Into the Stone, Poems 57–67, Whole Motion*) | footprint (*New Yorker*)

18: water (TS, *Poems 57–67, Whole Motion*) | water, (*New Yorker, Into the Stone*)

20: marsh-birds (TS, *Into the Stone, Poems 57–67, Whole Motion*) | marsh birds (*New Yorker*)

26: land, (TS, *Into the Stone, Poems 57–67, Whole Motion*) | land (*New Yorker*)

27: toes (TS, *Into the Stone, Poems 57–67, Whole Motion*) | toes, (*New Yorker*)

33: ship-wrecked (TS, *Into the Stone, Poems 57–67, Whole Motion*) | shipwrecked (*New Yorker*)

35: numb (TS, *Into the Stone, Poems 57–67, Whole Motion*) | numb, (*New Yorker*)

37: long (TS, *Into the Stone, Poems 57–67, Whole Motion*) | long, (*New Yorker*)

39: heads, (TS, *Into the Stone, Poems 57–67, Whole Motion*) | heads (*New Yorker*)

44: spell (TS, *Into the Stone, Poems 57–67, Whole Motion*) | spell— (*New Yorker*)

46: amazed, (TS, *Into the Stone, Poems 57–67, Whole Motion*) | amazed— (*New Yorker*)

47: And, (TS, *Into the Stone, Poems 57–67, Whole Motion*) | And (*New Yorker*)

47: enthrallment (TS, *Into the Stone, Poems 57–67, Whole Motion*) | enthrallment, (*New Yorker*)

48: hammer-headed (TS, *Into the Stone, Poems 57–67, Whole Motion*) | hammerheaded (*New Yorker*)

Trees and Cattle

FIRST PUBLICATION: *New Yorker* 36 (July 16, 1960): 34.

COLLECTED: *Into the Stone*, 75–76; *Poems 57–67*, 37–38; *Whole Motion*, 63–64.
REPRINTED: *New Poets*, 209–10.

A Birth

FIRST PUBLICATION: *New Yorker* 36 (August 13, 1960): 30.
COLLECTED: *Drowning*, 21; *Poems 57–67*, 61; *Whole Motion*, 80.
REPRINTED: Facsimile of MS printed as broadside (Pittsburgh International Poetry Forum, 1973)—follows text of *Drowning*, *Poems 57–67*, and *Whole Motion*—reprinted in *The International Poetry Forum Collectors' Deskbook 1984* following [p. 40]; *Earth, Air, Fire, and Water*, 63; *Footfalls* (North Fulton High School) (Spring 1969): [1]; *New Oxford Book of Modern Verse*, 859; *New York Times Book Review*, March 27, 1966, 2.
NOTES: "'A Birth' is a short poem about continuity and also about the capacity of the imagination to alter the real world. A man who wants to write a poem about a horse imagines a horse in a field. This is the way many poems start, I suppose. But then at a certain point the horse is no longer subject to the poet's mental restrictions and just walks away and becomes real. The poet finds himself in a room with his mother and his child, in the middle of three generations. He sits there, not saying anything, and feels the nature of reality changing, because the horse that he imagined has now been added to the totality of living existence" (*Self*, 110). Set to music (as "The Birth") by the Australian composer Robert Constable (b. 1958) in fall 1983; performed April 15, 1984.
VARIANTS:
4: fence posts (*Drowning, Poems 57–67, Whole Motion*) | fence-posts (*New Yorker*)
6: greenness (*Drowning, Poems 57–67, Whole Motion*) | pasture (*New Yorker*)
7: pasture (*Drowning, Poems 57–67, Whole Motion*) | greenness (*New Yorker*)
9: of (*Drowning, Poems 57–67, Whole Motion*) | from (*New Yorker*)
11: child (*Drowning, Poems 57–67, Whole Motion*) | son (*New Yorker*)

Between Two Prisoners

FIRST PUBLICATION: *Yale Review* 50 (Autumn 1960): 86–88.
COLLECTED: *Drowning*, 43–44; *Poems 57–67*, 78–80; *Early Motion*, 35–37; *Whole Motion*, 94–95.
REPRINTED: *American Poetry*, 1014–16; *Best Poems of 1960*, 37–38; *Norton Anthology of Poetry*, 1151–52; *Poetry and Its Conventions*, 354–55; *Reading Poetry*, 143–44.
NOTES: Dickey read in the December 6, 1945, issue of *Stars and Stripes* about a Japanese soldier named Takeo Kawaii on trial for the war crime of beheading one of two American prisoners kept in a schoolhouse on Cebu Island in March 1945 (see Hart, 114). Dickey had the title (if not the poem) as early as 1952 (*Striking*, 195, 201). It was finally realized as a companion-piece to "The Performance," with Lally and Armstrong "kept in an old schoolhouse and tied up with wire. . . . It seems terribly cruel to bind someone with wire. But the main thing is that they were put into a schoolhouse and evidently sat in desks. . . . There would be an enormous importance to words, because they couldn't act. . . . [The guard] would be affected even though he didn't understand a word. He would know that something essentially human was passing back and forth between these two bound, doomed men in the classroom. I didn't want to show the guard as an inhumane

person, but one who was simply caught in this situation. And although he might have been profoundly affected by the prisonership of these two fliers in the schoolhouse, and even changed, even made a saint by it, it didn't matter to the war crimes people" (*Self*, 114–15). See also *Summer*, 52.

46–48: On December 7, 1945, *Stars and Stripes* reported the conviction of Gen. Tomoyiku Yamashita (1885–1946) under the headline "'Bataan Butcher' Must Hang." He was hanged on February 23, 1946, eleven months after Lally's execution.

47: For the phrase, see "A Folk Singer of the Thirties," 141.

VARIANTS:

4: schoolhouse (*Drowning, Poems 57–67, Early Motion, Whole Motion*) | school-house (TS, *Yale Review*)

4, 12: palm tree (*Drowning, Poems 57–67, Early Motion, Whole Motion*) | palm-tree (TS, *Yale Review*)

7: yellow (*Drowning, Early Motion, Whole Motion*) | tousled (*Poems 57–67*)

19: desk tops (*Drowning, Poems 57–67, Early Motion, Whole Motion*) | desk-tops (TS, *Yale Review*)

24: wing feathers (*Drowning, Poems 57–67, Early Motion, Whole Motion*) | wing-feathers (TS, *Yale Review*)

26: light (TS, *Drowning, Poems 57–67, Early Motion, Whole Motion*)| light, (*Yale Review*)

28: palm leaf (*Drowning, Poems 57–67, Early Motion, Whole Motion*) | palm-leaf (TS, *Yale Review*)

40: Heaven (*Drowning, Poems 57–67, Early Motion, Whole Motion*) | heaven (TS, *Yale Review*)

41: sunlit (TS, *Drowning, Poems 57–67, Early Motion, Whole Motion*)| sunlight (*Yale Review*)

43: bloodletting (*Drowning, Poems 57–67, Early Motion, Whole Motion*) | blood-letting (TS, *Yale Review*)

48: horse stall (*Drowning, Poems 57–67, Early Motion, Whole Motion*) | horse-stall (TS, *Yale Review*)

Drowning with Others

FIRST PUBLICATION: *Partisan Review* 27 (Fall 1960): 636–37.

COLLECTED: *Drowning,* 49–50; *Poems 57–67,* 85–86; *Early Motion,* 44–45; *Whole Motion,* 99–100.

REPRINTED: *Controversy of Poets,* 77–78; *Reading Poetry,* 339–40.

NOTES: "But the general idea is that when there are a group of people in the middle of the ocean after a shipwreck with no life boats or life jackets, one by one they're going to drown. . . . they're going to go under your feet, and you will see them spiraling down under the sea. It seems to me that the essential human act is for you to try to keep somebody else up, even though you're all going to die. . . . That constitutes to me a symbol of the essential humanity of all of us at our best: that we can try to help someone even though nothing can save either of us" (*Self,* 116–17). See also Van Ness, 23; Baughman, 254.

VARIANTS:

4: shoulder bones (*Drowning, Poems 57–67, Early Motion, Whole Motion*) | shoulderbones (TS, *Partisan Review*)

20: wingblades (*Drowning, Poems 57–67, Early Motion, Whole Motion*) | wing-blades (TS, *Partisan Review*)

23: fisherbird (*Drowning, Poems 57–67, Early Motion, Whole Motion*) | fisher-bird (TS, *Partisan Review*)

35: laid out (*Drowning, Poems 57–67, Early Motion, Whole Motion*) | laid-out (TS, *Partisan Review*)

Mindoro, 1944

FIRST PUBLICATION: *Paris Review* 22 (Autumn–Winter 1960): 122–23.

COLLECTED: *Into the Stone*, 63–4.

REPRINTED: *The Paris Review Anthology*, edited by George Plimpton (New York: Norton, 1990), 74–75.

NOTES: Dickey arrived at Mindoro, the seventh largest island in the Philippines, on February 6, 1945, and stayed until June 1945. A working title was "Poem from an Old War" (TS and *Crux*, 158).

3: San Jose, a city of more than ten thousand on the southwestern coast of the island, is Mindoro's main commercial and entertainment port.

VARIANTS:

1: Six boys have slung a coffin by the ropes [is line 1 in TS and *Into the Stone*, line 4 in *Paris Review*.]

5: they, (TS, *Into the Stone*) | they (*Paris Review*)

5: it, (TS, *Into the Stone*) | it (*Paris Review*)

16: eye is equal (TS, *Into the Stone*) | equal eye is (*Paris Review*)

17: wheels, (*Into the Stone*) | wheels (*Paris Review*, TS)

19: *Wheels fall* (*Into the Stone*) | *Wheel falls* (*Paris Review*, TS)

34: down (TS, *Into the Stone*) | hair (*Paris Review*)

Autumn

FIRST PUBLICATION: *New Yorker* 36 (October 29, 1960): 42.

COLLECTED: *Drowning*, 83; *Early Motion*, 80; *Whole Motion*, 124.

VARIANTS:

7: die, (TS, *Drowning, Early Motion, Whole Motion*) | die (*New Yorker*)

Listening to Foxhounds

FIRST PUBLICATION: *New Yorker* 36 (November 26, 1960): 48.

COLLECTED: *Drowning*, 13–14; *Poems 57–67*, 53–54; *Early Motion*, 6–7; *Whole Motion*, 75–76.

REPRINTED: *Best Poems of 1960*, 39–40; *Introduction to Poetry* (Simpson), 352–53; *Life* 61 (July 22, 1966): 70; *Poetry: Points of Departure*, 278–79; *Southern Writing in the Sixties*, 14–16; *Selected*, 29–30; *The Wind Is Round*, edited by Sara Hannum and John Terry Chase (New York: Atheneum, 1970), 78–79.

NOTES: "The kind of fox-hunting I'm talking about does not involve people chasing foxes around on horseback. I'm talking about the kind that's done in Appalachia. You set your dogs loose on the trail of the fox, then build a fire in the woods and sit around drinking whiskey and listening to the dogs run the fox" (*Self,* 105). As Christopher Dickey wrote, "It's in 'Listening to Foxhounds' that he tells the truth about those trips he took with *his* father to the woods, about the loner-child sitting by the campfire with the men and listening to the baying of the dogs, and becoming the fox" (*Summer,* 93).

VARIANTS:

11: marvelous (*Drowning, Poems 57–67, Early Motion, Whole Motion*) | marvellous (*New Yorker,* TS)

Antipolis

FIRST PUBLICATION: *Poetry* 97 (December 1960): 153–54.

COLLECTED: *Drowning,* 80–81; *Early Motion,* 77–78; *Whole Motion,* 122–23.

NOTES: This poem is not set in a Greek town as some commentators have suggested. Antipolis is the Greek name of the small town on the southern French coast known today as Antibes, where the Dickeys lived from October 1954 to January 1955. The town is known for its market (line 2) and seafood (line 4). Its Port Vaubon, the heart of the ancient Greek Antipolis, is today the largest marina in Europe (lines 10–11). Dickey did not visit Greece on either of his European stays in 1954–55 and 1961–62.

20: Christopher Dickey had turned three in late 1954 and was not reading English, much less Homeric Greek.

34: A two-drachma coin from Metapontum in southern Italy from 340 B.C.E., was widely reproduced for tourists and collectors as depicting a head of Pericles (it is actually Leucippus). The Greek twenty-drachma coin with the head of Pericles on the obverse did not appear until 1976.

VARIANTS:

2: market place (*Drowning, Early Motion, Whole Motion*) | market-place (*Poetry,* TS)

21: answers; (*Poetry,* TS, *Drowning, Early Motion*) | answers: (*Whole Motion* ⌊typo⌋)

A View of Fujiyama after the War

FIRST PUBLICATION: *Poetry* 97 (December 1960): 154–56.

COLLECTED: *Drowning,* 51–52; *Early Motion,* 46–47; *Whole Motion,* 100–101.

NOTES: Following the Japanese surrender on September 2, 1945, Dickey remained in Okinawa until January 10, 1946. He and his friend Herbert Vaughn spent a week in Fujiyama, beginning Christmas Day 1945 (Hart, 115–16).

5: On the third day of Dickey's visit, it snowed.

VARIANTS:

11: cherry tree (*Drowning, Early Motion, Whole Motion*) | cherry-tree (*Poetry,* TS)

22: Heaven (TS, *Drowning, Early Motion, Whole Motion*) | heaven (*Poetry*)

33: wellspring (*Drowning, Early Motion, Whole Motion*) | well-spring (*Poetry,* TS)

Inside the River

First Publication: *Poetry* 97 (December 1960): 156–57.

Collected: *Drowning,* 91–92; *Poems 57–67,* 105–6; *Early Motion,* 88–89; *Whole Motion,* 128–29.

Reprinted: *Gathered Waters,* 38–39; Poetry *Anthology,* 372–73; *Poetry Southeast 1950–70,* 57–58; *Southern Album,* [125]; *Sports Poems,* 93–94.

Notes: This poem dates from Dickey's first canoe trips with his friends Lewis King and Al Braselton (dedicatees of *Deliverance*) in 1960–61. On Braselton, see "Drifting." The "red" Chattahoochee River—which rises from Chattahoochee Spring in the Blue Ridge Mountains of northeast Georgia—runs southwest toward Atlanta and its suburbs and then moves west to form the southern half of the Georgia/Alabama border, a total of 435 miles. Next the Chattahoochee joins the Flint River in Lake Seminole on the Florida border to form the Apalachicola River, which runs due south through the Florida panhandle. The Chattahoochee is partly a model for the river Dickey calls the "Cahulawassee" in *Deliverance,* which was filmed on the Chattooga River, a waterway Dickey never canoed. See John Lane, *Chattooga: Descending into the Myth of the Deliverance River* (Athens: University of Georgia Press, 2004). The opening image derives from Heraclitus's fragment 12: "Upon those who step into the same rivers different waters flow." See *Heraclitus: The Cosmic Fragments,* edited by G. S. Kirk (Cambridge: Cambridge University Press, 1954), 367–80. See also "The Rain Guitar," line 2, and, on the pre-Socratics, see *Sorties,* 32. For "red" river water, see "Root-Light."

The Magus

First Publication: *New Yorker* 36 (December 24, 1960): 30.

Collected: *Drowning,* 79; *Poems 57–67,* 102; *Early Motion,* 75–76; *Whole Motion,* 121.

Reprinted: *Formalist* 3, no. 1 (1992): 51–52; *The Gospels in Our Image: An Anthology of Twentieth Century Poetry Based on Biblical Texts,* edited by David Curzon (New York: Harcourt, Brace, 1995), 41; *Christmas at* The New Yorker, edited by *New Yorker* editors (New York: Modern Library, 2003) 281–82.

Notes: The story of the Magi is told in Matthew 2:1–13. Though the Gospel mentions three gifts, it does not specify the number of Magi. For "Annunciation" and "Virgin and Child," see *God's Images,* 60, 62.

8: For the "twelve-barred bed," see "A Child's Room," line 1.

—1961–1967—

Armor

First Publication: *Hudson Review* 14 (Winter 1961–62): 557–58.

Collected: *Drowning,* 45–46; *Poems 57–67,* 81–82; *Early Motion,* 38–40; *Whole Motion,* 96–97.

Reprinted: *Best Poems of 1962,* 43–44; *Contemporary American Poets,* 66–67.

Note:

37: See "The String."

The Change

FIRST PUBLICATION: *Kenyon Review* 23 (Winter 1961): 71.
COLLECTED: *Drowning*, 82; *Early Motion*, 79; *Whole Motion*, 123.
NOTE: For Dickey and sharks, see "The Shark's Parlor."
VARIANTS:

1: dreaming, (*Kenyon*, TS, *Drowning*, *Early Motion*) | dreaming. (*Whole Motion* [typo])
19: in (TS, *Drowning*, *Early Motion*, *Whole Motion*) | through (*Kenyon*)

Hunting Civil War Relics at Nimblewill Creek

FIRST PUBLICATION: *Sewanee Review* 69 (Winter 1961): 139–41.
COLLECTED: *Drowning*, 72–73; *Poems 57–67*, 98–99; *Early Motion*, 68–70; *Whole Motion*, 116–17.
REPRINTED: *American Literature*, 3684–86; *Contemporary American Poetry* (Hall), 78–80; *Lirică Americană Contemporană*, 104–6; *Many Worlds of Poetry*, 123–24; *Old Glory*, 92–94; *Selected*, 35–37; *Southern Partisan* 6 (Spring 1986): [27]; *Wesleyan Tradition*, 55–57.
NOTES: There was no Civil War activity at Nimblewill Creek in Lumpkin County in northern Georgia, near Dahlonega in the Blue Ridge Mountains. As boys, Jim and Tom ("The Sprinter at Forty") would accompany their father to the family's farm on Nickajack Creek in Cobb County, Georgia, where Gen. Joseph E. Johnston set up a line of defense for Atlanta on July 3, 1864, before skirmishes on July 4 and 5 (see "The Gamecocks" and "May Day Sermon," line 42). The boys easily found minié balls and belt buckles, which they proudly showed to their father at the end of each day. Using a World War II army mine detector, Tom searched Civil War battlefields throughout the 1950s and early 1960s, ultimately acquiring more than ten tons of artillery, which he stored in his or his parents' home (see Hart, 18–19). With his fellow collector, Sydney C. Kerksis, Tom Dickey wrote *Field Artillery Projectiles of the Civil War, 1861–1865* (Atlanta: Phoenix Press, 1968) and *Heavy Artillery Projectiles of the Civil War, 1861–1865* (Kennesaw, Ga.: Phoenix Press, 1972), and with Peter C. George, *Field Artillery Projectiles of the American Civil War* (Atlanta: Arsenal Press, 1980). On Tom Dickey's methods for seeking Civil War ordnance, see *Time* (March 24, 1967): 53, and *Atlanta Journal and Constitution*, October 6, 1967, 1–2. In 1974 his nephew Christopher ("A Child in Armor"), while a film student at Boston University, made a movie called *War under the Pinestraw* with David Goldenberg about his uncle and his hobby. The Thomas Swift Dickey Civil War Ordnance Collection is at the Atlanta History Center. On Tom and the Civil War, see "Last Hours."
VARIANTS:

1: mine detector (*Drowning*, *Poems 57–67*, *Early Motion*, *Whole Motion*) | mine-detector (TS, *Sewanee Review*)
21: battle lines (*Drowning*, *Poems 57–67*, *Early Motion*, *Whole Motion*) | battlelines (TS, *Sewanee Review*)
36–37: [stanza break] (*Sewanee Review*, *Poems 57–67*, *Early Motion*, *Whole Motion*) | [no stanza break] (*Drowning*)
64: mess tin (*Drowning*, *Poems 57–67*, *Early Motion*, *Whole Motion*) | mess-tin (TS, *Sewanee Review*)

Via Appia

First Publication: *Chicago Choice* 1 (Spring 1961): 50–51.

Collected: *Whole Motion*, 24–25.

Note: This poem about the ancient highway from Rome to Brindisi may have arisen from the Dickey family's three-week stay in Rome (with many side trips; see "In the Lupanar at Pompeii") in late April and early May 1955.

Variants:

23: rise (*Chicago Choice*) | arise (*Whole Motion*)

39: I almost hear . . . / I hear you. (*Chicago Choice*) | I still can make you. I am coming. (*Whole Motion*)

The Twin Falls

First Publication: *Chicago Choice* 1 (Spring 1961): 52.

Collected: *Drowning*, 74; *Early Motion*, 71; *Whole Motion*, 118.

Reprinted: *New Southern Poets*, 30–31; *Beach Glass*, 117.

Notes: Dickey may be describing the Anna Ruby Falls, twin falls of the York and Curtis Creeks in the Chattahoochee National Forest in Georgia.

The Summons

First Publication: *Virginia Quarterly Review* 37 (Spring 1961): 222–23.

Collected: *Drowning*, 24–25; *Poems 57–67*, 64–65; *Early Motion*, 17–18; *Whole Motion*, 81–82.

Reprinted: *Best Poems of 1961*, 45–46; *Poems from* The Virginia Quarterly Review, 91–92.

Variants:

1: sight, (*Virginia Quarterly, Drowning, Poems 57–67, Early Motion*) | sight (*Whole Motion* [typo])

2: grass-blade (*Drowning, Poems 57–67, Early Motion, Whole Motion*) | grassblade (*Virginia Quarterly*)

Fog Envelops the Animals

First Publication: *Virginia Quarterly Review* 37 (Spring 1961): 224–25.

Collected: *Drowning*, 22–23; *Poems 57–67*, 62–63; *Early Motion*, 15–16; *Whole Motion*, 80–81.

Reprinted: *Poems from* The Virginia Quarterly Review, 93–94.

Notes: Discussed in *Self*, 111; compare *Deliverance*, 83–84.

35: For another ending composed of one-word sentences, see "The Aura," and for another three-sentence, three-word final line, see "Uncle."

Variants:

9: tree trunks (*Drowning, Poems 57–67, Early Motion, Whole Motion*) | tree-trunks (*Virginia Quarterly*)

29: oak trees (*Drowning, Poems 57–67, Early Motion, Whole Motion*) | oak-trees (*Virginia Quarterly*)

31: snowflakes (*Drowning, Poems 57–67, Early Motion, Whole Motion*) | snow-flakes (*Virginia Quarterly*)

Facing Africa

First Publication: *Encounter* 16 (April 1961): 41.
Collected: *Drowning*, 89–90; *Poems 57–67*, 103–4; *Early Motion*, 86–87; *Whole Motion*, 127–28.
Reprinted: *Encounters*, 551–52.
Variants:
7: harbor (TS, *Drowning, Poems 57–67, Early Motion, Whole Motion*) | harbour (*Encounter*)
25: Into (TS, *Drowning, Poems 57–67, Early Motion, Whole Motion*) | In (*Encounter*)
35: rumor (TS, *Drowning, Poems 57–67, Early Motion, Whole Motion*) | rumour (*Encounter*)

In the Tree House at Night

First Publication: *New Yorker* 37 (June 24, 1961): 30.
Collected: *Drowning*, 26–27; *Poems 57–67*, 66–67; *Early Motion*, 19–20; *Whole Motion*, 82–84.
Reprinted: *Achievement*, 29–30; *Brother Songs*, 65–66; *Faber Book of Modern Verse*, 373–75; *Norton Anthology of Poetry*, 1150–51; *Poetry: An Introductory Anthology*, 342–43; *Selected*, 33–34; *Today's Poets*, 290–92; *Total Experience of Poetry*, 130–32.
Notes: This poem is "another way of getting at the continuity that exists in families by the passing of some kind of skill or enterprise from one member of the family to another. . . . [The middle brother] doesn't know whether his dead brother is actually present or not, but he feels that if he isn't present then, he's not likely to be present under any other conditions: he *has* to be there, with them, in their *place*" (*Self*, 111–12). Dickey's childhood friend Albert Roper built tree houses in the highest parts of trees, a challenge for young Dickey to climb (see Hart, 30–31).
13: On Eugene Dickey, Jr., see "The String" and "The Underground Stream," line 41.
41–42: Rilke, "Sonnets to Orpheus," 2:27. 7–8: "Is childhood, which is so deep, so full of promise, / Later stilled at its root?"
56: This line is the epitaph on Dickey's grave (along with the eye from the front cover of the first edition of *Deliverance*) at the All Saints Waccamaw Church, near Litchfield, South Carolina.
Variants:
4: dead, (TS, *Drowning, Poems 57–67, Early Motion, Whole Motion*) | dead (*New Yorker*)
13: I, (TS, *Drowning, Poems 57–67, Early Motion, Whole Motion*) | I— (*New Yorker*)
20: branches (TS, *Drowning, Poems 57–67, Early Motion, Whole Motion*) | branches, (*New Yorker*)
28: limbs, (TS, *Drowning, Poems 57–67, Early Motion, Whole Motion*) | limbs (*New Yorker*)
29: ascend, (TS, *Drowning, Poems 57–67, Early Motion, Whole Motion*) | ascend (*New Yorker*)
41: springs, (TS, *Drowning, Poems 57–67, Early Motion, Whole Motion*) | springs (*New Yorker*)

The Lifeguard

First Publication: *New Yorker* 37 (August 5, 1961): 24.
Collected: *Drowning*, 11–12; *Poems 57–67*, 51–52; *Early Motion*, 3–5; *Whole Motion*, 73–74.

REPRINTED: *Achievement,* 27–29; *American Literature,* 3683–84; *American Sports Poems,* 93; *American Tradition in Literature,* 1710–12; *Anthology,* 1748–49; *Aperture* 111 (1988): 42; *Best Poems of 1961,* 43–44; *Controversy of Poets,* 69–70; *Cosmos Club Poets,* 29–30; *Decade,* 61–63; *Distinctive Voice,* 228–29; *Georgia Voices,* 81–83; *Getting into Poetry,* 328–30; *Literature V,* general editor Albert R. Kitzhaber (New York: Holt, Rinehart, Winston, 1970), 651–62; *New York Times Book Review,* March 27, 1966, 2; *New Yorker Book of Poems,* 386–87; *Norton Anthology of Poetry,* 1149–50; *Now Voices,* 47–49; *One Hundred American Poems,* 277–79; *Poetry: A Closer Look,* 86–88; *Possibilities of Poetry,* 308–10; *Selected,* 31–32; *Shenandoah* 52 (Summer 2002): 27–92; *Self,* 103–5; *Sounds and Silences,* 88–90 (rev. ed., 80–82); *Total Experience of Poetry,* 132–34.

NOTES: "I was at a lake, near Atlanta, where a guy drowned, and they elicited all the people who were swimming to go down and help try to find the guy. I was one of them. I went down in the sightless darkness of the water and felt around, hoping I would not grab him or him grab me. I didn't find him. Nobody found him that day. But I remember the feeling of going down under there, trying to find something or someone, was eerie, terrifying" (Greiner, 8; see also *Self,* 101–3; *Babel,* 287–89). "Dickey often posed as a lifeguard, telling friends that during high school he had worked at Atlanta's Venetian swimming pool" (Hart, 285). Dickey actually claimed to have done so after his World War II service during the summer vacations from Vanderbilt: "[Actor] Dick Van Dyke [b. 1925] used to come out there—whom I never liked, . . . Harry Johnson [b. 1924], Mr. America, used to come out there" (Boleman-Herring, 15). Dickey spent summer vacations reading at the Brookwood Hills Community Club swimming pool in Buckhead from its founding in 1939. Located on East Wesley, it was an easy walk from his home at 166 West Wesley.

37–38: Dickey called these lines an example of his notion of "magical conjunction": "A moonlit lake would appear like a disappeared snowfield." See *NYQ* interview, 27; *Night,* 304.

59–60: Compare "The Night Pool," 15–17.

60: For another three-word repetition at the end of a poem, see "Uncle" and "Snow on a Southern State."

VARIANTS:

31: them (*Drowning, Poems 57–67, Early Motion, Whole Motion*) | them, (*New Yorker*)
38: snowfield (TS, *Drowning, Poems 57–67, Early Motion, Whole Motion*)| snow field (*New Yorker*)
53: ground (TS, *Drowning, Poems 57–67, Early Motion, Whole Motion*) | ground that (*New Yorker*)
56: grave (TS, *Drowning, Poems 57–67, Early Motion, Whole Motion*) | grave, (*New Yorker*)

The Salt Marsh

FIRST PUBLICATION: *New Yorker* 37 (September 16, 1961): 46.

COLLECTED: *Drowning,* 93–94; *Poems 57–67,* 107–8; *Early Motion,* 90–91; *Whole Motion,* 130–31.

REPRINTED: *Life* 61 (July 22, 1966): 70; *New Consciousness,* 519–20; *Poems,* 15–16; *Tricentennial Anthology,* 570–71.

NOTES: "If you go into a marsh, there's no possible way to know what your direction is, especially at noon. . . . When the wind begins to blow, though, all the [saw]grass leans to one side in an enormous whispering movement. . . . I tried to contrast these two feelings" (*Self,* 118–19).

VARIANTS:

6: sawgrass (*Drowning, Poems 57–67, Early Motion, Whole Motion*) | saw-grass (*New Yorker,* TS)

6: sawing, (*Drowning, Poems 57–67, Early Motion, Whole Motion*) | sawing (*New Yorker*)

17: touch (TS, *Drowning, Poems 57–67, Early Motion, Whole Motion*) | touch, (*New Yorker*)

28: sink, (TS, *Drowning, Poems 57–67, Early Motion, Whole Motion*) | sink (*New Yorker*)

39: swaying, (TS, *Drowning, Poems 57–67, Early Motion, Whole Motion*) | swaying (*New Yorker*)

46: marvelous (*Drowning, Poems 57–67, Early Motion, Whole Motion*) | marvellous (*New Yorker*, TS)

In the Lupanar at Pompeii

FIRST PUBLICATION: *Kenyon Review* 23 (Autumn 1961): 631–33.

COLLECTED: *Drowning*, 47–48; *Poems 57–67*, 83–84; *Early Motion*, 41–43; *Whole Motion*, 97–99.

REPRINTED: *Today's Poets*, 292–94.

NOTES: Dickey and his family visited Pompeii in May of 1955 (see *Self*, 115–16). There are now thought to have been about ten lupanars, or brothels, in Pompeii at the time Mount Vesuvius erupted and destroyed the city in 79 C.E. Dickey describes the largest, an establishment with ten bedrooms (five per floor), a bathroom, and a balcony, two blocks east of the forum at the intersection of Vico del Lupanare and Vico del Balcone Pensile. Archaeologists identify brothels by their obscene graffiti and erotic frescoes (though the latter are not exclusive to brothels).

10–11: There are several depictions of dogs at Pompeii, the best-known (rather like a painting described by Petronius in *Satyricon* 29) is at the "House of the Tragic Poet" and bears the warning "Cave canem" (Beware the Dog).

30–31: The eruption of Mount Vesuvius on August 24–25, 79 C.E., lasted for nineteen hours and destroyed the towns of Pompeii, Oplontis, and Herculaneum at the mountain's base.

43–44: Pliny the Younger witnessed the eruption (which killed his uncle, Pliny the Elder) and recounted it in a letter to the historian Tacitus, describing how the initial cone rose from the volcano's mouth as "more or less filled with earth and ash" (*Letters*, 6.16).

VARIANTS:

20: badly drawn (*Drowning, Poems 57–67, Early Motion, Whole Motion*) | badly-drawn (*Kenyon*)

35: stone-cutting (*Drowning, Poems 57–67, Early Motion, Whole Motion*) | stonecutting (*Kenyon*)

59: women (*Drowning, Poems 57–67, Early Motion, Whole Motion*) | woman (*Kenyon*)

The Movement of Fish

FIRST PUBLICATION: *New Yorker* 37 (October 7, 1961): 58.

COLLECTED: *Drowning*, 17–18; *Poems 57–67*, 57–58; *Early Motion*, 10–11; *Whole Motion*, 77–78.

REPRINTED: *New Consciousness*, 517–18; *New Yorker Book of Poems*, 451; *Voice That Is Great*, 491–92.

NOTES: On activity underwater, see "Winter Trout," and "The Driver."

44: "continue to work out your salvation with fear and trembling" (Philippians 2:1; see also 2 Corinthians 7:15, Ephesians 6:5). Søren Kierkegaard's *Fear and Trembling* (1843) presents an existential view of Abraham's response to God's order to kill his son Isaac.

VARIANTS:

22: sun (TS, *Drowning, Poems 57–67, Early Motion, Whole Motion*) | sun, (*New Yorker*)

In the Mountain Tent

FIRST PUBLICATION: *New Yorker* 37 (October 28, 1961): 54.

COLLECTED: *Drowning*, 95–96; *Poems 57–67*, 109–10; *Early Motion*, 92–93; *Whole Motion*, 131–32

REPRINTED: *Contemporary American Poetry* (Poulin), 65–66; *Decade*, 68–69; *Distinctive Voice*, 230; *Enduring Voice*, 385; *Georgia Voices*, 83–84; *Made Thing*, 75–76; *The Poem*, 487; *Poems*, 17–18; *Themes in American Literature*, 391–92; *Wesleyan Tradition*, 57–58.

NOTES: As the man drifts to sleep in his tent, "He knows that the only creatures around him are animals. As he's lying there, he begins to dream of his own death. I don't know whether he's a Christian or not, but being a product of Western culture, he's influenced by Christian doctrines and the belief in the Resurrection. And so he feels both a great kinship with the animals on the mountainside with him in the rain and a fundamental difference from them, because he realizes that he may rise from the dead and they'll only die" (*Self*, 120). For the man-beast revealing the nature of the human soul, compare "To His Children in Darkness"; for solitude, see "The Salt Marsh"; for the resurrection, see "To Be Edward Thomas," lines 105–6, and "The Heaven of Animals," with which "In the Mountain tent" may be contrasted.

VARIANTS:

19: midnight (TS, *Drowning, Poems 57–67, Early Motion, Whole Motion*) | midnight, (*New Yorker*)

24: wait (TS, *Drowning, Poems 57–67, Early Motion, Whole Motion*) | wait, (*New Yorker*)

25: half-smiling (TS, *Drowning, Poems 57–67, Early Motion, Whole Motion*) | half smiling (*New Yorker*)

29: ill-fitting, (TS, *Drowning, Poems 57–67, Early Motion, Whole Motion*) ill-fitting (*New Yorker*)

The Heaven of Animals

FIRST PUBLICATION: *New Yorker* 37 (November 18, 1961): 48.

COLLECTED: *Drowning*, 19–20; *Poems 57–67*, 59–60; *Early Motion*, 12–13; *Whole Motion*, 78–79.

REPRINTED: *Achievement*, 14–16; *American Poetry*, 1013–14; *Appreciating Poetry*, 255–56; *Columbia Anthology*, 585–86; *Contemporary American Poetry* (Poulin), 72–73; *Contemporary American Poets*, 64–65; *Contemporary Poetry in America*, 74–75; *Contemporary Southern Poetry*, 76–77; *Cosmos Club Poets*, 27–28; *Decade*, 64–66; *Faber Book of Modern Verse*, 372–73; *Forgotten Language*, 40; *Giant Book of Poetry*, 467–68; *Heath Introduction to Poetry*, 398–99; *Life* 61 (July 22, 1966): 70; *Made Thing*, 72–73; *Modern Age*, 658–59; *Modern American Poetry*, 691–92; *New Coasts and Strange Harbors*, 229–30; *New Consciousness*, 518–19; *New Oxford Book of Modern Verse*, 398–99; *Norton Anthology of Modern Poetry*, 1031–32; *Self*, 108–9; *Selected*, 31–32; *Themes in American Literature*, 88–89; *Things Appalachian*, 173–74; *Today's Poets*, 289–90; *Treasury of American Poetry*, 633–34; *Twentieth Century Poetry* (Marshall), 66–67; *Vintage*, 155–56; *Visions of America*, 42–43; *Workshop*, 200–201.

NOTES: "This poem . . . comes from a Walt Disney movie that I saw called *African Lion* [1955]. . . where they show a leopard fall from a tree onto the back of a wildebeest calf and drag it down and eat it—tears him to pieces. . . . St. Thomas Aquinas says animals have no souls, and therefore they're perishable, not like us wonderful human beings. But this always seemed grossly unfair to me. So, if you're a poet you try to imagine a heaven of animals. But it wouldn't really be a heaven if the animal were deprived of its nature. I mean the killer must still be able to kill, and the hunted should still be hunted" (Heyen, 143; *Night*, 284; discussed in *Self*, 106–8). Aquinas says in *Summa Theologiae* (1a, question 75, article 3 reply), "since souls of brute animals have no activity which is intrinsically of soul alone, they do not subsist." And (in 1a, 75, 6 reply): "brute souls pass away when the body does, while the human soul can not corrupt unless *per se*, that is, from within itself" (St. Thomas Aquinas, *Summa Theologiae*, translated by Timothy Suttor [Cambridge: Black-friars, 1964] 11:17, 29). The poem also bears affinity with Emerson's "Brahma," lines 1–4: "If the red slayer think he slays, / Or if the slain think he is slain, / They know not well the subtle ways / I keep, and pass, and turn again." On the resurrection theme see "To Be Edward Thomas," lines 105–6, and "In the Mountain Tent."

40–41: For the opposite action but similar asyndeton, see Isaiah 43.17: "Which bringeth forth the chariot and horse, the army and the power; they shall lie down together, they shall not rise: they are extinct, they are quenched as tow."

VARIANTS:

7: come, (*Drowning, Poems 57–67, Early Motion, Whole Motion*) | come (*New Yorker*)

9: bloom (*Drowning, Poems 57–67, Early Motion, Whole Motion*) | bloom, (*New Yorker*)

21: claws and teeth (*Drowning, Poems 57–67, Early Motion, Whole Motion*) | teeth and claws (*New Yorker*)

For the Nightly Ascent of the Hunter Orion over a Forest Clearing

FIRST PUBLICATION: *New Yorker* 37 (December 2, 1961): 58.
COLLECTED: *Drowning*, 28–29; *Poems 57–67*, 68–69; *Early Motion*, 21–22; *Whole Motion*, 84–85.
REPRINTED: *Twentieth Century Poetry* (Brinnin and Read), 88–90.
NOTES:

21–30: Dickey seems to have used Ovid's account of Orion (*Fasti* 5.493–544), in which the boy, miraculously conceived in the earth by Jupiter to be the son of a lowly farmer, grew to be handsome and powerful, boasting of his intention to clear the earth of beasts: "There is no wild animal I cannot slay." When Mother Earth sent a scorpion to attack Latona, Orion was killed by it, and the goddess set him in heaven as a constellation. As Homer says, his constellation is marked by a girdle, a lion skin, a sword, and a club (*Iliad* 28.486, 22.29) and is watched by the Bear (*Odyssey* 5.274). Orion is the brightest of the constellations, and his belt contains the star Alnilam. See "The Firebombing," lines 106–8; "The Zodiac," lines 75, 332–53; and "The Eagle's Mile," line 15.

24: An alternative version is that Orion tried to rape Artemis, who set the scorpion upon him. Both became constellations, with Orion always appearing to flee from the Scorpion (Horace, *Odes* 3.4.72).

28: Having fallen in love with Merope, the daughter of the king of the island Chios, Orion slew every animal on the island and presented them to Merope, but her father opposed the marriage. After Orion attempted to rape Merope, her father blinded the drunken Orion. Orion was given a young boy as a guide, who told him to turn his gaze to the rising sun. He walked east on water until his sight was restored.

32–33: On "the light / Of himself," see "The Owl King," lines 44, 61–62.
VARIANTS:
31: Who (TS, *Drowning, Poems 57–67, Early Motion, Whole Motion*) | Who, (*New Yorker*)

Under Oaks

FIRST PUBLICATION: *New York Times,* January 1, 1962, 22.
REPRINTED: *New York Times Book of Verse,* 122.

Adam in Winter

FIRST PUBLICATION: *Choice* 2 (1962): 14–15.
COLLECTED: *Whole Motion,* 17–19.
REPRINTED: *American Religious Poems,* 369–71.
NOTE: For an imaginative retelling of biblical stories, see "The Magus" and *God's Images.*
VARIANTS:
6: That (*Choice*) | The (*Whole Motion* [typo])

The Hospital Window

FIRST PUBLICATION: *Poetry* 99 (January 1962): 236–37.
COLLECTED: *Drowning,* 75–76; *Poems 57–67,* 100–101; *Early Motion,* 72–73; *Whole Motion,* 118–20.
REPRINTED: *Achievement,* 31–32; *American Literature,* 3683–84; *Beginnings in Poetry,* 165–66; *Controversy of Poets,* 78–80; *Decade,* 66–68; *Divided Light,* 94; *Harvard,* 132–33; *Heath Introduction to Poetry,* 399–401; *Made Thing,* 73–75; *Many Worlds of Poetry,* 59; *Possibilities of Poetry,* 311–12; *Vintage,* 156–58.
NOTES: "I think of [cancer] as the most dreadful thing to die of: a slow, wasting death. . . . [The son] takes renewed strength from the fact that he's his father's son and that he may himself have the qualities he imputes to his father, whether or not they really are there in either. I think illusion is a very great part of human existence; it enables you to bear up under the circumstances that you have to face" (*Self,* 117–18). For another poem on cancer, see "The First Morning of Cancer." For imaginative poems on the subject of his father's illness and death, see "Approaching Prayer," "Gamecock," and "Sled Burial, Dream Ceremony." Eugene Dickey, Sr. (1888–1974) died not of cancer, but of complications following a stroke, on January 12, 1974, in Piedmont Hospital, Atlanta, the same hospital where James Dickey was born. Dickey portrayed a father much like his own in his unpublished 1953 novel, "The Entrance to the Honeycomb," though he added a sadomasochistic streak to the fictional father's character. See "The Entrance to the Honeycomb," *Short Story* 1 (Spring 2007): 56–60.
10: For the glass-fronted hospital, see "The Escape."
VARIANTS:
[Changes from the text of *Poetry* at 21, 23, and 24 are restored by Dickey's hand in the TS of *Drowning.*]
21: Back, (TS, *Drowning, Poems 57–67, Early Motion, Whole Motion*) | Back (*Poetry*)

23: bright, erased (TS, *Drowning, Poems 57–67, Early Motion, Whole Motion*) | uprisen (*Poetry*)
24: there, (TS, *Drowning, Poems 57–67, Early Motion, Whole Motion*) | there (*Poetry*)
40: And (TS, *Drowning, Poems 57–67, Early Motion, Whole Motion*) | As (*Poetry*)

A Dog Sleeping on My Feet

FIRST PUBLICATION: *Poetry* 99 (January 1962): 238–39.
COLLECTED: *Drowning*, 15–16; *Poems 57–67*, 55–56; *Early Motion*, 8–9; *Whole Motion*, 76–77.
REPRINTED: *Decade*, 63–64; *Dog Music*, 64–65; *Many Worlds of Poetry*, 229; *Poems on Poetry*, 242–43; *Reading Poetry*, 340–41; *Southern Writing in the Sixties*, 13–14.
NOTES: Dickey discusses the composition of this poem as typical of his method of writing poems, novels, and screenplays in Greiner, 22–24.
VARIANTS:
1: resting place (*Drowning, Poems 57–67, Early Motion, Whole Motion*) | resting-place (TS, *Poetry*)
17: Marvelous (*Drowning, Poems 57–67, Early Motion, Whole Motion*) | Marvellous (TS, Poetry)
32–33: [no blank line] (*Poetry*, TS, *Drowning, Poems 57–67*) | [blank line inserted] (*Whole Motion* [typo])

After the Night Hunt

FIRST PUBLICATION: *Poetry* 99 (January 1962): 239–40.
REPRINTED: Poetry *Anthology*, 381–82.

The Gamecocks

FIRST PUBLICATION: *Poetry* 99 (January 1962): 240–42.
NOTES: Eugene Dickey, Sr., was passionately committed to fighting gamecocks. He kept a special farm for them off Nickajack Creek northwest of Atlanta (see "Hunting Civil War Relics at Nimblewill Creek"; "Approaching Prayer," line 17; and "May Day Sermon," line 42), but he also kept some at the Dickey residence at 166 West Wesley Road in Atlanta. According to the poet, "When I was no more than nine or ten years old, I went to my father and said, 'Dad, why are you doing this here chicken-fighting stuff when you could be providing for the family a little better some other way than gambling on your chickens?' He said, ''Cause, I tell you, it's *inspiring*. Every man that ever lived would like to have the *guts* those chickens have.'. . . All the chicken fights that I've seen—and it seems an awful gory business, but it seems to satisfy some kind of hidden instinct in people to watch this kind of thing go on. . . . you don't like to see a dog get torn up by another dog, but a chicken is just something you can't like. You don't care what happens to them" (Wayne Holmes, Joseph Costello, Mark Greenberg, and Randy McConnell, "James Dickey at Drury College," *James Dickey Newsletter* 5 (Fall 1988): 17; Baughman, 102). "I call 'em [gamecocks] chickens because my father had never heard the word 'cockfighting.' To him it was chicken-fighting" (Boleman-Herring, 14). See "False Youth: Winter," 19.
57: John 14:1, see "The Sheep Child," line 17.

The Owl King

FIRST PUBLICATION: "The Call," *Hudson Review* 12 (Winter 1959–60): 560; "The Owl King" ["The Owl King" & "The Blind Child's Story"], *Hudson Review* 14 (Winter 1961–62): 550–56.

COLLECTED: "The Call," *Into the Stone,* 42; thereafter the first part of "The Owl King" followed by "The Owl King" and "The Blind Child's Story" as "The Owl King" in *Drowning,* 32–40; *Poems 57–67,* 70–77; *Early Motion,* 25–34; *Whole Motion,* 86–93; published separately with illustrations by Ronald Keller (New York: Red Angel Press, 1977).

REPRINTED: "The Call," *New Poets,* 208; "The Owl King" (3 parts), *Controversy of Poets,* 70–77.

NOTES: "The Call": "The way you would call a blind son back from the woods probably would not be quite the way you would call a son who could see. It might be some kind of song that the father himself would become enamored of, not knowing he could make such a sound" (*Self,* 112). As birds of prey that keep nocturnal habits and live in nests unseen, owls were ominous in many cultures, particularly among the Romans who feared the owl-like *strix.* In *Hercules Furens,* Seneca placed these creatures at the margins of Tartarus.

3, 22: In his discussion of "The Owl King" in *Self,* 112, Dickey claimed that the title arose from a phrase of the French poet Loys Masson (1915–1970): "Le Roi des hiboux." In fact the first line of Masson's "Chanson d'Automne," is "J'entends chanter le roi des chats-huants" ("I hear the king of the wood-owls singing"). Dickey's library included Masson's *Les Vignes de Septembre* (Paris: Seghers, 1955), in which the poem appears on p. 73. Of the third part of Dickey's poem, he said: "The title . . . is a conscious parody on the kind of thing that Hollywood does all the time, *The Rocky Graziano Story* [*Somebody Up There Likes Me* (1956)] or *The Ernie Pyle Story* [*The Story of G.I. Joe* (1945)]; I took the convention and used it" (*Self,* 113). "The Blind Child's Story" has some affinity with Theodore Roethke's "The Lost Son" but differs in the need for a mentor; Roethke relied on the self for learning. "This is the Owl King, no ordinary owl; he's the quintessential owl, the immortal owl; the only thing he fears is the sun. Maybe I can make him a kind of Nietzschean owl who has taught himself to see by a long and extremely intense act of the will, so that he wakes up one evening in the woods and can see in the dark. . . . Whether or not the child really sees as a result of his encounter with the Owl King, or whether the owl is only a fantasy on the part of the child or the father or both of them, I would just as soon leave up to the reader" (*Self,* 113–14). On blindness, see "Reading Genesis to a Blind Child," "Why in London the Blind Are Saviors," "The Eye-Beaters," *Striking* (209), the headnote to "Cahill Is Blind" (*Esquire* 85 [February 1976]: 67), and *Alnilam.*

75–76: On touching the talon, see *Deliverance,* 87–89.

236: "The King of the Wood" is the first chapter of J. G. Frazer's *The Golden Bough* (1890); see "The Vegetable King."

VARIANTS:

48: outspread (TS, *Drowning, Poems 57–67, Early Motion, Whole Motion* | spread out (*Hudson*)

151: newborn (*Drowning, Poems 57–67, Early Motion, Whole Motion*) | new-born (*Hudson,* TS)

175: the same (TS, *Drowning, Poems 57–67, Early Motion, Whole Motion*) | it (*Hudson*)

The Rib

FIRST PUBLICATION: *Drowning,* 30–31 (*Drowning* published February 15, 1962).
COLLECTED: *Early Motion,* 23–24; *Whole Motion,* 85–86.
NOTES: Compare "Adam in Winter" and "The Magus."
1: "The Summons" also begins with the mysterious "Something" (lines 1 and 28).
33: See "The Other."

To His Children in Darkness

FIRST PUBLICATION: *Drowning,* 64–65.
COLLECTED: *Poems 57–67,* 94–95; *Early Motion,* 59–61; *Whole Motion,* 110–11.
NOTES: In 1962 Christopher was eleven, and Kevin was four.

A Screened Porch in the Country

FIRST PUBLICATION: *Drowning,* 66–67.
COLLECTED: *Poems 57–67,* 96–97; *Early Motion,* 62–63; *Whole Motion,* 112–13.
REPRINTED: *Wesleyan Tradition,* 54–55; *Shenandoah* 52 (Winter 2002): 36–37.
VARIANTS:
6: They (TS, *Drowning, Poems 57–67, Early Motion*) | The (*Whole Motion* [typo])

The Dream Flood

FIRST PUBLICATION: *Drowning,* 68–69.
COLLECTED: *Early Motion,* 64–65; *Whole Motion,* 113–14.

Snow on a Southern State

FIRST PUBLICATION: *Drowning,* 84–86.
COLLECTED: *Early Motion,* 81–83; *Whole Motion,* 124–26.
NOTE: For another triple repetition at the end of a poem, see "The Lifeguard" and "Uncle."
VARIANTS:
26: stares (TS, *Drowning, Early Motion*) | stars (*Whole Motion* [typo])

Fence Wire

FIRST PUBLICATION: *New Yorker* 38 (February 24, 1962): 36.
COLLECTED: *Helmets,* 11–12; *Poems 57–67,* 115–16, *Early Motion,* 99–100; *Whole Motion,* 136–37.
REPRINTED: *New York Times Book Review,* March 27, 1966, 2; *New Yorker Book of Poems,* 226; *Voice That Is Great,* 492–93.

NOTES: Written in Positano. The poem bears some affinity with Wallace Stevens's "Anecdote of the Jar."

VARIANTS:

4: right (*Helmets, Poems 57–67, Early Motion, Whole Motion*) | right, (*New Yorker*)

5: see (*Helmets, Poems 57–67, Early Motion, Whole Motion*) | see, (*New Yorker*)

29: highstrung (*Helmets, Poems 57–67, Early Motion, Whole Motion*) | high-strung (*New Yorker*)

40: psalm: (*Helmets, Poems 57–67, Early Motion, Whole Motion*) | psalm— (*New Yorker*)

The Step

FIRST PUBLICATION: *Literary Review* 5 (Summer 1962): 474–75.

NOTES:

21: "Knees" are characteristic woody projections of the cypress, rising above water level and then descending to the soil; knees are thought to give structural support ("to knee") to the swamp-grown trees.

32: Dickey's brother Eugene Dickey, Jr. ("The String") is buried in the Dickey crypt; his parents, Eugene Dickey, Sr. ("The Hospital Window") and Maibelle Swift Dickey ("The Sprinter's Mother"), are buried in the Swift-Burckhardt crypt at Oakland Cemetery (founded 1850) in downtown Atlanta. See also "The Escape."

A Letter

FIRST PUBLICATION: *Sewanee Review* 70 (Summer 1962): 416–17.

COLLECTED: *Poems 57–67*, 269–70; *Whole Motion*, 268–69.

REPRINTED: *Best Poems of 1962*, 41–42; *Poems*, 44–45.

NOTE: Intended for *Buckdancer* but omitted.

Springer Mountain [a]

FIRST PUBLICATION: *Virginia Quarterly Review* 38 (Summer 1962): 436–41.

REPRINTED: *Poems from* The Virginia Quarterly Review, 95–99.

NOTES: Written in Positano. Springer Mountain in Gilmer County, Georgia, is the beginning of the Appalachian Trail, not far from the Dickeys' ancestral home at Mineral Bluff. The mountain divides the northern and southern extensions of the Appalachians in Georgia; the north branch leads to the Cohutta Mountains (see "Under Buzzards"). This poem was important in Dickey's career, in that its publication in *Virginia Quarterly Review* attracted the notice of Theron Raines (1925–2012), who became Dickey's literary agent and encouraged the publication of *Deliverance*. For unexplained reasons the poem was so completely rewritten line by line in the two years between its first publication and its appearance in *Helmets*, that it is most efficient to treat the versions as two separate poems, "Springer Mountain [a]" and "Springer Mountain [b]." Discussed in *Self*, 125–26.

At the Home for Unwed Mothers

First Publication: *Quarterly Review of Literature* 12 (Fall–Winter 1962): 55–56.
Collected: *Whole Motion,* 39–40.
Variants:
7: lath (*Whole Motion*) | lathe (*Quarterly Review*) [Lathe is a machine; lath is a thin strip of wood.]
50: hers, (*Quarterly Review*) | hers. (*Whole Motion* [typo])

A Sound through the Floor

First Publication: *Quarterly Review of Literature* 12 (Fall–Winter 1962): 57–59.

On Discovering That My Hand Shakes

First Publication: *Quarterly Review of Literature* 12 (Fall–Winter 1962): 59–60.

At Darien Bridge

First Publication: As "At Darien Bridge, Georgia," *New Yorker* 38 (December 1, 1962): 60 (in group titled "Poems of North and South Georgia").
Collected: *Helmets,* 13–14; *Poems 57–67,* 117–18; *Early Motion,* 101–2; *Whole Motion,* 137–38.
Reprinted: *Norton Anthology of Poetry,* 1153.
Notes: Written in Rome. The actual bridge was an old railroad bridge that crossed the Darien River near the southeast coast of Georgia, near where the Dickey family vacationed at St. Simons Island in the summer. It was built in 1914 by prison labor, well before Dickey was born, but he would have heard the story of its construction. The bridge was torn down in 1944 and replaced by the present bridge at the same location. "It's a poem about a middle-aged man remembering how he thought things were when he was a child. In this case he's walking out by an old bridge down in the south coastal marshes of Georgia and remembering when he walked on the same places as a child and saw the convicts working to build the bridge that he now as a mature man, or a middle-aged man, sees falling into decay. . . . He remembers that as a child he thought it perfectly natural for the bird to be born of the flash of the convict's hammer in the sun. Now as a mature man, very much in the knowledge of his own impending death, he walks in the same place remembering how he felt as a child and the world of continuous miracle that the child inhabits" ("Comments," 9–10).
Variants:
18: Recalling (*Helmets, Poems 57–67, Early Motion, Whole Motion*) | Remembering (*New Yorker*)

In the Marble Quarry

First Publication: *New Yorker* 38 (December 1, 1962): 61 (in group titled "Poems of North and South Georgia").

COLLECTED: *Helmets*, 46–47; *Poems 57–67*, 147–48; *Early Motion*, 134–35; *Whole Motion*, 159–60.

REPRINTED: *Achievement*, 41–42; *Decade*, 74–76; *Life* 61 (July 22, 1966): 70; *Norton Anthology of Poetry*, 1153–54.

NOTES: Written in Positano. Discussed in *Self*, 132–33. The poem may have arisen from Dickey's memory of the Georgia Marble Quarry in Tate, Georgia. See "The Escape," 3.

11: Marble of a spectacular semitransparent whiteness was quarried on the north side of the island of Paros from the sixth century B.C.E. The Nike of Samothrace ("Winged Victory") and the Venus de Milo are made of Parian marble.

25–28: Dickey was fond of quoting Michelangelo's words to his students: "in every block of marble I see a statue" (see *Dictionary of Literary Biography: Documentary Series*, vol. 19: *James Dickey*, edited by Judith S. Baughman [Detroit & Columbia, S.C.: Gale, 1999], 319; and Henry Wadsworth Longfellow, *Michael Angelo* [1883], part 3.6).

VARIANTS:

24: tombstone (*Helmets, Poems 57–67, Early Motion, Whole Motion*) | tombstone, (*New Yorker*)

The Dusk of Horses

FIRST PUBLICATION: *New Yorker* 38 (December 1, 1962): 60–61 (in group titled "Poems of North and South Georgia").

COLLECTED: *Helmets*, 9–10; *Poems 57–67*, 113–14; *Early Motion*, 97–98, *Whole Motion*, 135–36.

REPRINTED: *Achievement*, 33–34; *American Poetry*, 1018–19; *Best Poems of 1962*, 47–48; *Columbia Anthology*, 586–87; *Decade*, 69–71; *New Yorker Book of Poems*, 182 (stanzas 1–6 only); *Selected*, 41–42; *Stained the Water Clear: A Festschrift for Lloyd J. Reynolds* (Portland Ore.: Reed College, 1966), 16; *Today's Poets*, 294–95; *Wesleyan Tradition*, 58–59.

NOTE: Written in Positano.

The Beholders

FIRST PUBLICATION: *New Yorker* 38 (December 1, 1962): 61 (in group titled "Poems of North and South Georgia").

COLLECTED: *Helmets*, 42–43; *Poems 57–67*, 143–44; *Early Motion*, 130–31; *Whole Motion*, 157–58.

REPRINTED: *American Poetry*, 1019–20; *Literature*, 444–45.

NOTE: Written in Positano.

VARIANTS:

17: cry (*Helmets, Poems 57–67, Early Motion, Whole Motion*) | cry something (*New Yorker*)

17: heads (*Helmets, Poems 57–67, Early Motion, Whole Motion*) | heads, (*New Yorker*)

39: men, (*Helmets, Poems 57–67, Early Motion, Whole Motion*) | men (*New Yorker*)

The Poisoned Man

FIRST PUBLICATION: *New Yorker* 38 (December 1, 1962): 61 (in group titled "Poems of North and South Georgia").

COLLECTED: *Helmets,* 44–45; *Poems 57–67,* 145–46; *Early Motion,* 132–33; *Whole Motion,* 158–59.

REPRINTED: *Fine Frenzy,* 240–41; *Literature in America,* 275–76; *Poems,* 25–26; *Today's Poets,* 297–98.

NOTES: Written in Positano. "The poem becomes an allegory—maybe too obvious an allegory—about the fall of Man, because the blood poisons the stream, and the trees and crops die, and he and his wife have to leave his farm like Adam and Eve leaving the Garden of Eden" (*Self,* 131). Dickey claimed to have been bitten by a water moccasin and to have sucked the venom out of his own hand (Hart, 272).

3–6: For cutting the skin to release venom after a snake bit, see "Snakebite," lines 36–42.

35: The expulsion from Eden is paralleled in Greek mythology by the end of the Golden and Silver Ages and the beginning of the Bronze Age, normally associated with the Mycenean Age of the Trojan War. (Bronze is an alloy of copper and usually tin). See Hesiod, *Works and Days,* 109–201, and Virgil, *Eclogue* 4. In many cultures, the Bronze Age is the earliest age of metalworking.

VARIANTS:

15: at (*Helmets, Poems 57–67, Early Motion, Whole Motion*) | from (*New Yorker*)

The Crows

FIRST PUBLICATION: *New World Writing* (Philadelphia: Lippincott, 1962), 50–51.

NOTES:

4: For the picture, see *Striking,* 38: "Illusion of a man crucified on side of moving freight car: seen through pines and brush"; and "A Folksinger of the Thirties," lines 22–40; and "Springer Mountain [b]," line 49.

49: An echo of Poe's "The Raven." For a picture of Dickey with a raven on his shoulder at the Poe Museum in Richmond, see Hart, 411.

Wall and Cloud

FIRST PUBLICATION: *New World Writing* (Philadelphia: Lippincott, 1962), 52.

COLLECTED: *Whole Motion,* 25.

VARIANTS:

16: wall, (*New World Writing*)| wall (*Whole Motion*)

A Poem about Bird-Catching by
One Who Has Never Caught a Bird

FIRST PUBLICATION: *New World Writing* (Philadelphia: Lippincott, 1962), 53–54.

Walking the Fire Line

FIRST PUBLICATION: *Mutiny,* no. 12 (1963): 96–97.

COLLECTED: *Whole Motion,* 29–30.

VARIANTS:
5: And (*Mutiny*) | and (*Whole Motion* [typo])
32: fire line (*Mutiny*) | line (*Whole Motion* [typo])
36: but (*Mutiny*) | or nearly (*Whole Motion*)

The Courtship

FIRST PUBLICATION: *Mutiny,* no. 12 (1963): 97–98.
COLLECTED: *Whole Motion,* 13–14.
NOTE: This is the first of Dickey's poems centered on the page, a practice he would return to in the later stages of his career.
VARIANTS:
5: quiet (*Mutiny*) | ragged (*Whole Motion*)
20: becalmed (*Mutiny*) | becalmed, (*Whole Motion*)

Paestum

FIRST PUBLICATION: *Shenandoah* 14 (Winter 1963): 7–10.
COLLECTED: *Whole Motion,* 20–23.
REPRINTED: *Shenandoah* 35 (1984): 121–22; *Strongly Spent,* 65–68.
NOTES: Dickey, his family, and their sixteen-year-old maid, Laura Rispoli, visited the ancient Campanian town of Paestum on the western coast of Italy, eighty miles south of Naples, during his Guggenheim semester in Italy (February–June 1962). Begun by Greeks in the seventh century B.C.E., Paestum (originally Poseidonia) is known today chiefly for the ruins of three sixth-century B.C.E. Doric temples standing side-by-side, two of them dedicated to Hera and the other to Athena. Dickey became *Shenandoah*'s advisory editor for poetry in the fall of 1963.
37–45: See "In the Marble Quarry," 25–28.
57–59: Presumably the temple of the virgin goddess Athena.
67: Only two or three steps give entrance to the temple, not stairs.
98: Piraeus is the ancient port for Athens, about ten miles from the city, and today it is the largest port in Europe.
VARIANTS:
13: The useless, blue-eyed (*Shenandoah*) | The blue-eyed (*Whole Motion*)
44: shrewd, (*Shenandoah*) | shrewd (*Whole Motion*)
106: Impossibly creative (*Shenandoah*) | Creative, impossible (*Whole Motion*)

Under Buzzards

FIRST PUBLICATION: *Granta* 67 (March 2, 1963): 9.
NOTES: The Cohutta Range is the Georgia extension of the Smoky Mountains, beginning in Fannin County, Georgia, "The Gateway to the Blue Ridge." See "Springer Mountain [a]." "Under Buzzards" is also used as a subtitle in "Diabetes."

VARIANTS:

[Holograph author's revisions on published copy at Emory]

17: opened (*Granta*) | coming open (Dickey)

18: comes (*Granta*) | rides (Dickey)

31: our [corrected by editor] | out (*Granta*)

Kudzu

FIRST PUBLICATION: *New Yorker* 39 (May 18, 1963): 44.

COLLECTED: *Helmets*, 38–41; *Poems 57–67*, 140–42; *Early Motion*, 126–29; *Whole Motion*, 154–57.

REPRINTED: *Poems of Our Moment*, 60–62; *Lyrikvännen* 4 (1980): 169–71 (Swedish translation).

NOTES: Written in Positano. "Kudzu" (*Pueraria lobata*) is a transcription of the Japanese name of this vine, which can grow up to one-hundred feet high in trees and spreads rapidly across the ground, up to one foot per day in season (see "Cherrylog Road," line 3). Introduced at the Philadelphia Centennial Exhibition in 1876 as an ornamental, it was widely planted by the Civilian Conservation Corps in the Southeast beginning in 1935, after the "Dust Bowl" era, to prevent soil erosion. Once it takes root, it kills off other vegetation, damages power lines, even attacks homes, and is difficult to extirpate. Unfortunately the South provided almost perfect growing conditions for the plant, and by 1953 it had been officially labeled a "pest weed." For examples see Richard J. Blaustein, "Kudzu's Invasion into Southern United States Life and Culture," in *The Great Reshuffling: Human Dimensions of Invasive Species*, edited by Jeffrey A. McNeely (Gland, Switzerland & Cambridge, U.K.: IUCN [International Union for Conservation of Nature and Natural Resources], 2001), 55–62, which begins with a quotation from this poem.

VARIANTS:

4: Up (*Helmets, Poems 57–67, Early Motion, Whole Motion*) | Up the (*New Yorker*)

13: fields. (*Helmets, Poems 57–67, Early Motion, Whole Motion*) | fields (*New Yorker*)

17: ground: (*Helmets, Poems 57–67, Early Motion, Whole Motion*) | ground; (*New Yorker*)

21: kneecap: (*Helmets, Poems 57–67, Early Motion, Whole Motion*) | kneecap— (*New Yorker*)

28: one (*Helmets, Poems 57–67, Early Motion, Whole Motion*) | one, (*New Yorker*)

49: leaf heads (*Helmets, Poems 57–67, Early Motion, Whole Motion*) | leaf-heads (*New Yorker*)

52–53: [blank line inserted] (*New Yorker, Helmets, Early Motion*) | [no blank line] (*Poems 57–67, Whole Motion* [typo])

70: warning: (*Helmets, Poems 57–67, Early Motion, Whole Motion*) | warning. (*New Yorker*)

74: though (*Helmets, Poems 57–67, Early Motion, Whole Motion*) | if (*New Yorker*)

79: cows—) (*Helmets, Poems 57–67, Early Motion, Whole Motion*) | cows (*New Yorker*)

80: Came in (*Helmets, Poems 57–67, Early Motion, Whole Motion*) | That grew to you (*New Yorker*)

81: sleep (*Helmets, Poems 57–67, Early Motion, Whole Motion*) | sleep, (*New Yorker*)

The Scarred Girl

FIRST PUBLICATION: *New Yorker* 39 (June 1, 1963): 36.

COLLECTED: *Helmets*, 36–37; *Poems 57–67*, 138–39; *Early Motion*, 124–25; *Whole Motion*, 153–54.

REPRINTED: *Hero's Way*, 409–10; *Poems*, 23–24; *Some Haystacks*, 69; *Today's Poets*, 295–97; *Total Experience of Poetry*, 134–35.

NOTES: Written in Positano. "I knew a girl who was the prettiest girl in Atlanta, by far. She was not pretty in a sexy way, but she had a Madonna-like beauty, that kind of soft, shining, lustrous-eyed quality—I never saw such eyes in a human head! . . . She went with a boy who was not in her class at all, I thought. Then of all things, he got into an automobile wreck, and she went through the windshield headfirst. It cut her face into absolute hamburger. . . . I've been brooding about it for thirty years. I had been reading in Plato about the Good, the True, and the Beautiful [for the phrase, *Phaedrus* 246e; for the "Theory of Forms," *Republic*, books 5–7]. This girl was true—although she seemed almost too good to be true—and good and beautiful she surely had been. . . . The beauty had been taken away by the wreck, but she still had this goodness, as I say at the end of the poem, that is now 'the only way'" (*Self*, 130–31).

VARIANTS:

1: whole (*Helmets, Poems 57–67, Early Motion, Whole Motion*) | whole, (*New Yorker*)

34: wrapping, (*Helmets, Poems 57–67, Early Motion, Whole Motion*) | wrapping— (*New Yorker*)

37: dreamed (*Helmets, Poems 57–67, Early Motion, Whole Motion*) | dreamed, (*New Yorker*)

46: sunlight (*Helmets, Poems 57–67, Early Motion, Whole Motion*) | sunlight, (*New Yorker*)

Drinking from a Helmet

FIRST PUBLICATION: *Sewanee Review* 71 (Summer 1963): 451–57.

COLLECTED: *Helmets*, 87–93; *Poems 57–67*, 173–78; *Early Motion*, 175–81; *Whole Motion*, 185–90.

REPRINTED: *Achievement*, 46–51; *Articles of War*, 118–23; *Georgia Voices*, 87–93.

NOTES: "I splintered the experience undergone in the poem into nineteen fragments of varying lengths, and by this means tried to get the lyric 'timeless-moment' intensity and the enveloping structure of a narrative into the same format" (*Early Motion*, viii). "I meant the reader to stop at each section and sort of reflect on that as a separate poem that related to the other poems, that it was all part of the sequence file" (Greiner, 10). See also *Self*, 123, 135–36.

18–20: Compare the refusal to put on the dead man's helmet with the assumption of boar's head in "Approaching Prayer," lines 36–40.

43: Dickey noted this line's "imaginative simplicity," which he learned from Ezra Pound (Suarez, 119).

97: In *The Tempest* Ariel is freed by Prospero from the tree in which he was imprisoned by the witch Sycorax.

168: for another tricolon ending, see "Fog Envelops the Animals."

169: See Walt Whitman, "Song of Myself," line 831: "I am the man—I suffer'd—I was there," and *Sorties*, 159.

VARIANTS:

60: oak rings (*Helmets, Poems 57–67, Early Motion, Whole Motion*) | oak-rings (*Sewanee Review*)

65: nearly dead (*Helmets, Poems 57–67, Early Motion, Whole Motion*) | nearly-dead (*Sewanee Review*)

The Being

FIRST PUBLICATION: *Poetry* 102 (August 1963): 281–84.

COLLECTED: *Helmets*, 55–58; *Poems 57–67*, 154–56; *Early Motion*, 143–46; *Whole Motion*, 166–68.

REPRINTED: *Intervisions*, 16–19; *New Modern Poetry*, 44–46; *Poetry: Premeditated Art*, 383–85; *Selected*, 52–54.

NOTES: Written in Positano. Discussed *Self*, 133–34: "Figure a man who is sleeping on a winter night and is being possessed by something. He doesn't know whether it's a human woman who gets into bed with him or a succubus . . . or whether it's an angel or some kind of renewing spirit of the year. I deliberately did not explain what it was, because when you have these visitations, as sometimes happens, the whole point is that you don't know whether it's a dream or what. It's all of those things and none of them. But the experience in the poem is definitely meant to be sexual and has not so much the effect of robbing the sleeper of his powers as being a kind of purgation of the winter's ills and a presage of the spring's renewal."

VARIANTS:

22: windowpane (*Helmets, Poems 57–67, Early Motion, Whole Motion*) | window-pane (*Poetry*)

26–27: [lines indented] (*Poetry*)

32: coal bed (*Helmets, Poems 57–67, Early Motion, Whole Motion*)| coal-bed (*Poetry*)

35–36: [blank line inserted] (*Poetry*)

44: liquefies (*Poetry, Helmets, Poems 57–67, Early Motion*) | liquifies (*Whole Motion* [typo])

50 windowpane (*Helmets, Poems 57–67, Early Motion, Whole Motion*) | window-pane (*Poetry*)

54: bottom two (*Helmets, Poems 57–67, Early Motion, Whole Motion*) | two bottom (*Poetry*)

61: half-dead (*Helmets, Poems 57–67, Early Motion, Whole Motion*) | sleep-walking (*Poetry*)

61–62: [no blank line inserted] (*Poetry, Helmets, Early Motion*)

62–63 [no blank line inserted] (*Poems 57–67*)

69: roof   wide   wider (*Poems 57–67, Early Motion, Whole Motion*) | roof, wide, wider (*Poetry, Helmets*)

Why in London the Blind Are Saviors

FIRST PUBLICATION: *Poetry* 102 (August 1963): 284–86.

NOTES: "a good idea bothered and botched by my inability to make it come off" (*Crux*, 213). On blindness see "Reading Genesis to a Blind Child," "The Owl King," "The Eye-Beaters," *Self* (209), headnote to "Cahill Is Blind" (*Esquire* 85 [February 1976]: 67), "False Youth: Winter," and *Alnilam.*

A Folk Singer of the Thirties

FIRST PUBLICATION: *Poetry* 102 (August 1963): 286–91.

COLLECTED: *Helmets*, 48–54; *Poems 57–67*, 149–53; *Early Motion*, 136–42; *Whole Motion*, 160–65.

NOTES: Written in Positano. "'A Folk Singer of the Thirties' came from reading Woody Guthrie's autobiography and reading Burl Ives's ghosted autobiography, *The Wayfaring Stranger*, and wondering what those guys must have had despite the deprivation and the poverty, in the Thirties, when they rode the rods and sang their songs for their meals in the little Depression-ridden towns all over the country—what the difference between that would be and what they have now in the great affluent society when they live in those uptown apartments and purvey their folksy humor on quiz shows and become actors and that sort of thing. . . . Something definitely has been lost. The music really has been lost. Burl Ives can sing 'Jimmy Crack Corn' all he likes in night clubs, but it won't be the same as when he was poor. It's not better that he should be poor, merely that it's closer to the true folk thing that he should wander and sing for his supper" (*Eclipse,* 10; Baughman, 17; see also *Self,* 65, and *Night,* 195–96). In 1976 Dickey reviewed Guthrie's *Seeds of Man: An Experience Lived and Dreamed* in the *New York Times Book Review* (October 3, 1976, 2–3). The first chapter in the autobiography of Woodrow Wilson "Woody" Guthrie (1912–1967), *Bound for Glory* (1943; reprinted, New York: Dutton, 1976), opens with Guthrie not alone but in a freight car with sixty-nine hobos, and they are subsequently set upon by railroad detectives. Guthrie lies on cement bags, not gravel. Ensuing chapters narrate his early life. The second half recounts a journey from Oklahoma to California by a southern route (not, as in this poem, via North Dakota), then back to New York, to Chicago, and the road beyond. Dickey added the perspective of the singer safe and comfortable in his apartment (probably Ives, not Guthrie), while in his book, Guthrie never wrote about settling down.

1–2: See *Bound for Glory,* 411.

8: This line echoes the title of *Into the Stone,* Dickey's first published book of poetry.

16–17: For "straining / Its breast," see "The Baggage King," line 40.

22–40: This crucifixion scene is presaged in *Striking,* 38 ("Illusion of a man crucified on side of moving freight car: seen through pines and brush") and "The Crows," line 4. A similar scene occurs at the end of Martin Scorsese's *Boxcar Bertha* (1972), when hobo Big Bill Shelley (David Carradine) is crucified on the side of a freight car by railroad detectives ("yard bulls").

27–28: See *Bound for Glory,* 418–19.

30–31: For hobo boys, see *Bound for Glory,* 416–18.

107–8: See *Bound for Glory,* 398.

113: In November 1930 Chicago's Grant Park was the site of one of the earliest Hoovervilles, a kind of Depression-era shantytown named for President Herbert Hoover, whom many blamed for the economic troubles of the period.

129: A.A. is Alcoholics Anonymous. Guthrie described his problems with alcohol and wrote of his need to watch his drinking.

141: For the phrase "A year later to the day," see ""Between Two Prisoners," line 47.

143: Burl Icle Ivanhoe Ives (1909–1995) sang folksongs before business groups and from 1940 led a comfortable life in New York, starring on Broadway and movies.

176: Guthrie's *Songs to Grow On for Mother and Child* was recorded in 1947 and released in 1956 by Folkways; Ives made several children's records for Decca in the 1950s and for Walt Disney in the 1960s.

178: Ives appeared as a guest on many television shows, including Jack Paar's in 1955 and Danny Kaye's in 1957, and later starred in two series of his own.

182: Guthrie auditioned at the swank Rainbow Room in Rockefeller Center, but refused to play there (*Bound for Glory,* 387–95).

VARIANTS:

13: freight yards (*Helmets, Poems 57–67, Early Motion, Whole Motion*) | freight-yards (*Poetry*)
14: gravel car (*Helmets, Poems 57–67, Early Motion, Whole Motion*) | gravel-car (*Poetry*)
109: choir boys (*Helmets, Poems 57–67, Early Motion, Whole Motion*) | choir-boys (*Poetry*)
119: lamp bulb (*Helmets, Poems 57–67, Early Motion, Whole Motion*) | lamp-bulb (*Poetry*)
135: shoe store (*Helmets, Poems 57–67, Early Motion, Whole Motion*) | shoe-store (*Poetry*)
150: coal beds (*Helmets, Poems 57–67, Early Motion, Whole Motion*) | coal-beds (*Poetry*)
156: with (*Helmets, Poems 57–67, Early Motion, Whole Motion*) | to (*Poetry*)
173: deathbed (*Helmets, Poems 57–67, Early Motion, Whole Motion*) | death-bed (*Poetry*)
178–79: [no blank line inserted] (*Whole Motion*)

Bums, on Waking

FIRST PUBLICATION: *New Yorker* 39 (September 7, 1963): 34.
COLLECTED: *Helmets*, 65–67; *Poems 57–67*, 159–60; *Early Motion*, 153–55; *Whole Motion*, 172–73.
REPRINTED: *Best Poems of 1963*, 42–43; *New Yorker Book of Poems*, 88; *Achievement*, 44–46; *To See the World Afresh*, 29–31.
NOTES: "You remember those two town bums in Positano that they used to find sleeping in the church? I wrote ["Bums, On Waking"] about them" (*Summer*, 117).
VARIANTS:
29: hedge, (*Helmets, Poems 57–67, Early Motion, Whole Motion*) | hedge (*New Yorker*)

Goodbye to Serpents

FIRST PUBLICATION: *New Yorker* 39 (September 21, 1963): 47.
COLLECTED: *Helmets*, 68–70; *Poems 57–67*, 161–62; *Early Motion*, 156–58; *Whole Motion*, 173–75.
NOTES: "That poem about the Jardin des Plantes—'I wrote [in Positano]'" (*Summer*, 117). Dickey loved going to zoos everywhere he visited, including London (see "Encounter in the Cage Country"), Paris, Rome, Portland, San Diego, and Columbia, South Carolina. In this case the French term *jardin* (garden) led him into another biblical story, the expulsion from the Garden of Eden (see "The Magus" and "Adam in Winter")
5–8: The Jardin des Plantes, occupying sixty-nine acres on the left bank of the Seine, is the main botanical garden in France. The rear entrance on rue Cuvier is undoubtedly the "hole in the wall." Among other exhibits the garden maintains a small zoo of animals (originally from the royal menagerie at Versailles). In the 1960s the zoo (including its reptile house, where Dickey was fond of the Gaboon viper) was depressing, holding the animals in small cages, often in disrepair, and in dirty malodorous conditions. The zoo has since been refurbished, and the animals are kept in simulated habitats. These lines are inscribed on a brass plaque on a bench dedicated to Dickey in front of the Vivarium at the Jardin des Plantes.
49: For Christopher Dickey and his father at a zoo, see "Encounter in the Cage Country."

6: Of (*New Yorker, Helmets, Poems 57–67, Early Motion*) | of (*Whole Motion* [typo])
24: curve (*Helmets, Poems 57–67, Early Motion, Whole Motion*) | curve, (*New Yorker*)

Horses and Prisoners

FIRST PUBLICATION: *Hudson Review* 16 (Autumn 1963): 384–5.
COLLECTED: *Helmets*, 84–86; *Poems 57–67*, 171–72; *Early Motion*, 172–74; *Whole Motion*, 183–85.
REPRINTED: *Best Poems of 1963*, 7–8.
VARIANTS:

37: with the (*Helmets, Poems 57–67, Early Motion, Whole Motion*) | with (*Hudson*)
38: long thighbones (*Helmets, Poems 57–67, Early Motion, Whole Motion*) | thighbones (*Hudson*)
56: air (*Helmets, Poems 57–67, Early Motion, Whole Motion*) | trained air (*Hudson*)
57: From (*Helmets, Poems 57–67, Early Motion, Whole Motion*) | Out of (*Hudson*)
57: tangled gate (*Helmets, Poems 57–67, Early Motion, Whole Motion*) | gate (*Hudson*)
62: Let (*Helmets, Poems 57–67, Early Motion, Whole Motion*) | Then let (*Hudson*)
62: the dead shirt from his chest (*Helmets, Poems 57–67, Early Motion, Whole Motion*)| off his dead
   shirt (*Hudson*)

Blowgun and Rattlesnake

FIRST PUBLICATION: *Texas Quarterly* 7 (Autumn 1963): 158–60.
COLLECTED: *Whole Motion*, 36–38.
NOTES: Written in Positano. "I've always had a very strong attraction to the *other*—the thing that's
most unlike humans and most unlike any kind of life that is close to us . . . (*Playboy* interview,
89; Baughman, 113). Dickey hated and feared snakes all his life, calling them "Universal Evil" and
"The Enemy from Eden." "They hate you and the human race instinctively hates them" (*Enemy*,
2). "Snakes seem to me to be the kind of ultimate other. . . . It's no wonder that we make the
snake the personification of evil, because he *is* so much the other, and that coupled with the fact
that some of them are poisonous is enough to make them the real nightmare creatures that we
somehow or other have got to come to terms with" (Arnett, 297–98). See "The Poisoned Man,"
"Victory," "Kudzu," "Goodbye to Serpents," "Cobra," and *Deliverance* (101). "The Poisoned Man"
and "Snakebite" both deal with cutting oneself after a snakebite to draw out the venom. See also
"Reincarnation (I)" and "Orpheus before Hades" (where Eurydice is killed by a snake). Dickey
wrote a prose version of events similar to those in this poem—"Blowjob on a Rattlesnake," *Esquire*
82 (October 1974): 177–78, 368; reprinted as *The Enemy from Eden* (1978)—including the purchase
of an eight-foot aluminum tube and fashioning of darts from typewriter paper and coat hangers
sharpened on the driveway pavement. On the eastern diamondback rattlesnake, see "Reincarna-
tion (I)."
7: See *Enemy*, 1–2.
12: Not mentioned in *Enemy*.
28: "The deep-pitted head is drawing back into the beautiful coils, and the tail is not quite visible"
   (*Enemy*, 9).

45–46: "He sweeps each piece over his gritty driveway in long strokes, turning the shaft" (*Enemy,* 3).

47: "Position those human lungs. You are trying to kill, with the breath of life" (*Enemy,* 11).

51–56: "[The rattlesnake] writhes, he turns over and over, he thrashes, he shows his obscene white belly, a terribly inadequate contrast to his beautiful back, he rattles hopelessly, he strikes at phantoms" (*Enemy,* 11–12).

71: Job 38:1, 40:6.

90: "The needle is in the brain. Universal Evil does not know what to do with it" (*Enemy,* 11).

Variants:

10: it (*Texas Quarterly*) | on it (*Whole Motion*)

11: bubble (*Texas Quarterly*) | air (*Whole Motion*)

13: lips; (*Texas Quarterly*) | lips: (*Whole Motion* [typo])

16: cone, (*Texas Quarterly*)| cone (*Whole Motion*)

21: Going back and back (*Texas Quarterly*) | Retreating, retreating (*Whole Motion*)

22: recoil (*Texas Quarterly*) | back up (*Whole Motion*)

25: and camouflage— (*Texas Quarterly*) | a camouflage (*Whole Motion*)

26: The (*Texas Quarterly*) | —the (*Whole Motion*)

27: Loses (*Texas Quarterly*)| Losing (*Whole Motion*)

In the Child's Night

First Publication: *Virginia Quarterly Review* 39 (Autumn 1963): 590–91.

Collected: *Helmets,* 71–72; *Early Motion,* 159–60; *Whole Motion,* 175–76.

Reprinted: Broadside (Winston-Salem, N.C.: Palaemon Press, 1981), follows *Helmets, Early Motion, Whole Motion.*

Variants:

4: Something thinks, "You (*Helmets, Early Motion, Whole Motion*) | You (*Virginia Quarterly*)

7: into the star-sea (*Helmets, Early Motion, Whole Motion*) | upstream (*Virginia Quarterly*)

7: sleep, (*Helmets, Early Motion, Whole Motion*) | sleep (*Virginia Quarterly*)

9: flowing." (*Helmets, Early Motion, Whole Motion*) | flowing. (*Virginia Quarterly*)

10–15: Yet levels of depth are wrestling / And rising from us; we are still. / The quilt pattern—a child's pink whale— // Has surfaced through ice at midnight / And now is dancing upon / The dead (*Helmets, Early Motion, Whole Motion*) | It would be, it is / That cold of space in this room. / The quilt-pattern—two facing peacocks— // Has somehow risen without us; / Two earthbound birds are dancing / In the dead (*Virginia Quarterly*)

20: evil. (*Helmets, Early Motion, Whole Motion*) | evil, (*Virginia Quarterly*)

21–33: I rise to do freezing battle // With my bare hands. / I enter the faraway other / Side of the struggling bed // And turn him to face me. / The stitched beast falls, and we / Are sewn warmly into a sea-shroud // It begins to haul through the dark. / Holding my son's / Best kicking foot in my hand, // I begin to move with the moon / As it must have felt when it went / From the sea to dwell in the sky, (*Helmets, Early Motion, Whole Motion*) | The "monster" that every child dreads // But by parents feared even more. / I rise to do freezing battle / With my bare hands. // I enter the faraway other / Side of the struggling bed / And turn him on his right side // Facing me. The peacocks hover / And fall in warm feathers upon us. / We all try to go away: // My son sets his blunt nose inward, / Upward, the tension dies out of his legs, / And, holding his best kicking foot, // I follow at some safe distance, / Sailing, drowning, growing, / Leaving the hallway lamp // To become a dim midnight sun / Among the innumerable others / All equidistant now / (*Virginia Quarterly*)

35: wellhead (*Helmets, Early Motion, Whole Motion*) | well-head (*Virginia Quarterly*)

Cherrylog Road

FIRST PUBLICATION: *New Yorker* 39 (October 12, 1963): 51.

COLLECTED: *Helmets*, 31–35; *Poems* 57–67, 134–37; *Early Motion*, 119–23; *Whole Motion*, 150–53.

REPRINTED: *Achievement*, 37–40; *America in Literature*, 213–16; *American Tradition in Literature*, 1712–14; *Appreciating Poetry*, 136–39; *Beginnings in Poetry*, 166–69; *Cambridge Poetry Magazine* 1 (Autumn 1983): 21–23; *College Anthology*, 651–64; *Columbia Anthology*, 587–90; *Contemporary American Poets*, 67–70; *Contemporary Poetry in America*, 73–74; *Contemporary Southern Poetry*, 73–75; *Decade*, 71–74; *Distinctive Voice*, 230–33; *Doors into Poetry*, 305–8; *Exploring Poetry*, 471–74; *Georgia Voices*, 84–87; *Grooving the Symbol*, 297–98; *Harvard*, 133–36; *Introduction to Poetry* (Simpson), 353–55; *Introduction to Poetry* (Kennedy), 444–46; *Logic of Poetry*, 272–73; *Made Thing*, 76–79; *Making It New*, 81–84; *New Yorker Book of Poems*, 114–16; *Pictures That Storm inside My Head*, 98; *Poems*, 19–22; *Selected*, 43–46; *Total Experience of Poetry*, 127–30; *Twentieth Century Poetry*, 90–94; *Workshop*, 202–5; (with comment by Dickey) *World on Wheels*, 447–50.

NOTES: "[Vanderbilt friend John] Hall once told Dickey about taking a high-school girlfriend into the middle of a junkyard in his hometown of Helena, Arkansas, and making love to her in a dilapidated car. He explained that this modus operandi helped them evade her stern, disapproving father, who happened to be a farmer" (Hart, 149). For Dickey's fantastical introduction to the poem, see Hart, 380. The motorcyclist may be based on Atlanta acquaintance Ed Van Valkenburg, "an extraordinary person" who would recite Kipling and Service while lifting weights with young Dickey (*Night*, 185; Hart, 44) or his friend Walter Armistead (See the poem "Walter Armistead"). Both boys had taught Dickey to ride motorcycles, which he would drive to his father's old homestead in Mineral Bluff (*Night*, 186). The motorcyclist reappears in "May Day Sermon." For an utterly fanciful description of the background and response to this poem, see "Comments," 10–11 (revised for *Self*, 130). Dickey first treated this subject in his unpublished 1953 novel, "The Entrance to the Honeycomb."

There is no "Cherrylog Road" in Atlanta, which—given the participation of Atlantan Charlotte Holbrook—might seem the ostensible setting of the poem. In Dickey's youth Gene Buchanan's junkyard covered many acres on either side of the only highway that ran due north from Atlanta, Old Georgia Route 5 (replaced today by Route 515) at the town of Cherry Log, which lies halfway between Mineral Bluff ("Slave Quarters") and Ellijay ("On the Coosawattee"). The enormous ancient junkyard contained some cars so old that not only had kudzu grown over them (line 4) but trees had grown through them. Hence two of the three cars named in this poem were out of production by the dramatic date of this poem. It was a local landmark that Dickey would have passed through on his family trips up to the old homestead in Mineral Bluff. The present-day "Cherrylog Street" and "Cherrylog Avenue" off Highway 515 did not exist then. The

Highway 106 that Dickey mentions runs north and south in eastern Georgia, from Athens to Toccoa, nowhere near Atlanta or Cherry Log.

4: See "Kudzu."

8: The Essex was an affordable car produced from 1918 to 1922 by the Essex Motor Company and from 1922 to 1932 by the Hudson Motor Company.

17, 50, 65: Hart (380) confuses Charlotte Sego Holbrook (1912–1963)—the wife of William Watt Neal (1908–1970), owner of the Liller, Neal, Battle, and Lindsey ad agency that Dickey joined as creative director in October 1959 after leaving McCann Erickson—with Charlotte Sheram Holbrook (b. 1922). Hart (380) claims that the name "Charlotte Holbrook" appears only "in early drafts," when in fact the name occurs in the *New Yorker* version of the poem. He further claims that Dickey chose the name of the wife of his former boss because of "its connection to the sort of authority figure he wanted to escape." It is far more likely that Dickey was thinking of the beautiful Charlotte Sheram Holbrook, one year ahead of him at North Fulton High School in Atlanta, where she was featured as the "Most Original" girl in her class (as Walter Armistead had been "Most Original" boy the year before). Dickey or any of the models for the teenaged narrator mentioned above would have been attracted to this Charlotte Holbrook. It is less likely that Dickey would have chosen to depict an assignation with a woman eleven years his senior who had already been married for four years at the dramatic date of the poem as a means of challenging the "authority figure" of an agency he had already "escaped" three years before the first publication of this poem. Moreover, Charlotte Neal died at the end of May 1963, tragically young at fifty, and Dickey would not have been cruel enough to refer to her so soon after her demise. In any case either William Neal complained directly to Dickey, or Dickey's friend Al Braselton (see "Drifting"), who was Charlotte Neal's son-in-law, mentioned it to Dickey after seeing the name in the *New Yorker,* and Dickey, though he originally intended no offense to Neal, nevertheless kindly changed the name to "Doris Holbrook."

35: The Pierce-Arrow was a luxury car manufactured between 1904 and 1938.

71: For the father whipping his daughter, see "May Day Sermon," line 6.

74: The shotgun may come from an incident related by another Dickey friend, Bill Barnwell, in which Dickey dated a girl whose stern father kept a shotgun on his living-room wall (Hart, 42).

Variants:

2: Road (*Helmets, Poems 57–67, Early Motion, Whole Motion*) | Road, (*New Yorker*)

7: then (*Helmets, Poems 57–67, Early Motion, Whole Motion*) | then, (*New Yorker*)

7: side (*Helmets, Poems 57–67, Early Motion, Whole Motion*) | side, (*New Yorker*)

9: leather (*Helmets, Poems 57–67, Early Motion, Whole Motion*) | leather, (*New Yorker*)

10: then (*Helmets, Poems 57–67, Early Motion, Whole Motion*) | then, (*New Yorker*)

16: junkyard (*Helmets, Poems 57–67, Early Motion, Whole Motion*) | junk yard (*New Yorker*)

17: Doris (*Helmets, Poems 57–67, Early Motion, Whole Motion*) | Charlotte (*New Yorker*)

23: forward (*Helmets, Poems 57–67, Early Motion, Whole Motion*) | forward, (*New Yorker*)

31: kingsnake (*Helmets, Poems 57–67, Early Motion, Whole Motion*) | kingsnake, (*New Yorker*)

50: Doris (*Helmets, Poems 57–67, Early Motion, Whole Motion*) | Charlotte (*New Yorker*)

51: southern-state (*Helmets, Poems 57–67, Early Motion, Whole Motion*) | Southern-state (*New Yorker*)

58: gear-knobs (*Helmets, Poems 57–67, Early Motion, Whole Motion*) | gear knobs (*New Yorker*)

65: Doris (*Helmets, Poems 57–67, Early Motion, Whole Motion*) | Charlotte (*New Yorker*)
69: father (*Helmets, Poems 57–67, Early Motion, Whole Motion*) | father, (*New Yorker*)
84: within: (*Helmets, Poems 57–67, Early Motion, Whole Motion*) | within. (*New Yorker*)
101: motorcycle (*Helmets, Poems 57–67, Early Motion, Whole Motion*) | motorcycle, (*New Yorker*)
102: junkyard (*Helmets, Poems 57–67, Early Motion, Whole Motion*) | junk yard (*New Yorker*)
107: handlebar (*Helmets, Poems 57–67, Early Motion, Whole Motion*) | handlebars (*New Yorker*)

Breath

First Publication: *New Yorker* 39 (November 9, 1963): 48.
Collected: *Helmets,* 59–61; *Early Motion,* 147–49; *Whole Motion,* 168–70.
Notes: Written in Positano.
35: See Genesis 1.2.
Variants:
1: Breath (*Helmets, Early Motion, Whole Motion*)| It (*New Yorker*)
2: neck. (*Helmets, Early Motion, Whole Motion*) | neck; (*New Yorker*)
4: Kept; (*Helmets, Early Motion, Whole Motion*) | Kept, (*New Yorker*)
4: back: (*Helmets, Early Motion, Whole Motion*) | back; (*New Yorker*)
10: sharks (*Helmets, Early Motion, Whole Motion*) | sharks, (*New Yorker*)
23: face (*Helmets, Early Motion, Whole Motion*) | face, (*New Yorker*)
40: song, (*Helmets, Early Motion, Whole Motion*) | song; (*New Yorker*)
41: body (*Helmets, Early Motion, Whole Motion*) | body, (*New Yorker*)
41: sea (*Helmets, Early Motion, Whole Motion*) | sea, (*New Yorker*)
42: smiling (*Helmets, Early Motion, Whole Motion*) | smiling, (*New Yorker*)
47: began (*Helmets, Early Motion, Whole Motion*) | began, (*New Yorker*)
48: seraphim, (*Helmets, Early Motion, Whole Motion*) | seraphim (*New Yorker*)
49: [line not indented] (*New Yorker*)
51: sons' (*Helmets, Early Motion, Whole Motion*) | son's (*New Yorker*)
52: stop: (*Helmets, Early Motion, Whole Motion*) | stop— (*New Yorker*)
53: the time (*Helmets, Early Motion, Whole Motion*) | its dark (*New Yorker*)
55: out of nowhere and anywhere (*Helmets, Early Motion, Whole Motion*) | as out of deep nothing-
ness (*New Yorker*)
56: Breathlessly (*Helmets, Early Motion, Whole Motion*) | Unlooked for, (*New Yorker*)

The Driver

First Publication: *New Yorker* 39 (December 7, 1963): 54.
Collected: *Helmets,* 81–3; *Poems 57–67,* 169–70; *Early Motion,* 169–71; *Whole Motion,* 182–83.
Reprinted: *American Poetry* 1965, 11–12; *Best Poems of 1963,* 44–45; *Voice That Is Great,* 494–95
Notes: Written in Positano. "I remember when I was in Okinawa and the war was over and we went out to one of the invasion beaches near Buckner Bay, me and my co-flyers, and we went swimming and there was an old amtrack there in ten feet of water that the Japanese had stove in—big holes in the side of it—and I swam down and sat in the driver's seat. The image stayed

with me and years later, twenty or twenty-five years later, I wrote "The Driver." (*Paris Review* 107 [Summer 1988]: 240—see also Arnett, 296; Baughman, 79). On activity underwater, see "The Movement of Fish" and "Winter Trout." Other poems set in Okinawa are "Amputee Ward, Okinawa 1945," "Victory," "The Coral Flight," "The Contest," and "The Work of Art." On Buckner Bay see "Victory," line 118.

VARIANTS:

10: then (*Helmets, Poems 57–67, Early Motion, Whole Motion*)| then, (*New Yorker*)

10: thistle (*Helmets, Poems 57–67, Early Motion, Whole Motion*)| thistle, (*New Yorker*)

15: halftrack (*Helmets, Poems 57–67, Early Motion, Whole Motion*) | half-track (*New Yorker*)

18: joy, (*Helmets, Poems 57–67, Early Motion, Whole Motion*) | joy (*New Yorker*)

18: sorrow, (*Helmets, Poems 57–67, Early Motion, Whole Motion*) | sorrow— (*New Yorker*)

The Ice Skin

FIRST PUBLICATION: *New Yorker* 39 (December 28, 1963): 37

COLLECTED: *Helmets,* 62–64; *Poems 57–67,* 157–58; *Early Motion,* 150–52; *Whole Motion,* 170–71.

REPRINTED: *Achievement,* 42–44; *Intervisions,* 35–36; *New Yorker Book of Poems,* 311–12; *Poems,* 27–28.

NOTES: "'The Ice Skin' . . . is about you [Christopher]" (*Summer,* 117–18).

VARIANTS:

25: Me (*Helmets, Poems 57–67, Early Motion, Whole Motion*) | Me, (*New Yorker*)

32: Rooms: (*Helmets, Poems 57–67, Early Motion, Whole Motion*) | Rooms— (*New Yorker*)

32: shining (*Helmets, Poems 57–67, Early Motion, Whole Motion*) | shining, (*New Yorker*)

37: kingdom: (*Helmets, Poems 57–67, Early Motion, Whole Motion*) | kingdom; (*New Yorker*)

38: ice (*Helmets, Poems 57–67, Early Motion, Whole Motion*) | ice, (*New Yorker*)

52: ice light (*Helmets, Poems 57–67, Early Motion, Whole Motion*) | ice-light (*New Yorker*)

The Leap

FIRST PUBLICATION: *North American Review,* n.s., 1 (Winter 1964): 31.

COLLECTED: *Poems 57–67,* 284–85; *Falling,* 54–55; *Whole Motion,* 279–80.

REPRINTED: *Poems,* 47–48; *Possibilities of Poetry,* 313–14; *Wesleyan Tradition,* 61–62.

NOTES: "In this poem I tried to ponder the relationship of her tomboyism in grade school, the athletic action of jumping to touch the decorations at the dance when she was committed to becoming a woman instead of a tomboy, and the results of her being a woman. . . . She married a man whom she didn't get along with, had his children, and eventually committed suicide because of it" (*Self,* 172). Mary Ann Robinson Young (1923–1961) attended a different grade school from Dickey, but they may have been in the same dancing class (line 2). She was one year ahead of Dickey (though seven months younger) at North Fulton High School and may be the "Mary Ann White" of *Striking,* 196. She graduated from the University of Georgia in 1944, married the supervisor of a hardware store, John Fant Young (1917–1998), had one child (not the "four" of line 28), and later divorced him. On Labor Day, September 4, 1961, at the age of thirty-eight, she left a note on the bed of her room and leapt unseen from the tenth floor of the Dinkler Plaza Hotel, in the 100 block of Forsyth Street in downtown Atlanta. Dickey, living in Atlanta before spending 1962 abroad, would have read on the front page of the next day's *Atlanta Constitution* that she "landed on the windshield of a taxicab parked on Williams Street, smashing the windshield and showering the driver with glass."

7–8: Mary Jane Brock, a year ahead of Dickey, may be the model for "Betty Lou Black"; Frances Long, in Dickey's class, may be "Frances Lane."

28–34: The *Constitution* published no photograph of Young's body. The image likely comes from an unforgettable full-page photograph published on page 43 of the May 12, 1947, issue of *Life*, showing the body of Evelyn McHale, a twenty-three-year-old bookkeeper from Babylon, Long Island, who had leapt from the observation deck of the Empire State Building and landed eighty-six floors below on the top of a sedan on West 33rd Street. Wearing pearls, white gloves, and stockings, she seems to be sleeping in the shimmering stoved-in roof of the car. One year before Dickey published this poem, the photograph so struck Andy Warhol (1928–1987) that he made a silkscreen painting of it, "Suicide (Fallen Body)," for his Suicide series. Dickey once told the Australian poet Tom Shapcott (b. 1935) that he had had an Australian wife who leapt to her death near Sydney (Hart, 387), and "Falling" dramatizes a similar event.

VARIANTS:

4: scrapbook (*Poems 57–67, Falling, Whole Motion*) | scrap-book (*North American Review*)

21: a brown (*Poems 57–67, Falling, Whole Motion*) | an orange (*North American Review*)

45: drawing paper (*Poems 57–67, Falling, Whole Motion*) | drawing-paper (*North American Review*)

Mary Sheffield

FIRST PUBLICATION: *Shenandoah* 15 (Winter 1964): 52–53.
COLLECTED: *Poems 57–67*, 281–82; *Falling*, 51–52; *Whole Motion*, 277–78.
REPRINTED: *Selected*, 116–17.
NOTES: During the war Dickey nearly married Gwendolyn Leege (Walti) and maintained a correspondence with her for the rest of his life (Hart, 76–78). See "Obstructions."
VARIANTS:

30: chord changes (*Poems 57–67, Falling, Whole Motion*) | chord-changes (*Shenandoah*)

30: river (*Poems 57–67, Falling, Whole Motion*) | rivers (*Shenandoah*)

Fox Blood

FIRST PUBLICATION: *Quarterly Review of Literature* 13 (Winter–Spring 1964): 37–38.
COLLECTED: *Buckdancer*, 46–47; *Poems 57–67*, 212–13; *Whole Motion*, 218–19.
REPRINTED: *New York Times Book Review*, March 27, 1966, 2; *Quarterly Review of Literature* 19 (Spring–Summer 1974): 264–25.
VARIANTS:

1: Blood blister (*Buckdancer, Poems 57–67, Whole Motion*) | Blood-blister (*Quarterly Review*)

20: *Hair tips* (*Buckdancer, Poems 57–67, Whole Motion*) | Hair-tips (*Quarterly Review*)

38: lopsided (*Buckdancer, Poems 57–67, Whole Motion*) | lop-sided (*Quarterly Review*)

40: half-moon (*Buckdancer, Poems 57–67, Whole Motion*) | halfmoon (*Quarterly Review*)
44: foreseen (*Buckdancer, Poems 57–67, Whole Motion*) | forseen (*Quarterly Review*)
47: nailbrush (*Buckdancer, Poems 57–67, Whole Motion*) |nail-brush (*Quarterly Review*)

For the Linden Moth

FIRST PUBLICATION: *Quarterly Review of Literature* 13 (Winter–Spring 1964): 38–40.
REPRINTED: *Quarterly Review of Literature* 19 (Spring–Summer 1974): 265–66.
NOTES: The linden moth (*Smerinthus tiliae*) was a threat to urban shade trees until the 1850s, when house sparrows imported from England devoured them in the caterpillar stage. In *Deliverance* Lewis describes to Ed "a mass hanging. A self-hanging of millions of 'em," explaining, "They let themselves down on threads. You can look anywhere you like and see 'em, wringing and twisting on the ends of the threads like men that can't die. Some of them are black and some are brown. And everything is quiet. It's so quiet. And they're there, twisting. But they're bad news. They eat the hardwood leaves. The government's trying to figure some way to get rid of 'em" (*Deliverance*, 54). On metamorphosis or resurrection, see also "Sleeping Out at Easter," "The Lifeguard," "A Folk Singer of the Thirties," and "The First Morning of Cancer." See Arnett, 289–90.
14–15: This famous question was not posed by the empiricist Bishop George Berkeley (1685–1753), but the essence may be found in his *Treatise Concerning the Principles of Human Knowledge*, §23, 24.

The Rafters

FIRST PUBLICATION: *Quarterly Review of Literature* 13 (Winter–Spring 1964): 40–42.
COLLECTED: *Whole Motion*, 26–27.
NOTES:
7: As Dickey's sister, Maibelle, was born in 1912 and his brother Eugene in 1914, they had seven years together before Eugene's death in 1921.
37: On Dickey's father and his beloved fighting birds, see "The Gamecocks."
VARIANTS:
29: roof, (*Quarterly Review*) | roof. (*Whole Motion* [typo])

Winter Trout

FIRST PUBLICATION: *Paris Review* 8 (Winter–Spring 1964): 98–99.
COLLECTED: *Helmets*, 24–26; *Poems 57–67*, 127–29; *Early Motion*, 112–14; *Whole Motion*, 145–47.
REPRINTED: *Best Poems of 1964*, 34–36.
NOTES: Written in Positano. On activity underwater see "The Movement of Fish" and "The Driver."
38–39: In book 21 of the *Odyssey*, Telemachus sets up twelve ax heads; his father, Odysseus, is able to shoot an arrow through them, but Penelope's suitors cannot.
40–41: Similarly Ed Gentry misses his first attempt to shoot a deer with a bow and arrow in *Deliverance*, 96–97.

35: dead beggar-lice (*Helmets, Poems 57–67, Early Motion, Whole Motion*) | beggar-lice (*Paris Review*)

39: ax heads (*Helmets, Poems 57–67, Early Motion, Whole Motion*) | ax-heads (*Paris Review*)

61: spring (*Helmets, Poems 57–67, Early Motion, Whole Motion*) | Spring (*Paris Review*)

61: wood (*Helmets, Poems 57–67, Early Motion, Whole Motion*) | woods (*Paris Review*)

Chenille

FIRST PUBLICATION: *Helmets*, 15–17. (*Helmets* published February 27, 1964)

COLLECTED: *Helmets*, 15–17; *Poems 57–67*, 119–21; *Early Motion*, 103–5; *Whole Motion*, 138–40.

REPRINTED: *American Poetry 1965*, 12–14; *Norton Anthology of Modern Poetry*, 1032–33; *Poetry Southeast 1950–70*, 55–57.

NOTES: Written in Positano. The popularity of the grandmother's craft of making chenille (French for "caterpillar") began in Dalton, Georgia, in 1895, when fifteen-year-old Catherine Evans Whitener used a French technique known in America as "tufting" (tying bunches of fuzzy cut threads together at their base) to create a raised pattern on a bedspread. By the 1920s machine-made chenille was an industry nationally centered in Dalton and memorialized in its Hamilton House Museum. In the 1930s and 1940s, it was a popular needlecraft for making personalized textiles. "I've known those old chenille mills and bedspreads all my life. But one winter I was hunting way up north of Atlanta, and I got lost, as usual. It was getting dark and cold and beginning to rain, so I went to a farmer's house and asked if I could stay there and pay for a bed. . . . His grandmother was living with his family, and she was making a design on a chenille spread. . . . It was a crazy-looking thing, like an elephant with great pink wings. I asked her what it was. 'Just something I made up,' she said. 'I thought it would be pretty.' Then I asked her, 'Ma'am, do you think things like this really exist in the world?' 'Of course they do,' she said, 'because they ought to. . . .' In writing the poem, I contrasted the industrial chenille spreads with the spreads produced by the half-demented imagination of this old lady. Maybe it's too obvious a contrast, but it seemed to me wonderfully symbolic of the artistic process, of art produced by the creative mind versus the officialized kind of beauty" (*Self*, 124–25).

61–62: For Adam see "Dust."

63–72: For Noah see *God's Images*, 10–11.

On the Coosawattee

FIRST PUBLICATION: "By Canoe Through the Fir Forest," *New Yorker* 38 (June 16, 1962): 32; "Below Ellijay," *Poetry* 101 (October–November 1962): 27–28; "On the Inundation of the Coosawattee Valley," *Yale Review* 52 (Winter 1963): 234–35.

COLLECTED: As "On the Coosawattee," *Helmets*, 18–23; *Poems 57–67*, 122–26; *Early Motion*, 106–11; *Whole Motion*, 140–45.

REPRINTED: "By Canoe Through the Fir Forest," *Best Poems of 1962*, 45–46, *Exile: Reed College Literary Magazine* (1981–82): 42–43, and *New Yorker Book of Poems*, 92–93; "Below Ellijay" *Poetry: Golden Anniversary*, 27–28.

NOTES: Begun in Positano. "Actually, they were written when I was in the advertising business in Atlanta and had just come back from the trip. That was an horrendous trip! I mean, that trip down the Coosawattee through the fir forest and those other places was the grimmest physical experience I'd had since I was in the service" (Arnett, 293; Baughman, 77). The Coosawattee rises just north of Ellijay, Georgia, at the junction of the Ellijay and Cartecay Rivers, about eighty miles north of Atlanta, flowing southwest about fifty miles to Carters Lake. Before the 1960s, it was one of the most dangerous whitewater canoeing sites in the country and was the chief model for the fictional "Cahulawassee" River in *Deliverance.* In 1962 it was decided to dam the river ("Carters Dam") and thus bury the rapids beneath what became Carters Lake in 1977. At a place on the Coosawattee, Dickey and his friend Al Braselton (see "Drifting") noticed chicken heads and entrails dumped into the river. "That was one of the most memorably disgusting things that I've ever seen. I think that is in Ellijay, Georgia. . . . We said, 'There's something wrong here.' And then we saw all these feathers and things and chicken heads" (Arnett, 293–94; Baughman, 77–78). Ellijay is the home of a Gold Kist Poultry Processing Plant and a Tyson Foods slaughterhouse and the model for the town of Aintry in *Deliverance* (Arnett, 293). A similar scene occurs in *Deliverance,* 69. See Broughton, 189, and Hart, 247.

NOTES:

105: Carters Lake

125: Lucas Gentry, the "strange woods boy" is a prototype of the memorable banjo-playing boy in *Deliverance.* His name is recalled in that of the narrator, Ed Gentry: "The boy's name was really, if I remember correctly, Ira Gentry, but I just changed it to Lucas for the poem . . ." (*Crux,* 358).

VARIANTS:

4: stones (*Helmets, Poems 57–67, Early Motion, Whole Motion*) | stones, (*New Yorker*)

5: To follow (*Helmets, Poems 57–67, Early Motion, Whole Motion*) | Following (*New Yorker*)

10: nerves (*Helmets, Poems 57–67, Early Motion, Whole Motion*) | nerves, (*New Yorker*)

11: ripples (*Helmets, Poems 57–67, Early Motion, Whole Motion*) | ripples, (*New Yorker*)

13: hard-pressed (*Helmets, Poems 57–67, Early Motion, Whole Motion*) | hard pressed (*New Yorker*)

13: up (*Helmets, Poems 57–67, Early Motion, Whole Motion*) | up, (*New Yorker*)

16: side (*Helmets, Poems 57–67, Early Motion, Whole Motion*) | side, (*New Yorker*)

23: water (*Helmets, Poems 57–67, Early Motion, Whole Motion*) | water, (*New Yorker*)

25: rowing muscles (*Helmets, Poems 57–67, Early Motion, Whole Motion*) | rowing-muscles (*New Yorker*)

29: hair (*Helmets, Poems 57–67, Early Motion, Whole Motion*) | hair, (*New Yorker*)

30: floor (*Helmets, Poems 57–67, Early Motion, Whole Motion*) | floor, (*New Yorker*)

31: eye (*Helmets, Poems 57–67, Early Motion, Whole Motion*) | eye, (*New Yorker*)

36: forever (*Helmets, Poems 57–67, Early Motion, Whole Motion*) | forever, (*New Yorker*)

40: As the (*Helmets, Poems 57–67, Early Motion, Whole Motion*) | As (*New Yorker*)

58: tool sheds (*Helmets, Poems 57–67, Early Motion, Whole Motion*) | tool-sheds (*Poetry*)

96: wing feathers (*Helmets, Poems 57–67, Early Motion, Whole Motion*) | wing-feathers (*Poetry*)

105: dam. (*Helmets, Poems 57–67, Early Motion, Whole Motion*) | dam, (*Yale Review*)

121: life preservers (*Helmets, Poems 57–67, Early Motion, Whole Motion*) | life-preservers (*Yale Review*)

128: looking (*Helmets, Poems 57–67, Early Motion, Whole Motion*) | and looked (*Yale Review*)

128: on the roaring (*Helmets, Poems 57–67, Early Motion, Whole Motion*) | upon the (*Yale Review*)

Springer Mountain [b]

FIRST PUBLICATION: *Helmets*, 27–30.

COLLECTED: *Poems 57–67*, 130–33; *Early Motion*, 115–18; *Whole Motion*, 147–49.

REPRINTED: *Appalachian Trail Reader*, 85–87; *Achievement*, 34–37; *Contemporary American Poetry*, 66–69; *Self*, 126–29; *Interviews*, 25–29.

NOTES: Rewritten version of "Springer Mountain [a]." "*I never took off my clothes and entered into a ritual dance with the animal I'd been trying to kill. I never did anything like this, but I aspire to it*" (*Self*, 126). "This poem concerns a bow hunter, very amateurish, first time he's been out. He really doesn't think he's going to see anything, but he's up there, dressed in warm clothes in the fall of the year at dawn, waiting for the deer to come down to drink. He thinks he's got a pretty good place picked out, but he doesn't know much about it. He's really not hoping for much. Just being there is enough for him, being there in the activity. A deer does come. And he seethes with a kind of frenzy, not to kill the deer with the arrow, but to join the deer in its world. So he takes off all his clothes in an attempt to do that, and he goes down, drinks from the mountain stream like the deer" (Greiner, 21).

45: A deer has antlers, not horns.

49: On crucifixion, see "The Crows," line 4.

54: On turning forty, see "Birthday Dream."

55: The narrator hangs his bow on a branch as Ike McCaslin sets his rifle against a fence in William Faulkner's "The Bear."

Approaching Prayer

FIRST PUBLICATION: *Helmets*, 73–80.

COLLECTED: *Poems 57–67*, 163–68; *Early Motion*, 161–68; *Whole Motion*, 176–81.

REPRINTED: *Selected*, 55–60; *Poems*, 29–34.

NOTES: Written in Positano. "The most complicated and far-fetched poem I've written. . . . I tried to imagine how a rather prosaic person would prepare himself for the miraculous event which will be the prayer he's going to try to pray" (*Self*, 134). On Dickey's one boar hunt, see Hart, 259. For murder of the father, see also "Dover: Believing in Kings" and "May Day Sermon." For a creature speaking in italics, see "The Sheep Child."

12: "I think that there are certain circumstances in a person's experience where it is better to participate in the experience by means of simple gut reactions and not through reasoning. Not through intellectualization about the experience but to just be in it and feel what you honestly feel as a response" (Suarez, 121).

17: On Eugene Dickey, Sr.'s fighting birds, see "The Gamecocks," line 4.

24: Possibly a punning allusion to the hogshead in which the cynic Diogenes was said to live.

62: Tushes are tusks.

158: Perhaps the pillars of fire that guided the Israelites through the desert (Exodus 13:21; Numbers 14:14; Nehemiah 9:12, 19). The Tower of Babel (Genesis 11:1–9) does not involve fire though it appears to do so in the famous engraving by Gustave Doré, *The Confusion of Tongues* (1865).

159: The seven years of plenty and of famine are described in Genesis 41:30.

160: Joseph sells corn to his brothers in Genesis 42. Locusts were the eighth plague of Egypt (Exodus 10:1–20). Moses and Aaron scattered ash to bring about the sixth plague, unhealable boils (Exodus 9:8).

161: Samson's riddle (Judges 14:8, 14–18).

162: The death of the first born is the tenth plague (Exodus 11:1–12:36).

163: Immaculate conception is described in Luke 1:28, 31.

165: Child of light: see Ephesians 5:8–10 and "children of light," Luke 16:1. See also "Genius, like a fallen child of light / Has filled the place with magic . . . ," Nathaniel Parker Willis, "Poem Delivered at Brown University, September 6, 1831," *The Poems, Sacred, Passionate and Humorous* (1831).

Reincarnation (I)

FIRST PUBLICATION: As "Reincarnation," *New Yorker* 40 (March 7, 1964): 51.

COLLECTED: As "Reincarnation," *Buckdancer*, 29–30; *Whole Motion*, 206–7; as "Reincarnation (I)," *Poems 57–67*, 196–97.

REPRINTED: *Anthology*, 1749–50; *Contemporary Poetry in America*, 70; *How Does a Poem Mean?*, 145–46; *Southern Writing in the Sixties*, 16–17.

NOTES: "I had been getting tired of the three-beat line, for I had already written the better part of three books in it. . . . So I put an arbitrary limit on the line of 'Reincarnation (I).' I simply wrote as far across the page as the typewriter would go, and that was essentially the line" (*Self*, 140). "I wrote the poem at the time when there began to be a lot of agitation in Mississippi. I don't know whether it was before or after the murder of those three civil rights workers involving Sheriff [Lawrence] Rainey and Deputy Cecil Price. It might have been a little before this, but the idea of the injustice of a great deal of Southern justice might have been on my mind to some extent. I thought it might be a good idea to leave a hint that the man who had been reincarnated as a rattlesnake was one of those kinds of people, because the symbol of the snake has to do with justice. . . . The justice of the Lord, in its most striking case, depended on the intervention of the snake" (*Self*, 140–41). For Dickey on reincarnation, see "Reincarnation (II)." The eastern diamondback rattlesnake (*Crotalus adamanteus*) is the most venomous snake and the largest rattlesnake (3'5"–6') in North America. It is found throughout the South from North Carolina to Florida. Its back features twenty-four to thirty-five diamond shapes (lines 21–22), and the triangular head has a "snub" appearance (line 24) enhanced by facial pits (hence "pit viper") used for detecting infrared heat. The snake reproduces ovoviviparously, meaning the young are gestated within an egg in the mother's body and then born live underground (line 5). Their diet is as Dickey describes it (lines 26–27), and they tend to lurk, waiting to strike passersby, rather than aggressively seeking food (line 28). In Georgia these snakes were so feared that there used to be annual "round-ups" of them (Laurence M. Klauber, *Rattlesnakes,* second edition [Berkeley & Los Angeles: University of California Press, 1972], 1:31, 449–50. See "Blowgun and Rattlesnake.")

VARIANTS:

5: sand (*Buckdancer, Poems 57–67, Whole Motion*) | sand, (*New Yorker*)

16: grass: (*Buckdancer, Poems 57–67, Whole Motion*) | grass; (*New Yorker*)

26: ice cold (*Buckdancer, Poems 57–67, Whole Motion*) | ice-cold (*New Yorker*)

29: river: (*Buckdancer, Poems 57–67, Whole Motion*) | river. (*New Yorker*) |

The Second Sleep

FIRST PUBLICATION: *Kenyon Review* 26 (Spring 1964): 302–3.

COLLECTED: With "The Aura" as "Fathers and Sons," *Buckdancer,* 48–49; *Poems 57–67,* 214–15; *Whole Motion,* 219–20.

NOTES: "I've always loved 'The Second Sleep,' but I don't think anybody else has ever paid much attention to it" (*Self,* 147).

VARIANTS:

3: arms; (*Kenyon, Buckdancer, Poems 57–67*) | arms. (*Whole Motion* [typo])

The Firebombing

FIRST PUBLICATION: *Poetry* 104 (May 1964): 63–72.

COLLECTED: *Buckdancer,* 11–20; *Poems 57–67,* 181–88; *Whole Motion,* 193–200.

REPRINTED: *50 Modern American and British Poets,* 140–49; *100 Postwar Poems,* 126–33; *Achievement,* 52–59; *Articles of War,* 110–17; *Because I Fly,* 8–11 (abbreviated version); *Contemporary American Poetry* (Poulin), 82–89; *Dickey Reader,* 62–70; *Selected,* 69–77; *Oxford Book of War Poetry,* 290–97; *Tricentennial Anthology,* 561–69; *Two Poems; Where is Vietnam?* (abridged), 28–29.

NOTES: The events in this poem seem to reflect the 418th Night Fighter Squadron's first bombing mission to Japan, on July 28, 1945, in which three planes bombed the island of Kyushu, but Dickey said, " 'The Firebombing' . . . is not based on any one mission I flew. It is a composite of several different ones, plus a lot of invention that seemed to go with the other stuff" (*Night,* 318). " 'The Firebombing' has to do with the aftermath of war, not the war itself, but the memory of the war" (Greiner, 11). See also "The Jewel." "The danger [facing pilots] is in the feeling of power it gives them to do these things and not be held accountable for the carnage and terror and bloodshed and mutilation. To not even *see* it. . . . That is what 'The Firebombing' is about—that you'll never have to face up to the carnage and death and mutilation you have wrought. To you it just looks like a beautiful spectacle. . . . 'The Firebombing' is about the worst guilt of all—the guilt of not being able to feel guilt over the things you ought to feel guilty about" (*Playboy* interview, 92; Baughman, 117). Dickey also described a firebombing raid from the ground in "Eye of the Fire," lines 62–64, and the aftermath of such a raid in *To the White Sea,* 42–76. In "[The Collapse of James Dickey] *Buckdancer's Choice*" (*Sixties* 9 [Spring 1967]: 74–75), Robert Bly touched off a major feud between the two poets by saying, "But this poem has no real anguish. . . . The poem emphasizes the picturesque quality of firebombing instead, the lordly and attractive isolation of the pilot, the spectacular colors unfolding beneath, and describes the way the fire spread. . . . Dickey in the poem appeared to be embarrassing the military establishment for its Japanese air raids, but he is actually performing a function for the establishment. . . . In short, if we read this poem right, we can go on living with napalm." Dickey wrote Diane Wakowski, on September 9, 1969: "But all one has to do is to read 'The Firebombing' to see that it has nothing to do with being a war mongering poem" (*Crux*, 309–10, 477). He later said that the poem "is based on a kind of paradox based on the sense of power one has as a pilot of an aircrew dropping bombs. This is a sense of power a person can otherwise never experience. Of course this sensation is humanly rep-rehensible, but so are many of the human emotions that one has. Judged by the general standard, such emotions are reprehensible, but they do happen, and that is the feeling. Then you come back from a war you won, and you're a civilian, and you begin to think about the implications of what you actually did do when you experienced this sense of power and remoteness and godlike vision. And you think of the exercise of authority via the machine that your own government has put at your disposal to do exactly what you did with it. Then you have a family yourself, and you think about these people twenty, thirty, forty years ago—I was dropping those bombs on them, on some of them. Suppose somebody did that to me?. . . You have fought for freedom and risked your life not once but many times for the cause of peace and freedom. . . . If you have a home in the sub-urbs and a lawn to cut, you are able to have it because forty years ago you had to do something else when the world's historical situation called for it. And you're not ashamed of it no matter who says what" (Suarez, 123). See *Babel*, 290–91, and *Self*, 137–39: "It's fashionable to talk about guilt in poems, like Sylvia Plath feeling guilty over the slaughter of the Jews. She didn't have anything to do with it. She can be *sorry*, but guilt is more personal than that: it has to do with something you have *done*, or could have done and didn't. It's a literary convention for her. To have guilt you've got to earn guilt, but sometimes when you earn it, you don't feel the guilt you ought to have. And that's what 'The Firebombing' is all about." In *To the White Sea* (39–45), Muldrow experiences a firebombing from the ground.

Epigraphs: Gunter Eich, "Denke daran," 22–23 ("One remembers that after great destruction / Everyone will prove that he was innocent."); Job 40:9: "Has thou an arm like God? Or canst thou thunder with a voice like him?"

17: Icarus's wings caught fire when he flew too close to the sun. Prometheus brought fire down from heaven to man.

95–97: The Prometheus image now turns into Vulcan, the god of the stithy, whose work took place deep within volcanoes.

106–8: For the Southern Cross, see "Reincarnation (II)"; for Orion and Scorpio, see "For the Nightly Ascent of the Hunter Orion over a Forest Clearing."

121: Beppu is a resort city on Kyushu Island in Japan famed for its more than three thousand sacred hot springs. The bombing run to Beppu was one of the "anti-morale" raids toward the close of the war.

276: Dickey was fond of Kant's phrase "Das Ding an sich," meaning the world itself beyond the grasp of human reason or understanding.

VARIANTS:

1: Homeowners (*Buckdancer, Poems 57–67, Whole Motion*) | Home-owners (*Poetry*)

9: coral sticks (*Buckdancer, Poems 57–67, Whole Motion*) | coral-sticks (*Poetry*)

10: cowl flaps (*Buckdancer, Poems 57–67, Whole Motion*) | cowl-flaps (*Poetry*)

10: tilt (*Buckdancer, Poems 57–67, Whole Motion*) | tilt' (*Poetry*)

41: nightwalkers (*Buckdancer, Poems 57–67, Whole Motion*) | night-walkers (*Poetry*)

70: that is (*Poetry, Buckdancer, Poems 57–67*) | this is (*Whole Motion*)

83: bus   where the new / Scoutmaster lives where (*Poetry, Buckdancer Poems 57–67*) | where (*Whole Motion* [typo, words omitted])

123: An (*Poetry, Buckdancer, Poems 57–67*) | And (*Whole Motion* [typo])

132: bathhouse (*Buckdancer, Poems 57–67, Whole Motion*) | bath-house (*Poetry*)

198: bar light (*Buckdancer, Poems 57–67, Whole Motion*) | bar-light (*Poetry*)

209: voice box (*Buckdancer, Poems 57–67, Whole Motion*) | voice-box (*Poetry*)

237: steppingstones (*Buckdancer, Poems 57–67, Whole Motion*) | stepping-stones (*Poetry*)

245: Beholding, beneath, (*Buckdancer, Poems 57–67, Whole Motion*) | Beholding beneath me (*Poetry*)

257: homeowners (*Buckdancer, Poems 57–67, Whole Motion*) | home-owners (*Poetry*)

272: easygoing (*Buckdancer, Poems 57–67, Whole Motion*) | easy-going (*Poetry*)

Them, Crying

First Publication: *New Yorker* 40 (May 9, 1964): 42.

Collected: *Buckdancer*, 31–33; *Poems 57–67*, 198–200; *Whole Motion*, 207–8.

Reprinted: *Best Poems of 1964*, 40–42; *Now Voices*, 216–18; *Teaching*, 38–40.

Notes: Dickey's favorite poem "in terms of its ending" (Broughton, 185). While riding his bicycle home for lunch on his last day in the seventh grade in Portland, Oregon, the eleven-year-old Christopher Dickey caught his pant leg in the bicycle's chain and pitched over the handlebars, landing on his chin and breaking his arm severely. Treated at the scene with a full anesthetic, young Dickey was taken to a hospital by ambulance and ultimately lay in a recovery room for a few hours while he regained consciousness. As he awoke he was aware of other patients in the room screaming in pain. Their screams must have been audible in the waiting room where his anxious father sat. Christopher was released that day with a cast on his arm and his face bandaged. In James Dickey's version of the events, his son was struck by a truck (perhaps the origin of the truck driver who barges into the recovery room) and remained in the hospital "two or three days before we ever caught a glimpse of him. I sat hour after hour after hour and day after day in the kind of antechamber there, . . . with other anxious parents who were waiting to get some word from the inner sanctum of the children's ward." (*Teaching*, 38). "I would sit there at one or two at night and could hear the children crying in there with no one to comfort them. And I thought, 'I'm going to get up my courage one of these days and go in there and see if I can do something for those children.' . . . I never did get the courage" (*Self*, 142). At three A.M., while Dickey was "trying to read Thomas Aquinas or somebody" an unshaven man came in "and sort of looked aggressively around to see if anybody was going to stop him. Nobody was there, so he went into the children's ward. . . . I thought about this as being one of those essentially brave and compassionate human acts, that this man, who probably didn't have anything to do with children, heard some kind of summons from these little voices, helpless with injuries or operations, and had been brought in, summoned from the outside world, to come to them" (*Teaching*, 38). See further *Self*, 141–43.

Variants:

6: wheels (*Buckdancer, Poems 57–67, Whole Motion*) | wheels, (*New Yorker*)

14: spiraling (*Buckdancer, Poems 57–67, Whole Motion*) | spiralling (*New Yorker*)

20: led: (*Buckdancer, Poems 57–67, Whole Motion*) | led— (*New Yorker*)

35: green-tiled (*Buckdancer, Poems 57–67, Whole Motion*) | green-tiled, (*New Yorker*)

64: *before,* (*Buckdancer, Poems 57–67, Whole Motion*) | *before—* (*New Yorker*)

67: *ward boys, pan handlers* (*Buckdancer, Poems 57–67, Whole Motion*) | *ward-boys, panhandlers* (*New Yorker*)

68: *nightwalkers* (*Buckdancer, Poems 57–67, Whole Motion*) | *night walkers* (*New Yorker*)

68: *drunkards* (*Buckdancer, Poems 57–67, Whole Motion*) | *drunkards,* (*New Yorker*)

The Escape

First Publication: *New Yorker* 40 (July 18, 1964): 30.

Collected: *Buckdancer,* 36–38; *Poems 57–67,* 203–4; *Whole Motion,* 211–12.

Reprinted: *Decade,* 76–78.

Notes: Dickey left Atlanta for good at the beginning of 1963, leaving behind many family landmarks. "I'm so claustrophobic that I have a horror of burial, especially in a cemetery—at least in an ordinary cemetery. . . . The cemetery in the city is a sad, sad environment where the hospital, textile mills, and the city have grown up around what used to be a village graveyard" (*Self,* 144).

1–3: Fairmount is a small town on the Coosawattee in Gordon County, Georgia. Dickey used the name for Oakland Cemetery in midtown Atlanta, where four generations of both sides of Dickey's family have mausoleums (see "The Step"). The Dickey mausoleum holds the remains of Dickey's grandfather James L. Dickey, Sr. ("The Angel of the Maze"), but neither of his great-grandmothers is at Oakland.

3: The small town of Tate (named for the Tate family) in Pickens County, Georgia, sits on "four square miles of marble" (*New York Times,* July 21, 1884, 2). It is the home of the Georgia Marble Company, begun by Col. Sam Tate (1860–1938) in the 1880s and carried on by his family (see "In the Marble Quarry"). At Oakland the Dickey structure is of granite, but the building for his mother's side, the Swift-Burckhardt family, built in 1891, is of Tate marble.

4–6: The Dickey mausoleum faces the Confederate memorial at Oakland and a burial ground for seven thousand soldiers, but there is no statue of "A Civil War general."

15–16: The Grady Memorial Hospital is near Oakland, while the one open window recalls "The Hospital Window," set at the Piedmont Hospital on Peachtree Road, where Dickey was born and his father died.

Variants:

8: him (*Buckdancer Poems 57–67 Whole Motion*) | him, (*New Yorker*)

30: [no blank line] (*Poems 57–67, Whole Motion*) | [blank line inserted] (*New Yorker, Buckdancer*)

43: hand-written (*Buckdancer, Poems 57–67, Whole Motion*) | handwritten (*New Yorker*)

54: buck, (*Buckdancer, Poems 57–67, Whole Motion*) | buck (*New Yorker*)

Faces Seen Once

FIRST PUBLICATION: *Hudson Review* 17 (Autumn 1964): 414–16.

COLLECTED: *Buckdancer,* 23–25; *Poems 57–67,* 191–93; *Whole Motion,* 202–4.

NOTES: "I began this poem in Edinburgh, Scotland, when I was in a taxi and a girl in a red tam crossed the street in front of me, in front of the cab at the red light. As Apollinaire said somewhere [in the poem "1909"], 'She was so beautiful she made me afraid' ['cette femme était si belle / Qu'elle me faisait peur']. And I never got over it. I started scribbling immediately. . . . It seems maybe that these faces that we see one time—as we get older we see more of them, just a snatch, just a glimpse here or a glimpse there—that they sort of amalgamate into one face and that at the moment of death this would be the thing that blazes up most urgently in the mind as being symbolic of all those human possibilities that we've never realized" ("Comments," 9).

17: Robertstown, in White County, Georgia, is ninety-five miles north-northeast of Atlanta, bordering Unicoi State Park and the Innsbruck Resort and Country Club.

VARIANTS:

44: coffee shops (*Buckdancer, Poems 57–67, Whole Motion*) | coffee-shops (*Hudson*)

44: filling stations (*Buckdancer, Poems 57–67, Whole Motion*) | filling-stations (*Hudson*)

51: pretesting (*Buckdancer, Poems 57–67, Whole Motion*) | pre-testing (*Hudson*)

Angina

FIRST PUBLICATION: *New Yorker* 40 (August 15, 1964): 30.

COLLECTED: *Buckdancer,* 63–65; *Poems 57–67,* 226–27; *Whole Motion,* 228–29.

NOTES: On Maibelle Swift Dickey's angina, see "Buckdancer's Choice" and "The Zodiac," lines 802–4.

24–25: Maibelle Swift Dickey (1888–1977) survived a childhood bout with rheumatic fever that left her heart with a mitral valve stenosis, but not angina pectoris, chest pain caused by lack of oxygen to the heart muscle. Her first child was Maibelle ("Power and Light"), born in 1912; she had Eugene ("The String") in 1914 and James in 1923.

41: Eugene Dickey, Sr., installed an electric chairlift on the staircase at the Dickey home at 166 West Wesley in Atlanta.

VARIANTS:

7: windowframed (*Buckdancer, Poems 57–67, Whole Motion*) | window-framed (*New Yorker*)

43: sun (*Buckdancer, Poems 57–67, Whole Motion*) | sun, (*New Yorker*)

44: steps (*Buckdancer, Poems 57–67, Whole Motion*) | steps, (*New Yorker*)

47: month: (*Buckdancer, Poems 57–67, Whole Motion*) | month, (*New Yorker*)

55: the (*Buckdancer, Poems 57–67, Whole Motion*) | those (*New Yorker*)

Pursuit from Under

FIRST PUBLICATION: *Hudson Review* 17 (Autumn 1964): 412–14.

COLLECTED: *Buckdancer,* 43–45; *Poems 57–67,* 209–11; *Whole Motion,* 216–18.

REPRINTED: *Achievement,* 63–65; *Best Poems 1964,* 37–39; *Georgia Voices,* 93–95; *Poetry Past and Present,* 428–30.

NOTES: "Some 6 or 7 killer whales, old and young, were skirting the vast floe edge ahead of the ship; they seemed excited and dived rapidly, almost touching the floe. . . . I had heard weird stories of these beasts, but had never associated serious danger with them. [Photographer H. G. Ponting] seized his camera and ran towards the floe edge to get a close picture of the beasts, which had momentarily disappeared. The next moment the whole floe under him and the dogs heaved up and split into fragments. One could hear the 'booming' noise as the whales rose under the ice and struck it with their backs. . . . Then it was clear that the whales shared our astonishment, for one after another their huge hideous heads shot vertically into the air through the cracks which they had made. As they reared them to a height of 6 or 8 feet it was possible to see their tawny head markings, their small glistening eyes, and their terrible array of teeth—by far the largest and most terrifying in the world" (*Scott's Last Expedition,* arranged by Leonard Huxley [New York: Dodd, Mead, 1913], 65–66). See "Angel of the Maze," 81.
VARIANTS:
3: week ends (*Buckdancer, Poems 57–67, Whole Motion*) | week-ends (*Hudson*)
17: seal holes (*Buckdancer, Poems 57–67, Whole Motion*) | seal-holes (*Hudson*)
20: icecap (*Buckdancer, Poems 57–67, Whole Motion*) | ice-cap (*Hudson*)

The War Wound

FIRST PUBLICATION: *New Yorker* 40 (12 September 1964) 54.
COLLECTED: *Buckdancer,* 58–59; *Poems 57–67,* 223; *Whole Motion,* 225–26.
REPRINTED: *Literature of America,* 731–32; *Pocket Book of Modern Verse,* 112–13.
NOTES: Dickey received a Purple Heart for an injury sustained when, during a wheel's-up landing, he put his hand through a glass dial in the cockpit. (He was sitting in the copilot's seat.) He wrote to his father on May 28, 1945: "I have a half-mooned-shaped cut on my hand that I got when I was in an airplane wreck. . . . It wasn't a bad cut; it didn't even require stitches. . . . I sometimes would look at my hand and think, 'Lord, the war that killed and mutilated so many people did only this to me!'" (*Self,* 151).
VARIANTS:
21: [indented] (*New Yorker, Poems 57–67*) | [not indented] (*Buckdancer, Whole Motion*)
21: And (*Buckdancer, Poems 57–67, Whole Motion*) | And, (*New Yorker*)
26: ago (*Buckdancer, Poems 57–67, Whole Motion*) | ago, (*New Yorker*)

Reincarnation (II)

FIRST PUBLICATION: As "Reincarnation," *Two Poems* (published September 1964), 39–84.
COLLECTED: *Poems 57–67,* 243–51; *Falling,* 15–23; *Whole Motion,* 250–58.
REPRINTED: *Contemporary American Poetry* (Poulin), 90–98; *Distinctive Voice,* 236–43; *Selected,* 99–108.
NOTES: "Reincarnation is one religious idea I have always loved believing in. I don't know whether the soul passes from one kind of creature to another; I hope it does. I would live this human life gladly if I knew I was going to be a bird—next time—or have any kind of consciousness at all"

(*Self,* 140). "I'd like to be some sort of bird—a migratory sea bird like a tern or a wandering alba-tross. But until death, until this either happens or doesn't happen, I'll have to keep trying to do it, to die and fly, by words" (*Self,* 79). "I would rather read "Reincarnation (II)" than any number of beautifully turned rhyming lyrics by other poets, or even by myself" (Friedmann, 31; Baughman, 171). Dickey used the trope of the observant flying bird (sea gull) for his coffee-table book *Jericho* (1974). Discussed in *Mademoiselle* interview, 142; *Self,* 163–64. As one who had navigated more than one hundred hours of combat in thirty-eight missions in World War II, Dickey was very familiar with the airborne perspective.

Dickey's M.A. thesis was "Symbol and Image in the Shorter Poems of Herman Melville" (Vanderbilt, 1950). Melville impressed him with "this sense of an apparently serene surface which masks some hidden horror, some unknown universal evil. There's the great chapter in *Moby-Dick,* on the whiteness of the whale, when he develops the idea that white is kind of the color that masks all the darkness" (*Playboy* interview, 89; Baughman, 112–13). Dickey addressed Melville's use of white in a chapter titled "The Pale Horse," reprinted in Ernest Suarez, "Dickey on Melville," *South Carolina Review* 26 (Spring 1994): 115–26. The chapter cites the passage that is the first epigraph for this poem, along with another passage, "Bethink thee of the albatross, whence come those clouds of spiritual wonderment and pale dread, in which that white phantom sails in all imaginations?" (ibid., 120.) For a white heron, see "The Ground of Killing," 10–11. For Melville see "Haunting the Maneuvers" and "Last Hours."

Epigraphs: "As Abraham before the angel, I bowed myself; the white thing was so white . . ." (Herman Melville, *Moby-Dick,* chapter 42, 194); "As apparitional . . ." (Hart Crane, "To Brooklyn Bridge," lines 6–7).

36: Draco is a northern constellation that from North America appears over the North Pole.

37: Leo is between Cancer and Virgo.

41: "Embued," var. of "Imbued."

42: The "Christmas Star," which led the Magi to the Christ child, was thought by Johannes Kepler to be a nova created by the conjunction of Jupiter and Saturn in 7 B.C.E. Today it is thought to be a supernova in the Andromeda Galaxy.

48: The Freudian dream is a "wish-fulfillment dream."

70: The flight past constellations is a zig-zag affair around the lower center of the southern hemi-sphere of the sky. The Southern Cross, also known as Crux (the title of the sequel to *Alnilam,* on which Dickey was working at the time of his death and the title of the collection of Dickey letters edited by Matthew J. Bruccoli and Judith S. Baughman), is the smallest of the eighty-eight constellations. The Centaur (line 111) surrounds it on three sides. Since there is no south-ern pole star, two stars in Crux are generally used to mark the Southern Celestial Pole.

75: The nearby False Cross is diamond-shaped, contains only four stars, and is dimmer than the kite-shaped, bright five-star Southern Cross.

111: Hydra is the largest of the constellations, adjacent on the north to Centaur.

112: Centaur is another southern constellation, lying just below Hydra. Lupus (the wolf) lies southwest of the Centaur. Virgo lies between Leo on the west and Libra on the east.

211–12: St. Elmo's Fire (named for St. Erasmus of Formiae, patron saint of sailors) is an electrical discharge that emanates a violet glow, commonly from the masts of ships during thunder-storms.

13: Born (*Two Poems*) | born (*Poems 57–67, Falling, Whole Motion*)

18: bubble (*Poems 57–67, Falling, Whole Motion*) | bubble— (*Two Poems*)

20: South (*Poems 57–67, Falling, Whole Motion*) | south (*Two Poems*)

37: Against (*Two Poems*) | Again (*Poems 57–67, Falling, Whole Motion* [typo])

52: *wingless*— (*Poems 57–67, Falling, Whole Motion*) | wingless   — (*Two Poems*)

69: Swan   he (*Poems 57–67, Falling, Whole Motion*) | Swan / he (*Two Poems*)

92–93: [blank line inserted] (*Two Poems*)

134–35: [blank line inserted] (*Two Poems*)

137: collected (*Poems 57–67, Falling, Whole Motion*) | uncollected (*Two Poems*)

155: sees something (*Poems 57–67, Falling, Whole Motion*) | sees   something (*Two Poems*)

157: bird word (*Poems 57–67, Falling, Whole Motion*) | bird-word (*Two Poems*)

163–64: [no blank line inserted] (*Two Poems*)

224: kingdoms (*Poems 57–67, Falling, Whole Motion*) | Kingdoms (*Two Poems*)

231: through. He (*Poems 57–67, Falling, Whole Motion*) | through.   He (*Two Poems*)

The Common Grave

FIRST PUBLICATION: *New Yorker* 40 (October 24, 1964): 54.

COLLECTED: *Buckdancer*, 26–28; *Poems 57–67*, 194–95; *Whole Motion*, 204–6.

REPRINTED: *Contemporary American Poets*, 70–72.

NOTES:

45: Oberon, the king of fairies, can retreat into an acorn in *A Midsummer Night's Dream*.

50: dumfoundedly, var. of dumbfoundedly.

VARIANTS:

2: though (*New Yorker, Buckdancer, Poems 57–67*) | through (*Whole Motion* [typo])

8: dark (*Buckdancer, Poems 57–67, Whole Motion*) | dark, (*New Yorker*)

18: Open-mouthed (*Buckdancer, Poems 57–67, Whole Motion*) | Open mouthed (*New Yorker*)

31: flyer (*Buckdancer, Poems 57–67, Whole Motion*) | flier (*New Yorker*)

42: sounds, (*Buckdancer, Poems 57–67, Whole Motion*) | sounds— (*New Yorker*)

Children Reading

FIRST PUBLICATION: *New York Times Book Review*, November 1, 1964, sect. 7, pt. 2, p. 1.

Sled Burial, Dream Ceremony

FIRST PUBLICATION: As "Sled Burial: Dream Ceremony," *Southern Review*, n.s., 1 (Winter 1965): 125–26.

COLLECTED: Buckdancer, 52–53; *Poems 57–67*, 218–19; *Whole Motion*, 222–23.

REPRINTED: *Decade*, 78–80.

NOTES: On the burial of Eugene Dickey, Sr., see Hart, 537. "Here I try to fathom what it was, what death is, essentially. I finally decided that it's being in the ultimate strange place, the thing that's most completely different from what you're accustomed to. So this is about a Southerner who dies, and death is—after death he both recognizes and doesn't recognize what it is that's happening to him—but death to a Southerner is to be in a place where it snows all the time, where people go fishing through the ice, where men wear scarves around their heads against the chill wind, where there are such things as sleds for transportation. That's the ultimate strange place for a Southerner" (Heyen, 149; *Night,* 290). See *Self,* 148.

VARIANTS:

20: coffin top (*Buckdancer, Poems 57–67, Whole Motion*) | coffin-top (*Southern Review*)

The Shark's Parlor

FIRST PUBLICATION: *New Yorker* 40 (January 30, 1965): 32–33.

COLLECTED: *Buckdancer,* 39–42; *Poems 57–67,* 205–8; *Whole Motion,* 212–15.

REPRINTED: *Achievement,* 60–63; *American Tradition in Literature,* 1714–18; *Anthology,* 1750–53; *Campfire,* 97–100; *Contemporary Southern Poetry,* 79–82; *Distinctive Voice,* 233–36; *Made Thing,* 79–81; *Mindscapes,* 116–17; *New Yorker Book of Poems,* 635–37; *Ways of the Poem,* 357–60.

NOTES: Dickey was fascinated with sharks. "Sharks . . . because they're primitive—they're perfect. . . . The shark has never even developed a skeleton. Because he worked so well like he was, there was no need to evolve. And those kind of perfect forms in nature are really very fascinating to me. They seem to me to demonstrate something important. You know, men are weak little creatures. That's the reason they developed one part of themselves—the head, the brain, and so on—. . . . But sharks didn't, and snakes didn't—very, very low mentality. But they get along fine, if men would just leave them alone" (Arnett, 298). "'The Shark's Parlor' is completely made up. I never heard of anything like it happening nor did I participate in anything like it. When I was a boy I did see some boys fishing with a sashcord in the south coastal part of Georgia. . . . when I was a kid all I ever used was a hand line" (*Self,* 145). "A shark has been made out of the few hammerheads I have ever seen in the water, those I have seen hanging up at docks, and one I found dead on a beach. It is not quite that these sharks combined into one in my mind, but that the dead one on the shore drew into himself, as my strongest mental hammerhead, all the others, so that the others became him and contributed to him in my mind, where I then attempted to place him in another kind of sea, in a poem, and cause him to live and act there. . . . The poem was also influenced, in what ways it is hard for me to tell, by a movie called *The Shark Fighters* [*The Sharkfighters* (1956)], which starred, if I remember correctly, Victor Mature. All of these things came together into the passionate and mysterious aura of association that this kind of fish had for *me.* And from these mixed sources I made a poem about an imaginary incident" (*Sorties,* 178–79). According to Dickey's friend and high-school classmate Bill Barnwell, he and Dickey as boys fished with chains and hooks with meat on them to attract sharks. Terrified when a large fin approached them, they made a hasty escape (Hart, 45–46). "The incident has a special place in the man's memory. It speaks to him in his middle age. It reminds him how close he was to the world of wild nature. Other people might remember a hurricane, a mountain-climbing trip—anything that tested them against the force of nature" (Nancy Malone, "Poet with Power: James Dickey," *Read* 17 [November 15, 1967]: 11; Baughman, 39). There was originally a first section, which the *New Yorker* did not publish and was not subsequently published (*Crux,* 237). Discussed in *Self,*

145–47; Malone, "Poet with Power," 10–12 (Baughman, 37–39). On the various stages of composition, see Gary Leising, "'More in Two Worlds than One': The Imagination and Writing Process of James Dickey," in *The Way We Read James Dickey: Critical Approaches for the Twenty-first Century*, edited by William B. Thesing and Theda Wrede (Columbia: University of South Carolina Press, 2009): 51–65. For other poems featuring sharks, see "The Shark at the Window," "Walking on Water," "The Change," and "Breath."

1: Cumberland Island, the southernmost of Georgia's barrier islands and south of St. Simons Island, is where Dickey taught his son Chris to fish with a handline (*Summer*, 23–24).

6: Glynn County contains the city of Brunswick, plus Jekyll Island, Sea Island, St. Simons, and Cumberland.

12: Ecclesiastes 11:1.

30: For the phrase see "Dover: Believing in Kings," line 202.

57: This is likely the smooth hammerhead (*Sphyrna zygaena*), which—unlike other hammerheads—prefers warmer southern waters. It can grow to sixteen feet in length (eight to twelve feet is normal) and migrates north in the summer in schools that often contain hundreds of thousands of fish.

62: Esso is the former name of Exxon Corporation (now Exxon/Mobil).

VARIANTS:

8: porch pillar (*Buckdancer, Poems 57–67, Whole Motion*) | porch-pillar (*New Yorker*)

11: shark hook (*Buckdancer, Poems 57–67, Whole Motion*) | shark-hook (*New Yorker*)

29: land wind (*Buckdancer, Poems 57–67, Whole Motion*) | land-wind (*New Yorker*)

30: porch pillars (*Buckdancer, Poems 57–67, Whole Motion*) | porch-pillars (*New Yorker*)

30: something   a (*New Yorker, Buckdancer, Poems 57–67*) | something, a (*Whole Motion*)

32: growing: in (*Buckdancer, Poems 57–67, Whole Motion*) | growing   in (*New Yorker*)

34: anyway: it (*Buckdancer, Poems 57–67, Whole Motion*) | anyway   it (*New Yorker*)

52: the (*Buckdancer, Poems 57–67, Whole Motion*) | a (*New Yorker*)

59: house: far (*Buckdancer, Poems 57–67, Whole Motion*) | house   far (*New Yorker*)

72: moment, throwing (*Buckdancer, Poems 57–67, Whole Motion*) | moment throwing (*New Yorker*)

73: buck teeth (*Buckdancer, Poems 57–67, Whole Motion*) | buckteeth (*New Yorker*)

78: log-rolling (*Buckdancer, Poems 57–67, Whole Motion*) | logrolling (*New Yorker*)

85: enough: all changes: (*Buckdancer, Poems 57–67, Whole Motion*) | enough. All changes. (*New Yorker*)

The Night Pool

FIRST PUBLICATION: *Virginia Quarterly Review* 41 (Spring 1965): 231–32.

COLLECTED: *Buckdancer*, 56–57; *Poems 57–67*, 222; *Whole Motion*, 224–25.

REPRINTED: *Self*, 150; *Poems from* The Virginia Quarterly Review, 100–101; *Teaching*, 41–42.

NOTES: Dickey regularly dreamed of "the happy swimming pool," like the one in the backyard of the house at 8950 Balboa Boulevard in Northridge, California, where he and his family lived during his 1964–65 tenure at San Fernando Valley State College (since 1972, California State University, Northridge). In the dream, friends sat and talked peacefully around the pool, a fantasy of "a sense of contentment, of being at ease with himself and the world, as if he had gotten a preview of heaven" (*Summer*, 128). The Northridge pool recurs in "The Olympian," and a scene like his dream makes up one of his happiest memories of James Wright sitting by the pool: "There by the blue waters of Sepulveda we would gather by the river and watch my wife swim up and down, streaming with California phosphorescence" (*Southern Review* 27 [Spring 1991]: 435). Dickey claimed, however, a different genesis for "The Night Pool": "In October several years ago a girl and I went swimming in a pool at the apartment complex where she lived in Atlanta" (see *Self*, 148–49). "It's about two sides of love, the side which is all good and the side which is horrible.... You have a court or mating dance, where you swim around.... That's the nice part, but then you have to get out and everything changes" (*Teaching*, 40–41).

15–17: Compare "The Lifeguard," 59–60.

Gamecock

FIRST PUBLICATION: *Virginia Quarterly Review* 41 (Spring 1965): 232–33.
COLLECTED: *Buckdancer*, 54–55; *Poems 57–67*, 220–21; *Whole Motion*, 223–24.
REPRINTED: *Southern Writing in the Sixties*, 12–13; *Decade*, 80–81; *How Does a Poem Mean?*, 273; *Tricentennial Anthology*, 574–75; *Poems from* The Virginia Quarterly Review, 102–3.
VARIANTS:
1: jealousy (*Buckdancer, Poems 57–67, Whole Motion*) | jealousy, (*Virginia Quarterly Review*)
10: chicken head cut off (*Buckdancer, Poems 57–67, Whole Motion*) | chicken-head cut-off (*Virginia Quarterly Review*)
29: women (*Buckdancer, Poems 57–67, Whole Motion*) | females (*Virginia Quarterly Review*)

The Head-Aim

FIRST PUBLICATION: *Virginia Quarterly Review* 41 (Spring 1965): 233–34.
COLLECTED: *Poems 57–67*, 271; *Falling*, 41; *Whole Motion*, 270.
REPRINTED: *James Dickey Reads His Poems* (London: American Embassy, 1968): 2; *Poems from* The Virginia Quarterly Review, 104.
VARIANTS:
2–3: [no blank line inserted] (*Virginia Quarterly Review*)
16: This (*Poems 57–67, Falling, Whole Motion*) | That (*Virginia Quarterly Review*)

The Fiend

FIRST PUBLICATION: *Partisan Review* 32 (Spring 1965): 206–9.
COLLECTED: *Buckdancer*, 68–72; *Poems 57–67*, 230–33; *Whole Motion*, 231–34.
REPRINTED: *Achievement*, 65–69; *Contemporary Poetry in America*, 71–73; *Experience of Literature*, 1310–13; *Galaxy*, 391–94; *Modern American Poetry*, 693–95; *Pocket Book of Modern Verse*, 516–21; *Poetry Past and Present*, 425–28; *Self*, 155–60.
NOTES: "I read an item in the paper about a guy who killed this girl. He was a voyeur, and he was frustrated because when she got to the crucial point of undressing, and he watched her night after

night, she would always pull the shade down just as she got, as they say, to the good part. He just got so frustrated, he went in there and killed her" (Greiner, 11). "I think women, who are explained endlessly to us, have that air of mystery and beatification and pedestal-dwelling for us, and can have it only in this kind of inaccessible state, such as you would behold them in if you looked in the window of an apartment when they were undressing. They have a marvelous, absolutely untouchable, transcendent quality there, and it seems to me that to say something about this would say something very real, not only about American life, but about the man-and-woman situation generally. One doesn't want a woman to be too accessible, one wants her to be beyond— beyond yet visible" (*Eclipse*, 11; Baughman, 18). See also *Self*, 153. "Aristotle, it was, who said that man contains both an angel and a monster. But I think you should give the monster a chance to speak as well. That's why I write poems like 'The Fiend'" (Broughton, 184). In *Politics* (1.2) Aristotle wrote: "Anyone who cannot form a community with others, or who does not need to because he is self-sufficient, is no part of a city-state—he is either a best or a god." In *Self* (153) Dickey commented, "It's important to the voyeur to have an invisibility that enables him to function in kind of a God-like way, as though he could be present at any scene, sexually or otherwise, that he wished to be present at." Compare the description of hawks in *To the White Sea*, 266: "They're always out there over the snow, over the woods and trees, over the rocks, with that superhuman eyesight, with power over everything they can see, or ever will see. I don't think God himself could ever want anything more." Dickey treated voyeurism in his unpublished 1953 novel, "The Entrance to the Honeycomb." "The best fan letter I ever got was from a police lieutenant who read 'The Fiend' in the *Partisan Review*, and he wrote to me and said, 'I've always had a sneaking sympathy with you guys. Please don't answer. I'm not going to sign this and I won't give you any return address, but I'm a member of the New York City Police Department.' . . . I was convinced that I'd said something that mattered to somebody, and, while maybe it shouldn't have mattered to him specifically, the fact that it did pleases me very much. . . . I think every male in America, and probably the world, is gorgeous material for a peeping tom anyway, don't you?" (*Eclipse*, 19; Baughman, 25–26).

11: Slithers: on Dickey and snakes, see "Blowgun and Rattlesnake."

16: "rarified," var. of "rarefied."

Variants:

12: And (*Partisan Review*) | and (*Buckdancer, Poems 57–67, Whole Motion* [typo])

19: shopgirl (*Buckdancer, Poems 57–67, Whole Motion*) | shop-girl (*Partisan Review*)

21: wind (*Buckdancer, Poems 57–67, Whole Motion*) | one wind (*Partisan Review*)

23: energy field (*Buckdancer, Poems 57–67, Whole Motion*) | energy-field (*Partisan Review*)

32: oak currents (*Buckdancer, Poems 57–67, Whole Motion*) | oak-currents (*Partisan Review*)

36: bathing cap (*Buckdancer, Poems 57–67, Whole Motion*) | bathing-cap (*Partisan Review*)

103–4: [blank line inserted] (*Partisan Review*)

109: window blinds (*Buckdancer, Poems 57–67, Whole Motion*) | window-blinds (*Partisan Review*)

Dust

First Publication: *Bulletin* (Sydney, Australia), May 8, 1965, 55.

Collected: *Buckdancer*, 66–67; *Poems 57–67*, 228–29; *Whole Motion*, 229–30.

Reprinted: *Intervisions*, 32–33; *Literature of America*, 732–33; *Workshop*, 208–9.
Notes: For Adam, see *God's Images*, 4.

Buckdancer's Choice

First Publication: *New Yorker* 41 (June 19, 1965): 36.
Collected: *Buckdancer*, 21–22; *Poems 57–67*, 189–90; *Whole Motion*, 201–2.
Reprinted: Broadside (Winston-Salem, N.C.: Palaemon Press, 1979); *Carnegie Magazine* 41 (February, 1967): 59; *Dickey Reader*, 70–72; *Modern American Poetry*, 692–93; *New Oxford Book of Modern Verse*, 859–60; *New Yorker Book of Poems*, 86–87; *Norton Anthology of Modern Poetry*, 1034; *Norton Anthology of Poetry*, 1155–56; *Selected*, 78–79; *The Poem*, 488; *Poetry of the Negro*, 579–80; *Poetry Pilot* (June 1982): 2; *Reading Modern Poetry*, 89–90; *Tricentennial Anthology*, 572–73.
Notes: "'Buckdancer's Choice' was just a song that I learned on the guitar which reminded me of a song I used to hear my mother whistle at home. I'm not sure it isn't the same, although I'm not sure that it is" (*Eclipse*, 10; Baughman, 17). Discussed in *Self*, 139–40. The buck dance (or "buck and wing") is thought to have been created in the southern Appalachian Mountains and was performed in minstrel and vaudeville shows as early as the 1830s by dancers imitating young African Americans, known as "bucks." The term "buckdancer" is thought to derive from the West Indies, where the captains of slave ships would "dance the slaves" for exercise, entertainment, and morale purposes. The Africans were referred to as "po' bockorau" or "buccaneer." The buck dance originally involved simply tapping the foot to the rhythm of the music; then it became a kind of countrified clog dancing; finally it evolved into the precursor of tap dancing, performed to syncopated rhythms as in African tribal rhythms. "Buckdancer's Choice," a term that may refer to the tap dancer's choice of song to dance to or lady to dance with, is a fiddle tune of unknown authorship, performed on the guitar on the first recording by the legendary country guitarist Sam McGee (1894–1975) in 1926. For the music, see Happy Traum, *Finger-Picking Styles for Guitar* (New York: Oak, 1966), 32–33.
3–4: See "False Youth: Winter," 18.
8: Blackface minstrelsy gave way to vaudeville about 1910 but survived in amateur and local productions through the 1950s.
9: The "wing" movement began as a shaking of the leg, then developed into a shooting out of the leg along with the tapping of the "buck dance." Among the "classic buck-and-wing men" were Master Juba in the 1840s, James McIntyre, who performed on the New York stage in 1880, and King and Rastus Brown in the 1920s and 1930s. In Jack London's *Martin Eden* (1909), a sailor claims to be a first-class buck-and-wing dancer.
12: On Dickey's mother's weakness, which was blamed on angina, see "Angina"; for her death see "The Sprinter's Mother."
Variants:
1: lungs, (*Buckdancer, Poems 57–67, Whole Motion*) | lungs— (*New Yorker*)
10: traveling (*Buckdancer, Poems 57–67, Whole Motion*) | travelling (*New Yorker*)
15: band, (*Buckdancer, Poems 57–67, Whole Motion*) | band— (*New Yorker*)
22: wall (*Buckdancer, Poems 57–67, Whole Motion*) | wall, (*New Yorker*)

The Celebration

FIRST PUBLICATION: *Harper's* 230 (June 1965): 50.

COLLECTED: *Buckdancer*, 34–35; *Poems 57–67*, 201–2; *Whole Motion*, 209–10.

REPRINTED: *Best Poems of 1965*, 5–6; *Literature in America*, 90–92; *Poetry Southeast 1950–70*, 58–59; *Voice That Is Great*, 495–96.

NOTES: Discussed in *Self*, 143–44. "That one really works. It's quite believable. I mean there aren't any literaryisms in it. That's something very few poets can say of anything they've written" (*Southern Partisan* 6 [Spring 1986]: 24).

10: Dodgem cars are also known as bumper cars or dashingcars.

28–51: The wheels seen by Ezekiel (Ezekiel 1) contained the throne of God (1:26), from which he surveyed the world (1:19): "And when the living creatures were lifted up from the earth, the wheels were lifted up." For "riding lights" see 1:13: "As for the likeness of the living creatures, their appearance was like burning coals of fire, and like the appearance of lamps."

52: "Ezekiel saw the wheel, way up in the middle of the air." For the various versions, see *Lyrics of the Afro-American Spiritual: A Documentary Collection*, edited by Erskine Peters (Westport, Conn.: Greenwood Press, 1993), 387–38, and for the music see *The Oxford Book of Spirituals*, edited by Moses Hogan (Oxford & New York: Oxford University Press, 2002), 37–45.

54: Lakewood Park opened in 1915 at the site of Atlanta's original waterworks on Lakewood Avenue. Its midway was the centerpiece of the Southeastern Fair from its opening until the park closed in 1974. The park was known for its wooden roller coaster, called "The Greyhound."

VARIANTS:

10: dodgem (*Buckdancer, Poems 57–67, Whole Motion*) | Dodgem (*Harper's*)

The Aura

FIRST PUBLICATION: *New Yorker* 41 (June 5, 1965): 38.

COLLECTED: With "The Second Sleep" in the group titled "Fathers and Sons," *Buckdancer*, 49–51; *Poems 57–67*, 215–17; *Whole Motion*, 220–22.

REPRINTED: *Invitation to Poetry*, 309–10; *Some Haystacks*, 55.

NOTES: "From my seventh-grade bicycle accident, Dickey extracted 'The Aura' about remembering a dead teenage son whose transistor-radio music followed him around the house wherever he went" (*Summer*, 135). "My own boy, Chris, was almost killed in a bicycle accident. I really was terrified he was going to die from shock or loss of blood. I would sit in the hospital—the same hospital that was more or less the background for 'Them, Crying'—and try desperately to characterize Chris to myself. What was it about him that I remembered the most? It finally turned out to be that he always had music around him, usually on his body, with a transistor radio. . . . Everywhere he went the Beatles went. It was this constant aura of music he carried on his body that was, to me, the most indicative thing about him, the most *him* (*Self*, 147). "I made 'Fathers and Sons' into a two-part sequence: one in which the father is killed and the son survives, and the other in which the son is killed and the father survives" (ibid.). Dickey wrote an early poem called "The Son," describing "the parricidal vision from the loin" (*Summer*, 67). Dickey sent Andrew Lytle a poem called "Fathers and Sons" (*One Voice 1,* 143, 230–32, 236–37; Hart, 177) but that is not this poem. Discussed in *Self,* 147–48.

54–55: Dickey may have had in mind Ramblin' Jack Elliott, born Elliott Charles Adnopoz in Brooklyn in 1931. He sang for and befriended two generations of folksingers from Woody Guthrie to Bob Dylan. The Juilliard-trained New Yorker Eric Weissberg (b. 1939) was the creator, with Marshall Brickman (b. 1941), of "Duelling Banjos," the popular theme song from the film of *Deliverance.*

59–60: For the concluding one-noun sentences, see "Fog Envelops the Animals," 35.

Variants:

27: traveling (*Buckdancer, Poems 57–67, Whole Motion*) | travelling (*New Yorker*)
30: places: (*Buckdancer, Poems 57–67, Whole Motion*) | places; (*New Yorker*)
40: joints (*Buckdancer, Poems 57–67, Whole Motion*) | joints, (*New Yorker*)
46: if (*Buckdancer, Poems 57–67, Whole Motion*) | though (*New Yorker*)
48: stomach: (*Buckdancer, Poems 57–67, Whole Motion*) | stomach. (*New Yorker*)
60: Something. Music. (*Buckdancer, Poems 57–67, Whole Motion*) | Music. (*New Yorker*)

Mangham

First Publication: *Kenyon Review* 27 (Summer 1965): 476–77.
Collected: *Buckdancer,* 60–62; *Poems 57–67,* 224–25; *Whole Motion,* 226–28.
Reprinted: *AWP Newsletter,* May 1981, 7.
Notes: Discussed in *Self,* 151–53: "I had a teacher at North Fulton High School named Mr. Mangham, a gray, undistinguished man but an extremely good mathematics teacher. What happens, though, when you're an extremely good mathematics teacher and nobody cares about learning mathematics? . . . he had a stroke one day in the classroom; he died a week later." William McKenzie Mangham, after teaching for five years at North Fulton High School, died on March 29, 1937. It is not clear if he was related to "Uncle Jim's" business partner, Samuel Mangham (see "The Angel of the Maze").

6–7: See Jeremiah 31:29 and Ezekiel 18.2.

Variants:

3: crooked (*Buckdancer, Poems 57–67, Whole Motion*) | crookèd (*Kenyon*)
17: hive sound (*Buckdancer, Poems 57–67, Whole Motion*) | hive-sound (*Kenyon*)
29: Lines (*Buckdancer, Poems 57–67, Whole Motion*) | The lines (*Kenyon*)
33: sixty-ninety (*Buckdancer, Poems 57–67, Whole Motion*) | Sixty-ninety (*Kenyon*)
35: colors (*Buckdancer, Poems 57–67, Whole Motion*) | Colors (*Kenyon*)
49: chalk motes (*Buckdancer, Poems 57–67, Whole Motion*) | chalk-motes (*Kenyon*)
52: a (*Buckdancer, Poems 57–67, Whole Motion*) | that (*Kenyon*)
62: ice (*Buckdancer, Poems 57–67, Whole Motion*) | ice, (*Kenyon*)

Sustainment

First Publication: *Yale Review* 54 (Summer 1965): 547–48.
Collected: *Poems 57–67,* 267–68; *Falling,* 37–38; *Whole Motion,* 267–68.

REPRINTED: *Best Poems of 1965*, 27–28.

VARIANTS:

4: path (*Poems 57–67, Falling, Whole Motion*) | earth (*Yale Review*)

30: out (*Poems 57–67, Falling, Whole Motion*) | out of (*Yale Review*)

30: lipsticked (*Poems 57–67, Falling, Whole Motion*) | lip-sticked (*Yale Review*)

Deer among Cattle

FIRST PUBLICATION: *Shenandoah* 16 (Summer 1965): 78.

COLLECTED: *Poems 57–67*, 283; *Falling*, 53; *Whole Motion*, 278–79.

REPRINTED: *Literature*, 443; *Mother Earth News*, March–April 1984): 170; *Poems*, 46; *Reading, Writing and Rhetoric*, 606; *Shake the Kaleidoscope*, 153; *Strongly Spent*, 64; *Twentieth Century Poetry* (Marshall), 67–68; *To See the World Afresh*, 69.

NOTES:

21: night of the hammer: Dickey told his friend James Mann (who told me) that he took this line from the title of a book of poems by Ned O'Gorman: *The Night of the Hammer* (New York: Harcourt Brace, 1959).

VARIANTS:

5: also is (*Poems 57–67, Falling, Whole Motion*) | is also (*Shenandoah*)

Slave Quarters

FIRST PUBLICATION: *New Yorker* 41 (August 14, 1965): 28–29.

COLLECTED: *Buckdancer*, 73–79; *Poems 57–67*, 234–39; *Whole Motion*, 235–40.

REPRINTED: *Contemporary American Poetry* (Poulin), 76–81; *Poems*, 35–39; *New Yorker Book of Poems*, 644–48.

NOTES: "This poem on slavery, 'Slave Quarters,' . . . has been in my notebook in one form or another for seven or eight years" (Roberts, 10; Baughman, 46). Dickey's ancestors George Dickey (1776–1842) and Hannah Taylor Dickey (1777–1868) were slaveholders who owned Hogback Plantation, near Mineral Bluff, Georgia. They are buried with twenty-six of their slaves at some distance from the plantation in a forty-by-fifty-foot cemetery atop Hogback Mountain ("Hogback Ridge," see "Diabetes") in a part of Gilmer County (see "A May Day Sermon") that is now Fannin County, Georgia. Dickey claimed that the ruins depicted in "Slave Quarters" were actually on St. Simons Island, off the coast of Georgia: "There really is a place on the coast of Georgia like this where there are remnants of slave quarters and you can see the approximate spot where the big house stood; there's nothing left of that. . . . In this poem I meant to strike right to the heart of the hypocrisy of slavery and show some of the pity and terror of it" (*Self*, 160) There were four great plantations and many others on the island, all involved in the production of fine Sea Island cotton. All the plantations were destroyed in the Civil War, but slave quarters at the Hamilton plantation stand to this day. For Dickey on race, see "Notes on the Decline of Outrage" in *Babel*, 274: "Not for a moment does he entertain the notion that these prejudices are just, fitting, or reasonable. But neither can he deny that they belong to him by inheritance, as they belong to other Southerners. Yet this does not mean that they cannot be seen for what they are, that they cannot be appraised and understood." For the fantasy of mating with a member of another race, see "The Enclosure."

109–10: "Michael Row the Boat Ashore" is a slave spiritual discovered on St. Helena, one of the Sea Islands of South Carolina, whose white inhabitants fled before the Union blockade was imposed. The song asks the archangel Michael to lead the people across a metaphorical river (Jordan/Ohio) to freedom. It was discovered by Charles Pickard Ware, who came from Massachusetts to supervise the plantations in 1862. He, his cousin William Francis Allen, and Lucy McKim Garrison published the song in *Slave Songs of the United States* (1867).

135: The eland is the largest antelope, native to Africa and distinguished by its spiral horns.

VARIANTS:

6: moonlight (*Buckdancer, Poems 57–67, Whole Motion*) | moonlight. (*New Yorker*)

7–14: [omitted (*New Yorker*); blank line precedes line 15]

18: sea wind (*Buckdancer, Poems 57–67, Whole Motion*) | sea-wind (*New Yorker*)

19: direction: (*Buckdancer, Poems 57–67, Whole Motion*) | direction. (*New Yorker*)

20: there (*Buckdancer, Poems 57–67, Whole Motion*) | There (*New Yorker*)

24: sea: (*Buckdancer, Poems 57–67, Whole Motion*) | sea (*New Yorker*)

25–26: [blank line inserted] (*New Yorker*)

29: sawgrass (*Buckdancer, Poems 57–67, Whole Motion*) | saw-grass (*New Yorker*)

39: absence: (*Buckdancer, Poems 57–67, Whole Motion*) | absence. (*New Yorker*)

39–40: [no blank line inserted] (*New Yorker*)

40: the (*Buckdancer, Poems 57–67, Whole Motion*) | The (*New Yorker*)

48: skins (*Buckdancer, Poems 57–67, Whole Motion*) | skins. (*New Yorker*)

49–53: [omitted] (*New Yorker*)

54–55: [blank line inserted] (*New Yorker*)

56: grass (*Buckdancer, Poems 57–67, Whole Motion*) | grass, (*New Yorker*)

59: wave (*Buckdancer, Poems 57–67, Whole Motion*) | wave. (*New Yorker*)

60–65: [omitted] (*New Yorker*)

66–67: [blank line inserted] (*New Yorker*)

73: sawgrass walking: (*Buckdancer, Poems 57–67, Whole Motion*) | saw-grass walking. (*New Yorker*)

76: tide—where (*Buckdancer, Poems 57–67, Whole Motion*) | tide where (*New Yorker*)

76: night sand (*Buckdancer, Poems 57–67, Whole Motion*) | night-sand (*New Yorker*)

77: outward (*Buckdancer, Poems 57–67, Whole Motion*) | outward, (*New Yorker*)

78: Feasting (*Buckdancer Poems 57–67 Whole Motion*) | Feeding (*New Yorker*)

81: jibes (*Buckdancer, Poems 57–67, Whole Motion*) | jibs (*New Yorker*)

82: wind, (*Buckdancer, Poems 57–67, Whole Motion*) | wind (*New Yorker*)

82–83: receives himself like a brother / As he [omitted in *New Yorker*]

83: reflection: (*Buckdancer, Poems 57–67, Whole Motion*) | reflection. (*New Yorker*)

84: freed: (*Buckdancer, Poems 57–67, Whole Motion*) | freed. (*New Yorker*)

86: off; (*Buckdancer, Poems 57–67, Whole Motion*) | off, (*New Yorker*)

92: ship.   Now (*Buckdancer, Poems 57–67, Whole Motion*) | ship. Now (*New Yorker*)

94: me   the fields (*Buckdancer, Poems 57–67, Whole Motion*) | me and I pass through the ghost of a slave / Born in this place of a white man the fields (*New Yorker*)

95–96: sea   and   not on a horse / I stoop to the soil   working (*Buckdancer, Poems 57–67, Whole Motion*) | sea   I stoop to the soil   working (*New Yorker*)

98: chains (*Buckdancer, Poems 57–67, Whole Motion*) | chains, (*New Yorker*)

101: though   the (*New Yorker, Buckdancer, Whole Motion*) | though the (*Poems 57–67*)

104–5: day: /   there (*Buckdancer, Poems 57–67, Whole Motion*) | day.   / But now I am here / In slave quarters, quarters,   am white   and know what I came for. / There (*New Yorker*)

106: walls (*Buckdancer, Poems 57–67, Whole Motion*) | walls, (*New Yorker*)

109–11: places   as faintly Michael rows / The boat ashore   his spiritual lungs / Entirely filling the sail.   How (*Buckdancer, Poems 57–67, Whole Motion*) | places. How (*New Yorker*)

118: rebirth (*Buckdancer, Poems 57–67, Whole Motion*) | rebirth, (*New Yorker*)

122: died with (*New Yorker, Buckdancer, Whole Motion*) | came in (*Poems 57–67*)

123: slaves, (*Buckdancer, Poems 57–67, Whole Motion*) | slaves (*New Yorker*)

125: Forgotten: the (*Buckdancer, Poems 57–67, Whole Motion*) | Forgotten: the (*New Yorker*)

132: Eden (*Buckdancer, Poems 57–67, Whole Motion*) | Eden, (*New Yorker*)

137: movement: (*Buckdancer, Poems 57–67, Whole Motion*) | movement, (*New Yorker*)

145: cave shadows (*Buckdancer, Poems 57–67, Whole Motion*) | cave-shadows (*New Yorker*)

146: him: a (*Buckdancer, Poems 57–67, Whole Motion*) | him. A (*New Yorker*)

149: eyes.   What (*Buckdancer, Poems 57–67, Whole Motion*) | eyes. What (*New Yorker*)

151: secret: into (*Buckdancer, Poems 57–67, Whole Motion*) | secret: into (*New Yorker*)

156: you, when (*Buckdancer, Poems 57–67, Whole Motion*) | you   when (*New Yorker*)

163: Of (*Buckdancer, Poems 57–67, Whole Motion*) | In (*New Yorker*)

164: spade (*New Yorker, Buckdancer, Whole Motion*) | hammer (*Poems 57–67*)

170–72: When Michael's voice is heard / Bending the sail like grass, / The real moon (*Buckdancer, Poems 57–67, Whole Motion*) | When the moon (*New Yorker*)

179: been (*Buckdancer, Poems 57–67, Whole Motion*) | been, (*New Yorker*)

Hedge Life

First Publication: *New Yorker* 41 (September 4, 1965): 34.
Collected: *Poems 57–67*, 261–62; *Falling*, 31–32; *Whole Motion*, 263–64.
Reprinted: *Longman*, 194.
Notes:
36: See "Looking for the Buckhead Boys," lines 11–12.
Variants:
6: who (*Poems 57–67, Falling, Whole Motion*) | that (*New Yorker*)

14–15: dawn / silver (*Poems 57–67, Falling, Whole Motion*) | dawn- / Silver (*New Yorker*)

18–19: [blank line inserted] (*New Yorker*)

25: us, (*Poems 57–67, Falling, Whole Motion*) | us (*New Yorker*)

29: feel, (*Poems 57–67, Falling, Whole Motion*) | feel— (*New Yorker*)

30: fur, (*Poems 57–67, Falling, Whole Motion*) | fur— (*New Yorker*)

32: That (*Poems 57–67, Falling, Whole Motion*) | that (*New Yorker*)

Coming Back to America

FIRST PUBLICATION: *New Yorker* 41 (September 18, 1965): 57.

COLLECTED: *Poems 57–67*, 286–87; *Falling*, 56–57; *Whole Motion*, 281–82.

REPRINTED: *New York: Poems*, 57–60; *New Yorker Book of Poems*, 135–36; *Splash*, 37–38; *Wesleyan Tradition*, 62–64.

NOTES: Discussed in *Mademoiselle* interview, 209; *Self*, 172–73.

14: "Sleep of a Thousand Years" was Gibbon's term for the Middle Ages. See "Hints of Some Subjects Fit for History," in *Miscellaneous Works of Edward Gibbon, Esq.* (London: B. Blake, 1837): 447.

VARIANTS:

6: barbaric rays (*Poems 57–67, Falling, Whole Motion*) | beams (*New Yorker*)

6: violent unavoidable (*Poems 57–67, Falling, Whole Motion*) | unavoidable violent (*New Yorker*)

24: talked   she (*Poems 57–67, Falling, Whole Motion*) | talked. She (*New Yorker*)

28: her: (*Poems 57–67, Falling, Whole Motion*) | her; (*New Yorker*)

37: Love-making (*Poems 57–67, Falling, Whole Motion*) | Lovemaking (*New Yorker*)

45: swirl (*Poems 57–67, Falling, Whole Motion*) | swirling (*New Yorker*)

48: exalting (*New Yorker*) | exhalting (*Poems 57–67, Falling, Whole Motion*)

54: The thing (*Poems 57–67, Falling, Whole Motion*) | the thing (*New Yorker*)

55: In (*New Yorker, Poems 57–67, Falling*) | in (*Whole Motion* [typo])

The Birthday Dream

FIRST PUBLICATION: *Nation* 201 (September 27, 1965): 170.

COLLECTED: *Poems 57–67*, 288–89; *Falling*, 58–59; *False Youth*, 3–5; *Whole Motion*, 282–84.

NOTES: Dickey turned forty on February 2, 1963. He had determined to learn to play guitar by this age, which he associated with physical decline ("The Sprinter at Forty"). Springer Mountain (a)" takes place when the narrator is forty. For Dickey's sixtieth birthday, see "Spring-Shock."

VARIANTS:

9: say (*Poems 57–67, Falling, False, Whole Motion*) | Say (*Nation*)

27: arm game (*Poems 57–67, Falling, False, Whole Motion*) | arm-game (*Nation*)

38: blood vessels (*Poems 57–67, Falling, False, Whole Motion*) | blood-vessels (*Nation*)

40: trumpet player's (*Poems 57–67, Falling, False, Whole Motion*) | trumpet-player's (*Nation*)

42: for. (*Poems 57–67, Falling, False, Whole Motion*) | for (*Nation*)

51: warning light (*Poems 57–67, Falling, False, Whole Motion*) | warning-light (*Nation*)

57: ice pick (*Poems 57–67, Falling, False, Whole Motion*) | ice-pick (*Nation*)

58: tire iron (*Poems 57–67, Falling, False, Whole Motion*) | tire-iron (*Nation*)

False Youth: Summer

FIRST PUBLICATION: *Harper's* 231 (September 1965): 115.

COLLECTED: As "I," grouped with "II: False Youth: Winter" as "False Youth: Two Seasons," *Poems 57–67*, 290–91; as "Summer," *Falling*, 60–61, and *Whole Motion*, 284–85; as "Summer: Porch-Wings" in *False Youth*, 21–23.

REPRINTED: *Kaleidoscope*, 103–5; *Best Poems of 1965*, 25–26.

NOTES: In the summer of 1951, Dickey spent a weekend in New Orleans with a woman first given the name Hunsinger, then Huntley (line 10), the name of Dickey's maternal grandmother, Lena Swift Burckhardt Huntley (1857–1934) (Hart, 167). Dickey similarly changed a woman's name in "Cherrylog Road." Discussed in *Mademoiselle* interview, 209; *Self*, 173–74.

VARIANTS:

10: Huntley (*Poems 57–67, Falling, False, Whole Motion*) | Hunsinger (*Harper's*)

32: Huntley (*Poems 57–67, Falling, False, Whole Motion*) | Hunsinger (*Harper's*)

Seeking the Chosen

FIRST PUBLICATION: "Poems of the Sixties—4," *Times Literary Supplement,* November 25, 1965, 1069.

COLLECTED: *Whole Motion*, 30–31.

VARIANTS:

19: up and down (*TLS*) | up down (*Whole Motion*)

33: but (*TLS*) | and (*Whole Motion*)

33: single (*TLS*) | simple (*Whole Motion*)

40: could still (*TLS*) | still could (*Whole Motion*)

Adultery

FIRST PUBLICATION: *Nation* 202 (February 28, 1966): 252.

COLLECTED: *Poems 57–67*, 259–60; *Falling*, 29–30; *Whole Motion*, 262–63.

REPRINTED: *Contemporary American Poetry* (Poulin), 73–74; *Contemporary Southern Poetry*, 78–79; *Man to Himself*, 316; *Made Thing*, 84; *Men-Talk*, 25; *Poems of Our Moment*, 63–64; *Poetry: Points of Departure*, 177–78; *Treasury of American Poetry*, 634–35.

NOTES: Written during his affair with Robin Jarecki (Hart, 340; see "Exchanges"). "I thought to myself that maybe one could write something enlightening on adultery and on all the illicit sexual relationships by writing about it from the standpoint of motivation. That is, why do people who are married reasonably happily to other people, and who have children and so on, and a certain degree of stability, risk everything by entering into an illicit relationship with somebody else's husband or wife, or some other person they're not married to?" ("Comments," 13) After many false starts on this poem, the key came to Dickey as he watched *Harlow* (1965), a film biography of Jean Harlow (played by Carol Lynley), whose husband, Paul Bern (played by Hurd Hatfield) says, "For the majority of the poor benighted race of mankind, human kind, sex is the only bulwark, the final stay against despair, death." Dickey noted that "it's in the very guilt of the adulterous relationship, in the heightening of sexuality by this added ingredient of guilt and uncertainty that there is a temporary alleviation of the terrible death fear that grows on people as they get older and older" ("Comments," 1). This was Dickey's favorite poem "in terms of honesty" (Broughton, 185). See also *Mademoiselle* interview, 143; *Self,* 166–68. On Chris Dickey's first hearing the poem, as he sat next to his mother in the audience at Rice University, see *Summer,* 136–37. The poem is discussed in "Comments," 13–14; revised for *Self,* 166–68.

5: Dickey began a long poem about Jarecki, "The Indian Maiden," which was never completed and whose drafts have been lost. "Indian Maiden," which Christopher Dickey referred to as "the dirty song he used to try to teach me when I was a little boy" (*Summer,* 138), was recorded by Sheb Wooley (1921–2003) in 1960.

VARIANTS:

13: wrist watch (*Poems 57–67, Falling, Whole Motion*) | wrist-watch (*Nation*)

False Youth: Winter

FIRST PUBLICATION: *New Yorker* 42 (February 26, 1966): 44.

COLLECTED: With "False Youth: Summer" as "False Youth: Two Seasons" (subtitled "II"), *Poems 57–67,* 291–92; (subtitled "Winter") *Falling,* 60–62, and *Whole Motion,* 284–86; as "Winter: Thumb-Fire" in *False Youth,* 31–33.

REPRINTED: *Kaleidoscope,* 103–5; as "False Youth: Winter," in *Achievement,* 76–77; *Literary Nashville,* 95–97.

NOTES: Discussed in *Self,* 174.

18: See "Angina," "Buckdancer's Choice," lines 3–4.

19: See "The Gamecocks."

45: Dickey's thirty-eighth year was 1961.

VARIANTS:

5: bone: brought (*Poems 57–67, Falling, False, Whole Motion*) | bone   brought (*New Yorker*)

32: you (*Poems 57–67, Falling, False, Whole Motion*) | You (*New Yorker*)

45: year (*Poems 57–67, Falling, False, Whole Motion*) | year— (*New Yorker*)

47: glass: (*Poems 57–67, Falling, False, Whole Motion*) | glass— (*New Yorker*)

The Bee

FIRST PUBLICATION: *Harper's,* 232 (June 1966): 80–81.

COLLECTED: *Poems 57–67,* 279–80; *Falling,* 49–50; *Whole Motion,* 275–77.

REPRINTED: *Selected,* 114–15; *Sound and Sense,* 307–9 (4th ed., 292–94); *Twentieth Century Treasury of Sports,* 145–47; *What's in a Poem?,* 259–61.

NOTES: "When I was six years old, we were on a routine family trip to the archery range . . . and were just finishing up and getting into the car. We were in one of those canyons above Los Angeles, near one of those mountain roads with many blind curves. Suddenly, this bee came out of the woods—not even woods. It came out of the grass over a picket fence. And I had the usual histrionic, childish reaction to a bee and ran off into the road. A little red pickup truck came around the bend, and I, in my frenzy, felt this vise-like grip on my right arm. It was my father's, and he pulled me back. Even though the poem embellishes upon the story, and makes it better, he was speechless at the time. But my mother wasn't" (Kevin Dickey, "Comments on 'The Sheep Child' and 'The Bee,'" *South Carolina Review* 37 [Spring 2005]: 46–47). "I want to get sports things into poetry. I don't think it has ever been done at all, not even by Pindar. Sports are among the most beautiful things on this earth to me. They represent the nearest thing that we can get to some kind of bodily perfection, especially in those 'use' situations which are also aesthetically pleasing" ("Things Happen," 4; Baughman, 32). "['The Bee' has] been misinterpreted lots of ways because coaches these days, with the now generation, are kind of looked on as proto-fascist figures, but I never had anything but the most intense gratitude to mine" (Heyen, 141; *Night,* 282). See also *Self,* 171; *Summer,* 134.

Dedication: The head football coach at Clemson was the legendary Frank Howard (1909–1996), and the ends' coach was Tom Rogers, but in 1942 Dickey played for the freshman team, coached by Absolom Willis "Rock" Norman (1893–1981). For Dickey's account of "Practice at Clemson," see *One Voice 1,* 51–53 and 32. Subsequent to the publication of this poem, Dickey ran into Norman at a Holiday Inn while at Clemson for a lecture (*One Voice 2,* 257).

8: The single-wing formation was invented by Glenn Scobey "Pop" Warner (1871–1954) at Carlisle College, as a vehicle for the athletic talents of Jim Thorpe (1888–1953). The formation featured an unbalanced line, a long snap from the center, and four players in the backfield, including a wingback, who lined up behind an end as a kind of wide receiver. It was the dominant offense in football during the first half of the twentieth century. Dickey was a reserve wingback at North Fulton High School and Darlington, but on the freshman team at Clemson he was a reserve T-formation quarterback (Hart, 49–51).

Variants:

9: knee action (*Poems 57–67, Falling, Whole Motion*) | knee-action (*Harper's*)
10: God damn (*Poems 57–67, Falling, Whole Motion*) | God-damn (*Harper's*)
59: son, (*Harper's*) | son (*Poems 57–67, Falling, Whole Motion*)

For the Last Wolverine

First Publication: *Atlantic* 217 (June 1966): 70–71.
Collected: *Poems 57–67,* 276–78; *Falling,* 46–48; *Whole Motion,* 273–75.
Reprinted: *Selected,* 111–13; *Deep Ecology,* 158–60; *From Three Sides,* 45–47; *Georgia Voices,* 99–102; *Forgotten Language,* 38–39.
Notes: "The theme of the poem, extinction, is one that has long haunted me, and when, years ago, I saw in the paper that the wolverine—which is kind of the ultimate wild animal, and along with the peregrine falcon and the barracuda is one of my totem creatures—had been put on the endangered species list, I knew I must write something about it" (*One Voice 2,* 468–49; see also Broughton, 174). Elsewhere Dickey commented that "dying is one thing, but dying out, having a whole species die out, is another thing. . . . I thought when I wrote this poem that there must be some special honor and power conferred on the last of any species. . . . So the last wolverine is given the power, magical power, to mate with the last eagle, and make a savage spirit, a spirit as savage as the wolverine's, that had wings, a new creature. And it would come back in revenge for its extinction, both the eagle and the wolverine now in one revenging creature never before seen" (Greiner, 19–20). "I just picked him out of my children's picture books as my totem animal. The

ultimate wild animal" (ibid., 20). Dickey also drew from the depiction of the wolverine in Walt Disney's *White Wilderness* (1958). Also discussed in *Mademoiselle* interview, 209; *Self,* 169–70. 66: "Carcajou" is the Algonquian name for the wolverine.

VARIANTS:

49: fibres (*Poems 57–67, Falling, Whole Motion*) | fibers (*Atlantic*)
67–68: [blank line inserted] (*Atlantic*)

Encounter in the Cage Country

FIRST PUBLICATION: *New Yorker* 42 (June 11, 1966): 34.
COLLECTED: *Poems 57–67,* 274–75; *Falling,* 44–45; *Whole Motion,* 272–73.
REPRINTED: *Achievement,* 75–76; *Contemporary American Poetry* (Poulin), 69–70; *Dickey Reader,* 91–92.
NOTES: According to Christopher Dickey, during a family trip to London in August 1962, the Dickeys visited Regent's Park Zoo: "We were just sort of strolling, as people do in zoos, through the building full of lions and tigers when the black panther saw my father in the crowd and dropped the bloody joint of meat he chewed and followed every step as we walked by. At first my father didn't notice. 'Daddy, look,' I said, spooked. 'Look.' Jim Dickey's eyes caught the animal's. Held them. Then, sensing the power of the moment, he walked back and forth in front of the cage. The big cat followed each move. My father looked at me and arched his brows. What was happening? Then he looked at the animal again, and the animal's eyes had never left him. Jim Dickey feinted in one direction, then jogged in the other like a broken-field runner, but he couldn't wrong-foot the panther. He moved out of sight of the cage. The cat waited, watching, his breath measured, his mouth open just enough to hint at the teeth within, his yellow-green eyes expectant, until my father came back into his view, and then, again, he followed him. . . . My father wasn't wearing green glasses that day" (*Summer,* 133–34). With that account, contrast James Dickey's fanciful account, with which he introduced the poem at readings. After several hours at a pub, he bought the "American dark glasses" at a "surplus house" with a check "from the *New Yorker* or some such publication," hoping that "people will mistake me for Marcello Mastroianni." Walking aimlessly, he found himself at the zoo. "I walked over to the lion cage and tried to relate to him. You know how poets do. But he wouldn't have any of that, so I walked down past the ocelots, jaguars, and tigers, until I came to the black leopard's cage. . . . He dropped the meat he was chewing and came over to the edge of the cage as though to say to me, 'Where have you been? Did you bring it?' And I didn't know whether I'd brought it or not. . . . To this day I don't know what he saw in me, whether it was my dark glasses, the way I dressed, the fact that I was an American, or my *soul.*" "It is supposed to be about one of those encounters where one of the parties, in this case a black leopard, knows what it is all about, and the other, in this case the man, has yet to find out what it is all signifying" ("Comments," 11–12; revised in *Mademoiselle* interview, 143, 209; *Self,* 168–69). For another zoo setting, see "Goodbye to Serpents."

VARIANTS:

10: beast house (*Poems 57–67, Falling, Whole Motion*) | beast-house (*New Yorker*)

The Sheep Child

FIRST PUBLICATION: As "The Sheep-Child," *Atlantic* 218 (August 1966): 86.
COLLECTED: *Poems* 57–67, 252–53; *Falling,* 13–14; *Whole Motion,* 248–49.
REPRINTED: *Achievement,* 69–71; *Best Poems of 1966,* 37–39; *Cambridge Poetry Magazine* 1 (Autumn 1983): 20–21; *Contemporary American Poetry* (Poulin), 70–72; *Contemporary Poetry in America,* 69–70; *Geography of Poets,* 323–24; *Giant Book of Poetry,* 468–70; *Great Ideas Today,* 108–9; *Harvard,* 136–38; *Men-Talk,* 26–27; *Modern Poems,* 379–80; *New Oxford Book of Modern Verse,* 860–62; *Norton Anthology of Modern Poetry,* 1034–36; *Made Thing,* 82–3; *Poems,* 40–41; *Preferences,* 53–54; *Self,* 176–83; *Treasury of American Poetry,* 635–37; *Tricentennial Anthology,* 559–60; *Vintage,* 158–60; *Yellow Silk II* (2000) 117–19.
NOTES: Dickey claimed that he was told the story of the sheep-child (hyphenated in the text of the poem but not in the title) by a boy named Dick Harris, "who came over from an adjacent farm on Sunday afternoon" (presumably near the Dickey farm on Nickajack Creek, Georgia): "What I intended to do, or tried to do, was to write a poem having something to do with the enormous need for contact that runs through all of sentient nature, and has no regard whatever for boundaries of species. . . . What survives in my mind is the image of the sort of ultimate horror that I personally possessed" ("Comments," 13; revised in *Mademoiselle* interview, 142–43; *Self,* 164–66). "What I intended was that this *contra naturam* creature born from this monstrous, clandestine marriage between a human being and an animal is not *contra naturam,* but very much *naturam*" (*Self,* 165; see Broughton, 180). Dickey showed an interest in "Beast and human in sexual congress poems" in the early 1950s (*Self,* 31). At readings he nearly always introduced this poem with these words from *Self:* "I don't know what other defects or virtues this poem might have, but I think it can hardly be faulted from the standpoint of originality of viewpoint, at least in the latter section!" (165). He would also tell the audience, "You cannot imagine the effect on the audience when I read this poem in New Zealand." For a creature speaking in italics, see "Approaching Prayer."
27, 49: John 14:2, see "The Gamecocks," line 57.

Turning Away: Variations on Estrangement

FIRST PUBLICATION: *Hudson Review* 19 (Autumn 1966): 361–68.
COLLECTED: *Eye-Beaters,* 56–63; *Central Motion,* 53–60; *Whole Motion,* 336–42.
NOTES: "We've all turned away from people that we cared for when we saw that it was no longer possible to swing. You turn away and things happen to you, you know? They don't know why you're turning away from them. They don't know why, but they've sensed it coming for a long time. And you turn away and things change. Everything begins to look like a military battlefield. It's a perfectly placid scene, nice country, beautiful weather, but because you did your act of turning away, the thing becomes a battlefield, and somebody behind you is crying" (*Unmuzzled Ox* interview, 84; Baughman, 91–92). Set to music by Robert C. Constable (see "A Birth") as "Variations on Estrangement" (ca. 1995).
59–60: See "Deborah, Moon, Mirror, Right Hand Rising," line 2.

Variants:
[All lines centered (*Eye-Beaters, Central Motion, Whole Motion*) | [all lines flush left] (*Hudson*)
116: desert: stands (TS, *Eye-Beaters, Central Motion, Whole Motion*) | desert: stands (*Hudson*)
117–18: [blank line inserted] (*Hudson*)
157: Double (TS, *Eye-Beaters, Central Motion, Whole Motion*) | Increase (*Hudson*)
196–97: [blank line inserted] (*Hudson*)
201–2: [blank line inserted] (*Hudson*)
202–3: [blank line inserted] (*Hudson*)

The Flash

First Publication: *Transatlantic Review*, no. 22 (Autumn 1966): 59.
Collected: *Poems 57–67*, 258; *Falling*, 28; *Whole Motion*, 261–62.
Reprinted: *James Dickey Reads His Poems* (London: American Embassy, 1968): 4; *Intervisions*, 31; SUNY–Brockport pamphlet advertising reading by Dickey (December 3, 1970); *Workshop*, 210.
Notes: "James Dickey: Worksheets," *Malahat Review*, no. 7 (July 1968): 113–17, contains five draft versions of "The Flash."
Variants:
8: hoe blade (*Poems 57–67, Falling, Whole Motion*) | hoe-blade (*Transatlantic*)

Sun

First Publication: *New Yorker* 42 (January 28, 1967): 32.
Collected: *Poems 57–67*, 254–55; *Falling*, 24–25; *Whole Motion*, 258–59.
Reprinted: *Achievement*, 71–73; *Contemporary American Poetry* (Poulin), 75–76.
Notes: For Dickey this poem presented "Dantean possibilities, two lovers who *can't*, and who can't *not*. . . . I minored in astronomy in college, at Vanderbilt, and it has always been a very great source of personal dissatisfaction to me that I was never able to get any astronomical imagery into poetry. . . . My excuse [for using it in this poem] was that I remembered the great dark field telescopic photograph that we made of solar surface phenomena on the sun, of these million mile long streamers of fire flying above the surface of the sun. . . . And I thought maybe that the two people that were supposed to be as sunburned as badly as these two were supposed to be, who had lain face up in the summer sun, . . . might catch a glimpse of these long fire things going above the surface of the sun. But really it isn't a poem about astronomy, it is a poem about sex and the pain that frequently attends it, and maybe always does" ("Comments," 12; revised in *Self*, 166).
Variants:
27: body halo (*Poems 57–67, Falling, Whole Motion*) | body-halo (*New Yorker*)
28: oxides: walked (*Poems 57–67, Falling, Whole Motion*) | oxides   walked (*New Yorker*)

Falling

First Publication: *New Yorker* 42 (February 11, 1967): 38–40.
Collected: *Poems 57–67*, 293–99; *Falling*, 3–9; *Whole Motion*, 243–47.

Reprinted: *Achievement,* 78–84; *Contemporary American and Australian Poetry,* edited by Thomas Shapcott (St. Lucia: University of Queensland Press, 1976) 41–45; *Great Ideas Today,* 110–13; *Dickey Reader,* 80–85; *Longman,* 195–200; *Made Thing,* 85–89; *New Yorker Book of Poems,* 216–20; *Of Time and Experience: Literary Themes,* edited by Richard H. Dodge and Peter D. Lindblom (Cambridge, Mass.: Winthrop, 1972), 701–6; *One Hundred American Poems,* 209–16; *Poems,* 49–55; *Poems of Our Moment,* 64–71; *Self,* 176–83; *Selected,* 118–23; *Zelo* 2, no. 2 (1987): 56–57.

Notes: "I was trying to write in a large, sort of block format where the lines are cut up into units, or what I call a 'word burst,' kind of like hand grenades. . . . It took me three or four years to write it—maybe not three or four, but at least two" (Greiner, 12). "In that poem I wanted to use a kind of Bergsonian time shift, in which time itself, that is as we know it, clock time, would not be real time. What we have in that poem is what Bergson referred to as *durée,* duration, lived time, rather than clock time, where things seem to stretch out longer than they ordinarily would. It seems to take an eternity to reach the earth, as it would do, I'm sure" (*Writer's Voice,* 230). See Henri Bergson, *Durée et simultanéité. À propos de la théorie d'Einstein* (1922).

"A 29-year-old stewardess fell 1,500 feet to her death tonight when she was swept through an emergency door that suddenly sprang open on an Allegheny Airlines plane. . . . The body of Françoise de Moriere [*sic*] was found near Red Oak Hill Road outside the town of Farmington three hours after the accident" (*New York Times,* October 20, 1962, 1). For the facts attending the fall of Françoise-Marie-Gabrielle Chabiel de Morière, see also ibid., October 21, 1962, 49; Jim Townsend, "Dickey," *Charlotte* 9 (March/April 1977): 22–23; Baughman, 148–49; and Hart, 367–38. Dickey claimed that Flannery O'Connor found the story and told him of it (Hart, 436; Townsend, 22; Baughman, 148). A facsimile of the first page of the MS was published in "James Dickey: The Art of Poetry XX," *Paris Review* 17 (Spring 1976): 52; *Writers at Work: The Paris Review Interviews,* 5th ser., edited by George Plimpton (New York: Viking, 1981), 200. See also *Mademoiselle* interview, 209–10; *Self,* 174–75. A "choral drama" of this poem by Libby Larsen was commissioned by the Sandlapper Singers of Columbia, South Carolina, and premiered on September 8, 2001.

12–13: Compare the well-dressed suicide in "The Leap," lines 31–32.

37–51: For Dickey taking the bird's perspective, see "Reincarnation (II)" and *Jericho.*

46–82: On the transference of owl instincts to man, see "The Owl King" and *Deliverance,* 87–89.

53: "stoop" is the downward swoop of a bird of prey.

72–74: The typical scenario of the sort of Coca-Cola commercials Dickey wrote for the *Eddie Fisher Show* in 1956. See Hart, 208–9.

78: Don Loper (1906–1972) was a Hollywood costume designer and sometime actor-producer. At the height of his fame, an episode of *I Love Lucy* ("The Fashion Show") took place in his salon with Lucy trying to obtain one of his dresses.

111–28: Compare the disrobing of the farm girl in "May Day Sermon," lines 265–69.

112–13: Jane McNaughton loses one shoe in "The Leap."

Variants:

Epigraph: [quotation in italic] (*Poems 57–67, Falling*) | [quotation in Roman] (*New Yorker, Whole Motion*)

Epigraph source: —*New York Times* (*Poems 57–67, Falling, Whole Motion*) | —*The Times* | (*New Yorker*)

1: black (*New Yorker, Poems 57–67, Falling*) | black and (*Whole Motion* [typo])

3: wingtip   some (*Poems 57–67, Falling, Whole Motion*) | wing tip. Some (*New Yorker*)

25: ways   and (*Poems 57–67, Falling, Whole Motion*) | ways   and, (*New Yorker*)

26: wider and (*Poems 57–67, Falling, Whole Motion*) | wider   and (*New Yorker*)

33: down seeing (*Poems 57–67, Falling, Whole Motion*) | down   seeing (*New Yorker*)

38: her no (*Poems 57–67, Falling, Whole Motion*) | her   no (*New Yorker*)

47: into the (*Poems 57–67, Falling, Whole Motion*) | into (*Whole Motion*)

48: lights of (*Poems 57–67, Falling, Whole Motion*) | lights   of (*New Yorker*)

50: midwest (*Poems 57–67, Falling, Whole Motion*) | Midwest (*New Yorker*)

51: above (*Poems 57–67, Falling, Whole Motion*) | within (*New Yorker*)

67: people (*Poems 57–67, Falling, Whole Motion*) | peoples (*New Yorker*)

75: so let me begin (*Poems 57–67, Falling, Whole Motion*) | *so let me begin* (*New Yorker*)

81: wool   revealing (*New Yorker, Poems 57–67, Falling*) | wool revealing (*Whole Motion*)

86: midwest (*Poems 57–67, Falling, Whole Motion*) | Midwest (*New Yorker*)

94: rise brooding (*Poems 57–67, Falling, Whole Motion*) | rise   brooding (*New Yorker*)

97: midwest (*Poems 57–67, Falling, Whole Motion*) | Midwest (*New Yorker*)

98: fires   burning (*Poems 57–67, Falling, Whole Motion*) | fires burning (*New Yorker*)

100: Stars.   For (*Poems 57–67, Falling, Whole Motion*) | Stars: for (*New Yorker*)

102: wheatfields she (*Poems 57–67, Falling, Whole Motion*) | wheatfields   she (*New Yorker*)

126: her ascending (*Poems 57–67, Falling, Whole Motion*) | her   ascending (*New Yorker*)

123: windsocks (*Poems 57–67, Falling, Whole Motion*) | wind-socks (*New Yorker*)

131: tassels thickly (*Poems 57–67, Falling, Whole Motion*) | tassels   thickly (*New Yorker*)

132: counting: will (*Poems 57–67, Falling, Whole Motion*) | counting   will (*New Yorker*)

155: back-breaking (*Poems 57–67, Falling, Whole Motion*) | backbreaking (*New Yorker*)

169: lightning (*New Yorker, Poems 57–67, Falling*) | lighting (*Whole Motion* [typo])

174–75: [blank line inserted] (*New Yorker*)

Snakebite

First Publication: *New Yorker* 43 (February 25, 1967): 44.

Collected: *Poems 57–67*, 263–64; *Falling*, 33–34; *Whole Motion*, 264–65.

Reprinted: *Poems*, 42–43.

Notes: On Dickey's fear of snakes, see "Blowgun and Rattlesnake."

36–42: For cutting the flesh to release the venom, see "The Poisoned Man," lines 3–6.

Variants:

8: surprise: (*Poems 57–67, Falling, Whole Motion*) | surprise— (*New Yorker*)

13: giving: at (*Poems 57–67, Falling, Whole Motion*) | giving   at (*New Yorker*)

18: pinestraw (*Poems 57–67, Falling, Whole Motion*) | pine straw (*New Yorker*)

20: chosen: (*Poems 57–67, Falling, Whole Motion*) | chosen; (*New Yorker*)

26: killing: hold (*Poems 57–67, Falling, Whole Motion*) | killing. Hold (*New Yorker*)

38: Blows: (*Poems 57–67, Falling, Whole Motion*) | Blows; (*New Yorker*)

Power and Light

First Publication: *New Yorker* 43 (March 11, 1967): 60–61.

Collected: *Poems 57–67*, 256–57; *Falling*, 26–27; *Whole Motion*, 260–61.

Reprinted: *Achievement*, 73–75.

Notes: Driving home drunk from a party in Atlanta, Dickey pulled over to the side of the road and his headlights illuminated a sign that said "Georgia Power and Light." The phrase stuck with him, and he began to consider the only "pole man" he knew, his brother-in-law, John Hodgins (1919–1999). "The only thing I know about John is that when he climbs down off the poles every day he gets a bottle of Jack Daniels Black Label, and he goes home and says a perfunctory 'Good evening' to his wife, my sister Maibelle, and then he retires into the cellar and turns all the lights out and he stays down there until he drinks a fifth of that liquor and then about three o'clock in the morning he staggers up the stairs and has a piece of bread in the kitchen and goes to bed. . . . [The poem] is really supposed to be about a man under these rather peculiar conditions who is justifying his own existence by what he does, by getting drunk until his profession of lineman becomes kind of an ecstatic vision to him and he is able to reconcile himself to his fate thereby. But it is really supposed to be a kind of affirmation under these rather special conditions of a man's own right to live, and justify himself by justifying the work he does" ("Comments," 14–15). *Epigraph:* "Only connect! That was the whole of her sermon. Only connect the prose and the passion, and both will be exalted, and human love will be seen at its highest." E. M. Forster, *Howards End* (1910), ch. 22.

2: my wife: Maibelle Dickey Hodgins (1912–1998) was Dickey's elder sister, a poet herself, and a noted rosarian, whose gardening is referred to in lines 5–6.

Variants:

13: bottle   like (*Poems 57–67, Falling, Whole Motion*) | bottle. Like (*New Yorker*)

55: way station (*Poems 57–67, Falling, Whole Motion*) | way-station (*New Yorker*)

Dark Ones

First Publication: *Saturday Evening Post* 240 (April 8, 1967): 72.

Collected: *Poems 57–67*, 272–73; *Falling*, 42–43; *Whole Motion*, 270–72.

Reprinted: *Intervisions*, 44–47; *Teaching in America*, 42–43.

Notes: "It is a poem about commuters, and the dilemma of the modern love relationship and marriage. You work all day in a conditional anxiety and pressure and you come home. . . . There is some anxiety at home, but it is not quite as bad as at the office. . . . I think it is a kind of terrible condemnation maybe of one factor about American life, in that many of us believe . . . that the only good time is in the dark and not in the light" (*Teaching in America*, 42).

The editor of the *Saturday Evening Post* at this time was the valedictorian of Dickey's high-school class, William Austin Emerson, Jr. (1923–2009), who later taught journalism at the University of South Carolina.

Variants:

21: beer cans (*Poems 57–67, Falling, Whole Motion*) | beer-cans (*Post*)

37–38: [no blank line inserted] (*Post*)
48: light: hold (*Poems 57–67, Falling, Whole Motion*) | light: / hold (*Post*)
51: light: O Glory, there (*Poems 57–67, Falling, Whole Motion*) | light: O / Glory: there (*Post*)
53: sun (*Poems 57–67, Falling, Whole Motion*) | day (*Post*)

Bread

First Publication: *Poems 57–67*, 265–66 (published April 24, 1967).
Collected: *Falling*, 35–36; *Whole Motion*, 266–67.
Reprinted: *Longman*, 191; *Norton Anthology of Poetry*, 1154–55.
Notes: The title likely comes from the word Dickey altered in his Coleridge allusion in the last line. Dickey's poem describes the crash landing on water of a B-25 by its pilot, 1st Lt. Ira M. Barnett, in the northwestern portion of New Guinea, called the Vogelkop or "Bird's Head" peninsula. The plane went down in the water on July 27, 1944. The crew slept on the plane's wings, eventually made it to shore, and with the help of natives returned to camp on August 19, 1944 (*History*, 36–37).
13: For another submerged airplane, see "Obstructions," lines 32–38. For another B-25, see "The Coral Flight."
14: The island of Ceram is part of the Moluccas (Maluku) archipelago of eastern Indonesia, located between the Ceram Sea (north) and the Banda Sea (south), west of New Guinea and east of Buru Island, across the Manipa Strait. Chester L. Patrick of Florida was a second lieutenant who served in the 418th from December 1944 to March 1945.
37: "It ate the bread it ne'er had eat" (Coleridge, "The Rime of the Ancient Mariner," 1.67).

May Day Sermon to the Women of Gilmer County, Georgia,
by a Woman Preacher Leaving the Baptist Church

First Publication: As "May Day Sermon to the Women of Gilmer County by a Lady Preacher Leaving the Baptist Church," *Atlantic* 219 (April 1967): 90–97.
Collected: *Poems 57–67*, 3–13; *Falling*, 65–75; *Whole Motion*, 287–96.
Reprinted: *Dickey Reader*, 92–102; *Selected*, 3–13; *America's 85 Greatest Living Authors*, 66–75; *Tricentennial Anthology*, 547–58.
Notes: Dickey claimed the stimulus for this poem was a statement by Edwin Arlington Robinson in a letter to Mrs. Laura E. Richards of June 2, 1924: "I have been reading the Old Testament, a most bloodthirsty and perilous book for the young. Jehovah is beyond a doubt the worst character in fiction" (*Selected Letters of Edwin Arlington Robinson* [New York: Macmillan, 1940], 135; see *Crux*, 285). "It hit me that God, whether by nature a villain or hero, can be <u>made</u> a villain by villainous people. . . . 'May Day Sermon' is about that, and about the malevolent power God has under certain circumstances: that is, when he is controlled and 'interpreted' by people of malevolent tendencies. In this case God is neither more nor less than a combination of the Old Testament and a half mad Georgia hill farmer. . . . What I wanted to do most in this poem was to make a kind of mythological framework for the action by casting the poem in the form of one of the legends that are prevalent in such communities" (*Crux*, 285–86). Indeed the working title of

this poem was "A Mayday Courtship Legend of Gilmer County" (*Crux,* 226). "If anything could be said good about that poem the best thing that I would like to have said about it is that in it, especially toward the end, there is an authentic frenzy" (*NYQ* interview, 30; *Night,* 306). "I could go on record as saying that's ["May Day Sermon"] the best thing that I've ever written (*NYQ* interview, 30; Dickey chose not to reprint this remark in *Night*). Discussed in *Crux,* 285–86; *Mademoiselle* interview, 210; *Self,* 183–84.

Gilmer County is a rural county in northern Georgia, about sixty miles north of Atlanta, adjacent to Fannin County. The county used to be the location of the Hogback Plantation of Dickey's ancestors. See "The Escape."

A short film based on this poem was made in 1969 by Len Richmond (Hart, 435). It was adapted for the stage in 1992 by John Gallogly and produced at Theatre West in Los Angeles starring Bridget Hanley.

6: "Croker sack" (originally "crocus sack") is a southern term for "gunnysack."

34–35: For a father whipping his daughter, see "Cherrylog Road," line 71.

39: In 1 Samuel 5:2–7 the Philistines captured the Ark of Yahweh and took it to the temple of Dagon, their god. On repeated mornings the image of Dagon was found prostrate before the ark.

42: For the Dickey farm on the Nickajack Creek outside Atlanta, see "Hunting Civil War Relics at Nimblewill Creek" and "The Gamecocks."

53: "From all inordinate and sinful affections; and from all the deceits of the world, the flesh, and the devil, Good Lord, deliver us" ("The Litany," *Book of Common Prayer*). *Flesh and the Devil* (1929) starred Greta Garbo and John Gilbert.

63: Grimes Nose is a cliff in White County, Georgia, adjacent to Gilmer County on the east.

64: Brasstown Bald is Georgia's highest mountain (elevation 4,784 feet) from which one can see four states (North Carolina, South Carolina, Tennessee, and Georgia).

74: Originally applied to the Styx, "The River of No Return" was the name Lewis and Clark gave the Salmon River in Idaho. Like *Flesh and the Devil, River of No Return* (1954), with Marilyn Monroe and Robert Mitchum, was a popular film.

77–78, 107: For this scene, see "Kudzu."

90: The lifespan of the *Dipterals,* commonly known as gnats, is about two to four months.

122: For David and Bathsheba, see 2 Samuel 11–12 and 1 Kings 1–2.

169: "Carolina Moon" was a popular song written in 1929 by Joe Burke and Benny Davis.

209: Ellijay (see "On the Coosawattee"), the seat of Gilmer County, has a population of barely sixteen hundred. It was the home of Hampton Mills.

221–22: Obadiah 1:3: "The pride of thine heart hath deceived thee, thou that dwellest in the clefts of the rock, whose habitation is high; that saith in his heart, Who shall bring me down to the ground?"

230: Matthew 19:24, Mark 10:25, Luke 18.25.

265–69: Compare the frenzied disrobing of the stewardess in "Falling," lines 111–28. For a similar "sermon" by a preaching folksinger, see "A Folk Singer of the Thirties."

292: Lindale is a town seventy miles southwest of Gilmer County, between Atlanta and Rome, home of Pepperell Mills, which produced rayon fabrics.

347: Jericho fell from the blowing of ram's horns (Joshua 6:1–21).

VARIANTS:

4: flying squirrel (*Poems 57–67, Falling, Whole Motion*) | flying-squirrel (*Atlantic*)

11: grease cans   lard cans (*Poems 57–67, Falling, Whole Motion*) | grease-cans   lard-cans (*Atlantic*)

15: stump chains (*Poems 57–67, Falling, Whole Motion*) | stump-chains (*Atlantic*)

45: whitefaced (*Poems 57–67, Falling, Whole Motion*) | white-faced (*Atlantic*)

69: lard cans (*Poems 57–67, Falling, Whole Motion*) | lard-cans (*Atlantic*)

70: mule bits (*Poems 57–67, Falling, Whole Motion*) | mule-bits (*Atlantic*)

94: cow chips (*Poems 57–67, Falling, Whole Motion*) | cow-chips (*Atlantic*)

98: stump chains (*Poems 57–67, Falling, Whole Motion*) | stump-chains (*Atlantic*)

98: shall (*Falling, Whole Motion*) | will (*Atlantic, Poems 57–67*)

102: speak, (*Poems 57–67, Falling, Whole Motion*) | speak; (*Atlantic*)

112: willow-leaves (*Poems 57–67, Falling, Whole Motion*) | willow leaves (*Atlantic*)

128: serpent (*Poems 57–67, Falling, Whole Motion*) | fox (*Atlantic*)

261: pinepoles (*Poems 57–67, Falling, Whole Motion*) | pine-poles (*Atlantic*)

262: crotchhair (*Poems 57–67, Falling, Whole Motion*) | crotch-hair (*Atlantic*)

290: scuppernong (*Atlantic, Poems 57–67, Falling*) | scuppermong (*Whole Motion* [typo])

325: ice-pick (*Poems 57–67, Falling, Whole Motion*) | ice pick (Atlantic)

328: you at (*Poems 57–67, Falling, Whole Motion*) | you (*Atlantic*)

351: blood: the (*Poems 57–67, Falling, Whole Motion*) | blood   (*Atlantic*)

The Christmas Towns

FIRST PUBLICATION: *American Christmas,* edited by Webster Schott and Robert J. Myers, 2nd ed. (Kansas City, Mo.: Hallmark, 1967), 79–80.

NOTES: Written on commission from Hallmark Cards, 1966 (Hart, 358).

15: Dickey published "Faces Seen Once" in 1964.

—1968–1973—

Victory

FIRST PUBLICATION: *Atlantic* 222 (August 1968): 48–50.

COLLECTED: *Eye-Beaters,* 38–41; *Central Motion,* 34–37; *Whole Motion,* 321–25.

REPRINTED: *Georgia* 16 (October 1972): 27–29; *Old Glory,* 225–28; *Selected,* 127–30.

NOTES: Okinawa, the setting of this poem, is the largest island of the Okinawa prefecture and sits some 340 miles from mainland Japan. In July 1945 more than five hundred thousand American troops and twelve hundred warships were deployed to secure this island. This action was the largest amphibious assault in the Pacific theater, roughly the size of D-day. The intention was to use the island as a staging ground for an assault on the mainland. Dickey arrived in Naha, the capital, on July 9. His squadron's camp was, as he wrote in his history of his squadron, "in the middle of one of the biggest battlefields of the war" (*One Voice 1,* 18). Dickey flew bombing and strafing missions in August. Following the dropping of atomic bombs on Hiroshima on August 6 and Nagasaki on August 9, the Japanese began suing for peace and announced acceptance of Allied terms on August 15, sparking wild celebrations on Okinawa. Dickey wrote of August 14 in the squadron history: "Everyone became violently excited with every news report on the radio or with liquor laid away against VJ Day" (*One Voice 1*, 19; see *Crux*, 24).

1: September 3rd: The formal signing of the Japanese surrender took place on board the USS *Missouri* on September 2, 1945 (VJ Day).

24: Dickey was born February 2, 1923.

36: For Maibelle Swift Dickey, see "The Sprinter's Mother." Dickey wrote her a series of letters from April to November 1945 describing his activities and asking for books and newspapers (*Crux*, 14–28).

41: After beginning the assault on Buna-Gona on November 16, 1942, a major battle in the New Guinea campaign, the Allies took control on January 22, 1943.

60: "Dead soldier" is a World War II term for an empty whiskey bottle.

71–72: "Detroit / Glass" is the Jeep windshield.

83–84: A Catherine Wheel is a pinwheel-type of fireworks, which is named after the wheel on which St. Catherine was martyred. From Dickey's squadron history: "As each outfit heard a fresh rumor, there were new outbursts of hilarity and fireworks until there was a greater display of ack ack in the sky than there had been for any Nip bomb raid" (*One Voice 1*, 19).

91: Yokohama, the chief port of Japan, was virtually destroyed after more than thirty U.S. bombing raids. On one day, May 29, 1945, American bombs destroyed more than one-third of the city in a little over an hour.

118: "Buckner Bay" was the Allied name for Nakagusuku Bay off the southern coast of Okinawa. It was named in honor of General Simon Bolivar Buckner, Jr. (1886–1945), killed in the later days of the Battle of Okinawa.

VARIANTS:

35: [indented] (*Atlantic*) | [not indented] (TS, *Eye-Beaters, Central Motion, Whole Motion*)

36: Yes (TS, *Eye-Beaters, Central Motion, Whole Motion*) | Yes, (*Atlantic*)

44: O (TS, *Eye-Beaters, Central Motion, Whole Motion*) | Oh (*Atlantic*)

44: you: the (TS, *Eye-Beaters, Central Motion, Whole Motion*) | you: the (*Atlantic*)

45–46: [blank line inserted] (*Atlantic*)

49: Seat (TS, *Eye-Beaters, Central Motion, Whole Motion*) | seat (*Atlantic*)

62: Out (TS, *Eye-Beaters, Central Motion, Whole Motion*) | out (*Atlantic*)

68: To (TS, *Eye-Beaters, Central Motion, Whole Motion*) | to (*Atlantic*)

79: [flush with preceding line] (*Atlantic*)

91: Yokohama (*Atlantic*) | Yokahama (TS, *Eye-Beaters, Central Motion, Whole Motion*)

115: Yokohama (*Atlantic*) | Yokahama (TS, *Eye-Beaters, Central Motion, Whole Motion*)

The Lord in the Air

FIRST PUBLICATION: *New Yorker* 44 (October 19, 1968): 56

COLLECTED: *Eye-Beaters*, 42–43; *Central Motion*, 38–39; *Whole Motion*, 325–26.

NOTES: "If the Spectator could Enter into these Images in his Imagination approaching them on the Fiery Chariot of his Contemplative Thought if he could Enter into Noah's Rainbow or into his bosom or could make a Friend & Companion of one of these Images of wonder which always intreats him to leave mortal things as he must know them would he arise from his Grave them would he meet the Lord in the Air & then he would be happy" (William Blake, "Visions of the Last Judgment" [1810], in *The Poetry and Prose of William Blake,* edited by David V. Erdman (Garden City, N.Y.: Doubleday, 1970), 550. Dickey read the quotation in Frank Kermode's *The Romantic Image* (London: Routledge & Kegan Paul, 1961). On the power and subsequent guilt of the bomber pilot, see "The Firebombing."

3, 36: For Christopher Dickey, see "The Child in Armor."

14: See "The Night Pool."

VARIANTS:

Epigraph: BLAKE (*Eye-Beaters, Central Motion*) | —*William Blake.* (*New Yorker*) | -Blake (TS) | —*Blake* (*Whole Motion*)

[All lines flush left] (*New Yorker*)

10: backyard (TS, *Eye-Beaters, Central Motion, Whole Motion*) | back yard (*New Yorker*)

17: Back, and (TS, *Eye-Beaters, Central Motion, Whole Motion*) | Back   and (*New Yorker*)

23: lungs, as (TS, *Eye-Beaters, Central Motion, Whole Motion*) | lungs   as (*New Yorker*)

28: air. The (TS, *Eye-Beaters, Central Motion, Whole Motion*) | air.   The (*New Yorker*)

32: crows (TS, *Eye-Beaters, Central Motion, Whole Motion*) | the crows (*New Yorker*)

33: belly-laughs (TS, *Eye-Beaters, Central Motion, Whole Motion*) | belly laughs (*New Yorker*)

36: warning, like marriage. O (TS, *Eye-Beaters, Central Motion, Whole Motion*) | warning,   like marriage.   O (*New Yorker*)

36: in, drop (TS, *Eye-Beaters, Central Motion, Whole Motion*) | in   drop (*New Yorker*)

37: wood, back (TS, *Eye-Beaters, Central Motion, Whole Motion*) | wood   back (*New Yorker*)

38: moment and (TS, *Eye-Beaters, Central Motion, Whole Motion*) | moment, and (*New Yorker*)

40: beasts: something (TS, *Eye-Beaters, Central Motion, Whole Motion*) | beasts   something (*New Yorker*)

41: betrayal, or (TS, *Eye-Beaters, Central Motion, Whole Motion*) | betrayal   or (*New Yorker*)

42: desire, but (TS, *Eye-Beaters, Central Motion, Whole Motion*) | desire   but (*New Yorker*)

The Eye-Beaters

FIRST PUBLICATION: *Harper's* 237 (November 1968): 134–36.

COLLECTED: *Eye-Beaters,* 50–55; *Central Motion,* 47–52; *Whole Motion,* 332–35.

REPRINTED: *Dickey Reader,* 103–7; *Selected,* 138–43.

NOTES: Mary Bookwalter (b. 1948) was a student at Carnegie Tech when Dickey gave a reading at the Pittsburgh Museum in 1966. At a reception following the reading, she told Dickey that during the previous spring she had visited the Muscatatuck State School for the Mentally Retarded near Columbus, Indiana, with her boyfriend, Mark Fuller, and his father, an audiologist who was testing the children, most of whom were deaf as well as blind. (In *One Voice 1,* 437, Dickey recalled the name of the school as the "Indiana Home for the Retarded and Blind.") The "school" (where no education of the inmates took place) warehoused the severely mentally handicapped of all ages, but Dr. Fuller wanted the two young people to see the children, who were capable of feeling only one sensation, pain. Because they tended to beat their heads and hands against walls and floors, they required helmets on their heads and heavy gauze bandages on their hands. They poked their own eyes to make images, much as Dickey described in "Reading Genesis to a Blind Child." Dickey told Bookwalter that the "Coleridge-like" marginal comments of "the therapist" were intended to replicate her responses (in masculine guise) to what Dr. Fuller (as "the Therapist") had told her when he took her around the "school." On blindness see also "Why in London the Blind Are Saviors"; "The Owl King"; *Self*, 209; the headnote to "Cahill Is Blind," *Esquire* 85 (February 1976) 67; and *Alnilam*. This was the last of Dickey's poems to employ the "block format" or "wall of words" technique (*Central Motion*, v).

41: The ibex is a wild goat with long backward-curving horns; it is native to the mountains of Eurasia and northern Africa. The quagga, a zebralike mammal of southern Africa, has been extinct since the nineteenth century.

42: The aurochs, or urus, the long-extinct ancestor of modern domestic cattle, was a wild ox of Europe, northern Africa, and western Asia.

140: See William Blake, "Jerusalem," line 11: "Bring me my spear."

VARIANTS:

48: [Dickey's typist broke this line at "its / stand" and the next line (unindented) at "fist / of"; I have arbitrarily decided to true up line 48 and break the line differently.]

49: [line not indented] (*Harper's*)

50–51: [blank line inserted] (*Harper's*)

55: conceived. The (*Eye-Beaters, Central Motion, Whole Motion*) | conceived.   The (*Harper's*)

57: make unrolling (*Eye-Beaters, Central Motion, Whole Motion*) | make   unrolling (*Harper's*)

58: itself clenching re-forming rising (*Eye-Beaters, Central Motion, Whole Motion*) | itself   clenching   re-forming   rising (*Harper's*)

66: *hunting* (*Harper's*) | *Hunting* (*Eye-Beaters, Central Motion, Whole Motion*)

68: *hands as* (*Eye-Beaters, Central Motion, Whole Motion*) | *hands   as* (*Harper's*)

79: indeed, (*Harper's*) | indeed (*Eye-Beaters, Central Motion, Whole Motion*)

100: sweat: It (*Eye-Beaters, Central Motion*) | sweat: it (TS, *Harper's*) | swear: it (*Whole Motion*) [typo]

140: Therapist (*Eye-Beaters, Central Motion, Whole Motion*) | Therapists (TS, *Harper's*)

Knock

FIRST PUBLICATION: *New Yorker* 44 (January 25, 1969): 92.

COLLECTED: *Eye-Beaters*, 37; *Central Motion*, 33; *Whole Motion*, 321.

REPRINTED: Broadside facsimile of manuscript (Washington, D.C.: Folger Shakespeare Library, 1977).

VARIANTS:

[All lines flush left] (*New Yorker*)

5: night, making (TS, *Eye-Beaters, Central Motion, Whole Motion*) | night,   making (*New Yorker*)

12 Anything? Have (TS, *Eye-Beaters, Central Motion, Whole Motion*) | Anything?   Have (*New Yorker*)

The Place

FIRST PUBLICATION: *New Yorker* 45 (March 1, 1969): 40.

COLLECTED: *Eye-Beaters,* 24; *Central Motion,* 21; *Whole Motion,* 313–14.

VARIANTS:

Subtitle: (Beside a Frozen Lake) (*New Yorker*)

2: Was (TS, *Eye-Beaters, Central Motion, Whole Motion*) | was (*New Yorker*)

3: Has (TS, *Eye-Beaters, Central Motion, Whole Motion*) | has (*New Yorker*)

4: Shaking (TS, *Eye-Beaters, Central Motion*) | shaking (*New Yorker, Whole Motion*)

7: Into (TS, *Eye-Beaters, Central Motion, Whole Motion*) | into (*New Yorker*)

8: On (TS, *Eye-Beaters, Central Motion, Whole Motion*) | on (*New Yorker*)

8: other   let (TS, *Eye-Beaters, Central Motion, Whole Motion*) | other—let (*New Yorker*)

9: Sweeping (TS, *Eye-Beaters, Central Motion, Whole Motion*) | sweeping (*New Yorker*)

10: Within (TS, *Eye-Beaters, Central Motion, Whole Motion*) | within (*New Yorker*)

10: impassable (TS, *Eye-Beaters, Central Motion, Whole Motion*) | impassible (*New Yorker*) ["impassable" means impossible to cross or overcome; "impassible" means not subject to pain]

11: Miles (TS, *Eye-Beaters, Central Motion, Whole Motion*) | miles (*New Yorker*)

12: Overwhelming (TS, *Eye-Beaters, Central Motion, Whole Motion*) | overwhelming (*New Yorker*)

14: Inside (TS, *Eye-Beaters, Central Motion, Whole Motion*) | inside (*New Yorker*)

16–17: [no blank line] (*New Yorker*)

Madness

FIRST PUBLICATION: *New Yorker* 45 (April 26, 1969): 40.

COLLECTED: *Eye-Beaters,* 47–9; *Central Motion,* 43–46; *Whole Motion,* 329–32.

REPRINTED: *New Yorker Book of Poems,* 407–10; *Selected,* 134–37.

NOTES: "[The poem] has a particular rhythm to it, which I haven't managed to reproduce anywhere else; I don't know whether I would want to. . . . [The poem has] some kind of peculiar linguistic structure" (*Unmuzzled Ox* interview, 80; Baughman, 89). Dickey may be referring to the absence in the opening lines of stated subjects for the verbs "Lay" (lines 1 and 3), "Had" (line 6),"Would lie" (line 8), "Would lap" (line 11). The poem also displays asyndeton and lacks the usual quotation punctuation. The quaint syntax and speech combine with the surprise in line 95 that it is not the fox but the dog that is hunted. From August 1966 to August 1968 Dickey and his family lived at 47 King Street in Leesville, Virginia.

3–4: See "A Dog Sleeping on My Feet."

VARIANTS:

12: Spring (TS, *Eye-Beaters, Central Motion, Whole Motion*) | spring (*New Yorker*)

20: [flush left] (*Whole Motion*)

29: children (*New Yorker, Eye-Beaters, Central Motion*) | chidlren (*Whole Motion* [typo])

29: Spring (TS, *Eye-Beaters, Central Motion, Whole Motion*) | spring (*New Yorker*)

31: wind (*New Yorker,* TS, *Eye-Beaters*) | winds (*Central Motion, Whole Motion*)

34: bushy-assed (TS, *Eye-Beaters, Central Motion, Whole Motion*) | bushy-tailed (*New Yorker*)

35: soap: (TS, *Eye-Beaters, Central Motion, Whole Motion*) | soap. (*New Yorker*)

43: hunted: (TS, *Eye-Beaters, Central Motion, Whole Motion*) | hunted; (*New Yorker*)

49: O (TS, *Eye-Beaters, Central Motion, Whole Motion*) | Oh, (*New Yorker*)

59: low-born (TS, *Eye-Beaters, Central Motion, Whole Motion*) | lowborn (*New Yorker*)

67: Spring (TS, *Eye-Beaters, Central Motion, Whole Motion*) | spring (*New Yorker*)

71: lips: (TS, *Eye-Beaters, Central Motion, Whole Motion*) | lips; (*New Yorker*)

78: Spring (TS, *Eye-Beaters, Central Motion, Whole Motion*) | spring (*New Yorker*)

98: shut: this (TS, *Eye-Beaters, Central Motion, Whole Motion*) | shut. This (*New Yorker*)

99: Spring (TS, *Eye-Beaters, Central Motion, Whole Motion*) | spring (*New Yorker*)

Living There

FIRST PUBLICATION: *Harper's* 238 (May 1969): 52–53.

COLLECTED: With "Looking for the Buckhead Boys" as "Two Poems of Going Home," *Eye-Beaters*, 17–19; *Central Motion*, 14–16; *Whole Motion*, 308–10.

VARIANTS:

21: this old one, the one (*Eye-Beaters, Central Motion, Whole Motion*) | these old ones, the ones (*Harper's*, TS)

22: is (*Eye-Beaters, Central Motion, Whole Motion*) | are (*Harper's*, TS)

23: it is (*Eye-Beaters, Central Motion, Whole Motion*) | they are (*Harper's*, TS)

24: a ghost. (*Eye-Beaters, Central Motion, Whole Motion*) | ghosts. (*Harper's*, TS)

Blood

FIRST PUBLICATION: *Poetry* 114 (June 1969): 149–50.

COLLECTED: *Eye-Beaters*, 34–35; *Central Motion*, 30–31; *Whole Motion*, 319–20.

NOTES: "In 'Blood' I tried to get an enormous dramatic compression in just a few lines" (*Unmuzzled Ox* interview, 75; Baughman, 84). Dickey said the poem concerns "screwing—you've been screwing, and you're drunk; you wake up, and there's blood all over the sheets, the room, and you think, My God, has someone been murdered—because, you know, you're drunk, you've been passed out; but then you realize, because you've been screwing, that she's having her period, and it's not the blood of death, but the blood of life—the blood of life" (David Havird, "In and Out of Class with James Dickey," *Virginia Quarterly Review* 76 [2000]: 463). Dickey also associated nosebleeds with male orgasm, see *Striking*, 198.

VARIANTS:

2: somebody. Is (TS, *Eye-Beaters, Central Motion, Whole Motion*) | somebody.   Is (*Poetry*)

3: Breath? What (TS, *Eye-Beaters, Central Motion, Whole Motion*) | Breath?   What (*Poetry*)

8: it? I (TS, *Eye-Beaters, Central Motion, Whole Motion*) | it?   I (*Poetry*)

10: what? And (TS, *Eye-Beaters, Central Motion, Whole Motion*) | what?   And (*Poetry*)

19: was it? Light (TS, *Eye-Beaters, Central Motion, Whole Motion*) | Was it?   Light (*Poetry*)

24: last? Who (TS, *Eye-Beaters, Central Motion, Whole Motion*) | last?   Who (*Poetry*)

25: girl? She (TS, *Eye-Beaters, Central Motion, Whole Motion*) | girl?   She (*Poetry*)

27: home: knife (TS, *Eye-Beaters, Central Motion, Whole Motion*) | home: knife (*Poetry*)

35: To (*Eye-Beaters, Central Motion, Whole Motion*) | to (*Poetry,* TS)

36: Will (*Eye-Beaters, Central Motion, Whole Motion*) | will (*Poetry,* TS)

38: woman? No (TS, *Eye-Beaters, Central Motion, Whole Motion*) | woman?   No (*Poetry*)

First Publication: *Poetry* 114 (June 1969): 151–55.

Collected: *Eye-Beaters,* 7–9; *Central Motion,* 3–6; *Whole Motion,* 299–301.

Reprinted: *Anthology,* 1753–56; as "Under Buzzards," *On Doctoring,* 251–52; *A Southern Renascence Man: Views of Robert Penn Warren,* edited by Walter Edgar (Baton Rouge: Louisiana State University Press, 1984), 92–93.

Notes: Dickey's beloved grandmother Lena Swift Burckhardt Huntley (see "False Youth: Summer") contracted diabetes, resulting in blindness and the loss of a leg. Sometime before 1966 a doctor told Dickey that he might be diabetic, but other doctors assured him he was not. He told interviewers in 1973 and 1975, "I'm a diabetic" (*Southern Review* 9 [Winter 1973]: 139; *Unmuzzled Ox* interview, 84; *Shenandoah* 18 [Autumn 1966]: 23; *Night,* 259). The fear of having to stop drinking because of diabetes terrified him, but he told friends he was determined to drink despite the disease (like Dylan Thomas and Brendan Behan), not to treat it into a comfortable old age (*Crux,* 341; Hart, 415–16). See Broughton, 167. Dickey dedicated this poem (as "Under Buzzards") to his friend Robert Penn Warren (1905–1989) because "I feel some root-deep kind of affinity with your poetic effort—that kind of yearning-toward in your poems is what I mean— . . . I think of you as the best of all of us" (*Crux,* 281). Dickey also dedicated *Värmland* to Warren. Dickey admired Warren's poems about eagles (which he emulated in "Eagles" and "The Eagle's Mile") but claimed his bird was the buzzard (see "Robert Penn Warren's Courage," *Saturday Review* 7 [August 1980]: 56–57; reprinted as "The Weathered Hand and Silent Space" in *Night,* 52–55).

37: The "companion" is to be taken as Warren.

55: For Hogback Ridge see "Slave Quarters."

Variants:

4: fire. I (TS, *Eye-Beaters, Central Motion, Whole Motion*) | fire.   I (*Poetry*)

5: sleep. In (TS, *Eye-Beaters, Central Motion, Whole Motion*) | sleep.   In (*Poetry*)

8: hell. Months (TS, *Eye-Beaters, Central Motion, Whole Motion*) | hell.   Months (*Poetry*)

9: me: I (TS, *Eye-Beaters, Central Motion, Whole Motion*) | me: I (*Poetry*)

10: way. The (TS, *Eye-Beaters, Central Motion, Whole Motion*) | way.   The (*Poetry*)

11: nice. He (TS, *Eye-Beaters, Central Motion, Whole Motion*) | nice.   He (*Poetry*)

13: exercise. You (TS, *Eye-Beaters, Central Motion, Whole Motion*) | exercise.   You (*Poetry*)

20: fury. Sleep (TS, *Eye-Beaters, Central Motion, Whole Motion*) | fury.   Sleep (*Poetry*)

21: own. Gangrene (TS, *Eye-Beaters, Central Motion, Whole Motion*) | own.   Gangrene (*Poetry*)

23: mountain. Moderation (TS, *Eye-Beaters, Central Motion, Whole Motion*) | mountain.   Moderation (*Poetry*)

24: exercise. Each (TS, *Eye-Beaters, Central Motion, Whole Motion*) | exercise.   Each (*Poetry*)

28: while. Not bad! I (TS, *Eye-Beaters, Central Motion, Whole Motion*) | while.   Not bad!   I (*Poetry*)

29: house: the (TS, *Eye-Beaters, Central Motion, Whole Motion*) | house: the (*Poetry*)

38: summer. Heavy. Companion (TS, *Eye-Beaters, Central Motion, Whole Motion*) | summer.   Heavy.   Companion (*Poetry*)

41: death. We (TS, *Eye-Beaters, Central Motion, Whole Motion*) | death.   We (*Poetry*)

42–43: [no blank line inserted] (TS, *Poetry*)

46: hill. We (TS, *Eye-Beaters, Central Motion, Whole Motion*) | hill.   We (*Poetry*)

47: moment; exactly (TS, *Eye-Beaters, Central Motion, Whole Motion*) | moment: exactly (*Poetry*)

52: is. Whirl (TS, *Eye-Beaters, Central Motion, Whole Motion*) | is.   Whirl (*Poetry*)

56: listen: what (TS, *Eye-Beaters, Central Motion, Whole Motion*) | listen: what (*Poetry*)

59–60: [no blank line inserted] (*Poetry*)

68: level. Tell (TS, *Eye-Beaters, Central Motion, Whole Motion*) | level.   Tell (*Poetry*)

70: world. O (TS, *Eye-Beaters, Central Motion, Whole Motion*) |world.   O (*Poetry*)

71: pine-woods, in (TS, *Eye-Beaters, Central Motion, Whole Motion*) | pine-woods,   in (*Poetry*)

72: die. When (TS, *Eye-Beaters, Central Motion, Whole Motion*) | die.   When (*Poetry*)

74: to (TS, *Eye-Beaters, Central Motion, Whole Motion*) | To (*Poetry*)

76: right! Physicians, witness! I TS (TS, *Eye-Beaters, Central Motion, Whole Motion*) | right!   Physicians, witness!   I (*Poetry*)

76–77: [blank line inserted] (*Poetry*)

82: summer. Heavy. My (TS, *Eye-Beaters, Central Motion, Whole Motion*) | summer.   Heavy.   My (*Poetry*)

83: time. Is (TS, *Eye-Beaters, Central Motion, Whole Motion*) | time.   Is (*Poetry*)

83: clear? Heat (TS, *Eye-Beaters, Central Motion, Whole Motion*) | clear?   Heat (*Poetry*)

84: birds. But (TS, *Eye-Beaters, Central Motion, Whole Motion*) | birds.   But (*Poetry*)

85: Friend. This (TS, *Eye-Beaters, Central Motion, Whole Motion*) | Friend.   This (*Poetry*)

85: sensible. Really (TS, *Eye-Beaters, Central Motion, Whole Motion*) | sensible.   Really (*Poetry*)

94: Everything: everything (TS, *Eye-Beaters, Central Motion, Whole Motion*) | Everything: everything (*Poetry*)

95: it: heavy (TS, *Eye-Beaters, Central Motion, Whole Motion*) | it: heavy (*Poetry*)

95: right (*Poetry, Eye-Beaters*) | right. (*Central Motion, Whole Motion* [typo; a penciled note not in Dickey's hand on the errata sheet for *Central Motion* notes that the period should be deleted, perhaps for a later printing.])

97: Feels (*Poetry, Eye-Beaters, Central Motion*) | Fells (*Whole Motion* [typo])

100: brother: my (TS, *Eye-Beaters, Central Motion, Whole Motion*) | brother: my (*Poetry*)

101: Sweetness (TS, *Poetry, Eye-Beaters*) | sweetness (*Central Motion, Whole Motion*)

Venom

First Publication: *Poetry* 114 (June 1969): 156–57.

Collected: *Eye-Beaters*, 33; *Central Motion*, 29; *Whole Motion*, 318–19.

Reprinted: *Poetry Anthology*, 418–19.

Notes: On Dickey and snakes, see "Blowgun and Rattlesnake." Dickey likely read about William E. Haast (1910–2011), "the priest of poison," the founder and director of the Miami Serpentarium in Florida, in *Life* in 1968. As a young man Haast began injecting himself with diluted cobra venom. By the age of sixty-seven he had survived 126 venomous bites, but he came perilously close to death several times, chiefly when he became the only man known to have survived the bite of the king cobra (twice). In the 1960s he was instrumental in developing antitoxin for American soldiers in Vietnam. He and Robert Anderson wrote *A Complete Guide to the Snakes of Florida* (Miami: Phoenix, 1981). See Marshall Smith, "The Most Snake-Bitten Man," *Life* 64 (June

21, 1968): 39–46, and Ben Funk, "Milking Cobras for Cures," *New York Times Magazine*, November 12, 1978, 68–70.

8–9: The bite of a Siamese cobra landed Haast in an iron lung. The fullest account of the bite and recovery is in Funk's article.

VARIANTS:

1: head. *Where* (TS, *Eye-Beaters, Central Motion, Whole Motion*) | head.   *Where* (*Poetry*)

2: blood. All (TS, *Eye-Beaters, Central Motion, Whole Motion*) | blood.   All (*Poetry*)

3: light. There (TS, *Eye-Beaters, Central Motion, Whole Motion*) | light.   There (*Poetry*)

5: *poison: where is he? Who* (TS, *Eye-Beaters, Central Motion, Whole Motion*) poison: *where is he?   Who* (*Poetry*)

18: low long (TS, *Eye-Beaters, Central Motion, Whole Motion*) | long low (*Poetry*)

The Cancer Match

FIRST PUBLICATION: *Poetry* 114 (June 1969): 158–59.

COLLECTED: *Eye-Beaters,* 31–32; *Central Motion,* 27–28; *Whole Motion,* 317–18.

REPRINTED: *Geography of Poets,* 322–23; *On Doctoring,* 254–55.

VARIANTS:

2: yourself. I (TS, *Eye-Beaters, Central Motion, Whole Motion*) | yourself.   I (*Poetry*)

4: drink. Two (TS, *Eye-Beaters, Central Motion, Whole Motion*) | drink.   Two (*Poetry*)

14: ground. They (TS, *Eye-Beaters, Central Motion, Whole Motion*) | ground.   They (*Poetry*)

15: dancing? I (TS, *Eye-Beaters, Central Motion, Whole Motion*) | dancing?   I (*Poetry*)

19: comes. You (TS, *Eye-Beaters, Central Motion, Whole Motion*) | comes.   You (*Poetry*)

20: growing. Why (TS, *Eye-Beaters, Central Motion, Whole Motion*) | growing.   Why (*Poetry*)

21: boys! They (TS, *Eye-Beaters, Central Motion, Whole Motion*) | boys!   They (*Poetry*)

29: street-lights! Internally (TS, *Eye-Beaters, Central Motion, Whole Motion*) | street-lights!   Internally (*Poetry*)

30: watch: and (TS, *Eye-Beaters, Central Motion, Whole Motion*) | watch: and (*Poetry*)

34: Alone. Swarm (TS, *Eye-Beaters, Central Motion, Whole Motion*) | Alone.   Swarm (*Poetry*)

35: Force! Let (TS, *Eye-Beaters, Central Motion, Whole Motion*) | Force!   Let (*Poetry*)

39: son! One (TS, *Eye-Beaters, Central Motion, Whole Motion*) | son!   One (*Poetry*)

39: time! Tonight (TS, *Eye-Beaters, Central Motion, Whole Motion*) | time!   Tonight (*Poetry*)

39: belovèd (TS, *Poetry, Central Motion, Whole Motion*) | beloved (*Eye-Beaters*)

Pine

FIRST PUBLICATION: Parts I and II as "Pine," *New Yorker* 45 (June 28, 1969): 89; parts III, IV, and V as "Taste, Touch and Sight," *Poetry* 114 (June 1969): 160–62.

COLLECTED: *Eye-Beaters,* 44–46; *Central Motion,* 40–42; *Whole Motion,* 326–29.

REPRINTED: *Selected,* 131–33.

NOTES: Published here as one poem because Dickey submitted it to the *New Yorker* as one poem. "The direction indicated by the 'Pine' poems is the one I want to explore now. This kind of associational imagery of a very special and wide-ranging sort can be applied to subjects either small or large, short or long. The thing may have tremendous depth and suggestibility. But I don't understand it yet" (*Sorties*, 96). "The 'Pine' poem is very artificial, but very interesting" (*Sorties*, 27); Dickey did not return to this experiment until the *Puella* poems. The epigraph comes from Immanuel Kant's *Critique of Pure Reason* (1790), pt. 2, div. 1, bk. 2, chap. 2, sec. 3.

VARIANTS:

I. (TS, *Eye-Beaters, Central Motion, Whole Motion*) | I. Sound (*New Yorker*)

1: whistles, changing (TS, *Eye-Beaters, Central Motion, Whole Motion*) | whistles,   changing (*New Yorker*)

2: you. How (TS, *Eye-Beaters, Central Motion, Whole Motion*) | you.   How (*New Yorker*)

4: near. Close (TS, *Eye-Beaters, Central Motion, Whole Motion*) | near.   Close (*New Yorker*)

5: by ear, so (TS, *Eye-Beaters, Central Motion, Whole Motion*) | be ear   so (*New Yorker*)

6: eyes. O (TS, *Eye-Beaters, Central Motion, Whole Motion*) | eyes.   O (*New Yorker*)

8: where. It (TS, *Eye-Beaters, Central Motion, Whole Motion*) | where.   It (*New Yorker*)

9: field: mid-whistling (TS, *Eye-Beaters, Central Motion, Whole Motion*) | field: mid-whistling (*New Yorker*)

9: life (TS, *Eye-Beaters, Central Motion, Whole Motion*) | life- (*New Yorker*)

10: sound. Overhead (TS, *Eye-Beaters, Central Motion, Whole Motion*) | sound.   Overhead (*New Yorker*)

17: to. O (TS, *Eye-Beaters, Central Motion, Whole Motion*) | to.   O (*New Yorker*)

19: right: O (TS, *Eye-Beaters, Central Motion, Whole Motion*) | right: O (*New Yorker*)

19: justice-scales (TS, *Eye-Beaters, Central Motion, Whole Motion*) | Justice-scales (*New Yorker*)

21: ax (TS, *Eye-Beaters, Central Motion, Whole Motion*) | axe (*New Yorker*)

22: shock. Nothing (TS, *Eye-Beaters, Central Motion, Whole Motion*) | shock.   Nothing (*New Yorker*)

II. (TS, *Eye-Beaters Central Motion Whole Motion*) | II. Smell (*New Yorker*)

33: overhead, steep-brewing (TS, *Eye-Beaters, Central Motion, Whole Motion*) | overhead steep-brewing (*New Yorker*)

36: iron (TS, *Eye-Beaters, Central Motion, Whole Motion*) | iron- (*New Yorker*)

40: sea-wall (TS, *Eye-Beaters, Central Motion, Whole Motion*) | seawall (*New Yorker*)

42: rosin (TS, *Eye-Beaters, Central Motion, Whole Motion*) | resin (*New Yorker*) [Rosin is the resin derived specifically from trees.]

54: own, for (TS, *Eye-Beaters, Central Motion, Whole Motion*) | own   for (*New Yorker*)

55: Food: windfalls (TS, *Eye-Beaters, Central Motion, Whole Motion*) | Food: windfalls (*New Yorker*)

57: more, through (TS, *Eye-Beaters, Central Motion, Whole Motion*) | more,   through (*Poetry*)

66–67: [blank line inserted] (*Poetry*)

69: eat? What (TS, *Eye-Beaters, Central Motion, Whole Motion*) | eat?   What (*Poetry*)

71: you? And (TS, *Eye-Beaters, Central Motion, Whole Motion*) | you?   And (*Poetry*)

76: insides. More (TS, *Eye-Beaters, Central Motion, Whole Motion*) | insides.   More (*Poetry*)

77: swaying. Rise (TS, *Eye-Beaters, Central Motion, Whole Motion*) | swaying.   Rise (*Poetry*)

80: points. The (TS, *Eye-Beaters, Central Motion, Whole Motion*) | points.   The (*Poetry*)

89: more. A (TS, *Eye-Beaters, Central Motion, Whole Motion*) | more.   A (*Poetry*)

First Publication: *New Yorker* 45 (August 2, 1969): 30.
Collected: *Eye-Beaters,* 10–13; *Central Motion,* 7–10; *Whole Motion,* 302–5.
Reprinted: As "Giving a Son to the Sea," *Twentieth Century Poetry* (Marshall), 82–84; lines 20–62, in *Writer's Voice,* 232–23.

Notes: "Butterflies": "I think one of the things that a parent should do is just get out and play with your child in abandon, do foolish things. . . . Encourage them to be as foolish as possible. And so my older boy, Chris, and I were doing that when he was around eleven or twelve years old. We were roaming around in the Virginia woods and unexpectedly came upon an open field of grass in the middle of these woods, and we just went out in that and started playing around. I sort of got tired out, and I sat down in the grass and he went by, down close to this little lake and sat down by himself. I found an old cow skull near where I was and just picked it up and looked at it. And some butterflies came from my son's direction, and came up over me and the cow skull and then flew on off. I thought about that as an emblem of something, a symbol of something, something beautiful, something that would just happen once" (Greiner, 21).

3, 36: On Christopher Dickey, see "The Child in Armor" and "To the Butterflies."

14: For entering the remains of a wild animal, see "Approaching Prayer."

39–48: Reminiscent of word placement on page to describe action by E. E. Cummings and the "poésie blanche" of André du Bouchet (see "Attempted Departure").

"Giving a Son to the Sea": "Now, this concerns my second son, Kevin ('The Signs'), who originally wanted to be a marine biologist and to cast his fate with the ocean. I thought, 'My God, this vulnerable little child wants to give his life to the ocean! What's down there, anyway? It's dark. And there's a lot of strange creatures down there'" (Greiner, 21).

63–64: "We were living in California, and I had given Kevin a Christmas present of a James Bond espionage kit. It had a gun, a pistol that fired a bullet with a special message in the bullet. When he played with it on Christmas day, he fired. He hit me with the bullet, and I read the secret message, which was, 'I love you.' I thought, '*This* is a child I'm going to give to the cold depths of the ocean? What has God wrought?'" (Greiner, 21).

Variants:

4: are. We (TS, *Eye-Beaters, Central Motion, Whole Motion*) | are.   We (*New Yorker*)
7: lake-water (TS, *Eye-Beaters, Central Motion, Whole Motion*) | lake water (*New Yorker*)
7: strain. Ah, (TS, *Eye-Beaters, Central Motion, Whole Motion*) | strain.   Ah, (*New Yorker*)
9: old! Ah (TS, *Eye-Beaters, Central Motion, Whole Motion*) | old!   Ah (*New Yorker*)
10: now! You (TS, *Eye-Beaters, Central Motion, Whole Motion*) | now!   You (*New Yorker*)
13: cow. O (TS, *Eye-Beaters, Central Motion, Whole Motion*) | cow.   O (*New Yorker*)
18: messages. I (TS, *Eye-Beaters, Central Motion, Whole Motion*) | messages.   I (*New Yorker*)
20: you. I (TS, *Eye-Beaters, Central Motion, Whole Motion*) | you.   I (*New Yorker*)
24: horns. They (TS, *Eye-Beaters, Central Motion, Whole Motion*) | horns.   They (*New Yorker*)
27: live. In (TS, *Eye-Beaters, Central Motion, Whole Motion*) | live.   In (*New Yorker*)
39: . . . Here (TS, *Eye-Beaters, Central Motion, Whole Motion*) | Here [flush left] (*New Yorker*)
46: here [flush left] (*New Yorker*)
48–56, 58, 60–62: [flush left] (*New Yorker*)

52: asleep: their (TS, *Eye-Beaters, Central Motion, Whole Motion*) | asleep   their (*New Yorker*)

59: In (TS, *Eye-Beaters, Central Motion, Whole Motion*) | in (*New Yorker*)

60: gamble. It (TS, *Eye-Beaters, Central Motion, Whole Motion*) | gamble.   It (*New Yorker*)

61: then. I (TS, *Eye-Beaters, Central Motion, Whole Motion*) | then.   I (*New Yorker*)

64: me (TS, *Eye-Beaters, Central Motion, Whole Motion*) | me, (*New Yorker*)

66: Spies: a (TS, *Eye-Beaters, Central Motion, Whole Motion*) | Spies   a (*New Yorker*)

67: Compartment. My (TS, *Eye-Beaters, Central Motion, Whole Motion*) | Compartment.   My (*New Yorker*)

74: [flush with preceding line] (*New Yorker*)

76: son. Out (TS, *Eye-Beaters, Central Motion, Whole Motion*) | son.   Out (*New Yorker*)

78: water into (TS, *Eye-Beaters, Central Motion, Whole Motion*) | water   into (*New Yorker*)

82: crowding. Many (TS, *Eye-Beaters, Central Motion, Whole Motion*) | crowding.   Many (*New Yorker*)

85: anywhere, there (TS, *Eye-Beaters, Central Motion, Whole Motion*) | anywhere,   there (*New Yorker*)

92: [indented from preceding line] (*New Yorker*)

94: [flush with preceding line] (*New Yorker*)

97: sea   lamp (TS, *Eye-Beaters, Central Motion, Whole Motion*) | sea-lamp (*New Yorker*)

99: Echoing. Your (TS, *Eye-Beaters, Central Motion, Whole Motion*) | Echoing.   Your (*New Yorker*)

101: bullet. When (TS, *Eye-Beaters, Central Motion, Whole Motion*) | bullet.   When (*New Yorker*)

In the Pocket

First Publication: As "The National Football League Celebrating its Fiftieth Season 1920–1969" (NFL), magazine advertising insert (before September 1969), 19.

Collected: *Eye-Beaters,* 36; *Central Motion,* 32; *Whole Motion,* 320–21.

Reprinted: *More Than a Game,* 175; *Writer's Voice,* 239.

Notes: Commissioned by David Boss (1932–1999), creative director of NFL Properties, who designed posters and programs for the first twenty-five Super Bowls (Hart, 60, 409). Dickey wrote Boss on March 16, 1969: "It is supposed to be a kind of rapid fire stream of action interior monologue about the sense impressions and thoughts of an NFL—or indeed any—T formation quarterback as he tries to find his receiver before the opposing linemen break through on him. . . . There are thoughts that link up not only with the play book but about man, fate, destiny, life, death, and probably a lot of other things too" (*One Voice 1,* 454). "One of the things I'm coming more and more to write about and to pay attention to is the dependency of men on each other. You find this in wars, in forward-zone combat action, probably at a more intense level than anywhere else. . . . This is a poem about that, except it's football instead of soldiering. Where the linemen form this pocket for the passer and everything. And they trust him; so it's really a kind of condition of trust. And they're going to keep the opposing linemen out until he can find his number one receiver, number two receiver, number three receiver. The first two may be covered, but the third one, even if he's got half a stride on the defensive halfback. . . ." (*Writer's Voice,* 238). For an early description of a quarterback passing (under pressure), see *Striking,* 200.

8: arm. Where (TS, *Eye-Beaters, Central Motion, Whole Motion*) | arm.   Where (NFL)

10: linebackers? I (TS, *Eye-Beaters, Central Motion, Whole Motion*) | linebackers?   I (NFL)

19: Three: throw (TS, *Eye-Beaters, Central Motion, Whole Motion*) | Three: throw (NFL)

22–23: [no blank line] (NFL)

Looking for the Buckhead Boys

First Publication: *Atlantic Monthly* 224 (October 1969): 53–56.

Collected: With "Living There" as "Two Poems of Going Home," *Eye-Beaters*, 20–23; *Central Motion*, 16–20; *Whole Motion*, 310–13.

Reprinted: *Georgia Voices*, 95–99; *Atlanta* (October 1980): 106–7; "From Looking for the Buckhead Boys" [broadside] (Atlanta: Chance Press, 1995) (lines 85–96, 51–60); lines 85–96 are the epigraph to Anne Rivers Siddons's novel of Buckhead, *Peachtree Road* (New York: Harper & Row, 1988).

Notes: "'The Buckhead Boys' is a sort of deliberate attempt to recapture that feeling of never having aged" (Broughton, 165). "You get that kind of desperate nostalgia for the old place, and you feel as though you must find somebody that you knew in those days" (Logue, 48; Baughman, 60).

The name "Buckhead" comes from a tavern and general store built in 1837 by Henry Irby (1807–1879) at what is now the corner of West Paces Ferry and Roswell Roads, which was then a hunting area. Irby mounted the head of a killed buck in front of, or above, the door and called the place "Buck's Head." In Dickey's day Buckhead was still separate from the city of Atlanta, and was the home of many Atlanta professionals. (It was not incorporated until 1952.) "Atlanta was just the city closest to us there in the County. But Buckhead was looked on as being pretty well out in the country. It was about ten, twelve miles to Atlanta, and there were no superhighways, or anything like that. . . . I wasn't there much at night. We went in the afternoons on the weekends. I don't remember much about the places where people got together. I don't think we did much of that" (Boleman-Herring, 14–15). In 1959, ten years before the composition of this poem, Lenox Square Shopping Mall eliminated many of Buckhead's small businesses, making the Buckhead of Dickey's youth virtually unrecognizable. The term "Buckhead Boys" was coined in the early 1960s by a group of North Fulton alumni of Dickey's vintage, who met informally once a year for lunch. "They once represented the best that privilege offered, a kind of monied hypermasculinity that strutted with the confidence of a time and place that viewed itself as manifestly special" (Drew Jubera, "The Buckhead Boys," *Atlanta Journal*, December 20, 1990, G1). Dickey wrote this poem at the end of the 1960s, and in 1971 he was named the first "Buckhead Boy of the Year."

Two of Dickey's favorite figures, Walter Armistead ("Walter Armistead") and Ed Van Valkenburg ("Cherrylog Road"), were in the class of 1939. On the identity of some of the characters in "Looking for the Buckhead Boys," see Hart, 45.

2, 8, 66: On blindness see "Reading Genesis to a Blind Child."

3–6: Dickey's home at 166 West Wesley was not razed.

12, 35, 47: "But if you do not find an intelligent companion, a wise and well-behaved person going the same way as yourself, then go on your way alone, like a king abandoning a conquered kingdom, or like a great elephant in the deep forest" (*Dhammapada* 23.329). See also Apocrypha,

Acts of Pilate 2–6, for the story of Jesus mistakenly walking "like a king" on a messenger's kerchief.

14: Wender and Roberts' Drug Store: In 1928 Lithuanian immigrant shopkeeper William Max Wender and Marvin Roberts bought a drugstore at 3073 Peachtree Road. The store's soda fountain specialized in Coca-Cola with crushed ice for five cents and peanut-butter sandwiches. A resident remembered that it "was the place to go. . . . it was a gathering place for young people" (Barnard, 130).

18: teen-ager: that is, a substance that ages teens and is thus inadvisable for athletes.

21–23: "Tommy Nichols" is likely Martin W. Nicholes, Jr. (b. 1922), in the class of 1940; he held the school broad-jump record and was on the successful 440-yard relay team. There was no mile relay team. Nicholes graduated from Georgia Tech, where he also played football and ran track, in 1944. He worked for an industrial management company in Atlanta, where he lived his entire life.

25–26: The 1939 relay team is pictured on page 83 (unnumbered) of *The Hi-Ways* (1939) running in tandem, with Dickey in the third position. Dickey is bare-chested in a photograph of the entire track team.

27–28, 67–68, 95–96: "The Book of the Dead is what the narrator calls the 1939 high school annual [*The Hi-Ways*], where he can open the pages and see pictures of himself and all these people as they used to be" (Logue, 49; Baughman, 61). Dickey was in the class of 1941.

30–34: The Buckhead Billiard Parlor at 26 Roswell Road was owned by Robert E. "Red" Dorough (1897–1973), a local character who in his twenties opened Atlanta's first drive-in restaurant, the Buckhead Drive-In, a popular gathering place for politicians (see *Atlanta Constitution,* September 6, 1973, 9-C; *Crux,* 312; Barnard, 181). James Howard Tyree (1919–2000) was in the class of 1939 and played on the football teams of 1938 and 1939. He drove a truck after high school before enlisting in January 1941, serving in World War II and Korea and rising to the rank of major. In her novel *Peachtree Road* (1988), 155, Anne Rivers Siddons mentions Tyree's Pool Hall, but it does not appear to have existed.

38, 43, 61, 66, 98–99: Charlie Gates is likely Charles Otis Cates, Jr. (1921–1996), the fullback from 1938 to 1940 and captain of the football team in 1941. He was originally in the class of 1940 but graduated in 1941. After the war he founded Cates Realty, but never owned a pool hall.

38–41: "'I said it,' Mr. Cates says, laughing. 'But I was never brave enough to use it'" (Jubera, "The Buckhead Boys").

50: Mr. Hamby is likely George P. Murray (1895–1971), owner of Buckhead Hardware Co. at 3059 Peachtree Road.

51: Prodigal's Crown is perhaps a reference to Joseph let out of prison and crowned by Pharaoh (Genesis 41) or to the crown given after death to the title character of "The Prodigal Daughter," an eighteenth-century American children's poem.

51–53: "We didn't play what was called the Georgia Interscholastic Athletic Association teams . . . but teams like Gainesville and Rome High, and little towns up in the hills—not in the Atlanta area" (Boleman-Herring, 15). North Fulton played the high schools of Gainesville (line 63), Rome, Decatur, Griffin, Newnan, and Marietta, as well as Russell High School in East Point (line 57), and R. E. Lee High School in Thomaston, Georgia.

56–57: In the fall of 1938, the football team lost to Russell, 27-7. The 1939 team defeated Russell for the first time in school history, 28-7.

71: Mont Black is likely Montague Lafitte "Mont" Boyd, Jr. (1922–1975), who joined the class of 1939 after attending school in Le Rosey, Switzerland. He was named "Handsomest" in his class and went to Princeton for three years before enlisting in the army.

73: Dick Shea is likely James Richard Gray, Jr. (1922–2002), quarterback and captain of the 1940 football team. He held the school record for the 100-yard dash and was a member of the 440- and 880-yard relay teams.

76: Punchy Henderson is likely Jack Holt "Punchy" Emerson (1923–1971), who played football, enlisted in the marines after graduation, and was wounded in World War II.

83: Harmon Quigley is perhaps E. Roy Hackney (1921–1997), who played on the "B" football squad in 1939.

88: Bobby Laster may be Charles Luther Rabun (1923–1970), an all-conference football player and short-distance track star in the class of 1940.

89: Bolton is in Fulton County, Georgia, nine or ten miles northwest of Atlanta.

90: Jack Siple is perhaps Ralph L. Slaten (1923–1992), who played on the line and moved to Alabama after the war.

92: The identity of Gordon Hamm is unknown.

102: This Gulf station was built in 1959 at the opening of Lenox Square Shopping Center, at the corner of East Paces Ferry and Lenox Roads; it appeared to many to resemble a UFO. Sandy Springs is sixteen miles north of Atlanta.

107–8: In 1968 Dickey bought a new white Jaguar XKE for his son Chris, but when Chris got married within the year, Dickey kept the car and gave him a station wagon instead.

VARIANTS:

9: Boys. If (TS, *Eye-Beaters, Central Motion, Whole Motion*) | Boys.   If (*Atlantic*)

11: die: it's (TS, *Eye-Beaters, Central Motion*) | die: it's (*Atlantic*) | die; it's (*Whole Motion*)

20: there. The (TS, *Eye-Beaters, Central Motion, Whole Motion*) | there.   The (*Atlantic*)

21: cosmetics. Tommy (TS, *Eye-Beaters, Central Motion, Whole Motion*) | cosmetics.   Tommy (*Atlantic*)

22: place: he (TS, *Eye-Beaters, Central Motion, Whole Motion*) | place: he (*Atlantic*)

27: it: the (TS, *Eye-Beaters, Central Motion, Whole Motion*) | it: the (*Atlantic*)

28: Annual. Go (TS, *Eye-Beaters, Central Motion, Whole Motion*) | Annual.   Go (*Atlantic*)

38: standing. Charlie (TS, *Eye-Beaters, Central Motion, Whole Motion*) | standing.   Charlie (*Atlantic*)

40: Buckhead. I'm (TS, *Eye-Beaters, Central Motion, Whole Motion*) | Buckhead.   I'm (*Atlantic*)

43: key: the (TS, *Eye-Beaters, Central Motion, Whole Motion*) | key: the (*Atlantic*)

44: Buckhead. Where (TS, *Eye-Beaters, Central Motion, Whole Motion*) | Buckhead.   Where (*Atlantic*)

45: Merchants. Why (TS, *Eye-Beaters, Central Motion, Whole Motion*) | Merchants.   Why (*Atlantic*)

48: Hardware. Hardware (TS, *Eye-Beaters, Central Motion, Whole Motion*) | Hardware.   Hardware (*Atlantic*)

50: wood-screws (TS, *Eye-Beaters, Central Motion, Whole Motion*) | wood screws (*Atlantic*)

56: A'Mighty (TS, *Eye-Beaters, Central Motion, Whole Motion*) | A'mighty (*Atlantic*)

61: fumbling. (TS, *Atlantic, Eye-Beaters*) | fumbling, (*Central Motion, Whole Motion*)

81: *windsprinters* (TS, *Eye-Beaters, Central Motion, Whole Motion*) | *wind sprinters* (*Atlantic*)

105: Roberts'. Do (TS, *Eye-Beaters, Central Motion, Whole Motion*) | Roberts'.   Do (*Atlantic*)

105: gas? No (TS, *Eye-Beaters, Central Motion, Whole Motion*) | gas?   No (*Atlantic*)

112: cue-stick (TS, *Eye-Beaters, Central Motion, Whole Motion*) | cue stick (*Atlantic*)

118: Gulf. I (TS, *Eye-Beaters, Central Motion, Whole Motion*) | gulf.   I (*Atlantic*)

119: out. His (TS, *Eye-Beaters, Central Motion, Whole Motion*) | out.   His (*Atlantic*)

120: baton-pass. He (TS, *Eye-Beaters, Central Motion, Whole Motion*) | baton-pass.   He (*Atlantic*)

121: line. Charlie (TS, *Eye-Beaters, Central Motion, Whole Motion*) | line.   Charlie (*Atlantic*)

123: minute. Can (TS, *Eye-Beaters, Central Motion, Whole Motion*) | minute.   Can (*Atlantic*)

123: me? You (TS, *Eye-Beaters, Central Motion, Whole Motion*) | me?   You (*Atlantic*)

124: say: where (TS, *Eye-Beaters, Central Motion, Whole Motion*) | say: where (*Atlantic*)

125: time? I (TS, *Eye-Beaters, Central Motion, Whole Motion*) | time?   I (*Atlantic*)

126: Charlie. I (TS, *Eye-Beaters, Central Motion, Whole Motion*) | Charlie.   I (*Atlantic*)

126: know. But (TS, *Eye-Beaters, Central Motion, Whole Motion*) | know.   But (*Atlantic*)

127: code. Understand (TS, *Eye-Beaters, Central Motion, Whole Motion*) | code.   Understand (*Atlantic*)

134 sons? No (TS, *Eye-Beaters, Central Motion, Whole Motion*) | sons?   No (*Atlantic*)

Root-light, or the Lawyer's Daughter

FIRST PUBLICATION: *New Yorker* 45 (November 8, 1969): 52.

COLLECTED: *Strength*, 13–14; *Central Motion*, 99; *Whole Motion*, 377.

NOTES: "'Root-light,' it's called, because the roots make the water sort of wine colored. Everything you see is red. Your hand is a wine red when you look at it in the water. The palmetto roots make it that way" (Greiner, 20). See "Inside the River." "This is about how a man acquires his image of ultimate sexual desirability . . . You have kind of an idealized form of a woman, that all others are going to have to be measured against as long as you live. This is how one man acquired his. He was a little boy. These things usually happen fairly early on in life. On Sunday afternoon after the sermon, he was swimming in one of those south Georgia rivers, where the water's red from palmetto roots. . . . He's swimming under a bridge, and a naked girl dives off and goes past him, shoots past him" ("Words That Work," *Papers from the 1973 Annual Meeting of the American Association of Advertising Agencies [May 19, 1973]* [White Sulphur Springs, W.Va.: Greenbrier, 1973], 3). Dickey called his condominium at Litchfield Plantation, South Carolina, "Root-Light."

5: St. Marys River rises in the Okefenokee Swamp, curves up into Georgia a few miles from Folkston, and then forms the eastern boundary of Georgia and Florida before debouching into the Atlantic between St. Marys, Georgia, and Fernandina Beach, Florida, which is about thirty miles east southeast of Folkston.

12–13: The Eugene Talmadge Bridge was a two-lane cantilever truss bridge built in 1954. It carried U.S. 17 Alternate across the Savannah River at a height of 136 feet, connecting Georgia and

South Carolina. It was replaced in 1991 by the new four-lane cable-stayed Talmadge Memorial Bridge. Both bridges memorialized Eugene Talmadge (1884–1946), governor of Georgia in 1933–37 and 1941–43.

16: Folkston, the county seat of Charlton County, Georgia, is 190 miles south of Savannah; it was known in Dickey's youth as the "Marriage Capital of the World," because of all the Floridians who were impatient about their state's marriage-license waiting period. The rail lines passing through Folkston channeled virtually all the train traffic entering and leaving Florida, hence the name the "Folkston Funnel." There is a J.C. Penney in St. Marys, but not in Folkston.

17: Exodus 3–4.

25–26: These distances, as the crow flies, overlap by a few miles; if Dickey means distances as the river flows, the location is somewhere between Colerain and a bend in the river called Flea Hill, near Greenville, Georgia.

26: Kingsland, Georgia, is twenty miles east of Folkston, in Camden County.

VARIANTS:

1–2: just to long for / The rest of my life (TS, *Strength, Central Motion, Whole Motion*) | just-to-long-for- / The-rest-of-my-life (*New Yorker*)

7: still, dividing (TS, *Strength, Central Motion, Whole Motion*) | still,   dividing (*New Yorker*)

11: light. She (TS, *Strength, Central Motion, Whole Motion*) | light.   She (*New Yorker*)

13: for as (TS, *Strength, Central Motion, Whole Motion*) | for, as (*New Yorker*)

25: wine. Be (TS, *Strength, Central Motion, Whole Motion*) | wine.   Be (*New Yorker*)

25: old (TS, *Strength, Central Motion, Whole Motion*) | old, (*New Yorker*)

25: ten (TS, *Strength, Central Motion, Whole Motion*) | ten, (*New Yorker*)

26: miles (TS, *Strength, Central Motion, Whole Motion*) | miles, (*New Yorker*)

26: clean (*New Yorker*, TS, *Strength, Central Motion*) | cleam (*Whole Motion* [typo])

30–31: [holograph notation to add blank line] (TS); [blank line inserted] (*Whole Motion*)

31: Head-down (TS, *Strength, Central Motion, Whole Motion*) | Head down (*New Yorker*)

Drums Where I Live

FIRST PUBLICATION: *New Yorker* 45 (November 29, 1969): 56.

COLLECTED: Collected with "Haunting the Maneuvers" as "Two Poems of the Military" in *Strength*, 21–22; *Central Motion*, 103–4; and *Whole Motion*, 381–82.

NOTES: At the end of 1968, Dickey moved into a house at 4620 Lelia's Court in Columbia, South Carolina, on the west bank of Lake Katherine, a private artificial lake (named for Katherine Manning, wife of the owner) that had formerly (as Bowers Beach) been the site of an amusement park on the trolley line from downtown to Fort Jackson, a chief basic training center for the army. Dickey's home was near the southwestern corner of the fort, whose grenade range was in its northwestern section. "With daybreak each day come the sounds of firing, of voices marching in unison, of bugles, of militaristic hymns, as though coming from a ghostly takeover army waiting for the day. After twelve years this is still vaguely disturbing to me . . ." ("Starry Place Beneath the Antlers"; *Night*, 23). "It's that business of living close to the war machine and that ghostly cadence count coming across the lake in the early morning, the drums, and so on. Some of the neighborhood ladies said, 'You know, it's very comforting to hear them over there, isn't it?' That's not the effect they had on me. I felt like I was right on the edge of a war" (*Playboy* interview, 216; Baughman, 130).

4: The family at that time consisted of Jim (age forty-five), his wife, Maxine (forty-two), sons Chris (seventeen) and Kevin (ten), a dachshund named Gretchen, and an Australian sheepdog named Thunderball. The poet's mother-in-law, Maxine Tipton (1903–1991), came as well but lived in an apartment downtown.

VARIANTS:

[Subtitled "(Across the Lake from a U.S. Army Base)" in *New Yorker*]

5: light (TS, *Strength, Central Motion, Whole Motion*) | light, (*New Yorker*)

10: to (TS, *Strength, Central Motion, Whole Motion*) | To (*New Yorker*)

13: Sun-up, neighbor: (TS, *Strength, Central Motion, Whole Motion*) | Sunup neighbor; (*New Yorker*)

18: know: he (*Strength, Central Motion, Whole Motion*) | know he (*New Yorker*, TS)

32: blood (TS, *Strength, Central Motion, Whole Motion*) | blood, (*New Yorker*)

33: barely-livable (TS, *Strength, Central Motion, Whole Motion*) | barely livable (*New Yorker*)

Mercy

FIRST PUBLICATION: As "At Mercy Manor," *Atlantic* 224 (December 1969): 75–76.

COLLECTED: *Eye-Beaters*, 14–16; *Central Motion*, 11–13; *Whole Motion*, 305–7.

NOTES: The property of the original St. Joseph's Hospital was given by "Uncle Jim" and his wife, Katherine Cox McWhorter Dickey (see "Angel of the Maze"), a devout Catholic who converted her husband. The nuns who served the hospital were Sisters of Mercy, who lived on the property in a dormitory which Dickey here called "Mercy Manor."

88: Arthur Morton Leo Godfrey (1903–1983) was a nearly ubiquitous presence on American radio in the late 1940s and television in the early 1950s. His radio variety show ran from after World War II until 1972, and his *Talent Scouts* program made him a television star.

VARIANTS:

3: Manor. Who (TS, *Eye-Beaters, Central Motion, Whole Motion*) | Manor.   Who (*Atlantic*)

3: cry? (*Eye-Beaters, Central Motion, Whole Motion*) | cry (*Atlantic*, TS)

5: Lot? O(TS, *Eye-Beaters, Central Motion, Whole Motion*) | Lot?   O (*Atlantic*)

9: Atlanta. I've (TS, *Eye-Beaters, Central Motion, Whole Motion*) | Atlanta   I've (*Atlantic*)

10: gin. She (TS, *Eye-Beaters, Central Motion, Whole Motion*) | gin.   She (*Atlantic*)

12: cry. Fay (TS, *Eye-Beaters, Central Motion, Whole Motion*) | cry.   Fay (*Atlantic*)

14: Evans. Television (TS, *Eye-Beaters, Central Motion, Whole Motion*) | Evans.   Television (*Atlantic*)

17: Looking. (TS, *Atlantic, Eye-Beaters, Central Motion*) | Loking. (*Whole Motion* [typo])

19: days. Some (TS, *Eye-Beaters, Central Motion, Whole Motion*) | days.   Some (*Atlantic*)

20: scream. Not (TS, *Eye-Beaters, Central Motion, Whole Motion*) | scream.   Not (*Atlantic*)

22: ask. No; (TS, *Eye-Beaters, Central Motion, Whole Motion*) | ask.   No; (*Atlantic*)

25: all: he(TS, *Eye-Beaters, Central Motion, Whole Motion*) | all: he (*Atlantic*)

27: me. And (TS, *Eye-Beaters, Central Motion, Whole Motion*) | me.   And (*Atlantic*)

28: Looking. And (TS, *Eye-Beaters, Central Motion, Whole Motion*) | Looking.   And (*Atlantic*)

32: book. You (TS, *Eye-Beaters, Central Motion, Whole Motion*) | book.   You (*Atlantic*)

33: O.K. (*Eye-Beaters, Central Motion, Whole Motion*) | OK. [on a separate line] (*Atlantic*) | O.K. [on a separate line] (TS)

33–34: [no blank line] (*Central Motion, Whole Motion*)

35: gin. The (TS, *Eye-Beaters, Central Motion, Whole Motion*) | gin.   The (*Atlantic*)

36: Fay. This (*Eye-Beaters, Central Motion, Whole Motion*) | Fay.   This (TS, *Atlantic*)

36: out. Who (TS, *Eye-Beaters, Central Motion, Whole Motion*) | out.   Who (*Atlantic*)

37: love? Whom (TS, *Eye-Beaters, Central Motion, Whole Motion*) | love?   Whom (*Atlantic*)

37: for? Is (TS, *Eye-Beaters, Central Motion, Whole Motion*) | for?   Is (*Atlantic*)

38: thigh? O (TS, *Eye-Beaters, Central Motion, Whole Motion*) | thigh?   O (*Atlantic*)

38: lysol (TS, *Eye-Beaters, Central Motion, Whole Motion*) | Lysol (*Atlantic*)

39: Vaseline. Died (TS, *Eye-Beaters, Central Motion, Whole Motion*) | Vaseline.   Died (*Atlantic*)

41: minute. These (TS, *Eye-Beaters, Central Motion, Whole Motion*) | minute.   These (*Atlantic*)

42: Says. Fay's (TS, *Eye-Beaters, Central Motion, Whole Motion*) | Says.   Fay's (*Atlantic*)

42: girl. She's (TS, *Eye-Beaters, Central Motion, Whole Motion*) | girl.   She's (*Atlantic*)

43: I do [on separate line] (*Atlantic*)

47: hair. She's (TS, *Eye-Beaters, Central Motion, Whole Motion*) | hair.   She's (*Atlantic*)

55: fit: Lord (TS, *Eye-Beaters, Central Motion, Whole Motion*) | fit: Lord (*Atlantic*)

56: Fay? O(TS, *Eye-Beaters, Central Motion, Whole Motion*) | Fay?   O (*Atlantic*)

57: O (*Atlantic*) | o (TS, *Eye-Beaters, Central Motion, Whole Motion*)

60: fatigue. Mother (TS, *Eye-Beaters, Central Motion, Whole Motion*) | fatigue.   Mother (*Atlantic*)

63: gin. The (TS, *Eye-Beaters, Central Motion, Whole Motion*) | gin.   The (*Atlantic*)

64: leaving. Turn (TS, *Eye-Beaters, Central Motion, Whole Motion*) | leaving.   Turn (*Atlantic*)

68: you. I'll (TS, *Eye-Beaters, Central Motion, Whole Motion*) | you.   I'll (*Atlantic*)

71: windows. O (TS, *Eye-Beaters, Central Motion, Whole Motion*) | windows.   O (*Atlantic*)

72: black. Without (TS, *Eye-Beaters, Central Motion, Whole Motion*) | black.   Without (*Atlantic*)

73: me. Hold (TS, *Eye-Beaters, Central Motion, Whole Motion*) | me.   Hold (*Atlantic*)

75: lips. I (TS, *Eye-Beaters, Central Motion, Whole Motion*) | lips.   I (*Atlantic*)

78: Collapsed (TS, *Atlantic, Eye-Beaters, Central Motion*) | collapsed (*Whole Motion* [typo])

83: help: She (TS, *Eye-Beaters, Central Motion, Whole Motion*) | help: She (*Atlantic*)

Haunting the Maneuvers

First Publication: *Harper's* 240 (January 1970): 95.

Collected: Collected with "Drums Where I Live" as "Two Poems of the Military," *Strength*, 18–20; *Central Motion*, 102–3; *Whole Motion*, 379–81.

Reprinted: *Best Poems of 1970*, 30–31.

Notes: Dickey loved the verb "haunt" ("To be at all is to haunt the world" ["The Flight," line 105]), and particularly Melville's use of "hauntedness" (see "Last Hours," 7). The title joins this favorite word with the Louisiana Maneuvers that took place in Louisiana and East Texas in the spring and autumn of 1940 and on a much larger scale during six weeks of August and September

1941 to test the readiness of the American army and prepare a proper training regimen for the war that had already begun in Europe. More than four hundred thousand troops were divided into two armies, the "Blue" army, the Third Army of Lt. Gen. Walter Krueger (1881–1967), and the "Red" army, the Second Army of Lt. Gen. Benjamin Lear (1879–1966). The maneuvers were widely covered in the press, reported on by notable newsmen such as Eric Sevareid and Drew Pearson, and referred to in the movie *A Walk in the Sun* (1945). The October 6, 1941, issue of *Life* devoted eleven photograph-packed pages to the games ("Big Maneuvers Test U.S. Army," 33–43). Since the games were initially directed by Lt. Gen. Stanley Embrick (1877–1957), commander of the Third Army stationed in Atlanta, there was wide coverage in the Georgia newspapers. All this took place during Dickey's postgraduate year at the Darlington School in Rome, Georgia, two years before he enlisted. See Mark Perry, "The Greatest War Games," *Military History* 25 (February–March 2009): 50–57.

Hart relates a story of Dickey's friend and fellow-poet James Seay (b. 1939), who invited Dickey to read at the University of Alabama in 1968. Dickey recalled his preflight training at the army's chief pilot-training center, Maxwell Field, near Montgomery, from July 28 to September 30, 1943, with the Eastern Flying Training Command, which in fact involved chiefly academic coursework and physical training, not the war games involving flour-sack "bombs" he described to Seay. (Dickey's basic training had been in Miami Beach in January and February.) Impressed, Seay suggested he write a poem about the experience using "the flour to suggest rising and resurrection," and offered the phrase "self-rising flour"; "As soon as he got to his motel, Dickey started writing the poem that would become 'Haunting the Maneuvers'" (Hart, 417).

2: Dwight David Eisenhower (1890–1969) was promoted to lieutenant colonel with the rest of his West Point class in 1936. Following his brilliant performance in the Louisiana Maneuvers, he was promoted to brigadier general.

4: The key event of the first part of the simulated "war" was a tank assault by the Second Armored Division under Maj. Gen. George S. Patton (1885–1945), which was thwarted by the defensive tactics devised for the occasion by Eisenhower, the chief of staff of the Blue Army. A later attack by Patton was more successful.

7: Dickey described to Seay how "bombers tried to hit the soldiers with sacks of flour. One of the first planes to fly over hit him, he said, so he had to join the other 'losers' in the 'dead and wounded' area" (Hart, 417). Although *Life* reported that "Planes bomb trucks with flour bags" (42), Perry wrote that the bags were filled with "white sand . . . to simulate the impact of artillery shells" ("The Greatest War Games," 54).

8: The maneuvers took place in part in the Kisatchie National Forest, filled with cypress groves and old growth pine (see line 33). Airplanes and artillery were parked beneath pine trees for cover (*Life,* 40).

18, 27: KP is "kitchen patrol."

43: Dickey trained with old Enfield rifles in Miami Beach (Hart, 66).

43: Martha White's Self-Rising Flour was a popular and highly advertised product in the South. Patented by Professor Eben Horsford of Harvard in 1864, this flour contained baking powder and salt.

48: As supreme commander of Allied forces in Europe, Eisenhower directed the Allied invasion of France and Germany from the Western Front in 1944–45.

VARIANTS:

4: Force.   The (*Strength, Central Motion, Whole Motion*) | Force. The (*Harper's*, TS)

7: Force.   Sacks (*Strength, Central Motion, Whole Motion*) | Force. Sacks (*Harper's*, TS)

11: it.   Yes Sir.   I (*Strength, Central Motion, Whole Motion*) | it. Yes Sir. I (*Harper's*, TS)

12: It.   One (*Strength, Central Motion, Whole Motion*) | It. One (*Harper's*, TS)

14: What.   Not (*Strength, Central Motion, Whole Motion*) | What. Not (*Harper's*, TS)

14: head,   though (*Strength, Central Motion, Whole Motion*) | head, though (*Harper's*, TS)

17: dead.   The (*Strength, Central Motion, Whole Motion*) | dead. The (*Harper's*, TS)

34–35: [blank line inserted] (*Harper's*)

45–46: [no blank line inserted] (*Harper's, Whole Motion*)

46–47: [blank line inserted] (*Harper's*)

50: you: I (*Strength, Central Motion, Whole Motion*) | you: I (*Harper's*, TS)

51: yeast: you (*Strength, Central Motion, Whole Motion*) | yeast: you (*Harper's*, TS)

52: me.   Where (*Strength, Central Motion, Whole Motion*) | me. Where (*Harper's*, TS)

58: best: the (*Strength, Central Motion, Whole Motion*) | best: the (*Harper's*, TS)

Apollo

FIRST PUBLICATION: "I. For the First Manned Moon Orbit" as "Discovery," *Life* 66 (January 10, 1969): 19–22; "II. The Moon Ground," as "The Moon Ground," *Life* 67 (July 4, 1969): 16c.

COLLECTED: As "Apollo," *Eye-Beaters*, 26–30; *Central Motion*, 22–26; *Whole Motion*, 314–17.

REPRINTED: Excerpted as "Discovery" (with black page missing), *America in Poetry*, 176–77; part of film score for *Anthem for Apollo*, by Carol Connor (1969); "I. For the First Manned Moon Orbit" adapted and set to music by Ronald Perera as *Apollo Circling: Four Lyric Songs for High Voice and Piano* (Boston: Schirmer, 1977). Perera set Dickey's poem "Math."

NOTES: *Life* asked Dickey to compose poems celebrating the Apollo 8 mission to orbit the moon (December 21, 1968) and the Apollo 11 manned mission to the moon (July 16–24, 1969) (Hart, 402–6). Apollo 8 astronauts James Lovell (b. 1928), the command module pilot, and William Anders (b. 1933), the lunar module pilot, were commanded by Capt. Frank Borman (b. 1928). The lunar mission was named for the Greek god of (among many other things) light and archery by NASA manager Abe Silverstein (1908–2001). After a three-day voyage out, the crew circled the moon ten times on Christmas Eve, during which they broadcast their reading of the first ten chapters of Genesis to a large American audience.

When the poem was collected in *Eye-Beaters* and subsequently, it was given the epigraph "Whoever lives out there in space must surely / call Earth 'the blue planet'. . . / *Ed White*." Astronaut Edward Higgins White (1930–1967) performed the first "space walk" as pilot of the crew of Gemini 4 in 1965. He died with fellow astronauts Virgil Ivan "Gus" Grissom (1926–1967) and Roger Bruce Chaffee (1935–1967) in a fire on the Apollo 1 launch pad at the Kennedy Space Center. Dickey kept a picture of White on the wall of his study. On White's "totemic" value for Dickey, see "Upthrust and Its Men" (*Night*, 175–76): "I like the fact that to me, if only to me, he has the look of a man who might well be thinking of the last line of Christopher Smart's great mad-poem, 'A Song to David': 'Determined, dared, and done.'" Although Dickey repeated the quotation about the earth as a "blue planet" and again attributed it to White in *Night* (176), White appears not to have said it. In a *Newsweek* article published on July 16, 1962, White's fellow astronaut Scott Carpenter (b. 1925) is quoted as saying that "the earth would appear to be a bright blue ring in the sky" (74); the article is titled "The Blue Planet."

36–37: The black leaf is meant to reflect the communications blackout that took place while Apollo 11 crossed the dark side of the moon.

"The Moon Ground" celebrates the Apollo 11 mission. The Apollo 11 astronauts were Neil Alden Armstrong (commander, 1930–2012), Edwin Eugene "Buzz" Aldrin, Jr. (b. 1930), and Michael Collins (b. 1930). The flight was launched on July 16, 1969, and landed on the moon on July 20: Other poems occasioned by this mission were W. H. Auden's "Moon Landing" and Archibald Macleish's "Voyage to the Moon."

48: This line again invokes Apollo, the god for whom the mission is named. The reference is likely to the reflection of the earth in the gold visors of the space suits (see note to line 19). Apollo's strike may refer to Apollo as sun god *striking* the visor with his beams ("The sunbeams are my shafts," Shelley, "Hymn to Apollo") or to his *striking* (and killing) his favorite, Hyacinthus, in the head with a discus (Euripides, *Helen*, 1469ff, and Apollodorus, 3.116).

52: Being one-fourth the size of the earth, the moon has one-sixth the earth's gravitational pull.

54–55: On July 21, Armstrong became the first man to set foot on the moon, saying: "That's one small step for man, one giant leap for mankind." Aldrin, the lunar-module pilot, joined him fifteen minutes later. They planted a flag, received a telephone call from President Nixon, and set up scientific instruments while the command-module pilot Collins stayed aloft.

58–59: Both astronauts had to learn to walk in the moon's light gravity and appeared at times be hopping, but as Dickey advised, they performed no leapfrog. Armstrong walked about sixty-five yards away from the landing module. The entire activity on the surface lasted about two and a half hours.

64: The helmet of the Apollo space suit ("Extra-Vehicular Mobility Unit") contained three visors, on the over-helmet a clear outside one to protect from meteorite damage and a second gold-covered retractable visor to block glare; a third was the basic plastic pressure helmet to seal the astronaut from the moon's atmosphere.

85–87: Thomas Gray, "Elegy Written in a Country Church Yard" (1751) lines 5–6. Dickey said privately that he hoped these would be the first words spoken by the man who landed on the moon.

VARIANTS:

1–2: [no blank line inserted] (*Eye-Beaters, Central Motion, Whole Motion*) | [blank line inserted] (*Life*)

25: computers (*Eye-Beaters, Central Motion, Whole Motion*) | computors (*Life*, TS)

27: split. (*Eye-Beaters, Central Motion, Whole Motion*) | split, (*Life*, TS)

35–36: [integral black leaf B6 (pages 27–28) between B5 and B7 in *Eye-Beaters*; remainder of page 23 black and page 24 black in *Central Motion*; remainder of unnumbered page following page 314 black, next unnumbered page black, and top half of page 315 black in *Whole Motion*]

37: Almighty! To come back! To (TS, *Eye-Beaters, Central Motion, Whole Motion*) | Almighty!   To come back!   To (*Life*)

Title: The Moon Ground (*Life, Eye-Beaters, Central Motion, Whole Motion*) | The Ground (TS)

52: ourselves (TS, *Eye-Beaters, Central Motion, Whole Motion*) | our weight (*Life*)

60: of (*Eye-Beaters, Central Motion, Whole Motion*) | Of (*Life*, TS)

FIRST PUBLICATION: *Virginia Quarterly Review* 46 (Spring 1970): 242–43.

COLLECTED: Collected with "Reunioning Dialogue" as "Two Poems of Flight-Sleep," *Strength*, 30–32; *Central Motion*, 110–11; *Whole Motion*, 385–86.

REPRINTED: *Because I Fly*, 6–7.

NOTES: Dickey had his preliminary flight training in Camden, South Carolina, from September 30, 1943, to January 6, 1944. On his first solo flight, he panicked and washed out of training as did all his roommates and some friends. On this flight he "feared the engine would fall out," so he made an abrupt and bumpy landing (Hart, 72–73).

5: The aircraft company of Lloyd Carlton Stearman (1898–1975) was taken over by Boeing in 1934, but Stearman's plant produced the Model 75 (called the "Kaydet" and PT-13, PT-17, or PT-18, depending on its engine) as its primary training plane. It was a propeller-driven biplane with two seats in tandem, one for the instructor and the other for the student-pilot. The two most common Stearman engines, the Continental R-670 and the Lycoming R-680, achieved between 210 and 255 horsepower.

22: In *Sorties* (38), Dickey wrote about a proposed novel with the title "Death's Baby Machine." The hero, dead in battle, will create a new order, a brotherhood of the elite to take over the world and resolve all the issues that were unsolved by the new generation of 1960s revolutionaries, who "can only offer unlimited sex, drugs, free stores, people's parks, and other unimaginative solutions."

VARIANTS:

31: No;   never (*Strength, Central Motion, Whole Motion*) | No; never (*Virginia Quarterly,* TS)

46: good.   I (*Strength, Central Motion, Whole Motion*) | good. I (*Virginia Quarterly,* TS)

52: uncaring (TS, *Strength, Central Motion, Whole Motion*) | uncaring, (*Virginia Quarterly*)

Exchanges

FIRST PUBLICATION: *Harvard Bulletin* 72 (July 6, 1970): 36–39.

COLLECTED: *Strength*, 48–56; *Central Motion*, 123–28; *Whole Motion*, 394–99.

REPRINTED: *Atlantic* 226 (September 1970): 63–67; *Forum* 70 (October 5, 1970) insert; *AS* [Association of Student Chapters/American Institute of Architects] no. 8 (October 5, 1970) as a poster on versos of pp. 5–8. Separately published with an introduction by Dickey as *Exchanges* (Bloomfield Hills, Mich.: Bruccoli Clark, 1971).

NOTES: As this poem was written for and delivered at Harvard's 1970 Phi Beta Kappa ceremony, the choice of interlocutor, Joseph Trumbull Stickney (1874–1904), himself a Phi Beta Kappa graduate of Harvard, was natural. Stickney, born in Geneva, Switzerland, received most of his early education in Latin and Greek at the feet of his father, Austin. As a young man, Stickney traveled widely across Europe, then graduated from Harvard in 1895, and in 1903 received the first non-Francophone *doctorat ès lettres* awarded by the University of Paris. He returned to Harvard to teach Greek but died of a brain tumor in October 1904 at the age of thirty. His book of poems, *Dramatic Verses* (1902), dedicated to his friend George Cabot "Bay" Lodge (1803–1909), was virtually unnoticed, but his posthumous collection *Poems* (1905), edited by Lodge, William

Vaughn Moody, and John Ellerton Lodge, brought him favorable notice from Edmund Wilson, Conrad Aiken, and John Hollander for his visionary qualities. Two years before Dickey wrote "Exchanges," the British poet James Morris (1909–1978), under the pseudonym James Reeves, and the poet-psychologist Seán Haldane (b. 1943) published *Homage to Trumbull Stickney: Poems* (London: Heinemann, 1968), containing Stickney's poems, a biographical note, and a plea for renewed appreciation of the poet. Two years later, Haldane published a collection of Stickney's letters, *The Fright of Time* (Ladysmith, Quebec: Ladysmith Press, 1970). Dickey said, "[Stickney] certainly is good. He wrote in an old-fangled way, but he had such an imagination. It's a wonder to behold, but mainly just in single lines and images" (Greiner, 4). "['Exchanges' is] a collaboration between someone in 1970 and someone who died in 1904. You take his lines and then you answer them back. Like we did in *Deliverance*, where there's a kind of musical dialogue" (*Unmuzzled Ox* interview, 81; Baughman, 90). The poem was written out of grief at the death of Dickey's lover Robin Lee Jarecki, whom he met in Rome in 1962; she lived with him in 1966, when he was in Northridge, California. She died on April 29, 1967, of Guillain-Barré syndrome at the same age Stickney died, thirty. She was, as the poem says, buried in Forest Lawn Cemetery in Glendale, California. "What matters is that Robin and I tried to make some kind of life, which was really outside of life" (*Sorties,* 70–71). On the composition of this poem, see *One Voice 2,* 69.

4–5: On January 29, 1969, an environmental catastrophe in the form of a natural gas "blowout" occurred at a Union Oil Company platform six miles off the coast of Summerland, near Santa Barbara, California. After the gas hole was capped, pressure built up along a fault line in the ocean floor resulted in a massive rupture that released natural gas and roughly two hundred thousand gallons of oil from beneath the ocean floor, creating an oil slick that covered nearly eight-hundred square miles, damaged thirty-five miles of coastline (including Zuma Beach), and devastated the wildlife population, especially those that needed to break the surface of the water to live: whales (line 5), dolphins, seals, and ten thousand seabirds ("birds black with corporations," line 61), cranes (line 15), and gulls (line 34). It was eleven days before the rupture could be sealed, and small leaks continued to bubble up afterwards. Two positive results of the disaster were the creation of Earth Day and the Environmental Protection Agency. See Robert Olney Easton, *Black Tide: The Santa Barbara Oil Spill and Its Consequences* (New York: Delacorte Press, 1972).

13–14: The smell of the petroleum caused irritation to lungs, throats, and eyes.

15: Stickney, "Oneiropolis," line 47.

18: Point Dume, at one end of Zuma Beach, is off the Pacific Coast Highway and Westward Road at Malibu, outside Los Angeles. Shorebirds such as plovers and willets abandoned the area, but diving birds such as cranes became fatally coated with the tarry oil.

19–23: Stickney, "Ralston," lines 4–8.

30: Stickney, "Oneiropolis," line 52.

37: Stickney, "Kalypso," line 14.

48: "Wildwood Flower" is a folk standard written and recorded in 1928 by the Carter Family.

48–49: Stickney, "Lodovico Martelli," line 46.

51–53: Stickney, "Prometheus Pyrphoros," lines 641–43: "and if I lived, / I was the cresting of the tide wherein / An endless motion rose exemplified."

55: Stickney, "Lodovico Martelli," line 174.

61–62: Stickney, "Driftwood," lines 25–26.

67: Stickney, "Oneiropolis," line 64.

70: Dickey wrote "Discovery" for *Life* 66 (January 10, 1969): 19–22, after witnessing the launch of Apollo 7, the first manned mission (earth orbiting) in the program, in October 1968 (see Hart, 402–6).

72: Stickney, "You Say, Columbus with His Argosies," lines 9–10: "The line / Of wizards and of saviours."

81: Stickney, "Lucretius: Sperata Voluptas Suavis Amicitiae," line 6.

89–90: Stickney, "Prometheus Pyrphoros," lines 420–21.

93: ibid., line 441.

94: ibid., lines 478–79: "firm-barred across / And bolted 'gainst the fearful universe."

96–97: Stickney, "Fragments of a Drama on the Life of the Emperor Julian," act 2, lines 21–22: "Still armoured in their visionary gold / Did human deeds."

106–7: Stickney, "Lodovico Martelli," lines 168–69.

110: Stickney, "Dramatic Fragments," IV.3: "Break desperate magic on the world I knew."

111–12: Glendale, California, is the site of Forest Lawn Cemetery, where Jarecki is buried. Stickney, "And, the Last Day Being Come, Man Stood Alone," lines 111–12: "All thro' the shadows crying grew, until / The wailing was like grass upon the ground."

122–23: Stickney, "Prometheus Pyrphoros," lines 281–82: "and behind / This endless shadow of my memory."

123–24: Stickney, "A Dramatic Scene," 253–54.

127: Stickney, "Music," line 11.

138: Stickney, "The Immortal Mixes with Mortality," line 19: "I feel a time-like tremor in my limbs."

143: Stickney, "My Ludovico, It Is Sad," line 26.

155–56: Stickney, "Kalypso," lines 7–8: "All the air / Was marvelous and sorrowful."

163: Stickney, "Live Blindly and upon the Hour. The Lord," line 13.

170: Stickney, "Now the Lovely Moon Is Wilted," line 12: "Let us softly speak of living."

Variants:

[Subtitle not printed in *Atlantic*.]

Headnote: (Phi Beta Kappa Poem, Harvard, 1970) [subtitle]—being in the form of a dead-living dialogue with Joseph Trumbull Stickney (1874–1904)— (Stickney's words are in italics) (*Strength* [italics], *Central Motion, Whole Motion*)—The Phi Beta Kappa Poem, by James Dickey, Poet in Residence at the University of South Carolina—Being in the form of a dialogue with Joseph Trumbull Stickney (1874–1904), a poet and member of the Harvard College class of 1895, whose lines appear in italics in his poem. (*Harvard Bulletin*) | —being in the form of a dialogue with Joseph Trumbull Stickney (1874–1904) (*Atlantic*) | being in the form of a dialogue with Joseph Trumbull Stickney (*Exchanges*)

4–5: horizon / And bubble (*Harvard Bulletin, Atlantic, Exchanges*, TS, *Strength*) | bubble / And horizon (*Central Motion, Whole Motion*)

6–7: [blank line inserted] (*Harvard Bulletin, Atlantic, Exchanges*)

30–31: [blank line inserted] (*Harvard Bulletin, Atlantic, Exchanges*)

37–38: [blank line inserted] (*Harvard Bulletin, Atlantic, Exchanges*)

69: Lawn. (*Harvard Bulletin, Atlantic, Exchanges, Strength, Central Motion*) | Lawn, (*Whole Motion*)

82–83: [blank line inserted] (*Atlantic, Exchanges*)

85–86: [blank line inserted] (*Atlantic, Exchanges*)

86: tomorrow: might (*Strength*, TS, *Central Motion, Whole Motion*) | tomorrow: might (*Harvard Bulletin, Atlantic, Exchanges*)

94–95: [no blank line inserted] (*Whole Motion*) | [cannot determine] (*Exchanges, Central Motion*)

120: smoldering (*Atlantic, Strength, Central Motion, Whole Motion*) | smouldering (*Harvard Bulletin, Exchanges*)

121: from (*Harvard Bulletin, Atlantic, Exchanges*, TS, *Strength, Central Motion*) | from the (*Whole Motion*)

138: —I (*Harvard Bulletin, Atlantic, Exchanges*, TS) | I (*Strength, Central Motion, Whole Motion*)

142: [flush left] (*Harvard Bulletin, Atlantic, Exchanges, Strength*) | [centered] (*Central Motion, Whole Motion*)

150: hardshell (TS, *Strength, Central Motion, Whole Motion*) | hard-shell (*Harvard Bulletin, Atlantic, Exchanges*)

156: *marvelous* (*Atlantic, Strength, Central Motion, Whole Motion*) | *marvellous* (*Harvard Bulletin, Exchanges*, TS)

The Angel

First Publication: *Translations by American Poets,* edited by Jean Garrigue (Athens: Ohio University Press, 1970), 80–89.

Notes: Translation of "L'Ange," by Louis Émié (1900–1967); French text on facing pages of Dickey's translation. "The best poets I know are little-known modern French poets like Louis Émié, Lucien Becker, and André Frénaud" (*Crux,* 359). In Dickey's personal library was *Louis Émié,* edited by Henri Amoroux and Albert Loranquin, *Poètes d'aujourd'hui,* 83 (Paris: Editions Pierre Seghers, 1961), 185–91. Émié's poem is dated "8–9 Novembre 1957" and contains the dedication "pour Pierre Sarrant," which neither Garrigue nor Dickey included.

Variants:

13: murmur [corrected by editor] | murmer (*Translations* [typo])

70: [comma added by editor]

Kamikaze

First Publication: *Playboy* 18 (October 1971): 152.

Reprinted: *New York Times,* October 8, 1971, 33; *Stolen Apples,* 103–5 (published October 22, 1971).

Notes: Anthony Kahn, a Harvard graduate who received an M.A. in Slavic studies from Columbia University, supplied Dickey with a literal translation of this and the following eleven poems by Yevgeny Yevtushenko (b. 1933) for publication in *Stolen Apples* (*Sorties,* 32–33). The Russian text is in *Stolen Apples,* 262–64. "From what I am able to tell, the guts of Yevtushenko's style is colloquialism. The best of the poems seem to be rattled off crazily in a very engaging youthful hell-for-leather manner. . . . The best of Yevtushenko's work has a true *seeming* spontaneity, and it is this quality that I am trying to get, or, if the original truly does not have this at all, to invent for him?" (*Sorties*, 33). Yevtushenko toured America in support of *Stolen Apples* from January 24 to February 18. 1972. He was introduced by Dickey at his first appearance, on January 24 in Columbia, South Carolina, where Dickey praised his "great releases of imagination" ("4,000 in South Carolina Charmed by Yevtushenko," *New York Times,* January 26, 1972, 30). Dickey also introduced the Russian poet at Madison Square Garden on January 28 ("5,000 Throng to Felt Forum for Poetry Reading by Yevtushenko," *New York Times,* January 29, 1972, 19).

5: Raskolnikov, the protagonist of Dostoyevsky's *Crime and Punishment* (1866), murders an elderly woman pawnbroker and her sister to help his family.

12: Shimose is an explosive largely composed of picric acid; it is named for its inventor, Masachika Shimose (1860–1911). Sergei Geogriyevich Lazo (1894–1921) helped the Bolsheviks gain control of Vladivostok in January 1920; in April of that year he was captured and either shot by Japanese troops or burned alive by the White Guard.

VARIANTS:

12: shimose (*Playboy*) | Shimonoze (*Stolen Apples*) [Yevtushenko used шимозы, the noun "shimose"]

28: hero-status (*Stolen Apples*) | hero status (*Playboy*)

32: god-damned (*Stolen Apples*) | goddamned (*Playboy*)

41: every (*Stolen Apples*) | Every (*Playboy*)

43: busted-up (*Stolen Apples*) | busted up (*Playboy*)

46: firewall (*Stolen Apples*) | fire-wall (*Playboy*)

48: battering ram (*Stolen Apples*) | battering-ram (*Playboy*)

49: But (*Stolen Apples*) | But, (*Playboy*)

57: lied-to (*Stolen Apples*) | lied to (*Playboy*)

58: And (*Stolen Apples*) | and (*Playboy*)

58: death- (*Stolen Apples*) | death (*Playboy*)

Pitching and Rolling

FIRST PUBLICATION: *Stolen Apples*, 17–19.

NOTES: With Anthony Kahn; Russian text, *Stolen Apples*, 205–26.

4: Spidola was a popular Latvian electronics company known for its inexpensive and reliable radios.

Assignation

FIRST PUBLICATION: *Stolen Apples*, 30–32.

COLLECTED: In "Three Poems with Yevtushenko": *Strength*, 80–83; *Central Motion*, 145–47; *Whole Motion*, 412–13.

NOTES: With Anthony Kahn; Russian text, *Stolen Apples*, 214–15.

56: The Wandering Jew of medieval myth was said to have been cursed to walk the earth until the Second Coming for having cursed Jesus on his way to the Crucifixion. See "[In aircraft, the newest . . .], 27.

VARIANTS:

29: come (*Strength, Central Motion, Whole Motion*) | have come (*Stolen Apples*)

[In aircraft, the newest inexorable models]

FIRST PUBLICATION: *Stolen Apples,* 37–38.
NOTES: With Anthony Kahn; Russian text, *Stolen Apples,* 218–19.
27: See "Assignment," line 56.

Doing the Twist on Nails

FIRST PUBLICATION: *Stolen Apples,* 39–40.
COLLECTED: In "Three Poems with Yevtushenko": *Strength,* 84–86; *Central Motion,* 147–48; *Whole Motion,* 414–15.
NOTES: With Anthony Kahn; Russian text, *Stolen Apples,* 219–20.
VARIANTS:

35: page (*Strength, Central Motion, Whole Motion*) | stage (*Stolen Apples*)

[I dreamed I already loved you]

FIRST PUBLICATION: *Stolen Apples,* 48–49.
COLLECTED: As "I Dreamed I Already Loved You" in "Three Poems with Yevtushenko": *Strength,* 78–79; *Central Motion,* 144–45; *Whole Motion,* 411–12.
NOTES: with Anthony Kahn; Russian text, *Stolen Apples,* 224–25.
VARIANTS:

3: form, (*Strength, Central Motion, Whole Motion*) | form, but you (*Stolen Apples*)
5: Naive (*Strength, Central Motion, Whole Motion*) | Naïve (*Stolen Apples*)
9: played out (*Strength, Central Motion, Whole Motion*) | played-out (*Stolen Apples*)
10: Hunchbacked (*Strength, Central Motion, Whole Motion*) | Hunch-backed (*Stolen Apples*)
29: so similar (*Stolen Apples, Strength*) | not similar (*Central Motion, Whole Motion*)

[Poetry gives off smoke]

FIRST PUBLICATION: *Stolen Apples,* 67–69.
NOTES: With Anthony Kahn; Russian text, *Stolen Apples,* 238–40.
Epigraph: "But as soon as the divine word reaches his keen hearing the poet's soul starts up like a wakened eagle" (Pushkin, "The Poet" [1827]; see Alexander Pushkin, *Collected Narrative and Lyrical Poetry,* translated by Walter Arndt [Ann Arbor, Mich.: Ardis, 1984], 80–81).
17: See "Living There," lines 51–52; "Reunioning Dialogue," line 114.

18: The protagonist of Ivan Goncharov's *Oblomov* (1859) was the model of the superfluous man.

19: On Apollo as the most beautiful of the gods, see "The Signs," line 57.

In the Wax Museum at Hamburg

FIRST PUBLICATION: *Stolen Apples*, 70–73.

NOTES: With Anthony Kahn; Russian text, *Stolen Apples*, 240–43.

Idol

FIRST PUBLICATION: *Stolen Apples*, 90–91.

NOTES: With Anthony Kahn, Russian text, *Stolen Apples*, 253–54.

3: The Evenk or Tungus are a largely nomadic Mongoloid people of eastern Siberia who practiced shamanism before contact with the Russians.

4: The *taiga* is the moist subarctic forest of spruce and firs bordering the tundra that runs from northern Siberia across Europe and North America.

Old Bookkeeper

FIRST PUBLICATION: *Stolen Apples*, 92–93.

NOTES: With Anthony Kahn; Russian text, *Stolen Apples*, 254–25.

24: Mytishchi, near Moscow, has an eighteenth-century aqueduct and is noted for arms manufacturing.

31: Prima was an old brand of unfiltered cigarette that occurs often in Yevtushenko's poetry. Perhaps the room is so still that one can smell stale cigarette smoke.

At the Military Registration and Enlistment Center

FIRST PUBLICATION: *Stolen Apples*, 108–10.

NOTES: With Anthony Kahn; Russian text, *Stolen Apples*, 265–66.

3: Zima, Yevtushenko's birthplace, is a small town located at the intersection of the Trans-Siberian Railway and the Oka River in southeastern Siberia.

The Heat in Rome

FIRST PUBLICATION: *Stolen Apples*, 119–23.

NOTES: With Anthony Kahn; Russian text, *Stolen Apples*, 272–75.

45: The Piazza dell'Indipendenza is near the train station in Rome.

False Youth: Autumn: Clothes of the Age

FIRST PUBLICATION: *Atlantic* 228 (November 1971): 67.

Collected: *Strength*, 43–44; *False Youth*, 27–28; *Central Motion*, 119–20; *Whole Motion*, 392–93.
Reprinted: *Made Thing*, 90; *Meaning*, 157.
Notes: Susan Tuckerman Dickey (b. 1951) was Dickey's daughter-in-law, the first wife of his son Christopher. She gave the poet a denim jacket that she had embroidered with the design Dickey describes.

3: Harden Street runs through Five Points, a bar and shopping area near the University of South Carolina. This poem is set in the Carolina Barber Shop at 2021 Devine Street, just off Harden, where Dickey frequently had his hair cut.

8: "I have a friend in New York who sent me a hat. . . . Yevtushenko stole the damn thing, the son of a bitch" ("Words that Work," *Papers from the 1973 Annual Meeting of the American Association of Advertising Agencies [May 19, 1973[* (White Sulphur Springs, W.Va.: Greenbrier, 1973): 5.

22: For James Bayard Tuckerman Dickey, see "The Little More" and "Tucky the Hunter."

Variants:

5: redneck (TS, *Strength, Central Motion, Whole Motion*) | red-neck (*Atlantic*)

17: softly, (TS, *Strength, Central Motion, Whole Motion*) | softly (*Atlantic*)

18: Goodbye (TS, *Strength, Central Motion, Whole Motion*) | Good-bye (*Atlantic*)

For the Death of Lombardi

First Publication: As "For the Death of Vince Lombardi," *Esquire* 76 (September 1971): 142.
Collected: *Strength*, 39–42; *Central Motion*, 116–18; *Whole Motion*, 390–92.
Reprinted: *American Sports Poems*, 15; *Motion*, 56–58; *Lombardi*, 206–10.
Notes: Vincent Thomas Lombardi (1913–1970), a member of Fordham University's offensive line famously called the "Seven Blocks of Granite," later coached the Green Bay Packers from 1959 to 1968 to a record of 98-30-4, winning six division and five National Football League championships, as well as the first two Super Bowls. He coached the Washington Redskins for one year before being diagnosed with intestinal cancer, from which he died on September 3, 1970. See David Maraniss, *When Pride Still Mattered: A Life of Vince Lombardi* (New York: Simon & Schuster, 1996). "But please don't think I approve wholeheartedly of the Vince Lombardis and George Pattons of this world. They are there, though, and their eternal fascination is that for some situations they are useful (if not indispensable), that they are spectacular, and that they do win" (*One Voice 2*, 312).

5: Paul Hornung (b. 1935) received the Heisman Trophy at Notre Dame in 1956 and was an all-pro halfback four times in his career with the Green Bay Packers (1957–67). Lombardi called him "the greatest clutch player I've ever seen." Hornung was inducted into the Pro Football Hall of Fame in 1986. See Paul Hornung with Billy Reed, *Lombardi and Me: Players, Coaches, and Colleagues Talk about the Man and the Myth* (Chicago: Triumph Books, 2006).

13: Bryan Bartlett "Bart" Starr (b. 1934) was the Green Bay quarterback from 1961 to 1967. He was the most valuable player in the NFL in 1966 and MVP of Super Bowls I and II. He was inducted into the Pro Football Hall of Fame in 1977. Lombardi thought that Donny "The Golden Palomino" Anderson (b. 1943) would be Hornung's replacement as halfback and punter. He was drafted from Texas Tech by the Packers in 1966, paid a then-unheard-of $600,000 bonus, and played for six seasons before being traded to the St. Louis Cardinals, with whom he played for three years. Raymond Edward Nitschke (1936–1998) played middle linebacker (1958–72), was all-pro in 1964–66, and was most valuable player in the 1962 NFL Championship game. He was elected to the Pro Football Hall of Fame in 1978. Gerald Louis Kramer (b. 1936) played guard for the Packers from 1958 to 1968. He was all-pro three times. See *The Green Bay Diary of Jerry Kramer* (New York: World, 1968).

27–31: Jim Marshall (b. 1937) played defensive end for the Minnesota Vikings in an NFL-record 282 consecutive games from 1960 to 1979. On January 30, 1971, Marshall and seventeen other snowmobilers were stranded near Cooke Mountain, Montana, when one-hundred-mph winds caused their machines to fail. Marshall and three others walked through waist-deep snow from noon until 2:30 A.M. the next day. In order to create a shelter in the drifting snow, Vikings tackle Paul Dickson "took out his lighter and we started the fire with five one-dollar bills, some candy wrappers, my checkbook and billfold." The fire melted enough snow to create a hole for them to sleep in and stay warm. "Dickson had some $20 bills to keep the fire going." Marshall described the experience as "the toughest thing I've ever encountered in my life," adding that it was not his physical conditioning that saved his life. "It was more the lessons of determination and competition one learns in football that helped me most" (Sid Hartman, "Marshall Burned Money to Keep Alive on Trek," *Minneapolis Star Tribune,* February 2, 1971).

33–34: On January 27, 1970, surgeons removed a two-foot section of Lombardi's rectosigmoid colon, near the malignant polypoid tumor that later killed him (Maraniss, *When Pride Still Mattered,* 489).

48–49: "The key to my attitude [about football] is in the one overt passage of abstraction, to the effect that 'love-hate is stronger / Than either love or hate.' I think that is true not only of Lombardi, football players, ex-football players and fans, but of people and situations, generally. In fact I cannot think of a single case in my own life that it has not been true" (*One Voice 2,* 312).

75–76: "Myself, I was the boy who wrapped his head in the red jersey and crammed it into the rusty locker. That's the side of football I know best" (ibid.).

78: "If you like, you can imagine the last line as being savagely and ironically muttered (or savagely and ironically mutter it yourself) by someone who feels bitter, cheapened and cheated by football, and by its irresponsible and self-righteous Satan, Lombardi and what he stands for. I intended to write about the baleful entrapment that football is—or of all sports—and the lifelong ambiguity it contains" (ibid.).

VARIANTS:

[Poem centered on page] (TS, *Strength, Central Motion, Whole Motion*) | [Poem flush left] (*Esquire*) | James Dickey February, 1971 [at end of poem] (*Lombardi*)

10: going":   pale (TS, *Strength, Central Motion, Whole Motion*) | going": pale (*Esquire*)

11: wall.   You (TS, *Strength, Central Motion, Whole Motion*) | wall. You (*Esquire*)

12: you, and (TS, *Strength, Central Motion, Whole Motion*) | you / And (*Esquire*)

13: Nitschke (*Esquire*) | Nitchke (TS, *Strength, Central Motion, Whole Motion* [typo])

19: home.   Here (TS, *Strength, Central Motion, Whole Motion*) | home. Here (*Esquire*)

20: snows.   Coach (TS, *Strength, Central Motion, Whole Motion*) | snows. Coach (*Esquire*)

20: up: we (TS, *Strength, Central Motion, Whole Motion*) | up: we (*Esquire*)

22: cancer. (*Esquire*, TS, *Strength, Central Motion*) | cancer (*Whole Motion* [typo])

28: plunging   burning (*Strength, Central Motion, Whole Motion*) | plunging burning (TS) | plunging, burning (*Esquire*)

31: us: (TS, *Strength, Central Motion, Whole Motion*) | us; (*Esquire*)

34: intestine, the (TS, *Strength, Central Motion*) | intestine / The (*Esquire*) | intenstine, the (*Whole Motion* [typo])

34: up (TS, *Strength, Central Motion, Whole Motion*) | up, (*Esquire*)

36: up.   Everyone's (TS, *Strength, Central Motion, Whole Motion*) | up. Everyone's (*Esquire*)

37: bed the (TS, *Strength, Central Motion, Whole Motion*) | bed / The (*Esquire*)

38: down   miles (TS, *Strength, Central Motion, Whole Motion*) | down miles (*Esquire*)

39: sweat blaze (TS, *Strength, Central Motion, Whole Motion*) | sweat / Blaze (*Esquire*)

41: you.   No (TS, *Strength, Central Motion, Whole Motion*) | you. No (*Esquire*)

43: life?   Everybody (TS, *Strength, Central Motion, Whole Motion*) | life? Everybody (*Esquire*)

43: win.   What (TS, *Strength, Central Motion, Whole Motion*) | win. What (*Esquire*)

44: Vince?   We (TS, *Strength, Central Motion, Whole Motion*) | Vince? We (*Esquire*)

45: lost.   And (TS, *Strength, Central Motion, Whole Motion*) | lost. / And (*Esquire*)

46: gray (TS, *Strength, Central Motion, Whole Motion*) | grey (*Esquire*)

47: here? It (TS, *Strength, Central Motion, Whole Motion*) | here / It (*Esquire*)

48: by.   Yes (TS, *Strength, Central Motion, Whole Motion*) | by? Yes (*Esquire*)

49: hate.   Into (TS, *Strength, Central Motion, Whole Motion*) | hate. Into (*Esquire*)

52: men.   Or (TS, *Strength, Central Motion, Whole Motion*) | men. Or (*Esquire*)

54: us: aggression   meanness   deception   delight (TS, *Strength, Central Motion, Whole Motion*) | us: aggression meanness deception delight (*Esquire*)

55: money?   Did (TS, *Strength, Central Motion, Whole Motion*) | money? Did (*Esquire*)

56: over-specialized (TS, *Strength, Central Motion, Whole Motion*) | over specialized (*Esquire*)

58: sense?   Have (TS, *Strength, Central Motion, Whole Motion*) | sense? Have (*Esquire*)

59: Nothing?   Does (TS, *Strength, Central Motion, Whole Motion*) | Nothing? Does (*Esquire*)

66: shower-water, unraveling (TS, *Strength, Central Motion, Whole Motion*) | shower water, / Unraveling (*Esquire*)

66: faceguards (TS, *Strength, Central Motion, Whole Motion*) | face guards (*Esquire*)

70: Either.   We've (TS, *Strength, Central Motion, Whole Motion*) | Either. We've (*Esquire*)

74: line-backer's (TS, *Strength, Central Motion, Whole Motion*) | linebacker's (*Esquire*)

74: knee-cartilage (TS, *Strength, Central Motion, Whole Motion*) | knee cartilage (*Esquire*)

The Rain Guitar

First Publication: *New Yorker* 47 (January 8, 1972): 36.

Collected: *Strength*, 25–27; *Central Motion*, 106–7; *Whole Motion*, 383–84.

Notes:

2: On Heraclitus see "Inside the River."

17: Men called "gandy dancers" positioned railroad track to be hammered into place, thanks to a tool called the "gandy." The songs they sang to accompany their work—such as "Linin' Track"—have been collected and recorded by scholars of the blues.

21: On the "buck dance," see "Buckdancer's Choice."

40: Compare "the gone depths" ("Remnant Water," line 9) and "my gone sight" ("Mexican Valley," line 16).

42: "reeled," as in "pulled in a fish," "staggered," and "danced."

VARIANTS:

10: thread (TS, *Strength, Central Motion, Whole Motion*) | Thread (*New Yorker*)

14: guitar, (TS, *Strength, Central Motion, Whole Motion*) | guitar (*New Yorker*)

22–23: this? /out (TS, *Strength, Central Motion, Whole Motion*) | this? Out (*New Yorker*)

26: liked: (TS, *Strength, Central Motion, Whole Motion*) | liked; (*New Yorker*)

28: years, (TS, *Strength, Central Motion, Whole Motion*) | years (*New Yorker*)

36: sang, (TS, *Strength, Central Motion, Whole Motion*) | sang; (*New Yorker*)

42: west (TS, *Strength, Central Motion, Whole Motion*) | West (*New Yorker*)

Reunioning Dialogue

FIRST PUBLICATION: *Atlantic* 231 (January 1973): 46–49.

COLLECTED: Collected with "Camden Town" as "Two Poems of Flight-Sleep," *Strength,* 33–38; *Central Motion* 111–15; *Whole Motion,* 387–90.

NOTES: First lieutenants Jack H. Egginton (b. 1924) of Bountiful, Utah, and Edward Falling "Salvo" Traverse (1922–2005) of Eureka, California, were pilots in Dickey's squadron. In his history of the squadron, Dickey reported that on March 16, 1945, Egginton landed his plane out of fuel with no instruments and no visual aid. Dickey used Traverse's memories of basic training and the operation of the aircraft in *Alnilam* (Hart, 522).

4: On the Southern Cross, see "Reincarnation (II)," line 70.

7: The Northrop XP-61 Black Widow was the largest and heaviest fighter aircraft to enter service with the U.S. Army Air Force during the Second World War. As Dickey wrote in his headnote for the *Atlantic Monthly,* it was also the first American aircraft specifically designed from the outset for night fighting. The plane made its operational debut in the South Pacific during the summer of 1944 and was the standard air force night fighter at the end of the war. See Garry R. Pape, John M. Campbell, and Donna Campbell, *The Northrop P-61 Black Widow: The Complete History and Combat Record* (Osceola, Wis.: Motorbooks International, 1991). Dickey's unit "reconverted" from B-25s to P-61s in September 1944; by October the unit was functioning fully as night fighters. To accomplish its mission, the plane was equipped with Airborne Intercept (AI) radar (the SCR [Signal Corps Radio]-720 was used in variously improved versions in the P-61 through the 1950s), so it could "see" enemy aircraft in the air without being reliant on instructions from the ground.

25: Dickey was radar observer on the night missions.

31–32: The SCR-720 was manufactured by General Electric Corporation. Hughes Electronics, founded by industrialist–film producer Howard Hughes (1905–1976), made its great leap forward in 1948 with a kind of radar that could intercept targets in all weather. The company made enormous profits supplying the system to the Lockheed F-94. See Donald L. Barlett and James B. Steele, *Howard Hughes: His Life and Madness* (New York: Norton, 2004), 171–72. The radar was used throughout the Korean War, when Dickey would have encountered it, not when he was in the Philippines.

36: The term "spinner" refers to the radar antenna, which would rotate or "spin" atop the plane and deliver the information to the radar screen, which had a green background with yellow markings and images.

71–72: "with no heads": see "The Performance."

102: The P-61 was built in Hawthorne, California.

104: For Cebu see "The Performance" and "Between Two Prisoners."

114: See "[Poetry gives off smoke]," line 17, and "Living There," lines 51–52.

Variants:

[headnote] (*Atlantic*) | [no headnote] (*Strength, Central Motion, Whole Motion*)

13–14 [blank line inserted] (*Atlantic*)

19–20 [blank line inserted] (*Atlantic*)

23: fresh (TS, *Strength, Central Motion, Whole Motion*) | the fresh (*Atlantic*, TS)

23: climb in (*Strength, Central Motion, Whole Motion*) | climb into (*Atlantic*, TS)

23–24 [blank line inserted] (*Atlantic*)

27–28 [no blank line inserted] (*Atlantic*)

30–31: [blank line inserted] (*Atlantic*)

32: [line .5" to left] (*Atlantic*)

33–34: [blank line inserted] (*Atlantic*, TS)

39: *chess-set* (TS, *Strength, Central Motion, Whole Motion*) | *chess set* (*Atlantic*)

67: Pacific.   Our (*Strength, Central Motion, Whole Motion*) | Pacific. Our (*Atlantic*, TS)

69: island.   Nothing.   But (TS, *Strength, Central Motion, Whole Motion*) | island. Nothing   but (*Atlantic*)

78: burn;   I'll (*Strength, Central Motion, Whole Motion*) | burn; I'll (*Atlantic*, TS)

80–81: [no blank line inserted] (*Atlantic*)

83: ground. I ((TS, *Strength, Central Motion, Whole Motion*) | ground.   I (*Atlantic*)

84: Buddy;   this (TS, *Strength, Central Motion, Whole Motion*) | Buddy; this (*Atlantic*) | Buddy, this (TS)

102–3: [no blank line](*Atlantic*)

103: me, (*Atlantic*, TS, *Strength, Central Motion*) | me (*Whole Motion* ⌊typo⌋)

106: million dollar (TS, *Strength, Central Motion, Whole Motion*) | million-dollar (*Atlantic*)

111: me.   We'd (*Strength, Central Motion, Whole Motion*) | me. We'd (*Atlantic*, TS)

122: then.   Ghosts and angels.   Nobody (TS, *Strength, Central Motion, Whole Motion*) | then. Ghosts and angels. Nobody (*Atlantic*)

123: guess   in (TS, *Strength, Central Motion*) | guess in   (*Atlantic*) | guess, in (*Whole Motion* [typo])

123: Park   I (TS, *Strength, Central Motion*) | Park I (*Atlantic*) | Park, (*Whole Motion* [typo])

124: years.   So (*Strength, Central Motion, Whole Motion*) | years. So (*Atlantic*, TS)

Remnant Water

First Publication: *New Yorker* 49 (March 10, 1973): 36.
Collected: *Strength*, 28–29; *Central Motion*, 108–9; *Whole Motion*, 384–85.

NOTES: The impetus for this poem may have been the draining in the early 1970s of Lake Katherine, the 153-acre man-made lake on which Dickey lived in Columbia, South Carolina. The speaker appears to be an Indian.

9: Compare "his gone leg" ("The Rain Guitar," line 40), "my gone sight" ("Mexican Valley," line 16).

VARIANTS:

17: green; (*Strength, Central Motion, Whole Motion*) | green: (*New Yorker*, TS)

18: canceled (*Strength, Central Motion, Whole Motion*) | cancelled (*New Yorker*, TS)

28–29: [no blank line inserted] (*Whole Motion*)

34: consequences, dying (TS, *Strength, Central Motion, Whole Motion*) | consequences   dying (*New Yorker*)

The Zodiac

FIRST PUBLICATION: *The Zodiac* (limited edition) (Bloomfield Hills & Columbia: Bruccoli Clark, [September 21] 1976).

COLLECTED: *The Zodiac; Central Motion*, 61–95; *Whole Motion*, 345–73.

REPRINTED: Section X in *Treasury of American Poetry*, 637–38.

NOTES: Dickey had great ambitions for *The Zodiac*, which he published in his maturity as an effort to enlarge his literary standing with a major long poem, as his admired Hart Crane had done with *The Bridge* (1930). "*The Zodiac* is at the same time a vindication of the demonic, drunken poet and the desperately serious artist: the clown, hopeful genius and wastrel, a man alone, and an affirmation of the European imaginative tradition, from which all creative literature in the western world stems. But above all it is a kind of chronicle of the creative last-ditch stand, where a rootless man who has come home—in this case to Amsterdam—tries to relate himself to the starry heavens, and, in a small, bare room, attempts to align his fragile, doomed human body with the forces of Creation, symbolized for him by the stars, the constellations: the Zodiac. He will fail; he will die. But he is trying. His is the eternal delusion of the artist: that he can read the universe. But in his trying is his triumph. Something is affirmed" (*The Zodiac* [limited edition] [ix]; see also *Central Motion*, v–vi).

While a student at Vanderbilt , Dickey read "The Zodiac," a translation by Adriaan J. Barnouw of "De Dierenriem" by Hendrik Marsman (1899–1940) in the *Sewanee Review* 55 (Spring 1947) 238–51 (*The Zodiac*, ix; see Monroe K. Spears, "Dionysus and the Galaxy: A Reading of James Dickey's *Zodiac*," in *The Vanderbilt Tradition: Essays in Honor of Daniel Thomas Young* [Baton Rouge: LSU Press, 1991], 94). Dickey had the poem in mind as early as 1953, citing line XII.16 (page 251) as a possible epigraph for a poem (*Self*, 185). He may also have reflected Marsman's vitalism when he wrote in 1971, "What I want to do most as a poet is to charge the world with vitality: with the vitality that it already has, if we could rise to it" (*Sorties*, 5).

In publicity for *The Zodiac*, Marsman was called "a Dutch sailor" who "on the verge of madness" wrote from "occasionally hallucinated experiences" the "fragments" on which this poem is based (Thomas Lask, "Long Poem by Dickey Due in Fall," *New York Times*, June 11, 1976, 73; dust jacket of *The Zodiac*). In fact Marsman, born in Zeist, Utrecht, Holland, to a well-to-do bookseller, was an attorney who gave up his practice for poetry. While living in Germany in the early 1920s, during a phase he called "vitalism" (a term that dates to the ancient physician Galen of the second century C.E.), he voiced in expressionistic imagery moderated by Dutch pictorialism and temperamental composure the antihumanist feelings of German youth following World War I in his collections *Verzen* (1923) and a book known by its English title, *Paradise Regained* (1927). In 1933 he declared vitalism finished. After marrying he lived for nearly a decade in France, Spain, Italy, Greece, and Austria. He moved to a simpler, more colloquial diction in *Parta Nigra* (1934). His *Verzameld Werk* (3 vols.) won the Groot Nederland of 1938, and Marsman was then established as one of the leading figures of his time in Dutch letters. He also made a considerable reputation as a critic. His most important work, *Tempel en kruise* (Temple and Cross, 1940), which contains "The Zodiac," is a collection of poems in a variety of forms that reflect the poet's intellectual struggle to understand the influence of Greek civilization and (to a lesser degree) the Christian religion on Western culture at a time when Europe was threatened by communism and fascism, though his long view of history kept the poems from political topicality. Thus Marsman was not a sailor, not mad or hallucinated, and he composed his zodiac poem not in fragments but in twelve sections corresponding to the constellations of the zodiac.

When Hitler invaded the Netherlands in 1940, Marsman, then living in France, tried to get to South Africa via England, but his ship was torpedoed shortly after leaving Bordeaux on June 21, 1940. His wife was one of only two survivors.

Dickey was probably attracted to Marsman's poem chiefly because of his long interest in astronomy, beginning with his service as a navigator in World War II and continuing through study late in life for a certificate in celestial navigation. Marsman's war was the horrifying opposite of Dickey's: Marsman was a civilian who tried to escape but died at the beginning of the war; Dickey was a flier who fought in the war and survived. Dickey served in the Pacific; Marsman's poem takes place in Amsterdam in 1938–39. Dickey survived the war as he had survived his older brother (lines 131–32), and more recently his wife (line 982), giving Marsman's attempt to make sense of the world more meaning for Dickey in his fifties than it had the Dutchman in his twenties.

Dickey translated poetry for most of his career—from languages he knew well, such as French, and those he knew not at all, such as Yevtushenko's Russian (see *Head-Deep in Strange Sounds* [1979]). But "The Zodiac" had already been translated, so Dickey set himself a different task; inventing a new literary genre that he called the "rewrite": not a translation nor a Robert Lowell–like "imitation" but "a complete reworking of another person's poem, with the personality and style of the present poet predominating, and only using the original as a kind of springboard off of which to launch into his own lines, his own verbal constructs, his own thresholds and anatomies, keyed but not detained by the original" (*The Zodiac*, ix). Dickey's rewrite is more than twice as long as Marsman's (6,880 words to 2,595), but most of the expansions are in the early sections of the poem (see Romy Heylen, "James Dickey's *The Zodiac*: A Self-Translation?" *James Dickey Newsletter* 6 [Spring 1990]: 5 and 14–15n4). Dickey introduced into Marsman's topics the extreme drunkenness of the narrator, whose hallucinations add another layer of perception in dealing with reality and the meaning of the zodiac; anger at Pythagoras; his continuing fascination with Orion (see "For the Nightly Ascent of the Hunter Orion over a Forest Clearing"); and the deeper investigation of the nature of time. Dickey perhaps drew from Arthur Rimbaud's "Le bateau ivre" (see lines 913–14). Mallarmé's poem "Un coup de dés" "was most influential for me on *The Zodiac*. He has a thing about sidereal distances and so on" (Compton, 35).

The poem takes place over three days, ending with the poet's resurrection. Dickey follows Marsman's arrangement of the poem into twelve sections, corresponding to the twelve signs of the zodiac. He mentions only four of the constellations: Cancer, Leo, Scorpio, and Capricorn. His attention is drawn to Orion and his imaginary Lobster. In 416 of the poem's 993 lines, part 1 portrays the protagonist as angry and taken to drink over his failure to understand the structure of the universe and the meaning of time. Parts 2–7 describe the failure of mathematics and philosophy to solve the questions. Parts 8–11 conclude that only art can make sense of it all. Part 12 finds the speaker comfortable at last with his resolution of the "intellect and madness" at the heart of his initial frustration.

In *Babel to Byzantium* (1968), Dickey described the "unwell-made poem" as a "conclusionless poem, the open or ungeneralizing poem" (291). He called *The Zodiac* "such an unwell-made piece of work" (Christensen, 4; *Night*, 222). A quarter-century later Dickey said, "I have a great fondness for *The Zodiac because it's a failure and I knew it would be. By any of the normal, traditional or current standards of appraisal, it's a failure. But it is something I wanted to do because it galvanized something about poetic creation which I had never seen anyone else do. And that is to come to terms with that part of creativity that depends on being drunk. Where you say things and you have attitudes that you do not ordinarily have. Some of them get down in words if you are a writer. You put all of them down and you think when you are doing it that they are all sublime, and then when you come out of it, when you sober up and you look at what you have put down and a lot of it is rot. I wanted to put that rot in there. But some of it, if not sublime, is at least very good and I wanted to mix up the bad stuff that's full of self-deludedness with the good stuff which would not be there if not for the self-deludedness. If I had taken all of the parts that were sheer foolishness out of *The Zodiac*, then it would not have had the effect I wanted. Whether it would have been better or not, I can't say. It's done now" (Compton, 40).

The limited edition of this poem is dedicated to Walter Marty Schirra, Jr. (1923–2007), one of the original Mercury 7 astronauts, the fifth American to ride in space, and the only astronaut to serve in the first three American space programs, Mercury, Gemini, and Apollo. That edition also contains an epigraph from Neil Armstrong's address to a joint session of the U.S. Congress on September 16, 1969 (see "Apollo," line 19): "The earth is travelling . . . in the direction of the constellation Hercules to some unknown destination in the cosmos" (*New York Times*, September 17, 1969, 30).

In the notes that follow, quotations followed by (*M*) are from Barnouw's translation of Marsman's poem (cited above). Line-by-line equivalents are noted by "~". Paraphrases are noted by a description of the subject/action.

1–34: "The man of whom I tell this narrative / Returned, some time ago, to his native land. . . . the city's unbombed neon . . ." (*M*, 1–17).

33–56: the walls of the cell (*M*, 18–24).

59: *Einfühlung*, ("empathy") is a term coined by the aesthetician Robert Vischer (1847–1933) in 1873 as a psychological theory of art that indicates the projection of personal feelings onto the subjects of paintings. Freud (following Theodor Lipps) discussed *Einfühlung* in *Humor and Its Relation to the Unconscious* (1905) as a means of understanding others by putting ourselves in their place. Dickey discusses the term in *Night* (193). Alnilam (also known as Epsilon Orionis) is the central star in the belt of the constellation Orion and, because it is one of the most luminous (energy-producing) stars in the heavens, it is one of the fifty-seven stars used in celestial navigation. *Alnilam* is also the title of Dickey's second novel (1987).

73: For Alnilam and Orion see lines 335–36.

75, 332–53: Orion is seen clearly in the northern sky during the winter months. For Orion blinded while drunk, see "For the Nightly Ascent of the Hunter Orion over a Forest Clearing," line 28.

78: In *The Zodiac* Dickey had originally written that the horse nebula was in Andromeda, but he subsequently corrected it in *Whole Motion* to Orion, leaving the feminine pronouns of the following lines without a referent.

89–95: ~ *M*, 25–30.

96: Dickey's friend Al Braselton (see "Drifting") was also an alcoholic and, according to Dickey, once hallucinated an alligator at his feet as he worked in his advertising-agency office. The beast was "singing 'Racing with the Moon' in the voice of Vaughn Monroe." Braselton, known as "Whitewater Al," was subsequently called "Alligator Al."

119–79: The lamp of three rods, the mobile (*M*, 31–39).

122: Aquavit is alcohol made from potatoes. Its name comes from Latin meaning "water of life" (see line 485). Marsman's protagonist drinks only gin and only once.

136–60: The three-part mobile corresponds to Pythagoras's three-part mechanical model of the universe as sun, moon, and stars hanging in the sky. The model explained the universe, which is the poet's job as much as the philosopher's.

163: The animals are constellations.

178–79: Perhaps a reference to the object of Pantagruel and Panurge's search in books 4 and 5 of Rabelais's *Pantagruel* (1532), "la dive bouteille." The bottle responds oracularly, "in vino veritas."

198: Leo is imagined as couchant in profile, so only one eye shows, but Scorpio is imagined as seen from above, with both eyes indicated by stars (see "The Eagle's Mile," 15–16).

202–19: ~ *M*, 43–9.

234–43: On Melville and whiteness see "Reincarnation (II)."

245–48, 355: Pythagoras of Samos (ca. 580–490 B.C.E.) was the first Greek to call himself a philosopher (Diogenes Laertius, *Lives of the Philosophers*, 1.12). Though he is chiefly known for his mathematics, Pythagoras was the first to assert that the earth was a spherical body, around which planets revolved on an axis. He later claimed that all the planets revolve around a "great fire." See Christoph Riedweg, *Pythagoras: His Life, Teaching and Influence* (Ithaca: Cornell University Press, 2005). On Pythagoras and the "music of the spheres" see "Vegetable King," lines 63–64.

265–70: Nearly repeated at lines 501–5.

270: Crab is the constellation Cancer.

271–98: The description of the elongated lobster is reminiscent of Scorpio, one of the longest of the constellations. The belt of Orion contains not only a very hot star ("blue" stars on the Hertzsprung-Russell color-magnitude chart) but a very cool one ("red") as well. White stars are of medium temperature (6000–7500° K). Dwarves turn from red to blue as they nearly deplete their hydrogen supply. When the supply is depleted, dwarves turn white. See Ian Ridpath, *Stars and Planets* (Princeton: Princeton University Press, 2001), 263–78.

299: Addressing Pythagoras, who opposed eating meat except on religious occasions.

316–17: For "triangular eyes," see line 948.

320–22: missal of blue and gold (*M*, 54–56).

323–24: cave-catacomb (*M*, 56–57).

336–45: See line 73.

351: "wedge script" (*M*, 59).

352–53: Though the etymology of "zodiac" suggests the Babylonian concept of a "circle of animals," the Greek zodiac, unlike the Babylonian, was composed of both animals and figures of myth (Gemini, Virgo, Libra), so presumably Orion might have been a candidate, had the movements of the heavens cooperated.

355: See lines 245–48.

362: Claudius Ptolemaeus (90–160 C.E.), either a Greek or a Hellenized Egyptian from Alexandria, is known for the *Almagest*, which gives in its thirteen books a geocentric model for the solar system, which was the accepted model for thirteen hundred years. He cataloged the known stars of his time (including Alnilam) along with forty-eight constellations (including Orion), as well as tables and theories for computing the positions of the sun, moon, planets, and stars. He is not mentioned by Marsman.

364: Edwin Powell Hubble (1889–1953), a pioneer of twentieth-century astronomy, discovered other galaxies apart from our own in 1924 and in 1929 gave a numerical value ("Hubble's Constant") to the relationship between the linear velocity of a galaxy's movement and their distance, proving that the universe was expanding.

365: The British astronomer Sir Fred Hoyle (1915–2001) accepted Hubble's view of the expanding universe, but as an atheist, he rejected creationism and especially the "Big-Bang Theory" of creation, preferring his "steady state" theory. See Hoyle's *Evolution from Space: A Theory of Cosmic Creationism* (1984). Hoyle would not have been known to Marsman.

369–70: "Sings *dies Irae* to the Trumpet's blast" (*M*, 62).

401: new metal (*M*, 69).

414–15: "grey thicket of the dusk" (*M*, 74).

418: "The tower clock strikes" (*M*, 75).

426: The "watchmaker" theory was used as a teleologic proof of God's existence by René Descartes (1596–1650) and Robert Boyle (1627–1691) but most famously by William Paley (1743–1805), provoking a prolonged response from Charles Darwin.

501–5: See lines 265–70.

454–55: "music box" (*M*, 94).

461–74: Cancer (*M*, 100–101).

479: Perhaps "Reunioning Dialogue," lines 39–40.

490: The phrase "bartending for God" echoes Dickey's widely publicized "Barnstorming for Poetry" tours of fall 1964 and fall 1965.

506–23: Lobster (*M*, 102–6).

520–23: On the affinity with the Tower of Babel, see Heylen, 5–6.

544: "standing at dawn" (*M*, 113).

560: "the Demetrian isle" (*M*, 115). Cyprus was the birthplace of St. Demetrian (885–912 C.E.).

564–65: "Uplifted by the strength / Of ancient colonnades" (*M*, 117–18).

565–71: peace of death (*M*, 119–22).

614: "palish moon" (*M*, 133).

620: "illumed ravine" (*M*, 137).

628–40: "without that mastodont . . ." (*M*, 143–49).

650: Venus is also called the morning or the evening star, the brightest heavenly body at dusk or dawn.

651–52: "Swaying along the sky" (*M*, 153).

658–63: "The faster I sleep, / The faster the universe sleeps, / The deeper I draw breath, / The higher the night / and the song of the nightingale" (*M*, 162–66).

681: "The candlestick, the book, and the lamb" (*M*, 173).

690–95: "The dreams cross his sleep / As monsters the universe; / The moon is a beast that dies / In the shameless valley of clouds" (*M*, 177–80).

699–705: "Like poison in a thirsty sponge / Feels at night the sweat of his thought / Break out in a crown of thorns / Like a fungus, a Venus wreath / Who shall lay a cloth on his head?" (*M*, 185–89).

710–16: "O flesh that sullies itself / With refinement's flaccid flesh, / Be a plant again, rushing weed / In the waters of Nature's black stream" (*M*, 193–96).

717–18: "All words evaporate" (*M*, 197).

718–29: hermaphrodite (*M*, 198–204).

722: The Goat is the Tropic of Capricorn.

738: moon and script (*M*, 209–10).

741–42: marrow and grass (*M*, 211–12).

758–59: lethargy, oblivion (*M*, 215–16).

765: "the old twilight" (*M*, 220).

767: Dickey was likely composing this passage in 1975, twenty-eight years after the publication of Barnouw's translation (1948). Coincidentally Dickey's first wife, Maxine, died on October 27, 1976, twenty-eight years after their marriage in 1948. (On Maxine Dickey see "Tomb Stone" and "The Drift-Spell.")

770–77: walking along "slain" canal (*M*, 222–24).

778–86: fish (*M*, 224–26).

786–93: trees tell unceasing story (*M*, 227–30).

793–99: stops at fort; moat; elm-heavy night; swans (*M*, 231–39).

802–4: illness of mother (*M*, 243–44), see "Angina."

806–7: father star gazing (*M*, 245–47).

806: see line 197 above.

808–13: ~*M*, 248–53.

811: "Sick with that same relentless slime" (*M*, 251).

814–36: dream of burying murdered rival in garden (*M*, 262–74).

837: "*Empty is the grave of youth*" (*M*, 275).

841–48: mother's advice (*M*, 279–89).

852–55: ~ *M*, 290–93.

856–78: dialogue with mother (*M*, 294–308).

879–94: ~ *M*, 315–30.

897–98: "He was silent, his arm around her waist" (*M*, 335).

911: "Past the window chase rain and wind" (*M*, 344).

913–21: Dickey added the color blue to Marsman's mention of Wassily Kandinsky (1866–1944), who believed in the power of the color blue to advance the spirituality of the spectator.

913–14: compare "Le bateau ivre," 25–28.

913–18: Kandinsky and friend's voice (*M*, 345–50).

917–18: red-hot stove and blue room (*M*, 353–54).

921–23: "He narrates. / He polar-bears through the room" (*M*, 357–58).

925: cheese and gin (*M*, 362).

932: ~ *M*, 373. The public market in Tetuan, Morocco, where people stock up before the Sabbath.

932: fish market (*M*, 373–76).

934: ~ *M*, 374; *chalif* is caliph (Arabic "Khalifah"), a Muslim political leader claiming a connection to the succession from Muhammad.

933–34: "Through a row of shimmering trumpets / Enter a little mosque" (*M*, 375–76).

939: "Full of jaundiced portraits" (*M*, 379).

941: "barrel organ" (*M*, 380).

944: "is back in his native land" (*M*, 381).

945–51: ~ *M*, 384–85.

954–73: ~ *M*, 388–89.

969–71: "For without ships the sea is not the sea" (*M*, 397).

972: Dickey added the solar boat, referring to the specific boat that the Pyramid Texts of Egypt state will carry the soul of the pharaoh to heaven to meet his father Re.

983: See above, line 767.

992–93: "As long as exaltation spans around space / A firmament of intellect and dream" (M, 411–12).

Variants: (limited and trade editions identical)

Headnote, paragraph 2: It (*Zodiac*) | That one (*Central Motion, Whole Motion*)

1: Man (*Central Motion, Whole Motion*) | man (*Zodiac*)

18: Hé (*Central Motion, Whole Motion*) | He (TS, *Zodiac*)

183: When (TS, *Zodiac, Central Motion*) | Where (*Whole Motion*)

203: *them!* (*Central Motion, Whole Motion*) | *that!* (*Zodiac*)

364: Hubble [corrected by editor] | Hubbell (*Zodiac, Central Motion, Whole Motion*)

375: die, (*Zodiac, Central Motion*) | die (*Whole Motion*)

396: Which (*Zodiac, Central Motion,*) | That (*Whole Motion*)

461: It's [corrected by editor (see line 434)] | Its (*Zodiac, Central Motion, Whole Motion*)

479: stadium (*Zodiac, Central Motion*) | stadium—I said this somewhere— (*Whole Motion*)

481: For (*Zodiac, Central Motion*) | for (*Whole Motion*)

563: Into (*Zodiac, Central Motion*) | into (*Whole Motion*)

706: skull's   broken (*Zodiac, Central Motion*) | skull's broken (*Whole Motion*)

837: *The* grave of (*Zodiac, Central Motion*) | The grave of (*Whole Motion*)

837: *I told you:* (*Zodiac, Central Motion*) | I told you: (*Whole Motion*)

848: remember." (*Whole Motion, Central Motion*) | remember. (*Zodiac*)

863: "that (*Whole Motion*) | that (*Zodiac, Central Motion*)

877: forgotten too (*Whole Motion*) | forgotten around too (*Zodiac, Central Motion*)

913–14: half-light one of Kandinsky's paintings / Squeezes art's blood (*Zodiac, Central Motion*) | half-light, framed, Kandinsky's blue pressure points, / Against their will, turn red, and swirl / Art's drunken blood (*Whole Motion*)

937–38: [blank line inserted] (*Whole Motion*)

962: want now (*Zodiac, Central Motion*) | want (*Whole Motion*)

—*1977–1997*—

The Strength of Fields

First Publication: *Washington Post Special Supplement—The Carter Presidency,* January 20, 1977, 3.

Collected: *Strength,* 15–17; *Central Motion,* 100–101; *Whole Motion,* 378–79.

Reprinted: Separate publication (Bloomfield Hills, Mich. & Columbia, S.C.: Bruccoli Clark, 1977); Broadside (Columbia, S.C.: South Carolina Educational Television, 1984), lines 37–49; *Chattahoochie Review* 17 (Winter 1997): 48–49; *High Roads Folio (Limited Edition)* 10 (1985): 20–21; *A New Spirit, A New Commitment, A New America* (New York: Bantam Books, January 1977), 90; *New York Times,* January 21, 1977, B6; *Vintage,* 160–61.

Notes: "[Carter] didn't ask me to 'write something for the occasion.' As it turns out I did write something that was sort of about the occasion, but I was under no pressure to" (Phil Patton, "Interview: James Dickey," *Sky* 6 (July 1977) 267; Baughman, 162). "I cast Jimmy Carter in his withdrawal from Washington and his return to his roots, his hometown, in the role of a mythical hero, and that is always the same. It doesn't make any difference if it's Theseus or Perseus or any one else" (*One Voice 2,* 37). "The role of President of the United States certainly qualifies a man as a hero, or at least as a potential hero. And I thought of the anthropological journey, the three-stage journey of the hero, which involves withdrawal from the world, a penetration to a source of power, and then a life-enhancing return. In this case, Jimmy's withdrawal from the world would be temporarily leaving the world of politics and going back to his hometown, Plains, Georgia, a small town surrounded by fields where things are growing, and walking in the small town at night with these growing things around him and the strength of fields—and then coming back into the arena with the renewed power that he had drawn from his source, which is the American small Southern town in a farming community" (Greiner, 20; see also Hart, 577).

Epigraph: Dickey told an interviewer: "If there's any literary precedent to *Deliverance,* it's that passage as I encountered it quoted by Hyman, referring to Van Gennep's concept of the 'rites de passage'" (Arnett, 295; Baughman, 79). Stanley Edgar Hyman's review of *The Hero with a Thousand Faces* (New York: Pantheon, 1949), by Joseph Campbell (1904–1987), and other books on ritual appeared as "Myth, Ritual, and Nonsense" in the *Kenyon Review* (11 [Summer 1949]: 455–75) and was influential on Dickey when he was studying anthropology at Vanderbilt (*Striking,* 187). Unfortunately Hyman did not quote *Les Rites de Passage* (1909) by Arnold van Gennep

(1873–1957) but Campbell's *Hero with a Thousand Faces* when he said: "It is Campbell's contention that all myth is one, 'the great myth,' 'the monomyth,' which can be described as an elaboration of the three stages of Van Gennep's *rites de passage,* thus: 'a separation from the world, a penetration to some source of power, and a life-enhancing return'" (455). The epigraph appears on page 35 of *The Hero with a Thousand Faces.*

49: "'My life belongs to the world,' he said, 'I will do what I can'" (Alun Lewis, "They Came," *The Last Inspection* [London: Allen & Unwin, 1942], 221). Welsh poet Alun Lewis (1915–1944) died in Burma during World War II. The quotation was apparently inadvertent (see *Night,* x).

VARIANTS:

22: You?   I?   What (*Strength, Central Motion, Whole Motion*) | You? I? What (*Post*)

27–28: [blank line inserted] (*Post*)

40–41: [blank line inserted] (*Post*)

44–45: green. / That (*Post, Strength*) | green.   That (*Central Motion, Whole Motion*)

The Voyage of the Needle

FIRST PUBLICATION: As "Water-Magic in Sunlight: The Voyage of the Needle," *Gentleman's Quarterly* 48 (Winter 1978–79): 146.

COLLECTED: *Strength,* 23–24; *Central Motion,* 105; *Whole Motion,* 382–83.

NOTES: Dickey's mother "invented a game of stillness" to calm her excitable children during their baths, and "fifty-five years later I wrote this poem because I realized that this game was a way to show her love for us and a concern for our well-being" (Mack Smith, "James Dickey's Varieties of Creation: The Voices of Narrative," *James Dickey Newsletter* 1 [Spring 1985]: 19). On Maibelle Swift Dickey, see "Angina" and "Buckdancer's Choice."

VARIANTS:

19: level (*Strength, Central Motion, Whole Motion*) | slanted (*Gentleman's Quarterly,* TS)

Mexican Valley

FIRST PUBLICATION: Broadside in portfolio *For Aaron Copeland on the Occasion of His Seventy-Eighth Birthday, 14 November 1978* (Winston-Salem, N.C.: Palaemon Press, 1978).

COLLECTED: *Four Poems,* [1–2]; *Head-Deep,* 19–20; *Strength,* 70–71; *Central Motion,* 138–39; *Whole Motion,* 407–8.

NOTES: Dickey's library contained *Les Poésies mexicaines,* edited by Jean-Clarence Lambert (Paris: Editions Seghers, 1961), with "Vallée de Mexico" by Octavio Paz (1914–1998) in French on page 275. The original, Spanish version of Paz's poem was published in *¿Aguila o sol?* (1951); see Octavio Paz, *Obra Poética (1935–1988)* (Barcelona: Seix Barral, 1990), 224. Dickey and Paz agreed informally to translate one another's poetry when they met in Mexico during Dickey's service on a cultural mission for President Jimmy Carter in April 1977 (*One Voice 2,* 208). Dickey regularly championed Paz as Mexico's greatest poet and deserving of the Nobel Prize, which Paz won in 1990 (Hart, 581). Of Paz's poetry, Dickey wrote: "He has a kind of interesting tropicalizing of surrealism that I like but am not crazy about" (*Crux,* 300).

8: Tlaloc is an important Aztec fertility, rain, and water divinity who—in four forms—holds up the four corners of the earth.

16: Compare "his gone leg" ("The Rain Guitar," line 40) and "the gone depths" ("Remnant Water," line 9).

VARIANTS:

2: body.   With (*Strength, Central Motion, Whole Motion*) | body. With (broadside, *Four Poems, Head-Deep*, TS)

4: on- (*Strength, Central Motion, Whole Motion*) | on— (broadside, *Four Poems, Head-Deep*, TS)

10: principal (*Four Poems, Head-Deep*) | principle (broadside, TS, *Strength, Central Motion, Whole Motion*)

20: That have (*Strength, Central Motion, Whole Motion*) | Have (broadside, *Four Poems, Head-Deep*, TS)

28: junk-hair (broadside, TS, *Strength, Central Motion, Whole Motion*) | junk hair (*Four Poems, Head-Deep*)

33: cross-glittering (broadside, TS, *Strength, Central Motion, Whole Motion*) | cross glittering (*Four Poems, Head-Deep*)

38: long-lost (broadside, TS, *Strength, Central Motion, Whole Motion*) | long lost (*Four Poems, Head-Deep*)

Undersea Fragment in Colons

FIRST PUBLICATION: *Four Poems* [3–4].

COLLECTED: *Head-Deep*, 17–18; *Strength*, 68–69; *Central Motion*, 137; *Whole Motion*, 406–7.

NOTES: Dickey's library contained Vicente Aleixandre (1898–1984), *Poesias Completas* (Madrid: Aguilar, 1960), with the original of this version, "Sin Luz," on pages 311–12.

VARIANTS:

26–27: [no blank line inserted] (*Head-Deep*)

When

FIRST PUBLICATION: *Four Poems* [5–6].

COLLECTED: *Head-Deep*, 23–24; *Strength*, 75–76; *Central Motion*, 142; *Whole Motion*, 410.

NOTES: Among the many books by Pierre Reverdy (1889–1960) in Dickey's library was *Main d'oeuvre: poèmes (1913–1949)* (Paris: Mercure de France, 1964), which contains on page 49 "À quand," the original of this version. The poem originally appeared in Reverdy's *La balle au bond* (1928).

VARIANTS:

13–14: [blank line inserted] (TS)

15: I (*Head-Deep*, TS, *Strength, Central Motion*) | I'll (*Whole Motion*)

Low Voice, Out Loud

FIRST PUBLICATION: *Four Poems* [7–8].
COLLECTED: *Head-Deep*, 21–22; *Strength*, 72–73; *Central Motion*, 140–41; *Whole Motion*, 408–9.
NOTES: Dickey owned Léon-Paul Fargue (1878–1947), *Poésies* (Paris: Editions Gallimard, 1963), which contains the source of this poem, "Voix du haut parleur," pages 246–47.

Purgation [first version]

FIRST PUBLICATION: *Head-Deep*, 11.
COLLECTED: *Strength*, 59–60; *Central Motion*, 131; *Whole Motion*, 403.
NOTES: Dickey's version of a poem by Po Chü-yi (772–846), number 69 in the Kiang Kang-hu text, whose title, roughly translated, is "Describing Again the Ancient Grass-Plain." The poem was translated by Witter Bynner as "Grasses" in his *The Jade Mountain: A Chinese Anthology, Being Three Hundred Poems of the T'ang Dynasty, 618–906* (New York: Knopf, 1929), 93—a volume in Dickey's library.
VARIANTS:
11: *on!* (*Head-Deep, Strength, Central Motion, Whole Motion*) | <u>On!</u> (TS)
12–13: [blank line inserted] (*Head-Deep*, TS)
15: Is what I want   both age-gazing living and dead (*Strength, Central Motion, Whole Motion*) | Is
    where I want to be (*Head-Deep*, TS)

The Ax-God: Sea-Pursuit

FIRST PUBLICATION: *Head-Deep*, 12.
COLLECTED: *Strength*, 61–62; *Central Motion*, 132; *Whole Motion*, 403–4.
REPRINTED: Broadside, in group of ten, under title *For Robert Penn Warren 24-IV-80* (Winston-Salem, N.C.: Palaemon Press, 1980).
NOTES: Dickey owned *Selected Works of Alfred Jarry [1873–1907]*, edited by Roger Shattuck and Simon Watson Taylor (New York: Grove, 1965), which contains Jarry's "L'Homme à la Hache" from *Les Minutes de Sable Mémorial* (1894). The dedication to Jarry's poem reads: "Après et pour P. Gauguin."
VARIANTS:
Title: Sea-Pursuit (*Head-Deep*, broadside, *Strength*) | Sea Pursuit (*Central Motion, Whole Motion*)

Nameless

FIRST PUBLICATION: *Head-Deep*, 13.
COLLECTED: *Strength*, 63; *Central Motion*, 133; *Whole Motion*, 404.
NOTES: "I think Montale is the greatest living poet and he hasn't even been translated over here" (Roberts, 9; Baughman, 43). Dickey's library contained two collections of poems by Eugenio Montale (1896–1981): *Ossi di Seppia (1920–1927)* (Milan: Mondadori, 1961)—with "Spesso il male di vivere" ("Often I have encountered the evil of living"), the source of this poem, on page 63— and *Poésies, I Os de seiche (Ossi di seppia) (1920–1927)*, translated into French by Patrice Angelini

(Paris: Gallimard, 1966)—with the original Italian version of "Spesso il male di vivere" on page 80 and a French translation on page 81.

VARIANTS:

9: religion-faking sun-blasted rack (TS, *Strength, Central Motion, Whole Motion*) | religion-fixing sand-blasting sun (*Head-Deep*)

Math

FIRST PUBLICATION: *Head-Deep,* 14.

COLLECTED: *Strength,* 64–65; *Central Motion,* 134; *Whole Motion,* 404–5.

NOTES: Dickey's library contained Comte de Lautréamont [Isidore Lucien Ducasse] (1846–1870) and Germain Nouveau (1851–1920), *Oeuvres Complètes* (Paris: Gallimard, 1970). This poem comes from Lautréamont's *Les Chants de Maldoror,* chant deuxième, strophe 10 ("Ô mathématiques sévères . . . triangle lumineux!," page 105). "If any one writer is responsible for the attitude known as 'surrealism' it was he. . . . He came originally from South America to Paris and went mad, died around thirty. He made up a phony thing as a nobleman, the 'Comte de Lautréamont.' Really he was a crazy Jew named Isidore Ducasse, from Montevideo. . . . His most famous statement is 'poetry must not be made by one but by all'" (Ron McFarland, "An Interview with James Dickey," *Slackwater Review* 3 [Winter 1979–80]: 30–31; Baughman, 184). Set to music for chamber ensemble and voice by Ronald Perera (who also set "Apollo") in "Crossing the Meridian" (1993). On Dickey's learning math in school, see "Mangham."

VARIANTS:

18: [line indented] (*Whole Motion*)

18: numbers. (*Strength, Central Motion, Whole Motion*) | numbers, (*Head-Deep,* TS)

20, 21: [lines not centered] (*Central Motion, Whole Motion*)

Judas

FIRST PUBLICATION: *Head-Deep,* 15.

COLLECTED: *Strength,* 66; *Central Motion,* 135; *Whole Motion,* 405.

NOTES: Dickey's library contained Georg Heym (1887–1912), *Gedichte* (Frankfurt am Main: Suhrkamp, 1966), which includes Heym's "Judas," on page 97. "Heym is such a violent writer that he is almost dangerous, and despite my indifferent German, I am very much moved by him, and solidly in his corner" (*One Voice 2,* 294; *Crux,* 391).

Headnote: On January 16, 1912, Heym and his friend Ernst Balcke went ice skating on the Havel River, a tributary of the Elbe that is frozen at that time of year. It appears that Balcke fell through the ice and Heym dived in to save him; both died and their bodies were not recovered until days later.

Small Song

FIRST PUBLICATION: *Head-Deep,* 16.

COLLECTED: *Strength,* 67; *Central Motion,* 136; *Whole Motion,* 406.

NOTES: Dickey owned *Hommage des poètes francais à Attila Jozsef,* introduction by Tristan Tzara (Paris: Pierre Seghers, 1955). On page 27 is "Chanson," a version of József's poem by Jean Cayrol (1911–2005) based on a translation by L. Gara.

Headnote: Attila József (1905–1937) was the most influential Hungarian poet between the two World Wars. He published his first book of poems at the age of seventeen, eight years after his first suicide attempt. His melancholy deepened as he grew into his thirties and on December 3, 1937, he threw himself under a passing freight train. See Ferenc Tóth, *Twentieth-Century Eastern European Writers First Series,* vol. 215 of *Dictionary of Literary Biography* (Detroit: Gale, 1999), 166–74.

Poem [b]

FIRST PUBLICATION: *Head-Deep,* 25.
COLLECTED: *Strength,* 74; *Central Motion,* 141; *Whole Motion,* 409.
NOTES: Dickey owned *Poètes finnois* (Paris: Pierre Seghers, 1951), with this poem by the Finnish poet Saima (Rauha Maria) Harmaja (1913–1937) translated into French as "Chère mort," by Henry G. Gröndahl (page 35). Harmaja died of tuberculosis at twenty-four.

A Saying of Farewell

FIRST PUBLICATION: *Head-Deep,* 26.
COLLECTED: *Strength,* 77; *Central Motion,* 143; *Whole Motion,* 410–11.
REPRINTED: *New Republic* 181 (October 20, 1979): 36.
NOTES: Dickey's library contained Nordahl Grieg (1902–1943), *Poèmes Choisis* (Paris: Pierre Seghers, 1954) with a French translation of the Norwegian dramatist and broadcaster's poem as "Adieu" by Marguerite Diehl (page 24).
VARIANTS:
Headnote: —homage, Nordahl Grieg— (*Strength, Central Motion, Whole Motion*) | —from the Norwegian of Nordahl Grieg (*Head-Deep*)
4: [line flush left] (*Head-Deep*)
[In place of lines 7–15, *Head-Deep* reads: "We could say that, but no other could. / In spite of this death, this death / Will stay with us. // The deepest of all wounds has closed over, / And the heart sleeps. But *does* it? / We're fooling ourselves. Face it squarely: there is no worse pain / Than to think that it does."]

For the Running of the
New York City Marathon

FIRST PUBLICATION: *Strength,* 45–47 [published February 1, 1977].
COLLECTED: *Central Motion,* 121–22; *Whole Motion,* 393–94.
REPRINTED: *New York: Poems,* 61–62.
NOTES: "But it struck me, looking at footage of these strange races through the city, that the whole point of almost anyone's participation in them <u>is</u> the participation—for any one of that rag-tag mob could run as much as he wanted to, by himself, at any time—and above all in the

finishing, the actual <u>finishing</u>, of the thing. Not more than ten of the contestants have any chance of winning the race, or even think they have, so the brute finishing, in each individual case, is the message, as Mr. McLuhan might say. Otherwise, I thought there were a couple of humorous things in it, particularly those about the reflections of the runners going by the stores where the mannequins and dummies are looking out at them" (*One Voice 2*, 312). On this theme see "The Sprinter at Forty," "The Sprinter's Mother," "The Sprinter's Sleep," and "The Olympian."

Variants:

42: and fall (*Strength, Central Motion*) | and (*Whole Motion* [typo])

Purgation (second version)

First Publication: As "Purgation," *Kenyon Review*, n.s., 2 (Spring 1980): 28–29.

Collected: *Night*, 9–10; *Eagle*, 63; *Whole Motion*, 472–73.

Notes: This version of the same poem by Po Chü-yi Dickey previously translated as "Purgation" in *Head-Deep* is thoroughly revised and expanded (from sixteen to thirty-one lines). Publication of this revision without reference to the first suggests that Dickey considered it a separate poem.

Variants:

Tag line: Chü (TS, *Kenyon, Eagle, Whole Motion*) | Chu (*Night*)

2: season (TS, *Kenyon, Eagle, Whole Motion*) | Season (*Night*)

3: though I (TS, *Kenyon, Night*) | though (*Eagle, Whole Motion*)

6–7: [one line] (*Kenyon*)

7–8: [no blank line inserted] (*Kenyon*)

10, 11: [As these lines are differently divided in *Kenyon Review, Night, Eagle,* and *Whole Motion,* it is assumed that these are very long lines that should be printed without breaks.]

11–12: [blank line inserted] (*Eagle, Whole Motion*)

14: leaned (*Eagle, Whole Motion*) | leant (TS, *Kenyon, Night*)

29: *over us   for us* (TS, *Night, Eagle, Whole Motion*) | over us   for us (*Kenyon*)

The Surround

First Publication: *Atlantic* 246 (July 1980): 58.

Collected: *Puella*, 45–46.

Reprinted: *Puella* (Pyracantha), 25.

Notes: "James Wright died while I was writing this poem. Originally the poem was just called 'The Surround' and it didn't have [James Wright] in it. It had the female figure—the procreative figure and not the destructive part—speaking at dusk. Wright becomes all of that. He is not only in the center of it, he is it. He is all of it" (Compton, 37–38). "The poem is a kind of elegy for the American poet James Wright, a close friend of mine for years, who feared the change from day to night and the coming of the predators, when the whole climate of fighting in the animal world changes to that of prey and predator, in the dark: he used to say that he feared the dark because he feared the change 'in the surround.' I am telling him in the poem that he is not to fear this any more, for he is the surround; the whole thing good and bad, and that the moon is beautiful on water, and that the tree grows its rings in the dark as well as the light" (*One Voice 2*, 291; see also 297). James Arlington Wright (1927–1980) and Dickey began a correspondence in 1958, when Wright strongly objected to Dickey's glancing characterization of Wright's poetry as "ploddingly 'sincere'" ("In the Prescence of Anthologies," *Sewanee Review* 66 [Spring 1958]: 297; comment cut from abridged reprint in *Babel to Byzantium*). Dickey responded more firmly, and Wright wrote back to apologize. By the time they met, sharing a stage with Robert Bly in 1959, they had begun a friendship that lasted twenty years, Dickey calling Wright "the best correspondent I have ever had" (*Crux*, 150). Wright gave Dickey great help in revising "Dover: Believing in Kings." Dickey later felt that Bly became too influential on Wright's work, but Wright's social conscience grew out of his witnessing the ravages of poverty as a youth in Martins Ferry, Ohio, where he was born to a southern family. Though he studied under the poets John Crowe Ransom (1888–1974) at Kenyon and Theodore Roethke (1908–1963) and Stanley Kunitz (1905–2006) at the University of Washington, Wright's chief influences were Thomas Hardy and Robert Frost. Dickey envied Wright his doctorate, his comfortable and secure teaching positions (University of Minnesota, Macalester College, and Hunter College), and probably the Pulitzer Prize his *Collected Poems* received in 1972, but he denigrated him as too influenced by Robert Bly. On the other hand Dickey lauded Wright's willingness to change style constantly in order to, in Pound's words, "make it new." Dickey and Wright shared a love of what Dickey called "country surrealism" (see introduction, p. xxxii). Wright figures in this poem and "Tapestry and Sail." Wright dedicated his poem "At the Executed Murderer's Grave" to Dickey. Although Dickey chose Wright's *Collected Poems* as one of his "favorite poetry books" (*Bookviews* 1 [February 1978]: 18–19), he claimed that Wright's widow took umbrage at his review of Wright's *Collected Poems* in the *Southern Review,* so Dickey did not include this poem in *Whole Motion* (*One Voice 2,* 483). Dickey did not review Wright's *Collected Poems;* in fact he contributed a complimentary blurb for the dust jacket. He may have been thinking of his 1958 *Sewanee Review* essay.

VARIANTS:

Headnote: James Wright Spoken-to at Sundown (*Atlantic*)

3: Dusk   seizure (*Atlantic*) | Dusk seizure (*Puella*)

8: with flame-threads (*Atlantic*) | with / flame-threads (*Puella*)

11: midnight: here (*Puella*) | midnight: here (*Atlantic*)

The Eagle's Mile

FIRST PUBLICATION: *Hastings Constitutional Law Quarterly* 8 (Fall 1980): 1–3.

COLLECTED: *Night*, 11–13; *Eagle*, 25–27; *Whole Motion*, 444–46.

REPRINTED: Broadside (Columbia, S.C. & Bloomfield Hills, Mich.: Bruccoli Clark, 1981); *Reckon* 1 (Winter 1996): 77.

NOTES: William Orville Douglas (1898–1980) was the longest-serving associate justice of the United States Supreme Court (thirty-six years, 1939–75). He was a noted environmentalist, and the Douglas Wilderness in Mount Rainier National Park in his home state of Washington was named for him. On his life see Bruce Allen Murphy, *Wild Bill: The Legend and Life of William O. Douglas* (New York: Random House, 2003). "[Douglas's wife] commissioned that poem. . . . He was a very old man when I knew him. . . . We talked about fishing and hunting and conservation, and I was very much in favor of him" (Greiner, 16). "I have concentrated on Douglas's stand on the issue of ecology and wildlife, and have written out of the belief that by his commitment he has thereby entered into the wild creatures—both predators and prey—and the wilderness he protected" (*One Voice 2,* 278). There is some affinity with Robinson Jeffers's "The Caged Eagle's Death-Dream." Dickey's poem reads as if it were a memorial, but Douglas was alive when Dickey submitted the poem to the *Hastings Constitutional Law Quarterly.* He died two weeks later to the day (Hart, 704).

Epigraph: "The emmet's inch and the eagle's mile / Make lame philosophy to smile." William Blake, *Auguries of Innocence,* lines 105–6.

12–13: "The phrase—and the image—of 'Adam in lightning' just alludes to the fact that a bolt of lightning, with all its off-branchings, looks something like an anatomical chart, a map of veins, a kind of instantaneous sketch of a human (because upright) vascular system, and it seems to me a much more dramatic and unexpected way of 'creating' Adam than the relatively commonplace traditional one, the matter of the molded clay into which God breathed life" (*One Voice 2,* 396). Dickey prized an incident in the early life of Lucien Becker (1911–1984)—found in Gaston Puel, *Lucien Becker* (Paris: Seghers, 1962), 16–17—when the young boy saw a stallion struck by lightning, creating a theme for much of Becker's later poetry. "My own fascination with lightning has been augmented by his," said Dickey, "and it was only with the greatest exercise of willpower that I was able to keep the figure of a horse out of . . . 'The Eagle's Mile'" ("Lightnings or Visuals," *South Atlantic Review* 57 [January 1992]: 5; *James Dickey Newsletter* 8 [Spring 1992]: 4–5).

15–16: The image may be of a one-eyed god, such as Wotan or Orion, or perhaps the one eye visible when an eagle crosses one's line of sight; nevertheless Dickey said, "I am not sure whether Douglas lost his eye in a fishing accident in England or Ireland . . ." (*One Voice 2,* 278). There is no evidence in his biographies that Douglas lost an eye in a fishing accident. (Dickey's admired friend Robert Penn Warren, who physically resembled Douglas, could see out of only one eye in his old age.)

27: Springer Mountain in Georgia is the beginning of the Appalachian Trail. See "Springer Mountain (a)."

80: For Brasstown Bald, see "May Day Sermon," line 64.

81: Compare W. B. Yeats, "Crazy Jane Talks with the Bishop," lines 17–18: "For nothing can be sole or whole / That has not been rent."

Variants:

Dedication: for Justice William Douglas (*Eagle, Whole Motion*) | - for William Douglas - (*Hastings*) | for William Douglas (*Night*)

1–2: [blank line inserted] (TS, *Hastings*)

14: leaves. Douglas, (*Night, Eagle, Whole Motion*)| leaves.   Douglas, (TS, *Hastings*)

17: thát (*Eagle, Whole Motion*) | that (TS, *Hastings, Night*)

25–26: [no blank line inserted] (*Whole Motion* [typo])

34: Clairvoyant (TS, *Night, Eagle, Whole Motion*) | Clairivoyant (*Hastings* [typo])

52: it. Douglas, (*Night, Eagle, Whole Motion*) | it.   Douglas, (TS, *Hastings*)

53–54: [no blank line inserted] (*Whole Motion* [typo])

62: all blades (TS, *Hastings, Eagle, Night*) | all the blades (*Whole Motion*)

Scion

FIRST PUBLICATION: *Scion* (published December 1980).

COLLECTED: As "Deborah as Scion," *Puella*, 31–34; *Whole Motion*, 421–24.

REPRINTED: *MSS* 1 (Spring 1981): 120–23; *Puella* (Pyracantha), 15–17; *Singular Voices*, 31–34.

NOTES: See "Concerning the Book *Puella* and Two of Its Poems," *Singular Voices*, 35–37.

65–79: "I think that the whaling sequence of "Deborah as Scion" demonstrates that you can do both things. I think it's the best thing I ever wrote" (Compton, 37).

VARIANTS:

1: Kin: quiet grasses.   Above, (*Puella, Whole Motion*) | kin: quiet grasses: Above (*Scion,* TS)

13: brows: in (*Puella, Whole Motion*) | brows: in (*Scion,* TS)

29: family plot (*Puella, Whole Motion*) | family-plot (*Scion,* TS)

33: alive: the (*Puella, Whole Motion*) | alive: the (*Scion,* TS)

35: peace.   My (*Puella, Whole Motion*) | peace. My (*Scion,* TS)

47: mystical: I (*Puella, Whole Motion*) | mystical: I (*Scion,* TS)

49: mother: I (*Puella, Whole Motion*) | mother: I (*Scion,* TS)

58: draw.   I (*Puella, Whole Motion*) | draw. I (*Scion,* TS)

59: cedar: ghost-smell (*Puella, Whole Motion*) | cedar: ghost-smell (*Scion,* TS)

62–63: broadening / world-wide (*Puella, Whole Motion*) | broadening world-wide (*Scion,* TS)

81: hand: the (*Puella, Whole Motion*) | hand: the (*Scion,* TS)

90: graze: I (*Puella, Whole Motion*) | graze: I (*Scion,* TS)

91–92: [blank line inserted] (*Scion,* TS)

94: animal: I (*Puella, Whole Motion*) | animal: I (*Scion,* TS)

102–3: [no blank line inserted] (*Scion,* TS)

108: possible: lamp (*Puella, Whole Motion*) | possible: lamp (*Scion,* TS)

From Time

FIRST PUBLICATION: *MSS* 1 (Spring 1981): 118–19.

COLLECTED: *Puella*, 39–40; *Whole Motion*, 425–26.

REPRINTED: *Carolina Lifestyles*, May 1982, 49; *Puella* (Pyracantha), 22.

VARIANTS:

2: struck (TS, *Puella, Whole Motion*) | stuck (*MSS* [typo])

4: cause: my (*Puella, Whole Motion*) | cause: my (*MSS,* TS)

7: Intercepting: that (*Puella, Whole Motion*) | Intercepting: that (*MSS,* TS)

11: slow (TS, *Puella, Whole Motion*) | show (*MSS* [typo])

15: wandering.   Here (*Puella, Whole Motion*) | wandering. Here (*MSS,* TS)

16: cousinly: are (*Puella, Whole Motion*) | cousinly: are (*MSS,* TS)

22–23: it, / then (*Puella, Whole Motion*) | it, then (*MSS,* TS)

24–25: and / wide-angle (*Puella*) | and wide-angle (*MSS,* TS, *Whole Motion*)

26: them!   How (*Puella, Whole Motion*) | them! How (*MSS,* TS)

26: Bach (*MSS,* TS, *Puella*) | Mozart (*Whole Motion*)

30: The past (*MSS,* TS, *Puella*) | Bach and his gist (*Whole Motion*)

31: overlook, the (*MSS,* TS, *Puella*) | overlook. You bet. The (*Whole Motion*)

Deborah Burning a Doll Made of House-Wood

FIRST PUBLICATION: In "Five Poems from 'Puella,'" *Poetry* 137 (March 1981): 313–14.

COLLECTED: *Puella*, 13–14.

REPRINTED: 45 *Contemporary Poems: The Creative Process*, edited by Alberta T. Turner (New York & London: Longman, 1985): 44–47; *Carolina Lifestyle*, May 1982, 48; *Dickey Reader*, 121–22; *Puella* (Pyracantha), 1–2.

NOTES: Rainer Maria Rilke, "Reflections on Dolls" ["Puppen: Zu den Wachs-Puppen von Lotte Pritzel"], *Sämtliche Werke* (Frankfurt am Main: Insel, 1965), 6:1067: "Ich weiß, ich weiß, wir mußten solche Dinge haben, die sich alles gefallen ließen."

VARIANTS:

9: leaving: I (*Puella*) | leaving: I (*Poetry*, TS)

16: stripped closet (*Puella*) | stripped / closet (*Poetry*, TS)

28–29: [lines centered] (*Poetry*)

44–45: [blank line inserted] (*Poetry*, TS)

Deborah, Moon, Mirror, Right Hand Rising

FIRST PUBLICATION: In "Five Poems from 'Puella,'" *Poetry* 137 (March 1981): 315.

COLLECTED: *Puella*, 15–16.

REPRINTED: *Puella* (Pyracantha), 3.

NOTE:

2: See "The Sheep Child," lines 59–60.

VARIANTS:

4: surface.   All (*Puella*) | surface. All (*Poetry*, TS)

7–8: [two lines centered] (*Poetry*)

18: of God-ruined (TS, *Puella*) | of / God-ruined (*Poetry*)

19: stone.   I (*Puella*) | stone. I (*Poetry*, TS)

19: time   at (*Puella*) | time at (*Poetry*, TS)

20: All-told.   The (*Puella*) | All-told. The (*Poetry*, TS)

23: air between/ the (*Puella*) | air / between the (*Poetry*)

Veer-Voices: Two Sisters under Crows

FIRST PUBLICATION: In "Five Poems from 'Puella,'" *Poetry* 137 (March 1981): 316–17.

COLLECTED: *Puella*, 19–20; *Whole Motion*, 419–20.

REPRINTED: *Puella* (Pyracantha), 5.

VARIANTS:

4: hawing in (TS, *Puella*, *Whole Motion*) | hawing / in (*Poetry*)

8: assertions   feeding (TS, *Puella*, *Whole Motion*) | assertions feeding (*Poetry*)

11: ground.   If (*Puella*, *Whole Motion*) | ground. If (*Poetry*, TS)

33: fences: come (*Puella*, *Whole Motion*) | fences: come (*Poetry*, TS)

Heraldic: Deborah and Horse in Morning Forest

FIRST PUBLICATION: In "Five Poems from 'Puella,'" *Poetry* 137 (March 1981): 317–19.
COLLECTED: *Puella*, 23–24.
REPRINTED: *Puella* (Pyracantha), 8–9.
NOTES:
Epigraph: Gerard Manley Hopkins (1844–1889) described the wind on July 22, 1873, as so hot that, when he went outdoors, "I seemed to put it on like a gown as a man puts on the shadow he walks into. . . . I mean it rippled and fluttered like light linen, one could feel the folds and braids of it—and indeed a floating flag. . . ." (*The Journals and Papers of Gerard Manley Hopkins*, edited by Humphry House, completed by Graham Storey [London: Oxford University Press, 1959], 233).
17, 37: For "head brass" see "To Be Edward Thomas," line 33.
VARIANTS:
5: leggèd (*Poetry,* TS) | leggéd (*Puella*)
11: ride.   This (*Puella*) | ride. This (*Poetry,* TS)
19: nails: the (*Puella*) | nails: the (*Poetry,* TS)
19: hidden log (TS, *Puella*) | hidden / log (*Poetry*)
27: hurtling: but (*Puella*) | hurtling: but (*Poetry,* TS)
38: their   speed (*Puella*) | their speed (*Poetry,* TS)
39: reins: Plan (*Puella*) | reins: Plan (*Poetry,* TS)

Springhouse, Menses, Held Apple, House and Beyond

FIRST PUBLICATION: In "Five Poems from 'Puella,'" *Poetry* 137 (March 1981): 319–20.
COLLECTED: *Puella*, 25–26; *Whole Motion*, 420–21.
REPRINTED: *Puella* (Pyracantha), 10.
VARIANTS:
1: life: all (*Puella, Whole Motion*) | life: all (*Poetry,* TS)
3: creek: territorially (*Puella, Whole Motion*) | creek: territorially (*Poetry,* TS)
20: and walk (*Puella*, TS, *Whole Motion*) |and / walk (*Poetry*)
43: house, a father, a (TS, *Puella, Whole Motion*) | house,   a father,   a (*Poetry*)
45–46: [blank line inserted] (*Poetry*)

The Lyric Beasts

FIRST PUBLICATION: *Paris Review* 23 (Spring 1981): 165–66.
COLLECTED: *Puella*, 35–36.
REPRINTED: *Puella* (Pyracantha), 18–19.
NOTES: Dickey said that this poem "is intended as a defense of illusion, and also a depiction of the essential detachment and cruelty of art, and the unearthly beauty that it may give to the human body" (Hart, 646).
VARIANTS:
6: this: is (*Puella*) | this: is (*Paris Review,* TS)

15: rarefy (*Puella*) | rarify (*Paris Review,* TS)

21: chasm-sweat, through (*Puella*) | chasm-sweat / through (*Paris Review,* TS)

26: Take (*Puella*) | take (*Paris Review*)

38: The go-devil (*Puella,* TS) | To go-devil (*Paris Review*)

48: us.   Rise (*Puella*) | us. Rise (*Paris Review,* TS)

49: Follow.   It (*Puella*) | Follow. It (*Paris Review,* TS)

Tapestry and Sail

First Publication: *Lone Star Review* 3 (July–August 1981): 4.
Collected: *Puella,* 43–44; *Whole Motion,* 427–28.
Reprinted: *Puella* (Pyracantha), 24.
Notes: On James Wright see "The Surround."
Variants:

Headnote: She imagines herself a figure upon them (TS, *Puella, Whole Motion*) | Imagining Herself as the Environment, She Speaks to James Wright at Sundown (*Lone Star*)

9: blazing.   Rigidly (*Puella, Whole Motion*) | blazing. Rigidly (*Lone Star,* TS)

The Olympian

First Publication: As "False Youth: Spring: The Olympian," *Amicus Journal* 4 (Summer 1982): 27.
Collected: As "Spring: The Olympian," *False Youth: Four Seasons,* 11–18; as "The Olympian," *Eagle,* 30–34, and *Whole Motion,* 448–52.
Notes: "I had a neighbor, a kind of neighbor, who was an Olympian, who taught mathematics at the school where my son went to junior high in Northridge, California. His name was Michael Larrabee, and he won the four hundred meters in the Tokyo Olympics. He was the oldest sprinter who ever won anything in the Olympics. . . . He never was very good in college, but he got good in his thirties by some strange means, and he won the gold in the Olympic Games. Hooray!" (Greiner, 16). Michael Denny Larrabee (1933–2003), a native of Ventura, California, won a track scholarship to the University of Southern California, but was hampered by injuries. He took a degree in geology and became a teacher of math and physics at James Madison High School in Sepulveda, California, where Chris Dickey was enrolled. At the age of thirty Larrabee developed a new training program, and in 1964 he tied the world record in the 400-meter run. At the Tokyo Olympics that year, he was in fifth place going into the final turn, but with a sudden sprint he won the gold medal. He also participated in the world-record-setting 4×400-meter relay team. He returned to teaching, ran a beverage-distribution company, and was track-and-field representative for Adidas (http://www.sports-reference.com/olympics/athletes/la/mike-larrabee-1.html [accessed February 2, 2012]). Dickey's close friend Michael Allin described an incident that may have inspired this poem: "It was a hot afternoon in 1965. Jim was wearing swimming trunks and a short-sleeved white sweatshirt with poetry emblazoned in black letters across the chest, a surprise gift from Maxine [Dickey]. Jim got to talking about his track career, which caused my friend and fellow wannabe poet Andy Wallace to remark that he had been undefeated in the 220. Jim waited through a few more beers, while Andy's remark percolated into a private challenge before

he organized the party, girls included, into a sprint competition across the backyard along the pool. Six-year-old Kevin did indeed start them off with his cap pistol and the brief run from cinderblock wall to cinderblock wall was more a beery stomping stampede than a race. Jim was by far the tallest competitor and most gloriously clad. Jim outran all the younger people except Andy, who outran him. Panting, Jim demanded, 'Let's go again!' And they all pounded back across the yard to the opposite wall. I remember the terrifying determination in Jim's face and how it seemed he wasn't going to slow down closing in on the wall; he hit the wall stopping himself with his outstretched hands and burst out laughing, panting, asking who won . . . but it was so close no one had noticed. 'Close enough!' Jim gasped" (letter to WB, February 10, 2011). "In the depiction of a fat, beer-guzzling California failed athlete's entrapment of an authentic Olympic champion into a steeplechase around the fat man's back-yard swimming pool, his involvement of the true winner of the world's gold medal in a kind of doomed Olympics in an environment of pleasure-culture where the very crows of the air are not black but gray with pollution from the freeways and the only rightful denizen is the rat. . . . 'The Olympian'—though I hope there are elements of grim humor in it—is intended as a depiction of culturally induced suicide" (*Amicus Journal* 4 [Summer 1982]: 28–29; see also *One Voice 2*, 375–76).

Dickey wrote a screenplay of Larrabee's story, "The Olympian," which may precede this poem (see Hart, 706). The copy in the Emory archive is undated.

Whether Dickey consciously tried to imitate a Pindaric victory ode in this poem, he said in 1966, "I want to get sports things into poetry. I don't think it has ever been done at all, not even by Pindar. Sports are among the most beautiful things on this earth to me" ("Things Happen," 4; Baughman, 32). On this theme see "The Sprinter at Forty," "The Sprinter's Mother," The Sprinter's Sleep," and "For the Running of the New York City Marathon." For the conviviality associated with Dickey's swimming pool, see "The Night Pool."

11: Dickey and his family lived at 8950 Balboa Boulevard while he was teaching at San Fernando Valley State College (after 1972, California State College at Northridge) in 1964–65.

14: Olympia Beer was produced from 1902 to 2003 at the Olympia Brewing Company in Olympia, Washington. Its trademark was "It's the water."

19: The steeplechase for men is usually three thousand meters with twenty-eight ordinary barriers to hurdle and seven water jumps.

26: The Sepulveda Basin Recreation Area and Dam lie to the south on Balboa Boulevard, past the Van Nuys Airport and Van Nuys Golf Course.

40: Pheidippides, a professional Athenian long-distance runner, is mentioned in Herodotus (*Histories* 105–6) as a courier sent to seek aid from the Spartans before the Battle of Marathon (490 B.C.E.). The popular myth, to which Dickey's poem refers, relates that after the battle, Pheidippides ran the 34.5 km (21.4 miles) from Marathon to Athens and having said "Nenikékamen!" (We have conquered!), expired on the spot. There is no ancient source for this story, but Robert Browning's "Pheidippides" (1879) may have inspired Baron Pierre de Coubertin (1863–1937) to found the modern Olympic Games with its marathon race.

41: "Hot gates" is a translation of Thermopylae, site of hot springs and of a narrow pass where in 480 B.C.E. Leonidas and his three-hundred Spartans made their stand against the invading Persians.

56–57: "The gray crows of Sepulveda, California, are a subtle sign of a pervasive sickness" (*Amicus Journal*, 29)

60: There was a Unimart, a discount department store, a precursor of the Walmart, specializing in groceries but selling a huge variety of items, at 8999 Balboa Boulevard, near Dickey's home. The chain closed in 1969. Cupid's Hotdog Stand on Victory Boulevard in Van Nuys, known as the "Victory Stand," was a local landmark.

67: The "Bringer of the Flame" is Prometheus.

VARIANTS:

17–18: Now . . . Champion! (TS, *Eagle, Whole Motion*) | *Now . . . Champion! (Amicus, False Youth)*

18–19: [blank line inserted] (*Amicus*)

19: me. Steeplechase. I (TS, *Eagle, Whole Motion*) | me.   Steeplechase.   I (*Amicus, False Youth*)

21: in. I (TS, *Eagle, Whole Motion*) | in.   I (*Amicus, False Youth*)

37: fury. My (TS, *Eagle, Whole Motion*) | fury.   My (*Amicus, False Youth*)

40: Athens! O (TS, *Eagle, Whole Motion*) | Athens!   O (*Amicus, False Youth*)

41: just-hurdlable (*Amicus*, TS, *False Youth, Eagle*) | just hurdlable (*Whole Motion*)

42: deck-chairs! Lounges! A (TS, *Eagle, Whole Motion*) | deck-chairs!   Lounges!   A (*Amicus, False Youth*)

43: laws! Here (TS, *Eagle, Whole Motion*) | laws!   Here (*Amicus, False Youth*)

51: play rafts (TS, *Eagle, Whole Motion*) | play-rafts (*Amicus, False Youth*)

54: wall. And (TS, *Eagle, Whole Motion*) | wall.   And (*Amicus, False Youth*)

69: set! You're (TS, *Eagle, Whole Motion*) | set!   You're (*Amicus, False Youth*)

70: everything!" James (TS, *Eagle, Whole Motion*) | everything!"   James (*Amicus, False Youth*)

71: together. We (TS, *Eagle, Whole Motion*) | together.   We (*Amicus, False Youth*)

82: mattering. I (TS, *Eagle, Whole Motion*) | mattering.   I (*Amicus, False Youth*)

96: Yes! My (TS, *Eagle, Whole Motion*) | Yes!   My (*Amicus, False Youth*)

109: no! My (TS, *Eagle, Whole Motion*) | no!   My (*Amicus, False Youth*)

114: blessèd (TS, *Eagle, Whole Motion*) | blessed (*Amicus, False Youth*)

118: glory. With (TS, *Eagle, Whole Motion*) | glory.   With (*Amicus, False Youth*)

Deborah in Mountain Sound: Bell, Glacier, Rose

FIRST PUBLICATION: In "Six Poems," *Kenyon Review,* n.s., 4 (Winter 1982): 1.
COLLECTED: *Puella,* 37.
REPRINTED: *Puella* (Pyracantha), 20.

Ray-Flowers I

FIRST PUBLICATION: In "Six Poems," *Kenyon Review,* n.s., 4 (Winter 1982) 2–3.
COLLECTED: *Puella,* 27–29.
REPRINTED: *Puella* (Pyracantha), 11–12.

NOTE:

35: "blurr" is presumably a variant of "blur" as in Coventry Patmore's "The Wedding Sermon," book 2 of *The Victories of Love* (8:19: "the still growth check and blurr / Of Contraries" (Coventry Patmore, *Poems* [London: Bell, 1909], 259). See "Summons," line 3.

VARIANTS:

3–4, 6–7, 10–11, 13–15, 18–19: [justified against center space] (*Kenyon*) | [not so justified] (*Puella*)

6: Unparalleled (*Puella*) | Unparallelled (*Kenyon*, TS)

20: unshakable (*Puella*) | unshakeable (*Kenyon*, TS)

22: crows: Come (*Puella*) | crows: Come (*Kenyon*, TS)

24: where.   Come (*Puella*) | where. Come (*Kenyon*, TS)

27–28: [blank line inserted] (*Kenyon*)

35: blurr (*Puella*, TS) | blur (*Kenyon*)

39: Elsewhere—:   pale-off (*Puella*) | Elsewhere—: pale-off (*Kenyon*, TS)

Ray-Flowers II

FIRST PUBLICATION: In "Six Poems," *Kenyon Review*, n.s., 4 (Winter 1982): 4.

COLLECTED: *Puella*, 30.

REPRINTED: *Puella* (Pyracantha), 13.

NOTES: As this poem was originally published with five others as "Six Poems," it is assumed that Dickey intended "Ray Flowers II" to be a separate poem, not the second part of "Ray-Flowers I."

VARIANTS:

5: lightness?   Is (*Puella*) | lightness? Is (*Kenyon*, TS)

16: fountains— (*Puella*, TS) | fountains: — (*Kenyon*)

Doorstep, Lightning, Waif-Dreaming

FIRST PUBLICATION: In "Six Poems," *Kenyon Review*, n.s., 4 (Winter 1982): 5.

COLLECTED: *Puella*, 38; *Whole Motion*, 425.

REPRINTED: *Puella* (Pyracantha), 21.

NOTES:

10: "spraddling," used in the sense of "sprawling"

VARIANTS:

13: time.   I (*Puella*, *Whole Motion*) | time. I (*Kenyon*, TS)

16: me: my (*Puella*, *Whole Motion*) | me: my (*Kenyon*, TS)

22: doorstep.   I (*Puella*, *Whole Motion*) | doorstep. I (*Kenyon*, TS)

Deborah in Ancient Lingerie, In Thin Oak over Creek

FIRST PUBLICATION: In "Six Poems," *Kenyon Review*, n.s., 4 (Winter 1982): 6–7.

COLLECTED: *Puella*, 21–22.

REPRINTED: *Puella* (Pyracantha), 6–7.

NOTES: On idealizing women in general and those in lingerie in particular, see "Complicity" (*Night*, 217.)

2: Dickey may invoke the description of the protagonist in Henry Fielding's *Tom Jones:* "it was the universal Opinion of all Mr. Allworthy's family, that he was certainly born to be hanged." The English proverb "He that is born to be hanged will never be drowned" is reflected in *The Tempest*, I.1.30–31: "his complexion is perfect gallows."

23: Salamanders were associated with fire by Aristotle and Pliny (*Natural History*, 10.86); Benvenuto Cellini claimed that salamanders were generated from fire when he saw one leap from a rotten log he had tossed onto a fire (see John Addington Symonds, *The Life of Benvenuto Cellini*, bk. 1, chap. 4).

VARIANTS:

20: do: a (*Puella*) | do: a (*Kenyon*, TS)

22: unparalleled (*Puella*) | unparallelled (*Kenyon*, TS)

27: do: reversal (*Puella*) | do: reversal (*Kenyon*, TS)

28: every day (*Puella*) | everyday (*Kenyon*, TS)

40: unparalleled (*Puella*) | unparallelled (*Kenyon*, TS)

The Lode

FIRST PUBLICATION: In "Six Poems," *Kenyon Review*, n.s., 4 (Winter 1982): 7–8.

COLLECTED: *Puella*, 41–42.

REPRINTED: *Puella* (Pyracantha), 23.

VARIANTS:

24: impulse.   There (*Puella*) | impulse. There (*Kenyon*, TS)

36: wanderer: every (*Puella*) | wanderer: every (*Kenyon*, TS)

39: breath.   Keep (*Puella*) | breath. Keep (*Kenyon*, TS)

Deborah and Deirdre as Drunk Bridesmaids
Foot-Racing at Daybreak

FIRST PUBLICATION: *Graham House Review*, no. 6 (Spring 1982): 5–6.

COLLECTED: *Puella*, 17–18.

REPRINTED: *Dickey Reader*, 123–24; *Puella* (Pyracantha), 4.

NOTES: Deirdre Elaine Dodson (b. 1953) is the younger sister of Dickey's second wife, Deborah. Dickey described the poem as "simply an evocation of the craziness of adolescence, and is just a depiction of two girls too full of sap and energy to go to sleep, blasting out of the house and running down a dirt road all out, in long gowns" (*Crux*, 409).

VARIANTS:

22: firebush [corrected by editor] | firebrush (*Graham, Puella*)

Summons

FIRST PUBLICATION: *Graham House Review*, no. 6 (Spring 1982): 7–8.

COLLECTED: *Puella*, 47–48.

REPRINTED: Broadside (Columbia, S.C.: Bruccoli Clark Layman, 1988), with revisions by Dickey; *Carolina Lifestyle*, May 1982, 49; *Puella* (Pyracantha), 26–27.

NOTES: Dickey described this poem as "a kind of spell which builds up image by image, and is meant to be spoken by a young girl to her first lover, somewhere out there in humanity with God knows what characteristics or what background; it is all right with the girl casting the spell: whoever comes will be all right, whatever he may be like: it will be him. The accumulative structure, where a line is added to each stanza, is also supposed to bear a parallel to imaginative process, generally, and to the mental associations that go to making up the composition of poetry. One thing calls forth another, and the process is endless, and should be" (*Crux*, 409).

1: See "The Rib," line 1.

3: For "blurr" see "Ray-Flowers I," line 35.

VARIANTS:

3: blurr (TS, *Puella*, broadside) | blur (*Graham*)

6: Sought (broadside) | Hanged (*Graham*, TS, *Puella*)

10–14 [added to broadside; see *One Voice 2*, 388]

34: unparalleled (*Puella*) | unparallelled (*Graham*, TS, broadside)

51: ice-dreams (*Puella*, broadside) | ice dreams (*Graham*, TS)

56: *invention* (*Graham*, TS, *Puella*) | *on-coming // invention // ongoing* (broadside)

Lakes of Värmland

FIRST PUBLICATION: *Värmland*, 5 (published December 1982).

COLLECTED: In "James Dickey with Others: Five Poems," *American Poetry Review* 12 (March/April 1983): 3; *Eagle*, 51; *Whole Motion*, 465.

NOTES: Dickey's library contained *Il n'y a pas de paradis* (Paris: Gallimard, 1967) by André Frénaud (1907–1993), "who seems to have—and let no one tell you this is not important—a personality somewhat like I conceive my own to be" (*Crux*, 284, see also 359). "Lacs du Värmland" appears on pages 93–94. Värmland is a *landskap* (province) of Sweden, set midway on the western border with Norway. It is known for its many lakes, ponds, and rivers; its largest lake is Vänern. Frénaud added a note that, according to a Swedish legend, the weaponry of the Caroline infantry of Charles XII (1682–1718), men who preferred to fight with swords and bayonets, is buried in the lakes of Värmland. Frénaud wrote this poem in 1939, two weeks before the beginning of World War II. The botanical name for bilberry is *Vaccinium myrtillus*.

VARIANTS:

[Title appears in regular type below tag line in *Värmland*.]

6: O (*Eagle*, *Whole Motion*) | o (TS, *Värmland*, *American Poetry Review*)

6: weapons, (TS, *Värmland*, *American Poetry Review*, *Eagle*) | weapons (*Whole Motion* [typo])

Form

FIRST PUBLICATION: *Värmland*, 6.

COLLECTED: *Eagle*, 52–53; *Whole Motion*, 465–66.

REPRINTED: *Ploughshares* 9 (Spring 1983): 16–17.
NOTES: Both parts are a version of André Frénaud's "Viens dans mon lit," from *Il n' y a pas Paradis* (Paris: Gallimard, 1967), 22. Dickey sent "Invitation," a version of part 2, to Robert Bly in 1962 for publication in the *Sixties,* but it was never published (*Crux,* 184).

13: "Carrara-piles" refers to the debris from mining Carrara marble in the Massa Carrara area of Tuscany, which is carried off and deposited in piles (*ravaneti*) that are landmarks of the Apuanian Alps.

VARIANTS:

7: booming: cliff-shudder   child (*Eagle, Whole Motion*) | booming: cliff-shudder child (TS, *Värmland, Ploughshares*)

10: ice-junk: here (*Eagle, Whole Motion*) | ice-junk: here (TS, *Värmland, Ploughshares*)

23: discovery: that (*Eagle, Whole Motion*) | discovery: that (TS, *Värmland, Ploughshares*)

Heads

FIRST PUBLICATION: *Värmland,* 7–8.

COLLECTED: In "James Dickey with Others: Five Poems," *American Poetry Review* 12 (March/April 1983): 3; *Eagle,* 54–55; *Whole Motion,* 466–67.

NOTES: Lucien Becker (1911–1984) said of his *Plein amour* (1954) that "in this collection woman and the outside world merge into one." Dickey was especially fond of Becker, whom he called "one of the best French poets of his generation" ("Lightnings or Visuals," *South Atlantic Review* 57 [January 1992]: 5; also in *James Dickey Newsletter* 8 [Spring 1992]: 4–5; *Crux,* 138, 359, 374). See "The Eagle's Mile," lines 12–13.

VARIANTS:

[All lines flush left] (TS, *Värmland, American Poetry Review*)

9: wellsprings (*Eagle, Whole Motion*) | well-springs (TS, *Värmland, American Poetry Review*)

Poem [c]

FIRST PUBLICATION: As "For Having Left the Birds," *Värmland,* 9–11.

COLLECTED: *Eagle,* 61–62; *Whole Motion,* 470–72.

NOTES: Dickey's library contained *Hibernales* (Paris: Gallimard, 1958) by Roland Bouhéret (1930–1995). "Pour avoir laissé les oiseaux," written in August 1953, is on pages 11–12. At line 13 Bouhéret described a dead "Jean," for whom Dickey substituted at line 12 the name of his father, Gene. Eugene Dickey died on March 12, 1974, not July, and was not a runner.

VARIANTS:

Headnote: through a French poet, Roland Bouhéret, and my running father (TS, *Eagle, Whole Motion*) | with Roland Bouhéret (*Värmland*)

15: Ten (TS, *Eagle, Whole Motion*) | Two (*Värmland*)

18: crock, (TS, *Eagle, Whole Motion*) | crock (*Värmland*)

37: advancing / / / / / / 2 (*Värmland*)

50–51: [blank line inserted] (*Värmland*)

54: singled and in-line (TS, *Eagle, Whole Motion*) | in-line and singled (*Värmland*)
57: grassblades (*Eagle, Whole Motion*) | grass-blades (TS, *Värmland*)

Attempted Departure

First Publication: *Värmland,* 12.

Collected: In "James Dickey with Others: Five Poems," *American Poetry Review* 12 (March/April 1983): 3; *Eagle,* 60; *Whole Motion,* 470.

Notes: "with André du Bouchet" (1924–2001). This poem derives from the latter portion of du Bouchet's poem "Sur le pas" (On the Threshold) in the volume *Dans la chaleur vacante* (Paris: Mercure de France, 1961), 87–93. The part related to Dickey's poem begins on page 91: "Je reviens, / sans être sorti, . . . L'air qui s'empare des lointains nous laisse vivants derrière lui," which may be translated as "I come back without having left. . . . The air that takes hold of faraway things, leaves us, the living, behind."

Crystal

First Publication: *Clockwatch Review* 2, no. 1 (1983): 16.

Notes: This poem is a "re-write" of Vicente Aleixandre's "Blancura," on page 283 in Dickey's copy of *Poesias completas* (Madrid: Aguilar, 1960). Aleixandre's poem originally appeared in his *Espadas como Labios* (1930–31) and was translated by Barnstone and Garrison in *Bird of Paper,* 20.

For a Time and Place

First Publication: Broadside (Columbia, S.C.: Bruccoli Clark, [January 12] 1983).

Collected: *Eagle,* 38–39; *Whole Motion,* 454–56.

Notes: Richard Wilson Riley (b. 1933) was governor of South Carolina (1979–87) and U.S. Secretary of Education (1993–2000). David Broder of the *Washington Post* called Riley one of the "most decent and honorable people in public life." The poem, however, is not about Riley but rather about the joys of living in the state of South Carolina. See Dickey's essay "The Starry Place Between the Antlers" (*Night,* 19–25).

Variants:

Headnote: A South Carolina inauguration of Richard Riley as governor (*Eagle, Whole Motion*) | —a South Carolina inauguration: Richard Riley as governor— (TS) | Commemorating the Inauguration of Richard W. Riley to his Second Term as Governor of South Carolina 12 January 1983 (broadside)

44: barreling (TS, *Eagle, Whole Motion*) | barrelling (broadside)
54: eelgrass (*Eagle, Whole Motion*) | eel-grass (TS, broadside)

Craters

First Publication: In "James Dickey with Others: Five Poems," *American Poetry Review* 12 (March/April 1983): 4.

COLLECTED: *Night,* 14–15; *Eagle,* 58–59; *Whole Motion,* 469–70.

NOTES: In Dickey's library was *Haut Mal. Collections Métamorphoses* (Paris: Gallimard, 1943) by Michel Leiris (1901–1990). Dickey's "Craters" was taken from "Chansons" on pages 32–33. In 1955 Dickey called Leiris "one of the best poets (an <u>ex</u>-surrealist) I have read over here [in Paris]" (*Crux,* 88). For Dickey's translation of another Leiris poem, see *Crux,* 88–89.

VARIANTS:

1: ongoing (*Eagle, Whole Motion*) | on-going (TS, *American Poetry Review, Night*)

2: wé (*Night, Eagle, Whole Motion*) | we (TS, *American Poetry Review*)

11: pasture (TS, *American Poetry Review, Night, Eagle*) | pastures (*Whole Motion*)

23: Pompeian (*Eagle, Whole Motion*) | Pompeiian (TS, *American Poetry Review, Night*)

26–27: [blank line inserted] (TS, *American Poetry Review, Night,*)

33: ín (*Night*) | iń (*Eagle, Whole Motion*) | in (TS, *American Poetry Review*)

Farmers: A Fragment

FIRST PUBLICATION: In "James Dickey with Others: Five Poems," *American Poetry Review* 12 (March/April 1983): 4.

COLLECTED: *Night,* 15–17; *Eagle,* 56–57; *Whole Motion,* 467–69.

NOTES: In Frénaud's *Il n'y a pas de paradis* (Paris: Gallimard, 1967), which includes "Les Paysans" (1949) on pages 73–79. Dickey's poem is a somewhat close translation of the first 39 lines of Frénaud's 151-line poem, though Dickey made some additions of his own (6–7: Even . . . up-toss; 10: To the grave; 15–16: as . . . well; 29: Slogger; 31: Less. . . real; 36–37: that . . . me; 44–48: For . . . again—). Dickey translated "Les Paysans" as early as 1960 (*Striking,* 178–79). He wrote James Wright on August 10, 1960, that while his son Christopher was in the hospital for a hernia operation, Dickey "spent about a week, . . . sitting with him and translating André Frénaud's long poem <u>Les Paysans</u>, which has some marvelous stuff in it." In the letter Dickey included a version of lines 7–9 (*One Voice 1,* 354).

Additions by Dickey:

15: Dickey's poem "The Underground Stream" dates from 1960, when he was translating "Les Paysans."

VARIANTS:

Heading: a fragment / with André Frénaud (*Eagle, Whole Motion*) | with André Frénaud / (a fragment) (*American Poetry Review*) | a fragment / (with André Frénaud) (*Night*) | –a fragment– / (with André Frénaud) (TS)

25: that (*Eagle, Whole Motion*) | which (TS, *American Poetry Review, Night*)

28: earth: (TS, *American Poetry Review, Eagle, Night*) | earth. (*Whole Motion*)

40: heartsick (*Eagle, Whole Motion*) | heart-sick (TS, *American Poetry Review, Night*)

43: that (*Night, Eagle, Whole Motion*) | which (TS, *American Poetry Review*)

52–54: *the furs . . . seed . . .* (TS, *Night, Eagle, Whole Motion*) | the furs. . .seed. . . (*American Poetry Review*)

To Be Done in Winter

First Publication: As "To Be Done in Winter by Those Surviving Truman Capote," *Dictionary of Literary Biography Yearbook 1984,* edited by Jean W. Ross (Detroit: Gale Research, 1984), 171.
Collected: As "To Be Done in Winter," *Eagle,* 44; *Whole Motion,* 459.
Reprinted: As "To Be Done in Winter by Those Surviving Truman Capote," in Dickey's Commemorative Tribute, "Truman Capote, 1924–1984," *Proceedings of the American Academy and Institute of Arts and Letters,* ser. 2, no. 35 (1984): 75; "Proceedings: Truman Capote," *Paris Review* 97 (Fall 1985): 190.
Notes: Dickey had no particular friendship with Capote (1924–1984), but both were southerners, had extraordinary memories, were identified with the *New Yorker,* had each written one blockbuster novel, and then had become victimized by their attraction to celebrity, alcohol, and, in Capote's case, drugs. "I like the idea of a sort of offbeat writer, who can command that sort of attention from the public and the press. But who, all in all, is very good too—who is a diligent craftsman and true to his gift when he chooses to exercise it" (*New York Times,* August 26, 1981, 42). Both men had little control over the destructive behavior their addictions caused. "It would be foolish to deny the International-Café-Society, jet-set, Beautiful-People, name-dropping Capote, or to downplay this aspect of his life. If we don't include it, we are not really talking about the person who existed . . . to wear a white sequined mask at one's own ball at the Plaza *and* to have written 'The Headless Hawk,' too, the real and private accomplishment underlying the publicity, the money and the pleasure! . . . This small childlike individual, this self-styled, self-made, self-taught country boy. . . . The sure-handed crystal-making detachment, the integrity of concentration, the craft of the artist by means of which the intently human thing is caught, Truman Capote had, and not just at certain times but at all times" (*Proceedings of the American Academy,* 69, 70–71, 72, 74; see also "Entering Scott's Night").
Variants:
[Not all lines are centered in TS.]

World

First Publication: In "Three Poems Improvised from Lines of Vicente Aleixandre (acknowledging the translation of Willis Barnstone and David Garrison)," *Kentucky Poetry Review* 20 (Fall 1984): 3–4.
Notes: Dickey's poem is a version of Aleixandre's "Mundo Inhumano," *Poesias Completas* (Madrid: Aguilar, 1960), 449–50; translated as "Inhuman World," *Bird of Paper,* 26–27.

Earth

First Publication: In "Three Poems Improvised from Lines of Vicente Aleixandre (acknowledging the translation of Willis Barnstone and David Garrison)," *Kentucky Poetry Review,* 20 (Fall 1984): 4.
Collected: With "Air" and "Sea" as "Immortals," *Eagle,* 11; *Whole Motion,* 437.
Notes: Dickey's poem is a version of Vicente Aleixandre's "La Tierra," from p. 536 in Dickey's copy of *Poésias completes* (Madrid: Aguilar, 1960), translated by Barnstone and Garrison in *Bird*

of Paper, 36. Aleixandre grouped poems translated by Dickey as "Earth," "Air," "Sea," "Sand," and "Sun" together as "Los Inmortales" in his *Sombra del Paraíso* (1944). Dickey's translations of "Sand" and "Sun" are grouped as "Two Women." In 1984 Dickey contemplated publishing an entire volume of these "re-writes" as *Immortals* (*One Voice 2*, 400–401).

VARIANTS:

3: in (TS, *Eagle, Whole Motion*) | in the (*Kentucky*)

6: infinite (TS, *Eagle, Whole Motion*) | indefinite (*Kentucky*)

Sea

FIRST PUBLICATION: In "Three Poems Improvised from Lines of Vicente Aleixandre (acknowledging the translation of Willis Barnstone and David Garrison)," *Kentucky Poetry Review* 20 (Fall 1984): 4.

COLLECTED: With "Earth" and "Air" as "Immortals," *Eagle*, 13; *Whole Motion*, 437.

REPRINTED: "Sea," in "James Dickey: Ten Poems," *American Poetry Review* 17 (March/April 1988): 38. *Best Verse: Ten Years of Poetry* 12, no. 2 (1995): 40.

NOTES: A version of Vicente Aleixandre's "El Mar," on page 539 of Dickey's copy of *Poésias completas* (Madrid: Aguilar, 1960), originally in Aleixandre's *Sombra del Paraíso* (1944) and translated by Barnstone and Garrison in *Bird of Paper*, 38. On the title "The Immortals," see "Earth."

Air

FIRST PUBLICATION: *Verse* (Citadel, Charleston, S.C.) 2 (1985): 3.

COLLECTED: With "Earth" and "Sea" as "Immortals," *Eagle*, 12; *Whole Motion*, 437.

NOTES: A version of Vicente Aleixandre's "El Aire," on page 538 of Dickey's copy of *Poésias completas* (Madrid: Aguilar, 1960), originally in Aleixandre's *Sombra del Paraíso* (1944) and translated by Barnstone and Garrison in *Bird of Paper*, 39. On the title "The Immortals," see "Earth."

VARIANTS:

1: sea— (*Eagle, Whole Motion*)| sea, (*Verse*)

2: thát (TS, *Eagle*) | that (*Verse, Whole Motion*)

7: keep (*Eagle, Whole Motion*) | keep, (TS, *Verse*)

Cobra

FIRST PUBLICATION: *New York Quarterly,* no. 27 (Summer 1985): 26.

NOTES: Dickey appended this note to the poem in *New York Quarterly:* "Though in no sense a translation, 'COBRA' takes off from an original by Vicente Aleixandre, and I acknowledge Willis Barnstone's and David Garrison's work; they did some straight translations of Aleixandre a few years ago." Dickey owned a copy of *Poésias completas de Vicente Aleixandre* (Madrid: Aguilar, 1960). "Cobra" is on pages 387–88; Barnstone and Garrison's translation is in *Bird of Paper* (24–25). On Dickey and snakes, see "Blowgun and Rattlesnake."

Spring-Shock

First Publication: *Paris Review* 28 (Summer/Fall 1986): 66–67.
Collected: *Eagle*, 23–24; *Whole Motion*, 443–44.
Reprinted: *Harper's* 274 (February 1987): 27.
Notes: See "The Birthday Dream," Dickey's fortieth-birthday poem.
Variants:

3: [no blank line following] (TS, *Paris Review*)
10: dreamlike but (*Eagle, Whole Motion*) | dream-like / But (TS, *Paris Review*)
18: shot (TS, *Eagle, Whole Motion*) | show (*Paris Review*)
23: Ín [corrected by editor] | Iń (TS, *Eagle, Whole Motion*) | In (*Paris Review*)
29: warehouses (*Eagle, Whole Motion*) | warehouses, (TS, *Paris Review*)

Two Women

First Publication: Part I as "Sand," *Clockwatch Review* 2, no. 1 (1983): 15; with Part II in "From the Low Country: Five Poems by James Dickey," *Southern Magazine* 1 (January 1987): 47.
Collected: *Eagle*, 9–10; *Whole Motion*, 436.
Notes:

Tag line: On Cumberland Island see "The Shark's Parlor," line 1.
Part I derives from Vicente Aleixandre's "Siempre" on page 256 in Dickey's copy of *Poesias completas* (Madrid: Aguilar, 1960). It originally appeared in Aleixandre's *Espadas como Labios* (1930–31) and was translated by Willis Barnstone in *Bird of Paper*, 18. Part II derives from Aleixandre's "El sol" on page 534 in Dickey's copy of *Poesias completas,* originally in *Espadas como Labios* (1930–31) and translated by Willis Barnstone in *Bird of Paper*, 34, as "Sun."
Variants:

Tag line: —*Cumberland Island*— [editor] | [no tag line] (*Eagle, Whole Motion*) | —*Cumberland Island* (*Southern*) | homage, Vicente Aleixandre / (and acknowledging translations / by Willis Barnstone and David Garrison) (*Clockwatch*)
Heading 1: I (*Eagle, Whole Motion*) | Woman I (*Southern*)
3: Sockets, sword-flats (TS, *Southern, Eagle, Whole Motion*) | Swords-flats, sockets (*Clockwatch*)
4: In (TS, *Southern, Eagle*) | On (*Whole Motion*)
4: sand, (TS, *Southern, Eagle, Whole Motion*) | sand (*Clockwatch*)
Heading 2: II (*Eagle, Whole Motion*) | Woman II (*Southern*)
20: here (*Eagle, Whole Motion*) | there (Southern) ["there" changed to "here" by hand in TS]

Daybreak

First Publication: "From the Low Country: Five Poems by James Dickey," *Southern Magazine* 1 (January 1987): 48.
Collected: *Eagle*, 8; *Whole Motion*, 435.
Notes: A jetty extends off the north end of Pawleys Island, South Carolina, near Dickey's vacation condo in Litchfield.

Tag line: —Pawley's Island— [editor] | [no tag line] (*Eagle, Whole Motion*) | —*Pawley's Jetty*
  (Southern)

2: difference (TS, *Southern, Eagle*) | different (*Whole Motion* [typo])

8: sounds (*Eagle, Whole Motion*) | sounds, (TS, *Southern*)

20: skylight, (*Eagle, Whole Motion*) | skylight (TS, *Southern*)

Vessels

FIRST PUBLICATION: In "From the Low Country: Five Poems by James Dickey," *Southern Maga-zine* 1 (January 1987): 48.

COLLECTED: *Eagle,* 40; *Whole Motion,* 456.

REPRINTED: *Los Angeles Times Book Review,* June 14, 1992, 6.

NOTES: Waccamaw Road is named for the Indian tribe native to Pawleys Island, South Carolina; the Waccamaw Trail runs along the east bank of the Waccamaw River in Pawleys Island.

11: On Tom Dickey, see "The Shark at the Window."

VARIANTS:

Tag line: —the Waccamaw Road— [editor] | [no tag line] (*Eagle, Whole Motion*) | —*the Wac-camaw Road (Southern)*

4: thén (TS, *Eagle, Whole Motion*) | then (*Southern*)

Meadow Bridge

FIRST PUBLICATION: As "Wetlands Bridge," in "From the Low Country: Five Poems by James Dickey," *Southern Magazine* 1 (January 1987): 49.

COLLECTED: *Eagle,* 42; *Whole Motion,* 457–58.

NOTES: This poem is a version of Vicente Aleixandre's "Epitafio," translated as "Epitaph" by Barn-stone and Garrison in *Bird of Paper,* 41. The bridges to Pawleys Island across the Waccamaw River are simply known as the North and South Causeways.

2: "Meditation on Being" refers to the work of Descartes and the French phenomenologists (and possibly Heidegger): "You just feel about Heidegger and his *dasein* and all of that business, that it's just philosophical jargon" (*NYQ* interview, 26; *Night,* 303).

VARIANTS:

10: crosscut (*Eagle, Whole Motion*) | cross-cut (TS, *Southern*)

Tomb Stone

FIRST PUBLICATION: In "From the Low Country: Five Poems by James Dickey," *Southern Maga-zine* 1 (January 1987): 49.

COLLECTED: *Eagle,* 43; *Whole Motion,* 458.

NOTES: Dickey's first wife, Maxine Webster Syerson (1926–1976), is buried in the churchyard of All Saints Waccamaw Episcopal Church (1739) and Cemetery Churchyard in Pawleys Island, South Carolina, as was her husband in 1997. See "The Drift-Spell."

4: "'Elegy': the living are 'the sleepers who do not fall' or 'the sleepers not yet fallen'" (*Striking*, 216).

17–19: A trope found in Martial 5.34 on the death of a child, the last lines "Let no harsh sod cover her tender bones, and press not heavy on her, earth; she pressed upon you only lightly." This was imitated by Oscar Wilde in his "Requiescat," an elegy for his sister, which begins: "Tread lightly, she is near / Under the snow, / Speak gently, she can hear / The daisies grow."

Variants:

Tag line: [no tag line] (*Eagle, Whole Motion*) | —*All Saints Churchyard* (*Southern*)

16: thém (*Whole Motion*) | them (*Southern*) | thém (TS, *Eagle*)

17: stand: Don't (TS, *Eagle, Whole Motion*) | stand: don't (*Southern*)

Eagles

First Publication: *American Poetry Review* 16 (March/April 1987): 56.

Collected: *Eagle*, 3–4; *Whole Motion*, 431–32.

Reprinted: *Body Electric*, 132–34; *Visions Decade* 30 (1989): 9–10.

Notes: A "re-write" of Vicente Aleixandre's "Las águilas."

Variants:

19: áll (*American Poetry Review*) | aĺl (TS, *Eagle*) | all (*Whole Motion*)

33–34: [blank line inserted] (*American Poetry Review*)

37–38: [no blank line inserted] (TS, *American Poetry Review*)

39: thís (*Eagle, Whole Motion*) | this (TS, *American Poetry Review*)

The Little More

First Publication: *Poetry* 150 (July 1987): 208–10.

Collected: *Eagle*, 35–37; *Whole Motion* 452–44.

Notes: JBTD is James Bayard Tuckerman Dickey (b. 1970), the only child of Christopher Dickey (see "A Child in Armor"), Dickey's older son, and his first wife, Susan Tuckerman (see "False Youth: Autumn: Clothes of the Age"). Dickey's children's poem "Tucky the Hunter" (1978) was written for him.

Variants:

16–17: [blank line inserted] (*Poetry*)

18: Thís (TS, *Poetry, Eagle*) | This (*Whole Motion*)

27–28: [blank line inserted] (TS, *Poetry*)

30–31: [no blank line inserted] (TS, *Poetry*)

Gila Bend

First Publication: *Poetry* 151 (October–November 1987): 40.

Collected: *Eagle*, 5; *Whole Motion*, 432–33.

NOTES: Gila Bend, Arizona, is the home of Luke Air Force Base, founded in 1941 and known as the "Home of the Fighter Pilot," for graduating more than twelve thousand fighter pilots during World War II. Dickey was never stationed at Gila Bend.

VARIANTS:

12: hím (*Poetry*, TS, *Eagle*) | him (*Whole Motion*)

The Six

FIRST PUBLICATION: *Poetry* 151 (October–November 1987): 41.
COLLECTED: *Eagle*, 20–21; *Whole Motion*, 441–42.
NOTES: A "re-write" of Vicente Aleixandre's "Las seis."
VARIANTS:

8: Breastbone (*Eagle, Whole Motion*) | Breast-bone (TS, *Poetry*)
26: The (*Eagle, Whole Motion*) | the (TS, *Poetry*)

Weeds

FIRST PUBLICATION: In "James Dickey: Ten Poems," *American Poetry Review* 17 (March/April 1988): 36.
COLLECTED: *Eagle*, 22; *Whole Motion*, 442–43.
REPRINTED: *Body Electric*, 134.

The One

FIRST PUBLICATION: In "James Dickey: Ten Poems," *American Poetry Review* 17 (March/April 1988): 36.
COLLECTED: *Eagle*, 17; *Whole Motion* 439–40.
REPRINTED: *Body Electric*, 135.
NOTES: A "re-write" of Vicente Aleixandre's "Las una."
VARIANTS:

6: color one (TS, *Eagle, Whole Motion*)| color One (*American Poetry Review*)

The Three

FIRST PUBLICATION: In "James Dickey: Ten Poems," *American Poetry Review* 17 (March/April 1988): 36.
COLLECTED: *Eagle*, 18–19; *Whole Motion*, 440–41.
REPRINTED: *Body Electric*, 135–36.
NOTES: A "re-write" of Vicente Aleixandre's "Las tres."

7: Dickey invented a verb form of Emerson's term "oversoul," which refers to the spiritual being in which human nature is perfected.
31: see "Circuit," line 26.

6: now (*Eagle, Whole Motion*) | Now (TS, *American Poetry Review*)

23: were (*Eagle, Whole Motion*) | were, (TS, *American Poetry Review*)

29: [no blank line inserted] (*Eagle, Whole Motion*)

Basics

First Publication: In "James Dickey: Ten Poems," *American Poetry Review* 17 (March/April 1988): 37.

Collected: With "III. Word" added, in *Eagle*, 64–66; *Whole Motion*, 473–75.

Reprinted: *Body Electric*, 136–38.

Notes: "Word" is a "re-write" of Vicente Aleixandre's "La Palabra," on page 535 in Dickey's copy of *Poésias completas* (Madrid: Aguilar, 1960), translated by Barnstone and Garrison in *Bird of Paper*, 35.

56: An echo of A. E. Housman, "Eight O'Clock" (lines 7– 8): "And then the clock collected in the tower / Its strength, and struck."

57: According to Dickey, "the last line of 'Word' is not from Aleixandre but from the notebooks of William Blake" (*One Voice 2*, 398). On page 67 of his manuscript notebook, Blake wrote "23 May 1810, found the Word Golden."

Variants:

4: spellbinder's (*Eagle, Whole Motion*) | spell-binder's (TS, *American Poetry Review*)

14: iń (*Eagle, Whole Motion*) | in (TS, *American Poetry Review*)

33: it: the (*American Poetry Review, Eagle, Whole Motion*) | it: the (TS)

Night Bird

First Publication: In "James Dickey: Ten Poems," *American Poetry Review* 17 (March/April 1988): 37.

Collected: *Eagle*, 7; *Whole Motion*, 434–45.

Reprinted: *Wesleyan Tradition*, 64.

Notes: On blindness, see "Reading Genesis to a Blind Child."

Sleepers

First Publication: In "James Dickey: Ten Poems," *American Poetry Review* 17 (March/April 1988): 37.

Collected: *Eagle*, 41; *Whole Motion*, 456–57.

Notes: Compare "Tomb Stone" and "'Elegy': the living are 'the sleepers who do not fall' or 'the sleepers not yet fallen'" (*Striking*, 216).

Snow Thickets

First Publication: In "James Dickey: Ten Poems," *American Poetry Review* 17 (March/April 1988): 38.

Collected: *Eagle*, 47; *Whole Motion*, 461.

Variants:

3: canceling (*Eagle, Whole Motion*) | cancelling (TS, *American Poetry Review*)

7–8: [blank line inserted] (TS, *American Poetry Review*)

15: cutthroat (*Eagle, Whole Motion*) | cut-throat (TS, *American Poetry Review*)

Expanses

First Publication: In "James Dickey: Ten Poems," *American Poetry Review* 17 (March/April 1988) 38.

Collected: *Eagle*, 48; *Whole Motion*, 461–62.

Variants:

18: trouble-free (*Eagle, Whole Motion*) | troublefree (TS, *American Poetry Review*)

Moon Flock

First Publication: In "James Dickey: Ten Poems," *American Poetry Review* 17 (March/April 1988): 38.

Collected: *Eagle*, 45–46; *Whole Motion*, 459–60.

Notes: "I am much attracted to what I am tempted to call 'word-radiance.' And find myself very often both fascinated by single words and by a possible context in which and by which they might, to use [Dylan] Thomas's phrase, be 'set.' There are words that have a this special aura for everyone, and I have two main ones which, for me, are so full of luminosity that I have never been able to conquer my fear of using them, lest it be misuse. These are a verb and a noun: 'swerve' and 'flock.'" ("Lightnings, or *Visuals*," *South Atlantic Review* 57 [January 1992]. 9, also in *James Dickey Newsletter* 8 [Spring 1992]: 9). The word "flock" or "flocking" occurs in "To Be Edward Thomas" (line 1), "Drinking from a Helmet" (line 115), "Mexican Valley" (line 12), "For the Running of the New York City Marathon" (line 5), "From Time" (line 10), "Tapestry and Sail" (line 27), "The Three" (line 21); "swerve" occurs only in "Lord in the Air" (line 18).

Variants:

3: ploughblade (*Eagle, Whole Motion*) | plough-blade (TS, *American Poetry Review*)

9: cannot (*Eagle, Whole Motion*) | can not (TS, *American Poetry Review*)

15: Overhead: overhead (TS, *Eagle, Whole Motion*) | Overhead: overhead (*American Poetry Review*)

16: [line right of center] (TS, *Eagle*) | [line centered] (*American Poetry Review*) | [line flush right] (*Whole Motion*)

23–24: [blank line inserted] (*American Poetry Review*)

30: [line flush left] (TS, *American Poetry Review*)

37: nothing: at (*Eagle, Whole Motion*) | nothing: at (*American Poetry Review*)

Daughter

First Publication: *Southpoint* 1 (November 1989): 88.
Collected: *Eagle*, 28–29; *Whole Motion.* 446–48.
Notes: Dickey's daughter, Bronwen Elaine, was born May 17, 1981 at 8:38 A.M. Dickey's friend and literary executor, Matthew J. Bruccoli (1931–2008), took him to the hospital and waited with him through the delivery. With them in the waiting room was a construction worker (Hart, 626–27).
58–9: See "Show Us the Sea," line 1. "Real god is what causes everything to exist, like the laws of motion. The humanization of God in the Bible I find absurd" (Suarez, 122).
Variants:
9: blessed (TS, *Eagle, Whole Motion*) | blessèd (*Southpoint*)
23: around (*Eagle, Whole Motion*) | around, (TS, *Southpoint*)
46–47: [blank line inserted] (*Southpoint*)

Circuit

First Publication: *Eagle*, 6.
Collected: *Whole Motion*, 433–44.
Notes: A "re-write" of Vicente Aleixandre's "Circuito."
26: See "The Three," line 31.
Variants:
6: ["(course)" added over "minds" by Dickey's hand in TS]

To the Butterflies

First Publication: *Eagle*, 14–16.
Collected: *Whole Motion*, 438–39.
Notes: Written for his son Christopher Dickey ("A Child in Armor") after reading his account of life among Nicaraguan rebels, *With the Contras* (1985): "It is maybe pretty slight, but at any rate I tried to get something said about the heat of the climate down there, which you so graphically and memorably describe, and also about the inter-connection between some of the good and bad elements of experience; in other words, if it weren't for the heat and humidity we wouldn't have the butterflies—or, a possible parallel with the butterflies—the colorful way the people dress down there" (*Crux,* 465).
21–24: See *Striking* (34): "Something you wish you could see, like a frozen tropic."
Variants:
2: To (TS, *Eagle*) | to (*Whole Motion* [typo])

Show Us the Sea

First Publication: *Partisan Review* 57 (Summer 1990): 428.
Notes:
1: "Real God, roll": compare "Daughter," lines 58–59. "I'm writing a long poem now, *Real God, Roll,* where a father watches his son pumping iron and exercising on the beach, and he feels it's all

part of the whole thing, or the real god. The waves coming in, his death, his father's death, the son's physique are all part of the whole thing. The real god is what causes everything to exist, like the laws of motion. The humanization of God in the Bible I find absurd" (Suarez, 122).

The Drift-Spell

First Publication: In *James Dickey at 70: A Tribute, September 17–November 29, 1993, An Exhibition at the Thomas Cooper Library, University of South Carolina, Columbia, South Carolina* (Columbia, S.C.: Thomas Cooper Library, 1993), 8–9.

Reprinted: *Princeton University Library Chronicle* 55 (Spring 1994): 457; *Atlanta* 35 (August 1995): 57.

Notes: Written after a visit with son Kevin ("The Signs," "Show Us the Sea") to the grave of the poet's first wife, Maxine (*Atlanta* [August 1995]: 57) as "a fragment from a much larger effort called 'Two Poems on the Survival of the Male Body'" (*One Voice 2*, 490, 531–32; see *Summer*, 262–63). On Maxine Dickey's gravesite, see notes to "Tomb Stone" above.

6: "stogged," meaning stuck.

23–29: A small owl is engraved in the center of Maxine Dickey's gravestone in the graveyard at All Saints Waccamaw Episcopal Church in Pawleys Island, South Carolina.

Variants:

21: swaying moss (*James Dickey at 70, Princeton*) | swaying-moss (*Atlanta*)

Last Hours

First Publication: *Southern Review* 30 (Autumn 1994): 693–98.

Notes: As an expert in Civil War artillery (lines 18–19) who had a major collection of projectile ordnance (see "Hunting Civil War Relics at Nimblewill Creek"), the poet's brother Tom Dickey was "fascinated by the Civil War and little else" (*Sorties*, 37). "He is a Civil War relic hunter: that is to say, a *maniac*" (*Night*, 186). As Tom lay dying in Atlanta of liver cancer, Dickey brought him a copy of Shelby Foote's three-volume *The Civil War: A Narrative* (1958–74), but Tom's daughter Dorian Marston Dickey (b. 1953) brought him a copy of *The Stranger beside Me* by Ann Rule (New York: Norton, 1980), about the charming serial killer Ted Bundy (1946–1989), who coincidentally had long been a subject of fascination for James Dickey. Bundy's later murders took place near the campus of Florida State University in Tallahassee. Dickey said of this poem, "I want to envision the death-bed situation in which the dying father, in his delirium, sees his own daughter as the murderer's victim" (*One Voice 2*, 490–91). Tom died on December 8, 1987.

9, 56, 65, 77, 93: Compare "Look, through the pines what line comes on? / Longstreet slants through the hauntedness?" (Herman Melville, "Armies of the Wilderness," ii.87–88, in *Battle-Pieces and Aspects of the War* [1866]). On Dickey and Melville, see "Reincarnation (II)."

23: The Battle of Malvern Hill, also known as the Battle of Poindexter's Farm, took place on July 1, 1862, in Henrico County, Virginia, the last of the Seven Days Battles. The divisions of Confederate generals James Longstreet (1821–1904), and A. P. Hill (1825–1865), having fought the day before at Glendale, were held in reserve. Shelby Foote's account is in volume 1: *Fort Sumter to Perryville* (508–14).

47: The buckle is in the Dickey Collection in Rare Books and Special Collections, Thomas Cooper Library, University of South Carolina.

49: The first major battle of the Civil War on Union soil, Antietam, known in the South as the Battle of Sharpsburg, took place on September 17, 1862, near Sharpsburg, Maryland, and resulted in more casualties (twenty-three thousand) than any battle in American history.

62: Theodore Robert Bundy confessed to killing more than thirty young women, usually by bludgeoning and strangling them, between 1974 and 1978 in Washington, Oregon, and Florida.

71: Chancellorsville was fought from April 30 to May 6, 1863, near Spotsylvania Court House, Virginia. The battle is notable for Lee's stunning tactic of dividing his army and for the accidental mortal wounding of Gen. Thomas "Stonewall" Jackson (1824–1863) by one of his own pickets. See Foote, volume 2: *Fredericksburg to Meridien* (278–317).

100: Bundy was electrocuted in the Florida State Prison in Starke on January 24, 1989.

Breaking the Field

FIRST PUBLICATION: *Super Bowl XXVIII: The Official Game Program* (Los Angeles: National Football League, 1994), 159.

NOTES: This poem was commissioned by Philip R. Barber (b. 1965), senior editor for NFL Publishing, for the program of the twenty-eighth Super Bowl. Dickey wanted to "give the essential fluidity and anarchy of the punt-return situation, as opposed to the rigidity, the straight-line formulations of the scrimmage, the rehearsed formations, and so on" (Hart, 724). According to his biographer, Dickey had often asked friends to "block" for him in literary matters and he transferred the notion to this poem (Hart, 725).

Conch

FIRST PUBLICATION: *Apostrophe* 1 (Spring/Summer 1996): 5.

REPRINTED: *New Yorker* 74 (July 13, 1998): 51.

NOTES: This poem appeared in the *New Yorker* accompanying Christopher Dickey's memoir of his father, "Summer of Deliverance" (38–51), an extract from his book of the same name. It is the last of the sixty Dickey poems published by the *New Yorker*. See "The Shark at the Window," line 43.

VARIANTS:

2: Forgot and empowered   intact both dead and alive: (*New Yorker*) | Too-much imprisoned   trapped and empowered: (*Apostrophe*)

5–6: infinitely encircling what the shudder- / dark under the mullet-field's spread (*New Yorker*) | taken neither alive nor dead from the down- / dark beneath the mullet-field's wide-spread (*Apostrophe*)

7: sun (*New Yorker*) | sun: (*Apostrophe*)

8: Says: inexhaustibly lost sound (*New Yorker*) | Eunuch-cry / / Delaying, unmarvelling, unmoralizing, / The found-forever lost sound (*Apostrophe*)

11–15: Delaying, unmarvelling, unmoralizing / Limitless last word / Released from spiraling. / There is no / Whole truth, (*New Yorker*) | direct, released from spiralling. /   The whole Truth / / Is lost, (*Apostrophe*)

18–19: [no blank line inserted] (*Apostrophe*)

19: As (*New Yorker*) | as (*Apostrophe*)

19: [line centered] (*New Yorker*) | [line flush right] (*Apostrophe*)

20–21: [blank line inserted] (*Apostrophe*)

21–24: the one voice, now, // For my son coming naked from the ocean, / Myself created new-human / / By limit, father-rooted (*New Yorker*) | the right voice / For mortality, for what may be coming, for myself / Watching my second son make it // Through hang-time this noon my self perishing / In the perishable feather-footed // Father-rooted (*Apostrophe*)

The Confederate Line at Ogeechee Creek

FIRST PUBLICATION: *Five Points* 1 (Winter 1997): 25.

NOTES: As General William Tecumseh Sherman (line 15) made his "final lap" of his march through Georgia in 1864, his men progressed up both sides of the Ogeechee River. His troops aimed for Fort Lawton, the Confederate prison camp at Millen's Junction, but the Southerners moved their Union prisoners to Savannah in advance. Sherman destroyed Millen anyway. On December 9, 1864, he fought a ragtag group of Confederate soldiers and Georgia state militiamen on the Ogeechee at Cuyler's Plantation and Monteith Swamp. The next day Sherman began investing Savannah, and on the thirteenth took Fort McAllister, whose 230 men were commanded by Major George W. Anderson. The fort lay on the right bank of the Ogeechee below Savannah and was the last obstacle to contact with the Union ships that carried supplies and food. Dickey would have read of these events in his copy of Shelby Foote's *The Civil War: A Narrative,* volume 3: *Red River to Appomattox* (New York: Random House, 1974), 648–52 (see also "Last Hours").

Entering Scott's Night

FIRST PUBLICATION: *New Yorker* 72 (February 3, 1997): 47.

NOTES: Dickey composed this poem at the request of Matthew Bruccoli (see "Daughter") for the centenary of Fitzgerald's birth, September 24, 1996. It was not completed in time for the celebration at the University of South Carolina, but Dickey submitted it to the *New Yorker,* where it appeared in the first issue published after Dickey's death on January 19, 1997. Like his poem about Truman Capote ("To Be Done in Winter"), Dickey's poem about F. Scott Fitzgerald seemed to offer a window into his own biography. He was amazed that Fitzgerald had not become a lyric poet like himself because he believed that Fitzgerald's "essential talent" lay in his lyric qualities: "The lyric instinct is out of time, timeless: a kind of immobilization, a penetration into an instant of perception fixed in words that illuminate the perception and make it possible in terms of those words and those only. I suggest that the best of Fitzgerald, mainly in the prose, but to some small extent also in the poems, has the quality of penetration and memorability that we associate with lyric success. In his use of what I am tempted to call a 'heartbreak' quality, in which a delicate irony and a kind of intelligent ruefulness are balanced by a strong sense that circumstances, given these people and these events, could not be otherwise" (foreword to *F. Scott Fitzgerald: Poems, 1911–1940,* edited by Matthew J. Bruccoli [Bloomfield Hills, Mich.: Bruccoli Clark, 1981], xiii; *Night,* 58). On another occasion Dickey told his wife, Maxine, in the context of Al Braselton's drinking: "But there's one thing worse than being an alcoholic and that's being a dried-up alcoholic. Look what it did to F. Scott Fitzgerald" (Hart, 527). "The triumph of Fitzgerald's life is not the story of his life, as fascinating and harrowing as that story is, but in his work, in the highly personal quality of his linguistic skill, his instinctive mastery of craft, his understanding of fictional people and their situations, and the larger implications of these. . . . Fitzgerald's biography is and will remain the story of a doomed, tragic talent—or, as I personally would say, genius—which underwent an almost unbelievable number of setbacks, but which survived, no matter what" (statement on *Some Sort of Epic Grandeur* [New York: Harcourt Brace Jovanovich, 1981], reproduced in Matthew J. Bruccoli and Judith S. Baughman, *James Dickey: A Descriptive Bibliography* [Pittsburgh: University of Pittsburgh Press, 1990], 212).

—Poems of Uncertain Date—

The Baggage King

FIRST PUBLICATION: *Whole Motion*, 3–4.
NOTES: Dickey arrived in New Guinea at Finschhafen in January 15, 1945.
7: The B-4 was a satchel-type canvas bag. The A-3 was a flyer's kit bag of nylon with a drawstring.
40: For "straining its breast," see "A Folk Singer of the Thirties," 16–17.
VARIANTS:
30: beseiging (*Whole Motion* [typo corrected by editor])

Patience: In the Mill

FIRST PUBLICATION: *Whole Motion*, 4–5.
NOTES: Dickey was working on this poem in 1957 (*Crux*, 117). He told Gordon Van Ness that it honors Mike Hall (see "The Mission"), whose name is echoed in "Mike Cole" (*Striking*, 222). Dickey said that Hall was killed in a plane behind Dickey's, but he is not listed among the casualties of the squadron and appears to have survived the war. Hall was chiefly responsible for the upkeep of the P-61 engines ("mills" in World War II slang); two of his assistants, Sgt. Andrew J. Cobb and Cpl. David Markowitz, were killed when a 20mm cannon went off while they were working on the mill of an aircraft on May 31, 1945. Dickey wrote in the squadron history, "The effect of this happening on the personnel of the 418th cannot be described" (*History*, 75). There is no record of a pilot in Dickey's squadron crashing into any of the many sugar mills in the Philippines. Dickey may have referred to this incident in "The Valley," line 27.
1–5: Compare *Striking* (222), lines originally written for the poem about Walter Armistead.

The Liberator Explodes

FIRST PUBLICATION: *Whole Motion*, 5–6.
REPRINTED: *Because I Fly*, 11–13.
NOTES: The B-24 Liberator, made by Consolidated Aircraft, was the mainstay bomber of the European and Pacific theaters in World War II. Though it was produced in greater numbers than any other aircraft before or since, it was called "The Flying Coffin" because it had only one exit

(in the rear), making it impossible for the flight crew to get out in an emergency. See Frederick A. Johnsen, *B-24 Liberator: Combat and Development History of the Liberator and Privateer* (Osceola, Wis.: Motorbooks International, 1993).

The Place of the Skull

FIRST PUBLICATION: *Whole Motion,* 7–8.

NOTES: No MS at Washington University.

26: Percy Bysshe Shelley drowned in a boating accident in 1822 and his body, having washed ashore later, was cremated on the beach at Viareggio, Italy. Hart Crane jumped off the SS *Orizaba* into the Gulf of Mexico in 1932. His body was never found. See "Hart Crane."

VARIANTS:

[In James Mann's copy of *Whole Motion,* Dickey made two corrections by hand at lines 5 and 6.]

5: head. [author's correction] | head, (*Whole Motion*)

6: others [author's correction] | other (*Whole Motion*)

45: at [corrected by editor] | as (*Whole Motion* [typo])

Obstructions

FIRST PUBLICATION: *Whole Motion,* 8–10.

NOTES: No MS at Washington University. The specific references to Dickey's wartime romances and subsequent career make one want to take the mention of his "two sons" as evidence for dating this poem after 1958.

22–23: In June 1944 Dickey was traveling by train to what he called "the best post in the Army," as a flight officer at Hammer Field in Fresno, California, when he met a beautiful and intelligent young woman returning home from the spring term at Bryn Mawr: Gwendolyn M. Leege (b. 1925) of Marin County, California. He fell deeply in love with her and visited her family's estate in Marin County (*Crux,* 9), but he was not ready to quit his bachelor ways. "She was rich and she was interested in some of the same things that I was. She knew literature pretty well, especially poetry, and she was multi-lingual [*sic*], which was an interesting thing about her. But she was a rich man's woman. She could never have survived the scruffy life I lived as a student. . . . I think she was the prettiest girl I ever had anything to do with . . . . She was not made for the nitty gritty of life, of getting in there and shoving with the rest of 'em like Maxine" (Van Ness, 20–21; Baughman, 251). Leege graduated from Stanford in the class of 1946. Dickey later described to his biographer a sexual encounter at about this time with "a nymphomaniac. . . . She was a sex nut" (Hart, 76–78).

34: Pratt & Whitney was founded in 1860 to make machinery for the Civil War and produced engines for many fighter planes in World War II. Four 14-cylinder R-1830 Pratt & Whitney engines powered the B-24 Liberator (see "The Liberator Explodes") while two 18-cylinder R-2800-10 Double Wasp engines powered Dickey's P-61 Nightfighter (see "Two Poems of Flight-Sleep").

51: Dickey spent the school year 1954–55 in France before assuming a job at the University of Florida.

58: Christopher Dickey was born in 1951; Kevin in 1958.

Canebrake

First Publication: *Striking*, 245–46.
Notes: Written "during the fifties" (*Striking*, 239).

The Wish to Be Buried Where One Has Made Love

First Publication: *Striking*, 246–47.
Notes: Written "during the fifties" (*Striking*, 239).

The Wheelchair Drunk

First Publication: *Sou'wester*, Summer 1968, 73–74.
Collected: *Striking*, 247–48.
Notes: Written "during the fifties" (*Striking*, 239). Found in 1967 by Dave Smith among Dickey's papers at Washington University and published in Smith's journal, *Sou'wester*.
Variants:
3: the thing I am in (*Striking*) | this damned thing (*Sou'wester*)

The Mission

First Publication: *Striking*, 256–57.
Notes: Written "during the fifties" (*Striking*, 239).
4: Mike Hall was Millard Frank Hall (1915–1982), of Beaver, Pennsylvania, the engineering officer for the 418th Night Fighter Squadron when the original squadron that deployed from Hampton Roads in October 1943; beginning as a first lieutenant, he was promoted to captain by August 1945. See "The Valley," line 10, and "Patience: In the Mill." On San Jose, see "Mindoro, 1944."
11: Following his first staged "landing" at Leyte, Gen. Douglas MacArthur (1880–1964) and Filipino soldiers staged a second on the beach at San Jose on December 15, 1944, to further the campaign to recapture the Philippines.
12: Tuba is a Filipino drink—known as "palm toddy" or "palm wine"—made from the sap (tuba) of palm trees and/or coconut juice, sometimes mixed with sweet potato for texture.

The Coral Flight

First Publication: *Striking*, 257–58.
Notes: Written "during the fifties" (*Striking*, 239), the poem springs from a hurricane that destroyed the camps of Dickey's 418th Night Fighter Squadron in Okinawa on October 16, 1945. Dickey slept in a B-25 (*One Voice 1*, 21). Other poems set in Okinawa include "Amputee Ward, Okinawa, 1945," "Victory," "The Driver," "The Contest," and "The Work of Art."
Variants:
23: creature's [corrected by editor] | creatures' (*Striking*)

The Valley

FIRST PUBLICATION: *Striking,* 258–59.

NOTES: Written "during the fifties" (*Striking,* 239). In April 1945 Dickey and his squadron built living quarters with wooden floors; shortly afterward the officers built an officers' club (*History,* 72–73). Though it has no bearing on the value of this poem, Dickey showed here that, although he departed from the facts in "The Performance" (as Dickey himself recorded them in his unit history), he knew that it was Lally who was beheaded and Donald Armstrong who died in the crash (see "The Performance").

10: For Mike Hall see "The Mission," line 5, and "Patience: In the Mill."

25: Presumably "Appleby" stands for Armstrong.

26: James J. Lally (not Lalley) was Armstrong's radar observer when Armstrong crashed his plane near San Jose, Panay, in March 1945. On the crash and Lally's likely beheading, see Hart (97–98).

27: This line may refer to the incident recounted in "Patience: In the Mill."

The Contest

FIRST PUBLICATION: With "The Work of Art" as "Two Versions of the Same Poem" in *Striking,* 263–66.

NOTES: Written "during the fifties" (*Striking,* 239).

44: "'I cannot preach, said Kenyon, 'with a page of heaven and a page of earth spread wide open before us" (Nathaniel Hawthorne, *The Marble Faun,* ch. 28).

Invitation au Voyage

FIRST PUBLICATION: *Striking,* 274.

NOTES: Written "during the fifties" (*Striking,* 239). Not a translation of Charles Baudelaire's famous poem of the same name, notably translated by Dickey's admired Roy Campbell (1952) and imitated by Edna St. Vincent Millay in *Flowers of Evil* (New York: Harper, 1936).

Hart Crane

FIRST PUBLICATION: As one of "Two Poems on Poets," *Striking,* 274–75.

NOTES: Written "during the fifties" (*Striking,* 239). On the morning of April 27, 1932, after being beaten for making advances toward a male crew member, poet Hart Crane jumped into the Gulf of Mexico from the deck of the SS *Orizaba,* bound from Mexico City to New York. For Dickey's notes on jazz and Crane's poetry, see *Striking* (22–23). See also "The Liberator Explodes." On February 7, 1962, Dickey delivered the twenty-fourth Peters Rushton Seminar in Contemporary Prose and Poetry at the University of Virginia. His address was "Hart Crane and the Peripheral in Poetry."

8: Some bystanders said that they thought they heard Crane say "Goodbye, everybody" before he jumped, but this is not mentioned in recent biographies.

The Archers

FIRST PUBLICATION: *Striking*, 280.
NOTES: Written "during the fifties" (*Striking*, 239).

Walter Armistead

FIRST PUBLICATION: *Whole Motion*, 43–44.
NOTES: Original title "On the Death of Walter Armistead" (*Striking*, 216). Probably written shortly after Armistead's death. Walter Moore Armistead (1921–1953) was a "rakish, motorcycle-riding friend," nicknamed "Crash Donovan II" after the 1936 movie about a motorcycle-riding California state trooper. Armistead's family had moved to Atlanta from Miami in 1934 and enrolled Walter at North Fulton High School in the class of 1939, two years ahead of Dickey. The older boy (named "Most Original" in his class) befriended the younger, and the two took particular pleasure in listening to records featuring the drummer Gene Krupa (Hart, 44). Armistead may have been the model for the motorcycling youth of "Cherrylog Road" and "May Day Sermon" (see also *Striking*, 222, 227). Dickey called him "an extraordinary boy whose enthusiasm for the swing music of the early 40s gave me my first notion of what genuine ecstasy might be. I never think of Blake's wonderful statement to the effect that 'exuberance is beauty' without thinking of Walter, who was killed in an airplane crash, . . . God rest his excitable soul" (*Night,* 186). See William Blake, "Proverbs of Hell," in *The Marriage of Heaven and Hell* (1790–93).

For Richard Wilbur

FIRST PUBLICATION: *Whole Motion*, 44.
NOTES: Dickey first met the poet Richard Wilbur (b. 1921) in Rome in April 1955 (Hart, 190–91). After Wilbur suffered a collapse in Rome, the Dickeys took care of their children, showing them the sights and amusements of Rome. "I do not wish to say anything in poetry *neatly.* That is the main trouble with Dick Wilbur's poetry: the sense of habitual dispatch. This is not only, in the end, tiresome, but even comes to seem a kind of poetical reflex. That is the wrong way to get a poem to behave" (*Sorties,* 45). In 1962 Dickey wrote, "When you open a book—a new book or an old book—by Wilbur, you relax as into a lively yet orderly conversation in which your greatest pleasure is in listening to your host talk disarmingly about his house, his grounds, and his reading. Such conversation proceeds with friendly modesty; there is a happy, tranquil marriage between words and things, there are charming surprises and satisfying disclosures, and every anecdote has its point; when you leave you hope to be invited again. Up to now though, there has been no *development,* or even change in Wilbur's work, and there is something vaguely disturbing about this . . ." (*Babel,* 171). This poem probably dates to Dickey's return to America in 1956.

Drifting

FIRST PUBLICATION: *Whole Motion*, 16–17.
NOTES: No date for this poem can be found, but Dickey first met Albert Boyd Braselton (1935–2002) in 1960 (Hart, 243–44). This poem was originally to be in *Buckdancer,* but it was omitted.

Shortly after graduating from Emory in 1957, Braselton married Pauline "Polly" Vance Neal, the daughter of William Neal (see "Cherrylog Road," 17, 50, 65), a partner in the established Atlanta advertising firm of Liller, Neal, Battle & Lindsey, which Braselton joined in 1959, the same year Dickey moved to that agency from McCann Erickson. Braselton was drawn to the older Dickey, and the two began a friendship chiefly characterized by poetry, canoeing trips on the Chattooga River, and alcohol. Braselton's canoeing prowess earned him the nickname "Whitewater Al" (see *The Zodiac,* line 96). In 1965 Dickey wrote to Maxine about Braselton's troubled marriage: "I now know exactly what is meant by shrewishness after seeing Polly needle Al continuously—and I mean by that, go out of her way to seek him out and needle him. Al is taking it out in drink; it is his best weapon in the war of wives against husbands, and he knows that it is the thing that irritates her the most" (*One Voice 1,* 417). Braselton accompanied Dickey on many canoe trips and is a co-dedicatee of *Deliverance.* He also enjoyed the dubious honor of having taught Dickey to play some guitar licks in return for Dickey's teaching him about poetry. Braselton wrote about his own memories of the "Buckhead Boys" in "Buckhead Revisited," *Atlanta* (October 1980): 109–10. Braselton left Liller Neal in 1964 to work for General Electric for two years as a salesman; then he became an account executive with D'Arcy Advertising (1966–68) and executive vice president of Scofield, Braselton & Williams (1968–71) before founding his own agency in 1972.

For the metaphor of a man as drifting boat, see Rimbaud, "Le Bateau ivre" and *Zodiac,* lines 913–14.

For Robert Bhain Campbell

First Publication: *Whole Motion,* 45–46.

Notes: Dickey was working on this poem in August 1960 (*Crux,* 167; *One Voice 1,* 356), in the course of his developing friendship with John Berryman (1914–1972), whom he called "the greatest American poet" and "the best living poet in English"; Dickey also considered Berryman's *77 Dream Songs* "the best poetry book" he'd seen in ten years (Paul L. Mariani, *Dream Song: A Life of John Berryman* [Amherst: University of Massachusetts Press, 1996], 393, 407). Berryman in turn considered Dickey "a sort of disciple" (Mariani, 396). Dickey had picked up *The Task* (1945) by Robert Bhain Campbell (1911–1940) at the remainder counter of a department store in Waco, Texas, when he finished his second tour with the air force in Korea. (*Crux,* 122). Campbell, a native of Michigan, met Berryman when both were at Columbia and became close the next year (1939–40), when Berryman taught at Wayne State University in Detroit and shared an apartment with Campbell and his wife. Campbell earned his tuition at the University of Michigan by working on a Detroit assembly line. After college he tried to enlist in the Abraham Lincoln Brigade during the Spanish Civil War, before returning to the United States, where he became known as a charismatic teacher, poet, and Marxist. He tried to raise Berryman's social conscience (see Campbell's "A Letter from the Airport" [Mariani, 114]) and loyally saw Berryman through his mental and physical illnesses. Campbell contracted testicular cancer in 1940 and was dead before the end of the year. Campbell's death affected Berryman nearly as much as that of his father when Berryman was twelve: "The marks of the only deaths I have undergone, my father's and Bhain's, I will carry always" (John Haffenden, *The Life of John Berryman* [Boston & London: Routledge & Kegan Paul, 1982], 125).

Berryman described Campbell as "an attractive man . . . [who] made no use of it; absolutely candid; considerate, & gay; uncontentious—indeed, innocent, for all his political wishes; loyal; I am obliged to say: virtuous; I never knew him to do an ill action; devoted to verse; brave" (Haffenden, 107). Berryman told Dickey that he was so involved with Campbell's poetry "that I should as soon think of beating a drum for my own" (117). Berryman described the dying Campbell to Dickey: "He was saffron-coloured, his eyes danced, his teeth shot from retreating gums like a madman's, and dying he was full of the senseless hopes (encouraged by his mother who sought quack remedies) that tubercular patients have at the end. . . . I thought life wd bring me nothing like this again" (Mariani, 127). For Dickey's relationship with Berryman, see "Damn You, Jim D., You Woke Me Up," in Berryman, *Collected Poems 1937–1971* (New York: Farrar, Straus & Giroux, 1989): 256–57.

23: Berryman in "A Poem for Bhain," compared himself and Campbell to "Two white birds following their profession / Of flight, together fly, loom, fall and rise, / Certain of the nature and station of their mission." For white birds in Dickey's poetry, see "Reincarnation (II)," "The Ground of Killing," and "Dover: Believing in Kings," line 188.

A Morning

First Publication: *Whole Motion*, 15.
Notes: Undated drafts at Washington University. This poem, with "Lazarus to the Assembled" and "The Sprinter at Forty," appears only in a section of *The Whole Motion* entitled "Peacetime: Seeking the Chosen." Of the fifteen poems in that section, ten were published in the 1960s, one ("Drifting") must date from after 1960, and one was published in 1955 ("The Angel of the Maze"). There is no other internal or external evidence for dating "A Morning" and "Lazarus to the Assembled," though "The Sprinter at Forty" seems clearly to date from the 1960s. I am therefore placing these poems with those that can definitely be dated in the 1960s.

Lazarus to the Assembled

First Publication: *Whole Motion*, 19–20.
Notes: No MS at Washington University. On the date, see "A Morning." For the Lazarus story, see John 11:41–44.
22–25: See "The First Morning of Cancer," lines 130–35.
42–45: See "The First Morning of Cancer," lines 124–29.

The Sprinter at Forty

First Publication: *Whole Motion*, 27–29.
Notes: No date on MS at Washington University. On the date, see "A Morning." The age of the protagonist may suggest a date at the time of "The Birthday Dream" (1965), since Dickey's brother Thomas Swift Dickey (1925–1987) would have been forty in that year and Dickey would have turned forty two years earlier. This would have been the dramatic date of "The Olympian" (1982), fall 1964 in Northridge, California. The three-beat anapestic lines might suggest the period of

Into the Stone (1960), and his other two "sprinter" poems date from the 1950s, but the age of the sprinter and the similarity in tone and event to "The Olympian" suggest a later date.

Dickey spoke of the "Image of sprinting (wish-fulfillment never attained)" in *Striking* (43 and 203–4). Tom Dickey ran the 100-yard dash at Louisiana State University and won the Southeastern Conference 100-yard dash and 220 titles in 1945. In 1948 he qualified for the Olympic trials in the 440 (Hart, 18). James Dickey set his high school's record in the 220 hurdles, but as he considered himself "an indifferent performer in the sports I liked best—football and track," he did not compete in college (see "Night Hurdling," *Night*, 185; Hart, 38). Other poems involving running include "The Sprinter's Mother," "The Sprinter's Sleep," "For the Running of the New York City Marathon," and "The Olympian."

—Poems for Children—

Tucky the Hunter

First Publication: October 11, 1978, with illustrations by Marie Angel (New York: Crown). Notes: Although poets of the modernist generation generally eschewed writing poems for (as opposed to about) children, poets of Dickey's generation, including Theodore Roethke, Randall Jarrell, Richard Wilbur, and Maxine Kumin, wrote many poetry books for children. James Bayard Tuckerman Dickey (see "The Little More") was born in June 1970, when his father, Chris Dickey, was nineteen, and Maxine and Jim Dickey, at forty-seven and forty-three respectively, were not ready to be called grandparents, so Dickey became known to his grandson as "Fun Man," a name by which Lt. Col. James B. T. Dickey still refers to his grandfather. This poem was written by the "Fun Man" for a boy who could convert anything of sticklike proportions into a gun and himself into either a soldier or hunter indoors or out. The boy shared with the poet a fascination with rare wild beasts (see for example "The Eye-beaters" and "For the Last Wolverine," line 66)—with which this poem abounds. According to Christopher Dickey, the germ of this poem may have arisen from a poem Dickey composed aloud during a drive he and his father shared in 1962–63, as they drove to Oregon following a spring on the beach at Positano: "He called it 'Kevin the Diver,' and with that conspiratorial-collaborative enthusiasm that was so wonderful about him as a father, friend or teacher, he encouraged me to make up some of the verses, too" (Christopher Dickey, letter to WB, November 12, 2010).
19–20: See "For the Last Wolverine."
21–22: See Edward Lear, "The Courtship of the Youghy-Boughy-Bò," 682–87.
30: The bintarong is the Asian bearcat.
56: For Susan Tuckerman Dickey, see "False Youth: Autumn: Clothes of an Age."

Bronwen, the Traw, and the Shape-Shifter

First Publication: September 10, 1986. Subtitle: "A Poem in Four Parts." Illustrations by Richard Jesse Watson. A Bruccoli Clark Book (San Diego, New York & London: Harcourt Brace Jovanovich).
Notes: Bronwen Elaine Dickey (see "Daughter") was born when Dickey was fifty-eight, approaching a grandfather's age. He doted on his daughter, dreamed up a two-person paper-plane air force,

played her in chess, and infused in her his love of the natural world and the fantasy world of his imagination. Various details of the young Bronwen are present: sunflower hat, zinc oxide (line 22), pigtails; her love of gardening, climbing (lines 423–30), and checkers, with a fondness for the red ones (line 483); and her mother kept a trowel (lines 18–19) that Bronwen sometimes used to tend her garden and rose bushes, an inheritance from her Aunt Maibelle, a noted Atlanta rosarian (see "Power and Light"). Other details—such as the blue rocks upon which the house sits (line 1), the greenhouse (line 25), the blue door (line 45), and the shape-shifter visions (lines 57ff)—are all Dickey's inventions. Like many children, Bronwen was afraid of the dark until about the age of seven. Dickey would tuck her in and compose fairy stories off the top of his head, often involving an adventurous duo, The Butterfly and The Bat (Dickey was fascinated by flying mammals) and climaxing in a battle against monsters. In one version the duo ended up at a castle made entirely of emeralds. (Bronwen was a fan of *The Wizard of Oz*.) She and her father watched a documentary on flying squirrels that may have influenced lines 97ff. (Bronwen Dickey, letter to WB, December 8, 2010).

NOTES:

33: For the phrase "all dark," see "Sleeping Out at Easter."

VARIANTS:

38: Bronwen [corrected by editor] | Brownwen (*Bronwen*)

Index of Titles

*In addition to listing titles of individual poems, this index includes titles of Dickey collections, each followed by its contents in the order in which the poems appear in that volume and the page numbers on which the poem appears in this edition. Single-poem books—*The Zodiac *(1976),* Tucky the Hunter *(1978), and* Bronwen, the Traw and the Shape-Shifter *(1986)—are not included, nor is* The Whole Motion *(1992).*

Fox Blood, 267–68; The Second Sleep, 292–93; The Aura, 342–44; Sled Burial, Dream Ceremony, 326–27; Gamecock, 331–32; The Night Pool, 330–31; The War Wound, 313; Mangham, 344–46; Angina, 308–10; Dust, 337–39; The Fiend, 334–37; Slave Quarters, 349–54

Bums, on Waking, 244–46

Camden Town, 457–59
Cancer Match, The, 433–34
Canebrake, 659–60
Celebration, The, 340–42
Change, The, 141
Chenille, 274–76
Cherrylog Road, 255–58
Child in Armor, The, 10–11
Children Reading, 325–26
Child's Room, A, 101–2
Christmas Shopping, 1947, 3
Christmas Towns, The, 405–6
Circuit, 633–34
Cobra, 606
Coming Back to America, 356–57
Common Grave, The, 323–25
Conch, 644–45
Confederate Line at Ogeechee Creek, The, 645–46
Confrontation of the Hero, The, 22–25
Contest, The, 668–72
Coral Flight, The, 665–66
Courtship, The, 217–18
Craters, 599–600
Crows, The, 211–12
Crystal, 596
Cypresses, The, 59–60

Dark Ones, 392–93
Daughter, 631–32
Daybreak, 609–10
Deborah and Deirdre as Drunk Bridesmaids Foot-Racing at Daybreak, 586–87

Deborah Burning a Doll Made of House-Wood, 563–64
Deborah in Ancient Lingerie, in Thin Oak over Creek, 583–84
Deborah in Mountain Sound: Bell, Glacier, Rose, 578–79
Deborah, Moon, Mirror, Right Hand Rising, 564–65
Deer among Cattle, 348–49
Diabetes, 428–31
Dog Sleeping on My Feet, A, 167–69
Doing the Twist on Nails, 476–77
Doorstep, Lightning, Waif-Dreaming, 582–83
Dover: Believing in Kings, 67–73
Dream Flood, The, 185–86
Drifting, 677–79
Drift-Spell, The, 637–38
Drinking from a Helmet, 228–34
Driver, The, 260–62
Drowning with Others, 124–25
Drowning with Others (1962)—The Lifeguard, 152–54; Listening to Foxhounds, 128–29; A Dog Sleeping on My Feet, 167–69; The Movement of Fish, 158–59; The Heaven of Animals, 160–62; A Birth, 122; Fog Envelops the Animals, 148–49; The Summons, 146–47; In the Tree House at Night, 150–52; For the Nightly Ascent of the Hunter Orion over a Forest Clearing, 162–63; The Rib, 180–81; The Owl King, 172–80 (The Call, 172–73; The Owl King, 173–75; The Blind Child's Story, 175–80); Between Two Prisoners, 122–24; Armor, 139–40; In the Lupanar at Pompeii, 156–57; Drowning with Others, 124–25; A View of Fujiyama after the War, 131–32; The Island 109–10; Dover: Believing in Kings, 67–73; To His Children in Darkness, 182–84; A Screened Porch in the Country, 184–85; The Dream Flood, 185–86; The Scratch, 105–7; Hunting Civil War Relics at Nimblewill Creek, 142–44; The Twin Falls, 145–46; The Hospital Window, 166–67;

Index of First Lines

I come back, 595
I don't have any pain. None at all, 485
I dreamed I already loved you, 477
I have had my time dressed up as something
    else, 359
I have just come down from my father, 166
I have on four black sweaters, 194
I lay at the edge of a well, 117
I lay in a twelve-barred cage, 101
I may even be, 390
I never had arms before, 661
I never played for you. You'd have thrown, 493
I see the tree think it will turn, 127
I set you level, 563
I used to get up, in the tent, 655
I would not wish to sit, 122
If he should lift his hand, 85
If I could believe it is, 203
If I told you I used to know the circular truth,
    614
If you would run, 550
I'm laughing, but being very quiet about it,
    548
In a cold night, 427
In a hushed, tremendous descent, 163
In a stable of boats I lie still, 152
In aircraft, the newest, inexorable models, 475
In such a tremendous window, 676
In the concrete cells of the hatchery, 272
In the great place the great house is gone from
    in the sun, 349
In the hurricane wind, 665
In the war where many men fell, 248
In the well-fed cage-sound of diesels, 301
In the world, or behind the world, 81
In under a flock of shade, 43
Interweaving, 646
Into the slain tons of needles, 277
Inventing a story with grass, 122
It could be that nothing you could do, 567
It is good, when leaving a place, 360
It is not as if it were painted, 59

It is there, above him, beyond, behind, 234
It is time for the others to come, 134
It is time for the trees in motionless flight in
    a ring, 26
It is worth it to get, 677
It is you who have made light crawl, 681
It may be the sea-moving moon, 104
It wounded well—one time and, 313

Japan invades. Far Eastern vines, 224
Just after the sun, 78

Kin: quiet grasses. Above, 558
Knowing that nothing is in it, 683

Lay in the house mostly living, 421
Light fails, in crossing a river, 96
Looking out of the dark of the town, 192
Lord, you've sent both, 433
Los Angeles back-yarding in its blue-eyed
    waters, 574
Low-cloudly it whistles, changing heads, 434
Lying at home, 337

Many trees can stand unshaded, 120
Mark. Hair, one strand of it, can curl, 548
May we be able to begin with ourselves, 597
Memory: I can take my head and strike it on
    a wall on Cumberland Island, 328
Monks, 488
Morning: it shows, 659
Moth-force a small town always has, 537
My father never finished, 270
My hands that were not born completely, 561

Name their traps, you feel them flutter, 214
No barometer but yellow, 621
No water is still, on top, 158
No, don't ask me to give you, 629
No, no! Believe me!, 473
Not Stonewall, 639
Nothing but one life: all stands, 569

Now I can be sure of my sleep, 93
Now secretness dies of the open, 162
Numbers who can't ever hear me, 547

O death, so dear to me, 549
O Lord, it was all night, 381
O sire, I dreamed, 10
Off Highway 106, 255
Often, in these blue meadows, 310
Often, when the almighty screen, 190
Old boys, the cracked boards spread before,
 394
On a bed of gravel moving, 239
On distant sides of the bed, 253
On every side, street lamps are burning
 deeply, 237
On side-showering wheels afloat, far off, 51
On such a day I see him at a window, 10
On the horizon, through the stream of
 exhausted blast-furnaces fog Yes, 545
On the way to a woman, I give, 94
Once hid in a fiery twist, 105
Once you have let the first blade, 154
One can do one begins to one can only, 314
One cry behind hunger, 13
One dot, 365
One harbor's history is the beam, 4
One man in a house, 116
One night I thirsted like a prince, 428
One sea. The present hour. One moon, 603
Open windows: we always have them, have,
 634
Over and around grass banked and packed
 short and holding back, 437

Poetry gives off smoke, 479
Prepared for death and unprepared, 451
Press of a thorn, quick, 596
Pull out the pissed-on clinkers, 590

Real God, roll, 636
Remember: not making, 675

Rest on the bright decks, 672
Right under their noses, the green, 207
Rising behind me, 564
Roots out of the ground and ongoing, 599

"See!" he cried, "the dead dust turns, 112
Sharing what sharing quickly who, 419
She is, she must be lying, 15
She is who, 11
Shook down shook up on these trees they
 have come, 413
Sick of your arms, 333
Sight, from the ocean dazzling, 673
Six boys have slung a coffin by the ropes, 126
So I would hear out those lungs, 339
So long, 453
So much of life is spent driving, 405
So that sleeping and waking, 447
Some beating in there, 625
Some fires are heard most truly, 250
Some of the time, going home, I go, 442
Some sit and stare, 323
Something far off buried deep and free, 380
Something for a long time has gone wrong,
 373
Something has left itself scattered, 180
Sometimes are living those who have been
 seen, 566
Somewhere between bells the right angles
 staggered, 344
Stars and grass, 620
Steady, the simple pleasures, 666
Still, passed through the spokes of an old
 wheel, on and around, 291
Still-down on all sides, 553
Sure. All the time I come up on the evil, 546
Swordfish, I know you are tired: tired out with
 the sharpness of your face, 541

That any just to long for, 446
That one who is the dreamer lies mostly in her
 left arm, 308

INDEX OF NAMES IN THE APPARATUS CRITICUS

Included here are proper names of real persons, things, and places. Most fictitious characters are not included. Titles of publications containing first appearances of Dickey poems are also listed.

Barnstone, Willis, 872, 874, 875, 876, 877, 880

Barnwell, Bill, 773, 790

Baudelaire, Charles, 889

Baughman, Judith S., 788

Becker, Lucien, 837, 861, 871

Behan, Brendan, 818

Beloit Poetry Journal, first appearance of poems in, 723, 725, 729

Beppu, Japan, 783

Bergson, Henri, 807

Berkeley, Bishop George, 777

Bern, Paul, 801

Berryman, John, 891–92

"Bird of Freedom," 719

Blake, William, 814, 815, 861, 880, 890

Bly, Robert, 782, 860, 871

Boeing, 834

Bolton, Ga., 828

Book of Common Prayer, 811

Bookwalter, Mary, 814–15

Borman, Capt. Frank, 832

Boss, David, 823

Bouhéret, Roland, 871

Boxcar Bertha, 768

Boyd, Montague Lafitte "Mont," 826

Boyle, Robert, 850

Braselton, Albert Boyd, 748, 773, 779, 849, 886, 890–91

Braselton, Polly Vance Neal, 891

Brasstown Bald, 811, 861

Brickman, Marshall, 796

Brindisi, 750

broadsides, first appearance of poems as, 854, 872

Brock, Mary Jane, 776

Broder, David, 872

Brookwood Hills Community Club swimming pool, 752

Brown, King, 794

Brown, Rastus, 794

Browning, Robert, 866

Bruccoli, Matthew J., 788, 882, 885–86

Brunswick, Ga., 791

B-24 Liberator, 886, 887

Buchanan, Gene, 772

Buck, Pearl S., 727

"Buckdancer's Choice" (song), 794

Buckhead, Atlanta, 824–25

Buckhead Billiard Parlor, 825

Buckhead Hardware Co., 825

Buckner, Gen. Simon Bolivar, 813

Buckner Bay, 774, 813

Bulletin (Sydney, Australia), first appearance of poem in, 793

Buna-Gona, New Guinea, 813

Bundy, Ted, 883, 884

Burke, Joe, 811

Bynner, Witter, 856

Caen, 720

Cahulawassee, 748, 779

Calais, 729

California State University, Northridge, 791, 866

Camden, S.C., 834

Campbell, Joseph, 853–54

Campbell, Robert Bhain, 891–92

Campbell, Roy, 889

Campion, Thomas, 742

Capote, Truman, 874, 885

Carolina Barber Shop, 841

"Carolina Moon," 811

Carpenter, Scott, 833

Carradine, David, 768

Cartecay River, 779

Carter, Jimmy, 853, 854

Carter family, 835

Carters Dam, 779

Carters Lake, 779

Cates, Charles Otis, Jr., 825

Catherine, Saint, 813

Cebu Island, 735, 744, 845

Cellini, Benvenuto, 869

Ceram Island, Indonesia, 810

Chadwick, Florence May, 729

Chaffee, Roger Bruce, 832

Chancellorsville, Battle of, 884

Charles II of England, 730

Charles XII of Sweden, 870

Charlton County, Ga., 828

Chattahoochee National Forest, 750

Chattahoochee River, 748

Chattooga River, 748, 891

Cherry Log, Ga., 772, 773

Chicago Choice, first appearance of poems in, 750

Chikao, Yusano, 735

Chios, 755

Choice, first appearance of poem in, 756

Civilian Conservation Corps, 765

Clausewitz, Carl von, 719

Clockwatch Review, first appearance of poems in, 872, 876

Cobb, Sgt. Andrew J., 886

Coca-Cola, 807

Cohutta Mountains, 760, 764

Colerain, Ga., 828

Coleridge, Samuel Taylor, 810, 815

collections, first appearance of poems in, 759, 778, 780, 787, 810, 855, 856, 857, 858, 862, 870, 871, 872, 882, 886, 887, 888, 889, 890, 891, 892

Collins, Michael, 833

Columbia, S.C., 769, 828, 838, 846

Commentary, first appearance of poem in, 729

Consolidated Aircraft, 886

Constable, Robert, 744, 805

Coosawattee River, 779, 785

Coraddi, first appearance of poems in, 718

Coubertin, Baron Pierre de, 866

Crane, Hart, 788, 846, 887, 889

Crawford Long Hospital, Atlanta, 734

Cromwell, Oliver, 730

Cumberland Island, Ga., 791, 876

Cummings, E. E., 822

Cupid's Hotdog Stand, Los Angeles, 867

Cyprus, 851

Dahlonega, Ga., 749

Daniell, Rosemary, 741–42

Dante, 734, 806

D'Arcy Advertising Co., 891

Darien, Ga., 739

Darien River, 761

Darlington School, Rome, Ga., 831

Darwin, Charles, 850

Davis, Benny, 811

Decatur, Ga., 825

Demetrian, Saint, 851

Descartes, René, 850, 877

Dickey, Bronwen Elaine (daughter), 882, 893–94

Dickey, Christopher Swift (son), 720, 721, 747, 759, 769, 775, 784, 791, 795, 804, 814, 822, 826, 829, 841, 865, 873, 878, 882, 884, 887, 893

Dickey, Deborah Dodson (wife), 869

Dickey, Dorian Marston (niece), 883

Dickey, Ervin (uncle), 722

Dickey, Eugene, Jr. (brother), 731, 736, 742, 751, 760, 777

Dickey, Eugene, Sr. (father), 741, 756–57, 760, 777, 780, 786, 789, 871

Dickey, George (ancestor), 797

Dickey, Hannah Taylor (ancestor), 797

Dickey, James Bayard Tuckerman (grandson), 841, 878, 893

Dickey, James Lafayette, Jr. (uncle), 722, 728, 740, 796, 829

Dickey, James Lafayette, Sr. (grandfather), 722, 785

Dickey, Katherine Cox McWhorter (aunt), 722, 829

Dickey, Kevin Webster (son), 734, 739, 759, 803, 822, 829, 883, 887

Dickey, Maibelle Swift (mother), 721, 760, 786, 813

Frénaud, André, 742, 837, 870, 871, 873

Freud, Sigmund, 849

Frost, Robert, 725, 726, 860

Fujiyama, 747

Fuller, Mark, 814

Gadfly, first appearance of poems in, 718,
    719

Gainesville, Fla., 726

Gainesville, Ga., 825

Galen, 847

Gallogly, John, 811

Garbo, Greta, 811

García Lorca, Federico, 721

Garrison, David, 874, 875, 876, 877, 880

Garrison, Lucy McKim, 798

Gemini 4 Mission, 832

General Electric, 844, 891

Gennep, Arnold van, 853–54

Gentleman's Quarterly, first appearance of
    poem in, 854

Gentry, Ira, 779

Georgia Marble Quarry, 762, 785

Gila Bend, Ariz., 879

Gilbert, John, 811

Gilmer County, Ga., 760, 797, 811

Glendale, Calif., 835

Glynn County, Ga., 791

Godfrey, Arthur, 829

Golden Warrior, The, 734

Goldenberg, David, 749

Goncharov, Ivan, 840

Gordon County, Ga., 785

Grady Memorial Hospital, Atlanta, 785

Graham House Review, first appearance of
    poems in, 869

Granta, first appearance of poem in, 764

Gray, James Richard, Jr., 826

Gray, Thomas, 833

Green Bay Packers, 841–42

Greenville, Ga., 828

Grieg, Nordahl, 858

Griffin, Ga., 825

Grimes Nose, Ga., 811

Grissom, Virgil Ivan "Gus," 832

Guthrie, Woodrow Wilson "Woody," 767–68,
    796

Guy, Landrum, 741–42

Haast, William E., 819–20

Hackney, E. Roy, 826

Haifa Bay, 720

Haldane, Seán, 835

Hall, John, 772

Hall, Capt. Mike, 886, 888, 889

Hallmark Cards, 812

Hamilton House Museum, Dalton, Ga., 778

Hammer Field, Fresno, Calif., 887

Hampton Mills, 811

Hanley, Bridget, 811

Harden Street, Columbia, S.C., 841

Hardy, Thomas, 860

Harlow, Jean, 801

Harmaja, Saima (Rauha Maria), 858

Harper's, first appearance of poems in, 795,
    800, 801, 802, 814, 817, 830

Harris, Dick, 805

Harvard Bulletin, first appearance of poem
    in, 834

Harvard University, 831, 834–36, 837

Hastings Constitutional Law Quarterly, first
    appearance of poem in, 860–61

Hatfield, Hurd, 801

Hawthorne, Calif., 845

Hawthorne, Nathaniel, 889

Heidegger, Martin, 877

Helen of Troy, 734

Hemans, Felicia Dorothea, 743

Hemingway, Ernest, 738

Hera, 764

Heraclitus, 748, 843

Herculaneum, 753

Hesiod, 763

Heym, Georg, 857

Hill, Lt. Gen. A. P., 883
Hiroshima, 719, 812
Hitler, Adolf, 847
Hodgins, John (brother-in-law), 809
Hodgins, Maibelle Swift Dickey (sister), 777, 786, 809, 894
Hogback Plantation, 797, 811
Hogback Ridge, 797, 818
Holbrook, Charlotte Sheram, 772, 773
Hollander, John, 835
Homer, 755
Hood, Edward M., 721
Hoover, Herbert, 768
Hopkins, Gerard Manley, 864
Hornung, Paul, 841
Horsford, Eben, 831
Horus, 732
House of Earth, The, 727
Housman, A. E., 880
Howard, Frank, 803
Hoyle, Sir Fred, 850
Hubble, Edwin Powell, 850
Hudson Motor Co., 773
Hudson Review, first appearance of poems in, 727, 748, 755, 770, 786, 805
Hughes, Howard, 844
Hunter College, 860
Huntley, Lena Swift Burckhardt (grand-mother), 801, 818
Hyman, Stanley Edgar, 853

I Love Lucy, 807
Icarus, 783
Impetus, first appearance of poem in, 731
"Indian Maiden, The," 802
Innsbruck Resort and Country Club, 786
Iphigenia, 734
Irby, Henry, 824
Isaac, 753
Isis, 732
Israel, 720
Ives, Burl Icle Ivanhoe, 767–68

Jackson, Gen. Thomas "Stonewall," 884
Jacob, 736
James Connally Air Force Base, Waco, Tex., 721
James Dickey at 70, first appearance of poem in, 883
Janus, 734
Jardin des Plantes, Paris, 769
Jarecki, Robin Lee, 801–2, 835–36
Jarrell, Randall, 893
Jarry, Alfred, 856
Jeffers, Robinson, 861
Jekyll Island, Ga., 791
Jesus Christ, 741, 743, 825, 839
Johnson, Harry, 752
Johnston, Gen. Joseph E., 749
Joseph, 736, 781, 825
József, Attila, 858
Juba, Master, 794

Kahn, Anthony, 837, 838, 839, 840
Kandinsky, Wassily, 852
Kant, Immanuel, 783, 821
Kawaii, Takeo, 735, 744
Kaye, Danny, 768
Kennedy Space Center, 832
Kentucky Poetry Review, first appearance of poems in, 874, 875
Kenyon College, 860
Kenyon Review, first appearance of poems in, 738, 749, 753, 782, 796, 859, 867, 868, 869
Kepler, Johannes, 788
Kerksis, Sydney C., 749
Kermode, Frank, 814
Kierkegaard, Søren, 753
King, Lewis, 748
King Lear, 729
Kingsland, Ga., 828
Kipling, Rudyard, 772
Kisatchie National Forest, 831
Kramer, Gerald Louis, 842
Krueger, Lt. Gen. Walter, 831
Krupa, Gene, 890

Robertstown, Ga., 786

Robinson, Edwin Arlington, 810

Robinson, Mary Ann. *See* Young, Mary Ann
    Robinson

Roethke, Theodore, 758, 860, 893

Rogers, Tom, 803

Rome, Ga., 811, 825, 831

Rome, Italy, 734, 750, 761, 840, 890

Roper, Albert, 751

Rule, Ann, 883

Ryukyu Islands, 719

St. Augustine lighthouse, Fla., 726

St. Joseph's Hospital, Atlanta, 722, 829

St. Marys River, 827

St. Simons Island, Ga., 739, 761, 791, 797

Saladin, 720

Salmon River, Idaho, 811

San Diego, Calif., 769

San Fernando Valley State College, 742, 791,
    866

San Jose, Panay, New Guinea, 735, 746, 888, 889

Sandlapper Singers, 807

Sandy Springs, Ga., 826

Santa Barbara, Calif., 835

Saturday Evening Post, first appearance of
    poem in, 809

Saturday Review, first appearance of poem in,
    733

Savannah, Ga., 885

Savannah River, 827

Schirra, Walter Marty, 848

Scofield, Braselton & Williams, 891

Scorpio, 783, 848, 849

Scorsese, Martin, 768

Scott, Robert Falcon, 722

Sea Island, Ga., 739, 791

Seay, James, 831

Sepulveda, Calif., 792, 865–67

Service Robert W., 772

Sevareid, Eric, 831

Seven Days Battles, 883

Sewanee Review, first appearance of poems in,
    719, 721, 722, 727, 732, 740, 749, 760, 766

Shapcott, Tom, 776

Sharkfighters, The, 790

Sharpsburg, Battle of, 884

Shelley, Percy Bysshe, 833, 887

Shenandoah, 721, 764; first appearance of
    poems in, 721, 764, 776, 797

Sherman, Gen. William Tecumseh, 885

Shimose, Masachika, 838

Shoeless Joe, 728

Siffleet, Leonard, 735

Silverstein, Abe, 832

Sisters of Mercy, 829

Skelton, John, 721

Slaten, Ralph L., 826

Smart, Christopher, 832

Somebody Up There Likes Me, 758

Sorrells, Helen, 742

Soundings, first appearance of poem in, 721

Southern Magazine, first appearance of poems
    in, 876, 877

Southern Review, first appearance of poems in,
    789, 883

Southpoint, first appearance of poems in, 882

Spears, Monroe K., 720

Spidola, 838

Spotsylvania Court House, Va., 884

Springer Mountain, 760, 861

Starr, Bryan Bartlett "Bart," 841

Stearman, Lloyd Carlton, 834

Stevens, Wallace, 760

Stickney, Austin, 834

Stickney, Joseph Trumbull, 834–36

Stolen Apples, first appearance of poems in,
    838, 839, 840

Story of G.I. Joe, The, 758

*Super Bowl XXVIII: The Official Game Pro-
    gram,* first appearance of poem in, 884

Tacitus, 753

Tacloban, 735

Talmadge, Eugene, 828
Tate, Ga., 762, 785
Tate, Col. Sam, 785
Telemachus, 777
Tempest, The, 766, 869
Tetuan, Morocco, 852
Texas Quarterly, first appearance of poem in,
    770
Thermopylae, 866
Thomas, Dylan, 818, 881
Thomas, Edward, 725, 726
Thomas, Helen, 726
Thomas, R. George, 725
Thomas Aquinas, Saint, 754–55, 784
Thomaston, Ga., 825
Thorpe, Jim, 803
Times Literary Supplement, first appearance
    of poem in, 801
Timon of Athens, 730
Tipton, Maxine (mother-in-law), 829
Tlaloc, 855
Toccoa, Ga., 773
Transatlantic Review, first appearance of
    poem in, 806
Translations by American Poets, first appear-
    ance of poem in, 837
Traverse, 1st Lt. Edward Falling "Salvo,"
    844
Tungus, 840
Tuxedo Park, Atlanta, 722
Tyree, James Howard, 825

Unicoi State Park, 786
Unimart, 867
Union Oil, 835
University of Alabama, 831
University of Florida, 723, 726, 887
University of Michigan, 891
University of Minnesota, 860
University of Paris, 834
University of South Carolina, 809, 836
University of Washington, 860

Van Dyke, Dick, 752
Van Ness, A. Gordon, 886
Van Valkenburg, Ed, 772, 824
Vanderbilt University, 733, 735, 806, 846, 853
Värmland, 870
Vaughn, Herbert, 735, 747
Venus, 851
Venus de Milo, 762
Verse, first appearance of poem in, 875
Vesuvius, Mount, 753
Viareggio, Italy, 887
Vico del Balcone Pensile, Pompeii, 753
Vico del Lupanare, Pompeii, 753
Villa Lou Galidou, Cap d'Antibes, 737
Vimy Ridge, 726
Virgil, 734, 738, 739, 763
Virginia Quarterly Review, first appearance of
    poems in, 741, 750, 760, 771, 791, 792, 834
Vischer, Robert, 848
Vladivostok, 838
Vogelkop, New Guinea, 810
Vulcan, 783

Waccamaw River, 877
Waco, Tex., 721
Wakowski, Diane, 783
Walk in the Sun, A, 831
Wallace, Andy, 865
Ware, Charles Pickard, 798
Warhol, Andy, 776
Warner, Glenn Scobey "Pop," 803
Warren, Robert Penn, 717, 818, 861
Washington and Lee University, 721
Washington Post, first appearance of poem in,
    853
Washington Redskins, 841
Wayne State University, 891
Weissberg, Eric, 796
Wender, William Max, 825
Wender & Roberts' Drug Store, 825
Wheelock, John Hall, 720. 721, 722, 724, 727,
    729

White, Edward Higgins, 832–33

White County, Ga., 786, 811

White Wilderness, 804

Whitener, Catherine Evans, 778

Whitman, Walt, 766

Whittern, Harold B., 719

Wilbur, Richard, 742, 890, 893

Wilde, Oscar, 878

Wilhelm II of Germany, 733

William the Conqueror, 720

Wilson, Edmund, 835

Wizard of Oz, The, 894

Woodhaven (Dickey estate), 722

Wooley, Sheb, 802

Wormwood Review, first appearance of poem
  in, 739

Wotan, 861

Wright, James, 729, 792, 859–60, 873

Yale Review, first appearance of poems in, 728,
  731, 744, 778, 796

Yamashita, Tomoyiku, 745

Yeats, William Butler, 861

Yevtushenko, Yevgeny, 837, 838, 839, 840, 841,
  847

Yokohama, 813

Young, John Fant, 775

Young, Mary Ann Robinson, 742, 775

Zeist, Utrecht, Holland, 846

Zima, Russia, 840

Zuma Beach, Calif., 835

About the Author and the Editor

James Dickey (1923–1997) is one of the great American poets of the twentieth century. After working in the advertising industry and teaching at several colleges and universities, Dickey received a National Book Award for *Buckdancer's Choice* in 1966 and served as consultant in poetry to the Library of Congress, a position that later became poet laureate, from 1966 to 1968. He then joined the University of South Carolina English department and served as poet in residence until his death. He became a member of the National Institute of Arts and Letters in 1972 and was elected to the American Academy of Arts and Letters in 1987.

Ward Briggs is Carolina Distinguished Professor of Classics Emeritus and Louis Fry Scudder Professor of Humanities Emeritus at the University of South Carolina. He has published widely on the history of American classical scholarship, the career of the classicist Basil Lanneau Gildersleeve, and the classical tradition. Briggs was a friend of James Dickey for more than thirty years.